MW01517869

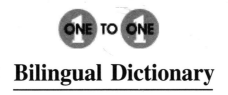

Bilingual Dictionary

English-Cantonese
Cantonese-English
Dictionary

Compiled by
Nisa Yang

ibs BOOKS (UK)

© Publishers

First Edition: 2011

ISBN : 978-1-905863-84-6

Published by
ibs BOOKS (UK)
55, Warren Street, London W1T 5NW (UK)
e-mail: indbooks@aol.com; starbooksuk@aol.com
www.starbooksuk.com

Printed in India at
Star Print-O-Bind, New Delhi-110020

Asian Puplications
7137-132 Street
Surrey, BC V3W 4M3
(604) 597-5837

About this Dictionary

Developments in science and technology today have narrowed down distances between countries, and have made the world a small place. A person living thousands of miles away can learn and understand the culture and lifestyle of another country with ease and without travelling to that country. Languages play an important role as facilitators of communication in this respect.

To promote such an understanding, **ibs BOOKS (UK)** has planned to bring out a series of bilingual dictionaries in which important English words have been translated into other languages, with Roman transliteration in case of languages that have different scripts. This is a humble attempt to bring people of the world closer through the medium of language, thus making communication easy and convenient.

These dictionaries have been compiled and edited by teachers and scholars of relative languages.

Bilingual Dictionaries in this Series

English-Arabic/Arabic-English	Rania-al-Qass
English-Bengali/Bengali-English	Amit Majumdar
English-Cantonese/Cantonese-English	Nisa Yang
English-Dari/Dari-English	Amir Khan
English-Farsi/Farsi-English	Maryam Zamankhani
English-Gujarati/Gujarati-English	Sujata Basaria
English-Hindi/Hindi-English	Sudhakar Chaturvedi
English-Hungarian/Hungarian-English	Lucy Mallows
English-Lithuanian/Lithuanian-English	Regina Kazakeviciute
English-Nepali/Nepali-English	Anil Mandal
English-Punjabi/Punjabi-English	Teja Singh Chatwal
English-Pashto/Pashto-English	Amir Khan
English-Polish/Polish-English	Magdalena Herok
English-Romanian/Romanian-English	Georgeta Laura Dutulescu
English-Somali/Somali-English	Ali Mohamud Omer
English-Tamil/Tamil-English	Sandhya Mahadevan
English-Turkish/Turkish-English	Nagme Yazgin
English-Urdu/Urdu-English	S.A Rahman

More languages in print

ibs BOOKS (UK)
London W1T 5NW (UK)

A

a *a.* 一 yat
aback *adv.* 向後 heurng ho
abaction *n* 強搶 keurng cheurng
abactor *n* 強搶者 keurng cheurng jeh
abandon *v.t.* 遺棄 way hey
abase *v.t.* 踩低 tai day
abasement *n* 踩低 tai day
abash *v.t.* 慚愧 tarm kwai
abate *v.t.* 減低 garm day
abatement *n.* 減低 garm day
abbey *n.* 寺院 ji yoon
abbreviate *v.t.* 簡稱 gan ting
abbreviation *n* 簡稱 gan ting
abdicate *v.t,* 放棄 forng hay
abdication *n* 放棄 forng hay
abdomen *n* 腹部 fuk bo
abdominal *a.* 腹部嘅 fuk bo geh
abduct *v.t.* 拐走 gwai jow
abduction *n* 綁架 borng ga
abed *adv.* 喺床度 hay chorng dow
aberrance *n.* 唔正常 hm jing seurng
abet *v.t.* 唆擺 sor bai
abetment *n.* 唆擺 sor bai
abeyance *n.* 擱置 gok ji
abhor *v.t.* 憎 jang
abhorrence *n.* 痛恨 tung han
abide *v.i* 容忍 yung yan
abiding *a* 永恆嘅 wing han geh
ability *n* 能力 lang lik
abject *a.* 賤格 jeen gak
ablactate *v.t* 戒奶 gai lai
ablactation *n* 戒奶 gai lai
ablaze *adv.* 着火 jeurk for
able *a* 可以 hor yi
ablepsy *n* 盲 mang
ablush *adv* 面紅 meen hung
ablution *n* 沐浴 muk yuk

abnegate *v.t* 否認 fow ying
abnegation *n* 否認 fow ying
abnormal *a* 唔正常 hm jing seurng
aboard *adv* 上咗 seurng jor
abode *n* 住所 ju sor
abolish *v.t.* 廢除 fay chuy
abolition *v* 廢除 fay chuy
abominable *a* 討厭 tow yeem
aboriginal *a* 本地 bwun day
aborigines *n. pl* 原住民 yoon ju man
abort *v.i* 終止 jung jee
abortion *n* 墮胎 dor toy
abortive *adv* 失敗 sat bai
abound *v.i.* 有好多 yow ho dor
about *adv* 大概 dai koy
about *prep* 關於 gwan yu
above *adv* 以上 yee seurng
above *prep.* 上面 seurng meen
abreast *adv* 並肩 bing geen
abridge *v.t* 縮短 suk doon
abridgement *n* 摘要 jak yiew
abroad *adv* 出國 chut gwok
abrogate *v. t.* 廢除 fay chuy
abrupt *a* 突然間 dak yeen gan
abruption *n* 中斷 jung toon
abscess *n* 膿腫 lung jung
absonant *adj* 唔一致 hm yat jee
abscond *v.i* 逃走 tow jow
absence *n* 缺席 koot tik
absent *a* 缺席 koot tik
absent *v.t* 缺席 koot tik
absolute *a* 絕對 joot duy
absolutely *adv* 絕對 joot duy
absolve *v.t* 解除 gai chuy
absorb *v.t* 吸收 kap sow
abstain *v.i.* 戒 gai
abstract *a* 抽象 tow jeurng
abstract *n* 摘要 jak yiew
abstract *v.t* 抽出 tow chut
abstraction *n.* 抽象嘅概念 tow

jeurng geh koy leem

absurd *a* 荒謬 forng mow
absurdity *n* 荒謬 forng mow
abundance *n* 充足 chung juk
abundant *a* 充足嘅 chung juk geh
abuse *v.t.* 虐待 yeurk doy
abuse *n* 濫用 larm yung
abusive *a* 侮辱嘅 mow yuk geh
abutted *v* 連接住 leen jeep ju
abyss *n* 深處 sam chu
academic *a* 學術嘅 hok sut geh
academy *n* 學院 hok yoon
acarpous *adj.* 無果嘅植物 mow gwor geh jik mat
accede *v.t.* 同意 tung yee
accelerate *v.t* 加速 ga chuk
acceleration *n* 加速 ga chuk
accent *n* 口音 ho yam
accent *v.t* 強調 keurng diew
accept & 接受 jeep sow
acceptable *a* 可以接受 hor yi jeep sow
acceptance *n* 接受 jeep sow
access *n* 用 yung
accession *n* 就任 jow yam
accessory *n* 飾物 sik mat
accident *n* 意外 yee ngoy
accidental *a* 唔小心 hm siew sam
acclaim *v.t* 讚 jan
acclaim *n* 讚 jan
acclamation *n* 歡呼 fwun fu
acclimatise *v.t* 適應 sik ying
accommodate *v.t* 容納 yung lap
accommodation *n.* 住宿 ju suk
accompaniment *n* 伴奏 bwun jow
accompany *v.t.* 伴 bwun
accomplice *n* 伴 bwun
accomplish *v.t.* 搞掂 gao deem
accomplished *a* 搞掂咗 gao deem jor
accomplishment *n.* 成就 sing

jow

accord *v.t.* 符合 fu hap
accord *n.* 一致 yat jee
accordingly *adv.* 按照 on jiew
account *n.* 戶口 wu ho
account *v.t.* 講明 gorng ming
accountable *a* 有責任 yow jak yam
accountancy *n.* 會計 wuy gey
accountant *n.* 會計師 wuy gey see
accredit *v.t.* 委任 way yam
accrementition *n* 增長 jang jeurng
accrete *v.t.* 增加 jang ga
accrue *v.i.* 增值 jang jik
accumulate *v.t.* 積累 jik luy
accumulation *n* 積累緊 jik luy gan
accuracy *n.* 準確性 jun kok sing
accurate *a.* 準確 jun kok
accursed *a.* 被詛咒嘅 bay juy jow geh
accusation *n* 控告 hung gow
accuse *v.t.* 控告 hung gow
accused *n.* 被人告 bay yan gow
accustom *v.t.* 習慣 jap gwan
accustomed *a.* 慣咗 gwan jor
ace *n* 高手 gow sow
acentric *adj* 唔正常 hm jing seurng
acephalous *adj.* 無首領嘅 mo sow ling geh
acephalus *n.* 無頭 mo tow
acetify *v.* 醋化 cho far
ache *n.* 痛 tung
ache *v.i.* 痛 tung
achieve *v.t.* 實現 yeen sat
achievement *n.* 成就 sing jow
achromatic *adj* 無色嘅 mo sik geh
acid *a* 酸味 shoon may

acid *n* 酸 shoon
acidity *n.* 酸性 shoon sing
acknowledge *v.* 承認 sing ying
acknowledgement *n.* 承認 sing ying
acne *n* 粉刺 fan tee
acorn *n.* 橡果 jeurng gwor
acoustic *a* 原聲 yoon seng
acoustics *n.* 音效 yam hao
acquaint *v.t.* 瞭解 liew gai
acquaintance *n.* 識嘅人 sik geh yan
acquest *n* 攞到 lor dow
acquiesce *v.i.* 順從 sun chuung
acquiescence *n.* 默然接受 mak yeen jeep sow
acquire *v.t.* 要 yiew
acquirement *n.* 需要嘅嘢 suy yiew geh yeh
acquisition *n.* 得到 dak dow
acquit *v.t.* 判無罪 pwun mow juy
acquittal *n.* 被判無罪 bay pwun mow juy
acre *n.* 英畝 ying mow
acreage *n.* 大幅田地 dai fuk teen day
acrimony *n* 尖刻嘅說話 jeem hak geh shoot wah
acrobat *n.* 雜技師 jap gey see
across *adv.* 橫過 wang gwor
across *prep.* 對面 duy meen
act *n.* 行爲 hang way
act *v.i.* 演 yeen
acting *n.* 演技 yeen gey
action *n.* 動作 dung jok
activate *v.t.* 開動 hoy dung
active *a.* 活躍 wut yeurk
activity *n.* 活動 wut dung
actor *n.* 演員 yeen yoon
actress *n.* 女演員 luy yeen yoon
actual *a.* 真正嘅 tan ting geh
actually *adv.* 其實 key sat

acumen *n.* 敏銳 man yuy
acute *a.* 嚴重 yeem jung
adage *n.* 格言 gak yeen
adamant *a.* 堅決 geen koot
adamant *n.* 堅決 geen koot
adapt *v.t.* 適應 sik ying
adaptation *n.* 改編嘅 goy peen geh
adays *adv* 日頭 yat tow
add *v.t.* 加 ga
addict *v.t.* 上癮 seurng yan
addict *n.* 上癮者 seurng yan jeh
addiction *n.* 癮 yan
addition *n.* 加上 ga seurng
additional *a.* 加上 ga seurng
addle *adj* 糊涂 wu tow
address *v.t.* 稱呼 ting fu
address *n.* 地址 day jee
addressee *n.* 收件人 sow geen yan
adduce *v.t.* 舉出 kuy chut
adept *n.* 擅長 seen cheurng
adept *a.* 熟練 suk leen
adequacy *n.* 恰當 hap dong
adequate *a.* 適合 sik hap
adhere *v.i.* 遵守 jun sow
adherence *n.* 遵守 jun sow
adhesion *n.* 黐住 tee ju
adhesive *n.* 膠水 gao suy
adhesive *a.* 黐 tee
adhibit *v.t.* 引入 yan yap
adieu *n.* 再見 joy geen
adieu *interj.* 再見 joy geen
adjacent *a.* 隔籬 gak lay
adjective *n.* 形容詞 ying yung tee
adjoin *v.t.* 連埋 leen mai
adjourn *v.t.* 押後 at ho
adjournment *n.* 延期 yeen kay
adjudge *v.t.* 裁定 choy ding
adjunct *n.* 附屬 fu suk
adjure *v.t.* 命令 ming ling
adjuration *n* 懇求 han ko

adjust *v.t.* 調整 tiew jing

adjustment *n.* 調整 tiew jing

administer *v.t.* 掌管 jeung gwun

administration *n.* 行政 hang jing

administrative *a.* 行政嘅 hang jing geh

administrator *n.* 行政人員 hang jing yan yoon

admirable *a.* 令人欣賞 ling yan yan seurng

admiral *n.* 司令 see ling

admiration *n.* 欣賞 yan seurng

admire *v.t.* 欣賞 yan seurng

admissible *a.* 可以接受 hor yi jeep sow

admission *n.* 收 sow

admit *v.t.* 承認 sing yan

admittance *n.* 入去 yap huy

admonish *v.t.* 責怪 jak gwai

admonition *n.* 警告 ging gow

adnascent *adj.* 寄生 gey sang

ado *n.* 事 see

adobe *n.* 黏土 leem tow

adolescence *n.* 青春期 ting chun kay

adolescent *a.* 青少年 ting siew leen

adopt *v.t.* 收養 sow yeurng

adoption *n* 收養 sow yeurng

adorable *a.* 可愛 hor ngoy

adoration *n.* 愛慕 ngoy mo

adore *v.t.* 愛 ngoy

adorn *v.t.* 裝扮 jorng ban

adscititious *adj* 後天性 ho teen sing

adscript *adj.* 後寫 ho seh

adulation *n* 奉承 fung sing

adult *a* 成熟 sing suk

adult *n.* 成年人 sing leen yan

adulterate *v.t.* 溝咗嘢 kow jor yeh

adulteration *n.* 溝嘢 kow yeh

adultery *n.* 通姦 tung garn

advance *v.t.* 進攻 jun gung

advance *n.* 預先 yu seen

advancement *n.* 晉升 jun sing

advantage *n.* 好處 ho chu

advantage *v.t.* 有利 yow lay

advantageous *a.* 着數 jerk sow

advent *n.* 出現 chut yeen

adventure *n* 冒險 mo heem

adventurous *a.* 大膽 dai dam

adverb *n.* 副詞 fu tee

adverbial *a.* 副詞嘅 fu tee geh

adversary *n.* 對手 duy sow

adverse *a* 不利 bat lay

adversity *n.* 困境 kwun ging

advert *v.* 廣告 gworng gow

advertise *v.t.* 推廣 tuy gworng

advertisement *n* 廣告 gworng gow

advice *n* 意見 yee geen

advisable *a.* 適宜 sik yee

advisability *n* 適當性 sik dong sing

advise *v.t.* 畀意見 bay yee geen

advocacy *n.* 支持 jee tee

advocate *n* 辯方律師 been forng lut see

advocate *v.t.* 支持 jee tee

aerial *a.* 空中嘅 hung jung geh

aerial *n.* 天線 teen seen

aeriform *adj.* 無形嘅 mo ying geh

aerify *v.t.* 氣體化 hey tay far

aerodrome *n* 機場 gey cheurng

aeronautics *n.pl.* 航空學 horn hung hok

aeroplane *n.* 飛機 fay gey

aesthetic *a.* 美學嘅 may hok geh

aesthetics *n.pl.* 美感 may gam

aestival *adj* 夏天嘅 har teen geh

afar *adv.* 遠 yoon

affable *a.* 好好人士 ho ho yan see

affair *n.* 婚外情 fan ngoy ting

affect *v.t.* 影響 ying heurng

affectation *n* 扮晒嘢 ban sai yeh
affection *n.* 感情 gam ting
affectionate *a.* 深情嘅 sam ting geh
affidavit *n* 誓章 say jeurng
affiliation *n.* 關係 gwan hay
affinity *n* 密切嘅關係 mat teet geh gwan hay
affirm *v.t.* 肯定 hang ding
affirmation *n* 證實 ting sat
affirmative *a* 肯定嘅 hang ding geh
affix *v.t.* 貼住 teep ju
afflict *v.t.* 折磨 jeet mor
affliction *n.* 痛苦 tung fu
affluence *n.* 富裕 fu yu
affluent *a.* 有錢 yow cheen
afford *v.t.* 負擔 fu dam
afforest *v.t.* 綠化 luk far
affray *n* 爭執 jang jap
affront *v.t.* 侮辱 mo yuk
affront *n* 侮辱 mo yuk
afield *adv.* 遠處 yoon chu
aflame *adv.* 燒緊 siew gan
afloat *adv.* 浮住 fow ju
afoot *adv.* 進行緊 jun hang gan
afore *prep.* 之前 jee teen
afraid *a.* 驚 geng
afresh *adv.* 重新 chung san
after *prep.* 之後 jee ho
after *adv* 後來 ho lay
after *conj.* 以後 yee ho
after *a* 後 ho
afterwards *adv.* 之後 ji ho
again *adv.* 再 joy
against *prep.* 反對 fan duy
agamist *n* 未婚人世 may fan yan see
agape *adv., 擘大個口 mak dai gor ho
agaze *adv* 望住 mong ju
age *n.* 年齡 leen ling

aged *a.* 老咗 lo jor
agency *n.* 代理處 doy lay chu
agenda *n.* 議程表 yee ting biew
agent *n* 經紀人 ging gey yan
aggravate *v.t.* 激嬲 gik lo
aggravation *n.* 激嬲 gik lo
aggregate *v.t.* 總數 jung so
aggression *n* 攻擊性 gung gik sing
aggressive *a.* 霸道 ba dow
aggressor *n.* 侵略者 tam leurk jeh
aggrieve *v.t.* 受委屈 sow way wat
aghast *a.* 嚇到傻咗 hak dow sor jor
agile *a.* 敏捷 man jeet
agility *n.* 敏捷度 man jeet dow
agitate *v.t.* 激動 gik dung
agitation *n* 憂慮 yow luy
agist *v.t.* 照顧馬匹 jiew gu ma pat
aglow *adv.* 發光 fat gwong
ago *adv.* 之前 jee teen
agog *adj.* 渴望 hot mong
agonist *n* 興奮劑 hing fan jay
agonize *v.t.* 苦悶 fu mun
agony *n.* 痛苦 tung fu
agronomy *n.* 農學 lung hok
agoraphobia *n.* 懼曠症 guy kwong jing
agrarian *a.* 農業嘅 lung yeep geh
agree *v.i.* 同意 tung yee
agreeable *a.* 可以接受 hor yi jeep sow
agreement *n.* 協議書 heep yee shu
agricultural *a* 農業嘅 lung yeep geh
agriculture *n* 農業 lung yeep
agriculturist *n.* 農業家 lung yeep ga
ague *n* 發冷 fat lang
ahead *adv.* 前面 teen meen
aheap *adv* 堆積嘅 duy jik geh

aid *n* 援助 woon jor
aid *v.t* 幫助 bong jor
aigrette *n* 白鷺 bak lo
ail *v.t.* 困擾 kwun yiew
ailment *n.* 小病 siew beng
aim *n.* 目標 muk biew
aim *v.i.* 瞄準 miew jun
air *n* 空氣 hung hey
aircraft *n.* 飛機 fay gey
airy *a.* 空氣流通 hung hey low tung
ajar *adv.* 半開 bun hoy
akin *a.* 類似 luy tee
alacrious *adj* 興奮 hing fan
alacrity *n.* 爽快 song fai
alamort *adj.* 去死 huy sey
alarm *n* 警報 ging bo
alarm *v.t* 驚動 ging dung
alas *interj.* 唉 ay
albeit *conj.* 就算 jow shoon
albion *n* 英國 ying gwok
album *n.* 專輯 joon tap
albumen *n* 蛋白 dan bak
alchemy *n.* 煉金術 leen gam sut
alcohol *n.* 酒精 jow jing
ale *n* 麥芽啤酒 mak ngar beh jow
alegar *n* 麥芽醋 mak ngar cho
alert *a.* 警覺 ging gok
alertness *n.* 警覺性 ging gok sing
algebra *n.* 代數 doy sing
alias *n.* 化名 far meng
alias *adv.* 化名 far meng
alibi *n.* 不在場證據 bat joy cheurng jing guy
alien *a.* 外國人 ngoy gwok yan
alienate *v.t.* 疏遠 sor yoon
aliferous *adj.* 有翼嘅 yow yik geh
alight *v.i.* 燒緊 siew gan
align *v.t.* 對齊 duy chay
alignment *n.* 形成直線 ying sing jik seen
alike *a.* 相同 seurng tung

alike *adv* 差唔多 cha hm dor
aliment *n.* 營養 ying yeurng
alimony *n.* 贍養費 seen yeurng fey
aliquot *n.* 徐得盡 chuy dak jun
alive *a* 在生 joy sang
alkali *n* 鹼 gan
all *a.* 全部 choon bo
all *n* 一切 yat chai
all *adv* 完全 yoon choon
all *pron* 所有 sor yow
allay *v.t.* 減輕 garm heng
allegation *n.* 指控 jee hung
allege *v.t.* 聲稱 sing ting
allegiance *n.* 忠誠 jung sing
allegorical *a.* 有意義嘅 yow yee yee geh
allegory *n.* 寓意 yu yee
allergy *n.* 敏感 man gam
alleviate *v.t.* 減輕 gam heng
alleviation *n.* 減輕 gam heng
alley *n.* 小巷 siew hong
alliance *n.* 聯盟 loon mang
alligator *n* 鈍吻鱷 dun man ok
alliterate *v.* 押頭韻 at tow wan
alliteration *n.* 押頭韻 at tow wan
allocate *v.t.* 分配 fan puy
allocation *n.* 分配到嘅嘢 fan puy dow geh yeh
allot *v.t.* 分配 fan puy
allotment *n.* 份 fan
allow *v.t.* 準 jun
allowance *n.* 津貼 jun teep
alloy *n.* 合金 hap gam
allude *v.i.* 暗示 am see
allure *v.t.* 誘惑 yow wak
allurement *n* 誘惑 yow wak
allusion *n* 暗示 am see
allusive *a.* 暗指 am jee
ally *v.t.* 結盟 geet mang
ally *n.* 盟國 mang gwok
almanac *n.* 通勝 tung sing
almighty *a.* 全能嘅 choon lang

ENGLISH-CANTONESE

About this Dictionary

Developments in science and technology today have narrowed down distances between countries, and have made the world a small place. A person living thousands of miles away can learn and understand the culture and lifestyle of another country with ease and without travelling to that country. Languages play an important role as facilitators of communication in this respect.

To promote such an understanding, **ibs BOOKS (UK)** has planned to bring out a series of bilingual dictionaries in which important English words have been translated into other languages, with Roman transliteration in case of languages that have different scripts. This is a humble attempt to bring people of the world closer through the medium of language, thus making communication easy and convenient.

These dictionaries have been compiled and edited by teachers and scholars of relative languages.

Bilingual Dictionaries in this Series

English-Arabic/Arabic-English	Rania-al-Qass
English-Bengali/Bengali-English	Amit Majumdar
English-Cantonese/Cantonese-English	Nisa Yang
English-Dari/Dari-English	Amir Khan
English-Farsi/Farsi-English	Maryam Zamankhani
English-Gujarati/Gujarati-English	Sujata Basaria
English-Hindi/Hindi-English	Sudhakar Chaturvedi
English-Hungarian/Hungarian-English	Lucy Mallows
English-Lithuanian/Lithuanian-English	Regina Kazakeviciute
English-Nepali/Nepali-English	Anil Mandal
English-Punjabi/Punjabi-English	Teja Singh Chatwal
English-Pashto/Pashto-English	Amir Khan
English-Polish/Polish-English	Magdalena Herok
English-Romanian/Romanian-English	Georgeta Laura Dutulescu
English-Somali/Somali-English	Ali Mohamud Omer
English-Tamil/Tamil-English	Sandhya Mahadevan
English-Turkish/Turkish-English	Nagme Yazgin
English-Urdu/Urdu-English	S.A Rahman

More languages in print

ibs BOOKS (UK)
London W1T 5NW (UK)

A

a *a.* 一 yat
aback *adv.* 向後 heurng ho
abaction *n* 強搶 keurng cheurng
abactor *n* 強搶者 keurng cheurng jeh
abandon *v.t.* 遺棄 way hey
abase *v.t.* 踩低 tai day
abasement *n* 踩低 tai day
abash *v.t.* 慚愧 tarm kwai
abate *v.t.* 減低 garm day
abatement *n.* 減低 garm day
abbey *n.* 寺院 ji yoon
abbreviate *v.t.* 簡稱 gan ting
abbreviation *n* 簡稱 gan ting
abdicate *v.t,* 放棄 forng hay
abdication *n* 放棄 forng hay
abdomen *n* 腹部 fuk bo
abdominal *a.* 腹部嘅 fuk bo geh
abduct *v.t.* 拐走 gwai jow
abduction *n* 綁架 borng ga
abed *adv.* 喺床度 hay chorng dow
aberrance *n.* 唔正常 hm jing seurng
abet *v.t.* 唆擺 sor bai
abetment *n.* 唆擺 sor bai
abeyance *n.* 擱置 gok ji
abhor *v.t.* 憎 jang
abhorrence *n.* 痛恨 tung han
abide *v.i* 容忍 yung yan
abiding *a* 永恆嘅 wing han geh
ability *n* 能力 lang lik
abject *a.* 賤格 jeen gak
ablactate *v. t* 戒奶 gai lai
ablactation *n* 戒奶 gai lai
ablaze *adv.* 着火 jeurk for
able *a* 可以 hor yi
ablepsy *n* 盲 mang
ablush *adv* 面紅 meen hung
ablution *n* 沐浴 muk yuk

abnegate *v. t* 否認 fow ying
abnegation *n* 否認 fow ying
abnormal *a* 唔正常 hm jing seurng
aboard *adv* 上咗 seurng jor
abode *n* 住所 ju sor
abolish *v.t* 廢除 fay chuy
abolition *v* 廢除 fay chuy
abominable *a* 討厭 tow yeem
aboriginal *a* 本地 bwun day
aborigines *n. pl* 原住民 yoon ju man
abort *v.i* 終止 jung jee
abortion *n* 墮胎 dor toy
abortive *adv* 失敗 sat bai
abound *v.i.* 有好多 yow ho dor
about *adv* 大概 dai koy
about *prep* 關於 gwan yu
above *adv* 以上 yee seurng
above *prep.* 上面 seurng meen
abreast *adv* 並肩 bing geen
abridge *v.t* 縮短 suk doon
abridgement *n* 摘要 jak yiew
abroad *adv* 出國 chut gwok
abrogate *v. t.* 廢除 fay chuy
abrupt *a* 突然間 dak yeen gan
abruption *n* 中斷 jung toon
abscess *n* 膿腫 lung jung
absonant *adj* 唔一致 hm yat jee
abscond *v.i* 逃走 tow jow
absence *n* 缺席 koot tik
absent *a* 缺席 koot tik
absent *v.t* 缺席 koot tik
absolute *a* 絕對 joot duy
absolutely *adv* 絕對 joot duy
absolve *v.t* 解除 gai chuy
absorb *v.t* 吸收 kap sow
abstain *v.i.* 戒 gai
abstract *a* 抽象 tow jeurng
abstract *n* 摘要 jak yiew
abstract *v.t* 抽出 tow chut
abstraction *n.* 抽象嘅概念 tow

jeurng geh koy leem

absurd *a* 荒謬 forng mow

absurdity *n* 荒謬 forng mow

abundance *n* 充足 chung juk

abundant *a* 充足嘅 chung juk geh

abuse *v.t.* 虐待 yeurk doy

abuse *n* 濫用 larm yung

abusive *a* 侮辱嘅 mow yuk geh

abutted *v* 連接住 leen jeep ju

abyss *n* 深處 sam chu

academic *a* 學術嘅 hok sut geh

academy *n* 學院 hok yoon

acarpous *adj.* 無果嘅植物 mow gwor geh jik mat

accede *v.t.* 同意 tung yee

accelerate *v.t* 加速 ga chuk

acceleration *n* 加速 ga chuk

accent *n* 口音 ho yam

accent *v.t* 強調 keurng diew

accept & 接受 jeep sow

acceptable *a* 可以接受 hor yi jeep sow

acceptance *n* 接受 jeep sow

access *n* 用 yung

accession *n* 就任 jow yam

accessory *n* 飾物 sik mat

accident *n* 意外 yee ngoy

accidental *a* 唔小心 hm siew sam

acclaim *v.t* 讚 jan

acclaim *n* 讚 jan

acclamation *n* 歡呼 fwun fu

acclimatise *v.t* 適應 sik ying

accommodate *v.t* 容納 yung lap

accommodation *n.* 住宿 ju suk

accompaniment *n* 伴奏 bwun jow

accompany *v.t.* 伴 bwun

accomplice *n* 伴 bwun

accomplish *v.t.* 搞掂 gao deem

accomplished *a* 搞掂咗 gao deem jor

accomplishment *n.* 成就 sing

jow

accord *v.t.* 符合 fu hap

accord *n.* 一致 yat jee

accordingly *adv.* 按照 on jiew

account *n.* 戶口 wu ho

account *v.t.* 講明 gorng ming

accountable *a* 有責任 yow jak yam

accountancy *n.* 會計 wuy gey

accountant *n.* 會計師 wuy gey see

accredit *v.t.* 委任 way yam

accrementition *n* 增長 jang jeurng

accrete *v.t.* 增加 jang ga

accrue *v.i.* 增值 jang jik

accumulate *v.t.* 積累 jik luy

accumulation *n* 積累緊 jik luy gan

accuracy *n.* 準確性 jun kok sing

accurate *a.* 準確 jun kok

accursed *a.* 被詛咒嘅 bay juy jow geh

accusation *n* 控告 hung gow

accuse *v.t.* 控告 hung gow

accused *n.* 被人告 bay yan gow

accustom *v.t.* 習慣 jap gwan

accustomed *a.* 慣咗 gwan jor

ace *n* 高手 gow sow

acentric *adj* 唔正常 hm jing seurng

acephalous *adj.* 無首領嘅 mo sow ling geh

acephalus *n.* 無頭 mo tow

acetify *v.* 醋化 cho far

ache *n.* 痛 tung

ache *v.i.* 痛 tung

achieve *v.t.* 實現 yeen sat

achievement *n.* 成就 sing jow

achromatic *adj* 無色嘅 mo sik geh

acid *a* 酸味 shoon may

acid *n* 酸 shoon
acidity *n.* 酸性 shoon sing
acknowledge *v.* 承認 sing ying
acknowledgement *n.* 承認 sing ying
acne *n* 粉刺 fan tee
acorn *n.* 橡果 jeurng gwor
acoustic *a* 原聲 yoon seng
acoustics *n.* 音效 yam hao
acquaint *v.t.* 瞭解 liew gai
acquaintance *n.* 識嘅人 sik geh yan
acquest *n* 攞到 lor dow
acquiesce *v.i.* 順從 sun chuung
acquiescence *n.* 默然接受 mak yeen jeep sow
acquire *v.t.* 要 yiew
acquirement *n.* 需要嘅嘢 suy yiew geh yeh
acquisition *n.* 得到 dak dow
acquit *v.t.* 判無罪 pwun mow juy
acquittal *n.* 被判無罪 bay pwun mow juy
acre *n.* 英畝 ying mow
acreage *n.* 大幅田地 dai fuk teen day
acrimony *n* 尖刻嘅說話 jeem hak geh shoot wah
acrobat *n.* 雜技師 jap gey see
across *adv.* 橫過 wang gwor
across *prep.* 對面 duy meen
act *n.* 行爲 hang way
act *v.i.* 演 yeen
acting *n.* 演技 yeen gey
action *n.* 動作 dung jok
activate *v.t.* 開動 hoy dung
active *a.* 活躍 wut yeurk
activity *n.* 活動 wut dung
actor *n.* 演員 yeen yoon
actress *n.* 女演員 luy yeen yoon
actual *a.* 真正嘅 tan ting geh
actually *adv.* 其實 key sat

acumen *n.* 敏銳 man yuy
acute *a.* 嚴重 yeem jung
adage *n.* 格言 gak yeen
adamant *a.* 堅決 geen koot
adamant *n.* 堅決 geen koot
adapt *v.t.* 適應 sik ying
adaptation *n.* 改編嘅 goy peen geh
adays *adv* 日頭 yat tow
add *v.t.* 加 ga
addict *v.t.* 上癮 seurng yan
addict *n.* 上癮者 seurng yan jeh
addiction *n.* 癮 yan
addition *n.* 加上 ga seurng
additional *a.* 加上 ga seurng
addle *adj* 糊涂 wu tow
address *v.t.* 稱呼 ting fu
address *n.* 地址 day jee
addressee *n.* 收件人 sow geen yan
adduce *v.t.* 舉出 kuy chut
adept *n.* 擅長 seen cheurng
adept *a.* 熟練 suk leen
adequacy *n.* 恰當 hap dong
adequate *a.* 適合 sik hap
adhere *v.i.* 遵守 jun sow
adherence *n.* 遵守 jun sow
adhesion *n.* 黐住 tee ju
adhesive *n.* 膠水 gao suy
adhesive *a.* 黐 tee
adhibit *v.t.* 引入 yan yap
adieu *n.* 再見 joy geen
adieu *interj.* 再見 joy geen
adjacent *a.* 隔籬 gak lay
adjective *n.* 形容詞 ying yung tee
adjoin *v.t.* 連埋 leen mai
adjourn *v.t.* 押後 at ho
adjournment *n.* 延期 yeen kay
adjudge *v.t.* 裁定 choy ding
adjunct *n.* 附屬 fu suk
adjure *v.t.* 命令 ming ling
adjuration *n* 懇求 han ko

adjust *v.t.* 調整 tiew jing
adjustment *n.* 調整 tiew jing
administer *v.t.* 掌管 jeung gwun
administration *n.* 行政 hang jing
administrative *a.* 行政嘅 hang jing geh
administrator *n.* 行政人員 hang jing yan yoon
admirable *a.* 令人欣賞 ling yan yan seurng
admiral *n.* 司令 see ling
admiration *n.* 欣賞 yan seurng
admire *v.t.* 欣賞 yan seurng
admissible *a.* 可以接受 hor yi jeep sow
admission *n.* 收 sow
admit *v.t.* 承認 sing yan
admittance *n.* 入去 yap huy
admonish *v.t.* 責怪 jak gwai
admonition *n.* 警告 ging gow
adnascent *adj.* 寄生 gey sang
ado *n.* 事 see
adobe *n.* 黏土 leem tow
adolescence *n.* 青春期 ting chun kay
adolescent *a.* 青少年 ting siew leen
adopt *v.t.* 收養 sow yeurng
adoption *n* 收養 sow yeurng
adorable *a.* 可愛 hor ngoy
adoration *n.* 愛慕 ngoy mo
adore *v.t.* 愛 ngoy
adorn *v.t.* 裝扮 jorng ban
adscititious *adj* 後天性 ho teen sing
adscript *adj.* 後寫 ho seh
adulation *n* 奉承 fung sing
adult *a* 成熟 sing suk
adult *n.* 成年人 sing leen yan
adulterate *v.t.* 溝咗嘢 kow jor yeh
adulteration *n.* 溝嘢 kow yeh
adultery *n.* 通姦 tung garn

advance *v.t.* 進攻 jun gung
advance *n.* 預先 yu seen
advancement *n.* 晉升 jun sing
advantage *n.* 好處 ho chu
advantage *v.t.* 有利 yow lay
advantageous *a.* 着數 jerk sow
advent *n.* 出現 chut yeen
adventure *n* 冒險 mo heem
adventurous *a.* 大膽 dai dam
adverb *n.* 副詞 fu tee
adverbial *a.* 副詞嘅 fu tee geh
adversary *n.* 對手 duy sow
adverse *a* 不利 bat lay
adversity *n.* 困境 kwun ging
advert *v.* 廣告 gworng gow
advertise *v.t.* 推廣 tuy gworng
advertisement *n* 廣告 gworng gow
advice *n* 意見 yee geen
advisable *a.* 適宜 sik yee
advisability *n* 適當性 sik dong sing
advise *v.t.* 畀意見 bay yee geen
advocacy *n.* 支持 jee tee
advocate *n* 辯方律師 been forng lut see
advocate *v.t.* 支持 jee tee
aerial *a.* 空中嘅 hung jung geh
aerial *n.* 天線 teen seen
aeriform *adj.* 無形嘅 mo ying geh
aerify *v.t.* 氣體化 hey tay far
aerodrome *n* 機場 gey cheurng
aeronautics *n.pl.* 航空學 horn hung hok
aeroplane *n.* 飛機 fay gey
aesthetic *a.* 美學嘅 may hok geh
aesthetics *n.pl.* 美感 may gam
aestival *adj* 夏天嘅 har teen geh
afar *adv.* 遠 yoon
affable *a.* 好好人士 ho ho yan see
affair *n.* 婚外情 fan ngoy ting
affect *v.t.* 影響 ying heurng

geh

almond *n.* 杏仁 hang yan
almost *adv.* 差唔多 cha hm dor
alms *n.* 救濟品 gao jay ban
aloft *adv.* 喺上面 hay seurng meen
alone *a.* 自己 jee gey
along *adv.* 一齊 yat chai
along *prep.* 順住 sun ju
aloof *adv.* 冷淡 lang dam
aloud *adv.* 大聲 dai seng
alp *n.* 高山 go san
alpha *n* 阿爾法 ah yee fat
alphabet *n.* 字母 jee mo
alphabetical *a.* 字母順序 jee mo sun juy
alpinist *n* 爬山家 pa san ga
already *adv.* 已經 yee ging
also *adv.* 而且 yee cher
altar *n.* 祭壇 jay tan
alter *v.t.* 改 goy
alteration *n* 修改 sow goy
altercation *n.* 爭論 jang lun
alternate *a.* 輪流 lun low
alternate *v.t.* 輪流 lun low
alternative *n.* 代替品 doy tay ban
alternative *a.* 代替 doy tay
although *conj.* 雖然 suy yeen
altimeter *n* 高度計 go dow gey
altitude *n.* 海拔 hoy bat
alto *n* 女低音 luy day yam
altogether *adv.* 一齊 yat chai
aluminate *n.* 鋁酸鹽 luy shoon yeem
aluminium *n.* 鋁 luy
alumna *n* 女畢業生 luy bat yeep sang
always *adv* 成日 sing yat
alveary *n* 蜂竇 fung dow
alvine *adj.* 腸嘅 cheurng geh
am 係 hay
amalgam *n* 混合體 wan hap tay
amalgamate *v.t.* 合併 hap ping

amalgamation *n* 合併 hap ping
amass *v.t.* 累積 luy jik
amateur *n.* 業餘愛好者 yeep yu ngoy ho jeh
amatory *adj* 戀愛嘅 loon ngoy geh
amaurosis *n* 黑內障 hak loy jeurng
amaze *v.t.* 驚奇 ging kay
amazement *n.* 驚奇 ging kay
ambassador *n.* 大使 dai see
amberite *n.* 琥珀炸藥 fu pak ja yeurk
ambient *adj.* 周圍嘅 jow way geh
ambiguity *n.* 模糊 mow wu
ambiguous *a.* 模糊 mow wu
ambition *n.* 理想 lay seurng
ambitious *a.* 恆心 hang sam
ambry *n.* 櫃 gway
ambulance *n.* 救護車 gao wu cher
ambulant *adj* 可以喐 hor yee yuk
ambulate *v.t* 行 hang
ambush *n.* 埋伏 mai fuk
ameliorate *v.t.* 改良 goy leurng
amelioration *n.* 改良 goy leurng
amen *interj.* 阿門 ah mun
amenable *a* 順從 sun chung
amend *v.t.* 修改 sow goy
amendment *n.* 修改 sow goy
amends *n.pl.* 修改 sow goy
amenorrhoea *n* 月經不調 yoot ging bat tiew
amiability *n.* 親切性 tan teet sing
amiable *a.* 平易近人 ping yee gan yan
amicable *adj.* 心平氣和 sam ping hay wor
amid *prep.* 中 jung
amiss *adv.* 唔正常 hm jing seurng
amity *n.* 和睦 wor muk
ammunition *n.* 彈藥 dan yeurk
amnesia *n* 失憶 sat yik
amnesty *n.* 大赦 dai she

among *prep.* 之中 jee jung
amongst *prep.* 之中 jee jung
amoral *a.* 唔遵守道德 hm jun sow dow dak
amount *n* 數額 sow ak
amount *v.i* 總計 jung gey
amount *v.* 等於 dang yu
amorous *a.* 性慾 sing yuk
amour *n* 私情 see ting
ampere *n* 安(培) on (puy)
amphibious *adj* 水陸兩棲 suy luk leurng chay
amphitheatre *n* 古羅馬劇場 gu lor ma kek cheurng
ample *a.* 足夠 juk gow
amplification *n* 擴大 kwong dai
amplifier *n* 擴音器 kwong yam hey
amplify *v.t.* 放大 fong dai
amuck *adv.* 癲狂 deem kwong
amulet *n.* 護身符 wu san fu
amuse *v.t.* 氹人 tam yan
amusement *n* 娛樂 yu lok
an *art* 一 yat
anabaptism *n* 再洗禮 joy say lay
anachronism *n* 過晒時 gwor sai see
anaclisis *n* 依賴 yee lai
anadem *n* 花冠 far gwun
anaemia *n* 貧血 pan hoot
anaesthesia *n* 麻醉 ma juy
anaesthetic *n.* 麻醉藥 ma juy yeurk
anal *adj.* 注重小事 ju jung siew see
analogous *a.* 相似 seurng tee
analogy *n.* 比喻 bei yu
analyse *v.t.* 分析 fan sik
analysis *n.* 分析結果 fan sik geet gwor
analyst *n* 分析員 fan sik yoon
analytical *a* 分析嘅 fan sik geh

anamnesis *n* 病歷 beng lik
anamorphous *adj* 再次形成 joy tee ying sing
anarchism *n.* 無政府主義 mo ting fu ju yee
anarchist *n* 無政府主義者 mo jing fu juu yee jeh
anarchy *n* 無政府 mo jing fu
anatomy *n.* 解剖學 gai fo hook
ancestor *n.* 祖先 jo seen
ancestral *a.* 祖先嘅 jo seen geh
ancestry *n.* 祖先 jo seen
anchor *n.* 錨 mao
anchorage *n* 停泊處 ting pak chu
ancient *a.* 古老 gu low
ancon *n* 肱木 gung muk
and *conj.* 同埋 tung mai
androphagi *n.* 食人族 sik yan juk
anecdote *n.* 短故事 doon gu see
anemometer *n* 風速計 fung chuk gey
anew *adv.* 重新 chung san
anfractuous *adj* 九曲十三彎 gow kuk sap sam wan
angel *n* 天使 teen see
anger *n.* 怒火 low for
angina *n* 心絞痛 sam gao tung
angle *n.* 角度 gok dow
angle *n* 觀點 gwoon deem
angry *a.* 嬲 low
anguish *n.* 苦惱 fu lo
angular *a.* 有角嘅 yow gok geh
anigh *adv.* 近 kan
animal *n.* 動物 dung mat
animate *v.t.* 製作成動畫片 jai jok sing dung wah peen
animate *a.* 變活躍 been wut yeurk
animation *n* 動畫 dung wah
animosity *n* 仇恨 sow han
animus *n* 敵意 dik yee
aniseed *n* 洋茴香 yeurng wuy heurng

ankle *n.* 腳踝 geurt ngan
anklet *n* 腳鍊 geurt leen
annalist *n.* 史官 see gwun
annals *n.pl.* 歷史記載 lik see gey joy
annectant *adj.* 連接緊 leen jeep gen
annex *v.t.* 吞併 tun ping
annexation *n* 吞併 tun ping
annihilate *v.t.* 毀滅 way meet
annihilation *n* 毀滅 way meet
anniversary *n.* 紀念日 gey leem yat
announce *v.t.* 宣佈 shoon bo
announcement *n.* 宣佈 shoon bo
annoy *v.t.* 煩 fan
annoyance *n.* 煩惱 fan lo
annual *a.* 一年一次嘅 yat leen yat tee geh
annuitant *n* 領養老金人 ling yeurng low gam yam
annuity *n.* 養老金 yeurng low gam
annul *v.t.* 廢除 fay chuy
annulet *n* 小環 siew wan
anoint *v.t.* 搽油 cha yow
anomalous *a* 異常嘅 yee seurng geh
anomaly *n* 異常 yee seurng
anon *adv.* 好快 ho fai
anonymity *n.* 匿名 lik ming
anonymous *a.* 匿名 lik ming
another *a* 另外 ling ngoy
answer *n* 答案 dap on
answer *v.t* 回答 wuy dap
answerable *a.* 負責 fu jak
ant *n* 蟻 ay
antacid *adj.* 抗酸劑 kong shoon jay
antagonism *n* 敵意 dik yee
antagonist *n.* 敵人 dik yan
antagonize *v.t.* 對抗 duy kong
antarctic *a.* 南極 larm gik

antecede *v.t.* 存在先過 choon jor seen gwor
antecedent *n.* 前因 teen yan
antecedent *a.* 之前嘅 jee teen geh
antedate *n* 預期 yu kay
antelope *n.* 羚羊 ling yeurng
antenatal *adj.* 產前嘅 chan teen geh
antennae *n.* 觸鬚 juk so
antenuptial *adj.* 結婚前嘅 geet fan teen geh
anthem *n* 國歌 gwok gor
anthology *n.* 選集 shoon jap
anthropoid *adj.* 似人嘅猿 chee yan geh yoon
anti *pref.* 反 fan
anti-aircraft *a.* 防空 forng hung
antic *n* 蠱惑 gu wak
anticardium *n* 腹上部 fuk seurng bo
anticipate *v.t.* 預料 yu liew
anticipation *n.* 預計 yu gey
antidote *n.* 解藥 gai yeurk
antinomy *n.* 矛盾 mao tun
antipathy *n.* 反感 fan gam
antiphony *n.* 輪住唱 lun ju cheurng
antipodes *n.* 剛剛相反 gong gong seurng fan
antiquarian *a.* 古文物嘅 gu man mat geh
antiquarian *n* 古物收藏家 gu mat sow chong gar
antiquary *n.* 古物收藏家 gu mat sow chong gar
antiquated *a.* 過晒時 gwor sai see
antique *a.* 古董 gu dung
antiquity *n.* 古代 gu doy
antiseptic *n.* 防腐劑 forng fu jay
antiseptic *a.* 消過毒嘅 siew gwor duk geh
antithesis *n.* 對立 duy lap

antitheist *n* 無神論者 mow san lun jeh

antler *n.* 鹿角 luk gok

antonym *n.* 反義詞 fan yee tee

anus *n.* 肛門 gong mun

anvil *n.* 鐵砧 teet tam

anxiety *a* 憂慮 yow luy

anxious *a.* 憂慮 yow luy

any *a.* 任何 yam hor

any *adv.* 任何 yam hor

anyhow *adv.* 點都好 deem dow ho

apace *adv.* 快 fai

apart *adv.* 分開 fan hoy

apartment *n.* 單位 dan way

apathy *n.* 冷漠 lang mok

ape *n* 猿 yoon

ape *v.t.* 模仿 mo fong

aperture *n.* 孔徑 hung ging

apex *n.* 窿 lung

aphorism *n* 格言 gak yeen

apiary *n.* 養蜂場 yeurng fung cheurng

apiculture *n.* 養蜂業 yeurng fung yeep

apish *a.* 好似猿咁 ho chee yoon gam

apnoea *n* 窒息 jat sik

apologize *v.i.* 道歉 dow heep

apologue *n* 寓言 yu yeen

apology *n.* 道歉 dow heep

apostle *n.* 信徒 sun tow

apostrophe *n.* 撇號 peet ho

apotheosis *n.* 高峰 go fung

apparatus *n.* 儀器 yee hey

apparel *n.* 服裝 fuk jorng

apparel *v.t.* 裝飾 jorng sik

apparent *a.* 明顯 ming heen

appeal *n.* 上訴 seurng so

appeal *v.t.* 吸引 kap yan

appear *v.i.* 出現 chut yeen

appearance *n* 外表 ngoy biew

appease *v.t.* 安撫 on fu

appellant *n.* 上訴人 seurng so yan

append *v.t.* 附加 fu ga

appendage *n.* 附件 fu geen

appendicitis *n.* 盲腸炎 mang cheurng yeem

appendix *n.* 闌尾 lan may

appendix *n.* 附錄 fu luk

appetence *n.* 慾望 yuk mong

appetent *adj.* 渴望 hot mong

appetite *n.* 胃口 way ho

appetite *n.* 慾望 yuk mong

appetizer *n* 頭盤 tow poon

applaud *v.t.* 鼓掌 gu jeurng

applause *n.* 掌聲 jeurng sing

apple *n.* 蘋果 ping gwor

appliance *n.* 器具 hay guy

applicable *a.* 適合 sik hap

applicant *n.* 申請人 san ting yan

application *n.* 申請表 san ting biew

apply *v.t.* 申請 san ting

appoint *v.t.* 委任 way yam

appointment *n.* 預約 yu yeurk

apportion *v.t.* 分配 fan puy

apposite *adj* 適合 sik hap

apposite *a.* 恰當 hap dong

appositely *adv* 貼切 teep teet

approbate *v.t* 批准 pay jun

appraise *v.t.* 評價 ping ga

appreciable *a.* 感覺到 gam gok dow

appreciate *v.t.* 欣賞 yan seurng

appreciation *n.* 感激 gam gik

apprehend *v.t.* 拉 lai

apprehension *n.* 擔心 dam sam

apprehensive *a.* 擔心嘅 dam sam geh

apprentice *n.* 徒弟 tow day

apprise *v.t.* 通知 tung jee

approach *v.t.* 接近 jeep gan

approach *n.* 方式 fong sik

approbation *n.* 認可 ying hor

appropriate *v.t.* 盜用 dow yung

appropriate *a.* 適當 sik dong

appropriation *n.* 經費 ging fay

approval *n.* 批准 pay jun

approve *v.t.* 批准 pay jun

approximate *a.* 大概 dai koy

apricot *n.* 杏子 hang jee

appurtenance *n* 附屬物 fu suk mat

apron *n.* 圍裙 way kwun

apt *a.* 適當嘅 sik dong geh

aptitude *n.* 天賦 teen fu

aquarium *n.* 水族館 suy juk gwun

aquarius *n.* 水瓶座 suy ping jor

aqueduct *n* 輸水管 shuy suy gwun

arable *adj* 適合耕種嘅 sik hap gang jung geh

arbiter *n.* 裁判 choy pwun

arbitrary *a.* 武斷 mo doon

arbitrate *v.t.* 裁判 choy poon

arbitration *n.* 仲裁 jung choy

arbitrator *n.* 仲裁人 jung choy yan

arc *n.* 弧 wu

arcade *n* 拱廊 gung long

arch *n.* 拱 gung

arch *v.t.* 弯曲 wan kuk

arch *a* 調皮 tiew pay

archaic *a.* 古代嘅 gu doy geh

archangel *n* 天使長 teen see jeurng

archbishop *n.* 大主教 dai ju gao

archer *n* 弓箭手 gung jeen sow

architect *n.* 建築師 geen juk see

architecture *n.* 建築學 geen juk hok

archives *n.pl.* 存檔 choon dong

Arctic *n* 北極 bat gik

ardent *a.* 熱情 yeet ting

ardour *n.* 熱情 yeet ting

arduous *a.* 艱難 garn lan

area *n* 地方 day forng

areca *n* 檳榔樹 ban long shu

arefaction *n* 乾 gon

arena *n* 舞台 mo toy

argil *n* 陶土 tow tow

argue *v.t.* 嗌交 ay gao

argument *n.* 鬧交 lao gao

argute *adj* 尖叫 jeem giew

arid *adj.* 乾燥 gorn cho

aries *n* 牡羊座 muk yeurng jor

aright *adv* 正確 jing kok

aright *adv.* 啱 ngam

arise *v.i.* 出現 chut yeen

aristocracy *n.* 貴族 gway juk

aristocrat *n.* 一個貴族 yat gor gway juk

aristophanic *adj* 諷刺喜劇風 fung chee hey kek fung

arithmetic *n.* 算術 shoon sut

arithmetical *a.* 算術嘅 shoon sut geh

ark *n* 方舟 forng jow

arm *n.* 手臂 sow bay

arm *v.t.* 裝備 jorng bay

armada *n.* 艦隊 lam duy

armament *n.* 軍備 gwan bay

armature *n.* 轉子 joon jee

armistlce *n.* 休戰 yow jeen

armlet *a* 臂釧 bay choon

armour *n.* 盔甲 kway gap

armoury *n.* 軍械庫 gwan hai fu

army *n.* 軍隊 gwan duy

around *prep.* 周圍 jow wey

around *adv* 到處 dow chu

arouse *v.t.* 激起 gik hey

arraign *v.* 提審 tay sam

arrange *v.t.* 安排 on pai

arrangement *n.* 安排 on pai

arrant *n.* 衰到徹尾 suy dow cheet mey

array *v.t.* 大堆 dai duy

array *n.* 佈置 bo jee

arrears *n.pl.* 債 jai

arrest *v.t.* 拉 lai

arrest *n.* 拘留 kuy low

arrival *n.* 到達 dow dat

arrive *v.i.* 到 dow

arrogance *n.* 自大 jee day

arrogant *a.* 囂張 hiew cheurng

arrow *n* 箭 jeen

arrowroot *n.* 竹芋 juk yu

arsenal *n.* 武器 mow hay

arsenic *n* 砒霜 pay seurng

arson *n* 縱火罪 jung for juy

art *n.* 藝術 ngay sut

artery *n.* 動脈 dung mak

artful *a.* 巧妙 hao miew

arthritis *n* 關節炎 gwan jeet yeem

artichoke *n.* 朝鮮薊 tiew seen ging

article *n* 文章 man jeurng

articulate *a.* 清楚表達 ting chor biew dat

artifice *n.* 手段 sow doon

artificial *a.* 人造嘅 yan jo geh

artillery *n.* 大炮 dai pao

artisan *n.* 工匠 gung jeurng

artist *n.* 藝術家 ngay sut ga

artistic *a.* 藝術嘅 ngay sut geh

artless *a.* 天真 teen jan

as *adv.* 同...一樣 tung...yat yeurng

as *conj.* 因為 yan way

as *prep..* 做 jow

asafoetida *n.* 阿魏樹脂 ah ay shu jee

asbestos *n.* 石棉 sek meen

ascend *v.t.* 升 sing

ascent *n.* 爬高 pa go

ascertain *v.t.* 查明 cha ming

ascetic *n.* 禁慾 gam yuk

ascetic *a.* 禁慾 gam yuk

ascribe *v.t.* 歸因於 gway yan yu

ash *n.* 灰 fuy

ashamed *a.* 慚愧 tarm kway

ashore *adv.* 上岸 seurng ngon

aside *adv.* 一邊 yat been

aside *n.* 旁邊 pong been

asinine *adj.* 蠢 chun

ask *v.t.* 問 man

asleep *adv.* 瞓咗覺 fan jor gao

aspect *n.* 方面 fong meen

asperse *v.* 誹謗 fey bong

aspirant *n.* 有上進心嘅人 yow seurng jun sam geh yan

aspiration *n.* 志向 jee heurng

aspire *v.t.* 立志做 lap jee jo

ass *n.* 驢 lo

assail *v.* 攻擊 gung gik

assassin *n.* 刺客 tee hak

assassinate *v.t.* 行刺 hang tee

assassination *n* 刺殺 tee sat

assault *n.* 襲擊 jap gik

assault *v.t.* 毆打 ow da

assemble *v.t.* 招集 jiew jap

assembly *n.* 晨會 san wuy

assent *v.i.* 贊成 jan sing

assent *n.* 同意 tung yee

assert *v.t.* 肯定 hang ding

assess *v.t.* 評估 ping gu

assessment *n.* 評價 ping ga

asset *n.* 資產 jee chan

assibilate *v.* 齒音化 tee yam far

assign *v.t.* 指派 jee pay

assignee *n.* 受託人 sow tok yan

assimilate *v.* 吸收 kap sow

assimilation *n* 吸收 kap sow

assist *v.t.* 幫助 bong jor

assistance *n.* 幫助 bong jor

assistant *n.* 助手 jor sow

associate *v.t.* 聯想 loon seurng

associate *a.* 有關係嘅 yow gwan hay geh

associate *n.* 同事 tung see

association *n.* 協會 heep wuy

assoil *v.t.* 赦免 seh meen

assort *v.t.* 分類 fan luy

assuage *v.t.* 減輕 garm heng

assume *v.t.* 假設 ga cheet
assumption *n.* 假設 ga cheet
assurance *n.* 保證 bo jing
assure *v.t.* 保證 bo jing
astatic *adj.* 唔穩定 hm wan ding
asterisk *n.* 星號 sing ho
asterism *n.* 星群 sing kwun
asteroid *adj.* 小行星 siu hang sing
asthma *n.* 哮喘 hao choon
astir *adv.* 轟動 gwun dung
astonish *v.t.* 驚訝 ging ngar
astonishment *n.* 驚訝 ging ngar
astound *v.t* 令到...驚訝 ling dow...
ging ngar
astray *adv.,* 當失路 dong sat lo
astrologer *n.* 占星師 jeem sing
see
astrology *n.* 占星學 jeem sing hok
astronaut *n.* 太空人 tai hung yan
astronomer *n.* 天文學家 teen man
hok ga
astronomy *n.* 天文學 teem man
hok
asunder *adv.* 碎 suy
asylum *n* 精神病院 jing san beng
yoon
at *prep.* 喺 hay
atheism *n* 無神論 mo san lun
atheist *n* 無神論者 mo san lun jeh
athirst *adj.* 渴望 hot mong
athlete *n.* 運動員 wan dung yoon
athletic *a.* 運動型 wan dung ying
athletics *n.* 田徑運動 teen ging
wan dung
athwart *prep.* 橫過 wang gwor
atlas *n.* 地圖 day tow
atmosphere *n.* 氣氛 hey fan
atoll *n.* 環狀珊瑚島 wan jorng san
wu dow
atom *n.* 原子 yoom jee
atomic *a.* 原子嘅 yoom jee geh
atone *v.i.* 彌補 lay bo

atonement *n.* 補償 bo seurng
atrocious *a.* 殘忍 tarn yan
atrocity *n* 殘暴行爲 tarn bo hang
way
attach *v.t.* 附加 fu gar
attache *n.* 使館館員 see gwun
gwun yoon
attachment *n.* 附件 fu geen
attack *n.* 襲擊 jap gik
attack *v.t.* 襲擊 jap gik
attain *v.t.* 獲得 wok dak
attainment *n.* 成就 sing jow
attaint *v.t.* 恥辱 tee yuk
attempt *v.t.* 嘗試 seurng see
attempt *n.* 嘗試 seurng see
attend *v.t.* 出席 chut jik
attendance *n.* 出席率 chut jik lut
attendant *n.* 服務員 fuk mo yoon
attention *n.* 注意 ju yee
attentive *a.* 留心 low sam
attest *v.t.* 證實 jing sat
attire *n.* 衫 sam
attire *v.t.* 打扮 da ban
attitude *n.* 態度 tai dow
attorney *n.* 受權人 sow koon yan
attract *v.t.* 吸引 kap yan
attraction *n.* 吸引 kap yan
attractive *a.* 好靚 ho leng
attribute *v.t.* 歸因於 gway yan yu
attribute *n.* 屬性 suk sing
auction *n* 拍賣 pak mai
auction *v.t.* 拍賣 pak mai
audible *a* 聽到嘅 teng dow geh
audience *n.* 觀眾 gwoon jung
audit *n.* 審查 sam ta
audit *v.t.* 審計 sam gey
auditive *adj.* 聽覺嘅 ting gok geh
auditor *n.* 審計員 sam gey yoon
auditorium *n.* 觀眾席 gwun jung
jik
auger *n.* 螺絲鑽 luy see joon
aught *n.* 任何嘢 yam hor yeh

augment v.t. 增加 jang ga
augmentation n. 增加 jang ga
August n. 八月 bat yoot
august n 威嚴 way yeem
aunt n. 姨 yee
auriform adj. 耳狀 yee jorng
aurilave n. 洗耳器 say yee hay
aurora n 極光 gik gwong
auspicate v.t. 做好意頭嘅嘢 jo ho
  yee tow geh yeh
auspice n. 預兆 yu siew
auspicious a. 吉利嘅 gat lay geh
austere a. 樸素 pok so
authentic a. 真正嘅 tan jing geh
author n. 作者 jok jeh
authoritative a. 有權威 yow koon
  way
authority n. 權力 koon lik
authorize v.t. 批准 pay jun
autobiography n. 自傳 jee joon
autocracy n 獨裁政治 duk choy
  jing ji
autocrat n 獨裁者 duk choy jeh
autocratic a 專橫 joon wang
autograph n. 簽名 teem meng
automatic a. 自動 ji dung
automobile n. 車 cher
autonomous a 自治 jee ji
autumn n. 秋天 chow teen
auxiliary a. 輔助嘅 fu jor geh
auxiliary n. 輔助人員 fu jor yan
  yoon
avale v.t. 下降 har gong
avail v.t. 有用 yow yung
available a 得閒 dak harn
avarice n. 貪錢 tarm teen
avenge v.t. 報仇 bo sow
avenue n. 大街 dai gai
average n. 平均數 ping gwun so
average a. 平均 ping gwun
average v.t. 平均爲 ping gwun
  way

averse a. 反對做 fan duy jo
aversion n. 反感 fan gam
avert v.t. 避免 bay meen
aviary n. 大雀籠 dai jeurk lung
aviation n. 航空 hong hung
aviator n. 飛機師 fey gey see
avid adj. 熱愛 yeet ngoi
avidity adv. 熱情 yeet ting
avidly adv 渴望咁 hot morn gam
avoid v.t. 避開 bay hoy
avoidance n. 避開 bay hoy
avow v.t. 聲明 sing ming
avulsion n. 撕裂 see leet
await v.t. 等緊 dang gan
awake v.t. 醒 seng
awake a 醒 seng
award v.t. 頒獎 barn jeurng
award n. 獎 jeurng
aware a. 知道 jee dow
away adv. 走 jow
awe n. 敬畏 ging way
awful a. 好衰 ho suy
awhile adv. 一陣 yat jan
awkward a. 尷尬 gam gai
axe n. 斧頭 fu tow
axis n. 軸 kuk
axle n. 車軸 cher kuk

babble n. 胡言亂語 wu yeen lun
  yu
babble v.i. 胡言亂語 wu yeen
  lun yu
babe n. 寶貝 bo bwuy
babel n 嘈雜聲 cho jap seng
baboon n. 狒狒 fut fut
baby n. BB BB
bachelor n. 單身男人 dan san
  larm yan

back *n.* 背脊 bwuy jek	**ballet** *sn.* 芭蕾舞 ba luy mo
back *adv.* 後面 how meen	**balloon** *n.* 氣球 hey kow
backbite *v.t.* 中傷 jung seurng	**ballot** *n* 選票 shoon piew
backbone *n.* 脊骨 jek gwut	**ballot** *v.i.* 無記名投票 mo gey meng tow piew
background *n.* 背景 bwuy ging	**balm** *n.* 香油 heurng yow
backhand *n.* 反手 fan sow	**balsam** *n.* 香脂 heurng jee
backslide *v.i.* 退步 tuy bo	**bam** *n.* 嘭 pang
backward *a.* 退後 tuy ho	**bamboo** *n.* 竹 juk
backward *adv.* 向後 heurng ho	**ban** *n.* 禁止 gam jee
bacon *n.* 煙肉 yeen yuk	**ban** *n* 禁令 gam ling
bacteria *n.* 細菌 sey kwun	**banal** *a.* 平凡 ping fan
bad *a.* 差 ta	**banana** *n.* 香蕉 heurng jiew
badge *n.* 徽章 fay jeurng	**band** *n.* 樂團 ngok toon
badger *n.* 獾 gwun	**bandage** ~*n.* 繃帶 bang dai
badly *adv.* 差 ta	**bandage** *v.t* 包紮 bao jat
badminton *n.* 羽毛球 yu mo kow	**bandit** *n.* 強盜 keurng dow
baffle *v.t.* 困擾 kwan yiew	**bang** *v.t.* 撞 jong
bag *n.* 袋 doy	**bang** *n.* 巨響 guy heurng
bag *v.i.* 入袋 yap doy	**bangle** *n.* 手鈪 sow ak
baggage *n.* 行李 hang lay	**banish** *v.t.* 驅逐 kuy juk
bagpipe *n.* 風笛 fung dek	**banishment** *n.* 驅逐 kuy juk
bail *n.* 保釋 bo sik	**banjo** *n.* 班卓琴 ban jeurk kam
bail *v.t.* 保釋 bo sik	**bank** *n.* 銀行 an hong
bailable *a.* 畀保釋嘅 bay bo sik geh	**bank** *v.t.* 存錢 choon teen
bailiff *n.* 執達員 jap dat yoon	**banker** *n.* 銀行家 an hong ga
bait *n* 餌 leay	**bankrupt** *n.* 破產 por tan
bait *v.t.* 放餌 forng lay	**bankruptcy** *n.* 破產 por tan
bake *v.t.* 焗 guk	**banner** *n.* 橫額 wang ak
baker *n.* 麵包師 meen bao see	**banquet** *n.* 宴會 yeen wuy
bakery *n* 餅店 beng deem	**banquet** *v.t.* 筵席 yeen jik
balance *n.* 餘額 yu ak	**bantam** *n.* 矮腳雞 doon geurt gey
balance *v.t.* 平衡 ping hang	**banter** *v.t.* 講笑 gong siew
balcony *n.* 陽台 yeurng toy	**banter** *n.* 玩笑 wun siew
bald *a.* 光頭 gwong tow	**bantling** *n.* 細路 say lo
bale *n.* 大包 dai bao	**banyan** *n.* 榕樹 yung shu
bale *v.t.* 打成大包 da sing dai bao	**baptism** *n.* 洗禮 say lay
baleful *a.* 有惡意 yow ok yee	**baptize** +*v.t.* 受洗 sow say
baleen *n.* 鯨鬚 king so	**bar** *n.* 酒吧 jow ba
ball *n.* 波 bor	**bar** *v.t* 封住 fung ju
ballad *n.* 情歌 ting gor	**barb** *n.* 倒鈎 dow oh
	barbarian *a.* 野蠻 yeh man

barbarian *n.* 野蠻人 yeh man yan

barbarism *n.* 野蠻 yeh man

barbarity *n* 殘忍 tan yan

barbarous *a.* 殘酷 tan huk

barbed *a.* 有刺 yow tee

barber *n.* 理髮師 lay fat see

bard *n.* 時人 see yan

bare *a.* 空 hung

bare *v.t.* 除 chuy

barely *adv.* 僅僅 gan gan

bargain *n.* 平貨 peng for

bargain *v.t.* 講價 gong ga

barge *n.* 駁船 bok shoon

bark *n.* 樹皮 shu pay

bark *v.t.* 吠叫聲 hoon giew seng

barley *n.* 大麥 dai mak

barn *n.* 穀倉 guk chorng

barnacles *n* 藤壺 tang wu

barometer *n* 氣壓計 hay ngat gey

barouche *n.* 馬車 ma cher

barrack *n.* 兵營 bing ying

barrage *n.* 彈幕射擊 dan mok she gik

barrator *ns.* 教唆犯 gao sor fan

barrel *n.* 桶 tung

barren *n* 不育 bat yuk

barricade *n.* 路障 lo jeurng

barrier *n.* 障礙 jeurng ngoy

barrister *n.* 大律師 dai lut see

barter1 *v.t.* 以物換物 yee mat wun mat

barter2 *n.* 交換 gao wun

barton *n.* 農場 lung cheurng

basal *adj.* 基礎 gey chor

base *n.* 根基 gan gey

base *a.* 卑鄙 bay pay

base *v.t.* 設喺 teet hay

baseless *a.* 無低 mo day

basement *n.* 地下室 day har sat

bashful *a.* 怕醜 pa cho

basic *a.* 基本 gey bwun

basil *n.* 羅勒 lor lak

basin *n.* 盆 pwun

basis *n.* 基礎 gey chor

bask *v.i.* 曬太陽 sai tai yeurng

basket *n.* 籃 larm

baslard *n.* 刀 dow

bass *n.* 男低音 larm day yam

bastard *n.* 私生子 see sang jee

bastard *a* 衰人 suy yan

bat *n* 蝙蝠 peen fuk

bat *n* 球拍 kow pak

bat *v.i* 拍 pak

batch *n* 批 pay

bath *n* 浴缸 yuk gong

bathe *v.t* 沖涼 chung leurng

baton *n* 接力棒 jeep lik pang

batsman *n.* 擊球手 gik kow so

battalion *n* 軍隊 gwan duy

battery *n* 電池 deem tee

battle *n* 戰鬥 jeen dow

battle *v.i.* 搏鬥 bok dow

bawd *n.* 妓女 gey luy

bawl *n.i.* 大喊 dai harm

bawn *n.* 圍牆 way cheurng

bay *n* 海灣 hoy wan

bayard *n.* 貝爾德 bwuy yee dak

bayonet *n* 刺刀 tee dow

be *v.t.* 存在 choon joy

be *pref.* 喺 hay

beach *n* 沙灘 sa tan

beacon *n* 燈塔 dang tap

bead *n* 珠 ju

beadle *n.* 儀仗官 yee jeurng gwun

beak *n* 鳥喙 niew

beaker *n* 燒杯 siew bwuy

beam *n* 光線 gwong seen

beam *v.i* 容光煥發 yung gwong wun fat

bean *n.* 豆 dow

bear *n* 熊 hung

bear *v.t* 承受 sing sow

beard *n* 鬍鬚 wu so

bearing *n* 方位 forng way

beast *n* 野獸 yeh so	**behalf** *n* 代表 doy biew
beastly *a* 野獸咁嘅 yeh so gam geh	**behave** *v. i.* 表現 biew yeem
beat *v. t.* 打 da	**behaviour** *n* 行為 hang way
beat *n* 拍子 pak jee	**behead** *v. t.* 斬頭 jam tow
beautiful *a* 靚 leng	**behind** *adv* 後面 ho meen
beautify *v. t* 美化 may far	**behind** *prep* 後面 ho meen
beauty *n* 美麗 mey lay	**behold** *v. t* 睇到 tay dow
beaver *n* 海狸 hoy lay	**being** *n* 生物 sang mat
because *conj.* 因為 yan way	**belabour** *v. t* 強調 keurng diew
beck *n.* 小溪 siew kay	**belated** *adj.* 遲咗嘅 tee jor geh
beckon *v.t.* 吸引 kap yan	**belch** *v. t* 打嗝 da ert
beckon *v. t* 招手 chiew so	**belch** *n* 打嗝聲 da ert seng
become *v. i* 變成 been sing	**belief** *n* 信仰 sun yeurng
becoming *a* 合適 hap sik	**believe** *v. t* 信 sun
bed *n* 床 chorng	**bell** *n* 鈴 ling
bedevil *v. t* 長期困擾 cheurng key kwan yiew	**belle** *n* 靚女 leng luy
bedding *n.* 寢具 tam guy	**bellicose** *a* 想鬥 seurng dow
bedight *v.t.* 裝飾 jorng sik	**belligerency** *n* 交戰 gao jeen
bed-time *n.* 瞓覺時間 fan gao see gan	**belligerent** *a* 好鬥 ho dow
bee *n.* 蜜蜂 mat fung	**belligerent** *n* 交戰國 gao jeen gwok
beech *n.* 山毛櫸 san mo guy	**bellow** *v. i* 呼喝 fu hot
beef *n* 牛肉 ngow yuk	**bellows** *n.* 叫聲 giew seng
beehlve *n.* 峰竇 fung dow	**belly** *n* 肚 tow
beer *n* 啤酒 beh jow	**belong** *v. i* 屬於 suk yu
beet *n* 甜菜 teem choy	**belongings** *n.* 財物 choy mat
beetle *n* 甲蟲 gap chung	**beloved** *a* 深愛嘅 sam ngoy geh
befall *v. t* 降臨到 gong lam dow	**beloved** *n* 心愛嘅人 sam ngoy geh yan
before *prep* 之前 jee teen	**below** *adv* 下面 ha meen
before *adv.* 以前 yee teen	**below** *prep* 少於 siew yu
before *conj* 之前 jee teen	**belt** *n* 皮帶 pay dai
beforehand *adv.* 事先 see seen	**belvedere** *n* 望景樓 morng ging low
befriend *v. t.* 做朋友 jo pang yow	**bemask** *v. t* 隱藏 yan chorng
beg *v. t.* 求 kow	**bemire** *v. t* 整到成身泥 jing dow sing san lay
beget *v. t* 引發 yan fat	**bemuse** *v. t* 困擾 kwan yiew
beggar *n* 乞兒 hat yee	**bench** *n* 長凳 cheurng dang
begin *n* 開始 hoy tee	**bend** *n* 彎 wan
beginning *n.* 開始 hoy tee	**bend** *v. t* 彎 wan
begird *v.t.* 圍繞 way yiew	**beneath** *adv* 下面 ha meen
beguile *v. t* 呃 ak	

beneath *prep* 下面 ha meen	**bewilder** *v. t* 混亂 wan loon
benefaction *n.* 捐款 goon fwun	**bewitch** *v.t* 迷惑 may wak
benefice *n* 聖俸 sing fung	**beyond** *prep.* 超出 tiew chut
beneficial *a* 有利嘅 yow lay geh	**beyond** *adv.* 更遠 gang yoon
benefit *n* 津貼 jun teep	**bi** *pref* 雙 seurng
benefit *v. t.* 有利於 yow lay yu	**biangular** *adj.* 雙角嘅 seurng gok
benevolence *n* 善心 seen sam	**bias** *n* 偏心 peen sam
benevolent *a* 有愛心 yow ngoy sam	**bias** *v. t* 有偏見 yow peen geen
benight *v. t* 落後 lok ho	**biaxial** *adj* 雙軸嘅 seurng kuk geh
benign *adj* 善良 seen leurng	**bibber** *n* 酒鬼 jow gway
benignly *adv* 善良咁 seen leurng gam	**bible** *n* 聖經 sing ging
benison *n* 祝福 juk fuk	**bibliography** *+n* 參考書目 tarm hao shu muk
bent *n* 彎咗 wan jor	**bibliographer** *n* 書目編著者 shu muk peen ju jeh
bequeath *v. t.* 遺留 way low	**bicentenary** *adj* 二百週年 yee bak jow leen
bereave *v. t.* 喪失 song sat	**biceps** *n* 二頭肌 yee tow gey
bereavement *n* 喪失親友 song sat tan yow	**bicker** *v. t* 拗 ai
berth *n* 鋪位 po way	**bicycle** *n.* 單車 dan cher
beside *prep.* 側邊 jak been	**bid** *v.t* 出價 chut ga
besides *prep* 徐咗 chuy jor	**bid** *n* 投標 tow biew
besides *adv* 而且 yee cher	**bidder** *n* 投家 tow ga
beslaver *v. t* 噴口水 pan ho suy	**bide** *v. t* 等 dang
besiege *v. t* 圍攻 way gung	**biennial** *adj* 兩年一次嘅 leurng leen yat chi geh
bestow *v.t* 賜贈 tee jang	**bier** *n* 棺材架 gwoon choy ga
bestrew *v. t* 散佈 san bo	**big** *a* 大 dai
bet *v.i* 賭 dow	**bigamy** *n* 重婚罪 chung fan juy
bet *n* 預計 yu gey	**bight** *n* 海灣 hoy wan
betel *n* 檳榔葉 ban long yeep	**bigot** *n* 頑固 wan gu
betray *v.t.* 背叛 bwuy bun	**bigotry** *n* 頑固 wan gu
betrayal *n* 背叛 bwuy bun	**bile** *n* 膽汁 dam jap
betroth *v. t* 許配 huy pwuy	**bilingual** *a* 雙語 seurng yu
betrothal *n.* 訂婚 ding fan	**bill** *n* 單 dan
better *a* 較好 gao ho	**billion** *n* 十億 sap yik
better *adv.* 更好 gang ho	**billow** *n* 巨浪 guy lorng
better *v. t* 叻過 lek gwor	**billow** *v.i* 大量冒出 dai leurng mo chut
betterment *n* 改善 goy seen	**biliteral** *adj* 兩個字母嘅 leurng gor jee mo geh
between *prep* 之間 jee gan	
beverage *n* 飲品 yam ban	**bilk** *v. t.* 呃 ak
bewail *v. t* 歎息 tan sik	
beware *v.i.* 提防 tay forng	

bimensal *adj* 每兩個月 mwuy leurng gor yoot

bimonthly *adj.* 隔個月嘅 gak gor yoot geh

binary *adj* 二進制 yee jun jay

bind *v.t* 綁 bong

binding *a* 必需遵守嘅 beet suy jun so geh

binocular *n.* 望遠鏡 mong yoon geng

biographer *n* 傳記作家 joon gey jok ga

biography *n* 傳記 joon gey

biologist *n* 生物學家 sang mat hok ga

biology *n* 生物學 sang mat hok

bioscope *n* 放映機 forng ying gey

biped *n* 兩足動物 leurng juk dung mat

birch *n.* 樺樹 wah shu

bird *n* 雀 jeurk

birdlime *n* 鳥膠 liew gao

birth *n.* 出生 chut sang

biscuit *n* 餅乾 beng gon

bisect *v. t* 平分 ping fan

bisexual *adj.* 雙性戀 seurng sing loon

bishop *n* 主教 ju gao

bison *n* 野牛 yeh ngow

bisque *n* 濃湯 lung tong

bit *n* 一啲 yat dee

bitch *n* 賤女人 jeen luy yan

bite *v. t.* 咬 ao

bite *n* 一啖 yat dam

bitter *a* 苦 fu

bi-weekly *adj* 兩星期一次 leurng sing kay yat tee

bizarre *adj* 奇怪 kay gwai

blab *v. t. & i* 亂嗡 loon ap

black *a* 黑色 hak sik

blacken *v. t.* 整黑 jing hak

blackmail *n* 勒索 lak sok

blackmail *v.t* 勒索 lak sok

blacksmith *n* 鐵匠 teet jeurng

bladder *n* 膀胱 pong gwong

blade *n.* 刀片 dow peen

blain *n* 水泡 suy pao

blame *v. t* 責怪 jak gwai

blame *n* 責任 jak yam

blanch *v. t. & i* 變白 been bak

bland *adj.* 無味 mo may

blank *a* 空白 hung bak

blank *n* 空格 hung gak

blanket *n* 毛氊 mo jeen

blare *v. t* 刺耳嘅聲 tee yee geh seng

blast *n* 爆炸 bao ja

blast *v.i* 炸爛 ja lan

blaze *n* 火焰 for yeem

blaze *v.i* 燃燒 yeen siew

bleach *v. t* 漂白水 piew bak suy

blear *v. t* 模糊 mo wu

bleat *n* 羊叫聲 yeurng giew seng

bleat *v. i* 咩咩叫 meh meh giew

bleb *n* 水泡 suy pao

bleed *v. i* 流血 low hoot

blemish *n* 瑕疵 har tee

blend *v. t* 溝勻 kow wan

blend *n* 混合品 wan hap ban

bless *v. t* 祝福 juk fuk

blether *v. i* 囉唆 lor sor

blight *n* 損害 shoon hoy

blind *a* 盲 mang

blindage *n* 掩體 yeem tay

blindfold *v. t* 蒙住眼 mung ju ngan

blindness *n* 失明 sat ming

blink *v. t. & i* 眨眼 jam ngan

bliss *n* 喜悅 hay yoot

blister *n* 水泡 suy pao

blizzard *n* 暴風雪 bo fung shoot

bloc *n* 國家集團 gwok ga jap toon

block *n* 一嚿 yat gow

block *v.t* 阻塞 jor sat

blockade *n* 封鎖 fung sor	**bogus** *a* 假嘅 gar geh
blockhead *n* 蠢材 chun choy	**boil** *n* 黃水瘡 wong suy chorng
blood *n* 血 hoot	**boil** *v.i.* 滾 gwun
bloodshed *n* 傷亡 seurng mong	**boiler** *n* 鍋爐 wok lo
bloody *a* 血淋淋 hoot lum lum	**bold** *a.* 大膽 dai dam
bloom *n* 花 fa	**boldness** *n* 膽量 dam leurng
bloom *v.i.* 開花 hoy fa	**bolt** *n* 門閂 mun san
blossom *n* 花朵 far dor	**bolt** *v. t* 鎖門 sor mun
blossom *v.i* 開花 hoy fa	**bomb** *n* 炸彈 ja dan
blot *n.* 污漬 wu jik	**bomb** *v. t* 炸 ja
blot *v. t* 吸乾 kap gorn	**bombard** *v. t* 轟炸 gwun ja
blouse *n* 襯衫 tan sam	**bombardment** *n* 轟炸 gwun ja
blow *v.i.* 吹 chuy	**bomber** *n* 放炸彈嘅人 forng ja
blow *n* 打擊 da gik	dan geh yan
blue *n* 藍色 larm sik	**bonafide** *adv* 誠實嘅 sing sat geh
blue *a* 憂鬱 yow wat	**bonafide** *a* 真正嘅 jan jing geh
bluff *v. t* 虛張聲勢 huy jeurng sing	**bond** *n* 關係 gwan hay
say	**bondage** *n* 束縛 chuk bok
bluff *n* 嚇人 hak yan	**bone** *n.* 骨 gwat
blunder *n* 錯 chor	**bonfire** *n* 大火堆 dai for duy
blunder *v.i* 做錯 jow chor	**bonnet** *n* 引擎蓋 yan king goy
blunt *a* 鈍 dun	**bontebok** *n* 南非羚羊 larm fay
blur *n* 模糊 mo wu	ling yeurng
blurt *v. t* 衝口而出 chung ho yee	**bonus** *n* 意外收穫 yee ngoy so
chut	wok
blush *n* 面紅 meen hung	**book** *n* 書 shu
blush *v.i* 面紅 meen hung	**book** *v. t.* 訂 deng
boar *n* 野豬 yeh ju	**book-keeper** *n* 記帳人 gey jeurng
board *n* 板 ban	yan
board *v. t.* 上 seurng	**book-mark** *n.* 書籤 shu teem
boast *v.i* 曬命 sai meng	**book-seller** *n* 書商 shu seurng
boast *n* 曬命 sai meng	**book-worm** *n* 書蟲 shu chung
boat *n* 船 shoon	**bookish** *n.* 蛀書蟲 ju shu chung
boat *v.i* 撐船 tang shoon	**booklet** *n* 小冊子 siew tak jee
bodice *n* 上身 seurng san	**boon** *n* 有利於 yow lay yu
bodily *a* 身體嘅 san tay geh	**boor** *n* 粗人 cho yan
bodily *adv.* 全身嘅 choon san geh	**boost** *n* 幫 borng
body *n* 身 san	**boost** *v. t* 提升 tay sing
bodyguard *n.* 保鑣 bo biew	**boot** *n* 靴 hur
bog *n* 沼澤 jiew jak	**booth** *n* 卡位 ka way
bog *v.i* 阻止 jor jee	**booty** *n* 贓物 jorng mat
bogle *n* 廁所 tee sor	**booze** *v. i* 狂飲酒 kwong yam jow

border *n* 邊界 been gai	**boyhood** *n* 童年 tung leen
border *v.t* 鑲邊 seurng been	**brace** *n* 牙箍 ngar ku
bore *v. t* 悶 mun	**bracelet** *n* 手鏈 sow leen
bore *n* 煩人 fan yan	**brag** *v. i* 吹水 chuy suy
born *v.* 出生 chut sang	**brag** *n* 曬 sai
born rich *adj.* 出生富裕 chut sang fu yu	**braille** *n* 盲文 mang man
borne *adj.* 攜帶 kway dai	**brain** *n* 腦 lo
borrow *v. t* 借 jeh	**brake** *n* 刹車 sat ter
bosom *n* 胸部 hung bo	**brake** *v. t* 刹車 sat ter
boss *n* 老細 lo say	**branch** *n* 樹枝 shu jee
botany *n* 植物學 jik mat hok	**brand** *n* 牌子 pai jee
botch *v. t* 輪盡 lun jun	**brandy** *n* 白蘭地 bak lan day
both *a* 雙方 seurng forng	**brangle** *v. t* 嗌交 ai gao
both *pron* 兩個 leurng gor	**brass** *n.* 黃銅 wong tung
both *conj* 而且 yee ter	**brave** *a* 大膽 dai dam
bother *v. t* 麻煩 ma fan	**bravery** *n* 膽量 dam leurng
botheration *n* 煩惱 fan lo	**brawl** *v. i. & n* 打鬥 da dow
bottle *n* 樽 jun	**bray** *n* 驢叫聲 lo giew seng
bottler *n* 裝樽機 jorng jun gey	**bray** *v. i* 刺耳 tee yee
bottom *n* 低 day	**breach** *n* 違法 way fat
bough *n* 大樹枝 dai shu jee	**bread** *n* 麵包 meen bao
boulder *n* 大石 dai sek	**breaden** *v. t. & i* 麵包整嘅 meen bao jing geh
bouncer *n* 保鏢 bo biew	**breadth** *n* 闊度 fwut dow
bound *n.* 跳 tiew	**break** *v. t* 整爛 ting lan
boundary *n* 邊界 been gai	**break** *n* 休息 yow sik
bountiful *a* 大方 dai forng	**breakage** *n* 破損 por shoon
bounty *n* 慷慨 hon koy	**breakdown** *n* 故障 gu jeurng
bouquet *n* 一紮花 yat jak fa	**breakfast** *n* 早餐 jo tan
bout *n* 一陣 yat jan	**breakneck** *n* 飛速 fay chuk
bow *v. t* 鞠躬 guk gung	**breast** *n* 胸 hung
bow *n* 鞠躬 guk gung	**breath** *n* 氣 hey
bow *n* 蝴蝶結 wu deep geet	**breathe** *v. i.* 唞氣 tow hey
bowel *n.* 腸 cheurng	**breeches** *n.* 半長褲 bwun cheurng fu
bower *n* 涼亭 leurng ting	**breed** *v.t* 交配繁殖 gao pwuy fan jik
bowl *n* 碗 wun	**breed** *n* 品種 ban jung
bowl *v.i* 投球 tow kow	**breeze** *n* 微風 may fung
box *n* 箱 seurng	**breviary** *n* 摘要 jak yiew
boxing *n* 拳擊 koon gik	**brevity** *n* 簡潔 gan geet
boy *n* 男仔 larm jai	**brew** *v. t.* 沖茶 chung cha
boycott *v. t.* 抵制 day jay	
boycott *n* 抵制 day jay	

brewery *n* 啤酒廠 beh jow chorng

bribe *n* 賄賂 kwuy lo

bribe *v. t.* 賄賂 kwuy lo

brick *n* 磚 joon

bride *n* 新娘 san leurng

bridegroom *n.* 新郎 san long

bridge *n* 橋 kiew

bridle *n* 馬勒 mah lak

brief *a.* 簡單 gan dan

brigade *n.* 陸軍 luk gwan

brigadier *n* 陸軍準將 luk gwan jun jeurng

bright *a* 光 gwong

brighten *v. t* 變光啲 been gwong dee

brilliance *n* 光彩 gwong choy

brilliant *a* 精彩 jing choy

brim *n* 邊沿 been yoon

brine *n* 鹽水 yeem suy

bring *v. t* 帶 dai

brinjal *n* 茄子 keh jee

brink *n.* 邊緣 been yoon

brisk *adj* 快 fai

bristle *n* 短而硬嘅毛 doon yee ngan geh mo

british *adj* 英國嘅 ying gwok geh

brittle *a.* 脆 chuy

broad *a* 闊 fwut

broadcast *n* 廣播 gwong bor

broadcast *v. t* 廣播 gwong bor

brocade *n* 錦緞 gam doon

broccoli *n.* 西蘭花 say lan far

brochure *n* 手冊 sow tak

brochure *n* 假日指南 ga yat jee larm

broker *n* 經紀人 ging gey yan

brood *n* 一竇 yat dow

brook *n.* 小溪 siew kay

broom *n* 掃把 so bar

bronze *n. & adj* 青銅 teng tung

broth *n* 肉湯 yuk tong

brothel *n* 妓院 gey yoon

brother *n* 兄弟 hing day

brotherhood *n* 手足之情 sow juk jee ting

brow *n* 額頭 ak tow

brown *a* 棕色 jung sik

brown *n* 棕色 jung sik

browse *n* 搜索 sow sok

bruise *n* 瘀 yu

bruit *n* 散播 san bor

brush *n* 掃 so

brustle *v. t* 摩擦 mor tat

brutal *a* 殘忍 tan yan

brute *n* 禽獸 kam so

bubble *n* 泡泡 pao pao

bucket *n* 水桶 suy tung

buckle *n* 扣住 kowju

bud *n* 花蕾 fa luy

budge *v. i. & n* 唧 yuk

budget *n* 預算 yu shoon

buff *n* 愛好者 ngoy ho jeh

buffalo *n.* 水牛 suy ngow

buffoon *n* 小丑 siew cho

bug *n.* 昆蟲 kwun chung

bugle *n* 號角 ho gok

build *v. t* 起 hey

build *n* 體格 tay gak

building *n* 建築 geen juk

bulb *n.* 燈泡 dang pao

bulk *n* 大部分 dai bo fan

bulky *a* 龐大 pong dai

bull *n* 牛 ngow

bulldog *n* 牛頭犬 ngow tow hoon

bull's eye *n* 靶心 ba sam

bullet *n* 子彈 jee dan

bulletin *n* 公告 gung go

bullock *n* 閹牛 yeem ngow

bully *n* 惡霸 ok ba

bully *v. t.* 蝦人 har yan

bulwark *n* 堡壘 bo luy

bumper *n.* 保險槓 bo heem gong

bumpy *adj* 崎嶇 kay kuy

bunch *n* 紮 jat

bundle *n* 包 bao
bungalow *n* 平房 ping forng
bungle *v. t* 失敗 sat bai
bungle *n* 失誤 sat hm
bunk *n* 臥鋪 ngor po
bunker *n* 地堡 day bo
buoy *n* 浮標 fow biew
buoyancy *n* 浮力 fow lik
burden *n* 包袱 bao fuk
burden *v. t* 負擔 fu dam
burdensome *a* 難以承擔 larn yee sing dam
bureau *n.* 事務處 see mo chu
Bureacuracy *n.* 官僚主義 gwun liew ju yee
bureaucrat *n* 官僚 gwun liew
burglar *n* 賊 tak
burglary *n* 盜竊 tow seet
burial *n* 葬禮 jorng lay
burk *v. t* 蠢材 chun choy
burn *v. t* 燒 siew
burn *n* 燒 siew
burrow *n* 地道 day dow
burst *v. i.* 爆 bao
burst *n* 爆破 bao por
bury *v. t.* 埋 mai
bus *n* 巴士 ba see
bush *n* 矮樹 ngai shu
business *n* 生意 sang yee
businessman *n* 生意人 sang yee yan
bustle *v. t* 催 chuy
busy *a* 忙 mong
but *prep* 但係 dan hay
but *conj.* 不過 bat gwor
butcher *n* 屠夫 tow fu
butcher *v. t* 屠殺 tow sat
butter *n* 牛油 ngow yow
butter *v. t* 搽牛油 ta ngow yow
butterfly *n* 蝴蝶 wu deep
buttermilk *n* 脫脂奶 toot jee lai
buttock *n* 屁股 pay gu

button *n* 鈕 low
button *v. t.* 扣鈕 kow low
buy *v. t.* 買 mai
buyer *n.* 買家 mai ga
buzz *v. i* 嗡嗡聲 wung wung seng
buzz *n.* 嗡嗡聲 wung wung seng
by *prep* 靠近 kao gan
by *adv* 經過 ging gwor
bye-bye *interj.* 拜拜 bai bai
by-election *n* 補選 bo shoon
bylaw, bye-law *n* 地方法 day forng fat
bypass *n* 旁路 pong lo
by-product *n* 副產品 fu tan ban
byre *n* 牛棚 ngow pang
byword *n* 俗語 juk yu

cab *n.* 的士 dik see
cabaret *n.* 歌舞表演 gor mo biew yeen
cabbage *n.* 生菜 sang choy
cabin *n.* 船艙 shoon chorng
cabinet *n.* 櫥櫃 chu gway
cable *n.* 電纜 deen larm
cable *v. t.* 打電報 da deen bo
cache *n* 隱藏物 chorng mat chu
cachet *n* 威信 way sun
cackle *v. i* 嘎嘎聲笑 ga ga seng siew
cactus *n.* 仙人掌 seen yan jeurng
cad *n* 無賴 mo lai
cadet *n.* 軍校生 gwan hao sang
cadge *v. i* 乞 hat
cadmium *n* 鎘 gak
cafe *n.* 咖啡店 ga feh deem
cage *n.* 籠 lung
cain *n* 殺兄弟者 sat hing day jeh
cake *n.* 蛋糕 dan go

calamity *n.* 災難 jor larn

calcium *n* 鈣 koy

calculate *v. t.* 計 gey

calculator *n* 計數機 gey so gey

calculation *n.* 計算 gey shoon

calendar *n.* 日曆 yat lik

calf *n.* 小腿 siew tuy

call *v. t.* 叫 giew

call *n.* 電話 deen wah

caller *n* 來電者 loy deen jeh

calligraphy *n* 書法 shu fat

calling *n.* 使命感 see ming gam

callow *adj* 幼稚 yow jee

callous *a.* 冷酷無情 lang huk mo ting

calm *n.* 冷靜 lang jing

calm *n.* 平靜 ping jing

calm *v. t.* 鎮靜 jan jing

calmative *adj* 鎮靜嘅 jan jing geh

calorie *n.* 卡路里 ka lo lay

calumniate *v. t.* 誹謗 fay borng

camel *n.* 駱駝 lok tor

camera *n.* 相機 seurng gey

camlet *n* 駝毛布 tor mo bo

camp *n.* 度假營 dow ga ying

camp *v. i.* 露營 lo ying

campaign *n.* 活動 wut dung

camphor *n.* 樟腦 jeurng lo

can *n.* 罐 gwun

can *v. t.* 可以 hor yi

can *v.* 裝罐 jorng gwun

canal *n.* 運河 wan hor

canard *n* 假新聞 ga san man

cancel *v. t.* 取消 chuy siew

cancellation *n* 取消 chuy siew

cancer *n.* 癌症 ngam jing

candid *a.* 公正 gung jing

candidate *n.* 申請人 san ting yan

candle *n.* 蠟燭 lap juk

candour *n.* 誠懇 sing han

candy *n.* 糖 tong

candy *v. t.* 用糖煮 yung tong ju

cane *n.* 藤條 tang tiew

cane *v. t.* 用藤條打 yung tang tiew da

canister *n.* 小罐 siew gwun

cannon *n.* 大炮 dai pao

cannonade *n. v. & t* 連續炮轟 leen juk pao gwun

canon *n* 原則 yoon jak

canopy *n.* 罩篷 jao fung

canteen *n.* 食堂 sik tong

canter *n* 騎馬慢跑 keh mah man pao

canton *n* 行政區 hang jing kuy

cantonment *n.* 兵營 bing ying

canvas *n.* 帆布 fan bo

canvass *v. t.* 拉票 lai piew

cap *n.* 帽 mo

cap *v. t.* 盒蓋 hap goy

capability *n.* 能力 lang lik

capable *a.* 有能力 yow lang lik

capacious *a.* 寬敞 fwun torng

capacity *n.* 容量 yung leurng

cape *n.* 披肩 pay geen

capital *n.* 首都 sow dow

capital *a.* 死刑嘅 say ying geh

capitalist *n.* 資本主義者 jee bun ju yee jeh

capitulate *v. t* 屈服 wat fuk

caprice *n.* 任性 yam sing

capricious *a.* 善變 seen been

Capricorn *n* 魔羯座 mor keet jor

capsicum *n* 辣椒 lat jiew

capsize *v. i.* 翻 fan

capsular *adj* 膠囊狀 gao lorng jorng

captain *n.* 隊長 duy jeurng

captaincy *n.* 隊長職位 duy jeurng jik way

caption *n.* 插圖說明 tap tow shoot ming

captivate *v. t.* 迷住 may ju

captive *n.* 俘虜 fu lo

captive *a.* 被監禁 bay garm gum

captivity *n.* 監禁 garm gum

capture *v. t.* 捉 juk

capture *n.* 捉 juk

car *n.* 車 cher

carat *n.* 卡 ka

caravan *n.* 旅行拖車 luy hang tor cher

carbide *n.* 碳化物 tan far mat

carbon *n.* 碳 tam

card *n.* 卡 ka

cardamom *n.* 豆蔻 dow kow

cardboard *n.* 紙皮 jee pay

cardiacal *adjs* 心臟嘅 sam jorng geh

cardinal *a.* 最重要 juy jung yiew

cardinal *n.* 樞機主教 shu gey ju gao

care *n.* 照顧 jiew gu

care *v. i.* 關心 gwan sam

career *n.* 職業生涯 jik yeep sang ngai

careful *a* 小心 siew sam

careless *a.* 大意 dai yee

caress *v. t.* 撫摩 fu mor

cargo *n.* 貨 for

caricature *n.* 諷刺畫 fung tee wah

carious *adj* 腐爛 fu lan

carl *n* 粗人 cho yan

carnage *n* 大屠殺 dai tow sat

carnival *n* 嘉年華 ka leen wah

carol *n* 頌歌 jung gor

carpal *n.* 腕骨 wun gwat

carpenter *n.* 木匠 muk jeurng

carpentry *n.* 木工 muk gung

carpet *n.* 地氈 dey jeen

carriage *n.* 車廂 cher seurng

carrier *n.* 運輸公司 wan shu gung see

carrot *n.* 紅蘿蔔 hung lor bak

carry *v. t.* 攞 lor

cart *n.* 馬車 ma cher

cartage *n.* 運輸費 wan shu fay

carton *n* 盒 hap

cartoon *n.* 動畫 dung wah

cartridge *n.* 盒 hap

carve *v. t.* 刻 hak

cascade *n.* 小瀑布 siew buk bo

case *n.* 箱 seurng

cash *n.* 現金 yeen gam

cash *v. t.* 兌現支票 duy yeen jee piew

cashier *n.* 收銀員 sow an yoon

casing *n.* 箱 seurng

cask *n* 木桶 muk tung

casket *n* 細盒 say hap

cassette *n.* 錄音帶 luk yam dai

cast *v. t.* 投射 tow she

cast *n.* 全體演員 choon tey yeen yoon

caste *n* 社會地位 seh wuy day way

castigate *v. t.* 嚴厲批評 yeem lay pay ping

casting *n* 角色分配 gok sik fan pwuy

cast-iron *n* 鑄鐵 ju teet

castle *n.* 城堡 sing bo

castor oll *n.* 蓖麻油 bay ma yow

castral *adj* 營嘅 ying geh

casual *a.* 平常 ping seurng

casualty *n.* 遇難者 yu lan jeh

cat *n.* 貓 mao

catalogue *n.* 目錄 muk luk

cataract *n.* 大瀑布 dai buk bo

catch *v. t.* 捉 chuk

catch *n.* 接 jeep

categorical *a.* 絕對 joot duy

category *n.* 種類 jung luy

cater *v. i* 提供飲食 tay gung yam sik

caterpillar *n* 毛蟲 mo chung

cathedral *n.* 大教堂 dai gao tong

catholic *a.* 天主教嘅 teen ju gao

geh
cattle *n.* 牛 ngow
cauliflower *n.* 椰菜花 yeh choy fa
causal *adj.* 因果關係 yan gwor gwan hay
causality *n* 因果關係 yan gwor gwan hay
cause *n.* 起因 hey yan
cause *v.t* 令到 ling dow
causeway *n* 堤道 tay dow
caustic *a.* 腐蝕性 fu sik sing
caution *n.* 警告 ging go
caution *v. t.* 提醒 tay sing
cautious *a.* 謹慎 gan san
cavalry *n.* 騎兵 keh bing
cave *n.* 山洞 san dung
cavern *n.* 大山洞 dai san dung
cavil *v. t* 抱怨 po yoon
cavity *n.* 窿 lung
caw *n.* 鴉叫聲 ngar giew seng
caw *v. i.* 鴉叫 ngar giew
cease *v. i.* 終止 jung jee
ceaseless *~a.* 不停嘅 bat ting geh
cedar *n.* 雪松 shu chung
ceiling *n.* 天花板 teen far ban
celebrate *v. t. & i.* 慶祝 hing juk
celebration *n.* 慶祝活動 hing juk wut dung
celebrity *n* 名人 ming yan
celestial *adj* 天上嘅 teen seurng geh
celibacy *n.* 獨身生活 duk san sang wut
celibacy *n.* 獨身 duk san
cell *n.* 細胞 say bao
cellar *n* 地窖 day gao
cellular *adj* 細胞嘅 say bao geh
cement *n.* 水泥 suy lay
cement *v. t.* 加強 ga keurng
cemetery *n.* 墓園 mo yoon
cense *v. t* 焚香致敬 fan heurng jee ging

censer *n* 香爐 heurng lo
censor *n.* 審查官 sam cha gwun
censor *v. t.* 刪剪 san jeen
censorious *adj* 奄尖 yeem jeem
censorship *n.* 審查 sam cha
censure *n.* 批評 pay ping
censure *v. t.* 譴責 heen jak
census *n.* 人口調查 yan ho tiew ta
cent *n* 仙 seen
centenarian *n* 人瑞 yan suy
centenary *n.* 一百週年 yat bak jow leen
centennial *adj.* 一百週年 yat bak jow leen
center *n* 中心 jung sam
centigrade *a.* 攝氏 seep see
centipede *n.* 蜈蚣 hm gung
central *a.* 中心 jung sam
centre *n* 中心 jung sam
centrifugal *adj.* 離心 lay sam
centuple *n. & adj* 百倍 bak pwuy
century *n.* 世紀 say gey
ceramics *n* 陶瓷 tow chee
cerated *adj.* 塗咗蠟嘅 tow jor lap geh
cereal *n.* 穀物 guk mat
cereal *a* 穀類 guk luy
cerebral *adj* 大腦嘅 dai lo geh
cerebral *a.* 禮儀 lay yee
ceremonious *a.* 講究禮儀 gong go lay yee
ceremony *n.* 儀式 yee sik
certain *a* 特定 dak ding
certainly *adv.* 當然 dong yeen
certainty *n.* 確定性 kok ding sing
certificate *n.* 獎狀 jeurng jorng
certify *v. t.* 證實 jing sat
cerumen *n* 耳垢 yee go
cesspool *n.* 垃圾坑 lap sap hang
chain *n* 鍊 leen
chair *n.* 凳 dang
chairman *n* 主席 ju jik

chaise *n* 馬車 ma cher
chaise *n* 躺椅 tong yee
challenge *n.* 挑戰 tiew jeen
challenge *v. t.* 挑戰 tiew jeen
chamber *n.* 會議廳 wuy yee teng
chamberlain *n* 管家 gwun ga
champion *n.* 冠軍 gwun gwan
champion *v. t.* 聲援 sing wun
chance *n.* 機會 gey wuy
chancellor *n.* 總理 jung lay
chancery *n* 檔案室 dong on sat
change *v. t.* 改變 goy been
change *n.* 改變 goy been
channel *n* 台 toy
chant *n* 反覆呼叫 fan fuk fu giew
chaos *n.* 混亂 wan loon
chaotic *adv.* 混亂 wan loon
chapel *n.* 細教堂 say gao tong
chapter *n.* 章 jeurng
character *n.* 角色 gok sik
charge *v. t.* 收費 so fay
charge *n.* 告 go
chariot *n* 戰車 jeen cher
charitable *a.* 慈善嘅 tee seen geh
charity *n.* 慈善 tee seen
charm1 *n.* 魅力 may lik
charm2 *v. t.* 吸引 kap yan
chart *n.* 圖表 tow biew
charter *n* 憲章 heen jeurng
chase1 *v. t.* 追 juy
chase2 *n.* 追捕 juy bo
chaste *a.* 純潔 sun geet
chastity *n.* 忠貞 jung jing
chat1 *n.* 傾偈 king gey
chat2 *v. i.* 傾偈 king gey
chatter *v. t.* 亂噏 look ap
chauffeur *n.* 司機 see gey
cheap *a* 平 peng
cheapen *v. t.* 降價 gorng ga
cheat *v. t.* 出貓 chut mao
cheat *n.* 騙子 peen jee
check *v. t.* 檢查 geem cha

check *n* 檢查 geem cha
checkmate *n* 將軍 jeurng gwan
cheek *n* 面珠 meen ju
cheep *v. i* 吱吱叫 jee jee giew
cheer *n.* 歡呼聲 fwun fu seng
cheer *v. t.* 喝彩 hot choy
cheerful *a.* 高興 go hing
cheerless *a* 陰暗 yam am
cheese *n.* 芝士 jee see
chemical *a.* 化學嘅 far hok geh
chemical *n.* 化學物品 far hok mat ban
chemise *n* 無袖連衣裙 mo jow leen yee kwan
chemist *n.* 化學家 far hok ga
chemistry *n.* 化學 far hok
cheque *n.* 支票 jee piew
cherish *v. t.* 珍惜 jan sik
cheroot *n* 雪茄煙 shoot ka yeen
chess *n.* 國際象棋 gwok jay jeurng kay
chest *n* 心口 sam ho
chestnut *n.* 栗子 lut jee
chew *v. t* chiew
chevalier *n* 騎士 keh see
chicken *n.* 雞 gey
chide *v. t.* 指責 jee jak
chief *a.* 首要嘅 sow yiew geh
chieftain *n.* 首領 sow ling
child *n* 細路仔 say lo jai
childhood *n.* 童年 tung leen
childish *a.* 幼稚 yow jee
chill *n.* 寒冷 hon lang
chilli *n.* 辣椒 lat jiew
chilly *a* 凍 dung
chiliad *n.* 一千 yat teen
chimney *n.* 煙囪 yeen tung
chimpanzee *n.* 黑猩猩 hak sing sing
chin *n.* 下巴 ha pa
china *n.* 瓷器 tee hay
chirp *v. i.* 吱喳叫 jee ja giew

chirp *n* 吱喳叫聲 jee ja giew seng
chisel *n* 鑿 jok
chisel *v. t.* 雕 diew
chit *n.* 欠單 heem dan
chivalrous *a.* 體貼 tay teep
chivalry *n.* 體貼 tay teep
chlorine *n* 氯氣 luk hay
chloroform *n* 氯仿 luk forng
choice *n.* 選擇 shoon jak
choir *n* 合唱團 hap cheurng toon
choke *v. t.* 哽 kang
cholera *n.* 霍亂 fok loon
chocolate *n* 朱古力 ju gu lik
choose *v. t.* 揀 gan
chop *v. t* 斬 jam
chord *n.* 和弦 wor yoon
choroid *n* 脈絡膜 mak lok mok
chorus *n.* 副歌 fu gor
Christ *n.* 耶穌 yeh so
Christendom *n.* 基督教徒 gey duk gao tow
Christian *n* 基督徒 gey duk tow
Christian *a.* 基督徒 gey duk tow
Christianity *n.* 基督教 gey duk gao
Christmas *n* 聖誕節 sing dan jeet
chrome *n* 鉻 gok
chronic *a.* 慢性 man sing
chronicle *n.* 編年史 peen leen see
chronology *n.* 年表 leen biew
chronograph *n* 記時器 gey see hay
chuckle *v. i* 笑 siew
chum *n* 好朋友 ho pang yow
church *n.* 教堂 gao tong
churchyard *n.* 教堂墓地 gao tong mo day
churl *n* 下賤嘅人 ha jeen geh yan
churn *v. t. & i.* 攪 gao
churn *n.* 攪乳機 gao yu gey
cigar *n.* 雪茄 shoot ka
cigarette *n.* 煙 yeen

cinema *n.* 戲院 hey yoon
cinnabar *n* 朱砂 ju sar
cinnamon *n* 肉桂粉 yuk gway fan
cipher, cipher *n.* 暗號 am ho
circle *n.* 圓圈 yoon hoon
circuit *n.* 線路 seen lo
circumfluence *n.* 環流 wan low
circumspect *adj.* 慎重 san jung
circular *a* 圓形 yoon ying
circular *n.* 傳單 choon dan
circulate *v. i.* 環繞 wan yiew
circulation *n* 循環 chun wan
circumference *n.* 圓周 yoon jow
circumstance *n* 情況 ting forng
circus *n.* 馬戲團 ma hay toon
cist *n* 石棺 sek gwun
citadel *n.* 堡壘 bo luy
cite *v. t* 舉出 guy chut
citizen *n* 市民 see man
citizenship *n* 公民權利 gung man koon lay
citric *adj.* 檸檬 ling mung
city *n* 城市 sing see
civic *a* 城市嘅 sing see geh
civics *n* 公民學 gung man hok
civil *a* 平民嘅 ping man geh
civilian *n* 平民 ping man
civilization *n.* 文明社會 man ming seh wuy
civilize *v. t* 開化 hoy far
clack *n. & v. i* 噼拍 pik pak
claim *n* 宣稱 shoon ting
claim *v. t* 聲稱 sing ting
claimant *n* 要求者 yiew kow jeh
clamber *v. i* 攀登 pan dang
clamour *n* 吵鬧聲 tao lao seng
clamour *v. i.* 大聲要求 dai seng yiew kow
clamp *n* 夾鉗 geep keem
clandestine *adj.* 秘密嘅 bay mat geh
clap *v. i.* 拍手 pak sow

clap *n* 鼓掌 gu jeurng

clarify *v. t* 澄清 ting ting

clarification *n* 澄清 ting ting

clarion *n.* 喇叭 la ba

clarity *n* 清晰 ting sik

clash *n.* 分歧 fan kay

clash *v. t.* 撞 jorng

clasp *n* 捉緊 juk gan

class *n* 班 ban

classic *a* 典型 deen ying

classic *n* 經典 ging deen

classical *a* 古典 gu deen

classification *n* 種類 jung luy

classify *v. t* 分類 fan luy

clause *n* 條款 tiew fwun

claw *n* 爪 jao

clay *n* 泥土 lay tow

clean *n.* 乾淨 gon jeng

clean *v. t* 清潔 ting geet

cleanliness *n* 乾淨 gon jeng

cleanse *v. t* 清洗 ting say

clear *a* 清楚 ting chor

clear *v. t* 搬走 bwun jow

clearance *n* 清除 ting chuy

clearly *adv* 明顯 ming heen

cleft *n* 裂口 leet ho

clergy *n* 牧師 muk see

clerical *a* 辦公室嘅 ban gung sat geh

clerk *n* 文員 man yoon

clever *a.* 叻 lek

clew *n.* 線毬 seen kow

click *n.* 點擊 deem gik

client *n..* 客 hak

cliff *n.* 懸崖 yoon ai

climate *n.* 氣候 hay ho

climax *n.* 高潮 go tiew

climb *n.* 攀登 pan dang

climb *v.i* 爬 pa

cling *v. i.* 捉緊 juk gan

clinic *n.* 診所 tan sor

clink *n.* 丁噹聲 ding dong seng

cloak *n.* 斗篷 dow fung

clock *n.* 鐘 jung

clod *n.* 泥塊 lay fai

cloister *n.* 修院 sow yoon

close *n.* 掘頭巷 gwat tow horng

close *a.* 近 kan

close *v. t* 閂 san

closet *n.* 壁櫃 bik gway

closure *n.* 停業 ting yeep

clot *n.* 蠢人 chun yan

clot *v. t* 凝結 ying geet

cloth *n* 布 bo

clothe *v. t* 着 jeurk

clothes *n.* 衫 sam

clothing *n* 衫 sam

cloud *n.* 雲 wan

cloudy *a* 多雲 dor wan

clove *n* 丁香 ding heurng

clown *n* 小丑 siew cho

club *n* 會 wuy

clue *n* 提示 tay see

clumsy *a* 輪盡 lun jun

cluster *n* 群 kwun

cluster *v. i.* 聚集 juy jap

clutch *n* 離合 lay hap

clutter *v. t* 亂 loon

coach *n* 大巴 dai ba

coachman *n* 馬車夫 ma cher fu

coal *n* 炭 tan

coalition *n* 聯合政府 loon hap jing fu

coarse *a* 粗 cho

coast *n* 海岸 hoy ngon

coat *n* 樓 lo

coating *n* 覆蓋層 fuk koy tang

coax *v. t* 氹 tam

cobalt *n* 鈷 gu

cobbler *n* 鞋匠 hai jeurng

cobra *n* 眼睛蛇 ngan geng seh

cobweb *n* 蜘蛛網 jee ju morng

cocaine *n* 可卡因 hor ka yan

cock *n* 公雞 gung gey

cocker *v. t* 嬌養 giew yeurng

cockle *v. i* 鳥蛤 liew ha

cock-pit *n.* 駕駛艙 ga say chorng

cockroach *n* 甲由 gat jat

coconut *n* 椰子 yeh jee

code *n* 密碼 mat ma

co-education *n.* 男女同校 larm luy tung hao

coefficient *n.* 係數 hay so

co-exist *v. i* 共存 gung choon

co-existence *n* 共存 gung choon

coffee *n* 咖啡 ga feh

coffin *n* 棺材 gwun choy

cog *n* 輪齒 lun tee

cogent *adj.* 有說服力 yow suy fuk lik

cognate *adj* 同族 tung juk

cognizance *n* 同族 ling hm

cohabit *v. t* 同居 tung guy

coherent *a* 合乎邏輯 hap fu lor tap

cohesive *adj* 有凝聚力 yow ying juy lik

coif *n* 頭巾 tow gan

coin *n* 銀仔 an jai

coinage *n* 硬幣 ang bay

coincide *v. i* 同時發生 tung see fat sang

coir *n* 椰殼纖維 yeh hok teem way

coke *v. t* 變焦炭 been jiew tan

cold *a* 凍 dung

cold *n* 感冒 gam mo

collaborate *v. i* 合作 hap jok

collaboration *n* 合作 hap jok

collapse *v. i* 暈低 wan day

collar *n* 領 leng

colleague *n* 同事 tung see

collect *v. t* 收集 so jap

collection *n* 系列 hay leet

collective *a* 集體 jap tay

collector *n* 收集家 so jap ga

college *n* 學院 hok yoon

collide *v. i.* 碰撞 pung jorng

collision *n* 碰撞 pung jorng

collusion *n* 串通 choon tung

colon *n* 冒號 mo ho

colon *n* 結腸 geet cheurng

colonel *n.* 上校 seurng gao

colonial *a* 殖民嘅 jik man geh

colony *n* 殖民地 jik man day

colour *n* 顏色 ngan sik

colour *v. t* 染色 yeem sik

colter *n* 犁刀 lay dow

column *n* 欄 lan

coma *n.* 昏迷 fan may

comb *n* 梳 sor

combat1 *n* 搏鬥 bok dow

combat *v. t.* 防止 forng jee

combatant1 *n* 戰士 jeen see

combatant *a.* 戰鬥 jeen dow

combination *n* 組合 jo hap

combine *v. t* 結合 geet hap

come *v. i.* 嚟 lay

comedian *n.* 喜劇家 hay kek ga

comedy *n.* 喜劇 hay kek

comet *n* 彗星 way sing

comfit *n.* 糖 tong

comfort1 *n.* 舒服 shu fuk

comfort *v. t* 安慰 on way

comfortable *a* 舒服 shu fuk

comic *a* 戲劇嘅 hay kek geh

comic *n* 漫畫 man wah

comical *a* 好笑嘅 ho siew geh

comma *n* 逗號 dow ho

command *n* 命令 ming ling

command *v. t* 命令 ming ling

commandant *n* 司令 see ling

commander *n* 指揮官 jee fay gwun

commemorate *v. t.* 紀念 gey leem

commemoration *n.* 紀念 gey leem

commence *v. t* 開始 hoy tee

commencement *n* 開始 hoy tee

commend *v. t* 表揚 biew yeurng

commendable *a.* 值得讚嘅 jik dak jan geh

commendation *n* 嘉許 ga huy

comment *v. i* 表達意見 biew dat yee geen

comment *n* 評論 ping lun

commentary *n* 評論 ping lun

commentator *n* 評論員 ping lun yoon

commerce *n* 貿易 mo yik

commercial *a* 商業嘅 seurng yeep geh

commiserate *v. t* 同情 tung ting

commission *n.* 佣金 yung gam

commissioner *n.* 委員 way yoon

commissure *n.* 接合處 jeep hap chu

commit *v. t.* 做 jow

committee *n* 委員會 way yoon wuy

commodity *n.* 貨 for

common *a.* 常見 seurng geen

commoner *n.* 平民 ping man

commonplace *a.* 普遍嘅 po peen geh

commonwealth *n.* 英聯邦 ying loon bong

commotion *n* 騷亂 so loon

commove *v. t* 激動 gik dung

communal *a* 共享嘅 gung heurng geh

commune *v. t* 群體 kwan tay

communicate *v. t* 溝通 kow tung

communication *n.* 通訊 tung sun

communiqué *n.* 公報 gung bo

communism *n* 共產主義 gung tan ju yee

community *n.* 社會 seh wuy

commute *v. t* 減刑 garm ying

compact *a.* 壓縮嘅 at suk geh

compact *n.* 合同 hap tung

companion *n.* 伴 bwun

company *n.* 公司 gung see

comparative *a* 相比 seurng bay

compare *v. t* 比較 bay gao

comparison *n* 比較 bay gao

compartment *n.* 間隔 gan gak

compass *n* 指南針 jee larm jam

compassion *n* 同情 tung ting

compel *v. t* 強迫 keurng bik

compensate *v.t* 賠償 pwuy seurng

compensation *n* 賠償 pwuy seurng

compete *v. i* 競爭 ging jang

competence *n* 能力 lang lik

competent *a* 有能力 yow lang lik

competition *n.* 比賽 bay choy

competitive *a* 競爭力 ging jang lik

compile *v. t* 編寫 peen she

complacent *adj.* 得戚 dak tik

complain *v. i* 投訴 tow so

complaint *n* 投訴 tow so

complaisance *n.* 殷勤 yan kan

complaisant *adj.* 順從 sun chung

complement *n* 補充物 bo chung mat

complementary *a* 互補 wu bo

complete *a* 完整 yoon jing

complete *v. t* 完成 yoon sing

completion *n* 完成 yoon sing

complex *a* 複雜 fuk jap

complex *n* 建築群 geen juk kwan

complexion *n* 膚色 fu sik

compliance *n.* 順從 sun chung

compliant *adj.* 順從 sun chung

complicate *v. t* 複雜化 fuk jap fa

complication *n.* 複雜化 fuk jap fa

compliment *n.* 讚揚 jan yeurng

compliment *v. t* 讚 jan
comply *v. i* 服從 fuk chung
component *n.* 組件 jo geen
compose *v. t* 作 jok
composition *n* 作品 jok ban
compositor *n.* 排版師 pai ban see
compost *n* 肥料 fay liew
composure *n.* 鎮定 jan ding
compound *n* 化合物 fa hap mat
compound *a* 混合 wan hap
compound *n* 復合詞 fuk hap tee
compound *v. i* 惡化 ok fa
compounder *n.* 製藥公司 jay yeurk gung see
comprehend *v. t* 理解 lay gai
comprehension *n* 領悟力 ling hm lik
comprehensive *a* 全部嘅 choon bo geh
compress *v. t.* 壓縮 at suk
compromise *n* 和解 wor gai
compromise *v. t* 妥協 tor heep
compulsion *n* 強迫 keurng bik
compulsory *a* 一定要 yat ding yiew
compunction *n.* 內疚 loy gow
computation *n.* 計算 gey shoon
compute *v.t.* 計算 gey shoon
comrade *n.* 戰友 jeen yow
conation *n.* 意圖 yee tow
concave *adj.* 凹 lup
conceal *v. t.* 隱瞞 yan mun
concede *v.t.* 承認 sing ying
conceit *n* 驕傲 giew oh
conceive *v. t* 想像 seurng jeurng
concentrate *v. t* 專心 joon sam
concentration *n.* 專心 joon sam
concept *n* 概念 koy leem
conception *n* 構思 kow see
concern *v. t* 涉及 seep kap
concern *n* 關心 gwan sum

concert *n.* 演唱會 yeen cheurng wuy
concert2 *v. t* 達成 dat sing
concession *n* 妥協 tor heep
conch *n.* 海螺殼 hoy lor hok
conciliate *v.t.* 安撫 on fu
concise *a* 簡潔 gan geet
conclude *v. t* 結束 geet chuk
conclusion *n.* 結論 geet lun
conclusive *a* 確鑿嘅 kok jok geh
concoct *v. t* 調製 tiew jay
concoction *n.* 調製品 tiew jay ban
concord *n.* 和諧 wor hai
concrescence *n.* 愈合 yu hap
concrete *n* 混凝土 wan ying tow
concrete *a* 確實嘅 kok sat geh
concrete *v. t* 用混凝土 yung wan ying tow
concubinage *n.* 同居 tung guy
concubine *n* 妾 teep
conculcate *v.t.* 踩 tai
condemn *v. t.* 指責 jee jak
condemnation *n* 譴責 heen jak
condense *v. t* 壓縮 at suk
condite *v.t.* 醃 yeep
condition *n* 條件 tiew geen
conditional *a* 附帶條件 fu dai tiew geen
condole *v. i.* 哀悼 oi dow
condolence *n* 慰問 way man
condonation *n.* 寬恕 fwun shu
conduct *n* 行爲舉止 hang way guy jee
conduct *v. t* 安排 on pai
conductor *n* 指揮家 jee fey ga
cone *n.* 圓錐形 yoon juy ying
confectioner *n* 甜食商 teem sik seurng
confectionery *n* 甜食 teem sik
confer *v. i* 商討 seurng tow
conference *n* 會議 wuy yee

confess *v. t.* 承認 sing yan
confession *n* 表白 biew bak
confidant *n* 知己 jee gey
confide *v. i* 透露 tow lo
confidence *n* 信心 sun sam
confident *a.* 有信心 yow sun sam
confidential *a.* 機密 gey mat
confine *v. t* 限制 han jay
confinement *n.* 監禁 garm gam
confirm *v. t* 確認 kok ying
confirmation *n* 確定 kok ding
confiscate *v. t* 充公 chung gung
confiscation *n* 沒收 mut so
conflict *n.* 爭論 jang lun
conflict *v. i* 衝突 chung dat
confluence *n* 匯流處 wuy low chu
confluent *adj.* 匯合 wuy hap
conformity *n.* 遵守 jun sow
conformity *n.* 同其他人一樣 tung kay ta yan yat yeurng
confraternity *n.* 團體 toon tay
confrontation *n.* 對質 duy jat
confuse *v. t* 混亂 wan loon
confusion *n* 混亂 wan loon
confute *v.t.* 駁 bok
conge *n.* 辭職 tee jik
congenial *a* 適合 sik hap
conglutinate *v.t.* 愈合 yu hao
congratulate *v. t* 恭喜 gung hey
congratulation *n* 祝賀 juk hor
congress *n* 國會 gwok wuy
conjecture *n* 猜測 tai tak
conjecture *v. t* 推測 tuy tak
conjugal *a* 夫妻間嘅 fu tay gan geh
conjugate *v.t. & i.* 動詞變化 dung tee been fa
conjunct *adj.* 結合 geet hap
conjunctiva *n.* 結膜 geet mok
conjuncture *n.* 緊急關頭 gan gao gwan tow

conjure *v.t.* 呼喚 fu wun
conjure *v.i.* 變魔術 been mor sut
connect *v. t.* 連接 leen jeep
connection *n* 關連 gwan leen
connivance *n.* 縱容 jung yung
conquer *v. t* 征服 jing fuk
conquest *n* 征服 jing fuk
conscience *n* 良心 leurng sam
conscious *a* 清醒 ting sing
consecrate *v.t.* 聖化 sing fa
consecutive *adj.* 連續 leen juk
consecutively *adv* 連續咁 leen juk gam
consensus *n.* 共識 gung sik
consent *n.* 允許 wan huy
consent *v. i* 同意 tung yee
consent3 *v.t.* 允許 wan huy
consequence *n* 後果 ho gwor
consequent *a* 後果 ho gwor
conservative *a* 保守 bo so
conservative *n* 保守黨支持者 bo so dong jee tee jeh
conserve *v. t* 保存 bo choon
consider *v. t* 考慮 hao luy
considerable *a* 相當大嘅 seurng dong dai geh
considerate *a.* 體貼 tay teep
consideration *n* 仔細考慮 jee say hao luy
considering *prep.* 考慮到 hao luy dow
consign *v.t.* 交畀 gao bay
consign *v. t.* 打發 da fat
consignment *n.* 運送貨 wan sung for
consist *v. i* 包含 bao ham
consistence,-cy *n.* 連貫性 leen gwan sing
consistent *a* 一直 yat jik
consolation *n* 安慰 on way
console *v. t* 安慰 on way
consolidate *v. t.* 加強 ga keurng

consolidation *n* 強化 keurng fa
consonance *n.* 和音 wor yam
consonant *n.* 輔音 fu yam
consort *n.* 配偶 pwuy oh
conspectus *n.* 大網 dai morng
conspicuous *a.* 明顯 ming heen
conspiracy *n.* 陰謀 yam mow
conspirator *n.* 共謀者 gung mo jeh
conspire *v. i.* 密謀 mat mo
constable *n* 警察 ging tat
constant *a* 一直 yat jik
constellation *n.* 星群 sing kwan
constipation *n.* 便秘 been bay
constituency *n* 選區 shoon kuy
constituent *n.* 選民 shoon man
constituent *adj.* 組成 jow sing
constitute *v. t* 被認爲 bay ying way
constitution *n* 憲法 heen fat
constrict *v.t.* 縮窄 suk jak
construct *v. t.* 起 hay
construction *n* 結構 geet kow
consult *v. t* 詢問 sun man
consultation *n* 商討會 seurng tow wuy
consume *v. t* 消耗 siew ho
consumption *n* 消耗量 siew ho leurng
consumption *n* 消費 siew fay
contact *n.* 接觸 jeep juk
contact *v. t* 聯絡 loon lok
contagious *a* 傳染 choon yeem
contain *v.t.* 有 yow
contaminate *v.t.* 污染 wu yeem
contemplate *v. t* 考慮 hao luy
contemplation *n* 考慮緊 hao luy gan
contemporary *a* 現代 yeen doy
contempt *n* 鄙視 pay see
contemptuous *a* 輕視 hing see
contend *v. i* 聲稱 sing ting

content *a.* 滿足 mun juk
content *v. t* 知足 jee juk
content *n* 內容 loy yung
content *n.* 目錄 muk luk
contention *n* 觀點 gwun deem
contentment *n* 滿意 mun yee
contest *v. t* 爭辯 jang been
contest *n.* 比賽 bay choy
context *n* 上下文 seurng har man
continent *n* 洲 jow
continental *a* 歐洲大陸嘅 oh jow dai luk geh
contingency *n.* 可能發生嘅事 hor lang fat sang geh see
continual *adj.* 連續 leen juk
continuation *n.* 持續 tee juk
continue *v. i.* 繼續 gey juk
continuity *n* 連續性 leen juk sing
continuous *a* 不斷嘅 bat doon geh
contour *n* 輪廓 lun kok
contra *pref.* 正相反 jing seurng fan
contraception *n.* 避孕 bay yan
contract *n* 合約 hap yeurk
contract *v. t* 伸縮 san suk
contrapose *v.t.* 對照 duy jiew
contractor *n* 承辦商 sing ban seurng
contradict *v. t* 反駁 fan bok
contradiction *n* 矛盾 mao tun
contrary *a* 相反 seurng fan
contrast *v. t* 對比 duy bay
contrast *n* 對照 duy jiew
contribute *v. t* 捐 goon
contribution *n* 貢獻 gung heen
control *n* 控制權 hung jay koon
control *v. t* 控制 hung jay
controller *n.* 遙控 yiew hung
controversy *n* 爭論 jang lun
contuse *v.t.* 挫傷 chor seurng
conundrum *n.* 難題 lan tay

convene *v. t* 召集 jiew jap
convener *n* 召集人 jiew jap yan
convenience *n.* 方便 forng been
convenient *a* 方便 forng been
convent *n* 女修道院 luy sow dow yoon
convention *n.* 集會 jap wuy
conversant *a* 熟悉 suk sik
conversant *adj.* 熟 suk
conversation *n* 傾偈 king gey
converse *v.t.* 傾 king
conversion *n* 轉換 joon wun
convert *v. t* 換 wun
convert *n* 轉宗教嘅人 joon jung gao geh yan
convey *v. t.* 表達 biew dat
conveyance *n* 傳送 choon sung
convict *v. t.* 宣判有罪 shoon pwun yow juy
convict *n* 罪犯 juy fan
conviction *n* 判罪 pwun juy
convince *v. t* 說服 suy fuk
convivial *adj.* 容易相處 yung yee seurng chu
convocation *n.* 集會 jap wuy
convoke *v.t.* 召集 jiew jap
convolve *v.t.* 捲 goon
coo *n* 細聲 say seng
coo *v. i* 咕咕叫 gu gu giew
cook *v. t* 煮 joo
cook *n* 廚師 choo see
cooker *n* 爐 lo
cool *a* 涼 leurng
cool *v. i.* 變涼 been leurng
cooler *n* 冷卻器 lang keurk hay
coolie *n* 苦力 fu lik
co-operate *v. i* 合作 hap jok
co-operation *n* 合作 hap jok
co-operative *a* 配合 pwuy hap
co-ordinate *a.* 協調 heep tiew
co-ordinate *v. t* 協調 heep tiew
co-ordination *n* 協調 heep tiew

coot *n.* 白骨頂 bak gwat ding
co-partner *n* 拍檔 pak dong
cope *v. i* 應付 ying fu
coper *n.* 馬販 ma fan
copper *n* 銅 tung
coppice *n.* 矮林 ay lam
coprology *n.* 糞石學 fan sek hok
copulate *v.i.* 交配 gao pwuy
copy *n* 複製品 fuk jay ban
copy *v. t* 複製 fuk jay
coral *n* 珊瑚 san wu
cord *n* 細繩 say sing
cordial *a* 好好人 ho ho yan
corbel *n.* 梁托 leurng tok
cordate *adj.* 心形 sam ying
core *n.* 果心 gwor sam
coriander *n.* 芫荽 yoon say
Corinth *n.* 科林斯 for see lam
cork *n.* 酒塞 jow sat
cormorant *n.* 鸕鷀 lo tee
corn *n* 粟米 suk may
cornea *n* 角膜 gok mok
corner *n* 角落 gok lok
cornet *n.* 短號 doon ho
cornicle *n.* 腹管 fuk gwun
coronation *n* 加冕典禮 ga meen dccn lay
coronet *n.* 冠冕 gwun meen
corporal *a* 身體嘅 san tay geh
corporate *adj.* 公司嘅 gung see geh
corporation *n* 大公司 dai gung see
corps *n* 兵團 bing toon
corpse *n* 屍體 see tay
correct *a* 正確 jing kok
correct *v. t* 更改 gang goy
correction *n* 改正 goy jing
correlate *v.t.* 互相依賴 wu seurng yee lai
correlation *n.* 相關 seurng gwan
correspond *v. i* 符合 fu hap

correspondence *n.* 通信 tung sun

correspondent *n.* 記者 gey jeh

corridor *n.* 走廊 jow long

corroborate *v.t.* 證實 jing sat

corrosive *adj.* 腐蝕性嘅 fu sik sing geh

corrupt *v. t.* 破壞 por wai

corrupt *a.* 唔誠實 hm sing sat

corruption *n.* 貪污 tam wu

cosier *n.* 更舒適 gang shu sik

cosmetic *a.* 表面 biew meen

cosmetic *n.* 化妝品 fa jorng ban

cosmic *adj.* 宇宙嘅 yu jow geh

cost *v.t.* 損失 shoon sat

cost *n.* 價格 gar gak

costal *adj.* 肋骨嘅 lak gwat geh

cote *n.* 小屋 siew uk

costly *a.* 貴 gway

costume *n.* 服裝 fuk jorng

cosy *a.* 舒適 shu sik

cot *n.* 幼兒床 yow yee chorng

cottage *n* 小屋 siew uk

cotton *n.* 棉 meen

couch *n.* 梳化 sor fa

cough *n.* 咳 kat

cough *v. i.* 咳 kat

council *n.* 政務委員會 jing mo way yoon wuy

councillor *n.* 市議員 see yee yoon

counsel *n.* 建議 geen yee

counsel *v. t.* 勸 hoon

counsellor *n.* 顧問 gu man

count *n.* 點數 deem so

count *v. t.* 數 so

countenance *n.* 面色 meen sik

counter *n.* 櫃台 gway toy

counter *v. t* 反駁 fan bok

counteract *v.t.* 抵消 day siew

countercharge *n.* 反控 fan hung

counterfeit *a.* 偽造 ay jow

counterfeiter *n.* 偽造者 ay jow jeh

countermand *v.t.* 撤銷 teet siew

counterpart *n.* 對應事物 duy ying see mat

countersign *v. t.* 副署 fu ju

countess *n.* 伯爵夫人 bak jeurk fu yan

countless *a.* 無數 mo so

country *n.* 國家 gwok ga

county *n.* 縣 yoon

coup *n.* 政變 jing been

couple *n* 一對 yat duy

couple *v. t* 連接 leen jeep

couplet *n.* 對聯 duy loon

coupon *n.* 優惠券 yow way goon

courage *n.* 勇氣 yung hey

courageous *a.* 勇敢 yung gam

courier *n.* 專遞公司 joon day gung see

course *n.* 課程 for ting

court *n.* 法庭 fat ting

court *v. t.* 討好 tow ho

courteous *a.* 有禮貌 yow lay mao

courtesan *n.* 情婦 ting fu

courtesy *n.* 禮貌 lay mao

courtier *n.* 朝臣 tiew san

courtship *n.* 求愛期 kow ngoy kay

courtyard *n.* 庭院 ting yoon

cousin *n.* 表親 biew tan

covenant *n.* 合同 hap tung

cover *v. t.* 遮住 jeh ju

cover *n.* 封面 fung meen

coverlet *n.* 床罩 chorng jao

covet *v.t.* 渴望 hot morng

cow *n.* 牛 ngow

cow *v. t.* 恐嚇 hung hak

coward *n.* 膽小鬼 dam siew gway

cowardice *n.* 懦弱 loy yeurk

cower *v.i.* 退縮 tuy suk

cozy *a.* 舒適 shu sik
crab *n* 蟹 hai
crack *n* 裂痕 leet han
crack *v. i* 裂開 leet hoy
cracker *n* 薄脆餅乾 bok chuy beng gon
crackle *v.t.* 劈里啪啦 pi lee pa la
cradle *n* 搖籃 yiew larm
craft *n* 手藝 sow ngay
craftsman *n* 工匠 gung jeurng
crafty *a* 狡猾 gao wat
cram *v. t* 塞 sat
crambo *n.* 對韻遊戲 duy wan yow hay
crane *n* 吊車 diew cher
crankle *v.t.* 彎曲 wan kuk
crash *v. i* 撞 jorng
crash *n* 碰撞 pung jorng
crass *adj.* 粗魯 cho lo
crate *n.* 板條箱 ban tiew seurng
crave *v.t.* 渴望 hot morng
craw *n.* 嗉囊 so long
crawl *v. t* 爬 pa
crawl *n* 慢速 man chuk
craze *n* 熱潮 yeet tiew
crazy *a* 黐線 tee seen
creak *v. i* 嘎吱聲 ga jee seng
creak *n* 嘎吱聲 ga jee seng
cream *n* 奶油 lai yow
crease *n* 摺痕 jeep han
create *v. t* 整 jing
creation *n* 作品 jok ban
creative *adj.* 創意 chorng yee
creator *n* 創作者 chorng jok jeh
creature *n* 生物 sang mat
credible *a* 可靠嘅 hor kao geh
credit *n* 信譽 sun yu
creditable *a* 值得讚嘅 jik dak jan geh
creditor *n* 債主 jai ju
credulity *adj.* 輕易相信 hing yee seurng sun

creed *n.* 原則 yoon jak
creed *n* 信念 sun leem
creek *n.* 小溪 siew kay
creep *v. i* 爬 pa
creeper *n* 攀緣植物 pan yoon jik mat
cremate *v. t* 火化 for far
cremation *n* 火化 for far
crest *n* 徽章 fay jeurng
crevet *n.* 熔爐 yung lo
crew *n.* 工作人員 gung jok yan yoon
crib *n.* 幼兒床 yow yee chorng
cricket *n* 板球 ban kow
crime *n* 罪 juy
crimp *n* 起皺 hay jow
crimple *v.t.* 蜷曲 goon kuk
criminal *n* 罪犯 juy fan
criminal *a* 犯法嘅 fan fat geh
crimson *n* 深紅色 sam hung sik
cringe *v. i.* 畏縮 way suk
cripple *n* 跛 bay
crisis *n* 危機 ngay gey
crisp *a* 脆 chuy
criterion *n* 標準 biew jun
critic *n* 批評家 pay ping ga
critical *a* 唔穩定 hm wan ding
criticism *n* 批評 pay ping
criticize *v. t* 批評 pay ping
croak *n.* 青蛙聲 ting wa seng
crockery *n.* 陶器 tow hay
crocodile *n* 鱷魚 ok yu
croesus *n.* 大富豪 dai fu yung
crook *a* 唔舒服 hm shu fuk
crop *n* 農作物 lung jok mat
cross *v. t* 過 gwor
cross *n* 十字架 sap jee ga
cross *a* 嬲 low
crossing *n.* 人行橫道 yan hang wang dow
crotchet *n.* 四分音符 say fan yam fu

crouch *v. i.* 跍低 mo day

crow *n* 烏鴉 wu ngar

crow *v. i* 得戚 dak tik

crowd *n* 一班人 yat ban yan

crown *n* 皇冠 wong gwun

crown *v. t* 加冕 ga meen

crucial *adj.* 決定性 koot ding sing

crude *a* 簡略 gan leurk

cruel *a* 殘忍 tan yan

cruelty *n* 殘暴行為 tan bo hang way

cruise *v.i.* 搭船遊覽 dap shoon yow larm

cruiser *n* 巡洋艦 chun yeurng larm

crumb *n* 碎 suy

crumble *v. t* 碎 suy

crump *adj.* 脆 chuy

crusade *n* 鬥爭 dow jang

crush *v. t* 壓 at

crust *n.* 麵包皮 meen bao pay

crutch *n* 腋杖 yik jeurng

cry *n* 叫聲 giew seng

cry *v. i* 喊 harm

cryptography *n.* 密碼學 mat ma hok

crystal *n* 水晶 suy jing

cub *n* 幼獸 yow sow

cube *n* 立方形 lap forng ying

cubical *a* 立方體 lap forng tay

cubiform *adj.* 立方形 lap forng ying

cuckold *n.* 戴綠帽嘅人 dai luk mo geh yan

cuckoo *n* 杜鵑鳥 dow goon liew

cucumber *n* 青瓜 teng gwa

cudgel *n* 棍棒 gwun pang

cue *n* 提示 tay see

cuff *n* 袖口 jow ho

cuff *v. t* 拍 pak

cuisine *n.* 風味 fung may

cullet *n.* 碎玻璃 suy bo lay

culminate *v.i.* 告終 go jung

culpable *a* 難辭其咎 lan tee kay gow

culprit *n* 罪犯 juy fan

cult *n* 時尚 see sseurng

cultivate *v. t* 耕 gang

cultrate *adj.* 尖銳 jeem yu

cultural *a* 文化嘅 man far geh

culture *n* 文化 man far

culvert *n.* 排水管 pai suy gwun

cunning *a* 狡猾嘅 gao wat geh

cunning *n* 狡猾 gao wat

cup *n.* 杯 bwuy

cupboard *n* 櫃 gway

Cupid *n* 邱比特 yow bay dak

cupidity *n* 貪心 tam sam

curable *a* 可以醫嘅 hor yi yee geh

curative *a* 有療效嘅 yow liew hao geh

curb *n* 控制 hung jay

curb *v. t* 控制 hung jay

curcuma *n.* 鬱金香 wat gam heurng

curd *n* 凝乳 ying yu

cure *n* 藥 yeurk

cure *v. t.* 醫好 yee ho

curfew *n* 宵禁令 siew gam ling

curiosity *n* 好奇心 ho kay sam

curious *a* 好奇 ho kay

curl *n.* 捲 goon

currant *n.* 提子乾 tay jee gon

currency *n* 貨幣 for bay

current *n* 水流 suy low

current *a* 流行嘅 low hang geh

curriculum *n* 課程 for ting

curse *n* 咒 jow

curse *v. t* 詛咒 juy jow

cursory *a* 倉促 chorng choot

curt *a* 簡短而無禮 gan doon yee mo lay

curtail *v. t* 限制 han jay

curtain *n* 窗簾 cheurng leêm
curve *n* 曲線 kuk seen
curve *v. t* 彎 wan
cushion *n* 墊 jeen
cushion *v. t* 緩和撞擊 wun wor jorng gik
custard *n* 奶油凍 lai yow dung
custodian *n* 監護人 garm wu yan
custody *v* 監護權 garm wu koon
custom *n.* 習俗 jap juk
customary *a* 習俗 jap juk
customer *n* 客 hak
cut *v. t* 剪 jeen
cut *n* 傷口 seurng ho
cutis *n.* 皮膚 pay fu
cuvette *n.* 細玻璃管 say bo lay gwun
cycle *n* 循環 chun wan
cyclic *a* 循環嘅 chun wan geh
cyclist *n* 單車手 dan cher sow
cyclone *n.* 旋風 shoon fung
cyclostyle *n* 復印機 fuk yan gey
cyclostyle *v. t* 複印 fuk yan
cylinder *n* 圓柱型 yoon chu ying
cynic *n* 憤世嫉俗者 fan say jat juk jeh
cypress *n* 柏樹 pak shu

D

dabble *v. i.* 玩 wan
dacoit *n.* 賊 tak
dacoity *n.* 搶劫 cheurng geep
dad, daddy *n* 爹地 deh dee
daffodil *n.* 黃水仙 wong suy seen
daft *adj.* 蠢 chun
dagger *n.* 匕首 bay sow
daily *a* 每日嘅 mwuy yat geh
daily *adv.* 每日 mwuy yat
daily *n.* 日報 yat bo

dainty *a.* 嬌小 giew siew
dainty *n.* 美食 may sik
dairy *n* 奶類 lai luy
dais *n.* 台 toy
daisy *n* 雛菊 chor guk
dale *n* 山谷 san guk
dam *n* 水壩 suy ba
damage *n.* 損壞 shoon wai
damage *v. t.* 破壞 por wai
dame *n.* 女爵士 luy jeurk see
damn *v. t.* 抵死 day say
damnation *n.* 天譴 teen heen
damp *a* 濕 sap
damp *n* 潮濕 tiew sap
damp *v. t.* 整濕 jing sap
damsel *n.* 少女 siew luy
dance *n* 舞 mo
dance *v. t.* 跳舞 tiew mo
dandelion *n.* 蒲公英 po gung ying
dandle *v.t.* 搖BB yiew bee bee
dandruff *n* 頭皮 tow pay
dandy *n* 花花公子 fa fa gung jee
danger *n.* 危險 ngay heem
dangerous *a* 危險 ngay heem
dangle *v. t* 吊 diew
dank *adj.* 陰濕 yam sap
dap *v.i.* 跳 tiew
dare *v. i.* 夠膽 gow dam
daring *n.* 大膽 dai dam
daring *a* 勇敢嘅 yung gam geh
dark *a* 黑 hak
dark *n* 黑暗 hak am
darkle *v.i.* 漸暗 jeem am
darling *n* 寶貝 bo bwuy
darling *a* 可愛嘅 hor ngoy geh
dart *n.* 飛鏢 fay biew
dash *v. i.* 閃 seem
dash *n* 快閃 fai seem
date *n* 日期 yat kay
date *v. t* 拍拖 pak tor
daub *n.* 塗料 tow liew
daub *v. t.* 搽 ta

daughter *n* 女 luy	**decade** *n* 十年 sap leen
daunt *v. t* 嚇 hak	**decadent** *a* 墮落 dorlok
dauntless *a* 勇敢嘅 yung gam geh	**decamp** *v. i* 逃走 tow jow
dawdle *v.i.* 慢吞吞 man tun tun	**decay** *n.* 腐爛 fu lan
dawn *n* 黎明 lay ming	**decay** *v. i* 腐爛 fu lan
dawn *v. i.* 變清楚 been ting chor	**decease** *n* 死亡 say morng
day *n* 日頭 yat tow	**decease** *v. i* 死 say
daze *n* 迷茫 may morng	**deceit** *n* 呃人 ak yan
daze *v. t* 凝視 ying see	**deceive** *v. t* 呃 ak
dazzle *n* 迷惑 may wak	**december** *n* 十二月 sap yee yoot
dazzle *v. t.* 迷惑 may wak	**decency** *n* 禮儀 lay yee
deacon *n.* 執事 jap see	**decennary** *n.* 十年 sap leep
dead *a* 死 say	**decent** *a* 似樣 tee yeurng
deadlock *n* 僵局 geurng guk	**deception** *n* 騙局 peen guk
deadly *a* 致命 jee ming	**decide** *v. t* 決定 koot ding
deaf *a* 聾 lung	**decillion** *n.* 千嘅十一乘方 teen geh sap yat sing forng
deal *n* 交易 gao yik	**decimal** *a* 十進位 sap jun way
deal *v. i* 發牌 fat pai	**decimate** *v.t.* 毀滅 way meet
dealer *n* 貿易商 mo yik seurng	**decision** *n* 決定 koot ding
dealing *n.* 處理 chu lay	**decisive** *a* 關鍵嘅 gwan geen geh
dean *n.* 主任 ju yam	**deck** *n* 甲板 gap ban
dear *a* 親愛 tan ngoi	**deck** *v. t* 佈置 bo jee
dearth *n* 缺乏 koot fat	**declaration** *n* 聲明 sing ming
death *n* 死亡 say morng	**declare** *v. t.* 宣佈 shoon bo
debar *v. t.* 禁止 gam jee	**decline** *n* 下降 ha gong
debase *v. t.* 降價 gorng ga	**decline** *v. t.* 拒絕 kuy joot
debate *n.* 爭論 jang lun	**declivous** *adj.* 傾斜嘅 king ter geh
debate *v. t.* 討論 tow lun	**decompose** *v. t.* 分解 fan gai
debauch *v. t.* 令人墮落 ling yan dor lok	**decomposition** *n.* 分解 fan gai
debauch *n* 放蕩 forng dong	**decontrol** *v.t.* 撤銷 teet siew
debauchee *n* 浪蕩者 lorng dong jeh	**decorate** *v. t* 裝修 jorng sow
debauchery *n* 放蕩 forng dong	**decoration** *n* 裝飾 jorng sik
debility *n* 虛弱 huy yeurk	**decorum** *n* 得體 dak tay
debit *n* 借記 jeh gey	**decrease** *v. t* 減少 garm siew
debit *v. t* 記入賬戶 gey yap jeurng wu	**decrease** *n* 降低 gorng day
debris *n* 殘骸 tan hai	**decree** *n* 裁決 choy koot
debt *n* 債 jai	**decree** *v. i* 裁定 choy ding
debtor *n* 債務人 jai mo yan	**decrement** *n.* 降低 gorng day
	dedicate *v. t.* 奉獻 fung heen
	dedication *n* 奉獻 fung heen

deduct *v.t.* 扣除 kow chuy
deed *n* 行爲 hang way
deem *v.i.* 認爲 ying way
deep *a.* 深 sam
deer *n* 鹿 luk
defamation *n* 誹謗 fay borng
defame *v. t.* 中傷 jung seurng
default *n.* 違約 way yeurk
defeat *n* 失敗 sat bai
defeat *v. t.* 擊敗 gik bai
defect *n* 缺點 koot deem
defence *n* 防禦 fong yu
defend *v. t* 防守 fong so
defendant *n* 被告 bay go
defensive *adv.* 自衛嘅 jee way geh
deference *n* 尊重 joon jung
defiance *n* 違抗 way korng
deficit *n* 赤字 tek jee
deficient *adj.* 有缺陷嘅 yow koot ham geh
defile *n.* 山路 san lo
define *v. t* 解釋 gai sik
definite *a* 肯定嘅 hang ding geh
definition *n* 解釋 gai sik
deflation *n.* 通貨緊縮 tung for gan suk
deflect *v.t. & i.* 轉移 joon yee
deft *adj.* 靈巧 ling hao
degrade *v. t* 降低身分 gorng day san fan
degree *n* 學位 hok way
dehort *v.i.* 勸阻 hoon jor
deist *n.* 自然神論者 jee yeen san lun jeh
deity *n.* 神 san
deject *v. t* 灰心 fwuy sam
dejection *n* 沮喪 juy sorng
delay *v.t. & i.* 延遲 yeen tee
delibate *v.t.* 試 see
deligate1 *n* 代表 doy biew
delegate *v. t* 委託 way tok

delegation *n* 代表團 doy biew toon
delete *v. t* 刪除 san chuy
deliberate *v. i* 仔細考慮 jee say hao luy
deliberate *a* 特登 dak dang
deliberation *n* 深思熟慮 sam see suk luy
delicate *a* 脆弱 chuy yeurk
delicious *a* 美味 mey mey
delight *n* 高興 go hing
delight *v. t.* 高興 go hing
deliver *v. t* 送 sung
delivery *n* 速遞 chuk day
delta *n* 三角洲 sam gok jow
delude *n.t.* 呃 at
delusion *n.* 錯覺 chor gok
demand *n* 需求 suy kow
demand *v. t* 強烈要求 keurng leet yiew kow
demarcation *n.* 界線 gai seen
dement *v.t* 發顛 fat deen
demerit *n* 過失 gwor sat
democracy *n* 民主 man ju
democratic *a* 民主 man ju
demolish *v. t.* 拆除 tak chuy
demon *n.* 魔鬼 mor gway
demonetize *v.t.* 停止通用 ting jee tung yung
demonstrate *v. t* 示範 see fan
demonstration *n.* 示範 see fan
demoralize *v. t.* 意志消沉 yee jee siew tam
demur *n* 猶豫 yow yee
demur *v. t* 反對 farn duy
demurrage *n.* 滯留費 jay low fay
den *n* 竇 dow
dengue *n.* 登革熱 dang gak yeet
denial *n* 否認 fow ying
denote *v. i* 象徵 jeurng jing
denounce *v. t* 指責 jee jak
dense *a* 濃密 lung mat

density *n* 密度 mat dow

dentist *n* 牙醫 ngar yee

denude *v.t.* 剝光 mok gwong

denunciation *n.* 指責 jee jak

deny *v. t.* 否認 fow ying

depart *v. i.* 離開 lay hoy

department *n* 部門 bo mun

departure *n* 離開 lay hoy

depauperate *v.t.* 變窮 been kung

depend *v. i.* 依賴 yee lai

dependant *n* 受養人 sow yeurng yan

dependence *n* 依賴 yee lai

dependent *a* 依靠嘅 yee kao geh

depict *v. t.* 描繪 miew kwuy

deplorable *a* 可悲 hor bay

deploy *v.t.* 部署 bo chu

deponent *n.* 證人 jing yan

deport *v.t.* 離境 lay ging

depose *v. t* 罷免 ba meen

deposit *n.* 按金 on gam

deposit *v. t* 放低 forng day

depot *n* 貨倉 for chorng

depreciate *v.t.i.* 跌價 deet ga

depredate *v.t.* 貶價 been ga

depress *v. t* 憂鬱 yow wat

depression *n* 抑鬱症 yik wat jing

deprive *v. t* 剝奪 mok doot

depth *n* 深度 sam dow

deputation *n* 代表團 doy biew toon

depute *v. t* 授權 sow koon

deputy *n* 副手 fu sow

derail *v. t.* 出軌 chut gway

derive *v. t.* 得到 dak dow

descend *v. i.* 降落 gorng lok

descendant *n* 後代 how doy

descent *n.* 降落 gorng lok

describe *v. t* 形容 ying yung

description *n* 描述 miew sut

descriptive *a* 描述 miew sut

desert *v. t.* 拋棄 pao hay

desert *n* 沙漠 sa mok

deserve *v. t.* 應得 ying dak

design *v. t.* 設計 teet gey

design *n.* 設計 teet gey

desirable *a* 值得做嘅 jik dak jow geh

desire *n* 渴望 hot morng

desire *v.t* 渴望 hot morng

desirous *a* 希望 hay morng

desk *n* 書枱 shu toy

despair *n* 絕望 joot morng

despair *v. i* 絕望 joot morng

desperate *a* 急 gap

despicable *a* 卑鄙 bay pay

despise *v. t* 憎 jang

despot *n* 暴君 bo gwan

destination *n* 目的地 muk di dey

destiny *n* 命運 ming wan

destroy *v. t* 破壞 por wai

destruction *n* 毀滅 way meet

detach *v. t* 分開 fan hoy

detachment *n* 分遣隊 fan heen duy

detail *n* 細節 say jeet

detail *v. t* 詳述 cheurng sut

detain *v. t* 扣留 kow low

detect *v. t* 探測 □□tak

detective *a* 偵探嘅 jing tam geh

detective *n.* 偵探 jing tam

determination *n.* 決心 koot sam

determine *v. t* 決定 koot ding

dethrone *v. t* 罷免 ba meen

develop *v. t.* 研發 yeen fat

development *n.* 成長 sing jeurng

deviate *v. i* 偏離 peen lay

deviation *n* 偏離 peen lay

device *n* 儀器 yee hay

devil *n* 魔鬼 mor gway

devise *v. t* 發明 fat ming

devoid *a* 完全無 yoon choon mo

devote *v. t* 專心 joon sam

devotee *n* 愛好者 ngoy ho jeh

devotion *n* 熱心 yeet sam
devour *v. t* 狼哽 lorng kang
dew *n.* 露水 lo suy
diabetes *n* 糖尿病 tong liew beng
diagnose *v. t* 診斷 tan doon
diagnosis *n* 診斷 tan doon
diagram *n* 圖表 tow biew
dial *n.* 打 da
dialect *n* 方言 fong yeen
dialogue *n* 錶盤 biew pwun
diameter *n* 直徑 jik ging
diamond *n* 鑽石 joon sek
diarrhoea *n* 肚屙 tow or
diary *n* 日記 yat gey
dice *n.* 骰 sik
dice *v. i.* 切粒 teet lap
dictate *v. t* 口述 ho sut
dictation *n* 口述 ho sut
dictator *n* 獨裁者 duk choy jeh
diction *n* 用詞 yung tee
dictionary *n* 字典 jee deen
dictum *n* 格言 gak yeen
didactic *a* 教誨 gao fwuy
die *v. i* 死 sey
die *n* 壓模 at mo
diet *n* 日常飲食 yat seurng yam sik
differ *v. i* 有差異 yow tar yee
difference *n* 差異 tar yee
different *a* 唔同 hm tung
difficult *a* 難 larn
difficulty *n* 難度 larn dow
dig *n* 輕撞 hing jorng
dig *v.t.* 掘 gwat
digest *v. t.* 消化 siew far
digest *n.* 摘要 jak yiew
digestion *n* 消化 siew far
digit *n* 數位 so way
dignify *v.t* 有尊嚴 yow joon yem
dignity *n* 尊嚴 joon yeem
dilemma *n* 困境 kwan ging
diligence *n* 努力 low lik

diligent *a* 勤力 kan lik
dilute *v. t* 稀釋 hey sik
dilute *a* 稀釋 hey sik
dim *a* 暗 am
dim *v. t* 變暗 been am
dimension *n* 尺寸 tek choon
diminish *v. t* 減少 garn siew
din *n* 嘈雜聲 cho jap seng
dine *v. t.* 食飯 sik fan
dinner *n* 飯 fan
dip *n.* 調味醬 tiew may jeurng
dip *v. t* 點 deem
diploma *n* 文憑課程 man pang for ting
diplomacy *n* 外交 ngoy gao
diplomat *n* 外交官 ngoy gao gwun
diplomatic *a* 外交嘅 ngoy gao geh
dire *a* 嚴重 yeem jung
direct *a* 直接 jik jeep
direct *v. t* 指導 jee dow
direction *n* 方向 forng heurng
director *n.* 導演 dow yeen
directory *n* 電話簿 deen wah bo
dirt *n* 泥 lay
dirty *a* 污糟 wu jow
disability *n* 缺陷 koot ham
disable *v. t* 令到無效 ling dow mow hao
disabled *a* 殘廢 tan fay
disadvantage *n* 不利因素 bat lay yan so
disagree *v. i* 唔同意 hm tung yee
disagreeable *a.* 乞人憎 hat yan jang
disagreement *n.* 分歧 fan kay
disappear *v. i* 消失 siew sat
disappearance *n* 失蹤 sat jung
disappoint *v. t.* 失望 sat morng
disapproval *n* 反對 fan duy
disapprove *v. t* 反對 fan duy

disarm *v. t* 繳械 giew hai

disarmament *n.* 裁減軍備 choy garm gwan bay

disaster *n* 災難 jor lan

disastrous *a* 極差 gik ta

disc *n.* 磁碟 tee deep

discard *v. t* 掟 deng

discharge *v. t* 釋放 sik forng

discharge *n.* 獲准離開 wok jun lay hoy

disciple *n* 信徒 sun tow

discipline *n* 紀律 gey lut

disclose *v. t* 透露 tow low

discomfort *n* 唔舒服 hm shu fuk

disconnect *v. t* 切斷 teet toon

discontent *n* 不滿 bat mun

discontinue *v. t* 停止 ting jee

discord *n* 紛爭 fan jang

discount *n* 折頭 jeet tow

discourage *v. t.* 阻止 jor jee

discourse *n* 論文 lun man

discourteous *a* 失禮 sat lay

discover *v. t* 發現 fat yeen

discovery *n.* 發現 fat yeen

discretion *n* 謹慎 gan san

discriminate *v. t.* 歧視 kay see

discrimination *n* 歧視 kay see

discuss *v. t.* 討論 tow lun

disdain *n* 鄙視 pay see

disdain *v. t.* 藐視 miew see

disease *n* 病 beng

disguise *n* 偽裝 ngay jorng

disguise *v. t* 假扮 gar ban

dish *n* 碟 deep

dishearten *v. t* 沮喪 juy sorng

dishonest *a* 唔誠實 hm sing sat

dishonesty *n.* 唔誠實 hm sing sat

dishonour *v. t* 違背 way bwuy

dishonour *n* 恥辱 tee yuk

dislike *v. t* 唔鐘意 hm jung yee

dislike *n* 反感 fan gam

disloyal *a* 唔忠心 hm jung sam

dismiss *v. t.* 解散 gai san

dismissal *n* 解雇 gai gu

disobey *v. t* 違抗 way korng

disorder *n* 失調 sat tiew

disparity *n* 差異 ta yee

dispensary *n* 藥房 yeurk forng

disperse *v. t* 分散 fan san

displace *v. t* 取代 chuy doy

display *v. t* 展示 jeen see

display *n* 展覽 jeen lan

displease *v. t* 得罪 dak juy

displeasure *n* 不滿 bat mun

disposal *n* 處理 chu lay

dispose *v. t* 揼 dum

disprove *v. t* 反駁 fan bok

dispute *n* 爭論 jang lun

dispute *v. i* 質疑 jat yee

disqualification *n* 取消資格 chut siew jee gak

disqualify *v. t.* 取消資格 chut siew jee gak

disquiet *n* 不安 bat on

disregard *n* 忽視 fat see

disregard *v. t* 唔理 hm lay

disrepute *n* 喪失名譽 sorng sat ming yu

disrespect *n* 唔尊敬 hm joon ging

disrupt *v. t* 打斷 da toon

dissatisfaction *n* 不滿 bat mun

dissatisfy *v. t.* 唔滿意 hm mun yee

dissect *v. t* 解剖 gai fow

dissection *n* 解剖 gai fow

dissimilar *a* 不同嘅 bat tung geh

dissolve *v.t* 溶解 yung gai

dissuade *v. t* 勸 hoon

distance *n* 距離 kuy lay

distant *a* 遠嘅 yoon geh

distil *v. t* 蒸餾 jing low

distillery *n* 釀酒廠 yeurng jow chorng

distinct *a* 明顯 ming heen
distinction *n* 差別 ta beet
distinguish *v. i* 分別 fan beet
distort *v. t* 扭曲 low kuk
distress *n* 憂慮 yow luy
distress *v. t* 憂慮 yow luy
distribute *v. t* 分配 fan pwuy
distribution *n* 分佈 fan bo
district *n* 地區 day kuy
distrust *n* 唔信 hm sun
distrust *v. t.* 唔信 hm sun
disturb *v. t* 騷擾 so yiew
ditch *n* 渠 kuy
ditto *n.* 同上 tung seurng
dive *v. i* 潛水 teem suy
dive *n* 潛水 teem suy
diverse *a* 唔同嘅 hm tung geh
divert *v. t* 轉移 joon yee
divide *v. t* 分 fan
divine *a* 神聖嘅 san sing geh
divinity *n* 神學 san hok
division *n* 除法 chuy fat
divorce *n* 離婚 lay fan
divorce *v. t* 離婚 lay fan
divulge *v. t* 爆料 bao liew
do *v. t* 做 jo
docile *a* 溫順 wan sun
dock *n.* 碼頭 ma tow
doctor *n* 醫生 yee sang
doctorate *n* 博士學位 bok see hok way
doctrine *n* 政策 jing tak
document *n* 文件 man geen
dodge *n* 詭計 gway gey
dodge *v. t* 避 bay
doe *n* 雌鹿 tee luk
dog *n* 狗 gow
dog *v. t* 折磨 jeet mor
dogma *n* 教條 gao tiew
dogmatic *a* 自以爲是 jee yee way see
doll *n* 公仔 gung jay

dollar *n* 蚊 man
domain *n* 領域 ling wik
dome *n* 圓頂屋 yoon deng uk
domestic *a* 家庭嘅 gar ting geh
domestic *n* 工人 gung yan
domicile *n* 住所 ju sor
dominant *a* 顯著嘅 heen ju geh
dominate *v. t* 控制 hung jay
domination *n* 控制 hung jay
dominion *n* 統治權 tung jee koon
donate *v. t* 捐 goon
donation *n.* 捐款 goon fwun
donkey *n* 驢 low
donor *n* 捐贈者 goon jang jeh
doom *n* 厄運 ak wan
doom *v. t.* 注定失敗 ju ding sat bai
door *n* 門 mun
dose *n* 一劑 yat jay
dot *n* 點 deem
dot *v. t* 加點 gar deem
double *a* 雙倍嘅 seurng pwuy geh
double *v. t.* 加倍 ga pwuy
double *n* 兩倍 leurng pwuy
doubt *v. i* 猶疑 yow yee
doubt *n* 疑問 yee man
dough *n* 麵團 meen toon
dove *n* 鴿 gap
down *adv* 向下 heurng har
down *prep* 下面 har meen
down *v. t* 飲 yam
downfall *n* 下滑 har wat
downpour *n* 大雨 dai yu
downright *adv* 徹底咁 teet day gam
downright *a* 完全 yoon choon
downward *a* 下降 har gorng
downward *adv* 向下 heurng har
downwards *adv* 向下 heurng har
dowry *n* 嫁妝 gar jorng
doze *n.* 瞓陣 fan jan

doze *v. i* 瞌眼瞓 hap ngan gan

dozen *n* 一打 yat da

draft *v. t* 草擬 cho yee

draft *n* 草稿 cho go

draftsman *n* 起草者 hay cho jeh

drag *n* 絆腳石 bwun geurt sek

drag *v. t* 拉 lai

dragon *n* 龍 lung

drain *n* 排水管 pai suy gwun

drain *v. t* 流 low

drainage *n* 排水 pai suy

dram *n* 少量嘅酒 siew leurng geh jow

drama *n* 戲劇 hay kek

dramatic *a* 戲劇化 hay kek fa

dramatist *n* 編劇 peen kek

draper *n* 布商 bo seurng

drastic *a* 極端 gik doon

draught *n* 通風 tung fung

draw *v.t* 畫 wak

draw *n* 打和 da wor

drawback *n* 缺點 koot deem

drawer *n* 櫃桶 gway tung

drawing *n* 畫 wah

drawing-room *n* 客廳 hak teng

dread *n* 恐懼 hung guy

dread *v.t* 擔心 dam sam

dread *a* 驚 geng

dream *n* 夢 mung

dream *v. i.* 夢 mung

drench *v. t* 濕晒 sap sai

dress *n* 裙 kwan

dress *v. t* 着 jeurk

dressing *n* 調料 tiew liew

drill *n* 鑽 joon

drill *v. t.* 鑽 joon

drink *n* 飲品 yam ban

drink *v. t* 飲 yam

drip *n* 滴 dik

drip *v. i* 滴 dik

drive *v. t* 揸車 ja cher

drive *n* 路程 lo ting

driver *n* 司機 see gey

drizzle *n* 細雨 sai yu

drizzle *v. i* 落細雨 lok sai yu

drop *n* 滴 dik

drop *v. i* 跌 deet

drought *n* 乾旱 gorn hon

drown *v.i* 沈 tam

drug *n* 毒品 duk ban

druggist *n* 藥劑師 yeurk jay see

drum *n* 鼓 gu

drum *v.i.* 打鼓 da gu

drunkard *n* 醉酒佬 juy jow low

dry *a* 乾 gon

dry *v. i.* 整乾 jing gon

dual *a* 雙 seurng

duck *n.* 鴨 ap

duck *v.i.* 跍低 mo day

due *a* 因爲 yan way

due *n* 應得嘅嘢 ying dak geh yeh

due *adv* 正向 jing heurng

duel *n* 決鬥 koot dow

duel *v. i* 決鬥 joot dow

duke *n* 公爵 gung jeurk

dull *a* 無聊 mo liew

dull *v. t.* 變麻木 been mar muk

duly *adv* 適當嘅 sik dorng geh

dumb *a* 蠢 chun

dunce *n* 遲鈍嘅人 tee dun gen yan

dung *n* 動物糞 dung mat fan

duplicate *a* 複製嘅 fuk jay ghe

duplicate *n* 副本 fu bwun

duplicate *v. t* 複製 fuk jay

duplicity *n* 奸詐行爲 gan ja hang way

durable *a* 耐用 loy yung

duration *n* 期間 kay gan

during *prep* 喺 hay

dusk *n* 黃昏 wong fan

dust *n* 塵 tan

dust *v.t.* 抹 mat

duster *n* 撢 tan

dutiful *a* 盡職嘅 jun jik geh

duty *n* 責任 jak yam

dwarf *n* 矮人 ai yan

dwell *v. i* 住 ju

dwelling *n* 住所 ju sor

dwindle *v. t* 減少 garm siew

dye *v. t* 染 yeem

dye *n* 染料 yeem liew

dynamic *a* 有活力嘅 yow wut lik geh

dynamics *n.* 動態 dung tai

dynamite *n* 炸藥 ja yeurk

dynamo *n* 發電機 fat deen gey

dynasty *n* 朝代 tiew doy

dysentery *n* 痢疾 lay jat

E

each *a* 每個 mwuy gor

each *pron.* 各自 gok jee

eager *a* 心急 sam gap

eagle *n* 鷹 ying

ear *n* 耳 yee

early *adv* 早 jow

early *a* 早 jow

earn *v. t* 賺 jan

earnest *a* 認真 ying tan

earth *n* 地球 dey kow

earthen *a* 土製嘅 tow jay geh

earthly *a* 人間嘅 yan gan geh

earthquake *n* 地震 dey jan

ease *n* 輕易 hing yee

ease *v. t* 舒緩 shu wun

east *n* 東 dung

east *adv* 向東 heurng dung

east *a* 東方嘅 dung forng geh

easter *n* 復活節 fuk wut jeet

eastern *a* 東方 dung fong

easy *a* 容易 yung yee

eat *v. t* 食 sik

eatable *n.* 食用 sik yung

eatable *a* 可以食嘅 hor yi sik geh

ebb *n* 退潮 tuy tiew

ebb *v. i* 衰弱 suy yeurk

ebony *n* 烏木 wu muk

echo *n* 回音 wuy yam

echo *v. t* 回音 wuy yam

eclipse *n* 日蝕 yat sik

economic *a* 經濟嘅 ging jay geh

economical *a* 經濟嘅 ging jay geh

economics *n.* 經濟學 ging jay hok

economy *n* 經濟 ging jay

edge *n* 邊 been

edible *a* 可以食嘅 hor yi sik geh

edifice *n* 大廈 dai har

edit *v. t* 修葺 so top

edition *n* 版 ban

editor *n* 編輯 peen top

editorial *a* 編輯嘅 peen top geh

editorial *n* 評論 ping lun

educate *v. t* 教 gao

education *n* 教育 gao yuk

efface *v. t* 消除 siew chuy

effect *n* 效果 hao gwor

effect *v. t* 引起 yan hey

effective *a* 有效 yow hao

effeminate *a* 好姆 ho la

efficacy *n* 功效 gung hao

efficiency *n* 效率 hao lut

efficient *a* 效率高 hao lut go

effigy *n* 雕像 diew jeurng

effort *n* 努力 lo lik

egg *n* 雞蛋 gey dan

ego *n* 自我 jee ngor

egotism *n* 自負 jee fu

eight *n* 八 bat

eighteen *a* 十八 sap bat

eighty *n* 八十 bat sap

either *a.,* 其中一個 kay jung yat gor

either *adv.* 或者 wak jeh

eject *v. t.* 噴出 pan chut

elaborate *v. t* 詳細描述 cheurng say miew sut

elaborate *a* 詳細嘅 cheurng say geh

elapse *v. t* 消逝 siew say

elastic *a* 有彈性 yow dan xing

elbow *n* 手踭 so jang

elder *a* 年長 leen jeurng

elder *n* 長者 jeurng jeh

elderly *a* 老人 lo yan

elect *v. t* 選 shoon

election *n* 選舉 shoon kuy

electorate *n* 全體選民 choon tay shoon man

electric *a* 電 deen

electricity *n* 電 deen

electrify *v. t* 興奮 hing fan

elegance *n* 優雅 yow ngar

elegant *adj* 優雅 yow ngar

elegy *n* 輓詩 wan see

element *n* 要素 yiew so

elementary *a* 基本嘅… gey bun geh

elephant *n* 大笨象 dai ban jeurng

elevate *v. t* 提高 tay go

elevation *n* 海拔 hoy bat

eleven *n* 十一 sap yat

elf *n* 精靈 jing ling

eligible *a* 有資格 yow jee gak

eliminate *v. t* 除去 chuy huy

elimination *n* 除去 chuy huy

elope *v. i* 私奔 see ban

eloquence *n* 口才 ho choy

eloquent *a* 流利 low lay

else *a* 唔同嘅 hm tung geh

else *adv* 其他 kay ta

elucidate *v. t* 講清楚 gorng ting chor

elude *v. t* 避開 bay hoy

elusion *n* 逃避 tow bay

elusive *a* 難以捉摸 larn yee juk

mor

emancipation *n.* 解放 gai forng

embalm *v. t* 防腐 forng fu

embankment *n* 堤 tay

embark *v. t* 開始 hoy tee

embarrass *v. t* 尷尬 gam gai

embassy *n* 使館 see gwun

embitter *v. t* 沮喪 juy sorng

emblem *n* 象徵 jeurng jing

embodiment *n* 典型 deen ying

embody *v. t.* 代表 doy biew

embolden *v. t.* 變大膽 been dai darm

embrace *v. t.* 抱 po

embrace *n* 接受 jeep sow

embroidery *n* 刺繡 tee sow

embryo *n* 胚胎 bwuy toy

emerald *n* 綠寶石 luk bo sek

emerge *v. i* 出現 chut yeen

emergency *n* 緊急 gan gap

eminance *n* 顯赫 heen hak

eminent *a* 著名嘅 ju ming geh

emissary *n* 密使 mat see

emit *v. t* 散發出 san fat chut

emolument *n* 糧 leurng

emotion *n* 感情 gam ting

emotional *a* 感情豐富 gam ting fung fu

emperor *n* 皇帝 wong day

emphasis *n* 強調 keurng diew

emphasize *v. t* 強調 keurng diew

emphatic *a* 強調嘅 keurng diew geh

empire *n* 帝國 day gwok

employ *v. t* 請 teng

employee *n* 僱員 gu yoon

employer *n* 僱主 gu joo

employment *n* 工作 gung jok

empower *v. t* 授權 sow koon

empress *n* 皇后 wong ho

empty *a* 空 hung

empty *v* 倒 dow

emulate *v. t* 模仿 mo forng

enable *v. t* 激活 gik wut

enact *v. t* 通過 tung gwor

enamel *n* 琺瑯質 fat lonrg jat

enamour *v. t* 傾心 king sam

encase *v. t* 圍住 way ju

enchant *v. t* 着迷 jeurk may

encircle *v. t.* 圍繞 way yiew

enclose *v. t* 附 fu

enclosure *n.* 附件 fu geen

encompass *v. t* 包含 bao ham

encounter *n.* 遭遇 jo yu

encounter *v. t* 相遇 seurng yu

encourage *v. t* 鼓勵 gu lay

encroach *v. i* 侵佔 tam jeem

encumber *v. t.* 阻礙 jor ngoy

encyclopaedia *n.* 百科全書 bak for choon shu

end *v. t* 結束 geet chuk

end *n.* 完 yoon

endanger *v. t.* 危及 ngay kap

endear *v.t* 受歡迎 sow fwun ying

endearment *n.* 愛 ngoy

endeavour *n* 嘗試 seurng see

endeavour *v.i* 盡力 jun lik

endorse *v. t.* 宣傳 shoon choon

endow *v. t* 資助 jee jor

endurable *a* 耐用嘅 loy yung geh

endurance *n.* 耐力 loy lik

endure *v.t.* 忍 yan

enemy *n* 敵人 dik yan

energetic *a* 有活力嘅 yow wut lik geh

energy *n.* 力量 lik leurng

enfeeble *v. t.* 變虛弱 been huy yeurk

enforce *v. t.* 執行 jap hang

enfranchise *v.t.* 授權投票 sow koon tow piew

engage *v. t* 吸引 kap yan

engagement *n.* 訂婚 ding fan

engine *n* 引擎 yan king

engineer *n* 工程師 gung ting see

English *n* 英文 ying man

engrave *v. t* 刻 hak

engross *v.t* 全神貫注 choon san gwun ju

engulf *v.t* 吞沒 tun mwut

enigma *n* 謎 may

enjoy *v. t* 享受 heurng so

enjoyment *n* 愉快 yu fai

enlarge *v. t* 放大 forng dai

enlighten *v. t.* 啓發 kay fat

enlist *v. t* 入伍 yap hm

enliven *v. t.* 搞生 gao sang

enmity *n* 仇恨 sow han

ennoble *v. t.* 封爲貴族 fung way gway juk

enormous *a* 好大嘅 ho dai geh

enough *a* 夠 gow

enough *adv* 足夠 juk gow

enrage *v. t* 激 gik

enrapture *v. t* 着迷 jeurk may

enrich *v. t* 變豐富 been fung fu

enrol *v. t* 入學 yap hok

enshrine *v. t* 放入神龕 forng yap san am

enslave *v.t.* 奴役 lo yik

ensue *v.i* 因而產生 yan yee tan sang

ensure *v. t* 保證 bo jing

entangle *v. t* 捲入 goon yap

enter *v. t* 入 yap

enterprise *n* 企業 kay yeep

entertain *v. t* 娛樂 yu lok

entertainment *n.* 娛樂 yu lok

enthrone *v. t* 登位 dang way

enthusiasm *n* 熱心 yeet sam

enthusiastic *a* 熱情 yeet ting

entice *v. t.* 引誘 yan yow

entire *a* 全部 choon bo

entirely *adv* 完全 yoon choon

entitle *v. t.* 有權 yow koon

entity *n* 實體 sat tay

entomology *n.* 昆蟲學 kwan chung hok

entrails *n.* 內臟 loy jorng

entrance *n* 入口 yap ho

entrap *v. t.* 設陷阱 teet ham jing

entreat *v. t.* 求 kow

entreaty *n.* 懇求 han kow

entrust *v. t* 委託 way tok

entry *n* 入 yap

enumerate *v. t.* 列舉 leet guy

envelop *v. t* 包 bao

envelope *n* 信封 sun fung

enviable *a* 令人羨慕 ling yan seen mo

envious *a* 妒忌 dow gey

environment *n.* 環境 wan ging

envy *v* 羨慕 seen mo

envy *v. t* 妒忌 dow gey

epic *n* 史詩 si see

epidemic *n* 流行病 low hang beng

epigram *n* 詼諧短詩 fwuy hai doon see

epilepsy *n* 羊癇症 yeurng gan jing

epilogue *n* 後記 ho gey

episode *n* 集 jap

epitaph *n* 碑文 bay man

epoch *n* 時代 see doy

equal *a* 相同嘅 seurng tung geh

equal *v. t* 等於 dang yu

equal *n* 同等 tung dang

equality *n* 平等 ping dang

equalize *v. t.* 變平等 been ping dang

equate *v. t* 相等於 seurng dang yu

equation *n* 方程式 fong ting sik

equator *n* 赤道 tek dow

equilateral *a* 等邊嘅 dang been geh

equip *v. t* 裝備 jorng bay

equipment *n* 器材 hey choy

equitable *a* 公平嘅 gung ping geh

equivalent *a* 相等於 seurng dang yu

equivocal *a* 說話模糊 shoot wah mo wu

era *n* 時代 see doy

eradicate *v. t* 鏟除 tan chuy

erase *v. t* 刪除 san chuy

erect *v. t* 創立 chorng lap

erect *a* 直立嘅 jik lap geh

erection *n* 建立 geen lap

erode *v. t* 侵蝕 tam sik

erosion *n* 侵蝕 tam sik

erotic *a* 性愛嘅 sing ngoy geh

err *v. i* 犯錯 fan chor

errand *n* 差事 tai see

erroneous *a* 錯嘅 chor geh

error *n* 錯誤 chor ng

erupt *v. i* 爆發 bao fat

eruption *n* 爆發 bao fat

escape *n* 逃避 tow bay

escape *v.i* 逃走 tow jow

escort *n* 護送者 wu sung jeh

escort *v. t* 護送 wu sung

especial *a* 特別嘅 dak beet geh

essay *n.* 論文 lun man

essay *v. t.* 企圖 kay tow

essayist *n* 散文家 san man ga

essence *n* 精髓 jing suy

essential *a* 必需嘅 beet suy geh

establish *v. t.* 成立 sing lap

establishment *n* 成立 sing lap

estate *n* 住宅區 ju jak kuy

esteem *n* 尊敬 joon ging

esteem *v. t* 尊敬 joon ging

estimate *n.* 估計 gu gey

estimate *v. t* 估 gu

estimation *n* 判斷 pwun doon

etcetera *adv.* 等等 dang dang

eternal *a.* 永遠 wing yoon

eternity *n* 永恒 wing hang

ether *n* 醚 may

ethical *a* 道德 dow dak

ethics *n.* 道德標準 dow dak biew jun

etiquette *n* 禮節 lay jeet

etymology *n.* 詞源學 tee yoon hok

eunuch *n* 太監 tai garm

evacuate *v. t* 疏散 sor san

evacuation *n* 疏散 sor san

evade *v. t* 避開 bay hoy

evaluate *v. t* 評估 ping gu

evaporate *v. i* 蒸發 jing fat

evasion *n* 逃避 tow bay

even *a* 平嘅 ping geh

even *v. t* 擺平 bai ping

even *adv* 甚至連 sam jee leen

evening *n* 挨晚 ai man

event *n* 活動 wut dung

eventually *adv.* 最終 juy jung

ever *adv* 曾 tang

evergreen *a* 常綠嘅 seurng luk geh

evergreen *n* 常綠樹 seurng luk shu

everlasting *a.* 永恆嘅 wing hang geh

every *a* 每個 mwuy gor

evict *v. t* 逐出 juk chut

eviction *n* 逐出 juk chut

evidence *n* 證據 jing guy

evident *a.* 清楚 ting chor

evil *n* 邪惡 ter ok

evil *a* 惡毒嘅 ok duk geh

evoke *v. t* 引起 yan hay

evolution *n* 進化 jun far

evolve *v.t* 進化 jun far

ewe *n* 母羊 mo yeurng

exact *a* 準確嘅 jun kok geh

exaggerate *v. t.* 誇大 kwa dai

exaggeration *n.* 誇張 kwa jeurng

exalt *v. t* 高度讚揚 go dow jan yeurng

examination *n.* 考試 hao see

examine *v. t* 檢查 geem cha

examinee *n* 考生 hao sang

examiner *n* 考官 hao gwun

example *n* 例子 lay jee

excavate *v. t.* 挖掘 wat gwut

excavation *n.* 挖掘 wat gwut

exceed *v.t* 超越 tiew yoot

excel *v.i* 超過 tiew gwor

excellence *n.* 優秀 yow sow

excellency *n* 優點 yow deem

excellent *a.* 優秀嘅 yow sow geh

except *v. t* 唔包括 hm bao kwut

except *prep* 徐咗 chuy jor

exception *n* 例外 lay ngoy

excess *n* 多餘 doryu

excess *a* 多餘嘅 dor yu geh

exchange *n* 交換 gao wun

exchange *v. t* 交換 gao wun

excise *n* 消費稅 siew fay suy

excite *v. t* 興奮 hing fan

exclaim *v.i* 叫 giew

exclamation *n* 感歎詞 gam tan tee

exclude *v. t* 撇除 peet chuy

exclusive *a* 獨有嘅 duk yow geh

excommunicate *v. t.* 逐出教會 juk chut gao wuy

excursion *n.* 遠足 yoon juk

excuse *v.t* 原諒 yoon leurng

excuse *n* 藉口 jik ho

execute *v. t* 執行 jap hang

execution *n* 處決 choo koot

executioner *n.* 行刑者 hang ying jeh

exempt *v. t.* 免除 meen chuy

exempt *a.* 免除 meen chuy

exercise *n.* 運動 wan dung

exercise *v. t* 鍛鍊 doon leen

exhaust *v. t.* 筋疲力盡 gan pay lik jun

exhibit *n.* 展覽品 jeen lam ban

exhibit *v. t* 展出 jeen chut

exhibition *n.* 展覽 jeen lam

exile *n.* 流放 low forng

exile *v. t* 放逐 forng juk

exist *v.i* 存在 choon joy

existence *n* 存在 choon joy

exit *n.* 出口 chut ho

expand *v.t.* 擴大 kwong dai

expansion *n.* 擴張 kwong jeurng

ex-parte *a* 單方面嘅 dan forng meen geh

ex-parte *adv* 單方 dan forng

expect *v. t* 預計 yu gey

expectation *n.* 期望 key morng

expedient *a* 權宜之計 koon yee jee gey

expedite *v. t.* 加速 gar chuk

expedition *n* 遠征 yoon jing

expel *v. t.* 趕出 gorn chut

expend *v. t* 花費 fa fay

expenditure *n* 消費 siew fay

expense *n.* 開支 hoy jee

expensive *a* 貴 gwey

experience *n* 經驗 ging yeem

experience *v. t.* 經歷 ging lik

experiment *n* 實驗 sat yeem

expert *a* 經驗豐富 ging yeem fung fu

expert *n* 專家 joon ga

expire *v.i.* 過期 gwor kay

expiry *n* 到期 dow kay

explain *v. t.* 解釋 gai sik

explanation *n* 解釋 gai sik

explicit *a.* 清楚 ting chor

explode *v. t.* 爆炸 bao ja

exploit *n* 英勇行爲 ying yung hang way

exploit *v. t* 利用 lay yung

exploration *n* 勘察 ham tat

explore *v.t* 探索 tam sok

explosion *n.* 爆炸 bao ja

explosive *n.* 炸藥 ja yeurk

explosive *a* 爆炸性 bao ja sing

exponent *n* 擁護者 yung wu jeh

export *n* 出口 chut ho

export *v. t.* 出口 chut ho

expose *v. t* 暴露 bo lo

express *v. t.* 表達 biew dat

express *a* 快 fai

express *n* 特快列車 dak fai leet cher

expression *n.* 表情 biew ting

expressive *a.* 表示 biew see

expulsion *n.* 逐出 juk chut gao wuy

extend *v. t* 延長 yeen cheurng

extent *n.* 限度 han dow

external *a* 外面嘅 ngoy meen geh

extinct *a* 絕種嘅 joot jung geh

extinguish *v.t* 撲熄 pok sik

extol *v. t.* 讚 jan

extra *a* 額外嘅 ak ngoy geh

extra *adv* 額外 ak ngoy

extract *n* 提取物 tay chuy mat

extract *v. t* 提煉 tey leen

extraordinary *a.* 異常嘅 yee seurng geh

extravagance *n* 大使 dai say

extravagant *a* 大使嘅 dai say geh

extreme *a* 偏激 peen gik

extreme *n* 極端 gik doon

extremist *n* 極端分子 gik doon fan jee

exult *v. i* 興奮 hing fan

eye *n* 眼 ngan

eyeball *n* 眼球 ngan kow

eyelash *n* 眼睫毛 ngan jeet mo

eyelet *n* 眼孔 ngan hung

eyewash *n* 洗眼液 say ngan yik

F

fable *n.* 寓言 yu yeen
fabric *n* 布料 bo liew
fabricate *v.t* 虛構 huy kow
fabrication *n* 製作 jay jok
fabulous *a* 太好啦 tai ho la
facade *n* 正面 jing meen
face *n* 面 meen
face *v.t* 面對 meen duy
facet *n* 方面 forng meen
facial *a* 面部嘅 meen bo geh
facile *a* 輕率 hing sut
facilitate *v.t* 幫 borng
facility *n* 設施 teet see
facsimile *n* 傳真 choon jan
fact *n* 事實 see sat
faction *n* 派 pai
factious *a* 派別嘅 pai beet geh
factor *n* 因素 yan so
factory *n* 工廠 gung chorng
faculty *n* 科系 for hay
fad *n* 短暫嘅狂熱 doon jam geh kwong yeet
fade *v.i* 甩色 lut sik
faggot *n* 柴把 tai ba
fail *v.i* 失敗 sat bai
failure *n* 失敗 sat bai
faint *a* 微弱 may yeurk
faint *v.i* 暈 wan
fair *a* 公平 gung ping
fair *n.* 露天遊樂場 lo teen yow lok cheurng
fairly *adv.* 公平 gung ping
fairy *n* 小仙女 siew seen luy
faith *n* 信念 sun leem
faithful *a* 忠誠嘅 jung sing geh
falcon *n* 獵鷹 leep ying
fall *v.i.* 跌 deet
fall *n* 跌 deet
fallacy *n* 謬論 mo lun

fallow *a* 休閒 yow han
false *a* 假 gar
falter *v.i* 衰退 suy tuy
fame *n* 名氣 ming hay
familiar *a* 熟 suk
family *n* 屋企人 uk kay yan
famine *n* 飢荒 gey forng
famous *a* 出名 chut meng
fan *n* 風扇 fung seen
fanatic *a* 入迷 yap may
fanatic *n* 狂迷 kwong may
fancy *n* 幻想 wan seurng
fancy *v.t* 鐘意 jung yee
fantastic *a* 太好啦 tai ho la
far *adv.* 遠 yoon
far *a* 遠 yoon
far *n* 小麥 siew mak
farce *n* 鬧劇 lao kek
fare *n* 票價 piew ga
farewell *n* 告別 go beet
farewell *interj.* 送別 sung beet
farm *n* 農場 lung cheurng
farmer *n* 農夫 lung fu
fascinate *v.t* 吸引 kap yap
fascination *n.* 吸引力 kap yan lik
fashion *n* 時裝 see jorng
fashionable *a* 流行嘅 low hang geh
fast *a* 快 fai
fast *adv* 快 fai
fast *n* 齋戒期 jai gai kay
fast *v.i* 齋戒 jai gai
fasten *v.t* 扣 kow
fat *a* 肥 fei
fat *n* 脂肪 jee forng
fatal *a* 致命嘅 jee ming geh
fate *n* 緣份 yoon fan
father *n* 爹地 deh dee
fathom *v.t* 理解 lay gai
fathom *n* 英尋 ying tam
fatigue *n* 疲勞 pay lo

fatigue *v.t* 厭 yeem
fault *n* 過錯 gwor chor
faulty *a* 壞嘅 wai geh
fauna *n* 動物群 dung mat kwan
favour1 *n* 事 see
favour *v.t* 比較鐘意 bay gao jung yee
favourable *a* 有利 yow lay
favourite *a* 最鐘意嘅 juy jung yee geh
favourite *n* 最鐘意嘅人 juy jung yee geh yan
fear *n* 恐懼 hung guy
fear *v.i* 驚 geng
fearful *a.* 驚 geng
feasible *a* 行得通嘅 hang dak tung geh
feast *n* 宴會 yeen wuy
feast *v.i* 盡情享用 jung ting heurng yung
feat *n* 功績 gung jik
feather *n* 羽毛 yu mo
feature *n* 特點 dak deem
February *n* 二月 yee yoot
federal *a* 聯邦嘅 loon borng geh
federation *n* 聯邦 loon borng
fee *n* 票價 piew ga
feeble *a* 虛弱 huy yeurk
feed *v.t* 餵 way
feed *n* 一餐 yat tan
feel *v.t* 摸 mor
feeling *n* 感覺 gam gok
feign *v.t* 扮 ban
felicitate *v.t* 祝賀 juk hor
felicity *n* 幸福 hang fuk
fell *v.t* 跌 deet
fellow *n* 同事 tung see
female *a* 女性嘅 luy sing geh
female *n* 女性 luy xing
feminine *a* 女性嘅 luy sing geh
fence *n* 圍欄 way lan
fence *v.t* 圍住 way ju
fend *v.t* 抵擋 day dorng
ferment *n* 政治騷動 jing jee so dung
ferment *v.t* 發酵 fat hao
fermentation *n* 發酵 fat hao
ferocious *a* 惡 ok
ferry *n* 郵輪 yow lun
ferry *v.t* 用船運送 yung shoon wan sung
fertile *a* 肥沃 fay yuk
fertility *n* 生育力 sang yuk lik
fertilize *v.t* 受精 sow jing
fertilizer *n* 肥料 fay liew
fervent *a* 熱烈 yeet leet
fervour *n* 熱情 yeet ting
festival *n* 節日 jeet yat
festive *a* 喜慶嘅 hay hing geh
festivity *n* 慶祝活動 hing juk wut dung
festoon *n* 花彩 fa choy
fetch *v.t* 攞 lor
fetter *n* 束縛 chuk bok
fetter *v.t* 限制 han jay
feud *n.* 世仇 say sow
feudal *a* 封建 fung geen
fever *n* 發燒 fat siew
few *a* 幾個 gey gor
fiasco *n* 慘敗 tarm bai
fibre *n* 纖維 teem way
fickle *a* 易變 yee been
fiction *n* 小說 siew shoot
fictitious *a* 虛構嘅 huy kow geh
fiddle *n* 騙局 peen guk
fiddle *v.i* 亂搞 loon gao
fidelity *n* 忠實 jung sat
fie *interj* 啤 ter
field *n* 田 teen
fiend *n* 惡魔 ok mor
fierce *a* 惡 ok
fiery *a* 暴躁 bo cho
fifteen *n* 十五 sap ng
fifty *n.* 五十 ng sap

fig *n* 無花果 mo fa gwor

fight *n* 打交 da gao

fight *v.t* 打 da

figment *n* 虛構 huy gou

figurative *a* 比如嘅 bay yu geh

figure *n* 身形 san ying

figure *v.t* 認爲 ying way

file *n* 文件 man gene

file *v.t* 提交 tay gao

file *n* 指甲銼 jee gap chor

file *v.t* 銼 chor

file *n* 一行人 yat horng yan

file *v.i.* 排成一行 pai sing yat horng

fill *v.t* 裝滿 jorng mun

film *n* 電影 deen ying

film *v.t* 錄影 luk ying

filter *n* 過濾器 gwor luy hay

filter *v.t* 過濾 gwor luy

filth *n* 污物 wu mat

filthy *a* 污糟 wu jo

fin *n* 鰭 kay

final *a* 最後 juy ho

finance *n* 財政 choy jing

finance *v.t* 提供資金 tay gung jee gam

financial *a* 財政嘅 choy jing geh

financier *n* 金融家 gam yung ga

find *v.t* 搵 wan

fine *n* 罰款 fat fwun

fine *v.t* 罰款 fat fwun

fine *a* 高質量 go jat leurng

finger *n* 手指 so jee

finger *v.t* 用手指摸 yung so jee mor

finish *v.t* 完成 yoon sing

finish *n* 結局 geet guk

finite *a* 有限嘅 yow han geh

fir *n* 冷杉 lang tam

fire *n* 火 for

fire *v.t* 發射 fat seh

firm *a* 結實 geet sat

firm *n.* 公司 gung see

first *a* 第一個 day yat gor

first *n* 第一個 day yat gor

first *adv* 首先 sow seen

fiscal *a* 財政嘅 choy jing geh

fish *n* 魚 yu

fish *v.i* 釣魚 diew yu

fisherman *n* 漁人 yu yan

fissure *n* 裂痕 leet han

fist *n* 拳頭 koon tow

fistula *n* 瘺管 low gwun

fit *v.t* 啱身 am san

fit *a* 健康 geen horng

fit *n* 發作 fat jok

fitful *a* 斷斷續續 toon toon juk juk

fitter *n* 安裝師傅 on jorng see fu

five *n* 五 ng

fix *v.t* 整好 jing ho

fix *n* 困境 kwun ging

flabby *a* 鬆弛 sung tee

flag *n* 旗 kay

flagrant *a* 明目張膽 ming muk jeurng darm

flame *n* 火焰 for yeem

flame *v.i* 燃燒 yeen siew

flannel *n* 法蘭絨 fat lan yung

flare *v.i* 燒 siew

flare *n* 火光 for gwong

flash *n* 閃光 seem gwong

flash *v.t* 閃 seem

flask *n* 燒瓶 siew ping

flat *a* 平嘅 ping geh

flat *n* 平嘅 ping geh

flatter *v.t* 討好 tow ho

flattery *n* 奉承 fung sing

flavour *n* 味道 mey dow

flaw *n* 瑕疵 har chee

flea *n.* 蚤 sat

flee *v.i* 閃人 seem yam

fleece *n* 羊毛 yeurng mo

fleece *v.t* 敲詐 hao ja

fleet *n* 艦隊 larm duy

flesh *n* 肉 yuk

flexible *a* 柔軟 yow yoon

flicker *n* 閃 seem

flicker *v.t* 閃閃下 seem ha

flight *n* 班機 ban gey

flimsy *a* 質地差 jat day ta

fling *v.t* 掟 deng

flippancy *n* 輕率 hing sut

flirt *n* 調情 tiew ting

flirt *v.i* 放電 forng deen

float *v.i* 漂 piew

flock *n* 群 kwan

flock *v.i* 擁埋 yung mai

flog *v.t* 賣 mai

flood *n* 水浸 suy jam

flood *v.t* 浸 jam

floor *n* 地下 dey ha

floor *v.t* 鋪地板 po day ban

flora *n* 植物群 jik mat kwan

florist *n* 花商 far seurng

flour *n* 麵粉 meen fan

flourish *v.i* 興旺 hing worng

flow *n* 流動 low dung

flow *v.i* 流 low

flower *n* 花 far

flowery *a* 花嘅 far geh

fluent *a* 流利 low lay

fluid *a* 流暢 low cheurng

fluid *n* 液體 yik tay

flush *v.i* 沖洗 chung say

flush *n* 面紅 meen hung

flute *n* 長笛 cheurng dek

flute *v.i* 吹笛 chuy dek

flutter *n* 飄動 piew dung

flutter *v.t* 飛 fay

fly *n* 烏蠅 wu ying

fly *v.i* 飛 fay

foam *n* 泡沫 po mut

foam *v.t* 起泡 hay po

focal *a* 重要嘅 jung yew geh

focus *n* 焦點 jiew deem

focus *v.t* 專注 joon ju

fodder *n* 飼料 jee liew

foe *n* 敵人 dik yan

fog *n* 霧 mo

foil *v.t* 制止 jay jee

fold *n* 摺 jeep

fold *v.t* 摺 jeep

foliage *n* 葉 yeep

follow *v.t* 跟住 gan ju

follower *n* 追隨者 juy chuy jeh

folly *n* 蠢 chun

foment *v.t* 挑起 tiew hay

fond *a* 鐘意 jung yee

fondle *v.t* 撫摸 fu mor

food *n* 食物 sik mat

fool *n* 蠢材 chun choy

foolish *a* 蠢嘅 chun geh

foolscap *n* 大頁紙 dai yeep jee

foot *n* 腳 geurt

for *prep* 畀 bay

for *conj.* 因為 yan way

forbid *v.t* 禁止 gam jee

force *n* 暴力 bo lik

force *v.t* 強迫 keurng bik

forceful *a* 堅強嘅 geen keurng geh

forcible *a* 強行嘅 keurng hang geh

forearm *n* 前臂 teen bay

forearm *v.t* 有備無患 yow bay mo wan

forecast *n* 預告 yu go

forecast *v.t* 預測 yu tak

forefather *n* 祖先 jo seen

forefinger *n* 食指 sik jee

forehead *n* 額頭 ak tow

foreign *a* 外國嘅 ngoy gwok geh

foreigner *n* 外國人 ngoy gwok yan

foreknowledge *n.* 預知 yu jee

foreleg *n* 前腳 teen geurt

forelock *n* 額髮 ak fat

foreman *n* 工頭 gung tow

foremost *a* 最重要嘅 juy jung yiew geh

forenoon *n* 上午 seurng hm
forerunner *n* 預兆 yu siew
foresee *v.t* 預見 yu geen
foresight *n* 先見之明 seen geen jee ming
forest *n* 森林 sam lam
forestall *v.t* 先發制人 seen fat jay yan
forester *n* 林務官 lam mo gwun
forestry *n* 林業 lam yeep
foretell *v.t* 預言 yu yeen
forethought *n* 預謀 yu mow
forever *adv* 永遠 wing yoon
forewarn *v.t* 預先警告 yu seen ging go
foreword *n* 序 juy
forfeit *v.t* 沒收 mwut sow
forfeit *n* 罰金 fat gam
forfeiture *n* 喪失 sorng sat
forge *n* 煉爐 leen lo
forge *v.t* 偽造 ngay jo
forgery *n* 偽造品 ngay jo ban
forget *v.t* 唔記得 hm gey dak
forgetful *a* 無記性 mo gey sing
forgive *v.t* 原諒 yoon leurng
forgo *v.t* 放棄 forng hay
forlorn *a* 孤苦伶仃 gu fu ling ding
form *n* 表格 biew gak
form *v.t.* 形成 ying sing
formal *a* 正式 jing sik
format *n* 格式 gak sik
formation *n* 隊形 duy ying
former *a* 昔日嘅 sik yat geh
former *pron* 前者 teen jeh
formerly *adv* 以前 yee teen
formidable *a* 可怕 hor pa
formula *n* 公式 gung sik
formulate *v.t* 規劃 kway wak
forsake *v.t.* 離棄 lay hay
forswear *v.t.* 放棄 forng hay
fort *n.* 堡壘 bo luy
forte *n.* 專長 joon cheurng

forth *adv.* 向前 heurng teen
forthcoming *a.* 即將發生嘅 jik jeurng fat sang geh
forthwith *adv.* 立刻 lap hak
fortify *v.t.* 增強 jang keurng
fortitude *n.* 耐力 loy lik
fort-night *n.* 兩個禮拜 leurng gor lay bai
fortress *n.* 城堡 sing bo
fortunate *a.* 好彩 ho choy
fortune *n.* 財產 choy tan
forty *n.* 四十 sey sap
forum *n.* 論壇 lun tan
forward *a.* 前 teen
forward *adv* 向前 heurng teen
forward *v.t* 轉寄 joon gey
fossil *n.* 化石 fa sek
foster *v.t.* 領養 ling yeurng
foul *a.* 臭 chow
found *v.t.* 搵到 wan dow
foundation *n.* 基礎 gey chor
founder *n.* 創立人 chorng lap yan
foundry *n.* 鑄造廠 ju jow chorng
fountain *n.* 噴水池 pan suy tee
four *n.* 四 sey
fourteen *n.* 十四 sap sey
fowl *n.* 家禽 ga kam
fowler *n.* 獵人 leep yan
fox *n.* 狐狸 wu lay
fraction *n.* 小部份 siew bo fan
fracture *n.* 骨折 gwat jeet
fracture *v.t* 折斷 jeet toon
fragile *a.* 脆弱 chuy yeurk
fragment *n.* 碎片 suy peen
fragrance *n.* 香味 heurng mey
fragrant *a.* 香嘅 heurng geh
frail *a.* 弱 yeurk
frame *v.t.* 鑲 seurng
frame *n* 框 kwang
frachise *n.* 特許經營權 dak huy ging ying koon
frank *a.* 坦白 tan bak

frantic *a.* 瘋狂 fung kwong	**frost** *n.* 霜 seurng
fraternal *a.* 兄弟嘅 hing day geh	**frown** *n.* 皺眉 jow mey
fraternity *n.* 群體 kwan tay	**frown** *v.i* 皺眉 jow mey
fratricide *n.* 殺兄弟姊妹罪 sat hing day jee mwuy juy	**frugal** *a.* 慳家 han ga
fraud *n.* 騙子 peen jee	**fruit** *n.* 生果 sang gwor
fraudulent *a.* 欺詐嘅 hay ja geh	**fruitful** *a.* 有效 yow hao
fraught *a.* 充滿 chung mun	**frustrate** *v.t.* 煩 fan
fray *n* 磨損 mor shoon	**frustration** *n.* 煩惱 fan lo
free *a.* 自由 jee yow	**fry** *v.t.* 炸 jar
free *v.t* 放 forng	**fry** *n* 魚苗 yu miew
freedom *n.* 自由 jee yow	**fuel** *n.* 燃料 yeen liew
freeze *v.i.* 凍結 dung geet	**fugitive** *a.* 走佬嘅 jow lo geh
freight *n.* 貨 for	**fugitive** *n.* 通緝犯 tung tap fan
French *a.* 法國嘅 fat gwok geh	**fulfil** *v.t.* 達成 dat sing
French *n* 法國人 fat gwok yan	**fulfilment** *n.* 成就感 sing jow gam
frenzy *n.* 狂熱 kwong yeet	**full** *a.* 滿 mun
frequency *n.* 頻率 pan lut	**full** *adv.* 滿嘅 mun geh
frequent *a.* 密 mat	**fullness** *n.* 豐滿度 fung mun dow
fresh *a.* 新鮮 san seen	**fully** *adv.* 完全 yoon choon
fret *n.* 煩惱 fan lo	**fumble** *v.i.* 亂摸 loon mor
fret *v.t.* 煩 fan	**fun** *n.* 好玩 ho wan
friction *n.* 摩擦力 mor chat lik	**function** *n.* 功能 gung lang
Friday *n.* 星期五 sing kay ng	**function** *v.i* 運作 wan jok
fridge *n.* 雪櫃 shoot gway	**functionary** *n.* 官員 gwun yoon
friend *n.* 朋友 pang yow	**fund** *n.* 資金 jee gam
fright *n.* 驚嚇 ging hak	**fundamental** *a.* 基本嘅 gey bwun geh
frighten *v.t.* 嚇 hak tan	**funeral** *n.* 喪禮 song lay
frigid *a.* 冷淡 lang dam	**fungus** *n.* 真菌 jan kwan
frill *n.* 褶邊 jeep been	**funny** *n.* 搞笑 gao siew
fringe *n.* 陰 yam	**fur** *n.* 毛 mo
fringe *v.t* 加緣飾 ga yoon sik	**furious** *a.* 超嬲 tiew low
frivolous *a.* 輕佻 hing tiew	**furl** *v.t.* 捲埋 goon mai
frock *n.* 裙 kwun	**furlong** *n.* 弗隆 fut lung
frog *n.* 青蛙 ting wa	**furnace** *n.* 火爐 for low
frolic *n.* 歡樂 fwun lok	**furnish** *v.t.* 佈置 bo jee
frolic *v.i.* 玩 wan	**furniture** *n.* 家私 ga see
from *prep.* 從 chung	**furrow** *n.* 皺紋 jow man
front *n.* 前 teen	**further** *adv.* 更遠嘅 gang yoon geh
front *a* 前面 teen meen	
front *v.t* 面向 meen heurng	
frontier *n.* 邊界 been gai	

further *a* 更進一步 gang jun yat bo	**gamble** *n* 賭博 dow bok
further *v.t* 增進 jang jun	**gambler** *n.* 賭仔 dow jay
fury *n.* 怒火 low for	**game** *n.* 遊戲 yow hai
fuse *v.t.* 結合 geet hap	**game** *v.i* 賭 dow
fuse *n* 保險絲 bo heem see	**gander** *n.* 雄鵝 hung or
fusion *n.* 結合 geet hap	**gang** *n.* 一班 yat ban
fuss *n.* 麻煩 ma fan	**gangster** *n.* 蠱惑仔 gu wak jay
fuss *v.i* 大驚小怪 dai geng siew gwai	**gap** *n* 罅 la
futile *a.* 無用 mo yung	**gape** *v.i.* 目定口呆 muk ding ho ngoy
futility *n.* 無益 mo yik	**garage** *n.* 車房 cher forng
future *a.* 未來嘅 may loy geh	**garb** *n.* 打扮 da ban
future *n* 將來 jeurng loy	**garb** *v.t* 着 jeurk
	garbage *n.* 垃圾 lap sap
	garden *n.* 花園 far yoon
	gardener *n.* 園藝家 yoon ngay ga

G

gabble *v.i.* 含糊不清 ham wu bat ting	**gargle** *v.i.* 口 lorng ho
gadfly *n.* 麻煩人 ma fan yan	**garland** *n.* 花環 far wan
gag *v.t.* 作嘔 jok oh	**garland** *v.t.* 戴花冠 dai far gwun
gag *n.* 笑話 siew wah	**garlic** *n.* 蒜蓉 shoon yung
gaiety *n.* 高興 go hing	**garment** *n.* 衫 sam
gain *v.t.* 增 jang	**garter** *n.* 吊襪帶 diew mat dai
gain *n* 好處 ho chu	**gas** *n.* 煤氣 mwuy hay
gainsay *v.t.* 唔認同 hm ying tung	**gasket** *n.* 墊圈 deen hoon
gait *n.* 行法 hang fat	**gasp** *n.* 深呼吸 sam fu kap
galaxy *n.* 星系 sing hay	**gasp** *v.i* 喘氣 choon hay
gale *n.* 颱風 toy fung	**gassy** *a.* 多氣體 dor hay tay
gallant *a.* 勇敢 yung gam	**gastric** *a.* 胃嘅 way geh
gallant *n* 型男 ying larm	**gate** *n.* 閘 jap
gallantry *n.* 勇敢 yung gam	**gather** *v.t.* 收集 sow jap
gallery *n.* 畫廊 wah lorng	**gaudy** *a.* 俗 juk
gallon *n.* 加侖 ga lun	**gauge** *n.* 計議器 gey yee hay
gallop *n.* 飛奔 fay ban	**gauntlet** *n.* 鐵手套 teet sow tow
gallop *v.t.* 奔跑 ban pao	**gay** *a.* 同性戀 tung sing loon
gallows *n.* . 絞刑架 gao ying ga	**gaze** *v.t.* 望住 morng ju
galore *adv.* 好多 ho dor	**gaze** *n* 凝視 ying see
galvanize *v.t.* 激勵 giklay	**gazette** *n.* 公報 gung bo
gamble *v.i.* 賭 dow	**gear** *n.* 檔 dorng
	geld *v.t.* 閹 yeem
	gem *n* 寶石 bo sek
	gender *n.* 性別 sing beet
	general *a.* 普遍嘅 po peen geh

generally *adv.* 通常 tung seurng

generate *v.t.* 產生 tan sang

generation *n.* 一代人 yat doy yan

generator *n.* 發電器 fat deen hay

generosity *n.* 寬宏大量 fwun wang dai leurng

generous *a.* 大方 dai forng

genius *n.* 天才 teen choy

gentle *a.* 溫柔 wan yow

gentleman *n.* 紳士 san see

gentry *n.* 上等人 seurng dang yan

genuine *a.* 真嘅 tan geh

geographer *n.* 地理學家 day lay hok ga

geographical *a.* 地理嘅 day lay geh

geography *n.* 地理學 day lay hok

geological *a.* 地質嘅 day jat geh

geologist *n.* 地質學家 day jat hok ga

geology *n.* 地質學 day jat hok

geometrical *a.* 幾何學嘅 gey hor hok geh

geometry *n.* 幾何學 gey hor hok

germ *n.* 病菌 beng kwan

germicide *n.* 殺菌劑 sat kwan jay

germinate *v.i.* 發芽 fat ngar

germination *n.* 成長 sing jeurng

gerund *n.* 動名詞 dung ming tee

gesture *n.* 手勢 sow say

get *v.t.* 攞 lor

ghastly *a.* 恐怖 hung bo

ghost *n.* 鬼 gway

giant *n.* 巨人 guy yan

gibbon *n.* 長臂猿 cheurng bay yoon

gibe *v.i.* 串人 choon yan

gibe *n* 侮辱 mo yuk

giddy *a.* 激動 gik dung

gift *n.* 禮物 lay mat

gifted *a.* 有才華嘅 yow choy wah

gigantic *a.* 巨大嘅 guy dai geh

giggle *v.i.* 格格笑 gak gak siew

gild *v.t.* 鍍金 dow gam

gilt *a.* 鍍金 dow gam

ginger *n.* 姜 geurng

giraffe *n.* 長頸鹿 cheurng geng luk

gird *v.t.* 準備 jun bay

girder *n.* 大梁 dai leurng

girdle *n.* 腰帶 yiew dai

girdle *v.t* 圍繞 way yiew

girl *n.* 女仔 luy jay

girlish *a.* 女性化 luy sing fa

gist *n.* 要點 yiew deem

give *v.t.* 畀 bay

glacier *n.* 冰河 bing hor

glad *a.* 高興 go hing

gladden *v.t.* 高興 go hing

glamour *n.* 吸引力 kap yan ik

glance *n.* 一眼 yat ngan

glance *v.i.* 望 morng

gland *n.* 腺 seen

glare *n.* 眼倔倔 ngan gwat gwat

glare *v.i* 眼倔倔咁望 ngan gwat gwat gam morng

glass *n.* 草 cho

glaucoma *n.* 青光眼 teng gwong ngan

glaze *v.t.* 發呆 fat ngoy

glaze *n* 釉 yow

glazier *n.* 玻璃工人 bor lay gung yan

glee *n.* 高興 go hing

glide *v.t.* 滑 wat

glider *n.* 滑翔機 wat cheurng gey

glimpse *n.* 一眼 yat ngan

glitter *v.i.* 閃 seem

glitter *n* 閃粒 seem lap

global *a.* 全球嘅 choon kow geh

globe *n.* 地球 day kow

gloom *n.* 幽暗 yow am

gloomy *a.* 陰暗 yam am

glorification *n.* 讚揚 jan yeurng

glorify *v.t.* 吹捧 chuy pung

glorious *a.* 光榮嘅 gwong wing geh

glory *n.* 榮譽 wing yu

gloss *n.* 光澤 gwong jak

glossary *n.* 詞彙表 tee wuy biew

glossy *a.* 光滑嘅 gwong wat geh

glove *n.* 手套 sow tow

glow *v.i.* 發光 fat gwong

glow *n* 暗光 am gwong

glucose *n.* 葡萄糖 po tow tong

glue *n.* 膠水 gao suy

glut *v.t.* 超量供應 tiew leurng gung ying

glut *n* 供過於求 gung gwor yu kow

glutton *n.* 爲食嘅人 way sik geh yan

gluttony *n.* 暴飲暴食 bo yam bo sik

glycerine *n.* 甘油 gam yow

go *v.i.* 去 huy

goad *n.* 激勵 gik lay

goad *v.t* 招惹 tiew yeh

goal *n.* 目標 muk biew

goat *n.* 山羊 san yeurng

gobble *n.* 狼吞虎嚥 lorng tun fu yeen

goblet *n.* 酒杯 jow bwuy

god *n.* 上帝 seurng day

goddess *n.* 女神 luy san

godhead *n.* 上帝 seurng day

godly *a.* 虔誠嘅 keen sing geh

godown *n.* 倉庫 chorng fu

godsend *n.* 天賜之物 tteen tee jee mat

goggles *n.* 護眼鏡 wu ngan geng

gold *n.* 金 gam

golden *a.* 金色嘅 gam sik geh

goldsmith *n.* 金匠 gam jeurng

golf *n.* 高爾夫球 go yee fu kow

gong *n.* 鑼 lor

good *a.* 好嘅 ho geh

good *n* 好處 ho chu

good-bye *interj.* 再見 joy geen

goodness *n.* 美德 may dak

goodwill *n.* 善意 seen yee

goose *n.* 鵝 or

gooseberry *n.* 醋栗 cho lut

gorgeous *a.* 好靚 ho leng

gorilla *n.* 猩猩 sing sing

gospel *n.* 福音 fuk yam

gossip *n.* 閒話 han wah

gourd *n.* 葫蘆 wu low

gout *n.* 通風病 tung fung beng

govern *v.t.* 統治 tung jee

governance *n.* 統治方式 tung jee forng sik

governess *n.* 家庭女教師 ga ting luy gao see

government *n.* 政府 jing fu

governor *n.* 州長 jow jeurng

gown *n.* 女禮服 luy lay fuk

grab *v.t.* 捉住 juk ju

grace *n.* 優美 yow may

grace *v.t.* 裝飾 jorng sik

gracious *a.* 仁慈 yan tee

gradation *n.* 階段 gai doon

grade *n.* 級 kap

grade *v.t* 分級 gan kap

gradual *a.* 逐漸 juk jeem

graduate *v.i.* 畢業 bat yeep

graduate *n* 畢業生 bat yeep sang

graft *n.* 移植物 yee jik mat

graft *v.t* 移植 yee jik

grain *n.* 一粒 yat lap

grammar *n.* 文法 man fat

grammarian *n.* 文法家 man fat ga

gramme *n.* 克 hak

gramophone *n.* 留聲機 low seng gey

granary *n.* 糧倉 leurng chorng	greet *v.t.* 打招呼 da jiew fu
grand *a.* 壯麗嘅 jorng lay geh	grenade *n.* 手榴彈 sow low dan
grandeur *n.* 宏偉 wang way	grey *a.* 灰色嘅 fwuy sik geh
grant *v.t.* 畀 bay	greyhound *n.* 灰狗 gwuy gow
grant *n* 撥款 pwut fwun	grief *n.* 悲痛 bay tung
grape *n.* 提子 tay jee	grievance *n.* 委屈 way wat
graph *n.* 圖表 tow biew	grieve *v.t.* 傷心 seurng sam
graphic *a.* 繪畫嘅 kwuy wah geh	grievous *a.* 令人痛苦 ling yan tung fu
grapple *n.* 格鬥 gak dow	
grapple *v.i.* 扭打 low da	grind *v.i.* 磨碎 mor suy
grasp *v.t.* 捉住 juk ju	grinder *n.* 磨碎機 mor suy gey
grasp *n* 掌握 jeurng ak	grip *v.t.* 捉實 juk sat
grass *n* 草 cho	grip *n* 控制 hung jay
grate *n.* 爐條 lo tiew	groan *v.i.* 嘆息 tan sik
grate *v.t* 磨碎 mor suy	groan *n* 呻吟聲 san yam seng
grateful *a.* 感激 gam gik	grocer *n.* 雜貨店 jap for deem
gratification *n.* 滿足感 mun juk gam	grocery *n.* 雜貨店 jap for deem
	groom *n.* 新郎 san lorng
gratis *adv.* 免費嘅 meen fay geh	groom *v.t* 梳毛 sormo
gratitude *n.* 感激 gam gik	groove *n.* 紋 man
gratuity *n.* 貼士 teep see	groove *v.t* 鍕 gai
grave *n.* 墳頭 fan tow	grope *v.t.* 猥瑣 wuy sor
grave *a.* 嚴肅 yeem suk	gross *n.* 總收入 jung sao yap
gravitate *v.i.* 被吸引到 bay kap yan dow	gross *a.* 核突 wat dat
	grotesque *a.* 荒謬嘅 forng mo geh
gravitation *n.* 引力 yan lik	
gravity *n.* 地心吸引力 day sam kap yan lik	ground *n.* 地 day
	group *n.* 一組 yat jow
graze *v.i.* 食草 sik cho	group *v.t.* 組成 jow sing
graze *n* 擦傷 tat seurng	grow *v.t.* 生 sang
grease *n* 油脂 yow jee	grower *n.* 種植者 jung jik jeh
grease *v.t* 擦油 tat yow	growl *v.i.* 吼叫 hung giew
greasy *a.* 多油 dor yow	growl *n* 吼叫聲 hung giew seng
great *a* 好好 ho ho	growth *n.* 發育 fat yuk
greed *n.* 貪慾 tam yuk	grudge *v.t.* 勉強做 meen keurng jo
greedy *a.* 貪心 tam sam	
Greek *n.* 希臘人 hay lap yan	grudge *n* 怨恨 yoon han
Greek *a* 希臘文 hay lap man	grumble *v.i.* 發牢騷 fat low sow
green *a.* 綠色嘅 luk sik geh	grunt *n.* 呼嚕 fu low
green *n* 綠色 luk sik	grunt *v.i.* 呼嚕聲 fu low seng
greenery *n.* 綠色植物 luk sik jik mat	guarantee *n.* 保養 bo yeurng
	guarantee *v.t* 擔保 dan bo

guard v.i. 守衛 sow way

guard n. 護衛 wu way

guardian n. 守護者 sow wu jeh

guava n. 番石榴 fan sek low

guerilla n. 游擊戰 yow gik jeen

guess n. 猜測 tai tak

guess v.i 估 gu

guest n. 嘉賓 gar ban

guidance n. 指導 jee dow

guide v.t. 指引 jee yan

guide n. 指南 jee lam

guild n. 協會 heep wuy

guile n. 蠱惑 gu wak

guilt n. 內疚 loy gow

guilty a. 內疚 loy gow

guise n. 外表 ngoy biew

guitar n. 結他 geet ta

gulf n. 海灣 hoy wan

gull n. 海鷗 hoy ow

gull n 受騙者 sow peen jeh

gull v.t 呃 ak

gulp n. 一大啖 yat dai dam

gum n. 牙肉 ngar yuk

gun n. 槍 cheurng

gust n. 一陣風 yat jan fung

gutter n. 水槽 suy cho

guttural a. 喉嚨嘅 ho lung geh

gymnasium n. 體育館 tay yuk gwun

gymnast n. 體操員 tay cho yoon

gymnastic a. 體操嘅 tay cho geh

gymnastics n. 體操 tay cho

habeas corpus n. 人身保護令 yan san bo wu ling

habit n. 習慣 jap gwan

habitable a. 適合住嘅 sik hap ju geh

habitat n. 棲息地 tay sik day

habitation n. 居住 guy ju

habituate v. t. 習慣咗 jap gwan jor

hack v.t. 侵入 tam yap

hag n. 醜女 tow luy

haggard a. 憔悴 tiew suy

haggle v.i. 講價 gorng ga

hail n. 冰雹 bing pao

hail v.i 讚 jan

hail v.t 招手 jiew sow

hair n 頭髮 tow fat

hale a. 硬朗 ang lorn

half n. 一半 yat bwun

half a 半 bwun

hall n. 禮堂 lay tong

hallmark n. 特徵 dak jing

hallow v.t. 崇敬 sung ging

halt v. t. 停止 ting jee

halt n 停止 ting jee

halve v.t. 分半 fan bwun

hamlet n. 細村莊 sai choon jorng

hammer n. 槌仔 chuy jay

hammer v.t 揼 dap

hand n 手 sow

hand v.t 畀 bay

handbill n. 傳單 choon dan

handbook n. 手冊 sow tak

handcuff n. 手扣 sow kow

handcuff v.t. 鎖 sor

handful n. 少數 siew sow

handicap v.t. 阻礙 jor ngoy

handicap n 殘疾 tan jat

handicraft n. 手工藝 sow gung ngay

handiwork n. 手工 sow gung

handkerchief n. 手巾 sow gan

handle n. 手柄 sow beng

handle v.t 處理 chu lay

handsome a. 靚仔 leng jay

handy a. 方便 forng been

hang v.t. 掛 gwa

hanker v.i. 渴望 hot morng

haphazard *a.* 無秩序 mo deet juy

happen *v.t.* 發生 fat sang

happening *n.* 事 see

happiness *n.* 快樂 fai lok

happy *a.* 開心 hoy sam

harass *v.t.* 騷擾 sow yiew

harassment *n.* 騷擾 sow yiew

harbour *n.* 港 gorng

harbour *v.t* 窩藏 wor chorng

hard *a.* 難 lan

harden *v.t.* 硬化 ang far

hardihood *n.* 大膽 dai dam

hardly *adv.* 幾乎無 gey fu mow

hardship *n.* 艱難 gan lan

hardy *adj.* 適應力強 sik ying lik keurng

hare *n.* 野兔 yeh tow

harm *n.* 損害 shoon hoy

harm *v.t* 傷害 seurng hoy

harmonious *a.* 和諧嘅 wor hai geh

harmonium *n.* 風琴 fung kam

harmony *n.* 和睦 wor muk

harness *n.* 馬具 ma guy

harness *v.t* 控制 hung jay

harp *n.* 豎琴 shu kam

harsh *a.* 刻薄 hak bok

harvest *n.* 收成 sow sing

havester *n.* 收割機 sow got gey

haste *n.* 匆忙 chung morng

hasten *v.i.* 促進 chuk jun

hasty *a.* 草率 cho sut

hat *n.* 帽 mo

hatchet *n.* 斧頭 fu tow

hate *n.* 仇恨 sow han

hate *v.t.* 憎 jang

haughty *a.* 高傲自大嘅 gow oh jee dai geh

haunt *v.t.* 鬼魂出沒 gway wan chut mwut

haunt *n* 成日去嘅地方 sing yat huy geh day forng

have *v.t,* 有 yow

haven *n.* 避難所 bay lan sor

havoc *n.* 浩劫 ho geep

hawk *n* 鷹 ying

hawker *n* 小販 siew fan

hawthorn *n.* 山楂樹 san ja shu

hay *n.* 乾草 gon cho

hazard *n.* 危險 ngay heem

hazard *v.t* 冒險 mo heem

haze *n.* 薄霧 bok mo

hazy *a.* 模糊 mo wu

he *pron.* 佢 kuy

head *n.* 頭 tow

head *v.t* 去 huy

headache *n.* 頭痛 tow tung

heading *n.* 標題 biew tay

headlong *adv.* 輕率 hing sut

headstrong *a.* 硬頸 ang geng

heal *v.i.* 醫好 yee ho

health *n.* 健康 geen horng

healthy *a.* 健康 geen horng

heap *n.* 一堆 yat duy

heap *v.t* 堆積 duy jik

hear *v.t.* 聽 teng

hearsay *n.* 傳聞 choon man

heart *n.* 心 sam

hearth *n.* 爐低 lo day

heartily *adv.* 盡情咁 jun ting gam

heat *n.* 熱 yeet

heat *v.t* 加熱 ga yeet

heave *v.i.* 搬 bwun

heaven *n.* 天堂 teen tong

heavenly *a.* 天堂嘅 teen tong geh

hedge *n.* 樹籬 shu lay

hedge *v.t* 轉彎抹角 joon wan mwut got

heed *v.t* 注意 ju yee

heed *n* 留心 low sam

heel *n.* 腳睜 geurt jang

hefty *a.* 重 chung

height *n.* 高度 go dow

heighten *v.t.* 增高 jang gow

heinous *a.* 非常惡毒嘅 fay seurng ok duk geh

heir *n.* 繼承人 gey sing yan

hell *a.* 地獄 dey yuk

helm *n.* 舵輪 tor lun

helmet *n.* 頭盔 tow kway

help *v.t.* 幫 borng

help *n* 幫助 borng jor

helpful *a.* 樂於助人 lok yu jor yan

helpless *a.* 無用嘅 mo yung geh

helpmate *n.* 伴侶 bwun luy

hemisphere *n.* 半球 bwun kow

hemp *n.* 大麻 dai ma

hen *n.* 母雞 mo gey

hence *adv.* 因此 yan tee

henceforth *adv.* 從此以後 chung tee yee ho

henceforward *adv.* 從今以後 chung gam yee ho

henchman *n.* 親信 tan sun

henpecked *a.* 怕老婆 pa lo por

her *pron.* 佢 kuy

her *a* 佢嘅 kuy geh

herald *n.* 宣佈 shoon bo

herald *v.t* 預兆 yu siew

herb *n.* 藥草 yeurk cho

herculean *a.* 力大無比嘅 lik dai mo bay geh

herd *n.* 一群 yat kwan

herdsman *n.* 牧人 muk yan

here *adv.* 呢度 lee dow

hereabouts *adv.* 呢頭附近 lee tow fu gan

hereafter *adv.* 從此以後 chung tee yee ho

hereditary *n.* 遺傳嘅 way choon geh

heredity *n.* 遺傳 way choon

heritable *a.* 可以遺傳嘅 hor yee way choon geh

heritage *n.* 遺產 way tan

hermit *n.* 隱士 yan see

hermitage *n.* 隱居處 yan guy chu

hernia *n.* 突出 dat chut

hero *n.* 英雄 ying hung

heroic *a.* 英勇嘅 ying yung geh

heroine *n.* 女主角 luy ju gok

heroism *n.* 英雄精神 ying hung jing san

herring *n.* 鯡魚 fay yu

hesitant *a.* 猶豫嘅 yow yee geh

hesitate *v.i.* 猶豫 yow yee

hesitation *n.* 猶豫 yow yee

hew *v.t.* 劈 pek

heyday *n.* 高峰時期 go fung see kay

hibernation *n.* 冬眠 dung meen

hiccup *n.* 打嗝 da gut

hide *n.* 藏身處 chorng san chu

hide *v.t* 收埋 sow mai

hideous *a.* 核突 wat dat

hierarchy *n.* 等級制度 dang kap jay dow

high *a.* 高 go

highly *adv.* 非常 fay seurng

Highness *n.* 殿下 deen ha

highway *n.* 大路 dai low

hilarious *a.* 好搞笑 ho gao siew

hilarity *n.* 高興 go hing

hill *n.* 山 san

hillock *n.* 小丘 siew yow

him *pron.* 佢 kuy

hinder *v.t.* 阻礙 jor ngoy

hindrance *n.* 防礙 forng ngoy

hint *n.* 提示 tay see

hint *v.i* 暗示 am see

hip *n* 臀部 toon bo

hire *n.* 租用 jow yung

hire *v.t* 租 jow

hireling *n.* 工人 gung yan

his *pron.* 佢嘅 kuy geh

hiss *n* 嘶嘶聲 see see seng

hiss *v.i* 發嘶嘶聲 fat see see seng

historian *n.* 歷史學家 lik see hok ga

historic *a.* 歷史性嘅 lik see sing geh

historical *a.* 歷史嘅 lik see geh

history *n.* 歷史 lik see

hit *v.t.* 打 da

hit *n* 打擊 da gik

hitch *n.* 故障 gu jeurng

hither *adv.* 到呢度 dow lee dow

hitherto *adv.* 直到而家 jik dow yee ga

hive *n.* 蜂房 fung forng

hoarse *a.* 沙啞 sar ngar

hoax *n.* 惡作劇 ok jok kek

hoax *v.t* 整蠱 jing gu

hobby *n.* 嗜好 see ho

hobby-horse *n.* 木馬 muk mah

hockey *n.* 曲棍球 kun gwan kow

hoist *v.t.* 吊起 diew hay

hold *n.* 控制 hung jay

hold *v.t* 揸住 ja ju

hole *n* 窿 lung

hole *v.t* 打窿 da lung

holiday *n.* 旅行 luy hang

hollow *a.* 空心嘅 hung sam geh

hollow *n.* 洞 dung

hollow *v.t* 整凹 jing lap

holocaust *n.* 大屠殺 dai tow sat

holy *a.* 神聖嘅 san sing geh

homage *n.* 敬意 ging yee

home *n.* 屋企 uk kay

homicide *n.* 殺人罪 sat yan juy

homoeopath *n.* 同種療法師 tung jung liew fat see

homeopathy *n.* 同種療法 tung jung liew fat

homogeneous *a.* 同類嘅 tung luy geh

honest *a.* 誠實 sing sat

honesty *n.* 誠實 sing sat

honey *n.* 蜜糖 mat torng

honeycomb *n.* 蜂巢 fung tao

honeymoon *n.* 度蜜月 dow may yoot

honorarium *n.* 酬金 chow gam

honorary *a.* 義務嘅 yee mo geh

honour *n.* 榮譽 wing yu

honour *v.t* 尊敬 joon ging

honourable *a.* 品加高尚 ban gak go seurng

hood *n.* 帽 mow

hoodwink *v.t.* 呃 ak

hoof *n.* 蹄 tay

hook *n.* 鉤 oh

hooligan *n.* 飛仔 fay jay

hoot *n.* 喇叭聲 la ba seng

hoot *v.i* 響 heurng

hop *v.i* 單腳跳 dan geurt tiew

hop *n* 單腳跳 dan geurt tiew

hope *v.t.* 希望 hay morng

hope *n* 希望 hay morng

hopeful *a.* 滿懷希望 mun wai hay morng

hopeless *a.* 無望 mo morng

horde *n.* 一大班人 yat dai ban yan

horizon *n.* 地平線 day ping seen

horn *n.* 角 gok

hornet *n.* 大黃峰 dai wong fung

horrible *a.* 恐怖嘅 hung bo geh

horrify *v.t.* 嚇 hak

horror *n.* 恐怖 hung bo

horse *n.* 馬 ma

horticulture *n.* 園藝 yoon ngay

hose *n.* 水管 suy gwun

hosiery *n.* 襪類 mat luy

hospitable *a.* 好客嘅 ho hak geh

hospital *n.* 醫院 yee yoon

hospitality *n.* 好客 ho hak

host *n.* 主持 ju tee

hostage *n.* 人質 yan jee

hostel *n.* 旅舍 luy she

hostile *a.* 強烈反對 keurng leet fan duy

hostility *n.* 對抗 duy korng	**hunt** *v.t.* 打獵 da leep
hot *a.* 熱 yeet	**hunt** *n* 搵 wan
hotchpotch *n.* 一大堆嘢 yat dai duy yeh	**hunter** *n.* 獵人 leep yan
hotel *n.* 酒店 jow deem	**huntsman** *n.* 獵人 leep yan
hound *n.* 獵犬 leep hoon	**hurdle1** *n.* 跨欄 kwa lan
hour *n.* 鐘頭 jung tow	**hurdle2** *v.t* 跳過 tiew gwor
house *n* 屋 uk	**hurl** *v.t.* 大力咁掟 dai lik gam deng
house *v.t* 收容 sow yung	**hurrah** *interj.* 好啊 ho ah
how *adv.* 點樣 deem yeurng	**hurricane** *n.* 颱風 toy fung
however *adv.* 不過 bat gwor	**hurry** *v.t.* 趕 gon
however *conj* 但係 dan hay	**hurry** *n* 急住 gap ju
howl *v.t.* 大聲叫 dai seng giew	**hurt** *v.t.* 受傷 sow seurng
howl *n* 喊叫聲 ham giew seng	**hurt** *n* 委屈 way wat
hub *n.* 輪轂	**husband** *n* 老公 lo gung
hubbub *n.* 嘈雜聲 cho jap seng	**husbandry** *n.* 農牧業 lung muk yeep
huge *a.* 好大嘅 ho dai geh	**hush** *n* 變安靜 been on jing
hum *v.i* 哼 hang	**hush** *v.i* 唔好講嘢 hm ho gorng yeh
hum *n* 嗡嗡聲 wung wung seng	
human *a.* 人類 yan luy	**husk** *n.* 外殼 ngoy hok
humane *a.* 有人性嘅 yow yan sing geh	**husky** *a.* 沙啞 sa ngar
humanitarian *a* 人道主義嘅 yan dow ju yee geh	**hut** *n.* 茅屋 mao uk
humanity *n.* 人類 yan luy	**hyaena, hyena** *n.* 鬣狗 leep gow
humanize *v.t.* 變得適合人 been dak sik hap yan	**hybrid** *a.* 雜種嘅 jap jung geh
humble *a.* 謙虛 heem huy	**hybrid** *n* 雜種 jap jung
humdrum *a.* 單調 dan diew	**hydrogen** *n.* 氫氣 hing hay
humid *a.* 焗 guk	**hygiene** *n.* 衛生 way sang
humidity *n.* 濕度 sap dow	**hygienic** *a.* 衛生嘅 way sang geh
humiliate *v.t.* 落面 lok meen	**hymn** *n.* 聖歌 sing gor
humiliation *n.* 恥辱 tee yuk	**hyperbole** *n.* 誇張 kwa jeurng
humility *n.* 謙虛 heem huy	**hypnotism** *n.* 催眠術 chuy meen suy
humorist *n.* 幽默作家 yow mak jok ga	**hypnotize** *v.t.* 催眠 chuy meen
humorous *a.* 幽默 yow mak	**hypocrisy** *n.* 虛偽 huy ngay
humour *n.* 幽默感 yow mak gam	**hypocrite** *n.* 偽君子 ngay gwan jee
hunch *n.* 直覺 jik gok	**hypocritical** *a.* 虛偽嘅 huy ngay geh
hundred *n.* 一百 yat bak	**hypothesis** *n.* 假設 ga teet
hunger *n* 渴望 hot morng	**hypothetical** *a.* 假設 ga teet
hungry *a.* 肚餓 tow or	

hysteria *n.* 大驚小怪 dai geng siew gwai

hysterical *a.* 情緒激動 ting suy gik dung

I *pron.* 我 ngor

ice *n.* 冰 bing

iceberg *n.* 冰山 bing san

icicle *n.* 冰柱 bing ju

icy *a.* 冰 bing

idea *n.* 想法 seurng fat

ideal *a.* 理想嘅 lay seurng geh

ideal *n* 理想 lay seurng

idealism *n.* 理想主義 lay seurng ju yee

idealist *n.* 理想主義者 lay seurng ju yee jeh

idealistic *a.* 理想主義 lay seurng ju yee

idealize *v.t.* 理想化 lay seurng far

identical *a.* 一樣嘅 yat yeurng geh

indentification *n.* 身分證明 san fan jing ming

identify *v.t.* 辨認 been ying

identity *n.* 身分 san fan

idiocy *n.* 愚蠢行爲 yu chun hang way

idiom *n.* 成語 sing yu

idiomatic *a.* 地道嘅 day dow geh

idiot *n.* 白癡 bak tee

idiotic *a.* 蠢嘅 chun geh

idle *a.* 無嘢做 mo yeh jow

idleness *n.* 閒散 han san

idler *n.* 遊手好閒嘅人 yow sow ho han geh yan

idol *n.* 偶像 oh jeurng

idolater *n.* 崇拜者 sung bai jeh

if *conj.* 如果 yu gwor

ignoble *a.* 唔光彩嘅 hm gwong choy geh

ignorance *n.* 無知 mo jee

ignorant *a.* 無知 mo jee

ignore *v.t.* 忽視 fat see

ill *a.* 病 beng

ill *adv.* 差 ta

ill *n* 病 beng

illegal *a.* 犯法 fan fat

illegibility *n.* 模糊不清 mow wu bat ting

illegible *a.* 難讀 lan duk

illegitimate *a.* 私生嘅 see sang geh

illicit *a.* 非法嘅 fay fat geh

illiteracy *n.* 文盲 man mang

illiterate *a.* 文盲 man mang

illness *n.* 病 beng

illogical *a.* 唔合邏輯嘅 hm hap lor tap geh

illuminate *v.t.* 照 jiew

illumination *n.* 光源 gwong yoon

illusion *n.* 錯覺 chor gok

illustrate *v.t.* 加圖 ga tow

illustration *n.* 插圖 tap tow

image *n.* 圖片 tow peen

imagery *n.* 意象 yee jeurng

imaginary *a.* 幻想 wan seurng

imagination *n.* 想像力 seurng jeurng lik

imaginative *a.* 有想像力 yow seurng jeurng lik

imagine *v.t.* 想像下 seurng jeurng ha

imitate *v.t.* 模仿 mo forng

imitation *n.* 模仿 mo forng

imitator *n.* 模仿者 mo forng jeh

immaterial *a.* 唔緊要 hm gan yiew

immature *a.* 幼稚 yow jee

immaturity *n.* 未成年 may sing

leen

immeasurable　*a.* 無限嘅 mo han geh

immediate　*a* 即刻 jik hak

immemorial　*a.* 古老嘅 gu low geh

immense　*a.* 巨大嘅 guy dai geh

immensity　*n.* 巨大 guy dai

immerse　*v.t.* 浸 jam

immersion　*n.* 浸 jam

immigrant　*n.* 移民 yee man

immigrate　*v.i.* 移民 yee man

immigration　*n.* 移民 yee man

imminent　*a.* 即將發生 jik jeurng fat sang

immodest　*a.* 唔謙虛 hm heem huy

immodesty　*n.* 唔謙虛 hm heem huy

immoral　*a.* 不道德 bat dow dak

immorality　*n.* 邪惡 ter ok

immortal　*a.* 不死嘅 bat say geh

immortality　*n.* 永生 wing sang

immortalize　*v.t.* 名垂千古 ming suy teen gu

immovable　*a.* 固定嘅 gu ding geh

immune　*a.* 有免疫力嘅 yow meen yik lik geh

immunity　*n.* 免疫力 meen yik lik

immunize　*v.t.* 免疫 meen yik

impact　*n.* 影響力 ying heurng lik

impart　*v.t.* 通知 tung jee

impartial　*a.* 中立嘅 jung lap geh

impartiality　*n.* 公平 gung ping

impassable　*a.* 過唔到 gwor hm dow

impasse　*n.* 死路 say low

impatience　*n.* 無耐性 mo loy sing

impatient　*a.* 無耐性 mo loy sing

impeach　*v.t.* 告 gow

impeachment　*n.* 告 gow

impede　*v.t.* 阻止 jor jee

impediment　*n.* 障礙 jeurng ngoy

impenetrable　*a.* 穿唔過嘅 choon hm gwor geh

imperative　*a.* 急嘅 gap geh

imperfect　*a.* 唔完美 hm yoon may

imperfection　*n.* 瑕疵 har tee

imperial　*a.* 皇帝嘅 worng day geh

imperialism　*n.* 帝國統治 day gwok tung jee

imperil　*v.t.* 陷入險境 ham yap heem ging

imperishable　*a.* 不死嘅 bat say geh

impersonal　*a.* 冷淡 lang dam

impersonate　*v.t.* 模仿 mo forng

impersonation　*n.* 模仿 mo forng

impertinence　*n.* 無禮嘅 mow lay geh

impertinent　*a.* 不敬 bat ging

impetuosity　*n.* 衝動 chung dung

impetuous　*a.* 輕率 hing sut

implement　*n.* 工具 gung guy

implement　*v.t.* 執行 jap hang

implicate　*v.t.* 牽涉 heen seep

implication　*n.* 牽連 heen leen

implicit　*a.* 唔懷疑 hm wai yee

implore　*v.t.* 求 kow

imply　*v.t.* 暗示 am see

impolite　*a.* 無禮貌 mow lay mao

import　*v.t.* 進入 jun yap

import　*n.* 引進 yan jun

importance　*n.* 重要性 jung yiew sing

important　*a.* 重要 jung yiew

impose　*v.t.* 推行 tuy hang

imposing　*a.* 令人印象深刻 ling yan yan jeurng sam hak

imposition　*n.* 實施 sat see

impossibility　*n.* 無可能性 mow

hor lang sing

impossible *a.* 無可能 mow hor lang

impostor *n.* 騙子 peen jee

imposture *n.* 假冒行騙 ga mow hang peen

impotence *n.* 無能 mo lang

impotent *a.* 性無能嘅 sing mo lang geh

impoverish *v.t.* 變窮 been kung

impracticability *n.* 無法事實 mo fat sat see

impracticable *a.* 不切實際嘅 bat teet sat jay geh

impress *v.t.* 驚喜 ging hay

impression *n.* 印象 yan jeurng

impressive *a.* 印象深刻 yan jeurng sam hak

imprint *v.t.* 印 yan

imprint *n.* 壓印 ngat yan

imprison *v.t.* 軟禁 yoon gam

improper *a.* 唔正當嘅 hm jing dong geh

impropriety *n.* 唔合適嘅行為 hm hap sik geh hang way

improve *v.t.* 進步 jun bo

improvement *n.* 進步 jun bo

imprudence *n.* 輕率 hing sut

imprudent *a.* 唔明智嘅 hm ming jee geh

impulse *n.* 衝動 chung dung

impulsive *a.* 衝動 chung dung

impunity *n.* 免責 meen jak

impure *a.* 唔純潔嘅 hm sun geet geh

impurity *n.* 雜質 jap jat

impute *v.t.* 歸咎於 gway gow yu

in *prep.* 喺 hay

inability *n.* 無能力 mo lang lik

inaccurate *a.* 唔準確 hm jun kok

inaction *n.* 唔做嘢 hm jow yeh

inactive *a.* 唔活躍 hm wut yeurk

inadmissible *a.* 唔允許 hm wan huy

inanimate *a.* 無生命嘅 mow sang ming geh

inapplicable *a.* 唔適合 hm sik hap geh

inattentive *a.* 無心裝載 mo sam jorng joy

inaudible *a.* 聽唔到 teng hm dow

inaugural *a.* 開創嘅 hoy chorng geh

inauguration *n.* 就職 jow jik

inauspicious *a.* 不祥嘅 bat cheurng geh

inborn *a.* 天生嘅 teen sang geh

incalculable *a.* 計唔到嘅 gey hm dow geh

incapable *a.* 無能力 mo lang lik

incapacity *n.* 無能力 mo lang lik

incarnate *a.* 人體化嘅 yan tay far geh

incarnate *v.t.* 具體化 guy tay far

incarnation *n.* 化身 far san

incense *v.t.* 激人 gikyan

incense *n.* 香 heurng

incentive *n.* 鼓勵 gu lay

inception *n.* 開始 hoy tee

inch *n.* 寸 choon

incident *n.* 事 see

incidental *a.* 唔重要嘅 hm jung yiew geh

incite *v.t.* 激發 gik fat

inclination *n.* 意願 yee yoon

incline *v.i.* 傾向 king heurng

include *v.t.* 包括 bao kwut

inclusion *n.* 包括 bao kwut

inclusive *a.* 包括 bao kwut

incoherent *a.* 唔清唔楚 hm ting hm chor

income *n.* 收入 sow yap

incomparable *a.* 無得比 mo dak bay

incompetent *a.* 無能力 mo lang lik

incomplete *a.* 未完成 may yoon sing

inconsiderate *a.* 唔體諒 hm tay leurng

inconvenient *a.* 唔方便 hm forng been

incorporate *v.t.* 加入 ga yap

incorporate *a.* 合併 hap ping

incorporation *n.* 納入 lap yap

incorrect *a.* 錯 chor

incorrigible *a.* 無藥可救 mo yeurk hor gow

incorruptible *a.* 清廉 ting leem

increase *v.t.* 增加 jang ga

increase *n* 增加 jang ga

incredible *a.* 難以置信 lan yee jee sun

increment *n.* 增值 jang jik

incriminate *v.t.* 牽連 heen leen

incubate *v.i.* 孵 fu

inculcate *v.t.* 灌輸 gwun shu

incumbent *n.* 現任者 yeen yam jeh

incumbent *a* 有責任 yow jak yam

incur *v.t.* 惹 yeh

incurable *a.* 無得醫 mo dak yee

indebted *a.* 感激 gam gik

indecency *n.* 不雅行為 bat ngar hang way

indecent *a.* 唔恰當 hm hap dong

indecision *n.* 優柔寡斷 yow yow gwa doon

indeed *adv.* 的確 dik kok

indefensible *a.* 無法防守 mo fat forng sow

indefinite *a.* 無限期 mo han kay

indemnity *n.* 保障 bo jeurng

independence *n.* 獨立 duk lap

independent *a.* 獨立 duk lap

indescribable *a.* 難以形容 lan yee ying yung

index *n.* 索引 sok yan

Indian *a.* 印度嘅 yan dow geh

indicate *v.t.* 指出 jee chut

indication *n.* 顯示 heen see

indicative *a.* 表示 biew see

indicator *n.* 跡象 jik jeurng

indict *v.t.* 起訴 hay sow

indictment *n.* 控告 hung gow

indifference *n.* 漠不關心 mok bat gwan sam

indifferent *a.* 唔好 hm how

indigenous *a.* 當地嘅 dorng day geh

indigestible *a.* 難消化 lan siew far

indigestion *n.* 消化不良 siew far bat leurng

indignant *a.* 憤慨 fan koy

indignation *n.* 憤慨 fan koy

indigo *n.* 靛藍 deen larm

indirect *a.* 間接 gan jeep

indiscipline *n.* 無紀律 mow gey lut

indiscreet *a.* 唔謹慎 hm gan san

indiscretion *n.* 唔檢點行為 hm geem deem hang way

indiscriminate *a.* 不加選擇 bat ga shoon jak

indispensable *a.* 不可缺乏嘅 bat hor koot fat geh

indisposed *a.* 唔舒服 hm shu fuk

indisputable *a.* 無得拗 mo dak ao

indistinct *a.* 模糊 mow wu

individual *a.* 個別嘅 gor beet geh

individualism *n.* 個性 gor sing

individuality *n.* 個性 gor sing

indivisible *a.* 分唔到 fan hm dow

indolent *a.* 懶 lan

indomitable *a.* 堅毅不屈 geen

ngay bat wat

indoor *a.* 室內嘅 sat loy geh

indoors *adv.* 室內 sat loy

induce *v.t.* 引起 yan hay

inducement *n.* 引誘 yan yow

induct *v.t.* 正式就職 jing sik jow jik

induction *n.* 就任 jow yam

indulge *v.t.* 沈迷 tam may

indulgence *n.* 縱容 jung yung

indulgent *a.* 縱容 jung yung

industrial *a.* 工業嘅 gung yeep geh

industrious *a.* 勤力 kan lik

industry *n.* 行業 horng yeep

ineffective *a.* 無效 mow hao

inert *a.* 惰性 dor sing

inertia *n.* 慣性 gwan sing

inevitable *a.* 無可避免 mow hor bay meen

inexact *a.* 唔準確 hm jun kok

inexorable *a.* 耳仔軟 yee jay yoon

inexpensive *a.* 唔貴 hm gway

inexperience *n.* 無經驗 mo ging yeem

inexplicable *a.* 無法解釋 mow fat gai sik

infallible *a.* 萬無一失 man mow yat sat

infamous *a.* 聲名狼藉 sing ming lorng jik

infamy *n.* 惡行 ok hang

infancy *n.* 初期 chor kay

infant *n.* 細路仔 say low jay

infanticide *n.* 殺嬰罪 sat ying juy

infantile *a.* 細佬仔 say low jay

infantry *n.* 步兵 bo ping

infatuate *v.t.* 迷戀 may loon

infatuation *n.* 著迷 jeurk may

infect *v.t.* 傳染 choon yeem

infection *n.* 感染 gam yeem

infectious *a.* 傳染性 choon yeem sing

infer *v.t.* 推斷 tuy doon

inference *n.* 結論 geet lun

inferior *a.* 較差 gao ta

inferiority *n.* 自卑感 jee bay gam

infernal *a.* 好討厭嘅 ho tow yeem geh

infinite *a.* 無限嘅 mow han geh

infinity *n.* 無限 mow han

infirm *a.* 體弱 tay yeurk

infirmity *n.* 體弱 tay yeurk

inflame *v.t.* 激起 gik hay

inflammable *a.* 易燃 yee yeen

inflammation *n.* 發炎 fat yeem

inflammatory *a.* 發炎 fat yeem

inflation *n.* 價格通脹 ga gak tung jeurng

inflexible *a.* 無彈性 mo dan sing

inflict *v.t.* 加害 ga hoy

influence *n.* 影響 ying heurng

influence *v.t.* 影響 ying heurng

influential *a.* 有影響力 yow ying heurng lik

influenza *n.* 流感 low gam

influx *n.* 湧入 yung yao

inform *v.t.* 通知 tung jee

informal *a.* 日常嘅 yat seurng geh

information *n.* 資料 jee liew

informative *a.* 提供資訊嘅 tay gung jee sun geh

informer *n.* 告密者 gow mat jeh

infringe *v.t.* 侵犯 tam fan

infringement *n.* 違反 way fan

infuriate *v.t.* 激 gik

infuse *v.t.* 注入 ju yap

infusion *n.* 灌輸 gwun shu

ingrained *a.* 日常 yat seurng

ingratitude *n.* 忘恩負義 morng yan fu yee

ingredient *n.* 材料 choy liew

inhabit *v.t.* 居住於 guy ju yu

inhabitable *a.* 適合住嘅 sik hap ju geh

inhabitant *n.* 居民 guy man

inhale *v.i.* 吸入 kap yap

inherent *a.* 固有嘅 gu yow geh

inherit *v.t.* 繼承 gey sing

inheritance *n.* 遺產 way tan

inhibit *v.t.* 阻止 jor jee

inhibition *n.* 拘謹 kuy gan

inhospitable *a.* 唔適合住嘅 hm sik hap ju geh

inhuman *a.* 冷酷無情 lang huk mo ting

inimical *a.* 不利 bat lay

inimitable *a.* 獨特嘅 duk dak geh

initial *a.* 最初 juy chor

initial *n.* 第一個字母 dai yat gor jee mow

initial *v.t* 草簽 cho teem

initiate *v.t.* 發起 fat hay

initiative *n.* 主動性 ju dung sing

inject *v.t.* 注射 ju she

injection *n.* 打針 da jam

injudicious *a.* 不當 bat dorng

injunction *n.* 禁制令 gam jay ling

injure *v.t.* 傷害 seurng hoy

injurious *a.* 有害 yow hoy

injury *n.* 傷 seurng

injustice *n.* 唔公正 hm gung jing

ink *n.* 墨 mak

inkling *n.* 略知 leurk jee

inland *a.* 陸地 luk day

inland *adv.* 陸地 luk day

in-laws *n.* 姻親 yan tan

inmate *n.* 同住者 tung ju jeh

inmost *a.* 內心深處 loy sam sam chu

inn *n.* 細旅館 say luy gwun

innate *a.* 天生嘅 teen sang geh

inner *a.* 裡面嘅 luy meen geh

innermost *a.* 內心深處 loy sam sam chu

innings *n.* 局 guk

innocence *n.* 天真 teen jan

innocent *a.* 無辜 mow gu

innovate *v.t.* 引入 yan yap

innovation *n.* 新思想 san see seurng

innovator *n.* 創新者 chorng san jeh

innumerable *a.* 無數嘅 mow sow geh

inoculate *v.t.* 打預防針 da yu forng jam

inoculation *n.* 預防接種 yu forng jeem jung

inoperative *a.* 無效 mow hao

inopportune *a.* 唔合時 hm hap see

input *n.* 投入 tow yap

inquest *n.* 審訊 sam sun

inquire *v.t.* 打聽 da ting

inquiry *n.* 詢問 sun man

inquisition *n.* 盤問 pwun man

inquisitive *a.* 八卦 bat gwa

insane *a.* 黐線 tee seen

insanity *n.* 精神病 jing san beng

insatiable *a.* 唔知足嘅 hm jee juk geh

inscribe *v.t.* 提 tay

inscription *n.* 題字 tan jee

insect *n.* 昆蟲 kwan chung

insecticide *n.* 殺蟲劑 sat chung jay

insecure *a.* 唔安全 hm on choon

insecurity *n.* 危險 ngay heem

insensibility *n.* 不省人事 bat sing yan see

insensible *a.* 無反應 mow fan ying

inseparable *a.* 分唔開 fan hm hoy

insert *v.t.* 插 tap

insertion *n.* 插入 tap yap

inside *n.* 內側 loy jak

inside *prep.* 入邊 yap been

inside *a* 入邊 yap been

inside *adv.* 入邊 yap been

insight *n.* 瞭解 liew gai

insignificance *n.* 唔重要 hm jung yiew

insignificant *a.* 唔重要 hm jung yiew

insincere *a.* 唔誠實 hm sing sat

insincerity *n.* 虛偽 huy ngay

insinuate *v.t.* 暗示 am see

insinuation *n.* 影射 ying she

insipid *a.* 無味 mow may

insipidity *n.* 無味 mow may

insist *v.t.* 堅持 geen tee

insistence *n.* 堅持 geen tee

insistent *a.* 堅決 geen koot

insolence *n.* 無禮 mow lay

insolent *a.* 無禮 mow lay

insoluble *n.* 唔溶 hm yung

insolvency *n.* 破產 por tan

insolvent *a.* 無力還 mow lik wan

inspect *v.t.* 視察 see tat

inspection *n.* 檢查 geem ta

inspector *n.* 檢察官 geem tat gwun

inspiration *n.* 靈感 ling gam

inspire *v.t.* 啓發 kay fat

instability *n.* 唔穩定性 hm wan ding sing

install *v.t.* 安裝 on jorng

installation *n.* 安裝 on jorng

instalment *n.* 一期付款 yat kay fu fwun

instance *n.* 例子 lay jee

instant *n.* 一刻 yat hak

instant *a.* 即刻 jik hak

instantaneous *a.* 立即 lap jik

instantly *adv.* 即刻 jik hak

instigate *v.t.* 煽動 seen dung

instigation *n.* 煽動 seen dung

instil *v.t.* 慢慢灌輸 man man gwun shu

instinct *n.* 直覺 jik gok

instinctive *a.* 直覺嘅 jik gok geh

institute *n.* 機構 gey gow

institution *n.* 機構 gey gow

instruct *v.t.* 指示 jee see

instruction *n.* 指示 jee see

instructor *n.* 教練 gao leen

instrument *n.* 樂器 ok hay

instrumental *a.* 樂器演奏 ok hay yeen jow

instrumentalist *n.* 樂器家 ok hay ga

insubordinate *a.* 唔順從嘅 hm sun chung geh

insubordination *n.* 犯上 dan seurng

insufficient *a.* 唔夠 hm gow

insular *a.* 保守 bo sow

insularity *n.* 孤立 gu lap

insulate *v.t.* 隔熱 gak yeet

insulation *n.* 隔離 gak lay

insulator *n.* 緣絕物 yoon joot mat

insult *n.* 侮辱 mow yuk

insult *v.t.* 侮辱 mow yuk

insupportable *a.* 難以接收 lan yee jeep sow

insurance *n.* 保險 bo heem

insure *v.t.* 投保 tow bo

insurgent *a.* 叛亂嘅 pwun loon geh

insurgent *n.* 作反者 jok fan jeh

insurmountable *a.* 克服唔到嘅 hak fuk hm dow geh

insurrection *n.* 叛亂 pwun loon

intact *a.* 完整 yoon jing

intangible *a.* 難以形容 lan yee ying yung

integral *a.* 必需嘅 beet suy geh

integrity *n.* 完整 yoon jing

intellect *n.* 智力 jee lik

intellectual *a.* 理智 lay jee

intellectual *n.* 知識分子 jee sik fan jee

intelligence *n.* 聰明才智 chung ming choy jee

intelligent *a.* 聰明 chung ming

intelligentsia *n.* 知識分子 jee sik fan jee

intelligible *a.* 易明嘅 yee ming geh

intend *v.t.* 打算 da shoon

intense *a.* 緊張 gan jeurng

intensify *v.t.* 加強 ga keurng

intensity *n.* 強度 keurng dow

intensive *a.* 密集嘅 mat jap geh

intent *n.* 目的 muk dik

intent *a.* 熱切 yeet teet

intention *n.* 目的 muk dik

intentional *a.* 故意 gu yee

intercept *v.t.* 截住 jeet ju

interception *n.* 攔截 lan jeet

interchange *n.* 交換 gao wun

interchange *v.* 交換 gao wun

intercourse *n.* 交流 gao low

interdependence *n.* 互相依賴 wu seurng yee lai

interdependent *a.* 互相依賴 wu seurng yee lai

interest *n.* 興趣 hing chuy

interested *a.* 有興趣 yow hing chuy

interesting *a.* 有興趣 yow hing chuy

interfere *v.i.* 干預 gorn yu

interference *n.* 干預 gorn yu

interim *n.* 間歇 gan keet

interior *a.* 室內嘅 sat loy geh

interior *n.* 室內 sat loy

interjection *n.* 感歎詞 gam tan tee

interlock *v.t.* 相連 seurng leen

interlude *n.* 間歇 gan keet

intermediary *n.* 中間人 jung gan yan

intermediate *a.* 中間嘅 jung gan geh

interminable *a.* 太長 tai cheurng

intermingle *v.t.* 混合 wan hap

intern *v.t.* 扣留 kow low

internal *a.* 內部嘅 loy bo geh

international *a.* 國際 gwok jay

interplay *n.* 互相影響 wu seurng ying heurng

interpret *v.t.* 翻譯 fan yik

interpreter *n.* 翻譯 fan yik

interrogate *v.t.* 審問 sam man

interrogation *n.* 審問 sam man

interrogative *a.* 提問 tay man

interrogative *n* 疑問詞 yee man tee

interrupt *v.t.* 插嘴 tap juy

interruption *n.* 打擾 da yiew

intersect *v.t.* 交叉 gao ta

intersection *n.* 交點 gao deem

interval *n.* 間隔 gan gak

intervene *v.i.* 介入 gai yap

intervention *n.* 介入 gai yap

interview *n.* 面試 meen see

interview *v.t.* 訪問 forng man

intestinal *a.* 腸嘅 cheurng geh

intestine *n.* 腸 cheurng

intimacy *n.* 親密 tan mat

intimate *a.* 密切 mat teet

intimate *v.t.* 暗示 am see

intimation *n.* 暗示 am see

intimidate *v.t.* 威脅 way heep

intimidation *n.* 恐嚇 hung hak

into *prep.* 入 yap

intolerable *a.* 頂唔順嘅 ding hm sun geh

intolerance *n.* 無法忍受 mo fat yan sow

intolerant *a.* 唔容忍 hm yung yan

intoxicant *n.* 酒類飲品 jow luy

yam ban

intoxicate *v.t.* 令人飲醉 ling yan yam juy

intoxication *n.* 醉 juy

intransitive *a. (verb)* 不及物 bat kap mat

interpid *a.* 勇敢 yung gam

intrepidity *n.* 大膽 dai dam

intricate *a.* 複雜 fuk jap

intrigue *v.t.* 激起興趣 gik hay hing chuy

intrigue *n* 陰謀 yam mow

intrinsic *a.* 內在嘅 loy joy geh

introduce *v.t.* 介紹 gai siew

introduction *n.* 介紹 gai siew

introductory *a.* 初步嘅 chor bo geh

introspect *v.i.* 反省 fan sing

introspection *n.* 反省 fan sing

intrude *v.t.* 闖入 chorng yap

intrusion *n.* 侵犯 tam fan

intuition *n.* 直覺 jik gok

intuitive *a.* 憑直覺嘅 pang jik gog geh

invade *v.t.* 侵略 tam leurk

invalid *a.* 無效 mow hao

invalid *a.* 令人退股 ling yan tuy gu

invalid *n* 病人 beng yan

invalidate *v.t.* 作廢 jok fay

invaluable *a.* 有用嘅 yow yung geh

invasion *n.* 侵略 tam leurk

invective *n.* 咒 jow

invent *v.t.* 發明 fat ming

invention *n.* 發明 fat ming

inventive *a.* 有創意 yow chorng yee

inventor *n.* 發明家 fat ming ga

invert *v.t.* 倒轉 dowjoon

invest *v.t.* 投資 tow jee

investigate *v.t.* 調查 tiew ta

investigation *n.* 調查 tiew ta

investment *n.* 投資 tow jee

invigilate *v.t.* 監考 gam hao

invigilation *n.* 監考 gam hao

invigilator *n.* 監考官 gam hao gwun

invincible *a.* 無敵嘅 mow dik geh

inviolable *a.* 不可侵犯 bat hor tam fan

invisible *a.* 隱形 yan ying

invitation *v.* 邀請 yiew ting

invite *v.t.* 邀請 yiew ting

invocation *n.* 祈禱 kay tow

invoice *n.* 單 dan

invoke *v.t.* 提及 tay kap

involve *v.t.* 關係到 gwan hay dow

inward *a.* 向內 heurng loy

inwards *adv.* 向內 heurng loy

irate *a.* 好嬲 how low

ire *n.* 憤怒 fan low

Irish *a.* 愛爾蘭嘅 ngoy yee lan geh

Irish *n.* 愛爾蘭人 ngoy yee lan yan

irksome *a.* 令人煩惱 ling yan fan low

iron *n.* 燙斗 torng dow

iron *v.t.* 燙 torng

ironical *a.* 諷刺 fung tee

irony *n.* 反話 fan wah

irradiate *v.i.* 輻照 fuk jiew

irrational *a.* 唔合邏輯 hm hap lor tap

irreconcilable *a.* 無法化解 mow fat far gai

irrecoverable *a.* 無法恢復 wu fat fwuy fuk

irrefutable *a.* 無可否認 mow hor fow ying

irregular *a.* 唔規則 hm kway jak

irregularity *n.* 唔規則性 hm kway jak sing

irrelevant *a.* 無關 mow gwan
irrespective *a.* 無關 mow gwan
irresponsible *a.* 不負責任 bat fu jak yam
irrigate *v.t.* 灌水 gwun suy
irrigation *n.* 灌溉 gwun koy
irritable *a.* 容易發嬲 yung yee fat low
irritant *a.* 好煩 ho fan
irritant *n.* 刺激嘢 tee gik mat
irritate *v.t.* 煩 fan
irritation *n.* 過敏 gwor man
irruption *n.* 闖入 chorng yap
island *n.* 島 dow
isle *n.* 島 dow
isobar *n.* 等壓線 dang ngat seen
isolate *v.t.* 隔離 gak lay
isolation *n.* 隔絕 gak joot
issue *v.i.* 派 pai
issue *n.* 問題 man tay
it *pron.* 佢 kuy
Italian *a.* 義大利嘅 yee dai lay geh
Italian *n.* 義大利人 yee dai lay yan
italic *a.* 斜體 ter tay
italics *n.* 斜體字 ter tay jee
itch *n.* 癢 yeurng
itch *v.i.* 癢 yeurng
item *n.* 物件 mat geen
ivory *n.* 象牙 jeung ngar
ivy *n* 常春藤 seurng chun tang

jab *v.t.* 拮 gat
jabber *v.t.* 急 gap
jack *n.* 千斤頂 teen gan ding
jack *v.t.* 決定放棄 koot ding forng hay

jackal *n.* 豺狼 tai lorng
jacket *n.* 外套 ngoy tow
jade *n.* 玉 yuk
jail *n.* 監牢 garm low
jailer *n.* 獄卒 yuk jut
jam *n.* 果醬 gwor jeurng
jam *v.t.* 塞 sak
jar *n.* 樽 jun
jargon *n.* 專業用詞 joon yeep yung tee
jasmine, jessamine *n.* 茉莉花 mwut lay far
jaundice *n.* 黃疸 worng dan
jaundice *v.t.* 影響 ying heurng
javelin *n.* 標槍 biew cheurng
jaw *n.* 下顎 har ok
jay *n.* 松鴉 chung ngar
jealous *a.* 妒忌 dow gey
jealousy *n.* 妒忌 dow gey
jean *n.* 牛仔褲 ngow jay fu
jeer *v.i.* 嘲笑 jao siew
jelly *n.* 啫哩 jeh lay
jeopardize *v.t.* 損害 shoon hoy
jeopardy *n.* 危險 ngay heem
jerk *n.* 猛烈動作 mang leet dung jok
jerkin *n.* 坎肩 ham geen
jerky *a.* 震 jan
jersey *n.* 運動衫 wan dung sam
jest *n.* 笑話 siew wah
jest *v.i.* 講笑 gorng siew
jet *n.* 噴氣式飛機 pan hay sik fay gey
Jew *n.* 猶太人 yow tai yan
jewel *n.* 寶石 bo sek
jewel *v.t.* 用寶石裝飾 yung bo sek jorng sik
jeweller *n.* 珠寶商 ju bo seurng
jewellery *n.* 首飾 sow sik
jingle *n.* 丁噹聲 ding dorng seng
jingle *v.i.* 丁噹 ding dong
job *n.* 工 gung

jobber *n.* 股票經紀 gu piew ging gey

jobbery *n.* 假公濟私 gar gung jay see

jocular *a.* 幽默 yow mak

jog *v.t.* 慢跑 man pao

join *v.t.* 參加 tam ga

joiner *n.* 木工 muk gung

joint *n.* 關節 gwan jeet

jointly *adv.* 聯合地 loon hap day

joke *n.* 笑話 siew wah

joke *v.i.* 講笑 gorng siew

joker *n.* 鐘意講笑嘅人 jung yee gorng siew geh yan

jollity *n.* 歡樂 fwun lok

jolly *a.* 愉快 yu fai

jolt *n.* 震動 jan dung

jolt *v.t.* 震 jan

jostle *n.* 推開 tuy hoy

jostle *v.t.* 推開 tuy hoy

jot *n.* 一啲 yat dee

jot *v.t.* 寫低 seh day

journal *n.* 日記 yat gey

journalism *n.* 新聞業 san man yeep

journalist *n.* 記者 gey jeh

journey *n.* 旅程 luy ting

journey *v.i.* 去旅行 huy luy hang

jovial *a.* 樂觀 lok gwun

joviality *n.* 快活 fai wut

joy *n.* 喜悅 hay yoot

joyful, joyous *n.* 高興 gow hing

jubilant *a.* 開心 hoy sam

jubilation *n.* 歡騰 fwun tang

jubilee *n.* 五十週年紀念 hm sap jow leen gey leem

judge *n.* 法官 fat gwun

judge *v.i.* 判斷 pwun doon

judgement *n.* 判斷 pwun doon

judicature *n.* 司法 see fat

judicial *a.* 司法 see fat

judiciary *n.* 法官 fat gwun

judicious *a.* 有見地 yow geen day

jug *n.* 壺 wu

juggle *v.t.* 耍雜耍 sa jap sa

juggler *n.* 表演者 biew yeen jeh

juice *n* 汁 jap

juicy *a.* 多汁 dor jap

jumble *n.* 亂堆 loon duy

jumble *v.t.* 整亂 jing loon

jump *n.* 跳 tiew

jump *v.i* 跳 tiew

junction *n.* 交叉路口 gao ta low ho

juncture *n.* 關頭 gwan tow

jungle *n.* 熱帶森林 yeet dai sam lam

junior *a.* 小學生嘅 siew hok sang geh

junior *n.* 小學生 siew hok sang

junk *n.* 垃圾 lap sap

jupiter *n.* 木星 muk sing

jurisdiction *n.* 司法權 see fat koon

jurisprudence *n.* 法律學 fat lut hok

jurist *n.* 法律家 fat lut ga

juror *n.* 陪審員 pwuy sam yoon

jury *n.* 陪審團 pwuy sam toon

juryman *n.* 陪審員 pwuy sam yoon

just *a.* 公正嘅 gung jing geh

just *adv.* 啱啱 ngarm ngarm

justice *n.* 公道 gung dow

justifiable *a.* 有理由嘅 yow lay yow geh

justification *n.* 正當理由 jing dorng lay yow

justify *v.t.* 證明 jing ming

justly *adv.* 公正 gung jing

jute *n.* 黃麻 worng ma

juvenile *a.* 幼稚嘅 yow jee geh

K

keen *a.* 熱心 yeet sam
keenness *n.* 熱情 yeet ting
keep *v.t.* 保管 bo gwun
keeper *n.* 保管人 bo gwun yan
keepsake *n.* 紀念品 gey leem ban
kennel *n.* 狗屋 gow uk
kerchief *n.* 方頭巾 forng tow gan
kernel *n.* 核 wat
kerosene *n.* 煤油 mwuy yow
ketchup *n.* 茄汁 keh jap
kettle *n.* 水壺 suy wu
key *n.* 鎖匙 sor see
key *v.t* 輸入 shu yap
kick *n.* 踢 tek
kick *v.t.* 踢 tek
kid *n.* 細佬仔 say low jay
kidnap *v.t.* 拐 gwai
kidney *n.* 腎 san
kill *v.t.* 殺 sat
kill *n.* 殺 sat
kiln *n.* 窰 yiew
kin *n.* 親戚 tan tik
kind *n.* 種 jung
kind *a* 善良 seen leurng
kindergarten ; *n.* 幼稚園 yow jee yoon
kindle *v.t.* 激起 gik hay
kindly *adv.* 善良咁 seen leurng gam
king *n.* 國王 gwok worng
kingdom *n.* 王國 worng gwok
kinship *n.* 親屬關係 tan suk gwan hay
kiss *n.* 錫 sek
kiss *v.t.* 錫 sek
kit *n.* 裝備 jorng bay
kitchen *n.* 廚房 chu forng
kite *n.* 紙鷂 jee yiew
kith *n.* 親戚朋友 tan tik pang yow

kitten *n.* 細貓 say mao
knave *n.* 無賴 mow lai
knavery *n.* 狡猾 gao wat
knee *n.* 膝頭哥 sat tow gor
kneel *v.i.* 跪 gway
knife *n.* 刀 dow
knight *n.* 騎士 keh see
knight *v.t.* 封...爲爵士 fung...way jeurk see
knit *v.t.* 織 jik
knock *v.t.* 敲 hao
knot *n.* 結 geet
knot *v.t.* 打結 da geet
know *v.t.* 知道 jee dow
knowledge *n.* 知識 jee sik

L

label *n.* 標籤 biew teem
label *v.t.* 貼標籤 teep biew teem
labial *a.* 唇音 sun yam
laboratory *n.* 實驗室 sat yeem sat
laborious *a.* 辛苦 san fu
labour *n.* 勞工 low gung
labour *v.i.* 努力做 low lik jow
laboured *a.* 辛苦 san fu
labourer *n.* 勞工 low gung
labyrinth *n.* 迷宮 may gung
lac, lakh *n* 蟲膠 chung gao
lace *n.* 花邊 far been
lace *v.t.* 穿鞋帶 choon hai dai
lacerate *v.t.* 鎅 gai
lachrymose *a.* 易喊 yee harm
lack *n.* 缺乏 koot fat
lack *v.t.* 唔夠 hm gow
lackey *n.* 跟班 gan ban
lacklustre *a.* 無趣味 mow chuy may
laconic *a.* 簡潔嘅 gan geet geh
lactate *v.i.* 哺乳 bo yu

lactometer *n.* 檢乳器 geem yu hay

lactose *n.* 乳糖 yu torng

lacuna *n.* 漏洞 low dung

lacy *a.* 蕾絲嘅 luy see geh

lad *n.* 男仔 larm jay

ladder *n.* 梯 tay

lade *v.t.* 裝載 jorng joy

iadle *n.* 湯殼 torng hok

ladle *v.t.* 不 bat

lady *n.* 女人 luy yan

lag *v.i.* 落後 lok how

laggard *n.* 遲鈍 tee dun

lagoon *n.* 環礁湖 wan jiew wu

lair *n.* 竇 dow

lake *n.* 湖 wu

lama *n.* 喇嘛 la ma

lamb *n.* 羔羊 gow yeurng

lambaste *v.t.* 毒打 duk da

lame *a.* 跛 bay

lame *v.t.* 整跛 jing bay

lament *v.i.* 失望 sat morng

lament *n* 悲歎 bay tan

lamentable *a.* 令人遺憾 ling yan way ham

lamentation *n.* 悲傷 bay seurng

lambkin *n.* 羊皮 yeurng pay

laminate *v.t.* 過塑 gwor sok

lamp *n.* 燈 dang

lampoon *n.* 諷刺文章 fung tee man jeurng

lampoon *v.t.* 諷刺 fung tee

lance *n.* 長矛 cheurng mao

lance *v.t.* 放膿 forng lung

lancer *n.* 槍騎兵 cheurng keh bing

lancet *a.* 柳葉刀 low yeep dow

land *n.* 地 day

land *v.i.* 降落 gorng lok

landing *n.* 降落 gorng lok

landscape *n.* 風景 fung ging

lane *n.* 小路 siew low

language *n.* 語言 yu yeen

languish *v.i.* 長期受苦 cheurng kay sow fu

lank *a.* 又高又瘦 yow gow yow sow

lantern *n.* 燈籠 dang lung

lap *n.* 一圈 yat hoon

lapse *v.i.* 衰弱 suy yeurk

lapse *n* 間隔時間 gan gak see gan

lard *n.* 豬油 ju yow

large *a.* 大 dai

largesse *n.* 贈款 jang fwun

lark *n.* 雲雀 wan jeurk

lascivious *a.* 淫蕩 yam dorng

lash *a.* 好 haow

lash *n* 鞭打 been da

lass *n.* 女仔 luy jay

last1 *a.* 最後 juy ho

last *adv.* 最後 juy ho

last *v.i.* 繼續 gey juk

last *n* 最後嘅人 juy ho geh yan

lastly *adv.* 最後 juy ho

lasting *a.* 繼續 gey juk

latch *n.* 插鎖 tap sor

late *a.* 晚年嘅 man leen geh

late *adv.* 遲 tee

lately 最近 juy gan

latent *a.* 潛伏 teem fuk

lath *n.* 板條 ban tiew

lathe *n.* 車床 cher chorng

lather *n.* 泡沫 pow mwut

latitude *n.* 緯度 way dow

latrine *n.* 坑廁 hang tee

latter *a.* 最後嘅 juy ho geh

lattice *n.* 格仔木架 gak jay muk ga

laud *v.t.* 讚 jan

laud *n* 讚揚 jan yeurng

.laudable *a.* 值得讚 jik dak jan

laugh *n.* 笑 siew

laugh *v.i* 笑 siew

laughable *a.* 有趣嘅 yow chuy

geh
laughter *n.* 笑聲 siew seng
launch *v.t.* 發行 fat hang
launch *n.* 發射 fat seh
launder *v.t.* 洗燙 say torng
laundress *n.* 洗衣女工 say yee luy gung
laundry *n.* 洗衫 say sarm
laureate *n.* 獲獎者 wok jeurng jeh
laureate *a.* 值得獲獎 jik dak wok jeurng
laurel *n* 月桂樹 yoot gway shu
lava *n.* 熔岩 yung ngam
lavatory *n.* 洗手間 say sow gan
lavender *n.* 薰衣草 fan yee cho
lavish *a.* 過度 gwor dow
lavish *v.t.* 印象深刻 yan jeurng sam hak
law *n.* 法律 fat lut
lawful *a.* 合法 hap fat
lawless *a.* 目無法紀 muk mow fat gey
lawn *n.* 草地 cho day
lawyer *n.* 律師 lut see
lax *a.* 馬虎 mah fu
laxative *n.* 通便嘅 tung been geh
laxative *a* 瀉藥 ser yeurk
laxity *n.* 散漫 san man
lay *v.t.* 民歌 man gor
lay *a.* 鋪 pow
lay *n* 外行嘅 ngoy horng geh
layer *n.* 層 tang
layman *n.* 外行 ngoy horng
laze *v.i.* 偷懶 tow lan
laziness *n.* 懶散 lan san
lazy *n.* 懶 lan
lea *n.* 草原 cho yoon
leach *v.t.* 過濾 gwor luy
lead *n.* 領先 ling seen
lead *v.t.* 帶 dai
lead *n.* 鉛 yoon
leaden *a.* 沈悶 tam mwun

leader *n.* 領隊 ling duy
leadership *n.* 領導才能 ling dow choy lang
leaf *n.* 葉 yeep
leaflet *n.* 傳單 choon dan
leafy *a.* 多樹葉 dor shu yeep
league *n.* 聯盟 loon mang
leak *n.* 漏洞 low dung
leak *v.i.* 漏 low
leakage *n.* 漏 low
lean *n.* 瘦肉 sow yuk
lean *v.i.* 挨 ai
leap *v.i.* 跳 tiew
leap *n* 跳高 tiew gow
learn *v.i.* 學 hok
learned *a.* 學咗 hok jor
learner *n.* 學生 hok sang
learning *n.* 學習 hok jap
lease *n.* 租約 jow yeurk
lease *v.t.* 租用 jow yung
least *a.* 最少 juy siew
least *adv.* 至少 jee siew
leather *n.* 皮 pay
leave *n.* 離開 lay hoy
leave *v.t.* 走 jow
lecture *n.* 演講 yeen gorng
lecture *v* 講課 gorng for
lecturer *n.* 講師 gorng see
ledger *n.* 賬簿 jeurng bo
lee *n.* 庇護所 bay wu sor
leech *n.* 水蛭 suy jat
leek *n.* 西芹 say kan
left *a.* 左 jor
left *n.* 左 jor
leftist *n* 左派分子 jor pai fan jee
leg *n.* 腳 geurk
legacy *n.* 遺產 way tan
legal *a.* 合法嘅 hap fat geh
legality *n.* 合法性 hap fat sing
legalize *v.t.* 變合法 been hap fat
legend *n.* 傳奇 joon kay

legendary *a.* 傳說嘅 choon shoot geh

leghorn *n.* 力行雞 lik horng gey

legible *a.* 清楚 ting chor

legibly *adv.* 易讀 yee duk

legion *n.* 軍團 gwan toon

legionary *n.* 軍團 gwan toon

legislate *v.i.* 立法 lap fat

legislation *n.* 立法 lap fat

legislative *a.* 立法嘅 lap fat geh

legislator *n.* 立法委員 lap fat way yoon

legislature *n.* 立法機關 lap fat gey gwan

legitimacy *n.* 合法性 hap fat sing

legitimate *a.* 合情合理 hap ting hap lay

leisure *n.* 空閒 hung han

leisure *a* 休閒嘅 yow han geh

leisurely *a.* 休閒咁 yow han gam

leisurely *adv.* 慢慢咁 man man gam

lemon *n.* 檸檬 ling mung

lemonade *n.* 檸檬水 ling mung suy

lend *v.t.* 借 jeh

length *n.* 長度 cheurng dow

lengthen *v.t.* 加長 ga cheurng

lengthy *a.* 幾長 gey cheurng

lenience, leniency *n.* 寬大 fwun dai

lenient *a.* 寬容 fwun yung

lens *n.* 鏡片 geng peen

lentil *n.* 扁豆 been dow

Leo *n.* 獅子座 see jee jor

leonine *a* 獅子嘅 see jee geh

leopard *n.* 豹 pao

leper *n.* 痲瘋病患者 ma fung beng wan jeh

leprosy *n.* 痲瘋 ma fung

leprous *a.* 痲瘋嘅 ma fung geh

less *a.* 比較少 bay gao siew

less *n* 少數 siew sow

less *adv.* 比較少 bay gao siew

less *prep.* 扣除 kow chuy

lessee *n.* 租戶 jow wu

lessen *v.t* 變少 been siew

lesser *a.* 更少 gang siew

lesson *n.* 堂 torng

lest *conj.* 費事 fay see

let *v.t.* 畀 bay

lethal *a.* 致命 jee ming

lethargic *a.* 眼瞓 ngan fan

lethargy *n.* 無精打采 mow jing da choy

letter *n* 信 sun

level *n.* 級 kap

level *a* 平嘅 ping geh

level *v.t.* 變平 been ping

lever *n.* 控制桿 hung jay gorn

lever *v.t.* 撬動 giew dung

leverage *n.* 影響力 ying heurng lik

levity *n.* 輕佻 hing tiew

levy *v.t.* 徵收 jing sow

levy *n.* 稅款 suy fwun

lewd *a.* 猥瑣 wuy sor

lexicography *n.* 詞典編纂 tee deen peen mow

lexicon *n.* 詞彙 tee wuy

liability *n.* 責任 jak yam

liable *a.* 信得過嘅 sun dak gwor geh

liaison *n.* 聯繫 loon hay

liar *n.* 講大話嘅人 gorng dai wah geh yan

libel *n.* 誹謗 fay borng

libel *v.t.* 中傷 jung seurng

liberal *a.* 開明 hoy ming

liberalism *n.* 自由主義 jee yow ju yee

liberality *n.* 慷慨 horng koy

liberate *v.t.* 解放 gai forng

liberation *n.* 解放 gai forng

liberator *n.* 解放者 gai forng jeh

libertine *n.* 放蕩嘅人 forng dong geh yan

liberty *n.* 自由 jee yow

librarian *n.* 圖書館館長 tow shu gwun gwun jeurng

library *n.* 圖書館 tow shu gwun

licence *n.* 牌 pai

license *v.t.* 批准 pay jun

licensee *n.* 持牌人 tee pai yan

licentious *a.* 放蕩 forng dong

lick *v.t.* lem

lick *n* 少量 siew leurng

lid *n.* 蓋 goy

lie *v.i.* 講大話 gorng dai wah

lie *v.i* 瞓 fan

lie *n* 大話 dai wah

lien *n.* 扣押權 kow ngat koon

lieu *n.* 代替 doy tay

lieutenant *n.* 上尉 seurng way

life *n* 生命 sang ming

lifeless *a.* 無生氣嘅 mow sang hay geh

lifelong *a.* 終身嘅 jung sang geh

lift *n.* leep

lift *v.t.* 攞起 lor hay

light *n.* 光 gwong

light *a* 輕 heng

light *v.t.* 點火 deem for

lighten *v.i.* 減輕 garm heng

lighter *n.* 打火機 da for gey

lightly *adv.* 輕輕 heng heng

lightening *n.* 閃電 seem deen

lignite *n.* 褐煤 keet mwuy

like *a.* 似 tee

like *n.* 喜好 hay ho

like *v.t.* 鐘意 jung yee

like *prep* 似 tee

likelihood *n.* 可能性 hor lang sing

likely *a.* 幾有可能 gey yow hor lang

liken *v.t.* 比 bay

likeness *n.* 相似 seurng tee

likewise *adv.* 同樣地 tung yeurng day

liking *n.* 愛好 ngoy ho

lilac *n.* 丁香 ding heurng

lily *n.* 百合花 bak hap far

limb *n.* 肢 tee

limber *v.t.* 熱身 yeet san

limber *n* 柔軟 yow yoon

lime *n.* 青檸 teng ling

lime *v.t* 傻石灰 sa sek fwuy

lime *n.* 石灰 sek fwuy

limelight *n.* 公眾嘅注目 gung jung geh ju muk

limit *n.* 限制 han jay

limit *v.t.* 限制 han jay

limitation *n.* 限制 han jay

limited *a.* 有限嘅 yow han geh

limitless *a.* 無限嘅 mow han geh

line *n.* 線 seen

line *v.t.* 加層 ga tang

line *v.t.* 襯 tan

lineage *n.* 血統 hoot tung

linen *n.* 亞麻布 ngar mar bo

linger *v.i.* 徘徊 pwuy wuy

lingo *n.* 語言 yu yeen

lingua franca *n.* 通用語 tung yung yu

lingual *a.* 語言嘅 yu yeen geh

linguist *n.* 語言學家 yu yeen hok ga

linguistic *a.* 語言嘅 yu yeen geh

linguistics *n.* 語言學 yu yeen hok

lining *n* 內襯 loy tan

link *n.* 關連 gwan leen

link *v.t* 連接 leen jeep

linseed *n.* 亞麻子 ngar mar jee

lintel *n.* 門框 mwun kwang

lion *n* 獅子 see jee

lioness *n.* 母獅 mow see

lip *n.* 嘴唇 juy sun

liquefy *v.t.* 液化 yik far

liquid *a.* 液體嘅 yik tay geh

liquid *n* 液體 yik tay

liquidate *v.t.* 清盤 ting pwun

liquidation *n.* 清盤 ting pwun

liquor *n.* 酒 jow

lisp *v.t.* 口齒不清 ho tee bat ting

lisp *n* 黐脷根 tee lay gan

list *n.* 清單 ting dan

list *v.t.* 列單 leet dan

listen *v.i.* 聽 teng

listener *n.* 聽者 teng jeh

listless *a.* 無精打采 mow jing da choy

lists *n.* 競技場 ging gey cheurng

literacy *n.* 讀寫能力 duk ser lang lik

literal *a.* 字面意義 jee meen yee yi

literary *a.* 文學嘅 man hok geh

literate *a.* 有文化嘅 yow man far geh

literature *n.* 文學 man hok

litigant *n.* 當事人 dorng see yan

litigate *v.t.* 打官司 da gwun see

litigation *n.* 訴訟 sow jung

litre *n.* 公升 gung sing

litter *n.* 垃圾 lap sap

litter *v.t.* 拋垃圾 pao lap sap

litterateur *n.* 文學家 man hok ga

little *a.* 細 say

little *adv.* 少少 siew siew

little *n.* 少量 siew leurng

littoral *a.* 海岸 hoy ngon

liturgical *a.* 禮拜儀式嘅 lay bai yee sik geh

live *v.i.* 住 ju

live *a.* 生嘅 sang geh

livelihood *n.* 生計 sang gey

lively *a.* 有生氣 yow sang hey

liver *n.* 肝 gorn

livery *n.* 制服 jay fuk

living *a.* 生嘅 sang geh

living *n* 生計 sang gey

lizard *n.* 蜥蜴 sik yik

load *n.* 大堆 dai duy

load *v.t.* 裝 jorng

loadstar *n.* 北極星 bak gik sing

loadstone *n.* 磁石 tee sek

loaf *n.* 一條 yat tiew

loaf *v.i.* 遊手好閒 yow sow ho han

loafer *n.* 拖鞋 tor hai

loan *n.* 貸款 tai fwun

loan *v.t.* 借 jeh

loath *a.* 唔情願 hm ting yoon

loathe *v.t.* 憎 jang

loathsome *a.* 乞人憎 hat yan jang

lobby *n.* 前廳 teen teng

lobe *n.* 耳垂 yee chuy

lobster *n.* 龍蝦 lung har

local *a.* 附近嘅 fu gan geh

locale *n.* 現場 yeen cheurng

locality *n.* 地區 day kuy

localize *v.t.* 局部化 guk bo far

locate *v.t.* 搵出確定位置 wan chut kok ding way jee

location *n.* 地點 day deem

lock *n.* 鎖 sor

lock *v.t* 鎖 sor

lock *n* 頭髮 tow fat

locker *n.* 儲物櫃 chu mat gway

locket *n.* 盒式頸鏈 hap sik geng leen

locomotive *n.* 火車頭 for cher tow

locus *n.* 中心 jung sam

locust *n.* 蝗蟲 worng chung

locution *n.* 語言風格 yu yeen fung gak

lodge *n.* 小屋 siew uk

lodge *v.t.* 寄宿 gey suk

lodging *n.* 租嘅房 jow geh forng

loft *n.* 閣樓 gok low
lofty *a.* 高嘅 gow geh
log *n.* 木頭 muk tow
logarithm *n.* 對數 duy sow
loggerhead *n.* 蠢材 chun choy
logic *n.* 邏輯 lor tap
logical *a.* 合乎邏輯 fu hap lor tap
logician *n.* 邏輯專家 lor tap joon ga
loin *n.* 腰肉 yiew yuk
loiter *v.i.* 徘徊 pwuy wuy
loll *v.i.* 懶散咁坐 lan san gam chor
lollipop *n.* 糖仔棍 tong jay gwan
lone *a.* 單獨嘅 dan duk geh
loneliness *n.* 孤單 gu dan
lonely *a.* 孤單 gu dan
lonesome *a.* 寂寞 jik mok
long *a.* 長 cheurng
long *adv* 長期 cheurng kay
long *v.i* 渴望 hot morng
longevity *n.* 長命 cheurng meng
longing *n.* 渴望 hot morng
longitude *n.* 經度 ging dow
look *v.i* 睇 tay
look *n.* 風格 fung gak
loom *n* 織布機 jik bo gey
loom *v.I.* 逼近 bik kan
loop *n.* 圓圈 yoon hoon
loop-hole *n.* 罅 la
loose *a.* 鬆嘅 sung geh
loose *v.t.* 鬆開 sung hoy
loosen *v.t.* 鬆開 sung hoy
loot *n.* 戰利品 jeen lay ban
loot *v.i.* 打劫 da geep
lop *v.t.* 斬 jam
lop *n.* 跳蚤 tiew sat
lord *n.* 勳爵 fan jeurk
lordly *a.* 宏偉 wang way
lordship *n.* 貴族權利 gway juk koon lay
lore *n.* 傳說 choon shoot
lorry *n.* 大貨車 dai for cher

lose *v.t.* 輸 shu
loss *n.* 損失 shoon sat
lot *n.* 全部 choon bo
lot *n* 一批 yat pay
lotion *n.* 護膚液 wu fuk yik
lottery *n.* 六合彩 luk hap choy
lotus *n.* 蓮花 leen far
loud *a.* 嘈 ccho
lounge *v.i.* 懶散咁坐 lan san gam chor
lounge *n.* 等候室 dang ho sat
louse *n.* 蝨 sat
lovable *a.* 惹人愛 yeh yan ngoy
love *n* 愛情 ngoy ting
love *v.t.* 愛 ngoy
lovely *a.* 好靚 ho leng
lover *n.* 情人 ting yan
loving *a.* 愛緊 ngoy gan
low *a.* 低嘅 day geh
low *adv.* 低 day
low *v.i.* 整低 jing day
low *n.* 低點 day deem
lower *v.t.* 降低 gorng day
lowliness *n.* 卑微 bay may
lowly *a.* 無足輕重 mow juk heng chung
loyal *a.* 忠心 jung sam
loyalist *n.* 忠心嘅人 jung sam geh yan
loyalty *n.* 忠心 jung sam
lubricant *n.* 潤滑油 yun wat yow
lubricate *v.t.* 上油 seurng yow
lubrication *n.* 潤滑 yun wat
lucent *a.* 發光嘅 fat gworng geh
lucerne *n.* 紫苜蓿 jee muk suk
lucid *a.* 易明嘅 yee ming geh
lucidity *n.* 清晰度 ting sik dow
luck *n.* 運氣 wan hay
luckily *adv.* 好彩 how choy
luckless *a.* 唔好彩 hm ho choy
lucky *a.* 好彩 ho choy

lucrative *a.* 賺大錢嘅 jan dai teen geh

lucre *n.* 利益 lay yik

luggage *n.* 行李 hang lay

lukewarm *a.* 暖嘅 loon geh

lull *v.t.* 令人放鬆 ling yan forng sung

lull *n.* 間歇 gan keet

lullaby *n.* 搖籃曲 yiew lam kuk

luminary *n.* 專家 joon ga

luminous *a.* 發光嘅 fat gworng geh

lump *n.* 一嚿 yat gow

lump *v.t.* 將就 jeurng jow

lunacy *n.* 精神錯亂 jing san chor loon

lunar *a.* 月亮嘅 yoot leurng geh

lunatic *n.* 顛佬 deen low

lunatic *a.* 黐線嘅 tee seen geh

lunch *n.* 晏晝 ngan jow

lunch *v.i.* 食晏 sik ngan

lung *n* 肺 fay

lunge *n.* 撲 pok

lunge *v.i* 撲 pok

lurch *n.* 前傾 teen king

lurch *v.i.* 浪下浪下 lorng ha lorng ha

lure *n.* 吸引力 kap yan lik

lure *v.t.* 誘惑 yow wak

lurk *v.i.* 埋伏 mai fuk

luscious *a.* 甜美嘅 teem may geh

lush *a.* 豪華 ho wah

lust *n.* 強烈嘅慾望 keurng leet geh yuk morng

lustful *a.* 貪慾 tam yuk

lustre *n.* 光澤 gworng jak

lustrous *a.* 有光澤 yow gworng jak

lusty *a.* 強壯 keurng jorng

lute *n.* 琵琶 pay pa

luxuriance *n.* 繁茂 fan mow

luxuriant *a.* 豐盛 fung sing

luxurious *a.* 豪華 ho wah

luxury *n.* 奢侈 ter tee

lynch *v.t.* 私刑處死 see ying chu say

lyre *n.* 七弦琴 tat yoon kam

lyric *a.* 抒情嘅 shu ting geh

lyric *n.* 歌詞 gor tee

lyrical *a.* 抒情嘅 shu ting geh

lyricist *n.* 填詞人 teen tee yan

M

magical *a.* 魔幻 mor wan

magician *n.* 魔術師 mor sut see

magisterial *a.* 權威嘅 koon way geh

magistracy *n.* 治安官 jee on gwun

magistrate *n.* 地方官 day forng gwun

magnanimity *n.* 寬大 fwun dai

magnanimous *a.* 寬宏 fwun wang

magnate *n.* 權貴 koon gway

magnet *n.* 磁石 tee sek

magnetic *a.* 有磁力嘅 yow tee lik geh

magnetism *n.* 磁力 tee lik

magnificent *a.* 宏偉 wang way

magnify *v.t.* 放大 forng dai

magnitude *n.* 幅度 fuk dow

magpie *n.* 喜鵲 hay jeurk

mahogany *n.* 桃花木 tow far muk

mahout *n.* 象夫 jeurng fu

maid *n.* 女僕 luy buk

maiden *n.* 處女 chu luy

maiden *a* 首次嘅 sow tee geh

mail *n.* 郵件 yow geen

mail *v.t.* 寄 gey

mail *n* 郵遞 yow day
main *a* 主要嘅 ju yiew geh
main *n* 電源 deen yoon
mainly *adv.* 主要 ju yiew
mainstay *n.* 支柱 jee chu
maintain *v.t.* 維持 way tee
maintenance *n.* 維修 way sow
maize *n.* 粟米 suk may
majestic *a.* 雄偉 hung way
majesty *n.* 陛下 bay ha
major *a.* 主要嘅 ju yiew geh
major *n* 主修課程 ju sow for ting
majority *n.* 大部分 dai bo fan
make *v.t.* 整 jing
make *n* 牌子 pai jee
maker *n.* 製造者 jay jow jeh
mal adjustment *n.* 失調 sat tiew
mal administration *n.* 管理不善
  gwun lay bat seen
malady *n.* 病 beng
malaria *n.* 瘧疾 yeurk jat
maladroit *a.* 輪盡 lun jun
malafide *a.* 唔誠實 hm sing sat
malafide *adv* 唔誠實 hm sing sat
malaise *n.* 唔舒服 hm shu fuk
malcontent *a.* 抱不平嘅 pow bat
  pɪng geh
malcontent *n* 反叛者 fan pwun
  jeh
male *a.* 男性嘅 larm sing geh
male *n* 男性 larm sing
malediction *n.* 詛咒 juy jow
malefactor *n.* 罪犯 juy fan
maleficent *a.* 作惡嘅 jok ok geh
malice *n.* 惡意 ok yee
malicious *a.* 惡毒嘅 ok duk geh
malign *v.t.* 誹謗 fay borng
malign *a* 有害嘅 yow hoy geh
malignancy *n.* 惡性 ok sing
malignant *a.* 惡性嘅 ok sing geh
malignity *n.* 惡意 ok yee
malleable *a.* 可塑嘅 hor sok geh

malmsey *n.* 馬姆齊甜酒 ma
  mow tay teem jow
malnutrition *n.* 營養不良 ying
  yeurng bat leurng
malpractice *n.* 不法行爲 bat fat
  hang way
malt *n.* 麥芽 mak ngar
mal-treatment *n.* 虐待 yeurk
  doy
mamma *n.* 媽媽 ma ma
mammal *n.* 哺乳類動物 bo yu
  luy dung mat
mammary *a.* 乳房嘅 yu forng geh
mammon *n.* 財富 choy fu
mammoth *n.* 毛象 mo jeurng
mammoth *a* 龐大嘅 porng dai geh
man *n.* 男人 larm yan
man *v.t.* 操縱 cho jung
manage *v.t.* 管理 gwun lay
manageable *a.* 可以處理嘅 hor
  yee chu lay geh
management *n.* 管理 gwun lay
manager *n.* 經理 ging lay
managerial *a.* 經理嘅 ging lay
  geh
mandate *n.* 命令 ming ling
mandatory *a.* 規定嘅 kway ding
  geh
mane *n.* 獅鬣 see leep
manes *n.* 鬃毛 jung mow
manful *a.* 陰間嘅諸神 yam gan
  geh ju san
manganese *n.* 錳 mang
manger *n.* 馬槽 ma cho
mangle *v.t.* 嚴重損壞 yeem jung
  shoon wai
mango *n* 芒果 morng gwor
manhandle *v.t.* 拉扯 lai ter
manhole *n.* 出入孔 chut yap
  hung
manhood *n.* 男人 larm yan
mania *n* 狂熱 kworng yeet

maniac *n.* 顛佬 deen low

manicure *n.* 指甲護理 jee gam wu lay

manifest *a.* 明顯嘅 ming heen geh

manifest *v.t.* 表示 biew see

manifestation *n.* 顯示 heen see

manifesto *n.* 宣言 shoon yeen

manifold *a.* 好多嘅 ho dor geh

manipulate *v.t.* 操控 cho hung

manipulation *n.* 操作 cho jok

mankind *n.* 人類 yan luy

manlike *a.* 有男子氣概 yow lam jee hay koy

manliness *n* 男子氣概 larm jee hay koy

manly *a.* 強壯嘅 keurng jorng geh

manna *n.* 及時雨 kap see yu

mannequin *n.* 人體模型 yan tay mow ying

manner *n.* 禮貌 lay mao

mannerism *n.* 言行舉止 yeen han guy jee

mannerly *a.* 客氣嘅 hak hay geh

manoeuvre *n.* 策略 tak leurk

manoeuvre *v.i.* 移動 yee dung

manor *n.* 莊園宅第 jorng yoon jak day

manorial *a.* 莊園嘅 jorng yoon geh

mansion *n.* 豪宅 ho jak

mantel *n.* 壁爐架 bik low ga

mantle *n* 責任 jak yam

mantle *v.t* 覆蓋 fuk koy

manual *a.* 用手嘅 yung sow geh

manual *n* 說明書 shoot ming shu

manufacture *v.t.* 大量生產 dai leurng sang tan

manufacture *n* 大量製造 dai leurng jay jow

manufacturer *n* 製造商 jay jow seurng

manumission *n.* 解放 gai forng

manumit *v.t.* 解放奴隸 gai forng low day

manure *n.* 肥料 fay liew

manure *v.t.* 施肥 see fay

manuscript *n.* 手稿 sow go

many *a.* 好多 ho dor

map *n* 地圖 day tow

map *v.t.* 繪製地圖 kwuy jay day tow

mar *v.t.* 破壞 por wai

marathon *n.* 馬拉松 ma lai chung

maraud *v.i.* 搶劫 cheurng geep

marauder *n.* 搶掠者 cheurng leurk jeh

marble *n.* 雲石 wan sek

march *n* 齊步走 tay bo jow

March *n.* 三月 sam yoot

march *v.i* 遊行 yow hang

mare *n.* 母馬 mow ma

margarine *n.* 人造奶油 yan jow lai yow

margin *n.* 頁邊 yeep been

marginal *a.* 唔重要嘅 hm jung yiew geh

marigold *n.* 萬壽菊 man sow guk

marine *a.* 海嘅 hoy geh

mariner *n.* 水手 suy sow

marionette *n.* 牽線木偶 heen seen muk oh

marital *a.* 婚姻嘅 fan yan geh

maritime *a.* 海嘅 hoy geh

mark *n.* 痕 han

mark *v.t* 畫記號 wak gey ho

marker *n.* 記號 gey ho

market *n* 街市 gai see

market *v.t* 推銷 tuy siew

marketable *a.* 暢銷嘅 cheurng siew geh

marksman *n.* 神槍手 san cheurng sow

marl *n.* 泥灰 lay fwuy

marmalade *n.* 橘子醬 gat jee jeurng
maroon *n.* 褐紅色 keet hung sik
maroon *a* 褐紅色嘅 keet hung geh
maroon *v.t* 困住 kwan ju
marriage *n.* 婚姻 fan yan
marriageable *a.* 適婚嘅 sik fan geh
marry *v.t.* 嫁 ga
Mars *n* 火星 for sing
marsh *n.* 濕地 sap day
marshal *n* 高級軍官 gow kap gwan gwun
marshal *v.t* 收集 sow jap
marshy *a.* 濕地嘅 sap day geh
marsupial *n.* 有袋類動物 yow doy luy dung mat
mart *n.* 貿易場所 mow yik cheurng sor
marten *n.* 貂 diew
martial *a.* 戰爭嘅 jeen jan geh
martinet *n.* 執法人 jap fat yan
martyr *n.* 烈士 leet see
martyrdom *n.* 殉職 sun jik
marvel *n.* 奇蹟 kay jik
marvel *v.i* 感到驚奇 gam dow ging kay
marvellous *a.* 好好嘅 ho ho geh
mascot *n.* 吉祥物 gat cheurng mat
masculine *a.* 男子漢嘅 larm jee hon geh
mash *n.* 薯仔泥 shu jay lay
mash *v.t* 整碎 jing suy
mask *n.* 面具 meen guy
mask *v.t.* 掩飾 yeem sik
mason *n.* 石匠 sek jeurng
masonry *n.* 磚石建築 joon sek geen juk
masquerade *n.* 掩飾 yeem sik
mass *n.* 一嚿 yat gow
mass *v.i* 聚集 juy jap

massacre *n.* 大屠殺 dai tow sat
massacre *v.t.* 屠殺 tow sat
massage *n.* 按摩 on mor
massage *v.t.* 按摩 on mor
masseur *n.* 按摩師 on mor see
massive *a.* 巨大嘅 guy dai geh
massy *a.* 沈重嘅 tam jung geh
mast *n.* 桅杆 ngay gorn
master *n.* 主人 ju yan
master *v.t.* 掌握 jeurng ak
masterly *a.* 技術精湛 gey sut jing jam
masterpiece *n.* 傑作 geet jok
mastery *n.* 精通 jing tung
masticate *v.t.* jiew
masturbate *v.i.* 手淫 sow yam
mat *n.* 細地氈 say day jeen
matador *n .* 鬥牛士 dow ngow see
match *n.* 比賽 bay choy
match *v.i.* 登對 dang duy
match *n* 火柴 for tai
matchless *a.* 無得比嘅 mow dak bay geh
mate *n.* 朋友 pang yow
mate *v.t.* 交配 gao pwuy
mate *n* 兄弟 hing day
material *a.* 物質嘅 mat jat geh
material *n* 質料 jat liew
materialism *n.* 物質主義 mat jat ju yee
materialize *v.t.* 實現 sat yeen
maternal *a.* 母親嘅 mow tan geh
maternity *n.* 懷孕 wai yan
mathematical *a.* 數學嘅 sow hok geh
mathematician *n.* 數學家 sow hok ga
mathematics *n* 數學 sow hok
matinee *n.* 午後場 hm ho cheurng
matriarch *n.* 女族長 luy juk jeurng

matricidal *a.* 弑母嘅 see mow geh
matricide *n.* 弑母罪 see mow juy
matriculate *v.t.* 正式錄取 jing sik luk chuy
matriculation *n.* 大學註冊 dai hok ju tak
matrimonial *a.* 婚姻嘅 fan yan geh
matrimony *n.* 婚姻 fan yin
matrix *n* 社會環境 ser wuy wan ging
matron *n.* 女護士長 luy wu see jeurng
matter *n.* 事 see
matter *v.i.* 緊要 gan yiew
mattock *n.* 鶴嘴鋤 hok juy chor
mattress *n.* 床褥 chorng yuk
mature *a.* 成熟嘅 sing suk geh
mature *v.i* 成熟 sing suk
maturity *n.* 成熟 sing suk
maudlin *a* 婆婆媽媽 por por ma ma
maul *n.* 大槌 dai chuy
maul *v.t* 打傷 da seurng
maulstick *n.* 腕杖 wun jeurng
maunder *v.t.* 徘徊 pwuy wuy
mausoleum *n.* 陵墓 ling mow
mawkish *a.* 婆婆媽媽 por por ma ma
maxilla *n.* 下顎 har ok
maxim *n.* 格言 gak yeen
maximize *v.t.* 放到最大 forng dow juy dai
maximum *a.* 最大限度 juy dai han dow
maximum *n* 最大限度 juy dai han dow
May *n.* 五月 hm yoot
may *v* 可能 hor lang
mayor *n.* 市長 see jeurng
maze *n.* 迷宮 may gung
me *pron.* 我 ngor

mead *n.* 蜂蜜酒 fung mat jow
meadow *n.* 草地 cho day
meagre *a.* 太少 tai siew
meal *n.* 一餐 yat tan
mealy *a.* 粉狀嘅 fan jorng geh
mean *a.* 衰 suy
mean *n.* 平均數 ping gwan sow
mean *v.t* 表示 biew see
meander *v.i.* 漫步 man bo
meaning *n.* 意思 yee see
meaningful *a.* 有意思 yow yee see
meaningless *a.* 無意思 mow yee see
meanness *n.* 卑鄙 bay pay
means *n* 方法 forng fat
meanwhile *adv.* 期間 kay gan
measles *n* 麻疹 ma tan
measurable *a.* 可以量度嘅 hor yee leurng dok geh
measure *n.* 措施 cho see
measure *v.t* 量度 leurng dok
measureless *a.* 無限嘅 mow han geh
measurement *n.* 長度 cheurng dow
meat *n.* 肉 yuk
mechanic *n.* 機械師 gey hai see
mechanic *a* 機械嘅 gey hai geh
mechanical *a.* 機械嘅 gey hai geh
mechanics *n.* 機械學 gey hai hok
mechanism *n.* 機械裝置 gey hai jorng jee
medal *n.* 獎牌 jeurng pai
medallist *n.* 獎牌獲得者 jeurng pai wok dak jeh
medieval *a.* 中世紀嘅 jung say gey geh
medieval *a.* 落後嘅 lok ho geh
median *a.* 中間嘅 jung gan geh
mediate *v.i.* 調停 tiew ting
mediation *n.* 調解 tiew gai

mediator *n.* 調停者 tiew ting jeh
medical *a.* 醫療嘅 yee liew geh
medicament *n.* 藥 yeurk
medicinal *a.* 藥嘅 yeurk geh
medicine *n.* 藥 yeurk
medico *n.* 醫生 yee sang
mediocre *a.* 普通嘅 pow tung ghe
mediocrity *n.* 普通 pow tung
meditate *v.t.* 冥想 ming seurng
meditation *n.* 冥想 ming seurng
meditative *a.* 深思嘅 sam see geh
medium *n* 形式 ying sik
medium *a* 中號 jung ho
meek *a.* 溫順嘅 wan sun geh
meet *n.* 運動會 wan dung wuy
meet *v.t.* 見 geen
meeting *n.* 會 wuy
megalith *n.* 巨石 guy sek
megalithic *a.* 巨石建造嘅 guy sek geen jow geh
megaphone *n.* 喇叭筒 la ba tung
melancholia *n.* 憂鬱症 yow wat jing
melancholic *a.* 憂鬱嘅 yow wat geh
melancholy *n.* 傷悲 seurng bay
melancholy *adj* 令人悲哀嘅 ling yan bay ngoy
melee *n.* 混亂 wan loon
meliorate *v.t.* 改善 goy seen
mellow *a.* 甘美嘅 gam may geh
melodious *a.* 動聽 dung ting
melodrama *n.* 情節劇 ting jeet kek
melodramatic *a.* 誇大嘅 kwa dai geh
melody *n.* 旋律 shoon lut
melon *n.* 瓜 gwa
melt *v.i.* 溶 yung
member *n.* 會員 wuy yoon

membership *n.* 會員身分 wuy yoon san fan
membrane *n.* 膜 mok
memento *n.* 紀念品 gey leem ban
memoir *n.* 回憶錄 wuy yik luk
memorable *a.* 難忘嘅 lan morng geh
memorandum *n* 備忘錄 bay morng luk
memorial *n.* 紀念碑 gey leem bay
memorial *a* 紀念嘅 gey leem geh
memory *n.* 記憶 gey yik
menace *n* 威脅 way heep
menace *v.t* 威脅到 way heep dow
mend *v.t.* 整 jing
mendacious *a.* 虛假 huy ga
menial *a.* 卑賤嘅 bay jeen geh
menial *n* 僕人 buk yan
meningitis *n.* 腦膜炎 low mok yeem
menopause *n.* 更年期 gang leen kay
menses *n.* 月經 yoot ging
menstrual *a.* 月經嘅 yoot ging geh
menstruation *n.* 經期 ging kay
mental *a.* 智力嘅 jee lik geh
mentality *n.* 心態 sam tai
mention *n.* 提及 tay kap
mention *v.t.* 提及 tay kap
mentor *n.* 導師 dow see
menu *n.* 餐牌 tan pai
mercantile *a.* 商業嘅 seurng yeep geh
mercenary *n.* 只係爲錢嘅 jee hay way teen geh
mercerize *v.t.* 絲光 see gworng
merchandise *n.* 推銷 tuy siew
merchant *n.* 商人 seurng yan
merciful *a.* 寬大嘅 fwun dai geh
merciless *adj.* 無情嘅 mow ting

mercurial *a.* 變幻莫測 been wan mok tak

mercury *n.* 水銀 suy an

mercy *n.* 寬恕 fwun shu

mere *a.* 僅僅 gan gan

merge *v.t.* 合併 hap ping

merger *n.* 合併 hap ping

meridian *a.* 子午線 jee hm seen

merit *n.* 優點 yow deem

merit *v.t* 值得 jik dak

meritorious *a.* 值得讚嘅 jik dak jan geh

mermaid *n.* 美人魚 may yan yu

merman *n.* 雄人魚 hung yan yu

merriment *n.* 歡樂 fwun lok

merry *a* 愉快嘅 yu fai geh

mesh *n.* 網狀物 morng jorng mat

mesh *v.t* 吻合 man hao

mesmerism *n.* 催眠術 chuy meen sut

mesmerize *v.t.* 迷惑 may wak

mess *n.* 亂 loon

mess *v.i* 整亂 jing loon

message *n.* 訊息 sun sik

messenger *n.* 送信人呢 sung sun yan

messiah *n.* 救星 gow sing

Messrs *n.* 先生 seen sang

metabolism *n.* 新陳代謝 san tan doy jeh

metal *n.* 金屬 gam suk

metallic *a.* 金屬嘅 gam suk geh

metallurgy *n.* 冶金學 jee gam hok

metamorphosis *n.* 變質 been jat

metaphor *n.* 暗喻 am yu

metaphysical *a.* 玄學嘅 yoon hok geh

metaphysics *n.* 玄學 yoon hok

mete *v.t* 責罰 jak fat

meteor *n.* 隕石 wan sek

meteoric *a.* 流星嘅 low sing geh

meteorologist *n.* 氣象學家 hay jeurng hok ga

meteorology *n.* 氣象學 hay jeurng hok

meter *n.* 計量器 gey leurng hay

method *n.* 方法 forng fat

methodical *a.* 有條理嘅 yow tiew lay geh

metre *n.* 米 may

metric *a.* 公制嘅 gung jay geh

metrical *a.* 格律嘅 gak lut geh

metropolis *n.* 首都 sow dow

metropolitan *a.* 大城市嘅 dai sing see ghe

metropolitan *n.* 大主教 dai ju gao

mettle *n.* 勇氣 yung hay

mettlesome *a.* 勇敢嘅 yung gam geh

mew *v.i.* 喵 miew

mew *n.* 貓叫聲 mao giew seng

mezzanine *n.* 夾樓層 gap low tang

mica *n.* 雲母 wan mow

microfilm *n.* 縮微膠卷 suk may gao gwun

micrology *n.* 微工藝學 may gung ngay hok

micrometer *n.* 千分尺 teen fan tek

microphone *n.* 咪 may

microscope *n.* 顯微鏡 heen may geng

microscopic *a.* 微細嘅 may say geh

microwave *n.* 微波爐 may bor low

mid *a.* 中間嘅 jung gan geh

midday *n.* 中午 jung hm

middle *a.* 中間嘅 jung gan geh

middle *n* 中間 jung gan

middleman *n.* 中間人 jung gan yan

middling *a.* 中等嘅 jung dang geh

midget *n.* 矮人 ngay yan

midland *n.* 中部地區 jung bo day kuy

midnight *n.* 午夜 hm yeh

mid-off *n.* 投球手左後 tow kow sow geh jor ho

mid-on *n.* 投球手嘅前右 tow kow sow geh teen yow

midriff *n.* 腹部 fuk bo

midst *n.* 中間 jung gan

midsummer *n.* 仲夏 jung ha

midwife *n.* 穩婆 wan por

might *n.* 力量 lik leurng

mighty *adj.* 大力嘅 dai lik geh

migraine *n.* 偏頭痛 peen tow tung

migrant *n.* 移民 yee man

migrate *v.i.* 移居 yee guy

migration *n.* 移居 yee guy

milch *a.* 有奶嘅 yow lai geh

mild *a.* 溫和嘅 wan wor geh

mildew *n.* 黴菌 may kwan

mile *n.* 英里 ying lay

mileage *n.* 英里數 ying lay sow

milestone *n.* 里程碑 lay ting bay

milieu *n.* 環境 wan ging

militant *a.* 好戰嘅 ho jeen geh

militant *n* 好戰嘅人 ho jeen geh yan

military *a.* 軍事嘅 gwan see geh

military *n* 軍隊 gwan duy

militate *v.i.* 影響 ying heurng

militia *n.* 民兵 man bing

milk *n.* 奶 lai

milk *v.t.* 揸奶 ja lai

milky *a.* 奶嘅 lai geh

mill *n.* 麵粉廠 meen fan chorng

mill *v.t.* 磨成粉 mor sing fan

millennium *n.* 千禧年 teen hay leen

miller *n.* 磨坊工人 mor forng gung yan

millet *n.* 粟 suk

milliner *n.* 女帽商 luy mow seurng

milliner *n.* 女帽設計師 luy mow teek gey see

millinery *n.* 女帽業 luy mow yeep

million *n.* 百萬 bak man

millionaire *n.* 百萬富翁 bak man fu yung

millipede *n.* 馬陸 ma luk

mime *n.* 啞劇表演 ngar kek biew yeen

mime *v.i* 用啞劇動作 yung ngar kek dung jok

mimesis *n.* 模仿 mow forng

mimic *a.* 模仿嘅 mow forng ghe

mimic *n* 識模仿嘅人 sik mow forng geh yan

mimic *v.t* 模仿 mow forng

mimicry *n* 模仿 mow forng

minaret *n.* 宣禮塔 shoon lay tap

mince *v.t.* 絞碎 gao suy

mind *n.* 頭腦 tow low

mind *v.t.* 介意 gai yee

mindful *a.* 考慮到 hao luy dow

mindless *a.* 盲目嘅 mang muk geh

mine *pron.* 我嘅 ngor geh

mine *n* 礦 kworng

miner *n.* 礦工 kworng gung

mineral *n.* 礦物質 kworng mat jat

mineral *a* 礦物質嘅 kworng mat jat geh

mineralogist *n.* 礦物學家 kworng mat hok ga

mineralogy *n.* 礦物學 kworng mat hok

mingle *v.t.* 混合 wan hap

miniature *n.* 微型畫 may ying

wah

miniature *a.* 小型嘅 siew ying geh

minim *n.* 半音符 bwun yan fu

minimal *a.* 最少嘅 juy siew geh

minimize *v.t.* 縮細 suk say

minimum *n.* 最低限度 juy day han dow

minimum *a* 最少嘅 juy siew geh

minion *n.* 下屬 har suk

minister *n.* 大臣 dai san

minister *v.i.* 服侍 fuk see

ministrant *a.* 服務嘅 fuk mow gch

ministry *n.* 政府部門 jing fu bo mun

mink *n.* 水貂 suy diew

minor *a.* 比較細嘅 bay gao say geh

minor *n* 未成年人 may sing leen yan

minority *n.* 少數 siew sow

minster *n.* 大教堂 dai gao tong

mint *n.* 薄荷 bok hor

mint *n* 鑄幣廠 ju bay chorng

mint *v.t.* 鑄造 ju jow

minus *prep.* 減除 garm chuy

minus *a* 負 fu

minus *n* 負號 fu ho

minuscule *a.* 好細嘅 ho say geh

minute *a.* 好細嘅 ho say geh

minute *n.* 分鐘 fan jung

minutely *adv.* 每分鐘嘅 mwuy fan jung geh

minx *n.* 狡猾嘅女仔 gao wat geh luy jay

miracle *n.* 奇蹟 kay jik

miraculous *a.* 神氣嘅 san kay geh

mirage *n.* 海市蜃樓 hoy see san low

mire *n.* 泥沼 lay jiew

mire *v.t.* 陷入 ham yap

mirror *n* 鏡 geng

mirror *v.t.* 反射 fan she

mirth *n.* 歡笑 fwun siew

mirthful *a.* 高興 gow hing

misadventure *n.* 不幸嘅遭遇 bat hang geh jow yu

misalliance *n.* 錯誤嘅結合 chor hm geh geet hap

misanthrope *n.* 厭世者 yeem say jeh

misapplication *n.* 濫用 larm yung

misapprehend *v.t.* 誤解 hm gai

misapprehension *n* 誤解 hm gai

misappropriate *v.t.* 私吞 see tun

misappropriation *n.* 落格 lok gak

misbehave *v.i.* 行文不端 hang way bat doon

misbehaviour *n.* 行爲不當 hang way bat dorng

misbelief *n.* 誤信 hm sun

miscalculate *v.t.* 算錯 shoon chor

miscalculation *n.* 誤算 hm shoon

miscall *v.t.* 叫錯 giew chor

miscarriage *n.* 小產 siew tan

miscarry *v.i.* 小產 siew tan

miscellaneous *a.* 各種各樣嘅 gok jung gok yeurng geh

miscellany *n.* 雜記 jap gey

mischance *n.* 不幸 bat hang

mischief *n* 惡作劇 ok jok kek

mischievous *a.* 搞鬼嘅 gao gway geh

misconceive *v.t.* 誤會 hm wuy

misconception *n.* 誤解 hm gai

misconduct *n.* 失職 sat jik

misconstrue *v.t.* 誤會 hm wuy

miscreant *n.* 不法之徒 bat fat jee tow

misdeed *n.* 惡行 ok hang

misdemeanour *n.* 行為不當 hang way bat dorng

misdirect *v.t.* 誤導 hm dow

misdirection *n.* 誤導 hm dow

miser *n.* 孤寒 gu horn

miserable *a.* 可憐 hor leen

miserly *a.* 孤寒嘅 gu horn geh

misery *n.* 痛苦 tung fu

misfire *v.i.* 唔起作用 hm hay jok yung

misfit *n.* 行為怪異嘅人 hang way gwai yee geh yan

misfortune *n.* 不幸 bat hang

misgive *v.t.* 令人擔心 ling yan dam sam

misgiving *n.* 疑慮 yee luy

misguide *v.t.* 誤入歧途 hm yap kay tow

mishap *n.* 不幸 bat hang

misjudge *v.t.* 睇錯 tay chor

mislead *v.t.* 誤導 hm dow

mismanagement *n.* 管理不善 gwun lay bat seen

mismatch *v.t.* 錯配 chor pwuy

misnomer *n.* 用詞不當 yung tee bat dorng

misplace *v.t.* 亂放 loon forng

misprint *n.* 印錯 yan chor

misprint *v.t.* 印錯 yan chor

misrepresent *v.t.* 歪曲 wai kuk

misrule *n.* 管治不當 gwun jee bat dorng

miss *n.* 小姐 siew jeh

miss *v.t.* 掛住 gwa ju

missile *n.* 導彈 dow dan

mission *n.* 任務 yam mow

missionary *n.* 傳教士 choon gao see

missis, missus *n..* 老婆 low por

missive *n.* 信 sun

mist *n.* 薄霧 bok mow

mistake *n.* 錯 chor

mistake *v.t.* 搞錯 gao chor

mister *n.* 先生 seen sang

mistletoe *n.* 槲寄生 huk gey sang

mistreat *v.t.* 虐待 yeurk doy

mistress *n.* 二奶 yee lai

mistrust *n.* 疑慮 yee luy

mistrust *v.t.* 唔信 hm sun

misty *a.* 多霧嘅 dor mow geh

misunderstand *v.t.* 誤會 hm wuy

misunderstanding *n.* 誤會 hm wuy

misuse *n.* 濫用 larm yung

misuse *v.t.* 濫用 larm yung

mite *n.* 蟎 mwun

mite *n* 可憐嘅細路 hor leen geh say low

mithridate *n.* 解藥 gai yeurk

mitigate *v.t.* 減輕 garm heng

mitigation *n.* 減輕 garm heng

mitre *n.* 牧冠 muk gwun

mitten *n.* 連指手套 leen jee sow tow

mix *v.i* 溝 kow

mixture *n.* 混合品 wan hap ban

moan *v.i.* 發牢騷 fat low sow

moan *n.* 牢騷 low sow

moat *n.* 護城河 wu sing hor

moat *v.t.* 減 wik

mob *n.* 暴民 bo man

mob *v.t.* 攻擊 gung gik

mobile *a.* 流動嘅 low dung geh

mobility *n.* 流動性 low dung sing

mobilize *v.t.* 調動 diew dung

mock *v.i.* 笑 siew

mock *adj* 虛假嘅 huy ga geh

mockery *n.* 笑柄 siew beng

modality *n.* 情態 ting tai

mode *n.* 方式 forng sik

model *n.* 模特兒 mo dak yee

model *v.t.* 展示 jeen see

moderate *a.* 適量嘅 sik leurng geh

moderate *v.t.* 緩和 wun wor

moderation *n.* 合理 hap lay

modern *a.* 現代嘅 yeen doy geh

modernity *n.* 現代性 yeen doy sing

modernize *v.t.* 現代化 yeen doy far

modest *a.* 謙虛 heem huy

modesty *n* 謙虛 heem huy

modicum *n.* 少量嘅 siew leurng geh

modification *n.* 更改 gang goy

modify *v.t.* 改 goy

modulate *v.t.* 調整 tiew jing

moil *v.i.* 忙 morng

moist *a.* 濕潤嘅 sap yun geh

moisten *v.t.* 整濕 jing sap

moisture *n.* 水分 suy fan

molar *n.* 大牙 dai ngar

molar *a* 大牙嘅 dai ngar geh

molasses *n* 糖漿 torng jeurng

mole *n.* 鼴鼠 yeem shu

molecular *a.* 分子嘅 fan jee geh

molecule *n.* 分子 fan jee

molest *v.t.* 性騷擾 sing sow yiew

molestation *n.* 性騷擾 sing sow yiew

molten *a.* 熔化嘅 yung far geh

moment *n.* 一刻 yat hak

momentary *a.* 一刻 yat hak

momentous *a.* 關鍵嘅 gwan geen geh

momentum *n.* 推動力 tuy dung lik

monarch *n.* 君主 gwan ju

monarchy *n.* 君主制 gwan ju gway

monastery *n.* 寺院 jee yoon

monasticism *n* 修道生活 sow dow sang wut

Monday *n.* 星期一 sing kay yat

monetary *a.* 錢銀嘅 teen ngan geh

money *n.* 錢 teen

monger *n.* 商人 seurng yan

mongoose *n.* 貓鼬 mao yow

mongrel *a* 雜種狗 jap jung gow

monitor *n.* 螢光幕 ying gworng mok

monitory *a.* 監察嘅 gam tat geh

monk *n.* 和尚 wor seurng

monkey *n.* 馬騮 mar low

monochromatic *a.* 單色嘅 dan sik geh

monocle *n.* 單片眼鏡 dan peen ngan geng

monocular *a.* 單眼嘅 dan ngan geh

monody *n.* 輓歌 wan gor

monogamy *n.* 一夫一妻制 yat fu yat tay jay

monogram *n.* 花押字 far ngat jee

monograph *n.* 專論 joon lun

monogynous *a.* 一妻制嘅 yat tay jay geh

monolatry *n.* 一神崇拜 yat san sung bai

monolith *n.* 巨石 guy sek

monologue *n.* 獨白 duk bak

monopolist *n.* 專營者 joon ying jeh

monopolize *v.t.* 獨佔 duk jeem

monopoly *n.* 獨家經營權 duk gar ging ying koon

monosyllable *n.* 單音節詞 dan yam jeet tee

monosyllabic *a.* 單音節嘅 dan yam jeet geh

monotheism *n.* 一神教 yat san gao

monotheist *n.* 一神教信徒 yat san gao sun tow

monotonous *a.* 單調嘅 dan diew geh

monotony *n* 單調 dan diew

monsoon *n.* 雨季 yu gway

monster *n.* 妖怪 yiew gwai

monstrous *a.* 嚇人嘅 hak yan geh

monostrous *n.* 長期單調 cheurng kay dan diew

month *n.* 月 yoot

monthly *a.* 每個月 mwuy gor yoot

monthly *adv* 每個月 mwuy gor yoot

monthly *n* 月刊 yoot hon

monument *n.* 歷史遺跡 lik see way jik

monumental *a.* 重要嘅 jung yiew geh

moo *v.i* 哞 mow

mood *n.* 心情 sam ting

moody *a.* 喜怒無常 hay low mow seurng

moon *n.* 月亮 yoot leurng

moor *n.* 荒野 forng yeh

moor *v.t* 停泊 ting bok

moorings *n.* 停船處 ting shoon chu

moot *n.* 爭論 jang lun

mop *n.* 地拖 day tor

mop *v.t.* 拖 tor

mope *v.i.* 悶悶不樂 mwun mwun bat lok

moral *a.* 道德嘅 dow dak geh

moral *n.* 道德 dow dak

morale *n.* 士氣 see hay

moralist *n.* 道德學家 dow dak hok ga

morality *n.* 道德 dow dak

moralize *v.t.* 訓話 fan wah

morbid *a.* 病態 beng tai

morbidity *n* 病態 beng tai

more *a.* 更多 gang dor

more *adv* 更多 gang dor

moreover *adv.* 而且 yee ter

morganatic *a.* 貴賤通婚嘅 gway jeen tung fan geh

morgue *n.* 殮房 leem forng

moribund *a.* 快頂唔住 fai ding hm ju

morning *n.* 上晝 seurng jow

moron *n.* 蠢材 chun choy

morose *a.* 悶悶不樂嘅 mwun mwun bat lok geh

morphia *n.* 嗎啡 ma feh

morrow *n.* 聽日 ting yat

morsel *n.* 少量 siew leurng

mortal *a.* 會死嘅 wuy say geh

mortal *n* 普通人 pow tung yan

mortality *n.* 死亡率 say morng lut

mortar *v.t.* 灰泥 fwuy lay

mortgage *n.* 貸款 tai fwun

mortgage *v.t.* 抵押 day ngat

mortagagee *n.* 承按人 sing ngon yan

mortgagor *n.* 抵押人 day ngat yan

mortify *v.t.* 難堪 lan ham

mortuary *n.* 殮房 leem forng

mosaic *n.* 馬賽克 ma choy hak

mosque *n.* 清真寺 ting jan jee

mosquito *n.* 蚊 man

moss *n.* 苔蘚 toy seen

most *pron.* 最 juy

most *adv.* 最多 juy dor

most *n* 最多 juy dor

mote *n.* 塵 tan

motel *n.* 旅館 luy gwun

moth *n.* 飛蛾 fay ngor

mother *n* 母親 mow tan

mother *v.t.* 照顧 jiew gu

motherhood *n.* 母性 mow sing

motherlike *a.* 似媽咪 tee ma mi

motherly *a.* 母性嘅 mow sing geh

motif *n.* 主題 ju tay

motion *n.* 動作 dong jok

motion *v.i.* 指示 jee see

motionless *a.* 嘟都唔嘟下 yuk dow hm yuk ha

motivate *v* 激勵 gik lay

motivation *n.* 推動 tuy dung

motive *n.* 動機 dung gey

motley *a.* 亂嘅 loon geh

motor *n.* 馬達 ma dat

motor *v.i.* 坐車 chor cher

motorist *n.* 駕駛者 ga say jeh

mottle *n.* 斑點 ban deem

motto *n.* 格言 gak yeen

mould *n.* 模具 mow guy

mould *v.t.* 塑造 sok jow

mould *n* 風格 fung gak

mould *n* 黴菌 may kwan

mouldy *a.* 發毛 fat mow

moult *v.i.* 蛻毛 tuy mow

mound *n.* 一堆 yat duy

mount *n.* 山 san

mount *v.t.* 裝 jorng

mount *n* 上馬 seurng ma

mountain *n.* 山 san

mountaineer *n.* 登山家 dang san ga

mountainous *a.* 多山 dor san

mourn *v.i.* 哀悼 oy diew

mourner *n.* 送葬者 sung jorng jeh

mournful *a* 憂傷嘅 yow seurng geh

mourning *n.* 哀悼 oy diew

mouse *n.* 老鼠 low shu

moustache *n.* 鬍鬚 wu sow

mouth *n.* 嘴 juy

mouth *v.t.* 無聲咁講 mow seng gam gorng

mouthful *n.* 成口 sing ho

movable *a.* 可以嘟嘅 hor yee yuk geh

movables *n.* 動產 dung tan

move *n.* 搬 bwun

move *v.t.* 嘟 yuk

movement *n.* 動作 dung jok

mover *n.* 搬運工 bwun wan gung

movies *n.* 電影 deen ying

mow *v.t.* 割草 got cho

much *a* 幾多 gey dor

much *adv* 更加 gang ga

mucilage *n.* 膠水 gao suy

muck *n.* 糞便 fan been

mucous *a.* 分泌液嘅 fan bay yik geh

mucus *n.* 黏液 leem yik

mud *n.* 泥 lay

muddle *n.* 混亂 wan loon

muddle *v.t.* 搞亂 gao loon

muffle *v.t.* 整細 jing say

muffler *n.* 頸巾 geng gan

mug *n.* 杯 bwuy

muggy *a.* 悶熱 mwun yeet

mulatto *n.* 黑白混血兒 hak bak wan hoot yee

mulberry *n.* 桑樹 sorng shu

mule *n.* 騾子 lor jee

mulish *a.* 騾似嘅 lor jee geh

mull *n.* 思考 see hao

mull *v.t.* 反覆思考 fan fuk see hao

mullah *n.* 毛拉 mo lai

mullion *n.* 豎框 shu kwang

multifarious *a.* 各種各樣嘅 gok jung gok yeurng geh

multiform *a* 多種形式嘅 dor jung ying sik geh

multilateral *a.* 多國嘅 dor gwok geh

multiparous *a.* 多胞胎 dor bao toy

multiple *a.* 多樣嘅 dor yeurng geh

multiple *n* 倍數 pwuy sow

multiped *n.* 多足動物 dor juk dung mat

multiplex *a.* 戲院 hay yoon
multiplicand *n.* 被乘數 bay sing sow
multiplication *n.* 乘數 sing sow
multiplicity *n.* 多重性 dor chung sing
multiply *v.t.* 乘 sing
multitude *n.* 眾多 jung dor
mum *a.* 保持沈默 bo tee tam mak
mum *n* 媽 ma
mumble *v.i.* 口齒不清 ho tee bat ting
mummer *n.* 啞劇演員 ngar kek yeen yoon
mummy *n.* 媽咪 ma mi
mummy *n* 木乃伊 muk lai yee
mumps *n.* 痄腮 ja soy
munch *v.t.* jiew
mundane *a.* 平凡嘅 ping fan geh
municipal *a.* 市政嘅 see jing geh
municipality *n.* 自治區 ji jee kuy
munificent *a.* 慷慨嘅 horng koy geh
muniment *n.* 證書 jing shu
munitions *n.* 軍火 gwan for
mural *a.* 牆嘅 cheurng geh
mural *n.* 壁畫 bik wah
murder *n.* 謀殺 mow sat
murder *v.t.* 謀殺 mow sat
murderer *n.* 殺人兇手 sat yan hung sow
murderous *a.* 兇殘嘅 hung tan geh
murmur *n.* 喃喃聲 am am seng
murmur *v.t.* 發牢騷 fat low sow
muscle *n.* 肌肉 gey yuk
muscovite *n.* 白雲母 bak wan mow
muscular *a.* 強壯嘅 keurng jorng geh
muse *v.i.* 冥想 ming seurng
muse *n* 靈感 ling gam

museum *n.* 博物館 bok mat gwun
mush *n.* 糊狀物 wu jorng mat
mushroom *n.* 蘑菇 mor gu
music *n.* 音樂 yam ok
musical *a.* 音樂嘅 yan ok geh
musician *n.* 音樂家 yam ok ga
musk *n.* 麝香 ser heurng
musket *n.* 火槍 for cheurng
musketeer *n.* 火槍手 for cheurng sow
muslin *n.* 平紋細布 ping man say bo
must *v.* 一定 yat ding
must *n.* 必需 beet suy
must *n* 一定 yat ding
mustache *n.* 鬍鬚 wu sow
mustang *n.* 北美野馬 bak may yeh ma
mustard *n.* 芥末 gai mwut
muster *v.t.* 聚集 juy jap
muster *n* 聚集嘅人群 juy jap geh yan kwan
musty *a.* 有霉味嘅 yow mwuy may geh
mutation *n.* 變化 been far
mutative *a.* 變化嘅 been far geh
mute *a.* 無聲嘅 mow seng geh
mute *n.* 啞巴 ngar ba
mutilate *v.t.* 變殘廢 been tan fay
mutilation *n.* 肢體殘缺 jee tay tan koot
mutinous *a.* 背叛 bwuy bwun
mutiny *n.* 暴動 bo dung
mutiny *v. i* 反抗 fan korng
mutter *v.i.* 發牢騷 fat low sow
mutton *n.* 羊肉 yeurng yuk
mutual *a.* 共同嘅 gung tung geh
muzzle *n.* 口鼻 ho bay
muzzle *v.t* 壓制 ngat jay
my *a.* 我嘅 ngor geh
myalgia *n.* 肌肉痛 gey yuk tung
myopia *n.* 近視 gan see

myopic *a.* 近視嘅 gan see geh

myosis *n.* 縮瞳症 suk tung jing

myriad *n.* 無數 mow sow

myriad *a* 無數嘅 mow sow geh

myrrh *n.* 沒藥 mwut yeurk

myrtle *n.* 香桃木 heurng tow muk

myself *pron.* 我自己 ngor jee gey

mysterious *a.* 神祕嘅 san bay geh

mystery *n.* 迷 may

mystic *a.* 神祕嘅 san bay geh

mystic *n* 神祕主義者 san bay ju yee jeh

mysticism *n.* 神主義意 san bay ju yee

mystify *v.t.* 故弄玄虛 gu lung yoon huy

myth *n.* 神話 san wah

mythical *a.* 神話嘅 san wah geh

mythological *a.* 神話嘅 san wah geh

mythology *n.* 神話 san wah

N

nab *v.t.* 捉住 juk ju

nabob *n.* 穆斯林官員 muk see lam gwun yoon

nadir *n.* 最低點 juy day deem

nag *n.* 馬 ma

nag *v.t.* 哦 or

nail *n.* 釘 deng

nail *v.t.* 釘 deng

naive *a.* 天真 teen jan

naivete *n.* 天真 teen jan

naivety *n.* 天真 teen jan

naked *a.* 裸體 lor tay

name *n.* 名 meng

name *v.t.* 改名 goy meng

namely *adv.* 就係 jow hay

namesake *n.* 同名人 tong meng yan

nap *v.i.* 瞓晏覺 fan ngan gao

nap *n.* 晏覺 ngan gao

nap *n* 短絨毛 doon yung mow

nape *n.* 後頸 how geng

napkin *n.* 餐巾 tan gan

narcissism *n.* 自憐 jee loon

narcissus *n* 水仙花 suy seen far

narcosis *n.* 麻醉 ma juy

narcotic *n.* 鎮靜劑 jan jing jay

narrate *v.t.* 講述 gorng sut

narration *n.* 旁白 porng bak

narrative *n.* 描述 miew sut

narrative *a.* 描述嘅 miew sut geh

narrator *n.* 旁白者 porng ban jeh

narrow *a.* 窄 jak

narrow *v.t.* 縮窄 suk jak

nasal *a.* 鼻嘅 bay geh

nasal *n* 鼻音 bay yam

nascent *a.* 初期嘅 chor kay geh

nasty *a.* 衰格 suy gak

natal *a.* 出生嘅 chut sang geh

natant *a.* 漂嘅 piew geh

nation *n.* 國家 gwok ga

national *a.* 全國嘅 choon gwok geh

nationalism *n.* 國家主義 gwok ga ju yee

nationalist *n.* 民族主義者 man juk ju yee jeh

nationality *n.* 國籍 gwok jik

nationalization *n.* 國有化 gwok yow far

nationalize *v.t.* 國有化 gwok yow far

native *a.* 本地嘅 bwun day geh

native *n* 本地人 bwun day yan

nativity *n.* 誕生 dan sang

natural *a.* 天然嘅 teen yeen geh

naturalist *n.* 博物學家 bok mat hok ga

naturalize *v.t.* 入籍 yap jik
naturally *adv.* 自然咁 jee yeen gam
nature *n.* 大自然 dai jee yeen
naughty *a.* 拽 yay
nausea *n.* 作嘔 jok oh
nautic(al) *a.* 船嘅 shoon geh
naval *a.* 海軍嘅 hoy gwan geh
nave *n.* 中殿 jung deen
navigable *a.* 可以通航嘅 hor yi tung horng geh
navigate *v.i.* 確定位置 kok ding way jee
navigation *n.* 導航 dow horng
navigator *n.* 導航儀 dow horng yee
navy *n.* 海軍 hoy gwan
nay *adv.* 唔係 hm hay
neap *a.* 小潮 siew tiew
near *a.* 近 kan
near *prep.* 附近 fu gan
near *adv.* 附近 fu gan
near *v.i.* 接近 jeep gan
nearly *adv.* 差唔多 ta hm dor
neat *a.* 整齊 jing tay
nebula *n.* 星雲 sing wan
necessary *n.* 必要 beet yiew
necessary *a* 需要嘅 suy yiew geh
necessitate *v.t.* 變成必要嘅 been sing bat yiew geh
necessity *n.* 必要 beet yiew
neck *n.* 頸 geng
necklace *n.* 頸鏈 geng leen
necklet *n.* 頸鏈 geng leen
necromancer *n.* 巫婆 mow por
necropolis *n.* 問米婆 man may por
nectar *n.* 花蜜 far mat
need *n.* 需要 suy yiew
need *v.t.* 要 yiew
needful *a.* 需要嘅 suy yiew geh
needle *n.* 針 jam

needless *a.* 唔需要嘅 hm suy yiew geh
needs *adv.* 需要 suy yiew
needy *a.* 窮嘅 kung geh
nefandous *a.* 唔似樣 hm tee yeurng
nefarious *a.* 惡毒 ok duk
negation *n.* 反面 fan meen
negative *a.* 有害嘅 yow hoy geh
negative *n.* 負面 fu meen
negative *v.t.* 拒絕 kuy joot
neglect *v.t.* 忽略 fat leurk
neglect *n* 忽略 fat leurk
negligence *n.* 疏忽 sor fat
negligent *a.* 疏忽嘅 sor fat geh
negligible *a.* 微不足道 may bat juk dow
negotiable *a.* 有得傾嘅 yow dak king geh
negotiate *v.t.* 傾 king
nagotiation *n.* 討論 tow lun
negotiator *n.* 談判人 tam pwun yan
negress *n.* 女黑人 luy hak yan
negro *n.* 黑人 hak yan
neigh *v.i.* 馬叫聲 ma giew seng
nelgh *n.* 馬叫聲 ma giew seng
neighbour *n.* 隔籬鄰舍 gak lay lun she
neighbourhood *n.* 附近 fu gan
neighbourly *a.* 住附近嘅 ju fu gan geh
neither *conj.* 亦都唔 yik dow hm
nemesis *n.* 報應 bo ying
neolithic *a.* 新石器時代嘅 san sek hay see doy geh
neon *n.* 氖氣 lai hay
nephew *n.* 姪仔 jat jay
nepotism *n.* 裙帶關係 kwan dai gwan hay
Neptune *n.* 海王星 hoy worng sing

nerve *n.* 神經 san ging
nerveless *a.* 麻木嘅 ma muk geh
nervous *a.* 緊張 gan jeurng
nescience *n.* 無知 mow jee
nest *n.* 雀巢 jeurk chao
nest *v.t.* 築巢 juk chao
nether *a.* 嘅下面 geh ha meen
nestle *v.i.* 抱 pow
nestling *n.* 未離巢嘅雀 may lay chao geh jeurk
net *n.* 網 morng
net *v.t.* 淨賺 jing jan
net *a* 淨低嘅 jing day geh
net *v.t.* 落網 lok morng
nettle *n.* 蕁麻 tam ma
nettle *v.t.* 激嬲 gik low
network *n.* 網絡 morng lok
neurologist *n.* 神經科醫生 san ging for yee sang
neurology *n.* 神經學 san ging hok
neurosis *n.* 恐懼症 hung kuy jing
neuter *a.* 中性嘅 jung sing geh
neuter *n* 閹割 yeem got
neutral *a.* 中立嘅 jung lap geh
neutralize *v.t.* 變無效 been mow hao
neutron *n.* 中子 jung jee
never *adv.* 永遠都唔會 wing yoon dow hm wuy
nevertheless *conj.* 不過 bat gowr
new *a.* 新 san
news *n.* 新聞 san man
next *a.* 隔籬 gak lay
next *adv.* 跟住 gan ju
nib *n.* 筆尖 bat jeem
nibble *v.t.* 細細噉食 say say dam sik
nibble *n* 一細噉 yat say dam
nice *a.* 好 how
nicety *n.* 仔細 jee say

niche *n.* 地位 day way
nick *n.* 監獄 gam yuk
nickel *n.* 鎳 leep
nickname *n.* 花名 far meng
nickname *v.t.* 起花名 hay far meng
nicotine *n.* 尼古丁 lay gu ding
niece *n.* 姪女 jat luy
niggard *n.* 孤寒鬼 gu horn gway
niggardly *a.* 孤寒 gu horn
nigger *n.* 黑鬼 hak gway
nigh *adv.* 差唔多 char hm dor
nigh *prep.* 近 kan
night *n.* 夜晚 yeh man
nightingale *n.* 夜鶯 yeh ang
nightly *adv.* 每晚 mwuy man
nightmare *n.* 惡夢 ok mung
nightie *n.* 睡衣 suy yee
nihilism *n.* 虛無主義 huy mow ju yee
nil *n.* 零 ling
nimble *a.* 靈活 ling wut
nimbus *n.* 雨雲 yu wan
nine *n.* 九 gow
nineteen *n.* 十九 sap gow
nineteenth *a.* 第十九 day sap gow
ninetieth *a.* 第九十 day gow sap
ninth *a.* 第九 day gow
ninety *n.* 九十 gow sap
nip *v.t* 好快去下 how fai huy ha
nipple *n.* 乳頭 yu tow
nitrogen *n.* 氮氣 dam hay
no *a.* 唔係 hm hay
no *adv.* 唔係 hm hay
no *n* 唔係 hm hay
nobility *n.* 貴族 gway juk
noble *a.* 高貴嘅 gow gway geh
noble *n.* 貴族 gway juk
nobleman *n.* 貴族 gway juk
nobody *pron.* 無人 mow yan
nocturnal *a.* 夜間活動嘅 yeh gan wut dung geh

nod *v.i.* 岌頭 ngap tow

node *n.* 節點 jeet deem

noise *n.* 聲 seng

noisy *a.* 嘈 cho

nomad *n.* 遊牧民 yow muk man

nomadic *a.* 遊牧嘅 yow muk geh

nomenclature *n.* 命名法 ming ming fat

nominal *a.* 名義上嘅 ming yee seurng geh

nominate *v.t.* 推展 tuy jeen

nomination *n.* 推展 tuy jeen

nominee *n* 被提名人 bay tay ming yan

non-alignment *n.* 唔結盟嘅 hm geeng mang geh

nonchalance *n.* 漠不關心 mok bat gwan sam

nonchalant *a.* 冷靜嘅 lang jing geh

none *pron.* 一啲都無 yat dee dow mow

none *adv.* 一啲都無 yat dee dow mow

nonentity *n.* 無成就嘅人 mow sing jow geh yan

nonetheless *adv.* 就算係咁 jow shoon hai gam

nonpareil *a.* 無得比嘅 mow dak bay geh

nonpareil *n.* 極品 gik ban

nonplus *v.t.* 困擾 kwan yiew

nonsense *n.* 廢話 fay wah

nonsensical *a.* 荒謬嘅 forng mow geh

nook *n.* 角落 gok lok

noon *n.* 正午 jing hm

noose *n.* 繩套 sing tow

noose *v.t.* 捉 juk

nor *conj* 亦都唔 yik dow hm

norm *n.* 正常 jing seurng

norm *n.* 標準 biew jun

normal *a.* 正常 jing seurng

normalcy *n.* 正常 jing seurng

normalize *v.t.* 正常化 jing seurng far

north *n.* 北 bak

north *a* 北方嘅 bak forng geh

north *adv.* 向北 heurng bak

northerly *a.* 北方嘅 bak forng geh

northerly *n.* 北風 bak fung

northern *a.* 北方嘅 bak forng geh

nose *n.* 鼻哥 bay gor

nose *v.t* 聞 man

nosegay *n.* 一細紮花 yat say jat far

nosey *a.* 八卦 bat gwa

nosy *a.* 八卦 bat gwa

nostalgia *n.* 念舊 leem gow

nostril *n.* 鼻 bay

nostrum *n.* 祕方 bay forng

not *adv.* 唔係 hm hay

notability *n.* 知名度 jee ming dow

notable *a.* 值得注意嘅 jing dak ju yee geh

notary *n.* 公證人 gung jing yan

notation *n.* 符號 fu ho

notch *n.* 級 kap

note *n.* 字條 jee tiew

note *v.t.* 寫低 seh day

noteworthy *a.* 值得注意嘅 jik dak ju yee geh

nothing *n.* 無嘢 mow yeh

nothing *adv.* 無嘢 mow yeh

notice *n.* 通知 tung jee

notice *v.t.* 注意 ju yee

notification *n.* 通知 tung jee

notify *v.t.* 通知 tung jee

notion *n.* 信念 sun leem

notional *a.* 理論上 lay lun seurng

notoriety *n.* 惡名 ok ming

notorious *a.* 聲名狼藉嘅 sing ming lorng jik geh

notwithstanding *prep.* 雖然 suy yeen

notwithstanding *adv.* 就算係咁 jow shoon hai gam

notwithstanding *conj.* 不過 bat gwor

nought *n.* 零 ling

noun *n.* 名詞 ming tee

nourish *v.t.* 滋潤 jee yun

nourishment *n.* 營養品 ying yeurng ban

novel *a.* 新穎嘅 san wing geh

novel *n* 小說 siew shoot

novelette *n.* 中篇小說 jung peen siew shoot

novelist *n.* 小說家 siew shoot ga

novelty *n.* 新穎 san wing

November *n.* 十一月 sap yat yoot

novice *n.* 新手 san sow

now *adv.* 而家 yee ga

now *conj.* 既然 gey yeen

nowhere *adv.* 無埞 mow deng

noxious *a.* 有害嘅 yow hoy geh

nozzle *n.* 管口 gwun ho

nuance *n.* 細微差別 say may tar beet

nubile *a.* 性感嘅 sing gam geh

nuclear *a.* 原子能嘅 yoon jee lang geh

nucleus *n.* 原子核 yoon jee wat

nude *a.* 赤裸嘅 tek lor geh

nude` *n* 裸體 lor tay

nudity *n.* 裸體 lor tay

nudge *v.t.* 輕推 heng tuy

nugget *n.* 一細嚿 yat say gow

nuisance *n.* 麻煩事 ma fan see

null *a.* 無效嘅 mow hao geh

nullification *n.* 無效 mow hao

nullify *v.t.* 作廢 jok fay

numb *a.* 無感覺嘅 mo gam gok geh

number *n.* 號碼 ho ma

number *v.t.* 編號 peen ho

numberless *a.* 無數嘅 mow sow geh

numeral *a.* 數字 sow jee

numerator *n.* 分子 fan jee

numerical *a.* 數字嘅 sow jee geh

numerous *a.* 好多嘅 ho dor geh

nun *n.* 修女 sow luy

nunnery *n.* 尼姑庵 lay gu am

nuptial *a.* 婚禮嘅 fan lay geh

nuptials *n.* 婚禮 fan lay

nurse *n.* 護士 wu see

nurse *v.t* 照顧 jiew gu

nursery *n.* 幼稚園 yow jee yoon

nurture *n.* 栽培 joy pwuy

nurture *v.t.* 栽培 joy pwuy

nut *n* 果仁 gwor yan

nutrition *n.* 營養 ying yeurng

nutritious *a.* 有營養 yow ying yeurng

nutritive *a.* 營養嘅 ying yeurng geh

nuzzle *v.* 用鼻摸 yung bay mor

nylon *n.* 尼龍 lay lung

nymph *n.* 仙女 seen luy

oak *n.* 橡樹 jeurng shu

oar *n.* 船槳 shoon jeurng

oarsman *n.* 撐艇手 tang teng sow

oasis *n.* 沙漠嘅綠洲 sa mok geh luk jow

oat *n.* 燕麥 yeen mak

oath *n.* 誓言 say yeen

obduracy *n.* 硬頸 ngan geng

obdurate *a.* 硬頸嘅 ngan geng geh

obedience *n.* 服從 fuk chung

obedient *a.* 聽話嘅 teng wah geh

obeisance *n.* 敬仰 ging yeurng

obesity *n.* 肥胖症 fay bwun jing

obey *v.t.* 遵從 jun chung

obituary *a.* 訃告 fu gow

object *n.* 物體 mat tay

object *v.t.* 反對 fan duy

objection *n.* 反對 fan duy

objectionable *a.* 令人反感嘅 ling yan fan gam geh

objective *n.* 目的 muk dik

objective *a.* 客觀嘅 hak gwun geh

oblation *n.* 祭品 jay ban

obligation *n.* 責任 jak yam

obligatory *a.* 一定要嘅 yat ding yiew geh

oblige *v.t.* 逼使 bik say

oblique *a.* 轉彎抹角 joon wan mwut gok

obliterate *v.t.* 消滅 siew meet

obliteration *n.* 消滅 siew meet

oblivion *n.* 無意識 mow yee sik

oblivious *a.* 唔注意嘅 hm ju yee geh

oblong *a.* 長方形嘅 cheurng forng ying geh

oblong *n.* 長方形 cheurng forng ying

obnoxious *a.* 令人作嘔嘅 ling yan jok oh geh

obscene *a.* 下流嘅 ha low geh

obscenity *n.* 下流嘅行為 ha low geh hang way

obscure *a.* 少為人知嘅 siew way yan jee geh

obscure *v.t.* 變模糊 been mow wu

obscurity *n.* 含糊 ham wu

observance *n.* 宗教儀式 jung gao ye sik

observant *a.* 觀察力強 gwun tat lik keurng

observation *n.* 觀察 gwun tat

observatory *n.* 天文台 teen man toy

observe *v.t.* 觀察 gwun tat

obsess *v.t.* 迷戀 may loon

obsession *n.* 沈迷 tam may

obsolete *a.* 淘汰咗嘅 tow tai jor geh

obstacle *n.* 障礙物 jeurng ngoy mat

obstinacy *n.* 固執 gu jap

obstinate *a.* 硬頸 ngan geng

obstruct *v.t.* 阻 jor

obstruction *n.* 阻擋 jor dorng

obstructive *a.* 阻止 jor jee

obtain *v.t.* 得到 dak dow

obtainable *a.* 可以得到嘅 hor yee dak dow geh

obtuse *a.* 遲鈍嘅 tee dun geh

obvious *a.* 明顯 ming heen

occasion *n.* 場合 cheurng hap

occasion *v.t* 導致 dow jee

occasional *a.* 間唔中 gan hm jung

occasionally *adv.* 耐唔中 loy hm jung

occident *n.* 西方 say forng

occidental *a.* 西方嘅 say forng geh

occult *a.* 神祕嘅 san bay geh

occupancy *n.* 佔有 jeem yow

occupant *n.* 佔有人 jeem yow yan

occupation *n.* 職業 jik yeep

occupier *n.* 佔有人 jeem yow yan

occupy *v.t.* 佔用 jeem uimg

occur *v.i.* 發生 fat sang

occurrence *n.* 出現 chut yeen

ocean *n.* 海洋 hoy yeurng

oceanic *a.* 海洋嘅 hoy yeurng geh

octagon *n.* 八角形 bat gok ying

octagonal *a.* 八角形嘅 bat gok ying geh

octave *n.* 八度 bat dow

October *n.* 十月 sap yoot

octogenarian *a.* 八旬老人 bat sun low yan

octroi *n.* 入市稅 yao see suy

ocular *a.* 眼嘅 ngan geh

oculist *n.* 眼科醫生 ngan for yee sang

odd *a.* 怪嘅 gwai geh

oddity *n.* 古怪 gu gwai

odds *n.* 可能性 hor lang sing

ode *n.* 頌歌 jung gor

odious *a.* 令人作嘔嘅 ling yan jok oh geh

odium *n.* 反感 fan gam

odorous *a.* 有味嘅 yow may geh

odour *n.* 臭味 chow may

offence *n.* 罪 juy

offend *v.t.* 得罪 dak juy

offender *n.* 犯罪人 fan juy yan

offensive *a.* 得罪人嘅 dak juy yan geh

offensive *n* 攻擊 gung gik

offer *v.t.* 提供 tay gung

offer *n* 提議 tay yee

offering *n.* 祭品 jay ban

office *n.* 寫字樓 seh jee low

officer *n.* 官員 gwun yoon

official *a.* 正式嘅 jing sik geh

official *n* 官員 gwun yoon

officially *adv.* 正式 jing sik

officiate *v.i.* 主持 ju tee

officious *a.* 多管閒事 dor gwun han see

offing *n.* 即將發生 jik jeurng fat sang

offset *v.t.* 抵消 day siew

offset *n* 抵消 day siew

offshoot *n.* 分枝 fan jee

offspring *n.* 仔女 jay luy

oft *adv.* 通常 tung seurng

often *adv.* 通常 tung seurng

ogle *v.t.* 眼甘甘 ngan gam gam

ogle *n* 凝望 ying morng

oil *n.* 油 yow

oil *v.t* 上油 seurng yow

oily *a.* 好油 ho yow

ointment *n.* 藥膏 yeurk gow

old *a.* 舊嘅 gow geh

oligarchy *n.* 寡頭政治 gwa tow jing jee

olive *n.* 橄欖 gam lam

olympiad *n.* 奧運會 oh wan wuy

omega *n.* 歐米加 oh may ga

omelette *n.* 煎蛋捲 jeen dan goon

omen *n.* 預兆 yu siew

ominous *a.* 唔吉利嘅 hm gat lay geh

omission *n.* 遺漏 way low

omit *v.t.* 發出 fat chut

omnipotence *n.* 全能 choon lang

omnipotent *a.* 無所不能嘅 mow sor bat lang geh

omnipresence *n.* 無所不在 mow sor bat joy

omnipresent *a.* 無所不在嘅 mow sor bat joy geh

omniscience *n.* 全知 choon jee

omniscient *a.* 無所不知嘅 mow sor bat jee geh

on *prep.* 喺...嘅上面 hay...geh seurng meen

on *adv.* 喺...嘅上面 hay...geh seurng meen

once *adv.* 一次 yat tee

one *a.* 一 yat

one *pron.* 一 yat
oneness *n.* 一致 yat jee
onerous *a.* 晒力嘅 sai lik gey
onion *n.* 蔥 chung
on-looker *n.* 旁觀者 porng gwun jeh
only *a.* 只有 jee yow
only *adv.* 只係 jee hay
only *conj.* 不過 bat gwor
onomatopoeia *n.* 象聲詞 jeurng sing tee
onrush *n.* 突如其來 dak yu kay loy
onset *n.* 開始 hoy tee
onslaught *n.* 攻擊 gung gik
onus *n.* 職責 jik jak
onward *a.* 向前 heurng teen
onwards *adv.* 向前 heurng teen
ooze *n.* 泥漿 lay jeurng
ooze *v.i.* 慢慢滲出 man man sam chut
opacity *n.* 透明度 tow ming dow
opal *n.* 貓眼石 mao ngan sek
opaque *a.* 唔透明嘅 hm tow ming geh
open *a.* 打開嘅 da hoy geh
open *v.t.* 打開 da hoy
opening *n.* 開頭 hoy tow
openly *adv.* 公開咁 gung hoy gam
opera *n.* 歌劇 gor kek
operate *v.t.* 操作 cho jok
operation *n.* 手術 sow sut
operative *a.* 用緊嘅 yung gan geh
operator *n.* 操作人 cho jok yan
opine *v.t.* 認為 ying way
opinion *n.* 意見 yee geen
opium *n.* 鴉片 ngar peen
opponent *n.* 對手 suy sow
opportune *a.* 適合嘅 sik hap geh
opportunism *n.* 機會主義 gey wuy ju yee

opportunity *n.* 機會 gey wuy
oppose *v.t.* 反對 fan duy
opposite *a.* 對住 duy ju
opposition *n.* 對立 duy lap
oppress *v.t.* 壓制 ngat jay
oppression *n.* 壓制 ngat jay
oppressive *a.* 壓制嘅 ngat jay geh
oppressor *n.* 壓迫者 ngat bik jeh
opt *v.i.* 揀 gan
optic *a.* 眼嘅 ngan geh
optician *n.* 眼鏡商 ngan geng seurng
optimism *n.* 樂觀 lok gwun
optimist *n.* 樂觀嘅人 lok gwun geh yan
optimistic *a.* 樂觀 lok gwun
optimum *n.* 最好 juy ho
optimum *a* 最佳嘅 juy gai geh
option *n.* 選擇 shoon jak
optional *a.* 可以揀嘅 hor yee gan geh
opulence *n.* 財富 choy fu
opulent *a.* 豪華嘅 ho wah geh
oracle *n.* 牧師 muk see
oracular *a.* 玄妙嘅 yoon miew geh
oral *a.* 口頭嘅 ho tow geh
orally *adv.* 口述嘅 ho sut geh
orange *n.* 橙 tang
orange *a* 橙色嘅 tang sik geh
oration *n.* 演講 yeen gorng
orator *n.* 演講家 yeen gorng ga
oratorical *a.* 演講嘅 yeen gorng geh
oratory *n.* 演講術 yeen gorng sut
orb *n.* 球體 kow tay
orbit *n.* 軌道 gway dow
orchard *n.* 果園 gwor yoon
orchestra *n.* 管弦樂隊 gwun yoon ok duy

orchestral *a.* 管弦樂嘅 gwun yoon ok geh

ordeal *n.* 折磨 jeet mor

order *n.* 次序 tee juy

order *v.t* 訂 deng

orderly *a.* 有條理嘅 yow tiew lay geh

orderly *n.* 護理員 wu lay yoon

ordinance *n.* 法令 fat ling

ordinarily *adv.* 平時咁 ping see gam

ordinary *a.* 普通 po tung

ordnance *n.* 軍用器材 gwan yung hay choy

ore *n.* 礦石 kworng sek

organ *n.* 器官 hay gwun

organic *a.* 有機嘅 yow gey geh

organism *n.* 生物 sang mat

organization *n.* 組織 jow jik

organize *v.t.* 安排 on pai

orient *n.* 東方 dung forng

orient *v.t.* 適應 sik ying

oriental *a.* 東方嘅 dung forng geh

oriental *n* 東方人 dung forng yan

orientate *v.t.* 面對 meen duy

origin *n.* 源頭 toon tow

original *a.* 原作嘅 yoon jok geh

original *n* 正本 jing bwun

originality *n.* 創意 chorng yee

originate *v.t.* 起源於 hay yoon yu

originator *n.* 創作人 chorng jok yan

ornament *n.* 裝飾品 jorng sik ban

ornament *v.t.* 裝飾 jorng sik

ornamental *a.* 裝飾嘅 jorng sik geh

ornamentation *n.* 裝飾 jorng sik

orphan *n.* 孤兒 gu yee

orphan *v.t* 成爲孤兒 sing way gu yee

orphanage *n.* 孤兒院 gu yee yoon

orthodox *a.* 正統嘅 jing tung geh

orthodoxy *n.* 正統觀念 jing tung gwun leem

oscillate *v.i.* 波動 bor dung

oscillation *n.* 擺動 bai dung

ossify *v.t.* 僵化 geurng far

ostracize *v.t.* 排斥 pai tik

ostrich *n.* 鴕鳥 torliew

other *a.* 其他 kay ta

other *pron.* 另外 ling ngoy

otherwise *adv.* 除此之外 chuy tee jee ngoy

otherwise *conj.* 如果唔係 yu gwor hm hay

otter *n.* 海獺 hoy lai

ottoman *n.* 長軟凳 cheurng yoon dang

ounce *n.* 安士 on see

our *pron.* 我哋 ngor day

oust *v.t.* 罷免 ba meen

out *adv.* 出去 chut huy

out-balance *v.t.* 重過 chung gwor

outbid *v.t.* 出高價 chut go ga

outbreak *n.* 爆發 bao fat

outburst *n.* 爆發 bao fat

outcast *n.* 被排斥者 bay pai tik jeh

outcast *a* 排斥 pai tik

outcome *n.* 結果 geet gwor

outcry *a.* 強烈抗議 keurng leet korng yee

outdated *a.* 過時 gwor see

outdo *v.t.* 勝過 sing gwor

outdoor *a.* 戶外嘅 woo ngoy geh

outer *a.* 外邊嘅 ngoy been geh

outfit *n.* 裝束 jorng chuk

outfit *v.t* 裝備 jorng bay

outgrow *v.t.* 着唔落 jeurk hm lok

outhouse *n.* 外圍建築 ngoy way geen juk

outing *n.* 郊遊 gao yow

outlandish *a.* 唔尋常嘅 hm tam seurng geh

outlaw *n.* 逃犯 tow fan

outlaw *v.t* 變爲非法 been way fay fat

outline *n.* 外型 ngoy ying

outline *v.t.* 講下 gorng har

outlive *v.i.* 比...長命 bay...cheurng meng

outlook *n.* 見解 geen gai

outmoded *a.* 過晒時嘅 gwor sai see geh

outnumber *v.t.* 壓倒 ngat dow

outpatient *n.* 門診病人 mun tan beng yan

outpost *n.* 前哨 teen sao

output *n.* 出產量 chut tan leurng

outrage *n.* 憤怒 fan low

outrage *v.t.* 發晒火 fat sai for

outright *adv.* 毫無保留咁 ho mo bo low gam

outright *a* 徹底嘅 teet day geh

outrun *v.t.* 超越 tiew yoot

outset *n.* 最初 chuy chor

outshine *v.t.* 勝過 sing gwor

outside *a.* 出邊嘅 chut been geh

outside *n* 出邊 chut been

outside *adv* 出邊嘅 chut been geh

outside *prep* 出邊 chut been

outsider *n.* 外來人 ngoy loy yan

outsize *a.* 特大 dak dai

outskirts *n.pl.* 市郊 see gao

outspoken *a.* 率直 sut jik

outstanding *a.* 優秀 yow sow

outward *a.* 向外 heurng ngoy

outward *adv* 外面 ngoy meen

outwards *adv* 向外 heurng ngoy

outwardly *adv.* 表面上 biew meen seurng

outweigh *v.t.* 重過 chung gwor

outwit *v.t.* 智勝 jee sing

oval *a.* 卵形嘅 lun ying geh

oval *n* 卵形 lun ying

ovary *n.* 卵巢 lun tao

ovation *n.* 熱烈歡迎 yeet leet fwun ying

oven *n.* 焗爐 guk low

over *prep.* 上面 seurng meen

over *adv* 過 gwor

over *n* 一輪投球 yat lun tow kow

overact *v.t.* 誇張 kwa jeurng

overall *n.* 外套 ngoy tow

overall *a* 總體嘅 jung tay geh

overawe *v.t.* 敬畏 ging way

overboard *adv.* 船外 shoon ngoy

overburden *v.t.* 負擔過重 fu dam gwor chung

overcast *a.* 多雲 dor wan

overcharge *v.t.* 收多錢 sow dor teen

overcharge *n* 收多錢 sow dor teen

overcoat *n.* 大樓 dai low

overcome *v.t.* 克服 hak fuk

overdo *v.t.* 做得過分 jow dak gwor fan

overdose *n.* 過量 gwor leurng

overdose *v.t.* 過量服用 gwor leung fuk yung

overdraft *n.* 透支 tow jee

overdraw *v.t.* 透支 tow jee

overdue *a.* 過期 gwor kay

overhaul *v.t.* 超越 tiew yoot

overhaul *n.* 改造 goy jow

overhear *v.t.* 無意中聽到 mo yee jung teng dow

overjoyed *a* 非常高興 fay seurng go hing

overlap *v.t.* 重疊 chung deep

overlap *n* 重疊 chung deep

overleaf *adv.* 下一頁 har yat yeep

overload *v.t.* 超載 tiew joy

overload *n* 過多 gwor dor

overlook *v.t.* 忽略 fat leurk

overnight *adv.* 一夜之間 yat yeh jee gan

overnight *a* 一夜之間 yat yeh jee gan

overpower *v.t.* 征服 jing fuk

overrate *v.t.* 高估 gow gu

overrule *v.t.* 駁回 bok wuy

overrun *v.t* 超時 tiew see

oversee *v.t.* 監督 gam duk

overseer *n.* 監工 gam gung

overshadow *v.t.* 掩蓋 yeem koy

oversight *n.* 疏忽 sor fat

overt *a.* 公開嘅 gung hoy geh

overtake *v.t.* 爬頭 pa tow

overthrow *v.t.* 推翻 tuy fan

overthrow *n* 推翻 tuy fan

overtime *adv.* 加班 gar ban

overtime *n* 加班 gar ban

overture *n.* 前奏曲 teen jow kuk

overwhelm *v.t.* 擊敗 gik bai

overwork *v.i.* 工作過度 gung jok gwor dow

overwork *n.* 工作過度 gung jok gwor dow

owe *v.t* 欠 heem

owl *n.* 貓頭鷹 mao tow ying

own *a.* 自己嘅 jee gey geh

own *v.t.* 擁有 yung yow

owner *n.* 物主 mat ju

ownership *n.* 產權 tan koon

ox *n.* 牛 ngow

oxygen *n.* 氧氣 yeurng hay

oyster *n.* 蠔 ho

P

pace *n* 速度 chuk dow

pace *v.i.* 節奏 jeet jow

pacific *a.* 平靜嘅 ping jing geh

pacify *v.t.* 平息 ping sik

pack *n.* 一包 yat bao

pack *v.t.* 執行李 jap hang lay

package *n.* 包裹 bao gwor

packet *n.* 一包 yat bao

packing *n.* 包裝 bao jorng

pact *n.* 協議 heep yee

pad *n.* 墊 deen

pad *v.t.* 加墊 ga deen

padding *n.* 墊 deen

paddle *v.i.* 撐船 tang shoon

paddle *n* 船槳 shoon jeurng

paddy *n.* 稻田 dow teen

page *n.* 頁 yeep

page *v.t.* 呼叫 fu giew

pageant *n.* 選美比賽 shoon may bay choy

pageantry *n.* 盛況 sing forng

pagoda *n.* 塔 tap

pail *n.* 桶 tung

pain *n.* 痛苦 tung fu

pain *v.t.* 痛 tung

painful *a.* 痛苦 tung fu

painstaking *a.* 辛苦嘅 san fu geh

paint *n.* 漆油 tat yow

paint *v.t.* 油 yow

painter *n.* 畫家 wah gar

painting *n.* 畫 wah

pair *n.* 一對 yat duy

pair *v.t.* 組成一對 jo sing yat duy

pal *n.* 朋友 pang yow

palace *n.* 皇宮 worng gung

palanquin *n.* 轎 kiew

palatable *a.* 好味嘅 ho may geh

palatal *a.* 顎嘅 ok geh

palate *n.* 上顎嘅 色哦口 geh

palatial *a.* 堂皇嘅 torng worng geh

pale *n.* 越軌 yoot gway

pale *a* 淺 teen

pale *v.i.* 變白 been bak

palette *n.* 調色板 tiew sik ban

palm *n.* 手板 sow ban

palm *v.t.* 收埋係手板 sow mai hay sow ban

palm *n.* 棕櫚樹 jung luy shu

palmist *n.* 手相術士 sow seurng sut see

palmistry *n.* 手相術 sow seurng sut

palpable *a.* 明顯嘅 ming heen geh

palpitate *v.i.* 急跳 gap tiew

palpitation *n.* 心悸 sam gway

palsy *n.* 痲痺 ma bay

paltry *a.* 無用嘅 mow yung ghe

pamper *v.t.* 縱容 jung yung

pamphlet *n.* 手冊 sow tak

pamphleteer *n.* 手冊作者 sow tak jok jeh

panacea *n.* 萬能之計 man lang jee gey

pandemonium *n.* 騷動 sow dung

pane *n.* 玻璃窗 bor lay cheurng

panegyric *n.* 頌文 jung man

panel *n.* 鑲板 seurng ban

panel *v.t.* 鑲板 seurng ban

pang *n.* 一陣劇痛 yat jan kek tung

panic *n.* 激動 gik dung

panorama *n.* 全景 choon ging

pant *v.i.* 喘氣 choon hay

pant *n.* 氣喘 hay choon

pantaloon *n.* 傻佬 sor low

pantheism *n.* 泛神論 fan san lun

pantheist *n.* 泛神論者 fan san lun jeh

panther *n.* 黑豹 hak pao

pantomime *n.* 童話劇 tung wah kek

pantry *n.* 食物室 sik mat sat

papacy *n.* 教宗嘅職位 gao jung geh jik way

papal *a.* 教宗嘅 gao jung geh

paper *n.* 紙 jee

par *n.* 標準杆數 biew jun gorn sow

parable *n.* 寓言 yu yeen

parachute *n.* 降落傘 gorng lok sna

parachutist *n.* 跳傘者 tiew san jeh

parade *n.* 遊行 yow hang

parade *v.t.* 遊行 yow hang

paradise *n.* 天堂 teen torng

paradox *n.* 矛盾 mao tun

paradoxical *a.* 自相矛盾嘅 jee seurng mao tun geh

paraffin *n.* 石蠟 sek lap

paragon *n.* 模範 mow fan

paragraph *n.* 段 don

parallel *a.* 平行嘅 ping hang geh

parallel *v.t.* 同時發生 tung see fat sang

parallelism *n.* 相似度 seurng tee dow

parallelogram *n.* 平行四角型 ping hang say gok ying

paralyse *v.t.* 變癱 been tan

paralysis *n.* 癱瘓 tan wun

paralytic *a.* 癱瘓嘅 tan wun geh

paramount *a.* 罪重要嘅 juy jung yiew geh

paramour *n.* 情人 ting yan

paraphernalia *n. pl* 裝備 jorng bay

paraphrase *n.* 解釋 gai sik

paraphrase *v.t.* 解釋 gai sik

parasite *n.* 寄生蟲 gey sang chung

parcel *n.* 包裹 bao gwor

parcel *v.t.* 包 bao

parch *v.t.* 烘 hung

pardon *v.t.* 赦免 ser meen

pardon *n.* 特赦 dak ser

pardonable *a.* 可以原諒嘅 hor yee yoon leurng geh

parent *n.* 父母 fu mow	**partition** *n.* 分區 fan kuy
parentage *n.* 出生 chut sang	**partition** *v.t.* 分割 fan got
parental *a.* 父母嘅 fu mow geh	**partner** *n.* 拍檔 pak dorng
parenthesis *n.* 插入語 tap yap yu	**partnership** *n.* 合作 hap jok
parish *n.* 教區 gao kuy	**party** *n.* 派對 pai duy
parity *n.* 平等 ping dang	**pass** *v.i.* 通過 tung gowr
park *n.* 公園 gung yoon	**pass** *n* 通行證 tung hang jing
park *v.t.* 泊 pak	**passage** *n.* 通到 tung dow
parlance *n.* 講法 gorng fat	**passenger** *n.* 乘客 sing hak
parley *n.* 對話 duy wah	**passion** *n.* 熱情 yeet ting
parley *v.i* 談判 tam pwun	**passionate** *a.* 熱情 yeet ting
parliament *n.* 國會 gwok wuy	**passive** *a.* 被動嘅 bay dung geh
parliamentarian *n.* 議員 yee yoon	**passport** *n.* 護照 wu jiew
parliamentary *a.* 國會嘅 gwok wuy geh	**past** *a.* 過去嘅 gwor huy geh
	past *n.* 過去 gwor huy
parlour *n.* 客廳 hak teng	**past** *prep.* 過 gwor
parody *n.* 模仿 mow forng	**paste** *n.* 肉醬 yuk jeurng
parody *v.t.* 模仿 mow forng	**paste** *v.t.* 貼 teep
parole *n.* 假釋 ga sik	**pastel** *n.* 蠟筆 lap bat
parole *v.t.* 假釋 ga sik	**pastime** *n.* 消遣 siew heen
parricide *n.* 殺父母罪 sat fu mow juy	**pastoral** *a.* 牧民嘅 muk man geh
parrot *n.* 鸚鵡 ying mow	**pasture** *n.* 牧場 muk cheurng
parry *v.t.* 擋開 dorng hoy	**pasture** *v.t.* 放牧 forng muk
parry *n.* 擋 dorng	**pat** *v.t.* 拍 pak
parson *n.* 牧師 muk see	**pat** *n* 拍 pak
part *n.* 部份 bo fan	**pat** *adv* 瞭如指掌 liew yu jee jeurng
part *v.t.* 分開 fan hoy	
partake *v.i.* 參與 tarm yu	**patch** *v.t.* 補 bo
partial *a.* 部份嘅 bo fan geh	**patch** *n* 一笪 yat dat
partiality *n.* 偏袒 peen tan	**patent** *a.* 明顯嘅 ming heen geh
participate *v.i.* 參與 tarm yu	**patent** *n* 專利權 joon lay koon
participant *n.* 參與者 tarm yu jeh	**patent** *v.t.* 申請專利 san ting joon lay
participation *n.* 參與 tarm yu	
particle *a.* 微粒 may lap	**paternal** *a.* 父親嘅 fu tan geh
particular *a.* 特別嘅 dak beet geh	**path** *n.* 小路 siew low
	pathetic *a.* 無用嘅 mow yung geh
particular *n.* 細節 say jeet	**pathos** *n.* 感染力 gam yeem lik
partisan *n.* 游擊隊員 yow gik duy yoon	**patience** *n.* 耐性 loy sing
	patient *a.* 有耐性嘅 yow loy sing geh
partisan *a.* 偏袒嘅 peen tan geh	**patient** *n* 病人 beng yan
	patricide *n.* 弒父罪 see fu juy

patrimony *n.* 遺產 yee tan	peck *n.* 錫 sek
patriot *n.* 愛國者 ngoy gwok jeh	peck *v.i.* 啄 deurk
patriotic *a.* 愛國嘅 ngoy gwok geh	peculiar *a.* 怪嘅 gwai geh
partiotism *n.* 愛國精神 ngoy gwok jing san	peculiarity *n.* 怪癖 gwai pik
	pecuniary *a.* 金錢嘅 gam teen geh
patrol *v.i.* 巡邏 chun lor	pedagogue *n.* 教師 gao see
patrol *n* 巡邏 chun lor	pedagogy *n.* 教育學 gao yuk hok
patron *n.* 贊助人 jan jor yan	pedal *n.* 踏板 dap ban
patronage *n.* 贊助 jan jor	pedal *v.t.* 踩 tai
patronize *v.t.* 扮晒嘢 ban sai yeh	pedant *n.* 講究 gorng gow
pattern *n.* 花樣 far yeurng	pedantic *a.* 太過講究 tai gwor gorng gow
paucity *n.* 少量 siew leurng	
pauper *n.* 窮人 kung yan	pedantry *n.* 迂腐 yu fu
pause *n.* 暫停 jam ting	pedestal *n.* 底座 day jor
pause *v.i.* 暫停 jam ting	pedestrian *n.* 行人 hang yan
pave *v.t.* 鋪 pow	pedigree *n.* 族譜 juk pow
pavement *n.* 行人路 hang yan low	peel *v.t.* 搣 meet
	peel *n.* 皮 pay
pavilion *n.* 涼亭 leurng ting	peep *v.i.* 偷睇 tow tay
paw *n.* 爪 jao	peep *n* 偷望 tow morng
paw *v.t.* 啷手啷腳 yuk sow yuk geurk	peer *n.* 同輩 tung pwuy
	peerless *a.* 無得比嘅 mow dak bay geh
pay *v.t.* 抓人 jao yan	
pay *n* 人工 yan gung	peg *n.* 夾 geep
payable *a.* 要畀嘅 yiew bay geh	peg *v.t.* 夾住 geep ju
payee *n.* 收款人 sow fwun yan	pelf *n.* 不義之財 bat yee jee choy
payment *n.* 款項 fwun horng	pell-mell *adv.* 趕 gorn
pea *n.* 綠豆 luk dow	pen *n.* 筆 bat
peace *n.* 和平 wor ping	pen *v.t.* 寫 she
peaceable *a.* 和平嘅 wor ping geh	penal *a.* 刑罰嘅 ying fat geh
	penalize *v.t.* 懲罰 ting fat
peaceful *a.* 安靜嘅 on jing geh	penalty *n.* 懲罰 ting fat
peach *n.* 桃 tow	pencil *n.* 鉛筆 yoon bat
peacock *n.* 孔雀 hung jeurk	pencil *v.t.* 畫 wak
peahen *n.* 雌孔雀 tee hung jeurk	pending *prep.* 等緊 dang gan
peak *n.* 頂峰 ding fung	pending *a* 待定嘅 doy ding geh
pear *n.* 梨 lay	pendulum *n.* 鐘擺 jung bai
pearl *n.* 珍珠 jan ju	penetrate *v.t.* 插入 tap yap
peasant *n.* 農民 lung man	penetration *n.* 插入 tap yap
peasantry *n.* 農民 lung man	penis *n.* 陰莖 yam ging
pebble *n.* 卵石 lun sek	

penniless *a.* 仙都唔仙下　seen dow hm seen ha

penny *n.* 便士　been see

pension *n.* 退休金　tuy yow gam

pension *v.t.* 強迫退休　keurng bik tuy yow

pensioner *n.* 退休人士　tuy yow yan see

pensive *a.* 沈思嘅　tam see geh

pentagon *n.* 五角型　hm gok ying

peon *n.* 苦功　fu gung

people *n.* 人　yan

people *v.t.* 住滿人　ju mwun yan

pepper *n.* 胡椒粉　wu jiew fan

pepper *v.t.* 加胡椒粉　ga wu jiew fan

per *prep.* 每　mwuy

perambulator *n.* BB車　bee bee cher

perceive *v.t.* 注意　ju yee

perceptible *adj* 睇得出嘅　tay dak chut geh

per cent *adv.* 百分之　bak fan jee

percentage *n.* 百分率　bak fan lut

perception *n.* 知覺　jee gok

perceptive *a.* 觀察力強嘅　gwun tat lik keurng geh

perch *n.* 棲息處　tay sik chu

perch *v.i.* 坐　chor

perennial *a.* 持續嘅　tee juk geh

perennial *n.* 多年生植物　dor leen sang jik mat

perfect *a.* 完美嘅　yoon may geh

perfect *v.t.* 整完美　jing yoon may

perfection *n.* 完美　yoon may

perfidy *n.* 背叛　bwuy bwun

perforate *v.t.* 大窿　da lung

perforce *adv.* 一定嘅　yat ding geh

perform *v.t.* 表演　biew yeen

performance *n.* 演出　yeen chut

performer *n.* 表演者　biew yeen jeh

perfume *n.* 香水　heurng suy

perfume *v.t.* 搽香水　ta heurng suy

perhaps *adv.* 或者　wak jeh

peril *n.* 危險　ngay heem

peril *v.t.* 禍害　wor hoy

perilous *a.* 危險嘅　ngay heem geh

period *n.* 時期　see kay

periodical *n.* 期刊　kay horn

periodical *a.* 定期嘅　ding kay geh

periphery *n.* 周圍　jow way

perish *v.i.* 死　say

perishable *a.* 易變質嘅　yee been jat geh

perjure *v.i.* 畀假口供　bay ga ho gung

perjury *n.* 偽證罪　ngay jing juy

permanence *n.* 永久性　wing gow sing

permanent *a.* 永久嘅　wing gow geh

permissible *a.* 容許嘅　yung huy geh

permission *n.* 批准　pay jun

permit *v.t.* 允許　wan huy

permit *n.* 許可證　huy hor jing

permutation *n.* 排列方式　pai leet forng sik

pernicious *a.* 有害嘅　yow hoy geh

perpendicular *a.* 垂直嘅　suy jik geh

perpendicular *n.* 垂直線　suy jik seen

perpetual *a.* 不斷嘅　bat doon geh

perpetuate *v.t.* 持續　tee juk

perplex *v.t.* 困擾　kwan yiew

perplexity *n.* 困擾　kwan yiew

persecute *v.t.* 逼害　bik hoy

persecution *n.* 逼害　bik hoy

perseverance *n.* 毅力　ngay lik

persevere *v.i.* 堅持 geen tee
persist *v.i.* 保持 bo tee
persistence *n.* 堅持 geen tee
persistent *a.* 執著嘅 jap jeurk geh
person *n.* 人 yan
personage *n.* 名人 ming yan
personal *a.* 私人嘅 see yan geh
personality *n.* 性格 sing gak
personification *n.* 人格化 yan gak far
personify *v.t.* 擬人化 yee yan far
personnel *n.* 人事部 yan see bo
perspective *n.* 觀點 gwun deem
perspiration *n.* 汗珠 horn ju
perspire *v.i.* 出汗 chut horn
persuade *v.t.* 說服 suy fuk
persuasion *n.* 說服力 suy fuk lik
pertain *v.i.* 關於 gwan yu
pertinent *a.* 有關嘅 yow gwan geh
perturb *v.t.* 感到不安 gam dow bat on
perusal *n.* 讀 duk
peruse *v.t.* 讀 duk
pervade *v.t.* 遍及 peen kap
perverse *a.* 任性嘅 yam sing geh
perversion *n.* 變態 been tai
perversity *n.* 倔強 gwat keurng
pervert *v.t.* 色狼 sik lorng
pessimism *n.* 悲觀 bay gwun
pessimist *n.* 悲觀嘅人 bay gwun geh yan
pessimistic *a.* 悲觀嘅 bay gwun geh
pest *n.* 害蟲 hoy chung
pesticide *n.* 殺蟲劑 sat chung jay
pestilence *n.* 瘟疫 wan yik
pet *n.* 寵物 chung mat
pet *v.t.* 調情 tiew ting
petal *n.* 花瓣 far fan
petition *n.* 請願書 ting yoon shu

petition *v.t.* 請願 ting yoon
petitioner *n.* 請願者 ting yoon jeh
petrol *n.* 汽油 hay yow
petroleum *n.* 石油 sek yow
petticoat *n.* 襯裙 tan kwan
petty *a.* 瑣碎嘅 sor suy geh
petulance *n.* 細路仔脾氣 say low jay pay hay
petulant *a.* 任性嘅 yam sing geh
phantom *n.* 鬼 gway
pharmacy *n.* 藥房 yeurk forng
phase *n.* 階段 gai doon
phenomenal *a.* 非凡嘅 fay fan geh
phenomenon *n.* 非凡嘅人 fay fan geh yan
phial *n.* 細藥樽 say yeurk jun
philanthropic *a.* 慈善嘅 tee seen geh
philanthropist *n.* 慈善家 tee seen ga
philanthropy *n.* 慈善 tee seen
philological *a.* 語言學 yu yeen hok
philologist *n.* 語言學家 yu yeen hok ga
philology *n.* 語言學 yu yeen hok
philosopher *n.* 哲學家 jeet hok ga
philosophical *a.* 哲學嘅 jeet hok geh
philosophy *n.* 哲學 jeet hok
phone *n.* 電話 deen wah
phonetic *a.* 拼音嘅 ping yam geh
phonetics *n.* 語音學 yu yam hok
phosphate *n.* 磷酸鹽 lun shoon yeem
phosphorus *n.* 磷 lun
photo *n* 相 seurng
photograph *v.t.* 影 ying
photograph *n* 相 seurng
photographer *n.* 攝影師 seep ying see

photographic *a.* 攝影嘅 seep ying geh

photography *n.* 攝影 seep ying

phrase *n.* 成語 sing yu

phrase *v.t.* 表達 biew dat

phraseology *n.* 措辭 chotee

physic *n.* 藥 yeurk

physic *v.t.* 醫 yee

physical *a.* 身體嘅 san tay geh

physician *n.* 醫師 yee see

physicist *n.* 物理學家 mat lay hok ga

physics *n.* 物理學 mat lay hok

physiognomy *n.* 容貌 yung mao

physique *n.* 體型 tay ying

pianist *n.* 鋼琴家 gorng kam ga

piano *n.* 鋼琴 gorng kam

pick *v.t.* 揀 gan

pick *n.* 選擇 shoon jak

picket *n.* 糾察人 dow tat yan

picket *v.t.* 抗議 korng yee

pickle *n.* 泡菜 pao choy

pickle *v.t* 醃 yeep

picnic *n.* 野餐 yeh tan

picnic *v.i.* 野餐 yeh tan

pictorial *a.* 圖畫嘅 tow wah geh

picture *n.* 圖畫 tow wah

picture *v.t.* 想像 seurng jeurng

picturesque *a.* 優美嘅 yow may geh

piece *n.* 塊 fai

piece *v.t.* 組合晒 jow hap sai

pierce *v.t.* 穿過 choon gwor

piety *n.* 虔誠 keen sing

pig *n.* 豬 ju

pigeon *n.* 白鴿 bak gap

pigmy *n.* 唔重要嘅人 hm jung yiew geh yan

pile *n.* 一堆 yat duy

pile *v.t.* 堆 duy

piles *n.* 痔瘡 jee chorng

pilfer *v.t.* 偷 tow

pilgrim *n.* 朝聖者 tiew sing jeh

pilgrimage *n.* 朝聖之旅 tiew sing jee luy

pill *n.* 藥丸 yeurk yoon

pillar *n.* 柱 chu

pillow *n* 枕頭 jam tow

pillow *v.t.* 墊住 deen ju

pilot *n.* 飛機師 fay gey see

pilot *v.t.* 揸 ja

pimple *n.* 粉刺 fan tee

pin *n.* 針 jam

pin *v.t.* 釘住 deng ju

pinch *v.t.* 捏 meet

pinch *v.* 捏 meet

pine *n.* 松樹 chung shu

pine *v.i.* 難過 lan gwor

pineapple *n.* 菠蘿 bor lor

pink *n.* 粉紅色 fan hung sik

pink *a* 粉紅色嘅 fan hung sik geh

pinkish *a.* 粉紅嘅 fan hung ghe

pinnacle *n.* 頂峰 ding fung

pioneer *n.* 開拓者 hoy tok jeh

pioneer *v.t.* 做先鋒 jow seen fung

pious *a.* 虔誠嘅 keen sing geh

pipe *n.* 管 gwun

pipe *v.i* 用管輸送 yung gwun shu sung

piquant *a.* 開胃嘅 hoy way geh

piracy *n.* 盜版行為 dow ban hang way

pirate *n.* 海盜 hoy dow

pirate *v.t* 盜印 dow yan

pistol *n.* 手槍 sow cheurng

piston *n.* 活塞 wut sat

pit *n.* 深坑 sam hang

pit *v.t.* 整坑 jing hang

pitch *n.* 球場 kow cheurng

pitch *v.t.* 用力掟 yung lik deng

pitcher *n.* 投球手 tow kow sow

piteous *a.* 可憐嘅 hor leen geh

pitfall *n.* 陷阱 ham jeng

pitiable *a.* 值得同情嘅 jik dak tung ting geh	**platonic** *a.* 純友誼嘅 sun yow yee geh
pitiful *a.* 可憐嘅 hor leen geh	**platoon** *n.* 排 pai
pitiless *a.* 無情嘅 mow ting geh	**play** *n.* 戲劇 hay kek
pitman *n.* 礦工 kworng gung	**play** *v.i.* 玩 wan
pittance *n.* 低人工 day yan gung	**player** *n.* 玩家 wan ga
pity *n.* 同情 tung ting	**plea** *n.* 請求 ting kow
pity *v.t.* 可憐 hor leen	**plead** *v.i.* 懇求 han kow
pivot *n.* 中心點 jung sam deem	**pleader** *n.* 答辯人 dap been yan
pivot *v.t.* 旋轉 shoon joon	**pleasant** *a.* 愉快嘅 yu fai geh
placard *n.* 標語牌 biew yu pai	**pleasantry** *n.* 客氣說話 hak hay shoot wah
place *n.* 地方 day forng	**please** *v.t.* 令人滿意 ling yan mwun yee
place *v.t.* 擺 bai	
placid *a.* 溫和嘅 wan wo geh	**pleasure** *n.* 愉快 yu fai
plague *a.* 疫病 yik beng	**plebiscite** *n.* 公民投票 gung man tow piew
plague *v.t.* 折磨 jeet mor	
plain *a.* 簡單嘅 gan dan geh	**pledge** *n.* 保證 bo jing
plain *n.* 平地 ping day	**pledge** *v.t.* 承諾 sing lok
plaintiff *n.* 原告 yoon gow	**plenty** *n.* 充裕 chung yu
plan *n.* 計劃 gey wak	**plight** *n.* 困難 kwan lan
plan *v.t.* 計劃 gey wak	**plod** *v.i.* 沈重咁行 tam chung gam hang
plane *n.* 飛機 fay gey	
plane *v.t.* 刨 pao	**plot** *n.* 故事情節 gu see ting jeet
plane *a.* 平嘅 ping geh	**plot** *v.t.* 密謀 mat mow
plane *n* 平面 ping meen	**plough** *n.* 犁 lay
planet *n.* 星球 sing kow	**plough** *v.l* 耕 gang
planetary *a.* 行星嘅 hang sing geh	**ploughman** *n.* 農夫 lung fu
	pluck *v.t.* 猛 mang
plank *n.* 木板 muk ban	**pluck** *n* 膽量 dam leurng
plank *v.t.* 用力擺 yung lik bai	**plug** *n.* 插蘇 tap sow
plant *n.* 植物 jik mat	**plug** *v.t.* 插 tap
plant *v.t.* 種 jung	**plum** *n.* 布冧 bo lam
plantain *n.* 車前草 cher teen cho	**plumber** *n.* 水工 suy gung
plantation *n.* 種植園 jung jik yoon	**plunder** *v.t.* 搶劫 cheurng geep
plaster *n.* 止血貼 jee hoot teep	**plunder** *n* 搶 cheurng
plaster *v.t.* 用灰泥鋪 yung fwuy lay pow	**plunge** *v.t.* 暴跌 bo deet
	plunge *n* 突然跌落 dak yeen deet lok
plate *n.* 碟 deep	
plate *v.t.* 電鍍 deen dow	**plural** *a.* 複數 fuk sow
plateau *n.* 高地 gow day	**plurality** *n.* 複數 fuk sow
platform *n.* 台 toy	**plus** *a.* 多 dor

plus *n* 好處 ho chu

ply *v.t.* 持續 tee juk

ply *n* 層 tang

pneumonia *n.* 肺炎 fay yeem

pocket *n.* 口袋 ho doy

pocket *v.t.* 袋 doy

pod *n.* 豆莢 sow gap

poem *n.* 詩 see

poesy *n.* 詩 see

poet *n.* 詩人 see yan

poetaster *n.* 差嘅詩人 ta geh see yan

poetess *n.* 女詩人 luy see yan

poetic *a.* 詩嘅 see geh

poetics *n.* 詩學 see hok

poetry *n.* 詩集 see jap

poignancy *n.* 悲慘 bay tarm

poignant *a.* 令人悲慘 ling yan bay tarm

point *n.* 點 deem

point *v.t.* 指 jee

poise *v.t.* 捉實 juk sat

poise *n* 儀態 yee tai

poison *n.* 毒 duk

poison *v.t.* 毒 duk

poisonous *a.* 有毒嘅 yow duk geh

poke *v.t.* 篤 duk

poke *n.* 篤 duk

polar *a* 極地嘅 gik day geh

pole *n.* 管 gwun

police *n.* 警察 ging tat

policeman *n.* 警察 ging tat

policy *n.* 方針 forng jam

polish *v.t.* 擦 tat

polish *n* 擦光劑 tat gworng jay

polite *a.* 有禮貌 yow lay mao

politeness *n.* 禮貌 lay mao

politic *a.* 明智嘅 ming jee geh

political *a.* 政治嘅 jing jee geh

politician *n.* 政治家 jing jee ga

politics *n.* 政治 jing jee

polity *n.* 國家組織 gwok ga jow jik

poll *n.* 投票 tow piew

poll *v.t.* 調查 diew ta

pollen *n.* 花粉 far fan

pollute *v.t.* 污染 wu yeem

pollution *n.* 污染 wu yeem

polo *n.* 馬球 ma kow

polygamous *a.* 一夫多妻嘅 yat fu dor tay geh

polygamy *n.* 一夫多妻 yat fu dor tay

polyglot1 *n.* 識多種語言嘅人 sik dor jung yu yeen geh yan

polyglot2 *a.* 多種語言寫成嘅 dor jung yu yeen seh sing geh

polytechnic *a.* 工藝嘅 gung ngay geh

polytechnic *n.* 理工學院 lay gung hok yoon

polytheism *n.* 多神信仰 dor san sun yeurng

polytheist *n.* 多神教徒 dor san gao tow

polytheistic *a.* 多神崇拜嘅 dor san sung bai geh

pomp *n.* 排場 pai cheurng

pomposity *n.* 自大 jee dai

pompous *a.* 誇大嘅 kwa dai geh

pond *n.* 池塘 tee tong

ponder *v.t.* 仔細考慮 jee say hao luy

pony *n.* 細馬 say ma

poor *a.* 窮 kung

pop *v.i.* 爆 bao

pop *n* 流行曲 low hang kuk

pope *n.* 教宗 gao jung

poplar *n.* 楊樹 yeurng shu

poplin *n.* 府綢 fu cho

populace *n.* 平民百姓 ping man bak sing

popular *a.* 受歡迎嘅 sow fwun ying geh

popularity *n.* 收歡迎度 sow fwun ying dow

popularize *v.t.* 宣傳 shoon choon

populate *v.t.* 填充 teen chung

population *n.* 人口 yan ho

populous *a.* 人口眾多嘅 yan ho jung dor geh

porcelain *n.* 瓷器 tee hay

porch *n.* 門廊 mwun lorng

pore *n.* 毛孔 mow hung

pork *n.* 豬肉 ju yuk

porridge *n.* 麥皮 mak pay

port *n.* 港口 gorng ho

portable *a.* 隨手攜帶嘅 chuy sow kway dai geh

portage *n.* 搬運 bwun wan

portal *n.* 入口 yap ho

portend *v.t.* 預兆 yu siew

porter *n.* 行李員 hang lay yoon

portfolio *n.* 文件夾 man geen gap

portico *n.* 柱廊 chu lorng

portion *n* 一份 yat fan

portion *v.t.* 分 fan

portrait *n.* 肖像 tiew jeurng

portraiture *n.* 畫像 wah jeurng

portray *v.t.* 顯得 heen dak

portrayal *n.* 描繪 miew kwuy

pose *v.i.* 擺姿勢 bai jee say

pose *n.* 姿勢 jee say

position *n.* 位置 way jee

position *v.t.* 擺 bai

positive *a.* 正面嘅 jing meen geh

possess *v.t.* 擁有 yung yow

possession *n.* 財物 choy mat

possibility *n.* 可能性 hor lang sing

possible *a.* 可能嘅 hor lang geh

post *n.* 郵政 yow jing

post *v.t.* 寄 gey

post *n* 職位 jik way

post *v.t.* 派人 pai yan

post *adv.* 快嘅 fai geh

postage *n.* 郵費 yow fay

postal *a.* 郵遞嘅 yow day geh

post-date *v.t.* 填遲日期 teen tee yat kay

poster *n.* 海報 hoy bo

posterity *n.* 後代 ho doy

posthumous *a.* 死後嘅 say ho geh

postman *n.* 郵差 yow tai

postmaster *n.* 郵政局長 yow jing guk jeurng

post-mortem *a.* 死後嘅 say ho geh

post-mortem *n.* 驗屍 yeem see

post-office *n.* 郵局 yow guk

postpone *v.t.* 延遲 yeen tee

postponement *n.* 延期 yeen kay

postscript *n.* 附言 fu yeen

posture *n.* 姿勢 jee say

pot *n.* 罐 gwun

pot *v.t.* 裝入盆度 jorng yao pwun dow

potash *n.* 碳酸鉀 tan shoon gap

potassium *n.* 鉀 gap

potato *n.* 薯仔 shu jay

potency *n.* 影響力 ying heurng lik

potent *a.* 有效嘅 yow hao geh

potential *a.* 有潛能 yow teem lang

potential *n.* 潛質 teem jat

potentiality *n.* 潛力 teem lik

potter *n.* 陶工 tow gung

pottery *n.* 陶器 tow hay

pouch *n.* 細袋 say doy

poultry *n.* 家禽肉 ga kam yuk

pounce *v.i.* 突襲 dak jap

pounce *n* 突襲 dak jap

pound *n.* 英鎊 ying borng

pound *v.t.* 怦怦咁跳 bung bung gam tiew

pour *v.i.* 倒 dow

poverty *n.* 貧窮 pan kung

powder *n.* 粉 fan

powder *v.t.* 加粉 ga fan

power *n.* 權力 koon lin

powerful *a.* 有權嘅 yow koon geh

practicability *n.* 實用性 sat yung sing

practicable *a.* 可行嘅 hor hang geh

practical *a.* 實際嘅 sat jay geh

practice *n.* 實際行動 sat jay hang dung

practise *v.t.* 練習 leen jap

practitioner *n.* 從業者 chung yeep jeh

pragmatic *a.* 實用嘅 sat yung geh

pragmatism *n.* 實用主義 sat yung ju yee

praise *n.* 稱讚 ting jan

praise *v.t.* 讚 jan

praiseworthy *a.* 值得讚嘅 jik dak jan geh

prank *n.* 惡作劇 ok jok kek

prattle *v.i.* 講廢話 gorng fay wah

prattle *n.* 廢話 fay wah

pray *v.i.* 祈禱 kay tow

prayer *n.* 禱告 tow gow

preach *v.i.* 宣揚 shoon yeurng

preacher *n.* 傳教者 choon dow jeh

preamble *n.* 開場白 hoy cheurng bak

precaution *n.* 預防 yu forng

precautionary *a.* 預防嘅 yu forng geh

precede *v.* 先於 seen yu

precedence *n.* 優先權 yow seen koon

precedent *n.* 先例 seen lay

precept *n.* 準則 jun jak

preceptor *n.* 訓導人 fan dow yan

precious *a.* 珍貴嘅 jan gway geh

precis *n.* 摘要 jak yiew

precise *a.* 準確嘅 jun kok geh

precision *n.* 準確度 jun kok dow

precursor *n.* 先驅 seen kuy

predecessor *n.* 前任 teen yam

predestination *n.* 宿命論 suk ming lun

predetermine *v.t.* 預先決定 yu seen koot ding

predicament *n.* 困境 kwan ging

predicate *n.* 謂語 way yu

predict *v.t.* 預計 yu gey

prediction *n.* 估計 gu gey

predominance *n.* 優勢 yow say

predominant *a.* 佔優勢嘅 jeem yow say geh

predominate *v.i.* 佔優勢 jeem yow say

pre-eminence *n.* 傑出 geet chut

pre-eminent *a.* 傑出嘅 geet chut geh

preface *n.* 序言 juy yeen

preface *v.t.* 寫序 ser juy

prefect *n.* 學長 hok jeurng

prefer *v.t.* 比較鐘意 bay gao jung yee

preference *n.* 喜好 hay ho

preferential *a.* 優先嘅 yow seen geh

prefix *n.* 前綴 teen juy

prefix *v.t.* 係...前面加 hay...teen meen ga

pregnancy *n.* 懷孕 wai yan

pregnant *a.* 有咗 yow jor

prehistoric *a.* 史前嘅 see teen geh

prejudice *n.* 偏見 peen geen

prelate *n.* 高級教士 gow kap gao see

preliminary *a.* 初步嘅 chor bo geh

preliminary *n* 預備措施 yu bay cho see

prelude *n.* 序曲 juy kuk

prelude *v.t.* 開始 hoy tee

premarital *a.* 婚前嘅 fan teen geh

premature *a.* 早產嘅 jow tan geh

premeditate *v.t.* 預先考慮 yu seen hao luy

premeditation *n.* 預謀 yu mow

premier *a.* 首要嘅 sow yiew geh

premier *n* 首相 sow seurng

premiere *n.* 首映 sow ying

premium *n.* 附加費 fu ga fay

premonition *n.* 預感 yu gam

preoccupation *n.* 盤算 pwun shoon

preoccupy *v.t.* 日夜思考 yat yeh see hao

preparation *n.* 準備 jun bay

preparatory *a.* 準備嘅 jun bay geh

prepare *v.t.* 準備 jun bay

preponderance *n.* 優勢 yow say

preponderate *v.i.* 佔優勢 jeem yow say

preposition *n.* 介詞 gai tee

prerequisite *a.* 必需嘅 beet suy geh

prerequisite *n* 條件 tiew geen

prerogative *n.* 特權 dak koon

prescience *n.* 預知 yu jee

prescribe *v.t.* 開 hoy

prescription *n.* 藥方 yeurk forng

presence *n.* 出現 chut yeen

present *a.* 而家嘅 yee ga geh

present *n.* 禮物 lay mat

present *v.t.* 頒 ban

presentation *n.* 演講 yeen gorng

presently *adv.* 而家 yee ga

preservation *n.* 保護 bo wu

preservative *n.* 防腐劑 forng fu jay

preservative *a.* 保存嘅 bo choon geh

preserve *v.t.* 保存 bo choon

preserve *n.* 果醬 gwor jeurng

preside *v.i.* 主持 ju tee

president *n.* 總統 jung tung

presidential *a.* 總統嘅 jung tung geh

press *v.t.* 　　　 gam

press *n* 傳媒 choon mwuy

pressure *n.* 壓力 ngat lik

pressurize *v.t.* 施壓 see ngat

prestige *n.* 威信 way sun

prestigious *a.* 有威望嘅 yow way morng geh

presume *v.t.* 估 gu

presumption *n.* 假設 ga teet

presuppose *v.t.* 預料 yu liew

presupposition *n.* 假設 ga teet

pretence *n.* 假象 ga jeurng

pretend *v.t.* 假扮 ga ban

pretension *n.* 自命 jee ming

pretentious *a.* 自命不凡嘅 jee ming bat fan geh

pretext *n* 藉口 jik ho

prettiness *n.* 美麗 may lay

pretty *a* 靚嘅 leng geh

pretty *adv.* 幾 gey

prevail *v.i.* 壓倒 ngat dow

prevalence *n.* 普遍 pow peen

prevalent *a.* 普遍嘅 pow peen geh

prevent *v.t.* 防止 forng jee

prevention *n.* 預防 yu forng

preventive *a.* 預防性嘅 yu forng sing geh

previous *a.* 之前嘅 jee teen geh

prey *n.* 獵物 leep mat

prey *v.i.* 捕食 bo sik

price *n.* 價錢 ga teen

price *v.t.* 定價 ding ga

prick *n.* 針拮 jam gat

prick *v.t.* 拮 gat

pride *n.* 驕傲 giew ow

pride *v.t.* 為...而驕傲 way...yee giew oh

priest *n.* 神父 san fu

priestess *n.* 女祭司 luy jay see

priesthood *n.* 神父職位 san fu jik way

prima facie *adv.* 初步印象 chor bo yan jeurng

primarily *adv.* 主要 ju yiew

primary *a.* 最重要嘅 juy jung yiew geh

prime *a.* 主要嘅 ju yiew geh

prime *n.* 盛年 sing leen

primer *n.* 低 day

primeval *a.* 原始嘅 yoon tee geh

primitive *a.* 落後嘅 lok ho geh

prince *n.* 王子 worng jee

princely *a.* 似王子咁嘅 tee worng jee gam geh

princess *n.* 公主 gung ju

principal *n.* 校長 hao jeurng

principal *a* 最重要嘅 juy jung yiew geh

principle *n.* 原則 yoon jak

print *v.t.* 印 yan

print *n* 複印 fuk yan

printer *n.* 印刷機 yan tat gey

prior *a.* 嘅之前 geh jee teen

prior *n* 會長 wuy jeurng

prioress *n.* 修女院院長 sow luy yoon yoon jeurng

priority *n.* 優先權 yow seen koon

prison *n.* 監獄 gam yuk

prisoner *n.* 囚犯 chow fan

privacy *n.* 私隱 see yan

private *a.* 私人嘅 see yan geh

privation *n.* 貧困 pan kwan

privilege *n.* 特權 dak koon

prize *n.* 獎品 jeurng ban

prize *v.t.* 珍惜 jan sik

probability *n.* 可能性 hor lang sing

probable *a.* 有可能嘅 yow hor lang geh

probably *adv.* 有可能 yow hor lang

probation *n.* 試用期 see yung kay

probationer *n.* 見習生 geen jap sang

probe *v.t.* 盤問 pwun man

probe *n* 探究 tam gow

problem *n.* 問題 man tay

problematic *a.* 有問題嘅 yow man tay geh

procedure *n.* 程序 ting juy

proceed *v.i.* 繼續做 gey juk jow

proceeding *n.* 過程 gwor ting

proceeds *n.* 收入 sow yap

process *n.* 程序 ting juy

procession *n.* 行列 horng leet

proclaim *v.t.* 宣佈 shoon bo

proclamation *n.* 聲名 sing ming

proclivity *n.* 癖好 pik ho

procrastinate *v.i.* 拖延 tor yeen

procrastination *n.* 延遲 yeen tee

proctor *n.* 監考官 garm hao gwun

procure *v.t.* 獲得 wok dak

procurement *n.* 採購 choy gow

prodigal *a.* 敗家嘅 bai ga geh

prodigality *n.* 浪費 lorng fay

produce *v.t.* 生產 sang tan

produce *n.* 產品 tan ban

product *n.* 產品 tan ban

production *n.* 製造 jay jok

productive *a.* 有效率嘅 yow hao lut geh

productivity *n.* 生產率 sang tan lut

profane *a.* 褻瀆神靈嘅 seet juk san ling geh

profane *v.t.* 褻瀆神靈 seet juk san ling

profess *v.t.* 聲稱 sing ting

profession *n.* 職業 jik yeep

professional *a.* 專業嘅 joon yeep geh

professor *n.* 教授 gao sow

proficiency *n.* 精通 jing tung

proficient *a.* 熟手嘅 suk sow geh

profile *n.* 簡介 gan gai

profile *v.t.* 寫簡介 seh gan gai

profit *n.* 利潤 lay yun

profit *v.t.* 得益 dak yik

profitable *a.* 有利潤嘅 yow lay yun geh

profiteer *n.* 奸商 gan seurng

profiteer *v.i.* 獲取暴利 wok chuy bo lay

profligacy *n.* 浪費 lorng fay

profligate *a.* 嘥嘅 sai geh

profound *a.* 深嘅 sam geh

profundity *n.* 深度 sam dow

profuse *a.* 大量嘅 dai leurng geh

profusion *n.* 大量 dai leurng

progeny *n.* 子孫 jee shoon

programme *n.* 節目 jeetmuk

programme *v.t.* 計劃 gey wak

progress *n.* 進度 jun dow

progress *v.i.* 進步 jun bo

progressive *a.* 有進度嘅 yow jun dow geh

prohibit *v.t.* 禁止 gam jee

prohibition *n.* 禁制令 gam jay ling

prohibitive *a.* 禁止嘅 gam jee geh

prohibitory *a.* 禁止嘅 gam jee geh

project *n.* 計劃 gey wak

project *v.t.* 放映 forng ying

projectile *n.* 投射物 tow she mat

projectile *a.* 發射嘅 fat seh geh

projection *n.* 放映嘅影像 forng ying geh ying jeurng

projector *n.* 放映機 forng ying gey

proliferate *v.i.* 激增 gik jang

proliferation *n.* 激增 gik jang

prolific *a.* 多產嘅 dor tan geh

prologue *n.* 序 juy

prolong *v.t.* 延長 yeen cheurng

prolongation *n.* 延長 yeen cheurng

prominence *n.* 突出 dak chut

prominent *a.* 突出嘅 dan chut geh

promise *n* 承諾 sing lok

promise *v.t* 應承 ying sing

promising *a.* 有希望嘅 yow hay morng geh

promissory *a.* 約好嘅 yeurk ho geh

promote *v.t.* 宣傳 shoon choon

promotion *n.* 宣傳 shoon choon

prompt *a.* 即刻 jik hak

prompt *v.t.* 提 tay

prompter *n.* 提示人 tay see yan

prone *a.* 容易感染到 yung yee gam yeem dow

pronoun *n.* 代名詞 doy ming tee

pronounce *v.t.* 發音 fat yam

pronunciation *n.* 發音 fat yam

proof *n.* 證據 jing guy

proof *a* 可以防護 hor yee forng wu

prop *n.* 道具 dow guy

prop *v.t.* 支撐 jee tang

propaganda *n.* 宣傳 shoon choon

propagandist *n.* 宣傳者 shoon choon jeh

propagate *v.t.* 傳播 choon bor

propagation *n.* 宣傳 shoon choon

propel *v.t.* 推動 tuy dung

proper *a.* 真正嘅 tan jing geh

property *n.* 財產 choy tan

prophecy *n.* 預言 yu yeen
prophesy *v.t.* 預告 yu gow
prophet *n.* 預言家 yu yeen ga
prophetic *a.* 預言嘅 yu yeen geh
proportion *n.* 比例 bay lay
proportion *v.t.* 分 fan
proportional *a.* 成比例嘅 sing bay lay geh
proportionate *a.* 成比例嘅 sing bay lay geh
proposal *n.* 計劃 gey wak
propose *v.t.* 求婚 kow fan
proposition *n.* 提議 tay yee
propound *v.t.* 提出 tay chut
proprietary *a.* 專有嘅 joon yow geh
proprietor *n.* 業主 yeep ju
propriety *n.* 得體 dak tay
prorogue *v.t.* 休會 yow wuy
prosaic *a.* 無聊嘅 mow liew geh
prose *n.* 散文 san man
prosecute *v.t.* 起訴 hay sow
prosecution *n.* 訴訟 sow jung
prosecutor *n.* 檢察官 geem tat gwun
prosody *n.* 韻律 wan lut
prospect *n.* 希望 hay morng
prospective *a.* 有望嘅 yow morng geh
prospsectus *n.* 簡介 gan gai
prosper *v.i.* 發達 fat dat
prosperity *n.* 興旺 hing worng
prosperous *a.* 繁榮嘅 fan wing geh
prostitute *n.* 妓女 gey luy
prostitute *v.t.* 賣淫 mai yam
prostitution *n.* 賣淫 mai yam
prostrate *a.* 趴低嘅 par day geh
prostrate *v.t.* 趴低 par day
prostration *n.* 衰竭 suy keet
protagonist *n.* 擁護者 yung wu jeh

protect *v.t.* 保護 bo wu
protection *n.* 保護 bo wu
protective *a.* 保護嘅 bo wu geh
protector *n.* 保護人 bo wu yan
protein *n.* 蛋白質 dan bak jatt
protest *n.* 抗議 korng yee
protest *v.i.* 反對 fan duy
protestation *n.* 鄭重聲明 jeng jung sing ming
prototype *n.* 樣板 yeurng ban
proud *a.* 驕傲嘅 giew oh geh
prove *v.t.* 證明 jing ming
proverb *n.* 格言 gak yeen
proverbial *a.* 眾所周知 jung sor jow jee
provide *v.i.* 提供 tay gung
providence *n.* 上帝 seurng day
provident *a.* 未雨綢繆 may yu tow mow
providential *a.* 及時嘅 kap see geh
province *n.* 省 sang
provincial *a.* 省嘅 sang geh
provincialism *n.* 固執 gu jap
provision *n.* 供應 gung ying
provisional *a.* 暫時嘅 jam see geh
provisonality *n.* 暫時性 jam see sing
provocation *n.* 刺激 tee gik
provocative *a.* 挑釁嘅 tiew yan geh
provoke *v.t.* 惹 yeh
prowess *n.* 威力 way lik
proximate *a.* 最接近嘅 juy jeep gan geh
proximity *n.* 近 kan
proxy *n.* 代理 doy lay
prude *n.* 正經過度嘅人 jing ging gwor dow geh yan
prudence *n.* 審慎 sam san
prudent *a.* 審慎嘅 sam san geh

prudential *a.* 謹慎嘅 gan san geh
prune *v.t.* 修剪 sow jeen
pry *v.i.* 打聽 da ting
psalm *n.* 讚美詩 jan may see
pseudonym *n.* 筆名 bat meng
psyche *n.* 心靈 sam ling
psychiatrist *n.* 精神科醫生 jing san for yee sang
psychiatry *n.* 精神病學 jing san beng hok
psychic *a.* 通靈嘅 tung ling geh
psychological *a.* 心靈嘅 sam ling geh
psychologist *n.* 心理學家 sam lay hok ga
psychology *n.* 心理學 sam lay hok
psychopath *n.* 精神病患者 jing san beng wan jeh
psychosis *n.* 精神病 jing san beng
psychotherapy *n.* 心裡治療 sam lay jee liew
puberty *n.* 青春期 ting chun kay
public *a.* 公眾嘅 gung jung geh
public *n.* 公眾 gung jung
publication *n.* 出版 chut ban
publicity *n.* 宣傳 shoon shoon
publicize *v.t.* 宣傳 shoon choon
publish *v.t.* 刊登 horn dang
publisher *n.* 出版人 chut ban yan
pudding *n.* 布丁 bo ding
puddle *n.* 水窪 suy tam
puddle *v.t.* 踩過水窪 tai gwor suy tam
puerile *a.* 幼稚嘅 yow jee geh
puff *n.* 吸 kap
puff *v.i.* 噴出 pan chut
pull *v.t.* 拉 lai
pull *n.* 拉 lai
pulley *n.* 滑輪 wat lun
pullover *n.* 過頭笠 gwor tow lap

pulp *n.* 紙漿 jee jeurng
pulp *v.t.* 攪成漿 gao sing jeurng
pulpit *a.* 講壇 gorng tan
pulpy *a.* 紙漿狀嘅 jee jeurng jorng geh
pulsate *v.i.* 搏動 bok dung
pulsation *n.* 震動 jan dung
pulse *n.* 脈搏 mak bok
pulse *v.i.* 跳動 tiew dung
pulse *n* 節拍 jeet bak
pump *n.* 泵 bung
pump *v.t.* 泵 bung
pumpkin *n.* 南瓜 lam gwa
pun *n.* 雙關語 seurng gwan yu
pun *v.i.* 用雙關語 yung seurng gwan yu
punch *n.* 拳擊 koon gik
punch *v.t.* 拳打 koon da
punctual *a.* 準時嘅 jun see geh
punctuality *n.* 準時率 jun see lut
punctuate *v.t.* 加標點符號 ga biew deem fu ho
punctuation *n.* 標點符號 biew deem fu ho
puncture *n.* 細窿 say lung
puncture *v.t.* 拮穿 gat choon
pungency *n.* 辛辣 san lat
pungent *a.* 強烈味道 keurng leet may dow
punish *v.t.* 罰 fat
punishment *n.* 懲罰 ting fat
punitive *a.* 懲罰嘅 ting fat geh
puny *a.* 孱弱孱弱 san yeurk geh
pupil *n.* 學生 hok sang
puppet *n.* 扯線公仔 ter seen gung jay
puppy *n.* 幼犬 yow hoon
purblind *n.* 半盲孱弱 bwun mang geh
purchase *n.* 購買 kow mai
purchase *v.t.* 買 mai
pure *a* 純嘅 sun geh

purgation *n.* 淨化 jing far

purgative *n.* 瀉藥 ser yeurk

purgative *a* 淨化嘅 jing far geh

purgatory *n.* 折磨 jeet mor

purge *v.t.* 清除 ting chuy

purification *n.* 淨化 jing far

purify *v.t.* 淨化 jing far

purist *n.* 純粹主義者 sun suy ju yee jeh

puritan *n.* 清教徒 ting gao tow

puritanical *a.* 清教徒式嘅 ting gao tow sik geh

purity *n.* 純潔 sun geet

purple *adj./n.* 紫色 jee sik

purport *n.* 大概意思 dai koy yee see

purport *v.t.* 自稱 jee ting

purpose *n.* 目的 muk dik

purpose *v.t.* 有目的 yow muk dik

purposely *adv.* 特登嘅 dak dang geh

purr *n.* 貓呼嚕聲 mao fu low seng

purr *v.i.* 貓打呼嚕 mao da fu low

purse *n.* 銀包 ngan bao

purse *v.t.* 撮起嘴唇 juy hay juy sun

pursuance *n.* 追求 juy kow

pursue *v.t.* 追求 juy kow

pursuit *n.* 追求 juy kow

purview *n.* 範圍嘅 fan way geh

pus *n.* 膿 lung

push *v.t.* 推 tuy

push *n.* 推 tuy

put *v.t.* 擺 bai

puzzle *n.* 謎 may

puzzle *v.t.* 令人煩嘅 ling yan fan geh

pygmy *n.* 侏儒 ju yu

pyorrhoea *n.* 膿漏 lung low

pyramid *n.* 金字塔 gam jee tap

pyre *n.* 柴堆 tai duy

python *n.* 蟒蛇 morng she

Q

quack *v.i.* 呱呱聲 gwa gwa seng

quack *n* 鴨叫聲 arp giew seng

quackery *n.* 江湖醫術 gorng wu yeet sut

quadrangle *n.* 四方院 say forng yoon

quadrangular *a.* 四角型嘅 say gok ying geh

quadrilateral *a. & n.* 四角型 say gok ying

quadruped *n.* 四足動物 say juk dung mat

quadruple *a.* 四倍嘅 say pwuy geh

quadruple *v.t.* 變為四倍 been way say pwuy

quail *n.* 鵪鶉 am chun

quaint *a.* 古色古香嘅 gu sik gu heurng ghe

quake *v.i.* 發抖 dat dow

quake *n* 地震 day jan

qualification *n.* 學歷 hok lik

qualify *v.i.* 有資格 yow jee gak

qualitative *a.* 質量嘅 jat leurng geh

quality *n.* 質量 jat leurng

quandary *n.* 困惑 kwan wak

quantitative *a.* 數量嘅 sow leurng geh

quantity *n.* 數量 sow leurng

quantum *n.* 量子 leurng jee

quarrel *n.* 嗌謝 ai sap

quarrel *v.i.* 頂頸 ding geng

quarrelsome *a.* 成日嗌謝 sing yat ai sap

quarry *n.* 採石場 choy sek cheurng

quarry *v.i.* 採 choy

quarter *n.* 四份一 say fan yat

133

quarter *v.t.* 分爲四份一 fan way say fan yat

quarterly *a.* 每季度嘅 mwuy gway dow geh

queen *n.* 女王 luy worng

queer *a.* 奇怪嘅 kay gwai geh

quell *v.t.* 鎮壓 jan ngat

quench *v.t.* 止 jee

query *n.* 疑問 yee man

query *v.t* 懷疑 wai yee

quest *n.* 探索 tam sok

quest *v.t.* 探索 tam sok

question *n.* 問題 man tay

question *v.t.* 質疑 jat yee

questionable *a.* 可疑嘅 hor yee geh

questionnaire *n.* 問卷 man goon

queue *n.* 一條長龍 yat tiew cheurng lung

quibble *n.* 嗌拗 ai sap

quibble *v.i.* 嗌拗 ai sap

quick *a.* 快嘅 fai geh

quick *n* 快 fai

quicksand *n.* 流沙 low sa

quicksilver *n.* 水銀 suy an

quiet *a.* 細聲嘅 say seng geh

quiet *n.* 靜 jing

quiet *v.t.* 平靜 ping jing

quilt *n.* 棉被 meen pay

quinine *n.* 奎寧 fwuy ling

quintessence *n.* 典範 deen fan

quit *v.t.* 退出 tuy chut

quite *adv.* 幾 gey

quiver *n.* 震動 jan dung

quiver *v.i.* 震 jan

quixotic *a.* 唔實際嘅 hm sat jay geh

quiz *n.* 小測驗 siew tak yeem

quiz *v.t.* 問 man

quorum *n.* 法定人數 fat ding yan sow

quota *n.* 配額 pwuy ak

quotation *n.* 報價 bo ga

quote *v.t.* 引用 yan yung

quotient *n.* 商數 seurng sow

R

rabbit *n.* 兔仔 tow jay

rabies *n.* 瘋狗症 fung gow jing

race *n.* 賽跑 choy pao

race *v.i* 比賽 bay choy

racial *a.* 種族嘅 jung juk geh

racialism *n.* 種族歧視 jung juk kay see

rack *v.t.* 受盡折磨 sow jun jeet mor

rack *n.* 架 ga

racket *n.* 吵鬧 tao lao

radiance *n.* 容光煥發 yung gwong wun fat

radiant *a.* 光芒四射 gwong morng say she

radiate *v.t.* 散發出 san fat chut

radiation *n.* 輻射 fuk she

radical *a.* 激進嘅 gik jun geh

radio *n.* 收音機 sow yam gey

radio *v.t.* 播 bor

radish *n.* 蘿蔔 lor bak

radium *n.* 鐳 luy

radius *n.* 半徑 bwun ging

rag *n.* 爛布 lan bo

rag *v.t.* 整蠱 jing gu

rage *n.* 火 for

rage *v.i.* 發火 fat for

raid *n.* 突襲 dak jap

raid *v.t.* 搜查 sow ta

rail *n.* 欄杆 lan gorn

rail *v.t.* 怒斥 low tik

raling *n.* 圍欄 way lan

raillery *n.* 講笑 gorng siew

railway *n.* 鐵路 teet low

rain *v.i.* 落雨 lok yu

rain *n* 雨 yu

rainy *a.* 多雨嘅 dor yu geh

raise *v.t.* 提高 tay gow

raisin *n.* 提子乾 tay jee gon

rally *v.t.* 集合 jap hap

rally *n* 公眾集會 gung jung jap wuy

ram *n.* 公羊 gung yeurng

ram *v.t.* 撞 jorng

ramble *v.t.* 亂講 loon gorng

ramble *n* 散步 san bo

rampage *v.i.* 橫衝直撞 wang chung jik jorng

rampage *n.* 亂鬧 loon lao

rampant *a.* 猖狂 cheurng kwong

rampart *n.* 城牆 sing cheurng

rancour *n.* 怨恨 yoon han

random *a.* 隨意嘅 chuy yee geh

range *v.t.* 變 been

range *n.* 系列 hay leet

ranger *n.* 護林人 wu lam yan

rank *n.* 地位 day way

rank *v.t.* 分級 fan kap

rank *a* 難聞嘅 lan man geh

ransack *v.t.* 洗劫 say geep

ransom *n.* 贖金 suk gam

ransom *v.t.* 交贖金 gao suk gam

rape *n.* 強姦罪 keurng gan juy

rape *v.t.* 強姦 keurng gan

rapid *a.* 快 fai

rapidity *n.* 迅速 sun chuk

rapier *n.* 長劍 cheurng geem

rapport *n.* 默契 mak kay

rapt *a.* 全神貫注 choon san gwun ju

rapture *n.* 歡天喜地 fwun teen hay day

rare *a.* 罕有 hon yow

rascal *n.* 無賴 mow lai

rash *a.* 皮疹 pay tan

rat *n.* 老鼠 low shu

rate *v.t.* 評估 ping gu

rate *n.* 率 lut

rather *adv.* 幾 gey

ratify *v.t.* 證實批准 jing sik pay jun

ratio *n.* 對比率 duy bay lut

ration *n.* 配額 pwuy ak

rational *a.* 理性 lay sing

rationale *n.* 原理 yoon lay

rationality *n.* 合理性 hap lay sing

rationalize *v.t.* 合理化 hap lay far

rattle *v.i.* 搖 yiew

rattle *n* 喀嗒聲 ka ta seng

ravage *n.* 損壞 shoon wai

ravage *v.t.* 毀壞 way wai

rave *v.i.* 亂嗡廿四 loop ap ya say

raven *n.* 渡鴉 dow ngar

ravine *n.* 深谷 sam guk

raw *a.* 生嘅 sang geh

ray *n.* 光線 gworng seen

raze *v.t.* 夷爲平地 yee way ping day

razor *n.* 剃刀 tay dow

reach *v.t.* 到 dow

react *v.i.* 反應 fan ying

reaction *n.* 反應 fan ying

reactinary *a.* 保守嘅 bo sow geh

read *v.t.* 讀 duk

reader *n.* 讀者 duk jeh

readily *adv.* 樂意 lok yee

readiness *n.* 準備 jun bay

ready *a.* 準備 jun bay

real *a.* 真嘅 jan geh

realism *n.* 逼真 bik tan

realist *n.* 現實主義者 yeen sat ju yee jeh

realistic *a.* 逼真嘅 bik tan geh

reality *n.* 現實生活 yeen sat sang wut

realization *n.* 領悟 ling hm

realize *v.t.* 意識到 yee sik dow

really *adv.* 真係 jan hay

realm *a.* 領域 ling wik

ream *n.* 令 ling

reap *v.t.* 收穫 sow wok

reaper *n.* 收割機 sow got gey

rear *n.* 後面 how meen

rear *v.t.* 養 yeurng

reason *n.* 原因 yoon yan

reason *v.i.* 講道理 gorng dow lay

reasonable *a.* 有道理 yow dow lay

reassure *v.t.* 向人保證 heurng yan bo jing

rabate *n.* 退款 tuy fwun

rebel *v.i.* 反 fan

rebel *n.* 作反 jok fan

rebellion *n.* 謀反 mow fan

rebellious *a.* 反叛嘅 fan bwun geh

rebirth *n.* 重生 chung sang

rebound *v.i.* 反彈 fan dan

rebound *n.* 籃板球 lam ban kow

rebuff *n.* 拒絕 kuy joot

rebuff *v.t.* 一口拒絕 yat ho kuy joot

rebuke *v.t.* 批評 pay ping

rebuke *n.* 批評 pay ping

recall *v.t.* 諗返起 lam fan hay

recall *n.* 記性 gey sing

recede *v.i.* 減弱 garm yeurk

receipt *n.* 單 dan

receive *v.t.* 收 sow

receiver *n.* 接收人 jeep sow yan

recent *a.* 近排 gan pai

recently *adv.* 近排 gan pai

reception *n.* 接待處 jeep doy chu

receptive *a.* 願意聆聽嘅 yoon yee ling ting geh

recess *n.* 休會期 yow wuy kay

recession *n.* 經濟衰退 ging jay suy tuy

recipe *n.* 食譜 sik po

recipient *n.* 收件人 sow geen yan

reciprocal *a.* 互惠互利 wu way wu lay

reciprocate *v.t.* 回報 wuy bo

recital *n.* 演奏會 yeen jow wuy

recitation *n.* 朗誦 lorng jung

recite *v.t.* 朗誦 lorng jung

reckless *a.* 不計後果 bat gey how gwor

reckon *v.t.* 認爲 ying way

reclaim *v.t.* 攞返 lor fan

reclamation *n* 開拓 hoy tok

recluse *n.* 隱士 yan see

recognition *n.* 認可 ying hor

recognize *v.t.* 認得 ying dak

recoil *v.i.* 退縮 tuy suk

recoil *adv.* 退縮 tuy suk

recollect *v.t.* 記得 gey dak

recollection *n.* 記憶 gey yik

recommend *v.t.* 推薦 tuy jeen

recommendation *n.* 提議 tay yee

recompense *v.t.* 賠 pwuy

recompense *n.* 賠償 pwuy seurng

reconcile *v.t.* 和解 wor gai

reconciliation *n.* 和解 wor gai

record *v.t.* 錄 luk

record *n.* 紀錄 gey luk

recorder *n.* 錄音機 luk yam gey

recount *v.t.* 講述 gorng sut

recoup *v.t.* 攞返 lor fan

recourse *n.* 依靠 yee kao

recover *v.t.* 恢復 fwuy fuk

recovery *n.* 恢復 fwuy fuk

recreation *n.* 消遣活動 siew heen wut dung

recruit *n.* 新人 san yan

recruit *v.t.* 招募 jiew mow

rectangle *n.* 長方形 cheurng forng ying

rectangular *a.* 長方形嘅 cheurng forng ying geh

rectification *n.* 改正 goy jing

rectify *v.i.* 矯正 giew jing

rectum *n.* 直腸 jik cheurng

recur *v.i.* 再發生 joy fat sang

recurrence *n.* 重現 chung yeen

recurrent *a.* 循環嘅 chun wan geh

red *a.* 紅色嘅 hung sik geh

red *n.* 紅色 hung sik

redden *v.t.* 變紅 been hung

reddish *a.* 紅紅哋 hung hung day

redeem *v.t.* 挽回 wan wuy

redemption *n.* 贖返 suk fan

redouble *v.t.* 加倍 ga pwuy

redress *v.t.* 糾正 gow jing

redress *n* 賠償 pwuy seurng

reduce *v.t.* 減 garm

reduction *n.* 減 garm

redundance *n.* 裁員 choy yoon

redundant *a.* 畀人炒嘅 bay yan tao geh

reel *n.* 捲筒 goon tung

reel *v.i.* 擺下擺下 yiew ha yiew ha

refer *v.t.* 提起 tay hay

referee *n.* 裁判 choy pwun

reference *n.* 提到 tay dow

referendum *n.* 全民投票 choon man tow piew

refine *v.t.* 去除雜質 huy chuy jap jat

refinement *n.* 改善 goy seen

refinery *n.* 提煉廠 tay leen chorng

reflect *v.t.* 反映 fan ying

reflection *n.* 倒映 dow ying

reflective *a.* 反光 fan gwong

reflector *n.* 反射器 fan seh hay

reflex *n.* 反應 fan ying

reflex *a* 反應嘅 fan ying geh

reflexive *a* 反射嘅 fan ser geh

reform *v.t.* 改 goy

reform *n.* 改善 goy seen

reformation *n.* 改革 goy gak

reformatory *n.* 感化院 gam far yoon

reformatory *a* 改革嘅 goy gak geh

reformer *n.* 改革者 goy gak jeh

refrain *v.i.* 克制 hak jay

refrain *n* 副歌 fu gor

refresh *v.t.* 提醒 tay seng

refreshment *n.* 飲品 yam ban

refrigerate *v.t.* 變冷 been lang

refrigeration *n.* 冷凍 lang dung

refrigerator *n.* 雪櫃 shoot gway

refuge *n.* 避難 bay lan

refugee *n.* 難民 lan man

refulgence *n.* 輝煌 fay worng

refulgent *a.* 燦爛嘅 tan lan geh

refund *v.t.* 退 tuy

refund *n.* 退款 tuy fwun

refusal *n.* 拒絕 kuy joot

refuse *v.t.* 拒絕 kuy joot

refuse *n.* 拒絕 kuy joot

refutation *n.* 反駁 fan bok

refute *v.t.* 反駁 fan bok

regal *a.* 豪華嘅 ho wah geh

regard *v.t.* 視爲 see way

regard *n.* 問候 man ho

regenerate *v.t.* 再生 jor sang

regeneration *n.* 重生 chung sang

regicide *n.* 弒君罪 see gwan juy

regime *n.* 統治方式 tung jee forng sik

regiment *n.* 軍團 gwan toon

regiment *v.t.* 組團 jow toon

region *n.* 地區 day kuy

regional *a.* 地區嘅 day kuy geh

register *n.* 登記簿 dang gey bo

register *v.t.* 登記 dang gey

registrar *n.* 登記員 dang gey yoon

registration *n.* 登記 dang gey

registry *n.* 註冊處 chu tak chu

regret *v.i.* 後悔 how fwut

regret *n* 遺憾 way han
regular *a.* 定時嘅 ding see geh
regularity *n.* 規律性 kway lut sing
regulate *v.t.* 約束 yeurk chuk
regulation *n.* 規則 kway jak
regulator *n.* 調節器 tiew jeet hay
rehabilitate *v.t.* 恢復 fwuy fuk
rehabilitation *n.* 復原 fuk yoon
rehearsal *n.* 彩排 choy pai
rehearse *v.t.* 排練 pai leen
reign *v.i.* 統治期 tung jee kay
reign *n* 統治 tung jee
reimburse *v.t.* 補償 bo seurng
rein *n.* 勒繩 lak sing
rein *v.t.* 勒住 lak ju
reinforce *v.t.* 加強 ga keurng
reinforcement *n.* 強化 keurng far
reinstate *v.t.* 復職 fuk jik
reinstatement *n.* 復職 fuk jik
reiterate *v.t.* 重複 chung fuk
reiteration *n.* 重複 chung fuk
reject *v.t.* 拒絕 kuy joot
rejection *n.* 拒絕 kuy joot
rejoice *v.i.* 高興 gow hing
rejoin *v.t.* 返去 fan huy
rejoinder *n.* 反駁 fan bok
rejuvenate *v.t.* 變後生 been ho sang
rejuvenation *n.* 恢復青春 fwuy fuk ting chun
relapse *v.i.* 復發 fuk fat
relapse *n.* 舊病復發 gow beng fuk fat
relate *v.t.* 聯繫 loon hay
relation *n.* 關係 gwan hay
relative *a.* 有關係嘅 yow gwan hay geh
relative *n.* 親戚 tan tik
relax *v.t.* 放鬆 forng sung
relaxation *n.* 放鬆 forng sung
relay *n.* 接力賽 jeep lik choy

relay *v.t.* 轉發 joon fat
release *v.t.* 放 forng
release *n* 發佈 fat bo
relent *v.i.* 終於應承 jung yu ying sing
relentless *a.* 持續嘅 tee juk geh
relevance *n.* 關係 gwan hay
relevant *a.* 有關嘅 yow gwan geh
reliable *a.* 信得過嘅 sun dak gwor geh
reliance *n.* 依賴 yee lai
relic *n.* 遺跡 way jik
relief *n.* 解脫 gai toot
relieve *v.t.* 減輕 garm heng
religion *n.* 宗教 jung gao
religious *a.* 虔誠嘅 keen sing geh
relinquish *v.t.* 放棄 forng hay
relish *v.t.* 享受 heurng sow
relish *n* 樂趣 lok chuy
reluctance *n.* 勉強 meen keurng
reluctant *a.* 勉強嘅 meen keurng geh
rely *v.i.* 依賴 yee lai
remain *v.i.* 保持 bo tee
remainder *n.* 剩低 jing day
remains *n.* 遺跡 way jik
remand *v.t.* 還押候審 wan ngat ho sam
remand *n* 還押 wan ngat
remark *n.* 言論 yeen lun
remark *v.t.* 講 gorng
remarkable *a.* 引人注目嘅 yarn yan ju muk geh
remedial *a.* 補救嘅 bo gow geh
remedy *n.* 藥 yeurk
remedy *v.t* 醫 yee
remember *v.t.* 記得 gey dak
remembrance *n.* 紀念 gey leem
remind *v.t.* 提 tay
reminder *n.* 提醒 tay seng
reminiscence *n.* 回憶 wuy yik
reminiscent *a.* 回憶返 wuy yik

fan

remission *n.* 緩解期 wun gai kay

remit *v.t.* 匯款 wuy fwun

remittance *n.* 匯款金額 wuy fwun gam ak

remorse *n.* 自責 jee jak

remote *a.* 偏遠嘅 peen yoon geh

removable *a.* 可以徐嘅 hor yee chuy geh

removal *n.* 消除 siew chuy

remove *v.t.* 清除 ting chuy

remunerate *v.t.* 出糧 chut leurng

remuneration *n.* 酬勞 chow low

remunerative *a.* 報酬豐厚嘅 bo chow fung ho geh

renaissance *n.* 復興 fuk hing

render *v.t.* 變得 been dak

rendezvous *n.* 約會 yeurk wuy

renew *v.t.* 更新 gang san

renewal *n.* 更新 gang san

renounce *v.t.* 宣佈放棄 shoon bo forng hay

renovate *v.t.* 翻新 fan san

renovation *n.* 翻新 fan san

renown *n.* 名望 ming morng

renowned *a.* 有名嘅 yow meng geh

rent *n.* 租金 jow gam

rent *v.t.* 租 jow

renunciation *n.* 宣佈放棄 shoon bo forng hay

repair *v.t.* 整返 jing fan

repair *n.* 修理 sow lay

raparable *a.* 有得整嘅 yow dak jing geh

repartee *n.* 巧妙嘅答案 hao miew geh dap on

repatriate *v.t.* 遣返 heen fan

repatriate *n* 遣返人 heen fan yan

repatriation *n.* 遣返 heen fan

repay *v.t.* 還返 wan fan

repayment *n.* 賠償 pwuy seurng

repeal *v.t.* 廢除 fay chuy

repeal *n* 廢除 fay chuy

repeat *v.t.* 重複 chung fuk

repel *v.t.* 擊退 gik tuy

repellent *a.* 令人討厭嘅 ling yan tow yeem geh

repellent *n* 殺蟲劑 sat chung jay

repent *v.i.* 後悔 ho fwuy

repentance *n.* 後悔 ho fwuy

repentant *a.* 後悔嘅 ho fwuy geh

repercussion *n.* 反應 fan ying

repetition *n.* 重複 chung fuk

replace *v.t.* 代替 doy tay

replacement *n.* 代替 doy tay

replenish *v.t.* 補充 bo chung

replete *a.* 充滿 chung mwun

replica *n.* 複製品 fuk jay ban

reply *v.i.* 回覆 wuy fuk

reply *n* 回覆 wuy fuk

report *v.t.* 報告 bo gow

report *n.* 報告 bo gow

reporter *n.* 記者 gey jeh

repose *n.* 休息 yow sik

repose *v.i.* 休息 yow sik

repository *n.* 倉庫 chorng fu

represent *v.t.* 代表 doy biew

representation *n.* 代表 doy biew

representative *n.* 代表 doy biew

representative *a.* 有代表性嘅 yow doy biew sing geh

repress *v.t.* 克制 hay jay

repression *n.* 壓制 ngat jay

reprimand *n.* 斥責 tik jak

reprimand *v.t.* 斥責 tik jak

reprint *v.t.* 重印 chung yan

reprint *n.* 重印 chung yan

reproach *v.t.* 指責 jee jak

reproach *n.* 批評 pay ping

reproduce *v.t.* 再造 joy jow

reproduction *n* 繁殖 fan jik

reproductive *a.* 生殖嘅 sang jik geh

reproof *n.* 責備 jay bay
reptile *n.* 爬行動物 pa hang dung mat
republic *n.* 共和國 gung wor gwok
republican *a.* 共和黨嘅 gung wor dorng geh
republican *n* 共和黨黨員 gung wor dorng dorng yoon
repudiate *v.t.* 拒絕 kuy joot
repudiation *n.* 拒絕 kuy joot
repugnance *n.* 反感 fan gam
repugnant *a.* 令人反感嘅 ling yan fan gam geh
repulse *v.t.* 擊退 gik tuy
repulse *n.* 拒絕 kuy joot
repulsion *n.* 反感 fan gam
repulsive *a.* 令人反感嘅 ling yan fan gam geh
reputation *n.* 名譽 ming yu
repute *v.t.* 認爲 ying way
repute *n.* 名氣 ming hay
request *v.t.* 要求 yiew kow
request *n* 請求 ting kow
requiem *n.* 安魂曲 on wan kuk
require *v.t.* 需要 suy yiew
requirement *n.* 需要 suy yiew
requisite *a.* 必需嘅 beet suy geh
requisite *n* 必需嘅嘢 beet suy geh yeh
requisition *n.* 徵用 jing yung
requisition *v.t.* 徵用 jing yung
requite *v.t.* 回報 wuy bo
rescue *v.t.* 救 gow
rescue *n* 搶救 cheurng gow
research *v.i.* 資料收集 jee liew sow jao
research *n* 調查 tiew ta
resemblance *n.* 似 tee
resemble *v.t.* 似 tee
resent *v.t.* 激氣 gik hay
resentment *n.* 怨恨 yoon han

reservation *n.* 預訂 yu deng
reserve *v.t.* 預約 yu yeurk
reservoir *n.* 水庫 suy fu
reside *v.i.* 住 ju
residence *n.* 住所 ju sor
resident *a.* 居住嘅 guy ju geh
resident *n* 居民 guy man
residual *a.* 殘留嘅 tan low geh
residue *n.* 殘留物質 tan low man jat
resign *v.t.* 辭職 tee jik
resignation *n.* 辭職 tee jik
resist *v.t.* 反抗 fan korng
resistance *n.* 反抗力 fan korng lik
resistant *a.* 有抵抗力 yow day korng lik
resolute *a.* 堅決嘅 geen koot geh
resolution *n.* 清晰度 ting sik dow
resolve *v.t.* 解決 gai koot
resonance *n.* 響亮 heurng leurng
resonant *a.* 響亮嘅 heurng leurng geh
resort *v.i.* 依靠 yee kao
resort *n* 旅遊勝地 luy yow sing day
resound *v.i.* 響 heurng
resource *n.* 資源 jee yoon
resourceful *a.* 機智嘅 gey jee geh
respect *v.t.* 尊重 joon jung
respect *n.* 尊重 joon jung
respectful *a.* 尊重嘅 joon jung geh
respective *a.* 分別嘅 fan beet geh
respiration *n.* 呼吸 fu kap
respire *v.i.* 呼吸 fu kap
resplendent *a.* 輝煌嘅 fay worng geh
respond *v.i.* 答 dap
respondent *n.* 回答人 wuy dap yan

response n. 答覆 dap fuk
responsibility n. 責任 jak yam
responsible a. 有責任感 yow jak yam gam
rest v.i. 休息 yow sik
rest n 其餘 kay yu
restaurant n. 餐廳 tan teng
restive a. 唔耐煩嘅 hm loy fan geh
restoration n. 復原 fuk yoon
restore v.t. 恢復 fwuy fuk
restrain v.t. 制止 jay jee
restrict v.t. 限 han
restriction n. 限制 han jay
restrictive a. 約束嘅 yeurk chuk geh
result v.i. 造成 jow sing
result n. 後果 ho gwor
resume v.t. 繼續 gey juk
resume n. 簡歷 gan lik
resumption n. 恢復 fwuy fuk
resurgence n. 復現 fuk yeen
resurgent a. 復興嘅 fuk hing geh
retail v.t. 賣 mai
retail n. 零售 ling sow
retail adv. 以零售方式 yee ling sow forng sik
retail a 零售嘅 ling sow geh
retailer n. 零售商 ling sow seurng
retain v.t. 保持 bo tee
retaliate v.i. 報復 bo fuk
retaliation n. 報復 bo fuk
retard v.t. 阻礙 jor ngoy
retardation n. 延滯 yeen jay
retention n. 維持 way tee
retentive a. 有記性 yow gey sing
reticence n. 沈默寡言 tam mak gwa yeen
reticent a. 沈默嘅 tam mak geh
retina n. 視網膜 see morng mok
retinue n. 隨從 chuy chung
retire v.i. 退休 tuy yow

retirement n. 退休 tuy yow
retort v.t. 駁嘴 bok juy
retort n. 駁嘴 bok juy
retouch v.t. 執下 jap ha
retrace v.t. 返轉頭 fan joon tow
retread v.t. 翻抄 fan tao
retread n. 翻抄 fan tao
retreat v.i. 撤退 teet tuy
retrench v.t. 節省開支 jeet sang hoy jee
retrenchment n. 節省開支 jeet sang hoy jee
retrieve v.t. 攞返 lor fan
retrospect n. 回想 wuy seurng
retrospection n. 回憶 wuy yik
retrospective a. 以前嘅 yee teen geh
return v.i. 返嚟 fan lay
return n. 回來 wuy loy
revel v.i. 陶醉 tow juy
revel n. 狂歡 kworng fwun
revelation n. 揭露 keet low
reveller n. 醉酒佬 juy jow low
revelry n. 狂歡作樂 kworng fwun jok lok
revenge v.t. 報仇 bo sow
revenge n. 報仇 bo sow
revengeful a. 報復嘅 bo fuk geh
revenue n. 財政收入 choy jing sow yap
revere v.t. 尊敬 joon ging
reverence n. 尊敬 joon ging
reverend a. 尊敬嘅 joon ging geh
reverent a. 非常尊敬嘅 fay seurng joon ging geh
reverential a. 充滿敬意嘅 chung mwun ging yee geh
reverie n. 幻想 wan seurng
reversal n. 倒轉 dow joon
reverse a. 相反嘅 seurng fan geh
reverse n 相反 seurng fan
reverse v.t. 倒轉 dow joon

reversible *a.* 可以翻轉嘅 hor yee fan joon geh
revert *v.i.* 回復 wuy fuk
review *v.t.* 回顧 wuy gu
review *n* 評價 ping ga
revise *v.t.* 溫習 wan jap
revision *n.* 溫習 wan jap
revival *n.* 復蘇 fuk sow
revive *v.i.* 復蘇 fuk sow
revocable *a.* 可以撤回嘅 hor yee teet wuy geh
revocation *n.* 廢除 fay chuy
revoke *v.t.* 取消 chuy siew
revolt *v.i.* 反抗 fan korng
revolt *n.* 反抗 fan korng
revolution *n.* 革命 gak ming
revolutionary *a.* 巨變嘅 guy been geh
revolutionary *n* 改革者 goy gak jeh
revolve *v.i.* 環繞 wan yiew
revolver *n.* 左輪槍 jor lun cheurng
reward *n.* 獎勵 jeurng lay
reward *v.t.* 獎 jeurng
rhetoric *n.* 修辭 sow tee
rhetorical *a.* 反問嘅 fan man geh
rheumatic *a.* 風濕病嘅 fung sap beng geh
rheumatism *n.* 風濕 fung sap
rhinoceros *n.* 犀牛 say ngow
rhyme *n.* 押韻 ngat wan
rhyme *v.i.* 押韻 ngat wan
rhymester *n.* 差嘅詩人 ta geh see yan
rhythm *n* 節奏 jeet jow
rhythmic *a.* 有節奏嘅 yow jeet jow geh
rib *n.* 肋骨 lak gwat
ribbon *n.* 絲帶 see dai
rice *n.* 米 may
rich *a.* 有錢嘅 yow teen geh

riches *n.* 財富 choy fu
richness *a.* 豐富 fung fu
rick *n.* 乾草堆 gorn cho duy
rickets *n.* 佝僂病 kuy low beng
rickety *a.* 唔穩固嘅 hm wan gu geh
rickshaw *n.* 人力車 yan lik cher
rid *v.t.* 擺脫 bay toot
riddle *n.* 謎語 may yu
riddle *v.i.* 充滿 chung mwun
ride *v.t.* 騎 keh
ride *n* 旅程 luy ting
rider *n.* 騎手 keh sow
ridge *n.* 山脊 san jek
ridicule *v.t.* 奚落 hai lok
ridicule *n.* 奚落 hai lok
ridiculous *a.* 荒謬嘅 forng mow geh
rifle *v.t.* 偷 tow
rifle *n* 來福槍 loy fuk cheurng
rift *n.* 裂縫 leet fung
right *a.* 啱嘅 ngam geh
right *adv* 向右 heurng yow
right *n* 權 koon
right *v.t.* 糾正 gow jing
righteous *a.* 正當嘅 jing dorng geh
rigid *a.* 死板嘅 say ban geh
rigorous *a.* 嚴格嘅 yeem gak geh
rigour *n.* 嚴厲 yeem lay
rim *n.* 邊緣 been yoon
ring *n.* 戒指 gai jee
ring *v.t.* 打界 da bay
ringlet *n.* 捲髮 goon fat
ringworm *n.* 癬 seen
rinse *v.t.* 沖洗 chung say
riot *n.* 騷亂 sow loon
riot *v.t.* 鬧事 lao see
rip *v.t.* 撕爛 see lan
ripe *a* 熟嘅 suk geh
ripen *v.i.* 成熟 sing suk
ripple *n.* 波浪 bor long

ripple *v.t.* 蕩漾 dorng yeurng	**roguery** *n.* 惡作劇 ok jok kek
rise *v.* 升 sing	**roguish** *a.* 蠱惑嘅 gu wak geh
rise *n.* 增加 jang ga	**role** *n.* 角色 gok sik
risk *v.t.* 冒險 mow heem	**roll** *n.* 卷 goon
risk *n.* 風險 fung hee,	**roll** *v.i.* 捲 goon
risky *a.* 危險嘅 ngay heem geh	**roll-call** *n.* 點名 deem meng
rite *n.* 儀式 yee sik	**roller** *n.* 滾筒 gwan tung
ritual *n.* 儀式 yee sik	**romance** *n.* 浪漫 lorng man
ritual *a.* 儀式上嘅 yee sik seurng geh	**romantic** *a.* 浪漫嘅 lorng man geh
rival *n.* 競爭對手 ging jang duy sow	**romp** *v.i.* 輕易咁取勝 hing yee gam chuy sing
rival *v.t.* 比得上 bay dak seurng	**romp** *n.* 風流韻事 fung low wan see
rivalry *n.* 競爭 ging jang	**rood** *n.* 十字架 sap jee ga
river *n.* 河 hor	**roof** *n.* 瓦面 ngar meen
rivet *n.* 鍋釘 wor deng	**roof** *v.t.* 整屋頂 jing uk deng
rivet *v.t.* 吸引住 kap yan ju	**rook** *n.* 禿鼻烏鴉 tuk bay wu ngar
rivulet *n.* 溪流 kay low	**rook** *v.t.* 呃 ak
road *n.* 路 low	**room** *n.* 房 forng
roam *v.i.* 漫步 man bo	**roomy** *a.* 寬敞嘅 fwun torng geh
roar *n.* 吼叫 hao giew	**roost** *n.* 棲息處 tay sik chu
roar *v.i.* 吼叫 hao giew	**roost** *v.i.* 棲息 tay sik
roast *v.t.* 烤 hao	**root** *n.* 根 gan
roast *a* 烤嘅 hao geh	**root** *v.i.* 搵 wan
roast *n* 烤肉 hao yuk	**rope** *n.* 繩 sing
rob *v.t.* 偷 tow	**rope** *v.t.* 綁 borng
robber *n.* 賊 tak	**rosary** *n.* 數珠 sow ju
robbery *n.* 搶劫 cheurng geep	**rose** *n.* 玫瑰 mwuy gway
robe *n.* 長袍 cheurng pow	**roseate** *a.* 粉紅色嘅 fan hung sik geh
robe *v.t.* 着長袍 jeurk cheurng pow	**rostrum** *n.* 講台 gorng toy
robot *n.* 機械人 gey hai yan	**rosy** *a.* 紅潤嘅 hung yun geh
robust *a.* 強壯嘅 keurng jorng geh	**rot** *n.* 腐爛 fu lan
rock *v.t.* 搖 yiew	**rot** *v.i.* 腐爛 fu lan
rock *n.* 石頭 sek tow	**rotary** *a.* 轉動嘅 joon dung geh
rocket *n.* 火箭 for jeen	**rotate** *v.i.* 轉 joon
rod *n.* 杆 gorn	**rotation** *n.* 轉動 joon dung
rodent *n.* 齧齒動物 jeet tee dung mat	**rote** *n.* 死記硬背 say gey ngang bwuy
roe *n.* 魚子 yu jee	**rouble** *n.* 盧布 low bo
rogue *n.* 無賴 mow lai	**rough** *a.* 諧霎霎 hai sap sap

round *a.* 圓形嘅 yoon ying geh
round *adv.* 環繞 wan yiew
round *n.* 局 guk
round *v.t.* 繞過 yiew gwor
rouse *v.i.* 叫醒 giew seng
rout *v.t.* 徹底打敗 teet day da bai
rout *n* 徹底打敗 teet day da bai
route *n.* 路線 low seen
routine *n.* 日常事務 yat seurng see mow
routine *a* 日常嘅 yat seurng geh
rove *v.i.* 流浪 low lorng
rover *n.* 流浪者 low lorng jeh
row *n.* 一行 yat horng
row *v.t.* 撐 tang
row *n* 糾紛 gow fan
row *n.* 一排 yat pai
rowdy *a.* 吵嘅 cho geh
royal *a.* 王室嘅 worng sat geh
royalist *n.* 保皇主義者 bo worng ju yee jeh
royalty *n.* 王室成員 worng sat sing yoon
rub *v.t.* 捽 jut
rub *n* 問題 man tay
rubber *n.* 橡膠 jeurng gao
rubbish *n.* 垃圾 lap sap
rubble *n.* 碎石 suy sek
ruby *n.* 紅寶石 hung bo sek
rude *a.* 無禮貌嘅 mow lay mao geh
rudiment *n.* 基礎 gey chor
rudimentary *a.* 基本嘅 gey bwun geh
rue *v.t.* 後悔 ho fwuy
rueful *a.* 後悔嘅 ho fwuy geh
ruffian *n.* 歹徒 dai tow
ruffle *v.t.* 整皺 jing tao
rug *n.* 細地氈 say day jeen
rugged *a.* 崎嶇嘅 kay kuy geh
ruin *n.* 廢墟 fay huy
ruin *v.t.* 破壞 por wai

rule *n.* 規矩 kway guy
rule *v.t.* 統治 tung jee
ruler *n.* 間尺 gan tek
ruling *n.* 裁決 choy koot
rum *n.* 朗姆酒 lorng mow jow
rum *a* 古怪嘅 gu gwai geh
rumble *v.i.* 發隆隆聲 fat lung lung seng
rumble *n.* 隆隆聲 lung lung seng
ruminant *a.* 反芻嘅 fan tow geh
ruminant *n.* 反芻動物 fan tow dung mat
ruminate *v.i.* 認真思考 ying jan see hao
rumination *n.* 思考 see hao
rummage *v.i.* 搜掠 sow leurk
rummage *n* 搜尋 sow tam
rummy *n.* 拉米紙牌 lai may jee pai
rumour *n.* 謠言 yiew yeen
rumour *v.t.* 傳 choon
run *v.i.* 跑 pao
run *n.* 跑步 pao bo
rung *n.* 梯級 tay kap
runner *n.* 跑手 pao sow
rupee *n.* 盧比 low bay
rupture *n.* 破裂 por leet
rupture *v.t.* 破裂 por leet
rural *a.* 鄉下嘅 heurng ha geh
ruse *n.* 詭計 gway gey
rush *n.* 趕時間 gorn see gan
rush *v.t.* 趕 gorn
rush *n* 衝 chung
rust *n.* 鐵鏽 teet sow
rust *v.i* 生鏽 sang sow
rustic *a.* 鄉下嘅 heurng ha geh
rustic *n* 鄉下人 heurng ha yan
rusticate *v.t.* 去鄉下 huy heurng ha
rustication *n.* 鄉村生活 heurng choon sang wut
rusticity *n.* 樸素 pok sow

rusty *a.* 生鏽 sang sow
rut *n.* 刻板生活 hak ban sang wut
ruthless *a.* 冷酷無情 lang huk
mo ting
rye *n.* 黑麥 hak mak

S

sabbath *n.* 安息日 on sik yat
sabotage *n.* 蓄意破壞 chuk yee
por wai
sabotage *v.t.* 蓄意破壞 chuk yee
por wai
sabre *n.* 佩劍 pwuy geem
sabre *v.t.* 殺 sat
saccharin *n.* 糖精 tong jing
saccharine *a.* 情緒化 ting suy far
sack *n.* 麻包袋 ma bao doy
sack *v.t.* 炒 tao
sacrament *n.* 聖禮 sing lay
sacred *a.* 神聖嘅 san sing geh
sacrifice *n.* 祭品 jay ban
sacrifice *v.t.* 犧牲 hay sang
sacrificial *a.* 犧牲嘅 hay sang geh
sacrilege *n.* 褻瀆 seet juk
sacrilegious *a.* 褻瀆 seet juk
sacrosanct *a.* 神聖不可侵犯 san
sing bat hor tam fan
sad *a.* 傷心 seurng sam
sadden *v.t.* 令人難過 ling yan lan
gwor
saddle *n.* 馬鞍 ma on
saddle *v.t.* 裝馬鞍 jorng ma on
sadism *n.* 虐待狂 yeurk doy
kwong
sadist *n.* 虐待狂 yeurk doy kwong
safe *a.* 安全 on choon
safe *n.* 保險箱 bo heem seurng
safeguard *n.* 保護 bo wu
safety *n.* 安全 on choon

saffron *n.* 藏紅花粉 jorng hung
far fan
saffron *a* 橙黃色 tang worng sik
sagacious *a.* 精明 jing ming
sagacity *n.* 聰慧 chung way
sage *n.* 智者 jee jeh
sage *a.* 聰明嘅 chung ming geh
sail *n.* 船帆 shoon fan
sail *v.i.* 坐船 chor shoon
sailor *n.* 船員 shoon yoon
saint *n.* 聖人 sing yan
saintly *a.* 聖潔嘅 sing geet geh
sake *n.* 爲咗 way jor
salable *a.* 暢銷 cheurng siew
salad *n.* 沙律 sa lut
salary *n.* 糧 leurng
sale *n.* 減價 garm ga
salesman *n.* 售貨員 sow for yoon
salient *a.* 最重要嘅 juy jung yiew
geh
saline *a.* 鹽嘅 yeem geh
salinity *n.* 鹽性 yeem sing
saliva *n.* 口水 ho suy
sally *n.* 突襲 dak jap
sally *v.i.* 衝出 chung chut
saloon *n.* 酒吧 jow ba
salt *n.* 鹽 yeem
salt *v.t* 加鹽 ga yeem
salty *a.* 鹹 harm
salutary *a.* 有益嘅 yow yik geh
salutation *n.* 問候 man ho
salute *v.t.* 敬禮 ging lay
salute *n* 敬禮 ging lay
salvage *n.* 搶救 cheurng gow
salvage *v.t.* 搶救 cheurng gow
salvation *n.* 救恩 gow yan
same *a.* 一樣嘅 yat yeurng geh
sample *n.* 樣本 yeurng bwun
sample *v.t.* 試下 see har
sanatorium *n.* 療養院 liew
yeurng yoon

sanctification *n.* 神聖化 san sing far

sanctify *v.t.* 神聖化 san sing far

sanction *n.* 制裁 jay choy

sanction *v.t.* 懲罰 ting fat

sanctity *n.* 神聖嘅 san sing geh

sanctuary *n.* 庇護所 bay wu sor

sand *n.* 沙 sa

sandal *n.* 涼鞋 leurng hai

sandalwood *n.* 檀香油 tan heurng yow

sandwich *n.* 三文治 sam man jee

sandwich *v.t.* 夾喺中間 geep hay jung gan

sandy *a.* 沙嘅 sa geh

sane *a.* 理智嘅 lay jee geh

sanguine *a.* 樂觀 lok gwun

sanitary *a.* 衛生嘅 way sang geh

sanity *n.* 理智 lay jee

sap *n.* 液 yik

sap *v.t.* 變虛弱 been huy yeurk

sapling *n.* 幼樹 yow shu

sapphire *n.* 藍寶石 lam bo sek

sarcasm *n.* 諷刺 fung tee

sarcastic *a.* 諷刺嘅 fung tee geh

sardonic *a.* 輕視嘅 hing see geh

satan *n.* 魔鬼 mor gway

satchel *n.* 書包 shu bao

satellite *n.* 衛星 way sing

satiable *a.* 滿足嘅 mun juk geh

satiate *v.t.* 厭 yeem

satiety *n.* 滿足 mun juk

satire *n.* 諷刺 fung tee

satirical *a.* 諷刺嘅 fung tee geh

satirist *n.* 諷刺作家 fung tee jok ga

satirize *v.t.* 諷刺 fung tee

satisfaction *n.* 滿意 mun yee

satisfactory *a.* 滿意嘅 mun yee geh

satisfy *v.t.* 滿足 mun juk

saturate *v.t.* 濕晒 sap sai

saturation *n.* 飽和度 bao wor dow

Saturday *n.* 星期六 sing kay luk

sauce *n.* 醬汁 jeurng jap

saucer *n.* 茶碟 ta deep

saunter *v.t.* 慢慢行 man man hang

savage *a.* 惡嘅 ok geh

savage *n* 野蠻人 yeh man yan

savagery *n.* 殘暴行爲 tan bo hang way

save *v.t.* 救 gow

save *prep* 徐咗 chuy jor

saviour *n.* 救星 gow sing

savour *n.* 味道 may dow

savour *v.t.* 品嘗 ban seurng

saw *n.* 鋸 guy

saw *v.t.* 睇到 tay dow

say *v.t.* 講 gorng

say *n.* 發言權 fat yeen koon

scabbard *n.* 鞘 tiew

scabies *n.* 疥癬 gai seen

scaffold *n.* 棚架 pang ga

scale *n.* 規模 kway mo

scale *v.t.* 攀登 pan dang

scalp *n* 頭皮 tow pay

scamper *v.i* 紮紮跳 jat jat tiew

scamper *n* 奔跑 ban pao

scan *v.t.* 掃描 sow miew

scandal *n* 醜聞 tow man

scandalize *v.t.* 令人震驚 ling yan jan ging

scant *a.* 少少 siew siew

scanty *a.* 唔夠 hm gow

scapegoat *n.* 代罪羔羊 doy juy gow yeurng

scar *n* 疤痕 ba han

scar *v.t.* 留疤痕 low ba han

scarce *a.* 稀有嘅 hay yow geh

scarcely *adv.* 勉強 meen keurng

scarcity *n.* 缺乏 koot fat

scare *n.* 嚇 hak

scare *v.t.* 嚇 hak

scarf *n.* 頸巾 geng gan

scatter *v.t.* 灑 sa

scavenger *n.* 食腐肉嘅動物 sik fu yuk geh dung mat

scene *n.* 鏡頭 geng tow

scenery *n.* 風景 fung ging

scenic *a.* 風景優美嘅 fung ging yow may geh

scent *n.* 味道 may dow

scent *v.t.* 聞到 man dow

sceptic *n.* 多疑嘅人 dor yee geh yan

sceptical *a.* 懷疑嘅 wai yee geh

scepticism *n.* 懷疑態度 wai yee tai dow

sceptre *n.* 權仗 koon jeurng

schedule *n.* 節目表 jeet muk biew

schedule *v.t.* 安排 on pai

scheme *n.* 計劃 gey wak

scheme *v.i.* 密謀 mat mow

schism *n.* 分裂 dan leet

scholar *n.* 學者 hok jeh

scholarly *a.* 有學問嘅 yow hok ham geh

scholarship *n.* 獎學金 jeurng hok gam

scholastic *a.* 學校嘅 hok hao geh

school *n.* 學校 hok hao

science *n.* 科學 for hok

scientific *a.* 科學嘅 for hok geh

scientist *n.* 科學家 for hok ga

scintillate *v.i.* 發出火花 fat chut for far

scintillation *n.* 閃 seem

scissors *n.* 鉸剪 gao jeen

scoff *n.* 整 jing

scoff *v.i.* 狼吞虎咽 lorng tun fur yeen

scold *v.t.* 鬧 lao

scooter *n.* 滑板車 wat ban cher

scope *n.* 機會 gey wuy

scorch *v.t.* 燒燶 siew lung

score *n.* 分數 fan sow

score *v.t.* 得分 dak fan

scorer *n.* 得分者 dak fan jeh

scorn *n.* 鄙視 pay see

scorn *v.t.* 鄙視 pay see

scorpion *n.* 蝎子 keet jee

Scot *n.* 蘇格蘭人 sow gak lan yan

scotch *a.* 蘇格蘭嘅 sow gak lan geh

scotch *n.* 蘇格蘭威士忌 sow gak lan way see gey

scot-free *adv.* 逍遙法外 siew yiew fat ngoy

scoundrel *n.* 無賴 mow lai

scourge *n.* 禍害 wor hoy

scourge *v.t.* 折磨 jeet mor

scout *n* 童子軍 tung jee gwan

scout *v.i* 物色 mat sik

scowl *v.i.* 皺眉頭 jow may tow

scowl *n.* 皺眉頭 jow may tow

scramble *v.i.* 爬 pa

scramble *n* 爬 pa

scrap *n.* 碎片 suy peen

scratch *n.* 抓 jao

scratch *v.t.* 抓 jao

scrawl *v.t.* 亂寫 loon she

scrawl *n* 潦草嘅字 liew cho geh jee

scream *v.i.* 叫 giew

scream *n* 叫聲 giew seng

screen *n.* 屏幕 ping mok

screen *v.t.* 檢查 geem ta

screw *n.* 螺絲 lor see

screw *v.t.* 上螺絲 seurng lor see

scribble *v.t.* 亂畫 loon wak

scribble *n.* 潦草嘅字 liew cho geh jee

script *n.* 劇本 kek bwun

scripture *n.* 聖經 sing ging

scroll *n.* 書卷 shu goon
scrutinize *v.t.* 仔細檢查 jee say geem ta
scrutiny *n.* 仔細檢查 jee say geem ta
scuffle *n.* 衝突 chung dat
scuffle *v.i.* 衝突 chung dat
sculptor *n.* 雕刻家 diew hak ga
sculptural *a.* 雕刻嘅 diew hak geh
sculpture *n.* 雕刻 diew hak
scythe *n.* 大鐮刀 dai leem dow
scythe *v.t.* 用大鐮刀割 yung dai leem dow got
sea *n.* 海 hoy
seal *n.* 海豹 hoy pao
seal *n.* 印章 yan jeurng
seal *v.t.* 封 fung
seam *n.* 線縫 色恩 fung
seam *v.t.* 接縫 jeep fung
seamy *a.* 污糟嘅 wu jow ghe
search *n.* 搜索 sow sok
search *v.t.* 搵 wan
season *n.* 季節 gway jeet
season *v.t.* 加調味料 ga iew may liew
seasonable *a.* 當令嘅 dorng ling geh
seasonal *a.* 季節嘅 gway jeet geh
seat *n.* 座位 jor way
seat *v.t.* 坐 chor
secede *v.i.* 脫離 toot lay
secession *n.* 脫離 toot lay
secessionist *n.* 脫離主義者 toot lay ju yee jeh
seclude *v.t.* 隔離 gak lay
secluded *a.* 與世隔絕嘅 yu say gak joot geh
seclusion *n.* 隱居 yan guy
second *a.* 第二嘅 day yee geh
second *n* 秒 miew
second *v.t.* 支持 jee tee

secondary *a.* 次要嘅 tee yiew geh
seconder *n.* 贊成人 jan sing yan
secrecy *n.* 保密 bo mat
secret *a.* 祕密嘅 bay mat geh
secret *n.* 祕密 bay may
secretariat (e) *n.* 秘書處 bay shu chu
secretary *n.* 秘書 bay shu
secrete *v.t.* 分泌 fan bay
secretion *n.* 分泌 fan bay
secretive *a.* 神祕嘅 san bay geh
sect *n.* 派別 pai beet
sectarian *a.* 教派嘅 gao pai geh
section *n.* 部份 bo fan
sector *n.* 部門 bo mwun
secure *a.* 安全嘅 on choon geh
secure *v.t.* 保護 bo wu
security *n.* 保安 bo on
sedan *n.* 轎車 giew cher
sedate *a.* 鎮定嘅 jan ding geh
sedate *v.t.* 畀鎮靜劑 bay jan jing jay
sedative *a.* 鎮靜嘅 jan jing geh
sedative *n* 鎮靜劑 jan jing jay
sedentary *a.* 成日坐嘅 sing yat chor geh
sediment *n.* 沈澱物 tam deen mat
sedition *n.* 煽動叛亂嘅詞 seen dung bwun loon geh tee
seditious *a.* 煽動性嘅 seen dung sing geh
seduce *v* 誘惑 yow wak
seduction *n.* 魅力 may lik
seductive *a* 性感嘅 sing gam geh
see *v.t.* 睇 tay
seed *n.* 種子 jung jee
seed *v.t.* 播種 bor jung
seek *v.t.* 搵 wan
seem *v.i.* 睇來 tay lay
seemly *a.* 得體嘅 dak tay geh
seep *v.i.* 滲入 sam yap

seer *n.* 預言家 yu yeen ga

seethe *v.i.* 激氣 gik hay

segment *n.* 部份 bo fan

segment *v.t.* 分割 fan got

segregate *v.t.* 分 fan

segregation *n.* 隔離措施 gak lay cho see

seismic *a.* 地震嘅 day jan geh

seize *v.t.* 捉住 juk ju

seizure *n.* 起獲 hay wok

seldom *adv.* 難得 lan dak

select *v.t.* 揀 gan

select *a* 精選嘅 jing shoon geh

selection *n.* 選擇 shoon jak

selective *a.* 有選擇嘅 yow shoon jak geh

self *n.* 自己 jee gey

selfish *a.* 自私 jee see

selfless *a.* 無私嘅 mow see geh

sell *v.t.* 賣 mai

seller *n.* 賣家 mai ga

semblance *n.* 假象 ga jeurng

semen *n.* 精液 jing yik

semester *n.* 學期 hok kay

seminal *a.* 影響深遠嘅 ying heurng sam yoon geh

seminar *n.* 研討會 yeen tow wuy

senate *n.* 參議院 tam yee yoon

senator *n.* 參議員 tam yee yoon

senatorial *a.* 參議員嘅 tam yee yoon geh

senatorial *a* 參議員嘅 tam yee yoon geh

send *v.t.* 寄 gey

senile *a.* 老糊塗嘅 low wu tow geh

senility *n.* 高齡 gow ling

senior *a.* 級別高嘅 kap beet gow geh

senior *n.* 上級 seurng kap

seniority *n.* 年長 leen jeurng

sensation *n.* 感覺 gam gok

sensational *a.* 轟動嘅 gwan dung geh

sense *n.* 五官 hm gwun

sense *v.t.* 感覺到 gam gok dow

senseless *a.* 無知覺嘅 mow jee gok geh

sensibility *n.* 敏感性 man gam sing

sensible *a.* 明智嘅 ming jee geh

sensitive *a.* 敏感嘅 man gam geh

sensual *a.* 感官嘅 gam gwun geh

sensualist *n.* 好色者 ho sik jeh

sensuality *n.* 享受 heurng sow

sensuous *a.* 感覺嘅 gam gok geh

sentence *n.* 句子 guy jee

sentence *v.t.* 判決 pwun koot

sentience *n.* 感覺性 gam gok sing

sentient *a.* 有感覺嘅 yow gam gok geh

sentiment *n.* 情緒 ting suy

sentimental *a.* 感情用事嘅 gam ting yung see geh

sentinel *n.* 哨兵 sao bing

sentry *n.* 哨兵 sao bing

separable *a.* 可以分開嘅 hor yee fan hoy geh

separate *v.t.* 分開 fan hoy

separate *a.* 分開嘅 fan hoy geh

separation *n.* 分離 fan lay

sepsis *n.* 膿毒病 lung duk beng

September *n.* 九月 gow yoot

septic *a.* 感染咗嘅 gam yeem jor geh

sepulchre *n.* 墳墓 fan mow

sepulture *n.* 墳墓 fan mow

sequel *n.* 續集 juk jap

sequence *n.* 一系列 yat hay leet

sequester *v.t.* 隔離 gak lay

serene *a.* 平靜嘅 ping jing geh

serenity *n.* 平靜 ping jing

serf *n.* 農奴 lung low

serge *n.* 嗶嘰 bat gey	**sew** *v.t.* 聯返 loon fan
sergeant *n.* 沙展 sa jeen	**sewage** *n.* 污水 wu suy
serial *a.* 連續嘅 leen juk geh	**sewer** *n* 污水道 wu suy dow
serial *n.* 連續劇 leen juk kek	**sewerage** *n.* 排水系統 pai suy
series *n.* 系列 hay leet	hay tung
serious *a* 嚴重嘅 yeem jung geh	**sex** *n.* 性行爲 sing hang way
sermon *n.* 講道 gorng dow	**sexual** *a.* 性嘅 sing geh
sermonize *v.i.* 說教 shoot gao	**sexuality** *n.* 性取向 sing chuy
serpent *n.* 蛇 seh	heurng
serpentine *a.* 彎彎曲曲 wan wan	**sexy** *n.* 性感 sing gam
kuk kuk	**shabby** *a.* 破舊嘅 por gow geh
servant *n.* 工人 gung yan	**shackle** *n.* 手扣 sow kow
serve *v.t.* 接待 jeep doy	**shackle** *v.t.* 扣住 kow ju
serve *n.* 發球 fat kow	**shade** *n.* 陰 yam
service *n.* 服務 fuk mow	**shade** *v.t.* 遮 jeh
service *v.t* 服務 fuk mow	**shadow** *n.* 影 ying
serviceable *a.* 有用嘅 yow yung	**shadow** *v.t* 射影 seh ying
geh	**shadowy** *a.* 陰暗嘅 yam am geh
servile *a.* 太順從嘅 tai sun chung	**shaft** *n.* 電梯蹧 deen tay cho
geh	**shake** *v.i.* 搖 yiew
servility *n.* 屈從 wat chung	**shake** *n* 搖動 yiew dung
session *n.* 堂 torng	**shaky** *a.* 唔穩陣嘅 hm wan jan
set *v.t* 設置 teet jee	geh
set *a* 固定嘅 gu ding geh	**shallow** *a.* 淺嘅 teen geh
set *n* 一套 yat tow	**sham** *v.i.* 冒充 mo chung
settle *v.i.* 解決 gai koot	**sham** *n* 假象 ga jeurng
settlement *n.* 協議 heep yee	**sham** *a* 假嘅 ga geh
settler *n.* 移民 yee man	**shame** *n.* 羞恥 sow tee
seven *n.* 七 tat	**shame** *v.t.* 羞恥 sow tee
seven *a* 七 tat	**shameful** *a.* 可恥嘅 hor tee geh
seventeen *n., a* 十七 sap tat	**shameless** *a.* 無恥嘅 mow tee
seventeenth *a.* 第十七 day sap	ghe
tat	**shampoo** *n.* 洗頭水 say tow suy
seventh *a.* 第七 day tat	**shampoo** *v.t.* 洗頭 say tow
seventieth *a.* 第七十 day tat sap	**shanty** *a.* 棚屋 pang uk
seventy *n., a* 七十 tat sap	**shape** *n.* 形狀 ying jorng
sever *v.t.* 切斷 teet toon	**shape** *v.t* 塑造 sok jow
several *a* 幾個 gey gor	**shapely** *a.* 有曲線嘅 yow kuk
severance *n.* 斷絕 toon joot	seen ghe
severe *a.* 嚴重嘅 yeem jung geh	**share** *n.* 股份 gu fan
severity *n.* 嚴重性 yeem jung	**share** *v.t.* 分 fan
sing	**share** *n* 一份 yat fan

shark *n.* 鯊魚 sa yu	**shine** *n* 光澤 gworng jak
sharp *a.* 尖嘅 jeem geh	**shiny** *a.* 閃嘅 seem geh
sharp *adv.* 正 jing	**ship** *n.* 船 shoon
sharpen *v.t.* 整尖 jing jeem	**ship** *v.t.* 運 wan
sharpener *n.* 鉛筆刨 yoon bat pao	**shipment** *n.* 運送嘅貨 wan sung geh for
sharper *n.* 騙子 peen jee	**shire** *n.* 郡 gwan
shatter *v.t.* 粉碎 fan suy	**shirk** *v.t.* 逃避 tow bay
shave *v.t.* 剃 tay	**shirker** *n.* 逃避者 tow bay jeh
shave *n* 剃 tay	**shirt** *n.* 裇衫 sut sam
shawl *n.* 被肩 pay geen	**shiver** *v.i.* 打冷震 da lang jan
she *pron.* 佢 kuy	**shoal** *n.* 魚群 yu kwan
sheaf *n.* 一沓 yat dap	**shoal** *n* 淺灘 teen tan
shear *v.t.* 剪 jeen	**shock** *n.* 嚇 hak
shears *n. pl.* 大剪刀 dai jeen dow	**shock** *v.t.* 嚇 hak
shed *v.t.* 落 lok	**shoe** *n.* 鞋 hai
shed *n* 棚 pang	**shoe** *v.t.* 釘蹄鐵 deng tay teet
sheep *n.* 羊 yeurng	**shoot** *v.t.* 射 she
sheepish *a.* 唔好意思嘅 hm ho yee see geh	**shoot** *n* 幼苗 yow miew
sheer *a.* 完全嘅 yoon choon geh	**shop** *n.* 店 deem
sheet *n.* 張 jeurng	**shop** *v.i.* 行街 hang gai
sheet *v.t.* 罩 jao	**shore** *n.* 岸 on
shelf *n.* 架 ga	**short** *a.* 短嘅 doon geh
shell *n.* 殼 hok	**short** *adv.* 唔夠 hm gow
shell *v.t.* 去殼 huy hok	**shortage** *n.* 短缺 doon koot
shelter *n.* 住所 ju sor	**shortcoming** *n.* 短處 doon chu
shelter *v.t.* 保護 bo wu	**shorten** *v.t.* 整短 jing doon
shelve *v.t.* 上架 seurng ga	**shortly** *adv.* 一陣 yat jan
shepherd *n.* 牧羊人 muk yeurng yan	**shorts** *n. pl.* 短褲 doon fu
shield *n.* 盾 tun	**shot** *n.* 射擊 seh gik
shield *v.t.* 擋住 dorng ju	**shoulder** *n.* 膊頭 bok tow
shift *v.t.* 轉移 joon yee	**shoulder** *v.t.* 承擔 sing dam
shift *n* 班 ban	**shout** *n.* 大叫 dai giew
shifty *a.* 唔可靠嘅 hm hor kao geh	**shout** *v.i.* 大叫 dai giew
shilling *n.* 先令 seen ling	**shove** *v.t.* 推 tuy
shilly-shally *v.i.* 猶豫 yow yee	**shove** *n.* 推 tuy
shilly-shally *n.* 猶豫 yow yee	**shovel** *n.* 鐵鏟 teet tan
shin *n.* 小腿 siew tuy	**shovel** *v.t.* 鏟 tan
shine *v.i.* 發光 fat gworng	**show** *v.t.* 證明 jing ming
	show *n.* 表演 biew yeen
	shower *n.* 沖涼 chung leurng
	shower *v.t.* 沖涼 chung leurng

shrew *n.* 老虎乸 low fu la
shrewd *a.* 精明嘅 jing ming ghe
shriek *n.* 尖叫聲 jeem giew seng
shriek *v.i.* 尖叫 jeem giew
shrill *a.* 尖聲嘅 jeem seng geh
shrine *n.* 聖地 sing day
shrink *v.i* 縮細 suk say
shrinkage *n.* 縮細 suk say
shroud *n.* 壽衣 sow yee
shroud *v.t.* 遮住 jeh ju
shrub *n.* 灌木 gwun muk
shrug *v.t.* 聳膊 sung bok
shrug *n* 聳膊 sung bok
shudder *v.i.* 打震 da jan
shudder *n* 打震 da jan
shuffle *v.i.* 拖住腳行 tor ju geurt hang
shuffle *n.* 洗牌 say pay
shun *v.t.* 避開 bay hoy
shunt *v.t.* 調去 diew huy
shut *v.t.* 閂 san
shutter *n.* 鐵閘 teet jap
shuttle *n.* 梭 sor
shuttle *v.t.* 兩地走 leurng day jow
shuttlecock *n.* 羽毛球 yu mow kow
shy *n.* 怕醜 pa tow
shy *v.i.* 怕醜 pa tow
sick *a.* 有病嘅 yow beng geh
sickle *n.* 鐮刀 leem dow
sickly *a.* 多病嘅 dor beng geh
sickness *n.* 疾病 jat beng
side *n.* 側邊 jat been
side *v.i.* 支持 jee tee
siege *n.* 包圍 bao way
siesta *n.* 晏覺 ngan goa
sieve *n.* 篩 say
sieve *v.t.* 篩 say
sift *v.t.* 篩 say
sigh *n.* 唉聲嘆氣 ai seng tan hay
sigh *v.i.* 唉聲嘆氣 ai seng tan hay
sight *n.* 視力 see lik

sight *v.t.* 見到 geen dow
sightly *a.* 少少 siew siew
sign *n.* 牌 pai
sign *v.t.* 簽 teem
signal *n.* 信號 sun ho
signal *a.* 重大嘅 jung dai geh
signal *v.t.* 發信號 fat sun ho
signatory *n.* 簽署方 teem chu forng
signature *n.* 簽名 teem meng
significance *n.* 重要性 jung yiew sing
significant *a.* 重要嘅 jung yiew geh
signification *n.* 意思 yee see
signify *v.t.* 表示 biew see
silence *n.* 無聲 mow seng
silence *v.t.* 變安靜 been on jing
silencer *n.* 消音器 siew yam hay
silent *a.* 無聲嘅 mow seng geh
silhouette *n.* 影 ying
silk *n.* 絲綢 see tow
silken *a.* 輕柔嘅 hing yow geh
silky *a.* 輕柔嘅 hing yow geh
silly *a.* 傻嘅 sor geh
silt *n.* 泥沙 lay sa
silt *v.t.* 塞 sak
silver *n.* 銀 ngan
silver *a* 銀色嘅 ngan sik geh
silver *v.t.* 鍍銀 dow ngan
similar *a.* 似 tee
similarity *n.* 相似度 seurng tee dow
simile *n.* 明喻 ming yu
similitude *n.* 相似度 seurng tee dow
simmer *v.i.* 燉 dun
simple *a.* 簡單 gan dan
simpleton *n.* 傻瓜 sor gwa
simplicity *n.* 簡單 gan dan
simplification *n.* 簡化 gan far
simplify *v.t.* 簡化 gan far

simultaneous *a.* 同時發生 tung see fat sang	**sixth** *a.* 第六 day luk
sin *n.* 罪惡 juy ok	**sixtieth** *a.* 第六十 day luk sap
sin *v.i.* 犯過失 fan gwor sat	**sixty** *n., a.* 六十 luk sap
since *prep.* 從 chung	**sizable** *a.* 幾大嘅 gey dai geh
since *conj.* 從 chung	**size** *n.* 大細 dai say
since *adv.* 從 chung	**size** *v.t.* 調大細 tiew dai say
sincere *a.* 衷心 chung sam	**sizzle** *v.i.* 煎 jeen
sincerity *n.* 真誠 jan sing	**sizzle** *n.* 嘶嘶聲 see see seng
sinful *a.* 邪惡嘅 ter ok geh	**skate** *n.* 溜冰鞋 low bing hai
sing *v.i.* 唱 cheurng	**skate** *v.t.* 溜冰 low bing
singe *v.t.* 燒燶 siew lung	**skein** *n.* 一紮 yat jat
singe *n* 燒傷 siew seurng	**skeleton** *n.* 骸骨 hai gwat
singer *n.* 歌手 gor sow	**sketch** *n.* 描繪 miew kwuy
single *a.* 單一嘅 dan yat geh	**sketch** *v.t.* 描繪 miew kwuy
single *n.* 單程票 dan ting piew	**sketchy** *a.* 粗略嘅 cho leurk geh
single *v.t.* 單獨挑出 dan duk tiew chut	**skid** *v.i.* 跌 seen
singular *a.* 單數嘅 dan sow geh	**skid** *n* 打滑 da wat
singularity *n.* 奇特 kay dak	**skilful** *a.* 有技術嘅 yow gey sut geh
singularly *adv.* 特別 dak beet	**skill** *n.* 技能 gey lang
sinister *a.* 險惡 heem ok	**skin** *n.* 皮膚 pay fu
sink *v.i.* 沈 tam	**skin** *v.t* 去皮 huy pay
sink *n* 洗手盤 say sow pwun	**skip** *v.i.* 跳繩 tiew sing
sinner *n.* 罪人 juy yan	**skip** *n* 廢料桶 fay liew tung
sinuous *a.* 彎曲嘅 wan kuk geh	**skipper** *n.* 船長 shoon jeurng
sip *v.t.* 細細啖飲 say say dam yam	**skirmish** *n.* 爭執 jang jap
sip *n.* 一細啖 yat say dam	**skirmish** *v.t.* 爭執 jang jap
sir *n.* 先生 seen sang	**skirt** *n.* 裙 kwan
siren *n.* 警報器 ging bo hay	**skirt** *v.t.* 環繞 wan yiew
sister *n.* 家姐 ga jeh	**skit** *n.* 滑稽短劇 wat kay doon kek
sisterhood *n.* 姐妹情誼 jeh mwuy ting yee	**skull** *n.* 頭骨 tow gwat
sisterly *a.* 姊妹咁嘅 jee mwuy gam geh	**sky** *n.* 天 teen
sit *v.i.* 坐 chor	**sky** *v.t.* 飛 fay
site *n.* 現場 yeen cheurng	**slab** *n.* 厚塊 ho fai
situation *n.* 情況 ting forng	**slack** *a.* 鬆弛嘅 sung tee geh
six *n., a* 六 luk	**slacken** *v.t.* 放慢 forng man
sixteen *n., a.* 十六 sap luk	**slacks** *n.* 休閒褲 yow han fu
sixteenth *a.* 第十六 day sap luk	**slake** *v.t.* 解渴 gai hot
	slam *v.t.* 砰 bung
	slam *n* 砰 bung
	slander *n.* 詆毀 day way
	slander *v.t.* 詆毀 day way

slanderous *a.* 中傷嘅 jung seurng geh

slang *n.* 俚語 lay yu

slant *v.t.* 傾斜 king ter

slant *n* 斜坡 ter bor

slap *n.* 一巴掌 yat ba jeurng

slap *v.t.* 摑 gwak

slash *v.t.* 劈 pek

slash *n* 劈 pek

slate *n.* 瓦塊 ngar fai

slattern *n.* 邋遢嘅女人 lat tat geh luy yan

slatternly *a.* 唔檢點嘅 hm geem deem geh

slaughter *n.* 屠殺 tow sat

slaughter *v.t.* 劏 torng

slave *n.* 奴隸 low day

slave *v.i.* 辛苦咁做嘢 san fu gam jow yeh

slavery *n.* 奴隸制 low day jay

slavish *a.* 盲目遵從 mang muk joon chung

slay *v.t.* 殺 sat

sleek *a.* 光滑嘅 gworng wat geh

sleep *v.i.* 瞓覺 fan gao

sleep *n.* 瞓覺 fan gao

sleeper *n.* 瞓得…嘅人 fan dak... geh yan

sleepy *a.* 眼瞓 ngan fan

sleeve *n* 衫袖 sam jow

sleight *n.* 敏捷手法 man jeet sow fat

slender *n.* 苗條 miew tiew

slice *n.* 一塊 yat fai

slice *v.t.* 切塊 teet fai

slick *a* 花言巧語嘅 far yeen hao yu geh

slide *v.i.* sur

slide *n* 滑梯 sur wat tay

slight *a.* 輕微嘅 hing may geh

slight *n.* 輕視 hing see

slight *v.t.* 輕視 hing see

slim *a.* 苗條嘅 miew tiew geh

slim *v.i.* 減肥 gam fay

slime *n.* 黏液 leem yik

slimy *a.* 粘住黏液嘅 tee ju leem yik geh

sling *n.* 吊帶 diew dai

slip *v.i.* 跣跌 seen deet

slip *n.* 跣 seen

slipper *n.* 拖鞋 tor hai

slippery *a.* 跣 seen

slipshod *a.* 馬虎嘅 ma fu geh

slit *n.* 裂縫 leet fung

slit *v.t.* 鍥 gai

slogan *n.* 口號 how ho

slope *n.* 斜坡 ter bor

slope *v.i.* 傾斜 king ter

sloth *n.* 樹懶 shu lan

slothful *n.* 懶散嘅 lan san geh

slough *n.* 蛻皮 tuy pay

slough *n.* 絕望 joot morng

slough *v.t.* 拋棄 pao hay

slovenly *a.* 邋遢嘅 lat tat geh

slow *a* 慢 man

slow *v.i.* 慢 man

slowly *adv.* 慢慢 man man

slowness *n.* 慢度 man dow

sluggard *n.* 遊手好閒嘅人 yow sow ho han geh yan

sluggish *a.* 懶嘅 lan geh

sluice *n.* 水閘 suy jap

slum *n.* 貧民窟 pan man fat

slumber *v.i.* 瞓 fan

slumber *n.* 瞓覺 fan gao

slump *n.* 驟降 jao gorng

slump *v.i.* 驟降 jao gorng

slur *n.* 含糊聲 ham wu seng

slush *n.* 雪泥 shoot lay

slushy *a.* 泥濘嘅 lay ling geh

slut *n.* 淫蕩嘅女人 yam dorng geh luy yan

sly *a.* 狡猾 gao wat

smack *n.* 摑 gwak

smack *v.i.* 摑 gwak

smack *n* 一巴掌 yat ba jeurng

smack *n.* 啪聲 pak seng

smack *v.t.* 撞 jorng

small *a.* 細嘅 say geh

small *n* 後腰 ho yiew

smallness *adv.* 細 say

smallpox *n.* 天花 teen far

smart *a.* 聰明嘅 chung ming geh

smart *v.i* 難過 lan gwor

smart *a.* 光鮮嘅 gworng seen geh

smash *v.t.* 打碎 da suy

smash *n* 撞車 jorng cher

smear *v.t.* 搽 ta

smear *n.* 污漬 wu jik

smell *n.* 氣味 hay may

smell *v.t.* 聞 man

smelt *v.t.* 聞到 man dow

smile *n.* 笑 siew

smile *v.i.* 笑 siew

smith *n.* 鐵匠 teet jeurng

smock *n.* 罩衣 jao yee

smog *n.* 煙霧 yeen mow

smoke *n.* 煙 yeen

smoke *v.i.* 食煙 sik yeen

smoky *a.* 多煙嘅 dor yeen geh

smooth *a.* 滑嘅 wat geh

smooth *v.t.* 整平 jing ping

smother *v.t.* 焗死人 guk say yan

smoulder *v.i.* 無明火燒 mow
ming for siew

smug *a.* 得戚 dak tik

smuggle *v.t.* 走私 jow see

smuggler *n.* 走私者 jow see jeh

snack *n.* 零食 ling sik

snag *n.* 問題 man tay

snail *n.* 蝸牛 wor ngoy

snake *n.* 蛇 seh

snake *v.i.* 曲折前行 kuk jeet teen
hang

snap *v.t.* 整斷 jing toon

snap *n* 相 seurng

snap *a* 倉促嘅 chorng choot geh

snare *n.* 陷阱 ham jeng

snare *v.t.* 設陷阱 teet ham jeng

snarl *n.* 低吼 day hao

snarl *v.i.* 低吼 day hao

snatch *v.t.* 搶 cheurng

snatch *n.* 搶 cheurng

sneak *v.i.* 偷偷咁走 tow tow gam
jow

sneak *n* 告狀人 gow jorng yan

sneer *v.i* 嘲笑 chao siew

sneer *n* 嘲笑 chao siew

sneeze *v.i.* 打乞嗤 da hat tee

sneeze *n* 乞嗤 hat tee

sniff *v.i.* 聞 man

sniff *n* 聞 man

snob *n.* 勢利鬼 say lay gway

snobbery *n.* 態度勢利 tai dow
say lay

snobbish *v* 勢利嘅 say lay geh

snore *v.i.* 打鼻鼾 da bay horn

snore *n* 鼻鼾聲 bay horn seng

snort *v.i.* 哼 hang

snort *n.* 哼 hang

snout *n.* 豬鼻 ju bay

snow *n.* 雪 shoot

snow *v.i.* 落雪 lok shoot

snowy *a.* 多雪嘅 dor shoot geh

snub *v.t.* 冷落 lang lok

snub *n.* 冷落 lang lok

snuff *n.* 鼻煙 bay yeem

snug *n.* 舒服 shu fuk

so *adv.* 所以 sor yee

so *conj.* 所以 sor yee

soak *v.t.* 整濕 jing sap

soak *n.* 濕晒 sap sai

soap *n.* 番梘 fan gan

soap *v.t.* 用番梘洗 yung fan gan
say

soapy *a.* 多番梘 dor fan gan

soar *v.i.* 急升 gap sing

sob *v.i.* 哭訴 huk sow

sob *n* 喊 ham
sober *a.* 清醒嘅 ting sing geh
sobriety *n.* 未醉 may juy
sociability *n.* 社交 seh gao
sociable *a.* 合群嘅 hap kwan geh
social *n.* 社會嘅 seh wuy geh
socialism *n* 社會主義 seh wuy ju yee
socialist *n,a* 社會主義者 seh wuy ju yee jeh
society *n.* 社會 seh wuy
sociology *n.* 社會學 seh wuy hok
sock *n.* 襪 mat
socket *n.* 插座 tap jor
sod *n.* 討厭鬼 tow yeem gway
sodomite *n.* 禽獸 jam sow
sodomy *n.* 雞姦 gey gan
sofa *n.* 梳化 sor fa
soft *n.* 軟 yoon
soften *v.t.* 整軟 jing yoon
soil *n.* 泥 lay
soil *v.t.* 整污糟 jing wu jow
sojourn *v.i.* 逗留 dow low
sojourn *n* 逗留 dow low
solace *v.t.* 安慰 on way
solace *n.* 安慰 on way
solar *a.* 太陽嘅 tai yeurng geh
solder *n.* 焊料 hon liew
solder *v.t.* 焊接 hon jeep
soldier *n.* 士兵 see bing
soldier *v.i.* 堅持 geen tee
sole *n.* 鞋底 hai day
sole *v.t* 換鞋底 wun hai day
sole *a* 唯一嘅 way yat geh
solemn *a.* 嚴肅嘅 yeem suk geh
solemnity *n.* 嚴肅 yeem suk
solemnize *v.t.* 舉行 guy hang
solicit *v.t.* 求 kow
solicitation *n.* 懇請 han ting
solicitor *n.* 律師 lut see
solicitous *a.* 操心 cho sam
solicitude *n.* 牽掛 heen gwa

solid *a.* 硬嘅 ngang geh
solid *n* 固體 gu tay
solidarity *n.* 團結 toon geet
soliloquy *n.* 獨白 duk bak
solitary *a.* 單獨嘅 dan duk geh
solitude *n.* 獨處 duk chu
solo *n* 獨唱 duk cheurng
solo *a.* 單獨嘅 dan duk geh
solo *adv.* 自己一個 jee gey yat gor
soloist *n.* 獨唱者 duk cheurng jeh
solubility *n.* 溶解度 yung gai dow
soluble *a.* 可以溶嘅 hor yee yung geh
solution *n.* 解決辦法 gai koot ban fat
solve *v.t.* 解開 gai hoy
solvency *n.* 付債能力 fu jai lang lik
solvent *a.* 可以溶嘅 hor yee yung geh
solvent *n* 溶劑 yung jay
sombre *a.* 沮喪嘅 juy sorng geh
some *adv.* 有啲 yow dee
some *pron.* 有啲 yow dee
somebody *pron.* 有人 yow yan
somebody *n.* 有人 yow yan
somehow *adv.* 唔知點解就 hm jee deem gai jow
someone *pron.* 有人 yow yan
somersault *n.* 空翻 hung fan
somersault *v.i.* 打空翻 da hung fan
something *pron.* 一啲嘢 yat dee yeh
something *adv.* 一啲嘢 yat dee yeh
sometime *adv.* 有時 yow see
sometimes *adv.* 有時 yow see
somewhat *adv.* 有啲 yow dee
somewhere *adv.* 某個地方 mow gor day forng

somnambulism *n.* 夢遊病 mung yow beng

somnambulist *n.* 夢遊病患者 mung yow beng wan jeh

somnolence *n.* 眼瞓 ngan fan

somnolent *n.* 眼瞓 ngan fan

son *n.* 仔 jay

song *n.* 歌 gor

songster *n.* 歌手 gor sow

sonic *a.* 聲音嘅 sing yam geh

sonnet *n.* 十四行詩 sap say horng see

sonority *n.* 響亮 heurng leurng

soon *adv.* 好快 ho fai

soot *n.* 油煙 yow yeen

soot *v.t.* 鋪滿油煙 pow mwun yow yeen

soothe *v.t.* 減輕 garm heng

sophism *n.* 詭辯 gway been

sophist *n.* 智者 jee jeh

sophisticate *v.t.* 複雜化 fuk jap far

sophisticated *a.* 複雜 fuk jap

sophistication *n.* 複雜 fuk jap

sorcerer *n.* 術士 sut see

sorcery *n.* 巫術 mow sut

sordid *a.* 卑鄙 bay pay

sore *a.* 痛嘅 tung geh

sore *n* 腫 jung

sorrow *n.* 悲傷 bay seurng

sorrow *v.i.* 悲傷 bay seurng

sorry *a.* 對唔住 duy hm ju

sort *n.* 種類 jung luy

sort *v.t* 整 jing

soul *n.* 心靈 sam ling

sound *a.* 合理嘅 hap lay geh

sound *v.i.* 聽起嚟 teng hay lay

sound *n* 聲 seng

soup *n.* 湯 torng

sour *a.* 酸 shoon

sour *v.t.* 惡化 ok far

source *n.* 來源 loy yoon

south *n.* 南 larm

south *a.* 南方嘅 larm forng geh

south *adv* 向南 heurng larm

southerly *a.* 南方嘅 larm forng geh

southern *a.* 南方嘅 larm forng geh

souvenir *n.* 手信 sow sun

sovereign *n.* 君主 gwan ju

sovereign *a* 獨立嘅 duk lap geh

sovereignty *n.* 主權 ju koon

sow *v.t.* 種 jung

sow *n.* 母豬 mow ju

space *n.* 空間 hung gan

space *v.t.* 隔開 gak hoy

spacious *a.* 寬敞 fwun torng

spade *n.* 鏟 tan

spade *v.t.* 鏟 tan

span *n.* 範圍 fan way

span *v.t.* 持續 tee juk

Spaniard *n.* 西班牙人 say ban ngar yan

spaniel *n.* 西班牙獵狗 say ban ngar leep gow

Spanish *a.* 西班牙嘅 say ban ngar geh

Spanish *n.* 西班牙人 say ban ngar yan

spanner *n.* 士巴拿 see ba la

spare *v.t.* 抽出 tow chut

spare *a* 多咗嘅 dor jor geh

spare *n.* 備用品 bay yung bam

spark *n.* 火花 for far

spark *v.i.* 引發 yan fat

spark *n.* 星火 sing for

sparkle *v.i.* 閃 seem

sparkle *n.* 閃 seem

sparrow *n.* 麻雀 ma jeurk

sparse *a.* 罕有嘅 hon yow geh

spasm *n.* 抽搐 tow chuk

spasmodic *a.* 斷斷續續 toon toon juk juk

spate *n.* 一連串 yat leen choon
spatial *a.* 空間 hung gan
spawn *n.* 卵 lun
spawn *v.i.* 造成 jow sing
speak *v.i.* 講 gorng
speaker *n.* 喇叭 la ba
spear *n.* 矛 mao
spear *v.t.* 用矛拮 yung mao gat
spearhead *n.* 領隊 ling duy
spearhead *v.t.* 帶頭 dai tow
special *a.* 特別 dak beet
specialist *n.* 專家 joon gar
speciality *n.* 專長 joon cheurng
specialization *n.* 專門化 joon mwun far
specialize *v.i.* 專攻 joon gung
species *n.* 種類 jung luy
specific *a.* 特定嘅 dak ding geh
specification *n.* 規範 kway fan
specify *v.t.* 詳述 cheurng sut
specimen *n.* 種類 jung luy
speck *n.* 一細點 yat say deem
spectacle *n.* 眼鏡 ngan geng
spectacular *a.* 壯觀 jorng gwun
spectator *n.* 觀眾 gwun jung
spectre *n.* 恐懼 hung guy
speculate *v.i.* 推測 tuy tak
speculation *n.* 推測 tuy tak
speech *n.* 台詞 toy tee
speed *n.* 速度 chuk dow
speed *v.i.* 加速 ga chuk
speedily *adv.* 快 fai
speedy *a.* 快 fai
spell *n.* 咒語 jow yu
spell *v.t.* 串 choon
spell *n.* 魅力 may lik
spend *v.t.* 使 say
spendthrift *n.* 大使嘅人 dai say geh yan
sperm *n.* 精子 jing jee
sphere *n.* 球形 kow ying
spherical *a.* 球形嘅 kow ying geh

spice *n.* 香料 heurng liew
spice *v.t.* 加香料 ga heurng liew
spicy *a.* 辣 lat
spider *n.* 蜘蛛 jee ju
spike *n.* 尖頭 jeem tow
spike *v.t.* 插 tap
spill *v.i.* 倒瀉 dow seh
spill *n* 瀉 seh
spin *v.i.* 轉 joon
spin *n.* 轉 joon
spinach *n.* 菠菜 bor choy
spinal *a.* 脊骨嘅 jek gwat geh
spindle *n.* 繞線杆 yiew seen gorn
spine *n.* 脊骨 jek gwat
spinner *n.* 紡紗工 forng sa gung
spinster *n.* 老姑婆 low gu por
spiral *n.* 螺旋型 lor shoon ying
spiral *a.* 螺旋形嘅 lor shoon ying geh
spirit *n.* 精心 jing san
spirited *a.* 堅定嘅 geen ding geh
spiritual *a.* 心靈嘅 sam ling geh
spiritualism *n.* 招魂術 jiew wan sut
spiritualist *n.* 信招魂嘅人 sun jiew wan geh yan
spirituality *n.* 精神性 jing san sing
spit *v.i.* 吐 tow
spit *n* 口水 ho suy
spite *n.* 怨恨 yoon han
spittle *n* 口水 ho suy
spittoon *n.* 痰罐 tam gwun
splash *v.i.* 潑 pwut
splash *n* 落水聲 lok suy seng
spleen *n.* 脾 pay
splendid *a.* 非常好嘅 fay seurng ho geh
splendour *n.* 華麗 wah lay
splinter *n.* 木刺 muk tee
splinter *v.t.* 碎 suy
split *v.i.* 分 fan

split *n* 裂口 leet ho

spoil *v.t.* 破壞 por wai

spoil *n* 贓物 jorng mat

spoke *n.* 講 gorng

spokesman *n.* 發言人 fat yeen yan

sponge *n.* 海綿 hoy meen

sponge *v.t.* 用海綿抹 yung hoy meen mat

sponsor *n.* 贊助商 jan jor seurng

sponsor *v.t.* 贊助 jan jor

spontaneity *n.* 衝動 chung dung

spontaneous *a.* 衝動 chung dung

spoon *n.* 匙羹 tee gang

spoon *v.t.* 舀 bat

spoonful *n.* 一匙羹 yat tee gang

sporadic *a.* 斷斷續續 toon toon juk juk

sport *n.* 運動 wan dung

sport *v.i.* 曬 sai

sportive *a.* 運動細胞 wan dung say bao

sportsman *n.* 運動員 wan dung yoon

spot *n.* 斑點 ban deem

spot *v.t.* 見到 geen dow

spotless *a.* 一塵不染 yat tan bat yeem

spousal *n.* 婚禮 fan lay

spouse *n.* 配偶 pwuy oh

spout *n.* 嘴 juy

spout *v.i.* 噴 pan

sprain *n.* 扭傷 low seurng

sprain *v.t.* 扭嚦 low tan

spray *n.* 噴劑 pan jay

spray *n* 水花 suy far

spray *v.t.* 噴 pan

spread *v.i.* 傳開 choon hoy

spread *n.* 傳播 choon bor

spree *n.* 歡狂 fwun kworng

sprig *n.* 帶葉嘅細枝 dai yeep geh

say jee

sprightly *a.* 精力充沛 jing lik chung pwuy

spring *v.i.* 彈 dan

spring *n* 春天 chun teen

sprinkle *v. t.* 灑 sa

sprint *v.i.* 快跑 fai pao

sprint *n* 短距離賽跑 doon kuy lay choy pao

sprout *v.i.* 發芽 fat ngar

sprout *n* 新芽 san ngar

spur *n.* 馬刺 ma tee

spur *v.t.* 鞭策 been tak

spurious *a.* 偽造嘅 ngay jow geh

spurn *v.t.* 拒絕 kuy joot

spurt *v.i.* 噴 pan

spurt *n* 湧出嘅 yung chut geh

sputnik *n.* 人造衛星 yan jow way sing

sputum *n.* 痰 tam

spy *n.* 間諜 gan deep

spy *v.i.* 監視 gam see

squad *n.* 小隊 siew duy

squadron *n.* 中隊 jung duy

squalid *a.* 邋遢 lat tat

squalor *n.* 邋遢 lat tat

squander *v.t.* 嘥 sai

square *n.* 四方形 say forng ying

square *a* 四方形嘅 say forng ying geh

square *v.t.* 平方 ping forng

squash *v.t.* 壓扁 ngat been

squash *n* 壁球 bik kow

squat *v.i.* 踎低 mow day

squeak *v.i.* 吱吱叫 jeet jeet giew

squeak *n* 吱吱聲 jeet jeet seng

squeeze *v.t.* 搾 ja

squint *v.i.*

squint *n* 斜視 ter see

squire *n.* 鄉紳 heurng san

squirrel *n.* 松鼠 chung shu

stab *v.t.* 捅 tung

stab *n.* 捅 tung
stability *n.* 穩定性 wan ding sing
stabilization *n.* 穩定 wan ding
stabilize *v.t.* 穩定 wan ding
stable *a.* 穩定嘅 wan ding geh
stable *n* 馬房 ma forng
stable *v.t.* 穩固嘅 wan gu geh
stadium *n.* 體育場 tay yuk cheurng
staff *n.* 工作人員 gung jok yan yoon
staff *n.* 職員 jik yoon
stag *n.* 雄鹿 hung luk
stage *n.* 舞台 mow toy
stage *v.t.* 上演 seurng yeen
stagger *v.i.* 搖搖擺擺 yiew yiew bai bai
stagger *n.* 搖晃 yiew forng
stagnant *a.* 無變化 mow been far
stagnate *v.i.* 停滯 ting jay
stagnation *n.* 停滯 ting jay
staid *a.* 古板嘅 gu ban geh
stain *n.* 污漬 wu jik
stain *v.t.* 整污糟 jing wu jow
stainless *a.* 無瑕疵 mow ha tee
stair *n.* 樓梯 low tay
stake *n* 股份 gu fan
stake *v.t.* 冒險 mow heem
stale *a.* 唔新鮮嘅 hm san seen geh
stale *v.t.* 過時 gwor see
stalemate *n.* 僵局 geurng guk
stalk *n.* 花梗 far gang
stalk *v.i.* 跟蹤 gan jung
stalk *n* 葉柄 yeep beng
stall *n.* 攤位 tan way
stall *v.t.* 死火 say for
stallion *n.* 種馬 jung ma
stalwart *a.* 忠實嘅 jung sat geh
stalwart *n* 忠實擁護者 jung sat yung wu jeh
stamina *n.* 耐力 loy lik

stammer *v.i.* 嚕口 low ho
stammer *n* 嚕口 low ho
stamp *n.* 郵票 yow piew
stamp *v.i.* 印 yan
stampede *n.* 風氣 fung hay
stampede *v.i* 狂跑 kworng pao
stand *v.i.* 企 kay
stand *n.* 貨攤 for tan
standard *n.* 標準 biew jun
standard *a* 普通嘅 pow tung geh
standardization *n.* 統一 tung yat
standardize *v.t.* 統一 tung yat
standing *n.* 地位 day way
standpoint *n.* 立場 lap cheurng
standstill *n.* 停滯 ting jay
stanza *n.* 節 jeet
staple *n.* 釘書釘 deng shu deng
staple *a* 基本嘅 gey bwun geh
star *n.* 星星 sing sing
star *v.t.* 主演 ju yeen
starch *n.* 澱粉 deen fan
starch *v.t.* 槳 jeurng
stare *v.i.* 瞪 dang
stare *n.* 凝視 ying see
stark *n.* 嚴厲 yeem lay
stark *adv.* 絕對 joot duy
starry *a.* 佈滿星星 bow mwun sing sing
start *v.t.* 開始 hoy tee
start *n* 開始 hoy tee
startle *v.t.* 嚇 hak
starvation *n.* 飢餓 gey or
starve *v.i.* 挨餓 ai or
state *n.* 狀況 jorng forng
state *v.t* 講明 gorng ming
stateliness *n.* 威嚴 way yeem
stately *a.* 壯觀嘅 jorng gwun geh
statement *n.* 銀行單 an horng dan
statesman *n.* 政治家 jing jee ga
static *n.* 干擾 gorn yiew
statics *n.* 靜力學 jing lik hok

station *n.* 車站 cher jam
station *v.t.* 派駐 pai ju
stationary *a.* 唔郁嘅 hm yuk geh
stationer *n.* 文具商 man guy seurng
stationery *n.* 文具 man guy
statistical *a.* 統計嘅 tung gey geh
statistician *n.* 統計學家 tung gey hok ga
statistics *n.* 統計 tung gey
statue *n.* 石像 sek jeurng
stature *n.* 身高 san gow
status *n.* 地位 day way
statute *n.* 法令 fat ling
statutory *a.* 法定嘅 fat ding geh
staunch *a.* 堅定嘅 geen ding geh
stay *v.i.* 留 low
stay *n* 逗留 dow low
steadfast *a.* 堅定嘅 geen ding geh
steadiness *n.* 穩定性 wan ding sing
steady *a.* 穩陣嘅 wan jan geh
steady *v.t.* 固定 gu ding
steal *v.i.* 偷 tow
stealthily *adv.* 暗地裡 am day luy
steam *n* 蒸氣 jing hay
steam *v.i.* 蒸 jing
steamer *n.* 蒸籠 jing lung
steed *n.* 駿馬 jun ma
steel *n.* 鋼 gorng
steep *a.* 斜 ter
steep *v.t.* 沈迷 tam may
steeple *n.* 尖塔 jeem tap
steer *v.t.* 揸 ja
stellar *a.* 星嘅 sing geh
stem *n.* 莖 ging
stem *v.i.* 封住 fung ju
stench *n.* 惡臭 ok tow
stencil *n.* 模板 mow ban
stencil *v.i.* 用模板印 yung mow ban yan

stenographer *n.* 速記員 chuk gey yoon
stenography *n.* 速記 chuk gey
step *n.* 腳步 geurt bo
step *v.i.* 行 hang
steppe *n.* 大草原 dai cho yoon
stereotype *n.* 刻板印象 hak ban yan jeurng
stereotype *v.t.* 類型化睇法 luy ying far tay fat
stereotyped *a.* 定型 ding ying
sterile *a.* 無菌嘅 mow kwan geh
sterility *n.* 不孕 bat yan
sterilization *n.* 消毒 siew duk
sterilize *v.t.* 消毒 siew duk
sterling *a.* 優秀嘅 yow sow geh
sterling *n.* 英鎊 ying borng
stern *a.* 嚴厲嘅 yeem lay geh
stern *n.* 嚴厲 yeem lay
stethoscope *n.* 聽筒 teng tung
stew *n.* 燜嘅菜 man geh choy
stew *v.t.* 燜 man
steward *n.* 服務員 fuk mow yoon
stick *n.* 棍 gwan
stick *v.t.* 黐 tee
sticker *n.* 貼紙 teep jee
stickler *n.* 堅持嘅人 geen tee geh yan
sticky *a.* 黐 tee
stiff *n.* 僵硬 geurng ang
stiffen *v.t.* 變僵硬 been geurng ang
stifle *v.t.* 壓制 ngat jay
stigma *n.* 恥辱 tee yuk
still *a.* 靜止 jing jee
still *adv.* 仲 jung
still *v.t.* 變平靜 been ping jing
still *n.* 劇照 kek jiew
stillness *n.* 靜止 jing jee
stilt *n.* 高蹺 gow kiew
stimulant *n.* 興奮劑 hing fan jay
stimulate *v.t.* 激發 gik fat

stimulus *n.* 刺激 tee gik	**stout** *a.* 肥嘅 fay geh
sting *v.t.* 刺 tee	**stove** *n.* 爐頭 low tow
sting *n.* 叮 deng	**stow** *v.t.* 收好 sow ho
stingy *a.* 小器嘅 siew hay geh	**straggle** *v.i.* 散佈 san bow
stink *v.i.* 臭 tow	**straggler** *n.* 落後嘅人 lok ho geh yan
stink *n* 惡臭 ok tow	
stipend *n.* 生活津貼 sang wut jun teep	**straight** *a.* 直嘅 jik geh
	straight *adv.* 直 jik
stipulate *v.t.* 規定 kway ding	**straighten** *v.t.* 整直 jing jik
stipulation *n.* 規定 kway ding	**straightforward** *a.* 率直 sut jik
stir *v.i.* 攪 gao	**straightway** *adv.* 即刻 jik hak
stirrup *n.* 馬鐙 ma dang	**strain** *v.t.* 拉傷 lai seurng
stitch *n.* 針腳 jam geurt	**strain** *n* 拉傷 lai seurng
stitch *v.t.* 聯 loon	**strait** *n.* 海峽 hoy hap
stock *n.* 存貨 choon for	**straiten** *v.t.* 變窄 been jak
stock *v.t.* 存貨 choon for	**strand** *v.i.* 滯留 jay low
stock *a.* 成日有 sing yat yow	**strand** *n* 一串 yat choon
stocking *n.* 絲襪 see mat	**strange** *a.* 古怪 gu gwai
stoic *n.* 堅強 geen keurng	**stranger** *n.* 陌生人 mak sang yan
stoke *v.t.* 激起 gik hay	**strangle** *v.t.* 勒死 lak say
stoker *n.* 司爐 see low	**strangulation** *n.* 勒死 lak say
stomach *n.* 肚 tow	**strap** *n.* 帶 dai
stomach *v.t.* 食得 sik dak	**strap** *v.t.* 綁 borng
stone *n.* 石頭 sek tow	**stratagem** *n.* 策略 tak leurk
stone *v.t.* 掟石 deng sek	**strategic** *a.* 戰略嘅 jeen leurk geh
stony *a.* 多石頭 dor sek tow	**strategist** *n.* 軍事家 gwan see ga
stool *n.* 褶凳 jeep dang	**strategy** *n.* 方法 fong fat
stoop *v.i.* 彎腰 wan yiew	**stratum** *n.* 層 tang
stoop *n* 駝背 tor bwuy	**straw** *n.* 吸管 kap gwun
stop *v.t.* 停 ting	**strawberry** *n.* 士多啤梨 see dor beh lay
stop *n* 車站 cher jam	
stoppage *n* 罷工 ba gung	**stray** *v.i.* 蕩失路 dorng sat low
storage *n.* 存放 choon forng	**stray** *a* 走失嘅 jow sat geh
store *n.* 士多 see dor	**stray** *n* 走散嘅動物 jow san geh dung mat
store *v.t.* 保存 bo choon	
storey *n.* 樓層 low tang	**stream** *n.* 小溪 siew kay
stork *n.* 鸛 gwun	**stream** *v.i.* 流 low
storm *n.* 暴風雨 bo fung yu	**streamer** *n.* 彩帶 choy dai
storm *v.i.* 突襲 dak jap	**streamlet** *n.* 小溪 siew kay
stormy *a.* 暴風雨嘅 bow fung yu geh	**street** *n.* 街 gai
	strength *n.* 力氣 lik hay
story *n.* 故事 gu see	**strengthen** *v.t.* 加強 ga keurng

strenuous *a.* 辛苦嘅 san fu geh

stress *n.* 壓力 ngat lik

stress *v.t* 強調 keurng diew

stretch *v.t.* 拉 lai

stretch *n* 彈性 dan sing

stretcher *n.* 擔架 dam ga

strew *v.t.* 佈滿 bo mwun

strict *a.* 嚴格 yeem gak

stricture *n.* 限制 han jay

stride *v.i.* 大步行 dai bo hang

stride *n* 大步 dai bo

strident *a.* 刺耳嘅 tee yee geh

strife *n.* 衝突 chung dat

strike *v.t.* 打 da

strike *n* 罷工 ba gung

striker *n.* 前鋒 teen fung

string *n.* 繩 sing

string *v.t.* 串 choon

stringency *n.* 緊縮 gan suk

stringent *a.* 嚴厲嘅 yeem lay geh

strip *n.* 一條 yat tiew

strip *v.t.* 徐衫 chuy sam

stripe *n.* 條紋 tiew man

stripe *v.t.* 加條紋 ga tiew man

strive *v.i.* 奮鬥 fan dow

stroke *n.* 一劃 yat wak

stroke *v.t.* 輕摸 heng mor

stroke *n* 擊球 gik kow

stroll *v.i.* 散步 san bo

stroll *n* 散步 san bo

strong *a.* 大力 dai lik

stronghold *n.* 堡壘 bo luy

structural *a.* 結構嘅 geet kow geh

structure *n.* 結構 geet kow

struggle *v.i.* 掙扎 jang jat

struggle *n* 難題 lan tay

strumpet *n.* 妓女 gey luy

strut *v.i.* 抬頭挺胸行 toy tow ting hung hang

strut *n* 支柱 jee chu

stub *n.* 煙頭 yeen tow

stubble *n.* 茬 ta

stubborn *a.* 硬頸 ngang geng

stud *n.* 釘 deng

stud *v.t.* 加釘 ga deng

student *n.* 學生 hok sang

studio *n.* 錄音室 luk yam sat

studious *a.* 好學嘅 ho hok geh

study *v.i.* 讀書 duk shu

study *n.* 書房 shu forng

stuff *n.* 嘢 yeh

stuff 2 *v.t.* 塞滿 sat mun

stuffy *a.* 焗 guk

stumble *v.i.* 棘嘅 kik tan

stumble *n.* 跌 deet

stump *n.* 樹墩 shu dun

stump *v.t* 難倒 lan dow

stun *v.t.* 打暈 da wan

stunt *v.t.* 阻礙生長 jor ngoy sang jeurng

stunt *n* 特技 dak gey

stupefy *v.t.* 令人驚訝 ling yan ging ngar

stupendous *a.* 極大嘅 gik dai geh

stupid *a* 蠢 chun

stupidity *n.* 蠢 chun

sturdy *a.* 紮實 jat sat

sty *n.* 豬場 ju cheurng

stye *n.* 麥粒腫 mak lap jung

style *n.* 風格 fung gak

subdue *v.t.* 制服 jay fuk

subject *n.* 主題 ju tay

subject *a* 影響嘅 ying heurng geh

subject *v.t.* 臣服 san fuk

subjection *n.* 制服 jay fuk

subjective *a.* 主觀 ju gwun

subjudice *n.* 懸案 yoon on

subjugate *v.t.* 征服 jing fuk

subjugation *n.* 制服 jay fuk

sublet *v.t.* 轉租 joon jow

sublimate *v.t.* 昇華 sing wah

sublime *a.* 崇高嘅 sung gow geh

sublime *n* 崇高嘅事 sung gow geh see

sublimity *n.* 高尚 gow seurng

submarine *n.* 潛艇 teem suy teng

submarine *a* 海底嘅 hoy day geh

submerge *v.i.* 潛入水裡度 teem yap suy dow

submission *n.* 屈服 wat fuk

submissive *a.* 聽話嘅 teng wah geh

submit *v.t.* 交 gao

subordinate *a.* 隸屬 day suk

subordinate *n* 部屬 bow suk

subordinate *v.t.* 屬於 suk yu

subordination *n.* 附屬 fu suk

subscribe *v.t.* 報名 bow meng

subscription *n.* 訂閱 deng yoot

subsequent *a.* 後嚟 ho lay

subservience *n.* 從屬 chung suk

subservient *a.* 次要 tee yiew

subside *v.i.* 減弱 garm yeurk

subsidiary *a.* 附帶嘅 fu dai geh

subsidize *v.t.* 資助 jee jor

subsidy *n.* 津貼 jun teep

subsist *v.i.* 維持生活 way tee sang wut

subsistence *n.* 勉強維持生活 meen keurng way tee sang wut

substance *n.* 物質 mat jat

substantial *a.* 大量嘅 dai leurng geh

substantially *adv.* 基本上 gey bwun seurng

substantiate *v.t.* 證明 jing ming

substantiation *n.* 證實 jing sat

substitute *n.* 代替人 doy tay yan

substitute *v.t.* 代替 doy tay

substitution *n.* 代替 doy tay

subterranean *a.* 地下嘅 day ha geh

subtle *n.* 唔明顯嘅 hm ming heen geh

subtlety *n.* 巧妙 hao miew

subtract *v.t.* 減 garm

subtraction *n.* 減 garm

suburb *n.* 郊區 gao kuy

suburban *a.* 郊區嘅 gao kuy geh

subversion *n.* 顛覆 deen fuk

subversive *a.* 破壞嘅 por wai geh

subvert *v.t.* 推翻 tuy fan

succeed *v.i.* 成功 sing gung

success *n.* 成就 sing jow

successful *a* 成功 sing gung

succession *n.* 繼承 gey sing

successive *a.* 連續嘅 leen juk geh

successor *n.* 繼承人 gey sing yan

succour *n.* 幫助 borng jor

succour *v.t.* 幫 borng

succumb *v.i.* 屈服 wat fuk

such *a.* 似 tee

such *pron.* 非常之 fay seurng jee

suck *v.t.* 啜 joot

suck *n.* 吸 kap

suckle *v.t.* 餵奶 way lai

sudden *n.* 突然 dat yeen

suddenly *adv.* 突然間 dat yeen gan

sue *v.t.* 告 go

suffer *v.t.* 受苦 so fu

suffice *v.i.* 足夠 juk gow

sufficiency *n.* 充足 chung juk

sufficient *a.* 足夠 juk go

suffix *n.* 後綴 ho joot

suffix *v.t.* 加後綴 ga ho joot

suffocate *v.t* 窒息 jat sik

suffocation *n.* 窒息 jat sik

suffrage *n.* 投票權 tow piew koon

sugar *n.* 糖 tong

sugar *v.t.* 加糖 ga torng

suggest *v.t.* 提議 tey yee
suggestion *n.* 提議 tay yee
suggestive *a.* 暗示嘅 am see geh
suicidal *a.* 有自殺傾向 yow jee sat king heurng
suicide *n.* 自殺 jee sat
suit *n.* 西裝 say jorng
suit *v.t.* 襯 tan
suitability *n.* 適合性 sik hap sing
suitable *a.* 適合 sik hap
suite *n.* 套房 tow forng
suitor *n.* 收購者 sow kow jeh
sullen *a.* 悶悶不樂 mun mun bat lok
sulphur *n.* 硫磺 low wong
sulphuric *a.* 硫酸 low shoon
sultry *a.* 悶熱 mun yeet
sum *n.* 總數 jung so
sum *v.t.* 總結 jung geet
summarily *adv.* 概要 koy yiew
summarize *v.t.* 總結 jung geet
summary *n.* 總結 jung geet
summary *a.* 總結性嘅 jung geet sing geh
summer *n.* 夏天 har teen
summit *n.* 山頂 san deng
summon *v.t.* 呼喚 fu wun
summons *n.* 傳票 choon piew
sumptuous *a.* 奢侈嘅 ter tee geh
sun *n.* 太陽 tai yeurng
sun *v.t.* 曬太陽 sai tai yeurng
Sunday *n.* 星期日 sing kay yat
sunder *v.t.* 分開 fan hoy
sundry *a.* 雜項嘅 jap horng ghe
sunny *a.* 好太陽 ho tai yeurng
sup *v.i.* 細細啖飲 say say dam yam
superabundance *n.* 過多 gwor dor
superabundant *a.* 大量嘅 dai leurng geh
superb *a.* 好極嘅 ho gik geh

superficial *a.* 粗枝大葉 cho jee dai yeep
superficiality *n.* 表面性 biew meen sing
superfine *a.* 精製嘅 jing jay geh
superfluity *n.* 奢侈品 ter tee ban
superfluous *a.* 過多嘅 gwor dor geh
superhuman *a.* 超出常人嘅 tiew chut seurng yan geh
superintend *v.t.* 主管 ju gwun
superintendence *n.* 監督 gam duk
superintendent *n.* 監管人 gam gwun yan
superior *a.* 優越 yow yoot
superiority *n.* 優越 yow yoot
superlative *a.* 卓越嘅 cheurk yoot geh
superlative *n.* 最高級 juy gow kap
superman *n.* 超人 tiew yan
supernatural *a.* 超自然嘅 tiew jee yeen geh
supersede *v.t.* 取代 chuy doy
supersonic *a.* 超音波嘅 tiew yam bor geh
superstition *n.* 迷信 mey sun
superstitious *a.* 迷信 mey sun
supertax *n.* 附加稅 fu ga suy
supervise *v.t.* 監督 gam duk
supervision *n.* 監督 gam duk
supervisor *n.* 主管 ju gwun
supper *n.* 宵夜 siew yeh
supple *a.* 柔軟 yow yoon
supplement *n.* 補充 bo chung
supplement *v.t.* 補充 bo chung
supplementary *a.* 額外嘅 ak ngoy geh
supplier *n.* 供應者 gung ying jeh
supply *v.t.* 提供 tey gung
supply *n* 供應量 gung ying leurng

support *v.t.* 支持 jee tee
support *n.* 支持 jee tee
suppose *v.t.* 估 gu
supposition *n.* 推測 tuy tak
suppress *v.t.* 鎮壓 jan ngat
suppression *n.* 鎮壓 jan ngat
supremacy *n.* 最大權利 juy dai koon lik
supreme *a.* 最高嘅 juy gow geh
surcharge *n.* 附加肥 fu ga fay
surcharge *v.t.* 收額外費 sow ak ngoy fay
sure *a.* 肯定 hang ding
surely *adv.* 想必 seurng beet
surety *n.* 擔保人 dam bo yan
surf *n.* 激浪 gik lorng
surface *n.* 表面 biew meen
surface *v.i* 露面 low meen
surfeit *n.* 過量 gwor leurng
surge *n.* 激增 gik jang
surge *v.i.* 湧 yung
surgeon *n.* 外科醫生 ngoy for yee sang
surgery *n.* 手術 sow sut
surmise *n.* 推測 tuy tak
surmise *v.t.* 推測 tuy tak
surmount *v.t.* 克服 hak fuk
surname *n.* 姓 sing
surpass *v.t.* 超過 tiew gwor
surplus *n.* 剩餘 jing yu
surprise *n.* 驚喜 ging hey
surprise *v.t.* 令人驚喜 ling yan ging hay
surrender *v.t.* 投降 tow horng
surrender *n* 投降 tow horng
surround *v.t.* 圍住 way ju
surroundings *n.* 周圍 jow way
surtax *n.* 附加稅 fu ga suy
surveillance *n.* 監視 gam see
survey *n.* 調查 tiew ta
survey *v.t.* 調查 tiew ta
survival *n.* 生存 sang choon

survive *v.i.* 生存 sang choon
suspect *v.t.* 懷疑 wai yee
suspect *a.* 唔可信嘅 hm hor sun geh
suspect *n* 嫌疑犯 yeem yee fan
suspend *v.t.* 暫停 jam ting
suspense *n.* 懸念 yoon leem
suspension *n.* 暫停職務 jam ting jik mow
suspicion *n.* 嫌疑 yeem yee
suspicious *a.* 可疑 hor yee
sustain *v.t.* 維持 way tee
sustenance *n.* 事務 sik mat
swagger *v.i.* 大搖大擺行 dai yiew dai bai hang
swagger *n* 大搖大擺 dai yiew dai bai
swallow *v.t.* 吞 tun
swallow *n.* 燕子 yeen jee
swallow *n.* 啖 dam
swamp *n.* 沼地 jiew day
swamp *v.t.* 浸 jam
swan *n.* 天鵝 teen ngor
swarm *n.* 一大群 yat dai kwan
swarm *v.i.* 飛嚟飛去 fay lay fay huy *f*
swarthy *a.* 皮膚黑嘅 pay fu hak geh
sway *v.i.* 搖擺 yiew bai
sway *n* 搖擺 yiew bai
swear *v.t.* 發誓 fat say
sweat *n.* 汗 horn
sweat *v.i.* 流汗 low horn
sweater *n.* 冷衫 larng sam
sweep *v.i.* 掃 sow
sweep *n.* 掃 sow
sweeper *n.* 清潔工 ting geet gung
sweet *a.* 甜 teem
sweet *n* 糖 tong
sweeten *v.t.* 整甜 jing teem
sweetmeat *n.* 糖 torng
sweetness *n.* 甜味 teem may

swell *v.i.* 腫 jung
swell *n* 腫 jung
swift *a.* 迅速嘅 sun chuk geh
swim *v.i.* 游水 yow suy
swim *n* 游水 yow suy
swimmer *n.* 游泳者 yow wing jeh
swindle *v.t.* 呃 ak
swindle *n.* 呃 ak
swindler *n.* 騙子 peen jeh
swine *n.* 豬 ju
swing *v.i.* 搖 yiew
swing *n* 鞦韆 teen tow
Swiss *n.* 瑞士人 suy scc yan
Swiss *a* 瑞士嘅 suy see geh
switch *n.* 掣 jay
switch *v.t.* 轉 joon
swoon *n.* 暈 wan
swoon *v.i* 迷戀 may loon
swoop *v.i.* 向下猛衝 heurng ha mang chung
swoop *n* 突擊搜查 dak gik sow ta
sword *n.* 劍 geem
sycamore *n.* 西卡莫 say ka mok
sycophancy *n.* 誹謗 fay borng
sycophant *n.* 擦鞋仔 tat hai jay
syllabic *a.* 音節嘅 yam jeet geh
syllable *n.* 音節 yam jeet
syllabus *n.* 教學大綱 gao hok dai gorng
sylph *n.* 窈窕淑女 miew tiew suk luy
sylvan *a.* 森林嘅 sam lam geh
symbol *n.* 標誌 biew jee
symbolic *a.* 代表性 doy biew sing
symbolism *n.* 象徵手法 jeurng jik sow fat
symbolize *v.t.* 象徵 jeurng jing
symmetrical *a.* 對稱嘅 duy ting ghe
symmetry *n.* 對稱 duy ting
sympathetic *a.* 同情嘅 tung ting geh

sympathize *v.i.* 同情 tong ting
sympathy *n.* 同情心 tung ting sam
symphony *n.* 交響曲 gao heurng kuk
symposium *n.* 討論會 tow lun wuy
symptom *n.* 症狀 jing jorng
symptomatic *a.* 症狀嘅 jing jorng geh
synonym *n.* 同義詞 tung yee tee
synonymous *a.* 等同於 dang tung yu
synopsis *n.* 概要 koy yiew
syntax *n.* 句法 guy fat
synthesis *n.* 綜合 jung hap
synthetic *a.* 人造嘅 yan jow geh
synthetic *n* 合成物 hap sing mat
syringe *n.* 注射器 ju seh hay
syringe *v.t.* 用注射器洗 yung ju seh hay say
syrup *n.* 糖漿 tong jeurng
system *n.* 系統 hay tung
systematic *a.* 有條理嘅 yow tiew lay geh
systematize *v.t.* 系統化 hay tung far

T

table *n.* 枱 toy
table *v.t.* 擱置 gok jee
tablet *n.* 藥 yeurk
taboo *n.* 禁忌 gam gey
taboo *a* 禁忌 gam gey
taboo *v.t.* 禁止 gam jee
tabular *a.* 表格式 biew gak sik
tabulate *v.t.* 列成表格 leet sing biew gak
tabulation *n.* 列表 leet biew

tabulator *n.* 製表員 jay biew yoon
tacit *a.* 默示 mak see
taciturn *a.* 沈默寡言 tam mak gwa yeen
tackle *n.* 應付 ying fu
tackle *v.t.* 阻截 jor jeet
tact *n.* 得體 dak tay
tactful *a.* 機智嘅 gey jee geh
tactician *n.* 策士 tak see
tactics *n.* 策略 tak leurk
tactile *a.* 觸覺 juk gok
tag *n.* 牌 pai
tag *v.t.* 標籤 biew teem
tail *n.* 尾 mey
tailor *n.* 裁縫 choy fung
tailor *v.t.* 訂做 deng jow
taint *n.* 污染 wu yeem
taint *v.t.* 污染 wu yeem
take *v.t* 攞 lor
tale *n.* 故事 gu see
talent *n.* 才華 choy wah
talisman *n.* 護身符 wu san fu
talk *v.i.* 講 gong
talk *n* 講座 gong jor
talkative *a.* 健談 geen tam
tall *a.* 高 go
tallow *n.* 動物油脂 dung mat yow jee
tally *n.* 紀錄 gey luk
tally *v.t.* 吻合 man hap
tamarind *n.* 羅望子 lor morng jee
tame *a.* 溫順 wan sun
tame *v.t.* 馴服 suk fuk
tamper *v.i.* 破壞 por wai
tan *v.i.* 曬黑 sai hak
tan *n., a.* 棕黃色 jung worng sik
tangent *n.* 切線 teet seen
tangible *a.* 實在嘅 sat joy geh
tangle *n.* 打結 da geet
tangle *v.t.* 打晒結 da sai geet
tank *n.* 缸 gong

tanker *n.* 油槽車 yow cho cher
tanner *n.* 製革工人 jay gak gung yan
tannery *n.* 皮革廠 pay gak chorng
tantalize *v.t.* 引 yan
tantamount *a.* 等於 dang yu
tap *n.* 水候 suy ho
tap *v.t.* 輕拍 heng pak
tape *n.* 錄影帶 luk ying dai
tape *v.t* 錄 luk
taper *v.i.* 變窄 been jak
taper *n* 木條 muk tiew
tapestry *n.* 織錦 jik gam
tar *n.* 瀝青 lik teng
tar *v.t.* 用瀝青鋪 yung lik teng pow
target *n.* 目標 muk biew
tariff *n.* 收費表 sow fay biew
tarnish *v.t.* 失去光澤 sat huy gworng jak
task *n.* 任務 yam mo
task *v.t.* 派任務 pai yam mow
taste *n.* 試 see
taste *v.t.* 試 see
tasteful *a.* 高雅嘅 gow ngar geh
tasty *a.* 好味 ho may
tatter *n.* 碎布 suy bo
tatter *v.t* 撕爛 see lan
tattoo *n.* 紋身 man san
tattoo *v.i.* 紋身 man san
taunt *v.t.* 辱罵 yuk ma
taunt *n* 嘲笑 jao siew
tavern *n.* 酒館 jow gwun
tax *n.* 稅 suy
tax *v.t.* 收稅 sow suy
taxable *a.* 應納稅嘅 ying lap suy geh
taxation *n.* 稅 suy
taxi *n.* 的士 dik see
taxi *v.i.* 滑行 wat hang
tea *n* 茶 ta
teach *v.t.* 教 gao

teacher *n.* 老師 lo see
teak *n.* 柚木 yow muk
team *n.* 隊 duy
tear *v.t.* 撕開 see hoy
tear *n.* 裂痕 leet han
tear *n.* 眼淚 ngan luy
tearful *a.* 眼濕濕 ngan sap sap
tease *v.t.* 整蠱 jing gu
teat *n.* 乳頭 yu tow
technical *a.* 技術嘅 gey sut geh
technicality *n.* 技術性細節 gey sut sing say jeet
technician *n.* 技師 gey see
technique *n.* 技巧 gey hao
technological *a.* 技術嘅 gey sut geh
technologist *n.* 技術專家 gey sut joon ga
technology *n.* 科技 for gey
tedious *a.* 囉唆 lor sor
tedium *n.* 囉唆 lor sor
teem *v.i.* 充滿 chung mun
teenager *n.* 青少年 ting siew leen
teens *n. pl.* 十幾歲 sap gey suy
teethe *v.i.* 生牙 sang ngar
teetotal *a.* 滴酒不沾 dik jow bat jeem
teetotaller *n.* 唔飲酒嘅人 hm yam jow geh yan
telecast *n.* 電視廣播 deen see gworng bor
telecast *v.t.* 廣播 gworng bor
telecommunications *n.* 電訊 deen sun
telegram *n.* 電報 deen bo
telegraph *n.* 電報 deen bo
telegraph *v.t.* 打電報 da deen bo
telegraphic *a.* 電報嘅 deen bo geh
telegraphist *n.* 電報員 deen bo yoon
telegraphy *n.* 電報學 deen bo hok

telepathic *a.* 心靈感應嘅 sam ling gam ying geh
telepathist *n.* 心靈感應者 sam ling gam ying jeh
telepathy *n.* 心靈感應 sam ling gam ying
telephone *n.* 電話 deem wah
telephone *v.t.* 打電話 da deen wah
telescope *n.* 望遠鏡 morng yoon geng
telescopic *a.* 放大嘅 forng dai geh
televise *v.t.* 廣播 gworng bor
television *n.* 電視 deen see
tell *v.t.* 講 gong
teller *n.* 出納員 chut lap yoon
temper *n.* 脾氣 pay hay
temper *v.t.* 變溫和 been wan wor
temperament *n.* 氣質 hay jat
temperamental *a.* 喜怒無常 hay low mow seurng
temperance *n.* 滴酒不沾 dik jow bat jeem
temperate *a.* 溫和嘅 wan wor geh
temperature *n.* 溫度 wan dow
tempest *n.* 暴風雨 bo fung yu
tempestuous *a.* 劇烈 kek leet
temple *n.* 太陽穴 tai yeurng yoot
temple *n* 廟 miew
temporal *a.* 世間嘅 say gan geh
temporary *a.* 暫時嘅 jam see geh
tempt *v.t.* 誘惑 yow wak
temptation *n.* 誘惑 yow wak
tempter *n.* 誘惑者 yow wak jeh
ten *n., a* 十 sap
tenable *a.* 講得過嘅 gorng dak gwor geh
tenacious *a.* 堅持嘅 geen tee geh
tenacity *n.* 固執 gu jap
tenancy *n.* 租期 jow kay

tenant *n.* 租戶 jow wu
tend *v.i.* 通常會 tung seurng wuy
tendency *n.* 傾向 king heurng
tender *n* 供應船 gung ying shoon
tender *v.t.* 提議 tay yee
tender *n* 投票 tow biew
tender *a* 溫柔 wan yow
tenet *n.* 原則 yoon jak
tennis *n.* 網球 mong kow
tense *n.* 時態 see tai
tense *a.* 緊張 gan jeurng
tension *n.* 緊張 gan jeurng
tent *n.* 帳篷 jeurng fung
tentative *a.* 唔肯定嘅 hm hang ding geh
tenure *n.* 任期 yam kay
term *n.* 學期 hok kay
term *v.t.* 叫做 giew jow
terminable *a.* 可以終止嘅 hor yee jung jee geh
terminal *a.* 末期嘅 mwut kay geh
terminal *n* 機場 gey cheurng
terminate *v.t.* 終止 jung jee
termination *n.* 終止 jung jee
terminological *a.* 專門名詞嘅 joon mun ming tee geh
terminology *n.* 術語 sut yu
terminus *n.* 終點站 jung deem jam
terrace *n.* 排屋 派uk
terrible *a.* 可怕 hor pa
terrier *n.* 小獵犬 siew leep hoon
terrific *a.* 好好 ho ho
terrify *v.t.* 嚇 hak
territorial *a.* 地盤 day pwun
territory *n.* 地盤 day pwun
terror *n.* 驚恐 ging hung
terrorism *n.* 恐怖主義 hung bo ju yee
terrorist *n.* 恐怖份子 hung bo fan jee
terrorize *v.t.* 恐嚇 hung hak

terse *a.* 簡要嘅 gan yiew geh
test *v.t.* 試 see
test *n* 測試 tak see
testament *n.* 證據 jing guy
testicle *n.* 睪丸 gow yoon
testify *v.i.* 證實 jing sat
testimonial *n.* 推薦信 tuy jeen sun
testimony *n.* 證據 jing guy
tete-a-tete *n.* 面對面 meen duy meen
tether *n.* 拴 san
tether *v.t.* 拴繩 san sing
text *n.* 字 jee
textile *a.* 紡織嘅 forng jik geh
textile *n* 紡織品 forng jik ban
textual *n.* 正文嘅 jing man geh
texture *n.* 質感 jat gam
thank *v.t.* 多謝 dor jeh
thanks *n.* 多謝 dor jeh
thankful *a.* 感謝 gam jeh
thankless *a.* 吃力不討好 hek lik bat tow ho
that *a.* 嗰個 gor gor
that *dem. pron.* 嗰個 gor gor
that *rel. pron.* 嗰 gor
that *adv.* 咁 gam
that *conj.* 以致 yee jee
thatch *n.* 稻草 dow cho
thatch *v.t.* 用茅草整屋頂 yung mao cho jing uk deng
thaw *v.i* 解凍 gai dung
thaw *n* 熔化季節 yung far gway jeet
theatre *n.* 劇院 kek yoon
theatrical *a.* 戲劇嘅 hay kek geh
theft *n.* 偷竊 tow seet
their *a.* 佢哋 kuy dey
theirs *pron.* 佢哋 kuy dey
theism *n.* 有神論 yow san lun
theist *n.* 有神論者 yow san lun jeh

them *pron.* 佢哋 kuy day	**think** *v.t.* 諗 lum
thematic *a.* 主題嘅 ju tay geh	**thinker** *n.* 思想家 see seurng ga
theme *n.* 主題 ju tay	**third** *a.* 第三 day sam
then *adv.* 跟住 gan ju	**third** *n.* 第三 day sam
then *a* 當時 dorng see	**thirdly** *adv.* 第三 day sam
thence *adv.* 然後 yeen ho	**thirst** *n.* 渴 hot
theocracy *n.* 神權政治 san koon jing jee	**thirst** *v.i.* 渴 hot
theologian *n.* 神學家 san hok ga	**thirsty** *a.* 口渴 ho hot
theological *a.* 神學嘅 san hok geh	**thirteen** *n.* 十三 sap sam
theology *n.* 宗教學 jung gao hok	**thirteen** *a* 十三 sap sam
theorem *n.* 定理 ding lay	**thirteenth** *a.* 第十三 day sap sam
theoretical *a.* 理論上 lay lun seurng	**thirtieth** *a.* 第三十 day sam sap
theorist *n.* 理論家 lay lun ga	**thirtieth** *n* 第三十 day sam sap
theorize *v.i.* 理論化 lay lun far	**thirty** *n.* 三十 sam sap
theory *n.* 理論 lay lun	**thirty** *a* 三十 sam sap
therapy *n.* 治療 jee liew	**thistle** *n.* 薊 gey
there *adv.* 嗰度 gor dow	**thither** *adv.* 向嗰度 heurng gor dow
thereabouts *adv.* 嗰度附近 gor dow fu gan	**thorn** *n.* 刺 tee
thereafter *adv.* 之後 jee ho	**thorny** *a.* 多刺 dor tee
thereby *adv.* 因此 yan tee	**thorough** *a* 仔細 jee say
therefore *adv.* 所以 sor yi	**thoroughfare** *n.* 大街 dai gai
thermal *a.* 保暖嘅 bo loon geh	**though** *conj.* 雖然 suy yeen
thermometer *n.* 探熱針 tam yeet jam	**though** *adv.* 不過 bat gwor
thermos (flask) *n.* 暖水壺 loon suy wu	**thought** *n* 諗 lum
	thoughtful *a.* 體貼 tay teep
thesis *n.* 論文 lun man	**thousand** *n.* 一千 yat teen
thick *a.* 厚 ho	**thousand** *a* 一千 teen
thick *n.* 艱難 gan lan	**thrall** *n.* 影響 ying heurng
thick *adv.* 厚厚咁 ho ho gam	**thralldom** *n.* 奴隸 low day
thicken *v.i.* 整厚 jing ho	**thrash** *v.t.* 連續打 leen juk da
thicket *n.* 樹叢 shu chung	**thread** *n.* 線 seen
thief *n.* 賊 tak	**thread** *v.t* 穿 choon
thigh *n.* 大髀 dai bay	**threadbare** *a.* 破舊 por gow
thimble *n.* 頂針 ding jam	**threat** *n.* 威脅 way heep
thin *a.* 瘦 so	**threaten** *v.t.* 恐嚇 hung hak
thin *v.t.* 稀釋 hay sik	**three** *n.* 三 sam
thing *n.* 嘢 yeh	**three** *a* 三 sam
	thresh *v.t.* 脫粒 toot lap
	thresher *n.* 打穀者 da guk jeh
	threshold *n.* 門口 mun ho
	thrice *adv.* 三次 sam tee

thrift *n.* 慳家 han ga	**tick** *n.* 剔 tik
thrifty *a.* 慳 han	**tick** *v.i.* 剔 tik
thrill *n.* 刺激 tee gik	**ticket** *n.* 票 piew
thrill *v.t.* 刺激 tee gik	**tickle** *v.t.* 搔 jeet
thrive *v.i.* 興旺 hing worng	**ticklish** *a.* 怕搔 pa jee
throat *n.* 喉嚨 ho lung	**tidal** *a.* 潮嘅 tiew geh
throaty *a.* 嘶啞嘅 see ngar geh	**tide** *n.* 潮 tiew
throb *v.i.* 抽搐 tow chuk	**tidings** *n. pl.* 消息 siew sik
throb *n.* 跳動 tiew dung	**tidiness** *n.* 整齊 jing tay
throe *n.* 劇痛 kek tung	**tidy** *a.* 整齊 jing tay
throne *n.* 王位 worng way	**tidy** *v.t.* 執 jap
throne *v.t.* 登位 dang way	**tie** *v.t.* 綁 borng
throng *n.* 一大班人 yat dai ban yan	**tie** *n* 呔 tai
throng *v.t.* 群集 kwan jap	**tier** *n.* 級 kap
throttle *n.* 油門 yow mun	**tiger** *n.* 老虎 lo fu
throttle *v.t.* 勒死 lak say	**tight** *a.* 緊 gan
through *prep.* 穿過 choon gwor	**tighten** *v.t.* 整緊 jing gan
through *adv.* 通過 tung gwor	**tigress** *n.* 老虎乸 low fu la
through *a* 全程嘅 choon ting geh	**tile** *n.* 瓷磚 tee joon
throughout *adv.* 遍及 peen kap	**tile** *v.t.* 鋪瓷磚 po tee joon
throughout *prep.* 由始至終 yow tee jee jung	**till** *prep.* 直到 jik dow
throw *v.t.* 掟 deng	**till** *n. conj.* 直到 jik dow
throw *n.* 掟 deng	**till** *v.t.* 耕 gang
thrust *v.t.* 猛推 mang tuy	**tilt** *v.i.* 斜 ter
thrust *n* 插 tap	**tilt** *n.* 斜 ter
thud *n.* 砰聲 pung seng	**timber** *n.* 木 muk
thud *v.i.* 砰 pung	**time** *n.* 時間 see gan
thug *n.* 死仔 say leng jay	**time** *v.t.* 計時 gey see
thumb *n.* 手指公 sow jee gung	**timely** *a.* 及時 kap see
thumb *v.t.* 用手指公評 yung sow jee gung ping	**timid** *a.* 細膽 say dam
thump *n.* 重擊 chung gik	**timidity** *n.* 無膽 mow dam
thump *v.t.* 重擊 chung gik	**timorous** *a.* 細膽 say dam
thunder *n.* 雷 luy	**tin** *n.* 罐 gwun
thunder *v.i.* 打雷 da luy	**tin** *v.t.* 裝罐 jorng gwun
thunderous *a.* 大聲 dai seng	**tincture** *n.* 藥酒 yeurk jow
Thursday *n.* 星期四 sing kay say	**tincture** *v.t.* 染 yeem
thus *adv.* 所以 sor yi	**tinge** *n.* 少少 siew siew
thwart *v.t.* 阻止 jor jee	**tinge** *v.t.* 染少少 yeem siew siew
tiara *n.* 皇冠 worng gwun	**tinker** *n.* 修補匠 sow bo jeurng
	tinsel *n.* 金屬絲 gam suk see
	tint *n.* 淺色 teen sik
	tint *v.t.* 稍微染 sao may yeem

tiny *a.* 細粒 say lap

tip *n.* 貼士 teep see

tip *v.t.* 畀貼士 bay teep see

tip *n.* 一堆垃圾 yat duy lap sap

tip *v.t.* 倒 dow

tip *n.* 頭 tow

tip *v.t.* 輕輕咁掂 heng heng gam deem

tipsy *a.* 少少醉 siew siew juy

tirade *n.* 長篇大論 cheurng peen dai lun

tire *v.t.* 劫 gwuy

tiresome *a.* 好煩 ho fan

tissue *n.* 紙巾 jee gan

Titanic *a.* 鐵達尼號 teet dat nay ho

tithe *n.* 捐稅 goon sut

title *n.* 名 meng

titular *a.* 有名無實 yow ming mow sat

toad *n.* 蟾蜍 siem chuy

toast *n.* 多士 dor see

toast *v.t.* 乾杯 gorn bwuy

tobacco *n.* 煙草 yeem cho

today *adv.* 今日 gam yat

today *n.* 今日 gam yat

toe *n.* 腳趾 geurt jee

toe *v.t.* 順從 sun chung

toffee *n.* 太妃糖 tai fay torng

toga *n.* 闊外袍 fwut ngoy pow

together *adv.* 一齊 yat chay

toil *n.* 苦工 fu gung

toil *v.i.* 辛苦做 san fu jow

toilet *n.* 廁所 tee sor

toils *n. pl.* 陷阱 ham jing

token *n.* 代幣 doy bay

tolerable *a.* 仲可以 jung hor yee

tolerance *n.* 耐力 loy lik

tolerant *a.* 忍受到嘅 yan sow dow geh

tolerate *v.t.* 忍 yan

toleration *n.* 容忍 yung yan

toll *n.* 通行費 tung hang fay

toll *n* 數目 sow muk

toll *v.t.* 敲 hao

tomato *n.* 番茄 fan keh

tomb *n.* 墓 mo

tomboy *n.* 男人婆 larm yan por

tomcat *n.* 公貓 gung mao

tome *n.* 厚書 ho shu

tomorrow *n.* 聽日 ting yat

tomorrow *adv.* 聽日 ting yat

ton *n.* 噸 dun

tone *n.* 語氣 yu hay

tone *v.t.* 變結實 been geet sat

tongs *n. pl.* 鉗 keem

tongue *n.* 脷 lay

tonic *a.* 補嘅 bo geh

tonic *n.* 湯力水 torng lik suy

tonight *n.* 今晚 gam man

tonight *adv.* 今晚 gam man

tonne *n.* 噸 dun

tonsil *n.* 扁桃體 been tow tay

tonsure *n.* 剃度 tay dow

too *adv.* 太過 tai gwor

tool *n.* 工具 gung guy

tooth *n.* 牙 ngar

toothache *n.* 牙痛 ngar tung

toothsome *a.* 好味嘅 ho may geh

top *n.* 頂 deng

top *v.t.* 超過 tiew gwor

top *n.* 上面 seurng meen

topaz *n.* 黃寶石 worng bo seng

topic *n.* 題目 tay muk

topical *a.* 有關嘅 yow gwan geh

topographer *n.* 地形學家 day ying hok ga

topographical *a.* 地形嘅 day ying geh

topography *n.* 地形 day ying

topple *v.i.* 倒塌 dow tap

topsy turvy *a.* 亂七八糟嘅 loon tat bat jow geh

topsy turvy *adv* 顛三倒四 deen sam dow say

torch *n.* 電筒 deen tung
torment *n.* 折磨 jeet mor
torment *v.t.* 折磨 jeet mor
tornado *n.* 龍捲風 lung goon fung
torpedo *n.* 魚雷 yu luy
torpedo *v.t.* 用魚雷襲擊 yung yu luy jap gik
torrent *n.* 急流 gap low
torrential *a.* 傾瀉嘅 king seh geh
torrid *a.* 乾燥嘅 gorn cho geh
tortoise *n.* 龜 gway
tortuous *a.* 彎彎曲曲嘅 wan wan kuk kuk geh
torture *n.* 折磨 jeet mor
torture *v.t.* 折磨 jeet mor
toss *v.t.* 掟 deng
toss *n* 擲銀決定 jak ngan koot ding
total *a.* 總計嘅 jung gey geh
total *n.* 總數 jung sow
total *v.t.* 計 gey
totality *n.* 全部 choon bo
touch *v.t.* 掂 deem
touch *n* 觸覺 juk gok
touchy *a.* 易嬲 yee low
tough *a.* 艱難 gan lan
toughen *v.t.* 強化 keurng far
tour *n.* 旅行 luy hang
tour *v.i.* 遊覽 yow lam
tourism *n.* 旅遊業 luy yow yeep
tourist *n.* 旅客 luy hak
tournament *n.* 錦標賽 gam biew choy
towards *prep.* 向 heurng
towel *n.* 毛巾 mo gan
towel *v.t.* 用毛巾抹 yung mo gan mat
tower *n.* 塔 tap
tower *v.i.* 超過 tiew gwor
town *n.* 市鎮 see jan
township *a.* 鎮區 jan kuy
toy *n.* 玩具 wun guy

toy *v.i.* 玩 wan
trace *n.* 痕跡 han jik
trace *v.t.* 跟蹤 gan jung
traceable *a.* 可以追溯嘅 hor yee juy sok geh
track *n.* 軌道 gway dow
track *v.t.* 追蹤 juy jung
tract *n.* 大片土地 dai peen tow day
tract *n* 宗教短文 jung gao doon man
traction *n.* 拉力 lai lik
tractor *n.* 拖拉機 tor lai gey
trade *n.* 買賣 mai mai
trade *v.i* 交易 gao yik
trader *n.* 商人 seurng yan
tradesman *n.* 商人 seurng yan
tradition *n.* 傳統 choon tung
traditional *a.* 傳統嘅 choon tung geh
traffic *n.* 交通 gao tung
traffic *v.i.* 非法做買賣 fay fat jow mai mai
tragedian *n.* 悲劇作家 bay kek jok ga
tragedy *n.* 悲劇 bay kek
tragic *a.* 悲慘嘅 bay tarm geh
trail *n.* 痕跡 han jik
trail *v.t.* 拉 lai
trailer *n.* 預告 yu go
train *n.* 火車 for cher
train *v.t.* 訓練 fan leen
trainee *n.* 練習生 leen jap sang
training *n.* 訓練 fan leen
trait *n.* 特徵 dak jing
traitor *n.* 叛徒 bwun tow
tram *n.* 電車 deen cher
trample *v.t.* 踩碎 tai suy
trance *n.* 發呆 fat oy
tranquil *a.* 安靜 on jing
tranquility *n.* 平靜 ping jing

tranquillize v.t. 變平靜 been ping jing

transact v.t. 辦理 ban lay

transaction n. 交易 gao yik

transcend v.t. 超越 tiew yoot

transcendent a. 傑出嘅 geet chut geh

transcribe v.t. 記錄 gey luk

transcription n. 抄寫 tao seh

transfer n. 轉 joon

transfer v.t. 轉 joon

transferable a. 可以轉嘅 hor yee joon geh

transfiguration n. 變形 been ying

transfigure v.t. 變形 been ying

transform v. 改變形態 goy been ying tai

transformation n. 變化 been far

transgress v.t. 越軌 yoot gway

transgression n. 違反 way fan

transit n. 運輸 wan shu

transition n. 轉變 joon been

transitive n. 轉遞 joon day

transitory a. 暫時 jam see

translate v.t. 翻譯 fan yik

translation n. 翻譯 fan yik

transmigration n. 轉世 joon say

transmission n. 傳染 choon yeem

transmit v.t. 傳送 choon sung

transmitter n. 發射機 fat seh gey

transparent a. 透明 tow ming

transplant v.t. 移植 yee jik

transport v. 運送 wan sung

transport n. 交通工具 gao tung gung guy

transportation n. 交通工具 gao tung gung guy

trap n. 陷阱 ham jeng

trap v.t. 捉 juk

trash n. 垃圾 lap sap

travel v.i. 旅遊 luy yow

travel n 旅行 luy hang

traveller n. 旅客 luy hao

tray n. 盤 pwun

treacherous a. 奸嘅 gan geh

treachery n. 背叛 bwuy bun

tread v.t. 踩 tai

tread n 步法 bo fat

treason n. 叛國罪 pwun gwok juy

treasure n. 寶藏 bo jorng

treasure v.t. 珍惜 jan sik

treasurer n. 財物主管 choy mow ju gwun

treasury n. 財政部 choy jing bo

treat v.t. 對待 duy doy

treat n 款待 fwun doy

treatise n. 論文 lun man

treatment n. 治療 jee liew

treaty n. 協定 heep ding

tree n. 樹 shu

trek v.i. 長途跋涉 cheurng tow bat seet

trek n. 長途跋涉 cheurng tow bat seet

tremble v.i. 震 jan

tremendous a. 巨大嘅 guy dai geh

tremor n. 微震 may jan

trench n. 溝 kow

trench v.t. 掘 gwat

trend n. 潮流 tiew lo

trespass v.i. 擅自侵入 seen jee tam yap

trespass n. 非法侵入 fay fat tam yap

trial n. 審訊 sam sun

triangle n. 三角形 sam gok ying

triangular a. 三角形 sam gok ying

tribal a. 部族嘅 bo juk geh

tribe n. 族 juk

tribulation n. 痛苦 tung fu

tribunal *n.* 法庭 fat ting	**troop** *v.i* 列隊行 leet duy hang
tributary *n.* 支流 jee low	**trooper** *n.* 騎兵 keh bing
tributary *a.* 支流嘅 jee low geh	**trophy** *n.* 獎座 jeurng jor
trick *n* 騙局 peen guk	**tropic** *n.* 熱帶 yeet dai
trick *v.t.* 呃 ak	**tropical** *a.* 熱帶 yeet dai
trickery *n.* 花招 far jiew	**trot** *v.i.* 快步行 fai bao hang
trickle *v.i.* 滴 dik	**trot** *n* 小步快跑 siew bo fai pao
trickster *n.* 騙子 peen jee	**trouble** *n.* 問題 man tay
tricky *a.* 難嘅 lan geh	**trouble** *v.t.* 煩 fan
tricolour *a.* 三色嘅 sam sik geh	**troublesome** *a.* 令人煩惱 ling
tricolour *n* 三色旗 sam sik kay	yan fan low
tricycle *n.* 三輪車 sam lun cher	**troupe** *n.* 戲團 hay toon
trifle *n.* 鬆糕 sung go	**trousers** *n. pl* 褲 fu
trifle *v.i* 睇小 tay siew	**trowel** *n.* 細鏟 say tan
trigger *n.* 板機 ban gey	**truce** *n.* 停戰協定 ting jeen heep
trim *a.* 苗條 miew tiew	ding
trim *n* 修剪 sow jeen	**truck** *n.* 卡車 ka cher
trim *v.t.* 修剪 sow jeen	**true** *a.* 啱 ngarm
trinity *n.* 三位一體 sam way yat	**trump** *n.* 王牌 worng pai
tay	**trump** *v.t.* 打敗 da bai
trio *n.* 三個人 sam gor yam	**trumpet** *n.* 喇叭 la ba
trip *v.t.* 棘嘅 kik tan	**trumpet** *v.i.* 宣揚 shoon yeurng
trip *n.* 旅行 luy hang	**trunk** *n.* 車尾箱 cher may seurng
tripartite *a.* 有三個部份 yow sam	**trust** *n.* 信任 sun yam
gor bo fan geh	**trust** *v.t* 信 sun
triple *a.* 三個部份 sam gor bo fan	**trustee** *n.* 受託人 sow tok yan
triple *v.t.,* 三倍 sam pwuy	**trustful** *a.* 信得過 sun dak gwor
triplicate *a.* 三個 sam gor	**trustworthy** *a.* 信得過 sun dak
triplicate *n* 一式三份 yat sik sam	gwor
fan	**trusty** *n.* 模範囚犯 mo fan tow fan
triplicate *v.t.* 三倍 sam pwuy	**truth** *n.* 真相 tan seurng
triplication *n.* 分成三份 fan sing	**truthful** *a.* 誠實 sing sat
sam fan	**try** *v.i.* 試 see
tripod *n.* 三腳架 sam geurt ga	**try** *n* 嘗試 seurng see
triumph *n.* 成就 sing jow	**trying** *a.* 麻煩 ma fan
triumph *v.i.* 打敗 da bai	**tryst** *n.* 幽會 yow wuy
triumphal *a.* 凱旋嘅 hoy shoon	**tub** *n.* 罐 gwun
geh	**tube** *n.* 管 gwun
triumphant *a.* 大獲全勝 dai wok	**tuberculosis** *n.* 肺癆 fay lo
choon sing	**tubular** *a.* 管狀 gwun jorng
trivial *a.* 瑣碎 sor suy	**tug** *v.t.* 拉 lai
troop *n.* 士兵 see bing	**tuition** *n.* 指導 jee dow

tumble *v.i.* 跌倒 deet dow

tumble *n.* 跌 deet

tumbler *n.* 玻璃杯 bor lay bwuy

tumour *n.* 腫瘤 jung lo

tumult *n.* 騷亂 sow loon

tumultuous *a.* 熱烈 yeet leet

tune *n.* 曲 kuk

tune *v.t.* 調音 tiew yam

tunnel *n.* 地下通到 day ha tung dow

tunnel *v.i.* 挖地道 gwat day dow

turban *n.* 包頭巾 bao tow gan

turbine *n.* 渦輪機 wor lun gey

turbulence *n.* 氣流 hay low

turbulent *a.* 混亂嘅 wan loon geh

turf *n.* 草皮 cho pay

turkey *n.* 火雞 for gey

turmeric *n.* 薑黃根粉 geurng worng gan fan

turmoil *n.* 騷動 sow dung

turn *v.i.* 轉 joon

turn *n* 彎 wan

turner *n.* 車工 cher gung

turnip *n.* 蘿蔔 lor bak

turpentine *n.* 松節油 chung jeet yow

turtle *n.* 烏龜 wu gway

tusk *n.* 象牙 jeurng ngar

tussle *n.* 爭鬥 jang dow

tussle *v.i.* 掙 jang

tutor *n.* 教師 gao see

tutorial *a.* 導師嘅 dow see geh

tutorial *n.* 輔導課 fu dow for

twelfth *a.* 第十二 day sap yee

twelfth *n.* 第十二 day sap yee

twelve *n.* 十二 sap yeet

twelve *a.* 十二 sup yee

twentieth *a.* 第二十 day yee sap

twentieth *n* 第二十 day yee sap

twenty *a.* 二十 yee sap

twenty *n* 二十 yee sup

twice *adv.* 兩次 leurng tee

twig *n.* 樹枝 shu jee

twilight *n* 暮色 mow sik

twin *n.* 雙胞胎之一 seurng bao toy jee yat

twin *a* 相連 seurng leen

twinkle *v.i.* 閃 seem

twinkle *n.* 閃亮 seem leurng

twist *v.t.* 扭 low

twist *n.* 轉變 joon been

twitter *n.* 吱吱聲 jee jee seng

twitter *v.i.* 吱喳 jee ja

two *n.* 二 yee

two *a.* 兩 leurng

twofold *a.* 有兩個部份 yow leurng gor bo fan

type *n.* 類型 luy ying

type *v.t.* 打字 da jee

typhoid *n.* 傷寒 seurng hon

typhoon *n.* 颱風 toy fung

typhus *n.* 斑疹傷寒 ban tan seurng hon

typical *a.* 典型嘅 deen ying geh

typify *v.t.* 做...嘅典範 jow...geh deen fa

typist *n.* 打字員 da jee yoon

tyranny *n.* 苛政 hor jing

tyrant *n.* 暴君 bo gwan

tyre *n.* 車胎 cher tai

U

udder *n.* 乳房 yu forng

uglify *v.t.* 醜化 tow far

ugliness *n.* 醜陋 tow low

ugly *a.* 醜 tow

ulcer *n.* 潰瘍 kwuy yeurng

ulcerous *a.* 潰瘍嘅 kwuy yeurng geh

ulterior *a.* 不可告人嘅 bat hor gow yan geh

ultimate *a.* 終極嘅 jung gik geh

ultimately *adv.* 最後 juy ho

ultimatum *n.* 最後通牒 juy ho tung deep

umbrella *n.* 遮 jeh

umpire *n.* 裁判員 choy pwun yoon

umpire *v.t.,* 做裁判 jow choy pwun

unable *a.* 唔可以 hm hor yi

unanimity *n.* 一致同意 yat jee tung yee

unanimous *a.* 一致嘅 yat jee geh

unaware *a.* 唔在意 hm joy yee

unawares *adv.* 未主義到 may ju yee dow

unburden *v.t.* 傾訴 king sow

uncanny *a.* 異常嘅 yee seurng geh

uncertain *a.* 唔肯定 hm han ding

uncle *n.* 阿叔 ah suk

uncouth *a.* 粗魯 cho low

under *prep.* 喺...嘅下面 hay...geh ha meen

under *adv* 少於 siew yu

under *a* 喺...嘅下面 hay...geh ha meen

undercurrent *n.* 暗流 am low

underdog *n* 唔被睇好嘅人 hm bay tay ho geh yan

undergo *v.t.* 經歷 ging lik

undergraduate *n.* 大學生 dai hok sang

underhand *a.* 祕密嘅 bay mat geh

underline *v.t.* 畫線 wak seen

undermine *v.t.* 逐漸減弱 juk jeen garm yeurk

underneath *adv.* 喺...嘅下面 hay...geh ha meen

underneath *prep.* 喺...嘅下面 hay...geh ha meen

understand *v.t.* 明白 ming bak

undertake *v.t.* 負責 fu jak

undertone *n.* 細聲 say seng

underwear *n.* 內衣 loy yee

underworld *n.* 陰曹地府 yam cho day fu

undo *v.t.* 解開 gai hoy

undue *a.* 過分 gwor fan

undulate *v.i.* 起伏 hay fuk

undulation *n.* 波浪形 bor lorng ying

unearth *v.t.* 發掘 fat gwat

uneasy *a.* 擔心 dam sam

unfair *a* 唔公平 hm gung ping

unfold *v.t.* 打開 da hoy

unfortunate *a.* 不幸 bat han

ungainly *a.* 笨手笨腳 ban sow ban geurt

unhappy *a.* 唔開心 hm hoy sam

unification *n.* 統一 tung yat

union *n.* 協會 heep wuy

unionist *n.* 聯合主義者 loon hap ju yee jeh

unique *a.* 獨特 duk tak

unison *n.* 一齊 yat tay

unit *n.* 單位 dan way

unite *v.t.* 團結 toon geet

unity *n.* 聯合 loon hap

universal *a.* 全世界嘅 choon say gai geh

universality *n.* 普遍性 pow peen sing

universe *n.* 宇宙 yu jow

university *n.* 大學 dai hok

unjust *a.* 唔公平嘅 hm gung ping geh

unless *conj.* 徐非 chuy fay

unlike *a* 唔同 hm tung

unlike *prep* 唔似 hm tee

unlikely *a.* 無咩可能 mow meh hor lang

unmanned *a.* 無人操作嘅 mow yan cho jok geh

unmannerly *a* 無禮貌嘅 mow lay moa geh

unprincipled *a.* 不道德嘅 bat dow dak geh

unreliable *a.* 唔信得過嘅 hm sun dak gwor geh

unrest *n* 騷動 sow dung

unruly *a.* 難控制嘅 lan hung jay geh

unsettle *v.t.* 擔憂 dam yow

unsheathe *v.t.* 拔出 bat chut

until *prep.* 直到 jik dow

until *conj* 直到 jik dow

untoward *a.* 意外嘅 yee ngoy geh

unwell *a.* 唔舒服 hm shu fuk

unwittingly *adv.* 無意咁 mow yee gam

up *adv.* 向上 heurng seurng

up *prep.* 沿着 yoon ju

upbraid *v.t* 鬧 lao

upheaval *n.* 劇變 kek been

uphold *v.t* 支持 jee tee

upkeep *n* 保養 bow yeurng

uplift *v.t.* 激勵 gik lay

uplift *n* 提高 tay gow

upon *prep* 上 seurng

upper *a.* 上嘅 seurng geh

upright *a.* 挺直嘅 ting jik geh

uprising *n.* 起義 hay yee

uproar *n.* 騷動 sow dung

uproarious *a.* 熱烈 yeet leet

uproot *v.t.* 連根拔起 leen gan bat hay

upset *v.t.* 令到唔開心 ling dow hm hoy sam

upshot *n.* 結果 geet gwor

upstart *n.* 暴發戶 bo fat wu

up-to-date *a.* 最新嘅 juy san geh

upward *a.* 向上嘅 heurng seurng geh

upwards *adv.* 上面 seurng meen

urban *a.* 城市嘅 sing see geh

urbane *a.* 彬彬有禮嘅 ban ban yow lay geh

urbanity *n.* 文雅 man ngar

urchin *n.* 頑童 wan tung

urge *v.t* 催 chuy

urge *n* 衝動 chung dung

urgency *n.* 急事 gap see

urgent *a.* 緊急 gan gap

urinal *n.* 尿兜 liew dow

urinary *a.* 尿嘅 liew geh

urinate *v.i.* 屙尿 or liew

urination *n.* 屙尿 or liew

urine *n.* 尿 liew

urn *n* 骨灰甕 gwat fwuy ang

usage *n.* 用法 yung fat

use *n.* 用處 yung chu

use *v.t.* 用 yung

useful *a.* 有用 yow yung

usher *n.* 門衛 mun way

usher *v.t.* 引導 yan dow

usual *a.* 平時 ping see

usually *adv.* 通常 tung seurng

usurer *n.* 大耳窿 dai yee lung

usurp *v.t.* 侵權 tam koon

usurpation *n.* 侵佔 tam jeem

usury *n.* 放貴利 forng gway lay

utensil *n.* 用具 yung guy

uterus *n.* 子宮 jee gung

utilitarian *a.* 實用嘅 sat yung geh

utility *n.* 效用 hao yung

utilization *n.* 利用 lay yung

utilize *v.t.* 用 yung

utmost *a.* 最大嘅 juy dai geh

utmost *n* 最大量 juy dai leurng

utopia *n*. 理想國 lay seurng gwok

utopian *a.* 不切實際 bat teet sat jay

utter *v.t.* 講 gorng

utter *a* 徹底 teet day

utterance *n.* 言論 yeen lun

utterly *adv.* 徹底咁 teet day gam

V

vacancy *n.* 空缺 hung koot

vacant *a.* 空嘅 hung geh

vacate *v.t.* 搬出 bwun chut

vacation *n.* 假期 ga kay

vaccinate *v.t.* 打疫苗 da yik miew

vaccination *n.* 接種 jeep jung

vaccinator *n.* 接種員 jeep jung yoon

vaccine *n.* 疫苗 yik miew

vacillate *v.i.* 成日轉軚 sing yat joon tai

vacuum *n.* 真空 jan hung

vagabond *n.* 流浪漢 low lorng hon

vagabond *a* 流浪嘅 low lorng geh

vagary *n.* 難測 lan tak

vagina *n.* 陰道 yam dow

vague *a.* 粗略嘅 cho leurk geh

vagueness *n.* 含糊度 ham wu dow

vain *a.* 自負 jee fu

vainglorious *a.* 自負 jee fu

vainglory *n.* 虛榮 huy wing

vainly *adv.* 嘥氣嘅 sai hay geh

vale *n.* 山谷 san guk

valiant *a.* 勇敢嘅 yung gam geh

valid *a.* 有效 yow hao

validate *v.t.* 證實 jing sat

validity *n.* 合法性 hap fat sing

valley *n.* 山谷 san guk

valour *n.* 勇氣 yung hay

valuable *a.* 有價值 yow ga jik

valuation *n.* 估價 gu ga

value *n.* 價值 ga jik

value *v.t.* 珍惜 jan sik

valve *n.* 氣門 hay mun

van *n.* 貨車 for cher

vanish *v.i.* 消失 siew sat

vanity *n.* 自負 jee fu

vanquish *v.t.* 徹底擊敗 teet day gik bai

vaporize *v.t.* 蒸發 jing fat

vaporous *a.* 充滿蒸氣 chung mwun jing hay

vapour *n.* 蒸氣 jing hay

variable *a.* 多變嘅 dor been geh

variance *n.* 差額 ta ak

variation *n.* 變化 been far

varied *a.* 不同嘅 bat tung geh

variety *n.* 不同類型 bat tug luy ying

various *a.* 幾種嘅 gey jung geh

varnish *n.* 清漆 ting tat

varnish *v.t.* 上清漆 seurng ting tat

vary *v.t.* 有唔同嘅 yow hm tung geh

vasectomy *n.* 輸精管切除手術 shu jing gwun teet chuy sow sut

vaseline *n.* 礦脂 kworng jee

vast *a.* 巨大嘅 guy dai geh

vault *n.* 保險庫 bo heem fu

vault *n.* 墓穴 mow yoot

vault *v.i.* 跳 tiew

vegetable *n.* 蔬菜 sor choy

vegetable *a.* 青菜 teng choy

vegetarian *n.* 素食者 sow sik jeh

vegetarian *a* 素食嘅 sow sik geh

vegetation *n.* 草木 cho muk

vehemence *n.* 強烈 keurng leet

vehement *a.* 強烈 keurng leet

vehicle *n.* 交通工具 gao tubg gung guy

vehicular *a.* 車輛嘅 cher leurng geh

veil *n.* 棉紗 meen sa

veil *v.t.* 遮 jeh

vein *n.* 靜脈 jing mak

velocity *n.* 速度 chuk dow

velvet *n.* 絲絨 see yung

velvety *a.* 絲絨嘅 see yung geh

venal *a.* 見利忘義 geen lay morng yee

venality *n.* 腐敗 fu bai

vendor *n.* 小販 siew fan

venerable *a.* 值得尊重嘅 jik dak joon jung geh

venerate *n.* 敬重 ging jung

veneration *n.* 尊敬 joon ging

vengeance *n.* 報復 bo fuk

venial *a.* 可以寬恕嘅 hor yee wun shu geh

venom *n.* 毒液 duk yik

venomous *a.* 有毒嘅 yow duk geh

vent *n.* 風口 fung ho

ventilate *v.t.* 通風 tung fung

ventilation *n.* 通風 tung fung

ventilator *n.* 通風口 tung fung ho

venture *n.* 企業 kay yeep

venture *v.t.* 敢去 gam huy

venturesome *a.* 大膽嘅 dai dam geh

venturous *a.* 大膽嘅 dai dam geh

venue *n.* 地點 dey deem

veracity *n.* 誠實 sing sat

veranda *n.* 陽台 yeurng tow

verb *n.* 動詞 dung tee

verbal *a.* 口講嘅 ho gorng geh

verbally *adv.* 口頭上嘅 ho tow seurng geh

verbatim *a.* 逐個字 juk gor jee

verbatim *adv.* 逐個字 juk gor jee

verbose *a.* 囉唆 lor sor

verbosity *n.* 囉唆 lor sor

verdant *a.* 碧綠嘅 bik luk geh

verdict *n.* 裁決 choy koot

verge *n.* 邊緣 been yoon

verification *n.* 確認 kok ying

verify *v.t.* 證實 ting sat

verisimilitude *n.* 逼真 bik jan

veritable *a.* 名副其實嘅 ming fu kay sat geh

vermillion *n.* 鮮紅色 seen hung sik

vermillion *a.* 鮮紅色嘅 seen hung sik geh

vernacular *n.* 本地話 bwun day wah

vernacular *a.* 本地嘅 bwun day geh

vernal *a.* 春天嘅 chun teen geh

versatile *a.* 多才多藝嘅 dor choy dor ngay geh

versatility *n.* 多用途 dor yung tow

verse *n.* 詩節 see jeet

versed *a.* 熟練嘅 suk leen geh

versification *n.* 詩律 see lut

versify *v.t.* 作詩 jok see

version *n.* 版本 ban bwun

versus *prep.* 對 duy

vertical *a.* 打直 da jik

verve *n.* 精力 jing lik

very *a.* 非常 fay seurng

vessel *n.* 大船 dai shoon

vest *n.* 背心 bwuy sam

vest *v.t.* 屬於 suk yu

vestige *n.* 遺跡 way jik

vestment *n.* 祭衣 jay yee

veteran *n.* 退伍軍人 tuy hm gwan yan

veteran *a.* 經驗豐富嘅 ging yeem fung fu geh

veterinary *a.* 獸醫嘅 sow yee geh

veto *n.* 否決 fow koot

veto *v.t.* 否決 for koot

vex *v.t.* 煩 fan

vexation *n* 煩惱 fan low

via *prep.* 經 ging

viable *a.* 可行嘅 hor hang ghe

vial *n.* 管形樽 gwun ying jun

vibrate *v.i.* 震 jan

vibration *n.* 震動 jan dung

vicar *n.* 牧師 muk see

vicarious *a.* 代替嘅 doy tay geh

vice *n.* 罪行 juy hang

viceroy *n.* 總督 jung duk

vice-versa *adv.* 反之亦然 fan jee yik yeen

vicinity *n.* 附近 fun gan

vicious *a.* 狠 han

vicissitude *n.* 變遷 been teen

victim *n.* 受害者 sow hoy jeh

victimize *v.t.* 令人受苦 ling yan sow fu

victor *n.* 勝利者 sing lay jeh

victorious *a.* 勝利嘅 sing lay geh

victory *n.* 勝利 sing lay

victuals *n. pl* 飲食 yam sik

vie *v.i.* 爭 jang

view *n.* 風景 fung ging

view *v.t.* 睇 tay

vigil *n.* 守夜 sow yeh

vigilance *n.* 警戒 ging gai

vigilant *a.* 警覺嘅 ging gok geh

vigorous *a.* 精力充沛 jing lik chung pwuy

vile *a.* 邪惡嘅 ter ok geh

vilify *v.t.* 中傷 jung seurng

villa *n.* 別墅 beet suy

village *n.* 村 choon

villager *n.* 村民 choon man

villain *n.* 衰人 suy yan

vindicate *v.t.* 證實 jing sat

vindication *n.* 證明無罪 jing ming mow juy

vine *n.* 葡萄藤 pow tow tang

vinegar *n.* 醋 cho

vintage *n.* 釀造年份 yeurng jow leen fan

violate *v.t.* 違反 way fan

violation *n.* 違反 way fan

violence *n.* 暴力 bo lik

violent *a.* 劇烈嘅 kek leet geh

violet *n.* 紫羅蘭 jee lor lan

violin *n.* 小提琴 siew tay kam

violinist *n.* 小提琴家 siew tay kam ga

virgin *n.* 處女 chu luy

virgin *n* 處男 chu larm

virginity *n.* 貞潔 jing geet

virile *a.* 強壯嘅 keurng jorng geh

virility *n.* 力量 lik leurng

virtual *a* 虛擬 huy yee

virtue *n.* 美德 may dak

virtuous *a.* 品德高 ban dak gow

virulence *n.* 毒性 duk sing

virulent *a.* 狠毒嘅 han duk geh

virus *n.* 病毒 beng duk

visage *n.* 面 meen

visibility *n.* 能見度 lang geen dow

visible *a.* 見到嘅 geen dow geh

vision *n.* 視力 see lik

visionary *a.* 有創意 yow chorng yee

visionary *n.* 有眼力嘅人 yow ngan lik geh yan

visit *n.* 參觀 tam gwun

visit *v.t.* 探 tarm

visitor *n.* 客人 hak yan

vista *n.* 景色 ging sik

visual *a.* 視覺嘅 see gok geh

visualize *v.t.* 想像 seurng jeurng

vital *a.* 好重要嘅 ho jung yiew geh

vitality *n.* 活力 wut lik

vitalize *v.t.* 激勵 gik lay

vitamin *n.* 維他命 way ta ming

vitiate *v.t.* 失效 sat hao

vivacious *a.* 活潑嘅 wut pwut geh

vivacity *n.* 活潑 wut pwut

viva-voce *adv.* 口頭上嘅 ho tow seurng geh

viva-voce *a* 口嘅嘅 ho tow geh

viva-voce *n* 口試 ho see

vivid *a.* 清晰嘅 ting sik geh

vixen *n.* 雌狐 tee wu

vocabulary *n.* 單詞 dan tee

vocal *a.* 聲嘅 seng geh

vocalist *n.* 歌手 gor sow

vocation *n.* 使命感 see ming gam

vogue *n.* 流行 low hang

voice *n.* 聲 seng

voice *v.t.* 表示 biew see

void *a.* 缺乏 koot fat

void *v.t.* 變無效 been mow hao

void *n.* 空間 hung gan

volcanic *a.* 火山嘅 for san geh

volcano *n.* 火山 for san

volition *n.* 意志力 yee jee lik

volley *n.* 擊球 gik kow

volley *v.t* 攔球 lan kow

volt *n.* 伏特 fuk dak

voltage *n.* 伏特 fuk dak

volume *n.* 音量 yam leurng

voluminous *a.* 肥大嘅 fay dai ghe

voluntarily *adv.* 自願咁 jee yoon gam

voluntary *a.* 自願 jee yoon

volunteer *n.* 志願者 jee yoon jeh

volunteer *v.t.* 主動建議 ju dung geen yee

voluptuary *n.* 沈迷酒色嘅 tam may jow sik geh

voluptuous *a.* 豐滿嘅 fung mun geh

vomit *v.t.* 嘔 oh

vomit *n* 嘔 oh

voracious *a.* 大食嘅 dai sik geh

votary *n.* 信徒 sun tow

vote *n.* 選舉 shoon guy

vote *v.i.* 投票 tow piew

voter *n.* 投票人 tow piew yan

vouch *v.i.* 擔保 dam bow

voucher *n.* 優惠券 yow way goon

vouchsafe *v.t.* 允許 wan huy

vow *n.* 承諾 sing lok

vow *v.t.* 許下諾言 huy ha lok yeen

vowel *n.* 元音 yoon yam

voyage *n.* 航行 horng hang

voyage *v.i.* 遠行 yoon hang

voyager *n.* 航行者 horng hang jeh

vulgar *a.* 粗魯嘅 cho low geh

vulgarity *n.* 粗魯 cho low

vulnerable *a.* 脆弱 chuy yeurk

vulture *n.* 禿鷲 tuk jow

W

wade *v.i.* 跋涉 pa seep

waddle *v.i.* 搖擺 yiew bai

waft *v.t.* 漂蕩 piew dorng

waft *n* 一股 yat gu

wag *v.i.* 搖 yiew

wag *n* 搖擺 yiew bai

wage *v.t.* 發動 fat dung

wage *n.* 糧 leurng

wager *n.* 打賭 da dow

wager *v.i.* 打賭 da dow

wagon *n.* 馬車 ma cher

wail *v.i.* 痛哭 tung huk

wail *n* 尖叫聲 jeem giew seng

wain *n.* 運貨馬車 wan for ma cher

waist *n.* 腰 yiew

waistband *n.* 腰頭 yiew tow

waistcoat *n.* 背心 bwuy sam

wait *v.i.* 等 dang

wait *n.* 等 dang

waiter *n.* 侍應 see ying

waitress *n.* 女侍應 luy see ying

waive *v.t.* 放棄 forng hay

wake *v.t.* 醒 seng

wake *n* 守靈 sow ling

wake *n* 船跡 shoon jik

wakeful *a.* 失眠 sat meen

walk *v.i.* 行 han

walk *n* 散步 san bo

wall *n.* 牆 cheurng
wall *v.t.* 圍住 way ju
wallet *n.* 銀包 an bao
wallop *v.t.* 猛擊 mang gik
wallow *v.i.* 翻滾 fan gwun
walnut *n.* 核桃 hat tow
walrus *n.* 海象 hoy jeurng
wan *a.* 憔悴 tiew suy
wand *n.* 魔法棒 mor fat pang
wander *v.i.* 遊蕩 yow dorng
wane *v.i.* 衰落 suy lok
wane *n* 變細 been say
want *v.t.* 想要 seurng yiew
want *n* 想要 seurng yiew
wanton *a.* 惡意嘅 ok yee geh
war *n.* 仗 jeurng
war *v.i.* 對抗 duy korng
warble *v.i.* 唱 cheurng
warble *n* 鳥鳴 liew ming
warbler *n.* 鶯 ang
ward *n.* 病房 beng forng
ward *v.t.* 防止 forng jee
warden *n.* 管理人 gwun lay yan
warder *n.* 守衛 sow way
wardrobe *n.* 衣櫃 yee gway
wardship *n.* 監護 gam wu
ware *n.* 物品 mat ban
warehouse *v.t* 倉庫 chorngfu
warfare *n.* 戰爭 jeen jang
warlike *a.* 好戰嘅 ho jeen geh
warm *a.* 暖 loon
warm *v.t.* 暖返 loon fan
warmth *n.* 溫暖 wan look
warn *v.t.* 警告 ging gow
warning *n.* 警告 ging gow
warrant *n.* 執行令 jap hang ling
warrant *v.t.* 保證 bo jing
warrantee *n.* 被保證人 bay bo jing yn
warrantor *n.* 保證人 bo jing yan
warranty *n.* 保養期 bo yeurng kay

warren *n.* 養兔場 yeurng tow cheurng
warrior *n.* 武士 mo see
wart *n.* 疣 yow
wary *a.* 謹慎 gan san
wash *v.t.* 洗 say
wash *n* 洗 say
washable *a.* 可以洗嘅 hor yi say geh
washer *n.* 洗衣機 say yee gey
wasp *n.* 黃蜂 worng fung
waspish *a.* 暴躁嘅 bo cho geh
wassail *n.* 酒宴 jow yeem
wastage *n.* 損耗 shoon ho
waste *a.* 無用嘅 mo yung geh
waste *n.* 垃圾 lap sap
waste *v.t.* 嘥 sai
wasteful *a.* 浪費 lorng fay
watch *v.t.* 睇 tay
watch *n.* 手錶 sow biew
watchful *a.* 眼利 ngan lay
watchword *n.* 口號 how ho
water *n.* 水 suy
water *v.t.* 淋水 lam suy
waterfall *n.* 瀑布 buk bo
water-melon *n.* 西瓜 say gwa
waterproof *a.* 防水嘅 forng suy geh
waterproof *n* 防水 forng suy
waterproof *v.t.* 變防水 been forng suy
watertight *a.* 水密嘅 suy mat geh
watery *a.* 似水嘅 tee suy geh
watt *n.* 瓦 ngar
wave *n.* 海浪 hoy lorng
wave *v.t.* 揮手 fay sow
waver *v.i.* 動搖 dung yiew
wax *n.* 蠟 lap
wax *v.t.* 打蠟 da lap
way *n.* 路 low
wayfarer *n.* 旅客 luy hak
waylay *v.t.* 攔住 lan ju

wayward *a.* 任性 yam sing	**weighty** *a.* 重 chung
weak *a.* 弱 yeurk	**weir** *n.* 堤壩 tay bar
weaken *v.t. & i* 削弱 seurk yeurk	**weird** *a.* 奇怪 kay gwai
weakling *n.* 弱者 yeurk jeh	**welcome** *a.* 歡迎 fwun ying
weakness *n.* 弱點 yeurk deem	**welcome** *n* 歡迎 fwun ying
weal *n.* 紅腫 hung jung	**welcome** *v.t* 歡迎 fwun ying
wealth *n.* 富裕 fu yu	**weld** *v.t.* 焊接 horn jeep
wealthy *a.* 有錢 yow teen	**weld** *n* 焊接點 horn jeep deem
wean *v.t.* 戒奶 gai lai	**welfare** *n.* 幸福 hang fuk
weapon *n.* 武器 mo hey	**well** *a.* 健康 geen horng
wear *v.t.* 着 jeurk	**well** *adv.* 好 ho
weary *a.* 劼 gwuy	**well** *n.* 水井 suy jeng
weary *v.t. & i* 劼 gwuy	**well** *v.i.* 流出 low chut
weary *a.* 無興趣 mo hing chuy	**wellington** *n.* 膝膠靴 tat gao hur
weary *v.t.* 無興趣 mo hing chuy	**well-known** *a.* 出名 chut meng
weather *n* 天氣 teen hey	**well-read** *a.* 博學 bok hok
weather *v.t.* 變 been	**well-timed** *a.* 及時 kap see
weave *v.t.* 織 jik	**well-to-do** *a.* 有錢 yow teen
weaver *n.* 織布工 jik bo gung	**welt** *n.* 紅腫 hung jung
web *n.* 蜘蛛網 jee ju mong	**welter** *n.* 一大堆 yat dai duy
webby *a.* 網狀嘅 morng jorng geh	**wen** *n.* 粉瘤 fan low
wed *v.t.* 結婚 geet fan	**wench** *n.* 少女 siew luy
wedding *n.* 婚禮 fan lay	**west** *n.* 西 say
wedge *n.* 楔 seet	**west** *a.* 西方嘅 say forng geh
wedge *v.t.* 楔位 seep way	**west** *adv.* 向西 heurng say
wedlock *n.* 婚姻 fan yan	**westerly** *a.* 西方嘅 say forng geh
Wednesday *n.* 星期三 sing kay sam	**westerly** *adv.* 向西嘅 heurng say geh
weed *n.* 雜草 jap cho	**western** *a.* 西方 say forng
weed *v.t.* 請雜草 ting jap cho	**wet** *a.* 濕 sap
week *n.* 禮拜 lay bai	**wet** *v.t.* 濕 sap
weekly *a.* 每個禮拜嘅 mwuy gor lay bai geh	**wetness** *n.* 濕度 sap dow
weekly *adv.* 每個禮拜 mwuy gor lay bai	**whack** *v.t.* 拍 pak
weekly *n.* 週刊 jow horn	**whale** *n.* 鯨魚 king yu
weep *v.i.* 流淚 low luy	**wharfage** *n.* 碼頭費 ma tow fay
weevil *n.* 象鼻蟲 jeurng bay chung	**what** *a.* 咩 meh
weigh *v.t.* 磅 bong	**what** *pron.* 咩 meh
weight *n.* 體重 tay chung	**what** *interj.* 咩 meh
weightage *n.* 權重 koon chung	**whatever** *pron.* 無論 mo lun
	wheat *n.* 小麥 siew mak
	wheedle *v.t.* 氹 tam
	wheel *a.* 轆 luk

wheel *v.t.* 推 tuy
whelm *v.t.* 淹沒 yeem mwut
whelp *n.* 狗仔 gow jay
when *adv.* 幾時 gey see
when *conj.* 幾時 gey see
whence *adv.* 從邊度 chung been dow
whenever *adv. conj.* 隨時 chuy see
where *adv.* 邊度 been dow
where *conj.* 喺 hay
whereabout *adv.* 喺邊度 hay been dow
whereas *conj.* 而 yee
whereat *conj.* 於是 yu see
wherein *adv.* 喺邊度 hay been dow
whereupon *conj.* 於是 yu see
wherever *adv.* 邊度 been dow
whet *v.t.* 增強興趣 jang keurng hing chuy
whether *conj.* 無論...定係 mo lun...ding hay
which *pron.* 邊個 been gor
which *a* 邊個 been gor
whichever *pron* 無論邊個 mo lun been gor
whiff *n.* 少少味 siew siew may
while *n.* 一陣 yat jan
while *conj.* 當...嘅時候 dong...geh see ho
while *v.t.* 消磨時間 siew mor see gan
whim *n.* 心血來潮 sam hoot loy tiew
whimper *v.i.* 抽泣 chow yap
whimsical *a.* 異想天開嘅 yee seurng teen hoy geh
whine *v.i.* 發牢騷 fat low sow
whine *n* 喊聲 ham seng
whip *v.t.* 鞭打 been da
whip *n.* 鞭 been

whipcord *n.* 鞭 been
whir *n.* 嗡嗡聲 wung wung seng
whirl *n.i.* 轉 joon
whirl *n* 旋轉 shoon joon
whirligig *n.* 旋轉木馬 shoon joon muk ma
whirlpool *n.* 旋渦 shoon wor
whirlwind *n.* 旋風 shoon fung
whisk *v.t.* 發 fat
whisk *n* 攪機 gao gey
whisker *n.* 鬚 sow
whisky *n.* 威士忌 way see gey
whisper *v.t.* 耳邊講 yee been gorng
whisper *n* 細聲講 say seng gorng
whistle *v.i.* 吹口哨 chuy ho sao
whistle *n* 口哨 ho sao
white *a.* 白色嘅 bak sik geh
white *n* 白色 bak sik
whiten *v.t.* 變白 been bak
whitewash *n.* 石灰水 sek fwuy suy
whitewash *v.t.* 掩飾 yeem sik
whither *adv.* 到邊度 dow been dow
whitish *a.* 白白嘅 bak bak geh
whittle *v.t.* 雕 diew
whiz *v.i.* 掠過 leurk gwor
who *pron.* 邊個 been gor
whoever *pron.* 邊個 been gor
whole *a.* 全部 choon bo
whole *n* 整個 jing gor
whole-hearted *a.* 全心全意 choon sam choon yee
wholesale *n.* 批發 pay fat
wholesale *a* 批發 pay fat
wholesale *adv.* 批發 pay fat
wholesaler *n.* 批發商 pay fat seurng
wholesome *a.* 有益 yow yik
wholly *adv.* 完全 yoon choon
whom *pron.* 邊個 been gor

whore *n.* 妓女 gey luy	**windlass** *v.t.* 降低 gorng day
whose *pron.* 邊個嘅 been gor geh	**windmill** *n.* 風車 fung ter
why *adv.* 點解 deem gai	**window** *n.* 窗 cheurng
wick *n.* 燭芯 juk sam	**windy** *a.* 大風 dai fung
wicked *a.* 邪惡嘅 ter ok geh	**wine** *n.* 酒 jow
wicker *n.* 柳條 low tiew	**wing** *n.* 翼 yik
wicket *n.* 板球 ban kow	**wink** *v.i.* 眨眼 jam ngan
wide *a.* 闊 fwut	**wink** *n* 眼色 ngan sik
wide *adv.* 闊 fwut	**winner** *n.* 贏家 yeng ga
widen *v.t.* 整闊 jing fwut	**winnow** *v.t.* 篩選 撒野shoon
widespread *a.* 普遍 po poeen	**winsome** *a.* 有魅力 yow may lik
widow *n.* 寡婦 gwa fu	**winter** *n.* 冬天 dung teen
widow *v.t.* 喪偶 song ow	**winter** *v.i* 過冬 gwor dung
widower *n.* 寡佬 gwa low	**wintry** *a.* 寒冷嘅 hon lang geh
width *n.* 闊度 fwut dow	**wipe** *v.t.* 抹 mat
wield *v.t.* 運用 wan yung	**wipe** *n.* 濕紙巾 sap jee gan
wife *n.* 老婆 lo por	**wire** *n.* 電線 deen seen
wig *n.* 假髮 ga fat	**wire** *v.t.* 接駁電線 jeep bok deen
wight *n.* 生物 sang mat	seen
wigwam *n.* 棚屋 pang uk	**wireless** *a.* 無線 mo seen
wild *a.* 野生嘅 yeh sang geh	**wireless** *n* 無線 mo seen
wilderness *n.* 荒野 forng yeh	**wiring** *n.* 線路 seen low
wile *n.* 詭計 gway gey	**wisdom** *n.* 智慧 jee way
will *n.* 遺囑 way juk	**wisdom-tooth** *n.* 智慧齒 jee way
will *v.t.* 會 wuy	tee
willing *a.* 樂意 lok yee	**wise** *a.* 有智慧 yow jee wey
willingness *n.* 自願 jee yoon	**wish** *n.* 願望 yoon mong
willow *n.* 柳樹 low shu	**wish** *v.t.* 許願 huy yoon
wily *a.* 狡猾嘅 gao wat geh	**wishful** *a.* 渴望嘅 hot morng geh
wimble *n.* 手搖鑽 sow yiew joon	**wisp** *n.* 一細紮 yat say jat
wimple *n.* 頭巾 tow gan	**wistful** *a.* 傷感 seurng gam
win *v.t.* 贏 yeng	**wit** *n.* 智慧 jee way
win *n* 贏 yeng	**witch** *n.* 女巫 luy mo
wince *v.i.* 畏縮 way suk	**witchcraft** *n.* 魔法 mor fat
winch *n.* 絞車 gao cher	**witchery** *n.* 巫術 mo sut
wind *n.* 風 fung	**with** *prep.* 同 tung
wind *v.t.* 上鏈 seurng leen	**withal** *adv.* 而且 yee ter
wind *v.t.* 環繞 wan yiew	**withdraw** *v.t.* 退出 tuy chut
windbag *n.* 多嘢講嘅人 dor yeh	**withdrawal** *n.* 退出 tuy chut
gorng geh yan	**withe** *n.* 枝 jee
winder *n.* 上鏈柄 seurng leen	**wither** *v.i.* 凋謝 diew jeh
beng	**withhold** *v.t.* 抑壓 yik at

within *prep.* 之內 jee loy	**word** *v.t* 話太多 wah tai dor
within *adv.* 裡面 luy meen	**wordy** *a.* 話太多 wah tai dor
within *n.* 入邊 yap been	**work** *n.* 工作 gung jok
without *prep.* 缺乏 koot fat	**work** *v.t.* 做嘢 jow yeh
without *adv.* 無 mo	**workable** *a.* 可行嘅 hor hang geh
without *n* 出邊 chut been	**workaday** *a.* 普通嘅 po tung geh
withstand *v.t.* 頂住 ding ju	**worker** *n.* 工人 gung yan
witless *a.* 唔明白事理 hm ming bak see lay	**workman** *n.* 工匠 gung jeurng
	workmanship *n.* 手藝 sow ngay
witness *n.* 目擊證人 muk gik ting yan	**workshop** *n.* 工場 gung cheurng
	world *n.* 世界 sey gai
witness *v.i.* 目擊 muk gik	**worldling** *n.* 俗人 juk yan
witticism *n.* 妙語 miew yu	**worldly** *a.* 世事嘅 sai see geh
witty *a.* 機智 gey jee	**worm** *n.* 蚯蚓 yow yan
wizard *n.* 魔法師 mor fat see	**wormwood** *n.* 蒿 ho
wobble *v.i* 搖 yiew	**worn** *a.* 殘晒 tan sai
woe *n.* 痛苦 tung fu	**worry** *n.* 擔憂 dam yow
woebegone *a.* 悲傷 bay seurng	**worry** *v.i.* 擔心 dam sam
woeful *n.* 悲哀 bay ngoy	**worsen** *v.t.* 變得更壞 been dak gang wai
wolf *n.* 狼 long	
woman *n.* 女人 luy yan	**worship** *n.* 信奉 sun fung
womanhood *n.* 女人 luy yan	**worship** *v.t.* 拜 bai
womanish *n.* 女人嘅 luy yan geh	**worshipper** *n.* 崇拜者 sun bai jeh
womanise *v.t.* 女性化 luy sing far	**worst** *n.* 最壞 juy wai
womb *n.* 子宮 jee gung	**worst** *a* 最壞嘅 juy wai geh
wonder *n* 驚訝 ging ngar	**worst** *v.t.* 戰勝 jeen sing
wonder *v.i.* 想知 seurng jee	**worsted** *n.* 精紡毛料 jing forng mo liew
wonderful *a.* 好好嘅 ho ho geh	
wondrous *a.* 奇異咗 kay yee geh	**worth** *n.* 價值 gah jik
wont *a.* 習慣咗 jap gwan jor	**worth** *a* 值得 jik dak
wont *n* 習慣 jap gwan	**worthless** *a.* 唔值得 hm jik dak
wonted *a.* 習慣嘅 jap gwan geh	**worthy** *a.* 值得 jik dak
woo *v.t.* 追求 juy kow	**would-be** *a.* 未來 may loy
wood *n.* 木 muk	**wound** *n.* 傷 seurng
woods *n.* 樹林 shu lam	**wound** *v.t.* 傷害 seurng hoy
wooden *a.* 木造嘅 muk jow geh	**wrack** *n.* 破壞 por wai
woodland *n.* 樹林 shu lam	**wraith** *n.* 鬼魂 gway wan
woof *n.* 狗吠聲 gow fay seng	**wrangle** *v.i.* 嘈 cho
wool *n.* 毛冷 mo larn	**wrangle** *n.* 爭論 jang lun
woollen *a.* 毛嘅 mo geh	**wrap** *v.t.* 包 bao
woollen *n* 冷衫 larn sam	**wrap** *n* 包裝料 bao jorng liew
word *n.* 字 jee	**wrapper** *n.* 包裝紙 bao jorng jee

wrath *n.* 怒火 low for
wreath *n.* 花圈 far hoon
wreathe *v.t.* 圍繞 way yiew
wreck *n.* 沈船 tam shoon
wreck *v.t.* 破壞 por wai
wreckage *n.* 殘骸 tan hai
wrecker *n.* 破壞者 por wai jeh
wren *n.* 鷦鷯 jiew liew
wrench *n.* 扳鉗 ban keem
wrench *v.t.* 大力擰 dai lik ling
wrest *v.t.* 搶 cheurng
wrestle *v.i.* 摔跤 sut gao
wrestler *n.* 摔跤選手 sut gao shoonsow
wretch *n.* 不幸嘅人 bat hang geh yan
wretched *a.* 難受 larn sow
wrick *n* 扭傷 low seurng
wriggle *v.i.* 扭嚟扭去 low lay low huy
wriggle *n* 扭動 low dung
wring *v.t* 擰出 ling chut
wrinkle *n.* 皺紋 jow man
wrinkle *v.t.* 皺 jow
wrist *n.* 手腕 sow wun
writ *n.* 書面命令 shu meen ming ling
write *v.t.* 寫 ser
writer *n.* 作者 jok jeh
writhe *v.i.* 扭動 low dung
wrong *a.* 錯嘅 chor geh
wrong *adv.* 錯嘅 chor geh
wrong *v.t.* 唔公正 hm gung jing
wrongful *a.* 唔正當嘅 hm jing dong geh
wry *a.* 諷刺 fung tee

X

xerox *n.* 影印機 ying yan gey
xerox *v.t.* 複印 fuk yan
Xmas *n.* 聖誕節 sing dan jeet
x-ray *n.* X光 ex gwong
x-ray *a.* X光嘅 ex gwong geh
x-ray *v.t.* X光檢查 ex gwong geem ta
xylophagous *a.* 蝕木嘅 sik muk geh
xylophilous *a.* 木生嘅 muk sang geh
xylophone *n.* 木琴 muk kam

Y

yacht *n.* 遊艇 yow teng
yacht *v.i* 揸遊艇 ja yow teng
yak *n.* 犛牛 mo ngow
yap *v.i.* 講嘢 gorng yeh
yap *n* 狗吠聲 gow fay seng
yard *n.* 碼 ma
yarn *n.* 冷線 larn seen
yawn *v.i.* 打喊路 da ham low
yawn *n.* 喊路 ham low
year *n.* 年 leen
yearly *a.* 每年嘅 mwuy leen geh
yearly *adv.* 一年一度嘅 yat leen yat dow geh
yearn *v.i.* 渴望 hot morng
yearning *n.* 渴望 hot morng
yeast *n.* 酵母菌 hao mo kwan
yell *v.i.* 嗌 ai

yell *n* 嗌 ai
yellow *a.* 黃色嘅 wong sik geh
yellow *n* 黃色 wong sik
yellow *v.t.* 變黃 been wong
yellowish *a.* 黃黃地 wong wong day
Yen *n.* 日元 yat yoon
yeoman *n.* 自由民 jee yow man
yes *adv.* 係 hay
yesterday *n.* 尋日 tam yat
yesterday *adv.* 尋日 tam yat
yet *adv.* 仲 jung
yet *conj.* 但係 dan hay
yield *v.t.* 屈服 wat fuk
yield *n* 產量 tan leurng
yoke *n.* 軛 ak
yoke *v.t.* 上軛 seurng ak
yolk *n.* 蛋黃 dan worng
yonder *a.* 嗰邊 gor been
yonder *adv.* 嗰邊 gor been
young *a.* 後生 ho sang
young *n* 青年人 ting leen yan
youngster *n.* 細路仔 say low jay
youth *n.* 少年 siew leen
youthful *a.* 後生嘅 ho sang geh

zephyr *n.* 微風 may fung
zero *n.* 零 ling
zest *n.* 熱情 yeet ting
zigzag *n.* 彎曲 wan kuk
zigzag *a.* 鋸齒形 guy chee ying
zigzag *v.i.* 曲折前進 kuk jeet teen jun
zinc *n.* 鋅 san
zip *n.* 拉鍊 lai leen
zip *v.t.* 拉 lai
zodiac *n* 生肖 sang chiew
zonal *a.* 區域嘅… kuy wik geh
zone *n.* 地區 day kuy
zoo *n.* 動物園 dung mat yoon
zoological *a.* 動物學嘅 dung mat hok geh
zoologist *n.* 動物學家 dung mat hok ga
zoology *n.* 動物學 dung mat hok
zoom *n.* 縮放 suk fong
zoom *v.i.* 快速 fai chuk

Z

zany *a.* 古怪嘅 gu gwai geh
zeal *n.* 熱情 yeet ting
zealot *n.* 發燒友 fat siew yow
zealous *a.* 熱情嘅 yeet ting geh
zebra *n.* 斑馬 ban ma
zenith *n.* 頂峰 ding fung

CANTONESE-ENGLISH

A

ah ay shu jee 阿魏樹脂 *n. asafoetida*
ah mun 阿門 *interj. amen*
ah suk 阿叔 *n. uncle*
ah yee fat 阿爾法 *n alpha*
ai 拗 *v. t bicker*
ai 挨 *v.i. lean*
ai 嗌 *v.i. yell*
ai 嗌 *n yell*
ai gao 嗌交 *v. t brangle*
ai man 挨晚 *n evening*
ai or 挨餓 *v.i. starve*
ai sap 嗌嚊 *n. quarrel*
ai sap 嗌嚊 *n. quibble*
ai sap 嗌嚊 *v.i. quibble*
ai seng tan hay 唉聲嘆氣 *n. sigh*
ai seng tan hay 唉聲嘆氣 *v.i. sigh*
ai yan 矮人 *n dwarf*
ak 呃 *v. t beguile*
ak 呃 *v. t. bilk*
ak 呃 *v. t deceive*
ak 呃 *v.t gull*
ak 呃 *v.t. hoodwink*
ak 呃 *v.t. rook*
ak 呃 *v.t. swindle*
ak 呃 *n. swindle*
ak 呃 *v.t. trick*
ak 軛 *n. yoke*
ak fat 額髮 *n forelock*
ak ngoy 額外 *adv extra*
ak ngoy geh 額外嘅 *a extra*
ak ngoy geh 額外嘅 *a. supplementary*
ak tow 額頭 *n brow*
ak tow 額頭 *n forehead*
ak wan 厄運 *n doom*
ak yan 呃人 *n deceit*
am 暗 *a dim*
am am seng 喃喃聲 *n. murmur*
am chun 鵪鶉 *n. quail*
am day luy 暗地裡 *adv. stealthily*
am gwong 暗光 *n glow*
am ho 暗號 *n. cipher, cipher*
am jee 暗指 *a. allusive*
am low 暗流 *n. undercurrent*
am san 啱身 *v.t fit*
am see 暗示 *v.i. allude*
am see 暗示 *n allusion*
am see 暗示 *v.i hint*
am see 暗示 *v.t. imply*
am see 暗示 *v.t. insinuate*
am see 暗示 *v.t. intimate*
am see 暗示 *n. intimation*
am see geh 暗示嘅 *a. suggestive*
am yu 暗喻 *n. metaphor*
an bao 銀包 *n. wallet*
an hong 銀行 *n. bank*
an hong ga 銀行家 *n. banker*
an horng dan 銀行單 *n. statement*
an jai 銀仔 *n coin*
ang 鶯 *n. warbler*
ang bay 硬幣 *n coinage*
ang far 硬化 *v.t. harden*
ang geng 硬頸 *a. headstrong*
ang lorn 硬朗 *a. hale*
ao 咬 *v. t. bite*
ap 鴨 *n. duck*
arp giew seng 鴨叫聲 *n quack*
at 壓 *v. t crush*
at 呃 *n.t. delude*
at ho 押後 *v.t. adjourn*
at mo 壓模 *n die*
at suk 壓縮 *v. t. compress*
at suk 壓縮 *v. t condense*
at suk geh 壓縮嘅 *a. compact*
at tow wan 押頭韻 *v.t. alliterate*
at tow wan 押頭韻 *n. alliteration*
ay 唉 *interj. alas*
ay 蟻 *n ant*
ay gao 嗌交 *v.t. argue*
ay jow 偽造 *a. counterfeit*

ay jow jeh 僞造者 n. counterfeiter
ay lam 矮林 n. coppice

B

B B B B n. baby
ba dow 霸道 a. aggressive
ba gung 罷工 n stoppage
ba gung 罷工 n strike
ba han 疤痕 n scar
ba luy mo 芭蕾舞 sn. ballet
ba meen 罷免 v. t depose
ba meen 罷免 v. t dethrone
ba meen 罷免 v.t. oust
ba sam 靶心 n bull's eye
ba see 巴士 n bus
bai 擺 v.t. place
bai 擺 v.t. position
bai 擺 v.t. put
bai 拜 v.t. worship
bai bai 拜拜 interj. bye-bye
bai dung 擺動 n. oscillation
bai ga geh 敗家嘅 a. prodigal
bai jee say 擺姿勢 v.i. pose
bai ping 擺平 v. t even
bak 北 n. north
bak bak geh 白白嘅 a. whitish
bak fan jee 百分之 adv. per cent
bak fan lut 百分率 n. percentage
bak for choon shu 百科全書 n. encyclopaedia
bak forng geh 北方嘅 a north
bak forng geh 北方嘅 a. northerly
bak forng geh 北方嘅 a. northern
bak fung 北風 n. northerly
bak gap 白鴿 n. pigeon
bak gik sing 北極星 n. loadstar
bak gwat ding 白骨頂 n. coot
bak hap far 百合花 n. lily

bak jeurk fu yan 伯爵夫人 n. countess
bak lan day 白蘭地 n brandy
bak lo 白鷺 n aigrette
bak man 百萬 n. million
bak man fu yung 百萬富翁 n. millionaire
bak may yeh ma 北美野馬 n. mustang
bak pwuy 百倍 n. & adj centuple
bak sik 白色 n white
bak sik geh 白色嘅 a. white
bak tee 白癡 n. idiot
bak wan mow 白雲母 n. muscovite
ban 板 n board
ban 班 n class
ban 版 n edition
ban 扮 v.t feign
ban 頒 v.t. present
ban 班 n shift
ban ban yow lay geh 彬彬有禮嘅 a. urbane
ban bwun 版本 n. version
ban dak gow 品德高 a. virtuous
ban deem 斑點 n. mottle
ban deem 斑點 n. spot
ban gak go seurng 品加高尚 a. honourable
ban gey 班機 n flight
ban gey 板機 n. trigger
ban gung sat geh 辦公室嘅 a clerical
ban jeurk kam 班卓琴 n. banjo
ban jung 品種 n breed
ban keem 扳鉗 n. wrench
ban kow 板球 n cricket
ban kow 板球 n. wicket
ban lay 辦理 v.t. transact
ban long shu 檳榔樹 n areca
ban long yeep 檳榔葉 n betel
ban ma 斑馬 n. zebra
ban pao 奔跑 v.t. gallop
ban pao 奔跑 n scamper

ban sai yeh 扮晒嘢 n affectation
ban sai yeh 扮晒嘢 v.t. patronize
ban seurng 品嘗 v.t. savour
ban sow ban geurt 笨手笨腳 a. ungainly
ban tan seurng hon 斑疹傷寒 n. typhus
ban tiew 板條 n. lath
ban tiew seurng 板條箱 n. crate
bang dai 繃帶 ~n. bandage
bao 爆 v. i. burst
bao 包 v. t envelop
bao 包 v.t. parcel
bao 爆 v.i. pop
bao 包 v.t. wrap
bao 包 n bundle
bao fat 爆發 v. i erupt
bao fat 爆發 n eruption
bao fat 爆發 n. outbreak
bao fat 爆發 n. outburst
bao fuk 包袱 n burden
bao gwor 包裹 n. package
bao gwor 包裹 n. parcel
bao ham 包含 v. i consist
bao ham 包含 v. t encompass
bao ja 爆炸 n blast
bao ja 爆炸 v. t. explode
bao ja 爆炸 n. explosion
bao ja sing 爆炸性 a explosive
bao jat 包紮 v.t bandage
bao jorng 包裝 n. packing
bao jorng jee 包裝紙 n. wrapper
bao jorng liew 包裝料 n wrap
bao kwut 包括 v.t. include
bao kwut 包括 n. inclusion
bao kwut 包括 a. inclusive
bao liew 爆料 v. t divulge
bao por 爆破 n burst
bao tow gan 包頭巾 n. turban
bao way 包圍 n. siege
bao wor dow 飽和度 n. saturation
barn jeurng 頒獎 v.t. award

bat 八 n eight
bat 不 v.t. ladle
bat 筆 n. pen
bat 不 v.t. spoon
bat cheurng geh 不祥嘅 a. inauspicious
bat chut 拔出 v.t. unsheathe
bat doon geh 不斷嘅 a continuous
bat doon geh 不斷嘅 a. perpetual
bat dorng 不當 a. injudicious
bat dow 八度 n. octave
bat dow dak 不道德 a. immoral
bat dow dak geh 不道德嘅 a. unprincipled
bat fat hang way 不法行為 n. malpractice
bat fat jee tow 不法之徒 n. miscreant
bat fu jak yam 不負責任 a. irresponsible
bat ga shoon jak 不加選擇 a. indiscriminate
bat gey 嗶嘰 n. serge
bat gey how gwor 不計後果 a. reckless
bat gik 北極 n Arctic
bat ging 不敬 a. impertinent
bat gok ying 八角形 n. octagon
bat gok ying geh 八角形嘅 a. octagonal
bat gowr 不過 conj. nevertheless
bat gwa 八卦 a. inquisitive
bat gwa 八卦 a. nosey
bat gwa 八卦 a. nosy
bat gwor 不過 conj. but
bat gwor 不過 adv. however
bat gwor 不過 conj. notwithstanding
bat gwor 不過 conj. only
bat gwor 不過 adv. though
bat han 不幸 a. unfortunate
bat hang 不幸 n. mischance
bat hang 不幸 n. misfortune

bat hang 不幸 n. mishap

bat hang geh jow yu 不幸嘅遭遇 n. misadventure

bat hang geh yan 不幸嘅人 n. wretch

bat hor gow yan geh 不可告人嘅 a. ulterior

bat hor koot fat geh 不可缺乏嘅 a. indispensable

bat hor tam fan 不可侵犯 a. inviolable

bat jeem 筆尖 n. nib

bat joy cheurng jing guy 不在場證據 n. alibi

bat kap mat 不及物 a. (verb) intransitive

bat lay 不利 a adverse

bat lay 不利 a. inimical

bat lay yan so 不利因素 n disadvantage

bat meng 筆名 n. pseudonym

bat mun 不滿 n discontent

bat mun 不滿 n displeasure

bat mun 不滿 n dissatisfaction

bat ngar hang way 不雅行為 n. indecency

bat on 不安 n disquiet

bat sap 八十 n eighty

bat say geh 不死嘅 a. immortal

bat say geh 不死嘅 a. imperishable

bat sing yan see 不省人事 n. insensibility

bat sun low yan 八旬老人 a. octogenarian

bat teet sat jay 不切實際 a. utopian

bat teet sat jay geh 不切實際嘅 a. impracticable

bat ting geh 不停嘅 ~a. ceaseless

bat tug luy ying 不同類型 n. variety

bat tung geh 不同嘅 a dissimilar

bat tung geh 不同嘅 a. varied

bat yan 不孕 n. sterility

bat yee jee choy 不義之財 n. pelf

bat yeep 畢業 v.i. graduate

bat yeep sang 畢業生 n graduate

bat yoot 八月 n. August

bat yuk 不育 n barren

bay 跛 n cripple

bay 避 v. t dodge

bay 畀 prep for

bay 畀 v.t. give

bay 畀 v.t. grant

bay 畀 v.t hand

bay 跛 a. lame

bay 畀 v.t. let

bay 比 v.t. liken

bay 鼻 n. nostril

bay bo jing yn 被保證人 n. warrantee

bay bo sik geh 畀保釋嘅 a. bailable

bay choon 臂釧 a armlet

bay choy 比賽 n. competition

bay choy 比賽 n. contest

bay choy 比賽 n. match

bay choy 比賽 v.i race

bay dak seurng 比得上 v.t. rival

bay dung geh 被動嘅 a. passive

bay forng 祕方 n. nostrum

bay ga ho gung 畀假口供 v.i. perjure

bay gao 比較 v. t compare

bay gao 比較 n comparison

bay gao jung yee 比較鐘意 v.t favour

bay gao jung yee 比較鐘意 v.t. prefer

bay gao say geh 比較細嘅 a. minor

bay gao siew 比較少 a. less

bay gao siew 比較少 adv. less

bay garm gum 被監禁 a. captive

bay geh 鼻嘅 a. nasal

bay go 被告 n defendant

bay gor 鼻哥 n. nose

bay gwun 悲觀 n. pessimism

bay gwun geh 悲觀嘅 a. pessimistic

bay gwun geh yan 悲觀嘅人 n. pessimist

bay ha 陛下 n. majesty

bay horn seng 鼻鼾聲 n snore

bay hoy 避開 v.t. avoid

bay hoy 避開 n. avoidance

bay hoy 避開 v. t elude

bay hoy 避開 v. t evade

bay hoy 避開 v.t. shun

bay jan jing jay 畀鎮靜劑 v.t. sedate

bay jeen geh 卑賤嘅 a. menial

bay juy jow geh 被詛咒嘅 a. accursed

bay kap yan dow 被吸引到 v.i. gravitate

bay kek 悲劇 n. tragedy

bay kek jok ga 悲劇作家 n. tragedian

bay lan 避難 n. refuge

bay lan sor 避難所 n. haven

bay lay 比例 n. proportion

bay ma yow 蓖麻油 n. castor oil

bay man 碑文 n epitaph

bay mat geh 秘密嘅 adj. clandestine

bay mat geh 祕密嘅 a. secret

bay mat geh 祕密嘅 a. underhand

bay may 卑微 n. lowliness

bay may 祕密 n. secret

bay meen 避免 v.t. avert

bay morng luk 備忘錄 n memorandum

bay ngoy 悲哀 n. woeful

bay pai tik jeh 被排斥者 n. outcast

bay pay 卑鄙 a. base

bay pay 卑鄙 a despicable

bay pay 卑鄙 n. meanness

bay pay 卑鄙 a. sordid

bay pwun mow juy 被判無罪 n. acquittal

bay seurng 悲傷 n. lamentation

bay seurng 悲傷 n. sorrow

bay seurng 悲傷 v.i. sorrow

bay seurng 悲傷 a. woebegone

bay shu 秘書 n. secretary

bay shu chu 秘書處 n. secretariat (e)

bay sing sow 被乘數 n. multiplicand

bay sow 匕首 n. dagger

bay tan 悲歎 n lament

bay tarm 悲慘 n. poignancy

bay tarm geh 悲慘嘅 a. tragic

bay tay ming yan 被提名人 n nominee

bay teep see 畀貼士 v.t. tip

bay toot 擺脫 v.t. rid

bay tung 悲痛 n. grief

bay wu sor 庇護所 n. lee

bay wu sor 庇護所 n. sanctuary

bay yam 鼻音 n nasal

bay yan 避孕 n. contraception

bay yan gow 被人告 n. accused

bay yan tao geh 畀人炒嘅 a. redundant

bay yee geen 畀意見 v.t. advise

bay yeem 鼻煙 n. snuff

bay ying way 被認爲 v. t constitute

bay yu geh 比如嘅 a figurative

bay yung bam 備用品 n. spare

bay...cheurng meng 比...長命 v.i. outlive

bee bee cher BB車 n. perambulator

been 邊 n edge

been 變 v.t. range

been 變 v.t. weather

been 鞭 n. whip

been 鞭 n. whipcord

been am 變暗 v. t dim

been bak 變白 v. t. & i blanch

been bak 變白 v.i. pale

been bak 變白 v.t. whiten

been bay 便秘 n. constipation

been da 鞭打 n lash

been da 鞭打 v.t. whip

been dai darm 變大膽 v. t. embolden

been dak 變得 v.t. render

been dak gang wai 變得更壞 *v.t. worsen*

been dak sik hap yan 變得適合人 *v.t. humanize*

been dow 扁豆 *n. lentil*

been dow 邊度 *adv. where*

been dow 邊度 *adv. wherever*

been far 變化 *n. mutation*

been far 變化 *n. transformation*

been far 變化 *n. variation*

been far geh 變化嘅 *a. mutative*

been forng lut see 辯方律師 *n advocate*

been forng suy 變防水 *v.t. waterproof*

been fung fu 變豐富 *v. t enrich*

been ga 貶價 *v.t. depredate*

been gai 邊界 *n border*

been gai 邊界 *n boundary*

been gai 邊界 *n. frontier*

been geet sat 變結實 *v.t. tone*

been geurng ang 變僵硬 *v.t. stiffen*

been gor 邊個 *pron. which*

been gor 邊個 *a which*

been gor 邊個 *pron. who*

been gor 邊個 *pron. whoever*

been gor 邊個 *pron. whom*

been gor geh 邊個嘅 *pron. whose*

been gwong dee 變光啲 *v. t brighten*

been hap fat 變合法 *v.t. legalize*

been ho sang 變後生 *v.t. rejuvenate*

been hung 變紅 *v.t. redden*

been huy yeurk 變虛弱 *v. t. enfeeble*

been huy yeurk 變虛弱 *v.t. sap*

been jak 變窄 *v.t. straiten*

been jak 變窄 *v.i. taper*

been jat 變質 *n. metamorphosis*

been jiew tan 變焦炭 *v. t coke*

been kung 變窮 *v.t. depauperate*

been kung 變窮 *v.t. impoverish*

been lang 變冷 *v.t. refrigerate*

been leurng 變涼 *v. i. cool*

been mar muk 變麻木 *v. t. dull*

been mor sut 變魔術 *v.i. conjure*

been mow hao 變無效 *v.t. neutralize*

been mow hao 變無效 *v.t. void*

been mow wu 變模糊 *v.t. obscure*

been on jing 變安靜 *n hush*

been on jing 變安靜 *v.t. silence*

been ping 變平 *v.t. level*

been ping dang 變平等 *v. t. equalize*

been ping jing 變平靜 *v.t. still*

been ping jing 變平靜 *v.t. tranquillize*

been say 變細 *n wane*

been see 便士 *n. penny*

been siew 變少 *v.t lessen*

been sing 變成 *v. i become*

been sing bat yiew geh 變成必要嘅 *v.t. necessitate*

been tai 變態 *n. perversion*

been tak 鞭策 *v.t. spur*

been tan 變癱 *v.t. paralyse*

been tan fay 變殘廢 *v.t. mutilate*

been teen 變遷 *n. vicissitude*

been ting chor 變清楚 *v. i. dawn*

been tow tay 扁桃體 *n. tonsil*

been wan mok tak 變幻莫測 *a. mercurial*

been wan wor 變溫和 *v.t. temper*

been way fay fat 變爲非法 *v.t outlaw*

been way say pwuy 變爲四倍 *v.t. quadruple*

been wong 變黃 *v.t. yellow*

been wut yeurk 變活躍 *a. animate*

been ying 辨認 *v.t. identify*

been ying 變形 *n. transfiguration*

been ying 變形 *v.t. transfigure*

been yoon 邊沿 *n brim*

been yoon 邊緣 *n. brink*

been yoon 邊緣 *n. rim*

been yoon 邊緣 *n. verge*

beet suy 必需 *n. must*

beet suy 別墅 *n. villa*

beet suy geh 必需嘅 a essential
beet suy geh 必需嘅 a. integral
beet suy geh 必需嘅 a. prerequisite
beet suy geh 必需嘅 a. requisite
beet suy geh yeh 必需嘅嘢 n requisite
beet suy jun so geh 必需遵守嘅 a binding
beet yiew 必要 n. necessary
beet yiew 必要 n. necessity
beh jow 啤酒 n beer
beh jow chorng 啤酒廠 n brewery
bei yu 比喻 n. analogy
beng 病 n disease
bcng 病 a. ill
beng 病 n ill
beng 病 n. illness
beng 病 n. malady
beng deem 餅店 n bakery
beng duk 病毒 n. virus
beng forng 病房 n. ward
beng gon 餅乾 n biscuit
beng kwan 病菌 n. germ
beng lik 病歷 n anamnesis
beng tai 病態 a. morbid
bcng tai 病態 n morbidity
beng yan 病人 n invalid
beng yan 病人 n patient
biew bak 表白 n confession
biew cheurng 標槍 n. javelin
biew dat 表達 v. t. convey
biew dat 表達 v. t. express
biew dat 表達 v.t. phrase
biew dat yee geen 表達意見 v. i comment
biew deem fu ho 標點符號 n. punctuation
biew gak 表格 n form
biew gak sik 表格式 a. tabular
biew jee 標誌 n. symbol
biew jun 標準 n criterion
biew jun 標準 n. norm

biew jun 標準 n. standard
biew jun gorn sow 標準杆數 n. par
biew meen 表面 a. cosmetic
biew meen 表面 n. surface
biew meen seurng 表面上 adv. outwardly
biew meen sing 表面性 n. superficiality
biew pwun 錶盤 n dialogue
biew see 表示 a. expressive
biew see 表示 a. indicative
biew see 表示 v.t. manifest
biew see 表示 v.t mean
biew see 表示 v.t. signify
biew see 表示 v.t. voice
biew tan 表親 n. cousin
biew tay 標題 n. heading
biew teem 標籤 n. label
biew teem 標籤 v.t. tag
biew ting 表情 n. expression
biew yeem 表現 v. i. behave
biew yeen 表演 v.t. perform
biew yeen 表演 n. show
biew yeen jeh 表演者 n. juggler
biew yeen jeh 表演者 n. performer
biew yeurng 表揚 v. t commend
biew yu pai 標語牌 n. placard
bik gway 壁櫃 n. closet
bik hoy 逼害 v.t. persecute
bik hoy 逼害 n. persecution
bik jan 逼真 n. verisimilitude
bik kan 逼近 v.i. loom
bik kow 壁球 n squash
bik low ga 壁爐架 n. mantel
bik luk geh 碧綠嘅 a. verdant
bik say 逼使 v.t. oblige
bik tan 逼真 n. realism
bik tan geh 逼真嘅 a. realistic
bik wah 壁畫 n. mural
bing 冰 n. ice
bing 冰 a. icy
bing geen 並肩 adv abreast

bing hor 冰河 n. glacier
bing ju 冰柱 n. icicle
bing pao 冰雹 n. hail
bing san 冰山 n. iceberg
bing toon 兵團 n corps
bing ying 兵營 n. barrack
bing ying 兵營 n. cantonment
bo 布 n cloth
bo 補 v.t. patch
bo biew 保鏢 n. bodyguard
bo biew 保鏢 n bouncer
bo bwuy 寶貝 n. babe
bo bwuy 寶貝 n darling
bo cho 暴躁 a fiery
bo cho geh 暴躁嘅 a. waspish
bo choon 保存 v. t conserve
bo choon 保存 v.t. preserve
bo choon 保存 v.t. store
bo choon geh 保存嘅 a. preservative
bo chow fung ho geh 報酬豐厚嘅 a.
  remunerative
bo chu 部署 v.t. deploy
bo chung 補充 v.t. replenish
bo chung 補充 n. supplement
bo chung 補充 v.t. supplement
bo chung mat 補充物 n complement
bo deet 暴跌 v.t. plunge
bo ding 布丁 n. pudding
bo dung 暴動 n. mutiny
bo fan 部份 n. part
bo fan 部份 n. section
bo fan 部份 n. segment
bo fan geh 部份嘅 a. partial
bo fat 步法 n tread
bo fat wu 暴發戶 n. upstart
bo fuk 報復 v.i. retaliate
bo fuk 報復 n. retaliation
bo fuk 報復 n. vengeance
bo fuk geh 報復嘅 a. revengeful
bo fung shoot 暴風雪 n blizzard
bo fung yu 暴風雨 n. storm
bo fung yu 暴風雨 n. tempest

bo ga 報價 n. quotation
bo geh 補嘅 a. tonic
bo gow 報告 v.t. report
bo gow 報告 n. report
bo gow geh 補救嘅 a. remedial
bo gwan 暴君 n despot
bo gwan 暴君 n. tyrant
bo gwun 保管 v.t. keep
bo gwun yan 保管人 n. keeper
bo heem 保險 n. insurance
bo heem fu 保險庫 n. vault
bo heem gong 保險槓 n. bumper
bo heem see 保險絲 n fuse
bo heem seurng 保險箱 n. safe
bo jee 佈置 n. array
bo jee 佈置 v. t deck
bo jee 佈置 v.t. furnish
bo jeurng 保障 n. indemnity
bo jing 保證 n. assurance
bo jing 保證 v.t. assure
bo jing 保證 v. t ensure
bo jing 保證 n. pledge
bo jing 保證 v.t. warrant
bo jing yan 保證人 n. warrantor
bo jorng 寶藏 n. treasure
bo juk geh 部族嘅 a. tribal
bo lam 布冧 n. plum
bo liew 布料 n fabric
bo lik 暴力 n force
bo lik 暴力 n. violence
bo lo 暴露 v. t expose
bo loon geh 保暖嘅 a. thermal
bo luy 堡壘 n bulwark
bo luy 堡壘 n. citadel
bo luy 堡壘 n. fort
bo luy 堡壘 n. stronghold
bo man 暴民 n. mob
bo mat 保密 n. secrecy
bo mun 部門 n department
bo mwun 部門 n. sector
bo mwun 佈滿 v.t. strew
bo on 保安 n. security

bo ping 步兵 *n. infantry*
bo sek 寶石 *n gem*
bo sek 寶石 *n. jewel*
bo seurng 補償 *n. atonement*
bo seurng 布商 *n draper*
bo seurng 補償 *v.t. reimburse*
bo shoon 補選 *n by-election*
bo sik 保釋 *n. bail*
bo sik 保釋 *v. t. bail*
bo sik 捕食 *v.i. prey*
bo so 保守 *a conservative*
bo so dong jee tee jeh 保守黨支持者 *n conservative*
bo sow 報仇 *v.t. avenge*
bo sow 保守 *a. insular*
bo sow 報仇 *v.t. revenge*
bo sow 報仇 *n. revenge*
bo sow geh 保守嘅 *a. reactinary*
bo tee 保持 *v.i. persist*
bo tee 保持 *v.i. remain*
bo tee 保持 *v.t. retain*
bo tee tam mak 保持沈默 *a. mum*
bo worng ju yee jeh 保皇主義者 *n. royalist*
bo wu 保護 *n. preservation*
bo wu 保護 *v.t. protect*
bo wu 保護 *n. protection*
bo wu 保護 *n. safeguard*
bo wu 保護 *v.t. secure*
bo wu 保護 *v.t. shelter*
bo wu geh 保護嘅 *a. protective*
bo wu yan 保護人 *n. protector*
bo yam bo sik 暴飲暴食 *n. gluttony*
bo yeurng 保養 *n. guarantee*
bo yeurng kay 保養期 *n. warranty*
bo ying 報應 *n. nemesis*
bo yu 哺乳 *v.i. lactate*
bo yu luy dung mat 哺乳類動物 *n. mammal*
bok 駁 *v.t. confute*
bok chuy beng gon 薄脆餅乾 *n cracker*

bok dow 搏鬥 *v. i. battle*
bok dow 搏鬥 *n combat1*
bok dung 搏動 *v.i. pulsate*
bok hok 博學 *a. well-read*
bok hor 薄荷 *n. mint*
bok juy 駁嘴 *v.t. retort*
bok juy 駁嘴 *n. retort*
bok mat gwun 博物館 *n. museum*
bok mat hok ga 博物學家 *n. naturalist*
bok mo 薄霧 *n. haze*
bok mow 薄霧 *n. mist*
bok see hok way 博士學位 *n doctorate*
bok shoon 駁船 *n. barge*
bok tow 膊頭 *n. shoulder*
bok wuy 駁回 *v.t. overrule*
bong 綁 *v.t bind*
bong 磅 *v.t. weigh*
bong jor 幫助 *v.t aid*
bong jor 幫助 *v.t. assist*
bong jor 幫助 *n. assistance*
bor 波 *n. ball*
bor 播 *v.t. radio*
bor choy 菠菜 *n. spinach*
bor dung 波動 *v.i. oscillate*
bor jung 播種 *v.t. seed*
bor lay bwuy 玻璃杯 *n. tumbler*
bor lay cheurng 玻璃窗 *n. pane*
bor lay gung yan 玻璃工人 *n. glazier*
bor long 波浪 *n. ripple*
bor lor 菠蘿 *n. pineapple*
bor lorng ying 波浪形 *n. undulation*
borng 幫 *n boost*
borng 幫 *v.t facilitate*
borng 幫 *v.t. help*
borng 綁 *v.t. rope*
borng 綁 *v.t. strap*
borng 幫 *v.t. succour*
borng 綁 *v.t. tie*
borng ga 綁架 *n abduction*

borng jor 幫助 n help
borng jor 幫助 n. succour
bow fung yu geh 暴風雨嘅 a. stormy
bow meng 報名 v.t. subscribe
bow mwun sing sing 佈滿星星 a. starry
bow suk 部屬 n subordinate
bow yeurng 保養 n upkeep
buk bo 瀑布 n. waterfall
buk yan 僕人 n menial
bun hoy 半開 adv. ajar
bung 泵 n. pump
bung 泵 v.t. pump
bung 砰 v.t. slam
bung 砰 n slam
bung bung gam tiew 怦怦咁跳 v.t. pound
bwun 伴 v.t. accompany
bwun 伴 n accomplice
bwun 伴 n. companion
bwun 半 a half
bwun 搬 v.i. heave
bwun 搬 n. move
bwun cheurng fu 半長褲 n. breeches
bwun chut 搬出 v.t. vacate
bwun day 本地 a aboriginal
bwun day geh 本地嘅 a. native
bwun day geh 本地嘅 a. vernacular
bwun day wah 本地話 n. vernacular
bwun day yan 本地人 n native
bwun geurt sek 絆腳石 n drag
bwun ging 半徑 n. radius
bwun jow 伴奏 n accompaniment
bwun jow 搬走 v. t clear
bwun kow 半球 n. hemisphere
bwun luy 伴侶 n. helpmate
bwun mang geh 半盲孱弱 n. purblind
bwun tow 叛徒 n. traitor
bwun wan 搬運 n. portage
bwun wan gung 搬運工 n. mover
bwun yan fu 半音符 n. minim

bwuy 杯 n. cup
bwuy 杯 n. mug
bwuy bun 背叛 v.t. betray
bwuy bun 背叛 n betrayal
bwuy bun 背叛 n. treachery
bwuy bwun 背叛 a. mutinous
bwuy bwun 背叛 n. perfidy
bwuy ging 背景 n. background
bwuy jek 背脊 n. back
bwuy sam 背心 n. vest
bwuy sam 背心 n. waistcoat
bwuy toy 胚胎 n embryo
bwuy yee dak 貝爾德 n. bayard

C

ccho 嘈 a. loud
cha hm dor 差唔多 adv alike
cha hm dor 差唔多 adv. almost
cha ming 查明 v.t. ascertain
cha yow 搽油 v.t. anoint
chan teen geh 產前嘅 adj. antenatal
chao siew 嘲笑 v.i sneer
chao siew 嘲笑 n sneer
char hm dor 差唔多 adv. nigh
chee yan geh yoon 似人嘅猿 adj. anthropoid
cher 車 n. automobile
cher 車 n. car
cher chorng 車床 n. lathe
cher forng 車房 n. garage
cher gung 車工 n. turner
cher jam 車站 n. station
cher jam 車站 n stop
cher kuk 車軸 n. axle
cher leurng geh 車輛嘅 a. vehicular
cher may seurng 車尾箱 n. trunk
cher seurng 車廂 n. carriage
cher tai 車胎 n. tyre

cher teen cho 車前草 n. plantain

cheurk yoot geh 卓越嘅 a. superlative

cheurng 腸 n. bowel

cheurng 槍 n. gun

cheurng 腸 n. intestine

cheurng 長 a. long

cheurng 搶 n plunder

cheurng 唱 v.i. sing

cheurng 搶 v.t. snatch

cheurng 搶 n. snatch

cheurng 牆 n. wall

cheurng 唱 v.i. warble

cheurng 窗 n. window

cheurng 搶 v.t. wrest

cheurng bay yoon 長臂猿 n. gibbon

cheurng dang 長凳 n bench

cheurng dek 長笛 n flute

cheurng dow 長度 n. length

cheurng dow 長度 n. measurement

cheurng forng ying 長方形 n. oblong

cheurng forng ying 長方形 n. rectangle

cheurng forng ying geh 長方形嘅 a. oblong

cheurng forng ying geh 長方形嘅 a. rectangular

cheurng geem 長劍 n. rapier

cheurng geep 搶劫 n. dacoity

cheurng geep 搶劫 v.i. maraud

cheurng geep 搶劫 v.t. plunder

cheurng geep 搶劫 n. robbery

cheurng geh 腸嘅 adj. alvine

cheurng geh 腸嘅 a. intestinal

cheurng geh 牆嘅 a. mural

cheurng geng luk 長頸鹿 n. giraffe

cheurng gow 搶救 n rescue

cheurng gow 搶救 n. salvage

cheurng gow 搶救 v.t. salvage

cheurng hap 場合 n. occasion

cheurng kay 長期 adv long

cheurng kay dan diew 長期單調 n.

monostrous

cheurng kay sow fu 長期受苦 v.i. languish

cheurng keh bing 槍騎兵 n. lancer

cheurng key kwan yiew 長期困擾 v. t bedevil

cheurng kwong 猖狂 a. rampant

cheurng leem 窗簾 n curtain

cheurng leurk jeh 搶掠者 n. marauder

cheurng mao 長矛 n. lance

cheurng meng 長命 n. longevity

cheurng peen dai lun 長篇大論 n. tirade

cheurng pow 長袍 n. robe

cheurng say geh 詳細嘅 a elaborate

cheurng say miew sut 詳細描述 v. t elaborate

cheurng siew 暢銷 a. salable

cheurng siew geh 暢銷嘅 a. marketable

cheurng sut 詳述 v. t detail

cheurng sut 詳述 v.t. specify

cheurng tow bat seet 長途跋涉 v.i. trek

cheurng tow bat seet 長途跋涉 n. trek

cheurng yoon dang 長軟凳 n. ottoman

chiew v. t chew

chiew so 招手 v. t beckon

cho 粗 a coarse

cho 草 n. glass

cho 草 n grass

cho 嘈 a. noisy

cho 醋 n. vinegar

cho 嘈 v.i. wrangle

cho day 草地 n. lawn

cho day 草地 n. meadow

cho far 醋化 v. acetify

cho geh 吵嘅 a. rowdy

cho go 草稿 n draft

cho hung 操控 *v.t. manipulate*
cho jap seng 嘈雜聲 *n babel*
cho jap seng 嘈雜聲 *n din*
cho jap seng 嘈雜聲 *n. hubbub*
cho jee dai yeep 粗枝大葉 *a. superficial*
cho jok 操作 *n. manipulation*
cho jok 操作 *v.t. operate*
cho jok yan 操作人 *n. operator*
cho jung 操縱 *v.t. man*
cho leurk geh 粗略嘅 *a. sketchy*
cho leurk geh 粗略嘅 *a. vague*
cho lo 粗魯 *adj. crass*
cho low 粗魯 *a. uncouth*
cho low 粗魯 *n. vulgarity*
cho low geh 粗魯嘅 *a. vulgar*
cho lut 醋栗 *n. gooseberry*
cho muk 草木 *n. vegetation*
cho pay 草皮 *n. turf*
cho sam 操心 *a. solicitous*
cho see 措施 *n. measure*
cho sut 草率 *a. hasty*
cho teem 草簽 *v.t initial*
cho yan 粗人 *n boor*
cho yan 粗人 *n carl*
cho yee 草擬 *v. t draft*
cho yoon 草原 *n. lea*
choo koot 處決 *n execution*
choo see 廚師 *n cook*
choon 寸 *n. inch*
choon 傳 *v.t. rumour*
choon 串 *v.t. spell*
choon 串 *v.t. string*
choon 穿 *v.t thread*
choon 村 *n. village*
choon bo 全部 *a. all*
choon bo 全部 *a entire*
choon bo 全部 *n. lot*
choon bo 全部 *n. totality*
choon bo 全部 *a. whole*
choon bo geh 全部嘅 *a comprehensive*

choon bor 傳播 *v.t. propagate*
choon bor 傳播 *n. spread*
choon dan 傳單 *n. circular*
choon dan 傳單 *n. handbill*
choon dan 傳單 *n. leaflet*
choon dong 存檔 *n.pl. archives*
choon dow jeh 傳教者 *n. preacher*
choon for 存貨 *n. stock*
choon for 存貨 *v.t. stock*
choon forng 存放 *n. storage*
choon gao see 傳教士 *n. missionary*
choon ging 全景 *n. panorama*
choon gwok geh 全國嘅 *a. national*
choon gwor 穿過 *v.t. pierce*
choon gwor 穿過 *prep. through*
choon hai dai 穿鞋帶 *v.t. lace*
choon hay 喘氣 *v.i gasp*
choon hay 喘氣 *v.i. pant*
choon hm gwor geh 穿唔過嘅 *a. impenetrable*
choon hoy 傳開 *v.i. spread*
choon jan 傳真 *n facsimile*
choon jee 全知 *n. omniscience*
choon jor seen gwor 存在先過 *v.t. antecede*
choon joy 存在 *v.t. be*
choon joy 存在 *v.i exist*
choon joy 存在 *n existence*
choon kow geh 全球嘅 *a. global*
choon lang 全能 *n. omnipotence*
choon lang geh 全能嘅 *a. almighty*
choon man 傳聞 *n. hearsay*
choon man 村民 *n. villager*
choon man tow piew 全民投票 *n. referendum*
choon mwuy 傳媒 *n press*
choon piew 傳票 *n. summons*
choon sam choon yee 全心全意 *a. whole-hearted*
choon san geh 全身嘅 *adv. bodily*
choon san gwun ju 全神貫注 *v.t engross*

choon san gwun ju 全神貫注 *a. rapt*

choon say gai geh 全世界嘅 *a. universal*

choon shoot 傳說 *n. lore*

choon shoot geh 傳說嘅 *a. legendary*

choon sung 傳送 *n conveyance*

choon sung 傳送 *v.t. transmit*

choon tay shoon man 全體選民 *n electorate*

choon teen 存錢 *v.t. bank*

choon tey yeen yoon 全體演員 *n. cast*

choon ting geh 全程嘅 *a through*

choon tung 串通 *n collusion*

choon tung 傳統 *n. tradition*

choon tung geh 傳統嘅 *a. traditional*

choon yan 串人 *v.i. gibe*

choon yeem 傳染 *a contagious*

choon yeem 傳染 *v.t. infect*

choon yeem 傳染 *n. transmission*

choon yeem sing 傳染性 *a. infectious*

chor 錯 *n blunder*

chor 銼 *v.t file*

chor 錯 *a. incorrect*

chor 錯 *n. mistake*

chor 坐 *v.i. perch*

chor 坐 *v.t. seat*

chor 坐 *v.i. sit*

chor bo geh 初步嘅 *a. introductory*

chor bo geh 初步嘅 *a. preliminary*

chor bo yan jeurng 初步印象 *adv. prima facie*

chor cher 坐車 *v.i. motor*

chor geh 錯嘅 *a erroneous*

chor geh 錯嘅 *a. wrong*

chor geh 錯嘅 *adv. wrong*

chor gok 錯覺 *n. delusion*

chor gok 錯覺 *n. illusion*

chor guk 雛菊 *n daisy*

chor hm geh geet hap 錯誤嘅結合 *n. misalliance*

chor kay 初期 *n. infancy*

chor kay geh 初期嘅 *a. nascent*

chor ng 錯誤 *n error*

chor pwuy 錯配 *v.t. mismatch*

chor seurng 挫傷 *v.t. contuse*

chor shoon 坐船 *v.i. sail*

chorng 床 *n bed*

chorng yuk 床褥 *n. mattress*

chorng choot 倉促 *a cursory*

chorng choot geh 倉促嘅 *a snap*

chorng fu 倉庫 *n. godown*

chorng fu 倉庫 *n. repository*

chorng jao 床罩 *n. coverlet*

chorng jok jeh 創作者 *n creator*

chorng jok yan 創作人 *n. originator*

chorng lap 創立 *v. t erect*

chorng lap yan 創立人 *n. founder*

chorng mat chu 隱藏物 *n cache*

chorng san chu 藏身處 *n. hide*

chorng san jeh 創新者 *n. innovator*

chorng yap 闖入 *v.t. intrude*

chorng yap 闖入 *n. irruption*

chorng yee 創意 *adj. creative*

chorng yee 創意 *n. originality*

chorngfu 倉庫 *v.t warehouse*

chotee 措辭 *n. phraseology*

chow 臭 *a. foul*

chow fan 囚犯 *n. prisoner*

chow gam 酬金 *n. honorarium*

chow low 酬勞 *n. remuneration*

chow may 臭味 *n. odour*

chow teen 秋天 *n. autumn*

chow yap 抽泣 *v.i. whimper*

choy 探 *v.i. quarry*

choy dai 彩帶 *n. streamer*

choy ding 裁定 *v.t. adjudge*

choy ding 裁定 *v. i decree*

choy fu 財富 *n. mammon*

choy fu 財富 *n. opulence*

choy fu 財富 *n. riches*

choy fung 裁縫 *n. tailor*

choy garm gwan bay 裁減軍備 *n. disarmament*

choy gow 採購 n. procurement

choy jing 財政 n finance

choy jing bo 財政部 n. treasury

choy jing geh 財政嘅 a financial

choy jing geh 財政嘅 a fiscal

choy jing sow yap 財政收入 n. revenue

choy koot 裁決 n decree

choy koot 裁決 n. ruling

choy koot 裁決 n. verdict

choy liew 材料 n. ingredient

choy mat 財物 n. belongings

choy mat 財物 n. possession

choy mow ju gwun 財物主管 n. treasurer

choy pai 彩排 n. rehearsal

choy pao 賽跑 n. race

choy poon 裁判 v.t. arbitrate

choy pwun 裁判 n. arbiter

choy pwun 裁判 n. referee

choy pwun yoon 裁判員 n. umpire

choy sek cheurng 採石場 n. quarry

choy tan 財產 n. fortune

choy tan 財產 n. property

choy wah 才華 n. talent

choy yoon 裁員 n. redundance

chu 柱 n. pillar

chu forng 廚房 n. kitchen

chu gway 櫥櫃 n. cabinet

chu larm 處男 n virgin

chu lay 處理 n. dealing

chu lay 處理 n disposal

chu lay 處理 v.t handle

chu lorng 柱廊 n. portico

chu luy 處女 n. maiden

chu luy 處女 n. virgin

chu mat gway 儲物櫃 n. locker

chu tak chu 註冊處 n. registry

chuk 捉 v. t. catch

chuk bok 束縛 n bondage

chuk bok 束縛 n fetter

chuk day 速遞 n delivery

chuk dow 速度 n pace

chuk dow 速度 n. speed

chuk dow 速度 n. velocity

chuk gey 速記 n. stenography

chuk gey yoon 速記員 n. stenographer

chuk jun 促進 v.i. hasten

chuk yee por wai 蓄意破壞 n. sabotage

chuk yee por wai 蓄意破壞 v.t. sabotage

chun 蠢 adj. asinine

chun 蠢 adj. daft

chun 蠢 a dumb

chun 蠢 n folly

chun 蠢 a stupid

chun 蠢 n. stupidity

chun choy 蠢材 n blockhead

chun choy 蠢材 v. t burk

chun choy 蠢材 n fool

chun choy 蠢材 n. loggerhead

chun choy 蠢材 n. moron

chun geh 蠢嘅 a foolish

chun geh 蠢嘅 a. idiotic

chun lor 巡邏 v.i. patrol

chun lor 巡邏 n patrol

chun teen 春天 n spring

chun teen geh 春天嘅 a. vernal

chun wan 循環 n circulation

chun wan 循環 n cycle

chun wan geh 循環嘅 a cyclic

chun wan geh 循環嘅 a. recurrent

chun yan 蠢人 n. clot

chun yeurng larm 巡洋艦 n cruiser

chung 從 prep. from

chung 重 a. hefty

chung 蔥 n. onion

chung 衝 n rush

chung 從 prep. since

chung 從 conj. since

chung 從 adv. since

chung 重 a. weighty

chung been dow 從邊度 *adv. whence*
chung cha 沖茶 *v. t. brew*
chung chut 衝出 *v.i. sally*
chung dat 衝突 *v. i conflict*
chung dat 衝突 *n. scuffle*
chung dat 衝突 *v.i. scuffle*
chung dat 衝突 *n. strife*
chung deep 重疊 *v.t. overlap*
chung deep 重疊 *n overlap*
chung dung 衝動 *n. impetuosity*
chung dung 衝動 *n. impulse*
chung dung 衝動 *a. impulsive*
chung dung 衝動 *n. spontaneity*
chung dung 衝動 *a. spontaneous*
chung dung 衝動 *n urge*
chung fan juy 重婚罪 *n bigamy*
chung fuk 重複 *v.t. reiterate*
chung fuk 重複 *n. reiteration*
chung fuk 重複 *v.t. repeat*
chung fuk 重複 *n. repetition*
chung gam yee ho 從今以後 *adv. henceforward*
chung gao 蟲膠 *n lac, lakh*
chung gik 重擊 *n. thump*
chung gik 重擊 *v.t. thump*
chung gung 充公 *v. t confiscate*
chung gwor 重過 *v.t. out-balance*
chung gwor 重過 *v.t. outweigh*
chung ho yee chut 衝口而出 *v. t blurt*
chung jeet yow 松節油 *n. turpentine*
chung juk 充足 *n abundance*
chung juk 充足 *n. sufficiency*
chung juk geh 充足嘅 *a abundant*
chung leurng 沖涼 *v. t bathe*
chung leurng 沖涼 *n. shower*
chung leurng 沖涼 *v.t. shower*
chung mat 寵物 *n. pet*
chung ming 聰明 *a. intelligent*
chung ming choy jee 聰明才智 *n. intelligence*
chung ming geh 聰明嘅 *a. sage*
chung ming geh 聰明嘅 *a. smart*

chung morng 匆忙 *n. haste*
chung mun 充滿 *v.i. teem*
chung mun 充滿 *a. fraught*
chung mwun 充滿 *a. replete*
chung mwun 充滿 *v.i. riddle*
chung mwun ging yee geh 充滿敬意嘅 *a. reverential*
chung mwun jing hay 充滿蒸氣 *a. vaporous*
chung ngar 松鴉 *n. jay*
chung sam 衷心 *a. sincere*
chung san 重新 *adv. afresh*
chung san 重新 *adv. anew*
chung sang 重生 *n. rebirth*
chung sang 重生 *n. regeneration*
chung say 沖洗 *v.i flush*
chung say 沖洗 *v.t. rinse*
chung shu 松樹 *n. pine*
chung shu 松鼠 *n. squirrel*
chung suk 從屬 *n. subservience*
chung tee yee ho 從此以後 *adv. henceforth*
chung tee yee ho 從此以後 *adv. hereafter*
chung way 聰慧 *n. sagacity*
chung yan 重印 *v.t. reprint*
chung yan 重印 *n. reprint*
chung yeen 重現 *n. recurrence*
chung yeep jeh 從業者 *n. practitioner*
chung yu 充裕 *n. plenty*
chut ban 出版 *n. publication*
chut ban yan 出版人 *n. publisher*
chut been 出邊 *n outside*
chut been 出邊 *prep outside*
chut been 出邊 *n without*
chut been geh 出邊嘅 *a. outside*
chut been geh 出邊嘅 *adv outside*
chut ga 出價 *v.t bid*
chut go ga 出高價 *v.t. outbid*
chut gway 出軌 *v. t. derail*
chut gwok 出國 *adv abroad*

chut ho 出口 *n. exit*
chut ho 出口 *n export*
chut ho 出口 *v. t. export*
chut horn 出汗 *v.i. perspire*
chut huy 出去 *adv. out*
chut jik 出席 *v.t. attend*
chut jik lut 出席率 *n. attendance*
chut lap yoon 出納員 *n. teller*
chut leurng 出糧 *v.t. remunerate*
chut mao 出貓 *v. t. cheat*
chut meng 出名 *a famous*
chut meng 出名 *a. well-known*
chut sang 出生 *n. birth*
chut sang 出生 *v. born*
chut sang 出生 *n. parentage*
chut sang fu yu 出生富裕 *adj. born rich*
chut sang geh 出生嘅 *a. natal*
chut siew jee gak 取消資格 *n disqualification*
chut siew jee gak 取消資格 *v. t. disqualify*
chut tan leurng 出產量 *n. output*
chut yap hung 出入孔 *n. manhole*
chut yeen 出現 *n. advent*
chut yeen 出現 *v.i. appear*
chut yeen 出現 *v.i. arise*
chut yeen 出現 *v. i emerge*
chut yeen 出現 *n. occurrence*
chut yeen 出現 *n. presence*
chuy 除 *v.t. bare*
chuy 吹 *v.i. blow*
chuy 脆 *a. brittle*
chuy 催 *v. t bustle*
chuy 脆 *a crisp*
chuy 脆 *adj. crump*
chuy 催 *v.t urge*
chuy ho sao 吹口哨 *v.i. whistle*
chuy chor 最初 *n. outset*
chuy chung 隨從 *n. retinue*
chuy dak jun 徐得盡 *n. aliquot*
chuy dek 吹笛 *v.i flute*

chuy doy 取代 *v. t displace*
chuy doy 取代 *v.t. supersede*
chuy fat 除法 *n division*
chuy fay 徐非 *conj. unless*
chuy huy 除去 *v. t eliminate*
chuy huy 除去 *n elimination*
chuy jay 槌仔 *n. hammer*
chuy jor 徐咗 *prep besides*
chuy jor 徐咗 *prep except*
chuy jor 徐咗 *prep save*
chuy meen 催眠 *v.t. hypnotize*
chuy meen sut 催眠術 *n. mesmerism*
chuy meen suy 催眠術 *n. hypnotism*
chuy pung 吹捧 *v.t. glorify*
chuy sam 徐衫 *v.t. strip*
chuy see 隨時 *adv. conj whenever*
chuy siew 取消 *v. t. cancel*
chuy siew 取消 *n cancellation*
chuy siew 取消 *v.t. revoke*
chuy sow kway dai geh 隨手攜帶嘅 *a. portable*
chuy suy 吹水 *v. i brag*
chuy tee jee ngoy 除此之外 *adv. otherwise*
chuy yee geh 隨意嘅 *a. random*
chuy yeurk 脆弱 *a delicate*
chuy yeurk 脆弱 *a. fragile*
chuy yeurk 脆弱 *a. vulnerable*

D

da 打 *v. t. beat*
da 打 *n. dial*
da 打 *v.t fight*
da 打 *v.t. hit*
da 打 *v.t. strike*
da bai 打敗 *v.i. triumph*
da bai 打敗 *v.t. trump*
da ban 打扮 *v.t. attire*

da ban 打扮 n. garb
da bay 打界 v.t. ring
da bay horn 打鼻鼾 v.i. snore
da deen bo 打電報 v. t. cable
da deen bo 打電報 v.t. telegraph
da deen wah 打電話 v.t. telephone
da dow 打鬥 v. i. & n brawl
da dow 打賭 n. wager
da dow 打賭 v.i. wager
da ert 打嗝 v. t belch
da ert seng 打嗝聲 n belch
da fat 打發 v. t. consign
da for gey 打火機 n. lighter
da gao 打交 n fight
da geep 打劫 v.i. loot
da geet 打結 v.t. knot
da geet 打結 n. tangle
da gik 打擊 n blow
da gik 打擊 n hit
da gu 打鼓 v.i. drum
da guk jeh 打穀者 n. thresher
da gut 打嗝 n. hiccup
da gwun see 打官司 v.t. litigate
da ham low 打喊路 v.i. yawn
da hat tee 打乞嚏 v.i. sneeze
da hoy 打開 v.t. open
da hoy 打開 v.t. unfold
da hoy geh 打開嘅 a. open
da hung fan 打空翻 v.i. somersault
da jam 打針 n. injection
da jan 打震 v.i. shudder
da jan 打震 n shudder
da jee 打字 v.t. type
da jee yoon 打字員 n. typist
da jiew fu 打招呼 v.t. greet
da jik 打直 a. vertical
da lang jan 打冷震 v.i. shiver
da lap 打蠟 v.t. wax
da leep 打獵 v.t. hunt
da lung 打窿 v.t hole
da lung 大窿 v.t. perforate
da luy 打雷 v.i. thunder

da sai geet 打晒結 v.t. tangle
da seurng 打傷 v.t maul
da shoon 打算 v.t. intend
da sing dai bao 打成大包 v.t. bale
da suy 打碎 v.t. smash
da ting 打聽 v.t. inquire
da ting 打聽 v.i. pry
da toon 打斷 v. t disrupt
da wan 打暈 v.t. stun
da wat 打滑 n skid
da wor 打和 n draw
da yiew 打擾 n. interruption
da yik miew 打疫苗 v.t. vaccinate
da yu forng jam 打預防針 v.t. inoculate
dai 大 a big
dai 帶 v. t bring
dai 大 a. large
dai 帶 v.t. lead
dai 帶 n. strap
dai ba 大巴 n coach
dai ban jeurng 大笨象 n elephant
dai bao 大包 n. bale
dai bay 大髀 n. thigh
dai bo 大步 n stride
dai bo fan 大部分 n bulk
dai bo fan 大部分 n. majority
dai bo hang 大步行 v.i. stride
dai buk bo 大瀑布 n. cataract
dai cho yoon 大草原 n. steppe
dai chuy 大槌 n. maul
dai dam 大膽 a. adventurous
dai dam 大膽 a. bold
dai dam 大膽 a brave
dai dam 大膽 n. daring
dai dam 大膽 n. hardihood
dai dam 大膽 n. intrepidity
dai dam geh 大膽嘅 a. venturesome
dai dam geh 大膽嘅 a. venturous
dai duy 大堆 v.t. array
dai duy 大堆 n. load
dai far gwun 戴花冠 v.t. garland

dai for cher 大貨車 n. lorry
dai for duy 大火堆 n bonfire
dai forng 大方 a bountiful
dai forng 大方 a. generous
dai fu yung 大富豪 n. croesus
dai fuk teen day 大幅田地 n. acreage
dai fung 大風 a. windy
dai gai 大街 n. avenue
dai gai 大街 n. thoroughfare
dai gao tong 大教堂 n. cathedral
dai gao tong 大教堂 n. minster
dai geng siew gwai 大驚小怪 v.i fuss
dai geng siew gwai 大驚小怪 n. hysteria
dai giew 大叫 n. shout
dai giew 大叫 v.i. shout
dai gung see 大公司 n corporation
dai har 大廈 n edifice
dai harm 大喊 n.i. bawl
dai hok 大學 n. university
dai hok ju tak 大學註冊 n. matriculation
dai hok sang 大學生 n. undergraduate
dai jee yeen 大自然 n. nature
dai jeen dow 大剪刀 n. pl. shears
dai jeurk lung 大雀籠 n. aviary
dai ju gao 大主教 n. archbishop
dai ju gao 大主教 n. metropolitan
dai koy 大概 adv about
dai koy 大概 a. approximate
dai koy yee see 大概意思 n. purport
dai leem dow 大鐮刀 n. scythe
dai leurng 大梁 n. girder
dai leurng 大量 n. profusion
dai leurng geh 大量嘅 a. profuse
dai leurng geh 大量嘅 a. substantial
dai leurng geh 大量嘅 a. superabundant
dai leurng jay jow 大量製造 n manufacture

dai leurng mo chut 大量冒出 v.i billow
dai leurng sang tan 大量生產 v.t. manufacture
dai lik 大力 a. strong
dai lik gam deng 大力咁掟 v.t. hurl
dai lik geh 大力嘅 adj. mighty
dai lik ling 大力擰 v.t. wrench
dai lo geh 大腦嘅 adj cerebral
dai low 大路 n. highway
dai low 大樓 n. overcoat
dai luk mo geh yan 戴綠帽嘅人 n. cuckold
dai lut see 大律師 n. barrister
dai ma 大麻 n. hemp
dai mak 大麥 n. barley
dai morng 大網 n. conspectus
dai ngar 大牙 n. molar
dai ngar geh 大牙嘅 a molar
dai pao 大炮 n. artillery
dai pao 大炮 n. cannon
dai peen tow day 大片土地 n. tract
dai san 大臣 n. minister
dai san dung 大山洞 n. cavern
dai say 大使 n extravagance
dai say 大細 n. size
dai say geh 大使嘅 a extravagant
dai say geh yan 大使嘅人 n. spendthrift
dai see 大使 n. ambassador
dai sek 大石 n boulder
dai seng 大聲 adv. aloud
dai seng 大聲 a. thunderous
dai seng giew 大聲叫 v.t. howl
dai seng yiew kow 大聲要求 v. i. clamour
dai she 大赦 n. amnesty
dai shoon 大船 n. vessel
dai shu jee 大樹枝 n bough
dai sik geh 大食嘅 a. voracious
dai sing see ghe 大城市嘅 a. metropolitan

dai tow 歹徒 *n. ruffian*
dai tow 帶頭 *v.t. spearhead*
dai tow sat 大屠殺 *n carnage*
dai tow sat 大屠殺 *n. holocaust*
dai tow sat 大屠殺 *n. massacre*
dai wah 大話 *n lie*
dai wok choon sing 大獲全勝 *a. triumphant*
dai wong fung 大黃峰 *n. hornet*
dai yat gor jee mow 第一個字母 *n. initial*
dai yee 大意 *a. careless*
dai yee lung 大耳窿 *n. usurer*
dai yeep geh say jee 帶葉嘅細枝 *n. sprig*
dai yeep jee 大頁紙 *n foolscap*
dai yiew dai bai 大搖大擺 *n swagger*
dai yiew dai bai hang 大搖大擺行 *v.i. swagger*
dai yu 大雨 *n downpour*
dak beet 特別 *adv. singularly*
dak beet 特別 *a. special*
dak beet geh 特別嘅 *a especial*
dak beet geh 特別嘅 *a. particular*
dak chut 突出 *n. prominence*
dak dai 特大 *a. outsize*
dak dang 特登 *a deliberate*
dak dang geh 特登嘅 *adv. purposely*
dak deem 特點 *n feature*
dak ding 特定 *a certain*
dak ding geh 特定嘅 *a. specific*
dak dow 得到 *n. acquisition*
dak dow 得到 *v. t. derive*
dak dow 得到 *v.t. obtain*
dak fai leet cher 特快列車 *n express*
dak fan 得分 *v.t. score*
dak fan jeh 得分者 *n. scorer*
dak gey 特技 *n stunt*
dak gik sow ta 突擊搜查 *n swoop*
dak harn 得閒 *a available*
dak huy ging ying koon 特許經營權 *n. frachise*

dak jap 突襲 *v.i. pounce*
dak jap 突襲 *n pounce*
dak jap 突襲 *n. raid*
dak jap 突襲 *n. sally*
dak jap 突襲 *v.i. storm*
dak jing 特徵 *n. hallmark*
dak jing 特徵 *n. trait*
dak juy 得罪 *v. t displease*
dak juy 得罪 *v.t. offend*
dak juy yan geh 得罪人嘅 *a. offensive*
dak koon 特權 *n. prerogative*
dak koon 特權 *n. privilege*
dak ser 特赦 *n. pardon*
dak tay 得體 *n decorum*
dak tay 得體 *n. propriety*
dak tay 得體 *n. tact*
dak tay geh 得體嘅 *a. seemly*
dak tik 得戚 *adj. complacent*
dak tik 得戚 *v. i crow*
dak tik 得戚 *a. smug*
dak yeen deet lok 突然跌落 *n plunge*
dak yeen gan 突然間 *a abrupt*
dak yik 得益 *v.t. profit*
dak yu kay loy 突如其來 *n. onrush*
dam 啖 *n. swallow*
dam bo yan 擔保人 *n. surety*
dam bow 擔保 *v.i. vouch*
dam ga 擔架 *n. stretcher*
dam hay 氮氣 *n. nitrogen*
dam jap 膽汁 *n bile*
dam leurng 膽量 *n boldness*
dam leurng 膽量 *n bravery*
dam leurng 膽量 *n pluck*
dam sam 擔心 *n. apprehension*
dam sam 擔心 *v.t dread*
dam sam 擔心 *a. uneasy*
dam sam 擔心 *v.i. worry*
dam sam geh 擔心嘅 *a. apprehensive*
dam siew gway 膽小鬼 *n. coward*
dam yow 擔憂 *v.t. unsettle*
dam yow 擔憂 *n. worry*

dan 單 *n* bill
dan 單 *n. invoice*
dan 單 *n. receipt*
dan 彈 *v.i. spring*
dan bak 蛋白 *n albumen*
dan bak jatt 蛋白質 *n. protein*
dan bo 擔保 *v.t guarantee*
dan cher 單車 *n. bicycle*
dan cher sow 單車手 *n cyclist*
dan chut geh 突出嘅 *a. prominent*
dan diew 單調 *a. humdrum*
dan diew 單調 *n monotony*
dan diew geh 單調嘅 *a. monotonous*
dan duk geh 單獨嘅 *a. lone*
dan duk geh 單獨嘅 *a. solitary*
dan duk geh 單獨嘅 *a. solo*
dan duk tiew chut 單獨挑出 *v.t. single*
dan forng 單方 *adv ex-parte*
dan forng meen geh 單方面嘅 *a ex-parte*
dan geurt tiew 單腳跳 *v. i hop*
dan geurt tiew 單腳跳 *n hop*
dan go 蛋糕 *n. cake*
dan hay 但係 *prep but*
dan hay 但係 *conj however*
dan hay 但係 *conj. yet*
dan leet 分裂 *n. schism*
dan mok she gik 彈幕射擊 *n. barrage*
dan ngan geh 單眼嘅 *a. monocular*
dan peen ngan geng 單片眼鏡 *n. monocle*
dan san larm yan 單身男人 *n. bachelor*
dan sang 誕生 *n. nativity*
dan seurng 犯上 *n. insubordination*
dan sik geh 單色嘅 *a. monochromatic*
dan sing 彈性 *n stretch*
dan sow geh 單數嘅 *a. singular*
dan tee 單詞 *n. vocabulary*

dan ting piew 單程票 *n. single*
dan way 單位 *n. apartment*
dan way 單位 *n. unit*
dan worng 蛋黃 *n. yolk*
dan yam jeet geh 單音節嘅 *a. monosyllabic*
dan yam jeet tee 單音節詞 *n. monosyllable*
dan yat geh 單一嘅 *a. single*
dan yeurk 彈藥 *n. ammunition*
dang 等 *v. t bide*
dang 凳 *n. chair*
dang 燈 *n. lamp*
dang 等 *v.i. wait*
dang 等 *n. wait*
dang 瞪 *v.i. stare*
dang been geh 等邊嘅 *a equilateral*
dang dang 等等 *adv. etcetera*
dang duy 登對 *v.i. match*
dang gak yeet 登革熱 *n. dengue*
dang gan 等緊 *v.t. await*
dang gan 等緊 *prep. pending*
dang gey 登記 *v.t. register*
dang gey 登記 *n. registration*
dang gey bo 登記簿 *n. register*
dang gey yoon 登記員 *n. registrar*
dang ho sat 等候室 *n. lounge*
dang kap jay dow 等級制度 *n. hierarchy*
dang lung 燈籠 *n. lantern*
dang ngat seen 等壓線 *n. isobar*
dang pao 燈泡 *n. bulb*
dang san ga 登山家 *n. mountaineer*
dang tap 燈塔 *n beacon*
dang tung yu 等同於 *a. synonymous*
dang way 登位 *v. t enthrone*
dang way 登位 *v.t. throne*
dang yu 等於 *v. amount*
dang yu 等於 *v. t equal*
dang yu 等於 *a. tantamount*
dap 揼 *v.t hammer*
dap 答 *v.i. respond*

dap ban 踏板 *n. pedal*

dap been yan 答辯人 *n. pleader*

dap fuk 答覆 *n. response*

dap on 答案 *n answer*

dap shoon yow larm 搭船遊覽 *v.i. cruise*

dat chut 突出 *n. hernia*

dat dow 發抖 *v.i. quake*

dat sing 達成 *v. t concert2*

dat sing 達成 *v.t. fulfil*

dat yeen 突然 *n. sudden*

dat yeen gan 突然間 *adv. suddenly*

day 低 *n bottom*

day 地 *n. ground*

day 地 *n. land*

day 低 *adv. low*

day 低 *n. primer*

day bo 地堡 *n.bunker*

day deem 地點 *n. location*

day deem 低點 *n. low*

day dorng 抵擋 *v.t fend*

day dow geh 地道嘅 *a. idiomatic*

day forng 地方 *n area*

day forng 地方 *n. place*

day forng fat 地方法 *n bylaw, bye-law*

day forng gwun 地方官 *n. magistrate*

day gao 地窖 *n cellar*

day geh 低嘅 *a. low*

day gow 第九 *a. ninth*

day gow sap 第九十 *a. ninetieth*

day gwok 帝國 *n empire*

day gwok tung jee 帝國統治 *n. imperialism*

day ha geh 地下嘅 *a. subterranean*

day ha tung dow 地下通到 *n. tunnel*

day hao 低吼 *n. snarl*

day hao 低吼 *v.i. snarl*

day har sat 地下室 *n. basement*

day jan 地震 *n quake*

day jan geh 地震嘅 *a. seismic*

day jat geh 地質嘅 *a. geological*

day jat hok 地質學 *n. geology*

day jat hok ga 地質學家 *n. geologist*

day jay 抵制 *v. t. boycott*

day jay 抵制 *n boycott*

day jee 地址 *n. address*

day jor 底座 *n. pedestal*

day kow 地球 *n. globe*

day kuy 地區 *n district*

day kuy 地區 *n. locality*

day kuy 地區 *n. region*

day kuy 地區 *n. zone*

day kuy geh 地區嘅 *a. regional*

day lay geh 地理嘅 *a. geographical*

day lay hok 地理學 *n. geography*

day lay hok ga 地理學家 *n. geographer*

day luk 第六 *a. sixth*

day luk sap 第六十 *a. sixtieth*

day ngat 抵押 *v.t. mortgage*

day ngat yan 抵押人 *n. mortgagor*

day ping seen 地平線 *n. horizon*

day pwun 地盤 *a. territorial*

day pwun 地盤 *n. territory*

day sam 第三 *a. third*

day sam 第三 *n. third*

day sam 第三 *adv. thirdly*

day sam kap yan lik 地心吸引力 *n. gravity*

day sam sap 第三十 *a. thirtieth*

day sam sap 第三十 *n thirtieth*

day sap gow 第十九 *a. nineteenth*

day sap luk 第十六 *a. sixteenth*

day sap sam 第十三 *a. thirteenth*

day sap tat 第十七 *a. seventeenth*

day sap yee 第十二 *a. twelfth*

day sap yee 第十二 *n. twelfth*

day say 抵死 *v. t. damn*

day siew 抵消 *v.t. counteract*

day siew 抵消 *v.t. offset*

day siew 抵消 *n offset*

day suk 隸屬 *a. subordinate*

day tat 第七 *a. seventh*
day tat sap 第七十 *a. seventieth*
day tor 地拖 *n. mop*
day tow 地圖 *n. atlas*
day tow 地圖 *n map*
day way 地位 *n. niche*
day way 地位 *n. rank*
day way 詆毀 *n. slander*
day way 詆毀 *v.t. slander*
day way 地位 *n. standing*
day way 地位 *n. status*
day yan gung 低人工 *n. pittance*
day yat gor 第一個 *a first*
day yat gor 第一個 *n first*
day yee geh 第二嘅 *a. second*
day yee sap 第二十 *a. twentieth*
day yee sap 第二十 *n twentieth*
day ying 地形 *n. topography*
day ying geh 地形嘅 *a. topographical*
day ying hok ga 地形學家 *n. topographer*
deem 點 *v. t dip*
deem 點 *n dot*
deem 點 *n. point*
deem 店 *n. shop*
deem 掂 *v.t. touch*
deem dow ho 點都好 *adv. anyhow*
deem for 點火 *v.t. light*
deem gai 點解 *adv. why*
deem gik 點擊 *n. click*
deem kwong 癲狂 *adv. amuck*
deem meng 點名 *n. roll-call*
deem so 點數 *n. count*
deem tee 電池 *n battery*
deem wah 電話 *n. telephone*
deem yeurng 點樣 *adv. how*
deen 電 *a electric*
deen 電 *n electricity*
deen 墊 *n. pad*
deen 墊 *n. padding*
deen bo 電報 *n. telegram*

deen bo 電報 *n. telegraph*
deen bo geh 電報嘅 *a. telegraphic*
deen bo hok 電報學 *n. telegraphy*
deen bo yoon 電報員 *n. telegraphist*
deen cher 電車 *n. tram*
deen dow 電鍍 *v.t. plate*
deen fan 典範 *n. quintessence*
deen fan 澱粉 *n. starch*
deen fuk 顛覆 *n. subversion*
deen ha 殿下 *n. Highness*
deen hoon 墊圈 *n. gasket*
deen ju 墊住 *v.t. pillow*
deen larm 電纜 *n. cable*
deen larm 靛藍 *n. indigo*
deen low 顛佬 *n. lunatic*
deen low 顛佬 *n. maniac*
deen sam dow say 顛三倒四 *adv topsy turvy*
deen see 電視 *n. television*
deen see gworng bor 電視廣播 *n. telecast*
deen seen 電線 *n. wire*
deen sun 電訊 *n. telecommunications*
deen tay cho 電梯蹭 *n. shaft*
deen tung 電筒 *n. torch*
deen wah 電話 *n. call*
deen wah 電話 *n. phone*
deen wah bo 電話簿 *n directory*
deen ying 典型 *a classic*
deen ying 典型 *n embodiment*
deen ying 電影 *n film*
deen ying 電影 *n. movies*
deen ying geh 典型嘅 *a. typical*
deen yoon 電源 *n main*
deep 碟 *n dish*
deep 碟 *n. plate*
deet 跌 *v. i drop*
deet 跌 *v.i. fall*
deet 跌 *n fall*
deet 跌 *v.t fell*
deet 跌 *n. stumble*
deet 跌 *n. tumble*

deet dow 跌倒 *v.i.* tumble
deet ga 跌價 *v.t.i.* depreciate
deh dee 爹地 *n* dad, daddy
deh dee 爹地 *n father*
deng 訂 *v. t. book*
deng 揼 *v. t discard*
deng 揼 *v.t fling*
deng 釘 *n. nail*
deng 釘 *v.t. nail*
deng 訂 *v.t order*
deng 叮 *n. sting*
deng 釘 *n. stud*
deng 揼 *v.t. throw*
deng 揼 *n. throw*
deng 頂 *n. top*
deng 揼 *v.t. toss*
deng jow 訂做 *v.t. tailor*
deng ju 釘住 *v.t. pin*
deng sek 揼石 *v.t. stone*
deng shu deng 釘書釘 *n. staple*
deng tay teet 釘蹄鐵 *v.t. shoe*
deng yoot 訂閱 *n. subscription*
deurk 啄 *v.i. peck*
dey deem 地點 *n. venue*
dey ha 地下 *n floor*
dey jan 地震 *n earthquake*
dey jeen 地氈 *n. carpet*
dey kow 地球 *n earth*
dey yuk 地獄 *a. hell*
diew 雕 *v. t. chisel*
diew 吊 *v. t dangle*
diew 貂 *n. marten*
diew 雕 *v.t. whittle*
diew cher 吊車 *n crane*
diew dai 吊帶 *n. sling*
diew dung 調動 *v.t. mobilize*
diew hak 雕刻 *n. sculpture*
diew hak ga 雕刻家 *n. sculptor*
diew hak geh 雕刻嘅 *a. sculptural*
diew hay 吊起 *v.t. hoist*
diew huy 調去 *v.t. shunt*
diew jeh 凋謝 *v.i. wither*

diew jeurng 雕像 *n effigy*
diew mat dai 吊襪帶 *n. garter*
diew ta 調查 *v.t. poll*
diew yu 釣魚 *v.i fish*
dik 滴 *n drip*
dik 滴 *v. i drip*
dik 滴 *n drop*
dik 滴 *v.i. trickle*
dik jow bat jeem 滴酒不沾 *a. teetotal*
dik jow bat jeem 滴酒不沾 *n. temperance*
dik kok 的確 *adv. indeed*
dik see 的士 *n. cab*
dik see 的士 *n. taxi*
dik yan 敵人 *n. antagonist*
dik yan 敵人 *n enemy*
dik yan 敵人 *n foe*
dik yee 敵意 *n animus*
dik yee 敵意 *n antagonism*
ding dong 丁噹 *v.i. jingle*
ding dong seng 丁噹聲 *n. clink*
ding dorng seng 丁噹聲 *n. jingle*
ding fan 訂婚 *n. betrothal*
ding fan 訂婚 *n. engagement*
ding fung 頂峰 *n. peak*
ding fung 頂峰 *n. pinnacle*
ding fung 頂峰 *n. zenith*
ding ga 定價 *v.t. price*
ding geng 頂頸 *v.i. quarrel*
ding heurng 丁香 *n clove*
ding heurng 丁香 *n. lilac*
ding hm sun geh 頂唔順嘅 *a. intolerable*
ding jam 頂針 *n. thimble*
ding ju 頂住 *v.t. withstand*
ding kay geh 定期嘅 *a. periodical*
ding lay 定理 *n. theorem*
ding see geh 定時嘅 *a. regular*
ding ying 定型 *a. stereotyped*
don 段 *n. paragraph*
dong jok 動作 *n. motion*

dong on sat 檔案室 *n chancery*
dong sat lo 當失路 *adv., astray*
dong yeen 當然 *adv. certainly*
dong...geh see ho 當...嘅時候 *conj. while*
doon chu 短處 *n. shortcoming*
doon fu 短褲 *n. pl. shorts*
doon geh 短嘅 *a. short*
doon geurt gey 矮腳雞 *n. bantam*
doon gu see 短故事 *n. anecdote*
doon ho 短號 *n. cornet*
doon jam geh kwong yeet 短暫嘅狂熱 *n fad*
doon koot 短缺 *n. shortage*
doon kuy lay choy pao 短距離賽跑 *n sprint*
doon leen 鍛鍊 *v. t exercise*
doon yee ngan geh mo 短而硬嘅毛 *n bristle*
doon yung mow 短絨毛 *n nap*
dor 多 *a. plus*
dor bao toy 多胞胎 *a. multiparous*
dor been geh 多變嘅 *a. variable*
dor beng geh 多病嘅 *a. sickly*
dor choy dor ngay geh 多才多藝嘅 *a. versatile*
dor chung sing 多重性 *n. multiplicity*
dor fan gan 多番梘 *a. soapy*
dor gwok geh 多國嘅 *a. multilateral*
dor gwun han see 多管閒事 *a. officious*
dor hay tay 多氣體 *a. gassy*
dor jap 多汁 *a. juicy*
dor jeh 多謝 *v.t. thank*
dor jeh 多謝 *n. thanks*
dor jor geh 多咗嘅 *a spare*
dor juk dung mat 多足動物 *n. multiped*
dor jung ying sik geh 多種形式嘅 *a multiform*
dor jung yu yeen seh sing geh 多種語言寫成嘅 *a. polyglot2*

dor leen sang jik mat 多年生植物 *n. perennial*
dor mow geh 多霧嘅 *a. misty*
dor san 多山 *a. mountainous*
dor san gao tow 多神教徒 *n. polytheist*
dor san sun yeurng 多神信仰 *n. polytheism*
dor san sung bai geh 多神崇拜嘅 *a. polytheistic*
dor see 多士 *n. toast*
dor sek tow 多石頭 *a. stony*
dor shoot geh 多雪嘅 *a. snowy*
dor shu yeep 多樹葉 *a. leafy*
dor sing 惰性 *a. inert*
dor tan geh 多產嘅 *a. prolific*
dor tee 多刺 *a. thorny*
dor toy 墮胎 *n abortion*
dor wan 多雲 *a cloudy*
dor wan 多雲 *a. overcast*
dor yee geh yan 多疑嘅人 *n. sceptic*
dor yeen geh 多煙嘅 *a. smoky*
dor yeh gorng geh yan 多嘢講嘅人 *n. windbag*
dor yeurng geh 多樣嘅 *a. multiple*
dor yow 多油 *a. greasy*
dor yu geh 多餘嘅 *a excess*
dor yu geh 多雨嘅 *a. rainy*
dor yung tow 多用途 *n. versatility*
dorlok 墮落 *a decadent*
dorng 檔 *n. gear*
dorng 擋 *n. parry*
dorng day geh 當地嘅 *a. indigenous*
dorng hoy 擋開 *v.t. parry*
dorng ju 擋住 *v.t. shield*
dorng ling geh 當令嘅 *a. seasonable*
dorng sat low 蕩失路 *v.i. stray*
dorng see 當時 *a then*
dorng see yan 當事人 *n. litigant*
dorng yeurng 蕩漾 *v.t. ripple*
doryu 多餘 *n excess*
dow 到 *v.i. arrive*

dow 刀 n. baslard
dow 豆 n. bean
dow 賭 v.i bet
dow 竇 n den
dow 倒 v empty
dow 賭 v.i. gamble
dow 賭 v.i game
dow 島 n. island
dow 島 n. isle
dow 刀 n. knife
dow 竇 n. lair
dow 倒 v.i. pour
dow 到 v.t. reach
dow 倒 v.t. tip
dow ban hang way 盜版行為 n. piracy
dow been dow 到邊度 adv. whither
dow bok 賭博 n gamble
dow cho 稻草 n. thatch
dow chu 到處 adv around
dow dak 道德 a ethical
dow dak 道德 n. moral
dow dak 道德 n. morality
dow dak biew jun 道德標準 n. ethics
dow dak geh 道德嘅 a. moral
dow dak hok ga 道德學家 n moralist
dow dan 導彈 n. missile
dow dat 到達 n. arrival
dow fung 斗篷 n. cloak
dow ga ying 度假營 n. camp
dow gam 鍍金 v.t. gild
dow gam 鍍金 a. gilt
dow gey 妒忌 a envious
dow gey 妒忌 v. t envy
dow gey 妒忌 a. jealous
dow gey 妒忌 n. jealousy
dow goon liew 杜鵑鳥 n cuckoo
dow guy 道具 n. prop
dow heep 道歉 v.i. apologize
dow heep 道歉 n. apology
dow ho 逗號 n comma

dow horng 導航 n. navigation
dow horng yee 導航儀 n. navigator
dow jang 鬥爭 n crusade
dow jay 賭仔 n. gambler
dow jee 導致 v.t occasion
dow joon 倒轉 n. reversal
dow joon 倒轉 v.t. reverse
dow kay 到期 n expiry
dow kow 豆蔻 n. cardamom
dow lee dow 到呢度 adv. hither
dow low 逗留 v.i. sojourn
dow low 逗留 n sojourn
dow low 逗留 n stay
dow may yoot 度蜜月 n. honeymoon
dow ngan 鍍銀 v.t. silver
dow ngar 渡鴉 n. raven
dow ngow see 鬥牛士 n. matador
dow oh 倒鈎 n. barb
dow peen 刀片 n. blade
dow see 導師 n. mentor
dow see geh 導師嘅 a. tutorial
dow seh 倒瀉 v.i. spill
dow tap 倒塌 v.i. topple
dow tat yan 糾察人 n. picket
dow teen 稻田 n. paddy
dow yan 盜印 v.t pirate
dow yeen 導演 n. director
dow ying 倒映 n. reflection
dow yung 盜用 v.t. appropriate
dowjoon 倒轉 v.t. invert
doy 袋 n. bag
doy 袋 v.t. pocket
doy bay 代幣 n. token
doy biew 代表 n behalf
doy biew 代表 n deligate1
doy biew 代表 v. t. embody
doy biew 代表 v.t. represent
doy biew 代表 n. representation
doy biew 代表 n. representative
doy biew sing 代表性 a. symbolic
doy biew toon 代表團 n delegation
doy biew toon 代表團 n deputation

doy ding geh 待定嘅 *a pending*

doy juy gow yeurng 代罪羔羊 *n. scapegoat*

doy lay 代理 *n. proxy*

doy lay chu 代理處 *n. agency*

doy ming tee 代名詞 *n. pronoun*

doy sing 代數 *n. algebra*

doy tay 代替 *a. alternative*

doy tay 代替 *n. lieu*

doy tay 代替 *v.t. replace*

doy tay 代替 *n. replacement*

doy tay 代替 *v.t. substitute*

doy tay 代替 *n. substitution*

doy tay ban 代替品 *n. alternative*

doy tay geh 代替嘅 *a. vicarious*

doy tay yan 代替人 *n. substitute*

duk 讀 *n. perusal*

duk 讀 *v.t. peruse*

duk 毒 *n. poison*

duk 毒 *v.t. poison*

duk 篤 *v.t. poke*

duk 篤 *n. poke*

duk 讀 *v.t. read*

duk bak 獨白 *n. monologue*

duk bak 獨白 *n. soliloquy*

duk ban 毒品 *n drug*

duk cheurng 獨唱 *n solo*

duk cheurng jeh 獨唱者 *n. soloist*

duk choy jeh 獨裁者 *n autocrat*

duk choy jeh 獨裁者 *n dictator*

duk choy jing ji 獨裁政治 *n autocracy*

duk chu 獨處 *n. solitude*

duk da 毒打 *v.t. lambaste*

duk dak geh 獨特嘅 *a. inimitable*

duk gar ging ying koon 獨家經營權 *n. monopoly*

duk jeem 獨佔 *v.t. monopolize*

duk jeh 讀者 *n. reader*

duk lap 獨立 *n. independence*

duk lap 獨立 *a. independent*

duk lap geh 獨立嘅 *a sovereign*

duk san 獨身 *n. celibacy*

duk san sang wut 獨身生活 *n. celibacy*

duk ser lang lik 讀寫能力 *n. literacy*

duk shu 讀書 *v.i. study*

duk sing 毒性 *n. virulence*

duk tak 獨特 *a. unique*

duk yik 毒液 *n. venom*

duk yow geh 獨有嘅 *a exclusive*

dum 揼 *v. t dispose*

dun 鈍 *a blunt*

dun 燉 *v.i. simmer*

dun 噸 *n. ton*

dun 噸 *n. tonne*

dun man ok 鈍吻鱷 *n alligator*

dung 凍 *a chilly*

dung 凍 *a cold*

dung 東 *n east*

dung 洞 *n. hollow*

dung fong 東方 *a eastern*

dung forng 東方 *n. orient*

dung forng geh 東方嘅 *a east*

dung forng geh 東方嘅 *a. oriental*

dung forng yan 東方人 *n oriental*

dung geet 凍結 *v.i. freeze*

dung gey 動機 *n. motive*

dung jok 動作 *n. action*

dung jok 動作 *n. movement*

dung mak 動脈 *n. artery*

dung mat 動物 *n. animal*

dung mat fan 動物糞 *n dung*

dung mat hok 動物學 *n. zoology*

dung mat hok ga 動物學家 *n. zoologist*

dung mat hok geh 動物學嘅 *a. zoological*

dung mat kwan 動物群 *n fauna*

dung mat yoon 動物園 *n. zoo*

dung mat yow jee 動物油脂 *n. tallow*

dung meen 冬眠 *n. hibernation*

dung ming tee 動名詞 *n. gerund*

dung tai 動態 n. dynamics
dung tan 動產 n. movables
dung tee 動詞 n. verb
dung tee been fa 動詞變化 v.t. & i. conjugate
dung teen 冬天 n. winter
dung ting 動聽 a. melodious
dung wah 動畫 n animation
dung wah 動畫 n. cartoon
dung yiew 動搖 v.i. waver
duy 堆 v.t. pile
duy 隊 n. team
duy 對 prep. versus
duy bay 對比 v. t contrast
duy bay lut 對比率 n. ratio
duy chay 對齊 v.t. align
duy doy 對待 v.t. treat
duy hm ju 對唔住 a. sorry
duy jat 對質 n. confrontation
duy jeurng 隊長 n. captain
duy jeurng jik way 隊長職位 n. captaincy
duy jiew 對照 v.t. contrapose
duy jiew 對照 n contrast
duy jik 堆積 v.t heap
duy jik geh 堆積嘅 adv aheap
duy ju 對住 a. opposite
duy kong 對抗 v.t. antagonize
duy korng 對抗 n. hostility
duy korng 對抗 v.i. war
duy lap 對立 n. antithesis
duy lap 對立 n. opposition
duy loon 對聯 n. couplet
duy meen 對面 prep. across
duy sow 對手 n. adversary
duy sow 對數 n. logarithm
duy ting 對稱 n. symmetry
duy ting ghe 對稱嘅 a. symmetrical
duy wah 對話 n. parley
duy wan yow hay 對韻遊戲 n. crambo
duy yeen jee piew 兌現支票 v. t. cash

duy ying 隊形 n formation
duy ying see mat 對應事物 n. counterpart

E

ex gwong X光 n. x-ray
ex gwong geem ta X光檢查 v.t. x-ray
ex gwong geh X光嘅 a. x-ray

F

fa 花 n bloom
fa choy 花彩 n festoon
fa fa gung jee 花花公子 n dandy
fa fay 花費 v. t expend
fa hap mat 化合物 n compound
fa jorng ban 化妝品 n. cosmetic
fa luy 花蕾 n bud
fa sek 化石 n. fossil
fai 快 adv. apace
fai 快 adj brisk
fai 快 a express
fai 快 a fast
fai 快 adv fast
fai 塊 n. piece
fai 快 n quick
fai 快 a. rapid
fai 快 adv. speedily
fai 快 a. speedy
fai bao hang 快步行 v.i. trot
fai chuk 快速 v.i. zoom
fai ding hm ju 快頂唔住 a. moribund
fai geh 快嘅 adv. post
fai geh 快嘅 a. quick
fai lok 快樂 n. happiness

fai pao 快跑 *v.i. sprint*	**fan dan** 反彈 *v.i. rebound*
fai seem 快閃 *n dash*	**fan dow** 奮鬥 *v.i. strive*
fai wut 快活 *n. joviality*	**fan dow yan** 訓導人 *n. preceptor*
fan 份 *n. allotment*	**fan duy** 反對 *prep. against*
fan 煩 *v.t. annoy*	**fan duy** 反對 *n disapproval*
fan 反 *pref. anti*	**fan duy** 反對 *v. t disapprove*
fan 翻 *v. i. capsize*	**fan duy** 反對 *v.t. object*
fan 飯 *n dinner*	**fan duy** 反對 *n. objection*
fan 分 *v. t divide*	**fan duy** 反對 *v.t. oppose*
fan 煩 *v.t. fret*	**fan duy** 反對 *v.i. protest*
fan 瞓 *v.i lie*	**fan duy jo** 反對做 *a. averse*
fan 分 *v.t. portion*	**fan fat** 犯法 *a. illegal*
fan 粉 *n. powder*	**fan fat geh** 犯法嘅 *a criminal*
fan 分 *v.t. proportion*	**fan fuk fu giew** 反覆呼叫 *n chant*
fan 反 *v.i. rebel*	**fan fuk see hao** 反覆思考 *v.t. mull*
fan 分 *v.t. segregate*	**fan gai** 分解 *v. t. decompose*
fan 分 *v.t. share*	**fan gai** 分解 *n. decomposition*
fan 瞓 *v.i. slumber*	**fan gam** 反感 *n. antipathy*
fan 分 *v.i. split*	**fan gam** 反感 *n. aversion*
fan 煩 *v.t. trouble*	**fan gam** 反感 *n dislike*
fan 煩 *v.t. vex*	**fan gam** 反感 *n. odium*
fan 煩 *v.t. irritate*	**fan gam** 反感 *n. repugnance*
fan bay 分泌 *v.t. secrete*	**fan gam** 反感 *n. repulsion*
fan bay 分泌 *n. secretion*	**fan gan** 番梘 *n. soap*
fan bay yik geh 分泌液嘅 *a. mucous*	**fan gao** 瞓覺 *v.i. sleep*
fan been 糞便 *n. muck*	**fan gao** 瞓覺 *n. sleep*
fan beet 分別 *v. i distinguish*	**fan gao** 瞓覺 *n. slumber*
fan beet geh 分別嘅 *a. respective*	**fan gao see gan** 瞓覺時間 *n. bed-time*
fan bo 帆布 *n. canvas*	**fan got** 分割 *v.t. partition*
fan bo 分佈 *n distribution*	**fan got** 分割 *v.t. segment*
fan bok 反駁 *v. t contradict*	**fan gwong** 反光 *a. reflective*
fan bok 反駁 *v. t counter*	**fan gwor sat** 犯過失 *v.i. sin*
fan bok 反駁 *v. t disprove*	**fan gwun** 翻滾 *v.i. wallow*
fan bok 反駁 *n. refutation*	**fan heen duy** 分遣隊 *n detachment*
fan bok 反駁 *v.t. refute*	**fan heurng jee ging** 焚香致敬 *v. t cense*
fan bok 反駁 *n. rejoinder*	**fan hm dow** 分唔到 *a. indivisible*
fan bwun 分半 *v.t. halve*	**fan hm hoy** 分唔開 *a. inseparable*
fan bwun geh 反叛嘅 *a. rebellious*	**fan hoy** 分開 *adv. apart*
fan chor 犯錯 *v. i err*	**fan hoy** 分開 *v. t detach*
fan dak...geh yan 瞓得…嘅人 *n. sleeper*	**fan hoy** 分開 *v.t. part*
	fan hoy 分開 *v.t. separate*

fan hoy 分開 *v.t. sunder*
fan hoy geh 分開嘅 *a. separate*
fan hung 反控 *n. countercharge*
fan hung ghe 粉紅色嘅 *a. pinkish*
fan hung sik 粉紅色 *n. pink*
fan hung sik geh 粉紅色嘅 *a pink*
fan hung sik geh 粉紅色嘅 *a. roseate*
fan huy 返去 *v.t. rejoin*
fan jan 瞓陣 *n. doze*
fan jang 紛爭 *n discord*
fan jee 分子 *n. molecule*
fan jee 分子 *n. numerator*
fan jee 分枝 *n. offshoot*
fan jee geh 分子嘅 *a. molecular*
fan jee yik yeen 反之亦然 *adv. vice-versa*
fan jeurk 勳爵 *n. lord*
fan jik 繁殖 *n reproduction*
fan joon tow 返轉頭 *v.t. retrace*
fan jor gao 瞓咗覺 *adv. asleep*
fan jorng geh 粉狀嘅 *a. mealy*
fan jung 分鐘 *n. minute*
fan juy yan 犯罪人 *n. offender*
fan kap 分級 *v.t. rank*
fan kay 分歧 *n. clash*
fan kay 分歧 *n. disagreement*
fan keh 番茄 *n. tomato*
fan korng 反抗 *v. i mutiny*
fan korng 反抗 *v.t. resist*
fan korng 反抗 *v.i. revolt*
fan korng 反抗 *n. revolt*
fan korng lik 反抗力 *n. resistance*
fan koy 憤慨 *a. indignant*
fan koy 憤慨 *n. indignation*
fan kuy 分區 *n. partition*
fan lay 婚禮 *n. nuptials*
fan lay 返嚟 *v.i. return*
fan lay 分離 *n. separation*
fan lay 婚禮 *n. spousal*
fan lay 婚禮 *n. wedding*
fan lay geh 婚禮嘅 *a. nuptial*

fan leen 訓練 *v.t. train*
fan leen 訓練 *n. training*
fan lo 煩惱 *n. annoyance*
fan lo 煩惱 *n botheration*
fan lo 煩惱 *n. fret*
fan lo 煩惱 *n. frustration*
fan low 憤怒 *n. ire*
fan low 憤怒 *n. outrage*
fan low 煩惱 *n vexation*
fan low 粉瘤 *n. wen*
fan luy 分類 *v.t. assort*
fan luy 分類 *v. t classify*
fan man geh 反問嘅 *a. rhetorical*
fan may 昏迷 *n. coma*
fan meen 反面 *n. negation*
fan mow 繁茂 *n. luxuriance*
fan mow 墳墓 *n. sepulchre*
fan mow 墳墓 *n. sepulture*
fan ngan gao 瞓晏覺 *v.i. nap*
fan ngoy ting 婚外情 *n. affair*
fan puy 分配 *v.t. allocate*
fan puy 分配 *v.t. allot*
fan puy 分配 *v.t. apportion*
fan puy dow geh yeh 分配到嘅嘢 *n. allocation*
fan pwun jeh 反叛者 *n malcontent*
fan pwuy 分配 *v. t distribute*
fan san 分散 *v. t disperse*
fan san 翻新 *v.t. renovate*
fan san 翻新 *n. renovation*
fan san lun 泛神論 *n. pantheism*
fan san lun jeh 泛神論者 *n. pantheist*
fan say jat juk jeh 憤世嫉俗者 *n cynic*
fan seh hay 反射器 *n. reflector*
fan sek hok 糞石學 *n. coprology*
fan sek low 番石榴 *n. guava*
fan ser geh 反射嘅 *a reflexive*
fan she 反射 *v.t. mirror*
fan sik 分析 *v.t. analyse*

fan sik geet gwor 分析結果 *n. analysis*

fan sik geh 分析嘅 *a analytical*

fan sik yoon 分析員 *n analyst*

fan sing 反省 *v.i. introspect*

fan sing 反省 *n. introspection*

fan sing sam fan 分成三份 *n. triplication*

fan sow 反手 *n. backhand*

fan sow 分數 *n. score*

fan suy 粉碎 *v.t. shatter*

fan tao 翻抄 *v.t. retread*

fan tao 翻抄 *n. retread*

fan tee 粉刺 *n acne*

fan tee 粉刺 *n. pimple*

fan teen geh 婚前嘅 *a. premarital*

fan tow 墳頭 *n. grave*

fan tow dung mat 反芻動物 *n. ruminant*

fan tow geh 反芻嘅 *a. ruminant*

fan wah 反話 *n. irony*

fan wah 訓話 *v.t. moralize*

fan way 範圍 *n. span*

fan way geh 範圍嘅 *n. purview*

fan way say fan yat 分爲四份一 *v.t. quarter*

fan wing geh 繁榮嘅 *a. prosperous*

fan yan 煩人 *n bore*

fan yan 婚姻 *n. marriage*

fan yan 婚姻 *n. wedlock*

fan yan geh 婚姻嘅 *a. marital*

fan yan geh 婚姻嘅 *a. matrimonial*

fan yee cho 薰衣草 *n. lavender*

fan yee tee 反義詞 *n. antonym*

fan yik 翻譯 *v.t. interpret*

fan yik 翻譯 *n. interpreter*

fan yik 翻譯 *v.t. translate*

fan yik 翻譯 *n. translation*

fan yin 婚姻 *n. matrimony*

fan ying 反應 *v.i. react*

fan ying 反應 *n. reaction*

fan ying 反映 *v.t. reflect*

fan ying 反應 *n. reflex*

fan ying 反應 *n. repercussion*

fan ying geh 反應嘅 *a reflex*

far 花 *n flower*

far been 花邊 *n. lace*

far dor 花朵 *n blossom*

far fan 花瓣 *n. petal*

far fan 花粉 *n. pollen*

far gang 花梗 *n. stalk*

far geh 花嘅 *a flowery*

far gwun 花冠 *n anadem*

far hok 化學 *n. chemistry*

far hok ga 化學家 *n. chemist*

far hok geh 化學嘅 *a. chemical*

far hok mat ban 化學物品 *n. chemical*

far hoon 花圈 *n. wreath*

far jiew 花招 *n. trickery*

far mat 花蜜 *n. nectar*

far meng 化名 *n. alias*

far meng 化名 *adv. alias*

far meng 花名 *n. nickname*

far ngat jee 花押字 *n. monogram*

far san 化身 *n. incarnation*

far seurng 花商 *n florist*

far wan 花環 *n. garland*

far yeen hao yu geh 花言巧語嘅 *a slick*

far yeurng 花樣 *n. pattern*

far yoon 花園 *n. garden*

farn duy 反對 *v. t demur*

fat 罰 *v.t. punish*

fat 發 *v.t. whisk*

fat bo 發佈 *n release*

fat chut 發出 *v.t. omit*

fat chut for far 發出火花 *v.i. scintillate*

fat dat 發達 *v.i. prosper*

fat deen 發顛 *v.t dement*

fat deen gey 發電機 *n dynamo*

fat deen hay 發電器 *n. generator*

fat ding geh 法定嘅 *a. statutory*

fat ding yan sow 法定人數 n. quorum

fat dung 發動 v.t. wage

fat for 發火 v.i. rage

fat fwun 罰款 n fine

fat fwun 罰款 v.t fine

fat gam 罰金 n forfeit

fat gwat 發掘 v.t. unearth

fat gwok geh 法國嘅 a. French

fat gwok yan 法國人 n French

fat gwong 發光 adv. aglow

fat gwong 發光 v.i. glow

fat gworng 發光 v.i. shine

fat gworng geh 發光嘅 a. lucent

fat gworng geh 發光嘅 a. luminous

fat gwun 法官 n. judge

fat gwun 法官 n. judiciary

fat hang 發行 v.t. launch

fat hao 發酵 v.t ferment

fat hao 發酵 n fermentation

fat hay 發起 v.t. initiate

fat jok 發作 n fit

fat kow 發球 n. serve

fat lan yung 法蘭絨 n flannel

fat lang 發冷 n ague

fat leurk 忽略 v.t. neglect

fat leurk 忽略 n neglect

fat leurk 忽略 v.t. overlook

fat ling 法令 n. ordinance

fat ling 法令 n. statute

fat lonrg jat 琺瑯質 n enamel

fat low sow 發牢騷 v.i. grumble

fat low sow 發牢騷 v.i. moan

fat low sow 發牢騷 v.t. murmur

fat low sow 發牢騷 v.i. mutter

fat low sow 發牢騷 v.i. whine

fat lung lung seng 發隆隆聲 v.i. rumble

fat lut 法律 n. law

fat lut ga 法律家 n. jurist

fat lut hok 法律學 n. jurisprudence

fat ming 發明 v.t devise

fat ming 發明 v.t. invent

fat ming 發明 n. invention

fat ming ga 發明家 n. inventor

fat mow 發毛 a. mouldy

fat ngar 發芽 v.i. germinate

fat ngar 發芽 v.i. sprout

fat ngoy 發呆 v.t. glaze

fat oy 發呆 n. trance

fat pai 發牌 v.i deal

fat sai for 發晒火 v.t. outrage

fat sang 發生 v.t. happen

fat sang 發生 v.i. occur

fat say 發誓 v.t. swear

fat see 忽視 n disregard

fat see 忽視 v.t. ignore

fat see see seng 發嘶嘶聲 v.i hiss

fat seh 發射 v.t fire

fat seh 發射 n. launch

fat seh geh 發射嘅 a projectile

fat seh gey 發射機 n. transmitter

fat siew 發燒 n fever

fat siew yow 發燒友 n. zealot

fat sun ho 發信號 v.t. signal

fat ting 法庭 n. court

fat ting 法庭 n. tribunal

fat yam 發音 v.t. pronounce

fat yam 發音 n. pronunciation

fat yeem 發炎 n. inflammation

fat yeem 發炎 a. inflammatory

fat yeen 發現 v.t discover

fat yeen 發現 n. discovery

fat yeen koon 發言權 n. say

fat yeen yan 發言人 n. spokesman

fat yuk 發育 n. growth

fay 飛 v.t flutter

fay 飛 v.i fly

fay 肺 n lung

fay 飛 v.t. sky

fay ban 飛奔 n. gallop

fay biew 飛鏢 n. dart

fay borng 誹謗 v.t. calumniate

fay borng 誹謗 n defamation

fay borng 誹謗 *n. libel*
fay borng 誹謗 *v.t. malign*
fay borng 誹謗 *n. sycophancy*
fay bwun jing 肥胖症 *n. obesity*
fay chuk 飛速 *n breakneck*
fay chuy 廢除 *v.t abolish*
fay chuy 廢除 *v abolition*
fay chuy 廢除 *v. t. abrogate*
fay chuy 廢除 *v.t. annul*
fay chuy 廢除 *v.t. repeal*
fay chuy 廢除 *n repeal*
fay chuy 廢除 *n. revocation*
fay dai ghe 肥大嘅 *a. voluminous*
fay fan geh 非凡嘅 *a. phenomenal*
fay fan geh yan 非凡嘅人 *n. phenomenon*
fay fat geh 非法嘅 *a. illicit*
fay fat jow mai mai 非法做買賣 *v.i. traffic*
fay fat tam yap 非法侵入 *n. trespass*
fay geh 肥嘅 *a. stout*
fay gey 飛機 *n. aeroplane*
fay gey 飛機 *n. aircraft*
fay gey 飛機 *n. plane*
fay gey see 飛機師 *n. pilot*
fay huy 廢墟 *n. ruin*
fay jay 飛仔 *n. hooligan*
fay jeurng 徽章 *n. badge*
fay jeurng 徽章 *n crest*
fay lay fay huy 飛嚟飛去 *v.i. swarm*
fay liew 肥料 *n compost*
fay liew 肥料 *n fertilizer*
fay liew 肥料 *n. manure*
fay liew tung 廢料桶 *n skip*
fay lo 肺癆 *n. tuberculosis*
fay ngor 飛蛾 *n. moth*
fay see 費事 *conj. lest*
fay seurng 非常 *adv. highly*
fay seurng 非常 *a. very*
fay seurng go hing 非常高興 *a overjoyed*

fay seurng ho geh 非常好嘅 *a. splendid*
fay seurng jee 非常之 *pron. such*
fay seurng joon ging geh 非常尊敬嘅 *a. reverent*
fay seurng ok duk geh 非常惡毒嘅 *a. heinous*
fay sow 揮手 *v.t. wave*
fay wah 廢話 *n. nonsense*
fay wah 廢話 *n. prattle*
fay worng 輝煌 *n. refulgence*
fay worng geh 輝煌嘅 *a. resplendent*
fay yeem 肺炎 *n. pneumonia*
fay yu 鯡魚 *n. herring*
fay yuk 肥沃 *a fertile*
fei 肥 *a fat*
fey bong 誹謗 *v. asperse*
fey gey see 飛機師 *n. aviator*
fok loon 霍亂 *n. cholera*
fong dai 放大 *v.t. amplify*
fong fat 方法 *n. strategy*
fong meen 方面 *n. aspect*
fong sik 方式 *n. approach*
fong so 防守 *v. t defend*
fong ting sik 方程式 *n equation*
fong yeen 方言 *n dialect*
fong yu 防禦 *n defence*
for 貨 *n. cargo*
for 貨 *n. commodity*
for 火 *n fire*
for 貨 *n. freight*
for 火 *n. rage*
for bay 貨幣 *n currency*
for cher 火車 *n. train*
for cher 貨車 *n. van*
for cher tow 火車頭 *n. locomotive*
for cheurng 火槍 *n. musket*
for cheurng sow 火槍手 *n. musketeer*
for chorng 貨倉 *n depot*
for far 火化 *v. t cremate*
for far 火化 *n cremation*
for far 火花 *n. spark*

for gey 科技 *n. technology*
for gey 火雞 *n. turkey*
for gwong 火光 *n flare*
for hay 科系 *n faculty*
for hok 科學 *n. science*
for hok ga 科學家 *n. scientist*
for hok geh 科學嘅 *a. scientific*
for jeen 火箭 *n. rocket*
for koot 否決 *v.t. veto*
for low 火爐 *n. furnace*
for san 火山 *n. volcano*
for san geh 火山嘅 *a. volcanic*
for see lam 科林斯 *n. Corinth*
for sing 火星 *n Mars*
for tai 火柴 *n match*
for tan 貨攤 *n. stand*
for ting 課程 *n. course*
for ting 課程 *n curriculum*
for yeem 火焰 *n blaze*
for yeem 火焰 *n flame*
forng 放 *v.t free*
forng 放 *v.t. release*
forng 房 *n. room*
forng been 方便 *n. convenience*
forng been 方便 *a convenient*
forng been 方便 *a. handy*
forng dai 放大 *v. t enlarge*
forng dai 放大 *v.t. magnify*
forng dai geh 放大嘅 *a. telescopic*
forng day 放低 *v. t deposit*
forng deen 放電 *v.i flirt*
forng dong 放蕩 *n debauch*
forng dong 放蕩 *n debauchery*
forng dong 放蕩 *a. licentious*
forng dong geh yan 放蕩嘅人 *n. libertine*
forng dow juy dai 放到最大 *v.t. maximize*
forng fat 方法 *n means*
forng fat 方法 *n. method*
forng fu 防腐 *v. t embalm*
forng fu jay 防腐劑 *n. antiseptic*

forng fu jay 防腐劑 *n. preservative*
forng gway lay 放貴利 *n. usury*
forng hay 放棄 *v.t, abdicate*
forng hay 放棄 *n abdication*
forng hay 放棄 *v.t forgo*
forng hay 放棄 *v.t. forswear*
forng hay 放棄 *v.t. relinquish*
forng hay 放棄 *v.t. waive*
forng heurng 方向 *n direction*
forng hung 防空 *a. anti-aircraft*
forng ja dan geh yan 放炸彈嘅人 *n bomber*
forng jam 方針 *n. policy*
forng jee 防止 *v. t. combat*
forng jee 防止 *v.t. prevent*
forng jee 防止 *v.t. ward*
forng jik ban 紡織品 *n textile*
forng jik geh 紡織嘅 *a. textile*
forng jow 方舟 *n ark*
forng juk 放逐 *v. t exile*
forng lay 放餌 *v.t. bait*
forng lung 放膿 *v.t. lance*
forng man 訪問 *v.t. interview*
forng man 放慢 *v.t. slacken*
forng meen 方面 *n facet*
forng mo geh 荒謬嘅 *a. grotesque*
forng mow 荒謬 *a absurd*
forng mow 荒謬 *n absurdity*
forng mow geh 荒謬嘅 *a. nonsensical*
forng mow geh 荒謬嘅 *a. ridiculous*
forng muk 放牧 *v.t. pasture*
forng ngoy 防礙 *n. hindrance*
forng sa gung 紡紗工 *n. spinner*
forng sik 方式 *n. mode*
forng sung 放鬆 *v.t. relax*
forng sung 放鬆 *n. relaxation*
forng suy 防水 *n waterproof*
forng suy geh 防水嘅 *a. waterproof*
forng tow gan 方頭巾 *n. kerchief*
forng way 方位 *n bearing*

forng yap san am 放入神龕 *v. t* enshrine

forng yeh 荒野 *n. moor*

forng yeh 荒野 *n. wilderness*

forng ying 放映 *v.t. project*

forng ying geh ying jeurng 放映嘅影像 *n. projection*

forng ying gey 放映機 *n bioscope*

forng ying gey 放映機 *n. projector*

fow biew 浮標 *n buoy*

fow ju 浮住 *adv. afloat*

fow koot 否決 *n. veto*

fow lik 浮力 *n buoyancy*

fow ying 否認 *v. t abnegate*

fow ying 否認 *n abnegation*

fow ying 否認 *n denial*

fow ying 否認 *v. t. deny*

fu 苦 *a bitter*

fu 附 *v. t enclose*

fu 孵 *v.i. incubate*

fu 負 *a minus*

fu 褲 *n. pl trousers*

fu bai 腐敗 *n. venality*

fu bwun 副本 *n duplicate*

fu cho 府綢 *n. poplin*

fu dai geh 附帶嘅 *a. subsidiary*

fu dai tiew geen 附帶條件 *a conditional*

fu dam 負擔 *v.t. afford*

fu dam 負擔 *v. t burden*

fu dam gwor chung 負擔過重 *v.t. overburden*

fu dow for 輔導課 *n. tutorial*

fu ga 附加 *v.t. append*

fu ga fay 附加費 *n. premium*

fu ga fay 附加肥 *n. surcharge*

fu ga suy 附加稅 *n. supertax*

fu ga suy 附加稅 *n. surtax*

fu gan 附近 *prep. near*

fu gan 附近 *adv. near*

fu gan 附近 *n. neighbourhood*

fu gan geh 附近嘅 *a. local*

fu gar 附加 *v.t. attach*

fu geen 附件 *n. appendage*

fu geen 附件 *n. attachment*

fu geen 附件 *n. enclosure*

fu giew 呼叫 *v.t. page*

fu gor 副歌 *n. chorus*

fu gor 副歌 *n refrain*

fu gow 訃告 *a. obituary*

fu gung 苦功 *n. peon*

fu gung 苦工 *n. toil*

fu hap 符合 *v.t. accord*

fu hap 符合 *v. i correspond*

fu hap lor tap 合乎邏輯 *a. logical*

fu ho 負號 *n minus*

fu ho 符號 *n. notation*

fu hot 呼喝 *v. i bellow*

fu jai lang lik 付債能力 *n. solvency*

fu jak 負責 *a. answerable*

fu jak 負責 *v.t. undertake*

fu jor geh 輔助嘅 *a. auxiliary*

fu jor yan yoon 輔助人員 *n. auxiliary*

fu ju 副署 *v. t. countersign*

fu kap 呼吸 *n. respiration*

fu kap 呼吸 *v.i. respire*

fu lan 腐爛 *adj carious*

fu lan 腐爛 *n. decay*

fu lan 腐爛 *v. i decay*

fu lan 腐爛 *n. rot*

fu lan 腐爛 *v.i. rot*

fu lik 苦力 *n coolie*

fu lo 苦惱 *n. anguish*

fu lo 俘虜 *n. captive*

fu low 呼嚕 *n. grunt*

fu low seng 呼嚕聲 *v.i. grunt*

fu luk 附錄 *n. appendix*

fu meen 負面 *n. negative*

fu mor 撫摩 *v. t. caress*

fu mor 撫摸 *v.t fondle*

fu mow 父母 *n. parent*

fu mow geh 父母嘅 *a. parental*

fu mun 苦悶 *v.t. agonize*

fu pak ja yeurk 琥珀炸藥 *n. amberite*

fu sik 膚色 *n complexion*
fu sik sing 腐蝕性 *a. caustic*
fu sik sing geh 腐蝕性嘅 *adj. corrosive*
fu sow 副手 *n deputy*
fu suk 附屬 *n. adjunct*
fu suk 附屬 *n. subordination*
fu suk mat 附屬物 *n appurtenance*
fu tan ban 副產品 *n by-product*
fu tan geh 父親嘅 *a. paternal*
fu tay gan geh 夫妻間嘅 *a conjugal*
fu tee 副詞 *n. adverb*
fu tee geh 副詞嘅 *a. adverbial*
fu tow 斧頭 *n. axe*
fu tow 斧頭 *n. hatchet*
fu wun 呼喚 *v.t. conjure*
fu wun 呼喚 *v.t. summon*
fu yam 輔音 *n. consonant*
fu yeen 附言 *n. postscript*
fu yu 富裕 *n. affluence*
fu yu 富裕 *n. wealth*
fuk bo 腹部 *n abdomen*
fuk bo 腹部 *n. midriff*
fuk bo geh 腹部嘅 *a. abdominal*
fuk chung 服從 *v. i comply*
fuk chung 服從 *n. obedience*
fuk dak 伏特 *n. volt*
fuk dak 伏特 *n. voltage*
fuk dow 幅度 *n. magnitude*
fuk fat 復發 *v.i. relapse*
fuk gwun 腹管 *n. cornicle*
fuk hap tee 復合詞 *n compound*
fuk hing 復興 *n. renaissance*
fuk hing geh 復興嘅 *a. resurgent*
fuk jap 複雜 *a complex*
fuk jap 複雜 *a. intricate*
fuk jap 複雜 *a. sophisticated*
fuk jap 複雜 *n. sophistication*
fuk jap fa 複雜化 *v. t complicate*
fuk jap fa 複雜化 *n. complication*
fuk jap far 複雜化 *v.t. sophisticate*
fuk jay 複製 *v. t copy*

fuk jay 複製 *v. t duplicate*
fuk jay ban 複製品 *n copy*
fuk jay ban 複製品 *n. replica*
fuk jay ghe 複製嘅 *a duplicate*
fuk jiew 輻照 *v.i. irradiate*
fuk jik 復職 *v.t. reinstate*
fuk jik 復職 *n. reinstatement*
fuk jorng 服裝 *n. apparel*
fuk jorng 服裝 *n. costume*
fuk koy 覆蓋 *v.t mantle*
fuk koy tang 覆蓋層 *n coating*
fuk mo yoon 服務員 *n. attendant*
fuk mow 服務 *n. service*
fuk mow 服務 *v.t service*
fuk mow geh 服務嘅 *a. ministrant*
fuk mow yoon 服務員 *n. steward*
fuk see 服侍 *v.i. minister*
fuk seurng bo 腹上部 *n anticardium*
fuk she 輻射 *n. radiation*
fuk sow 複數 *a. plural*
fuk sow 複數 *n. plurality*
fuk sow 復蘇 *n. revival*
fuk sow 復蘇 *v.i. revive*
fuk wut jeet 復活節 *n easter*
fuk yam 福音 *n. gospel*
fuk yan 複印 *v. t cyclostyle*
fuk yan 複印 *n print*
fuk yan 複印 *v.t. xerox*
fuk yan gey 復印機 *n cyclostyle*
fuk yeen 復現 *n. resurgence*
fuk yoon 復原 *n. rehabilitation*
fuk yoon 復原 *n. restoration*
fun gan 附近 *n. vicinity*
fung 封 *v.t. seal*
fung 風 *n. wind*
fung chee hey kek fung 諷刺喜劇風 *adj aristophanic*
fung chuk gey 風速計 *n anemometer*
fung dek 風笛 *n. bagpipe*
fung dow 蜂竇 *n alveary*
fung dow 峰竇 *n. beehive*
fung forng 蜂房 *n. hive*

fung fu 豐富 *a. richness*
fung gak 風格 *n. look*
fung gak 風格 *n mould*
fung gak 風格 *n. style*
fung geen 封建 *a feudal*
fung ging 風景 *n. landscape*
fung ging 風景 *n. scenery*
fung ging 風景 *n. view*
fung ging yow may geh 風景優美嘅 *a. scenic*
fung gow jing 瘋狗症 *n. rabies*
fung hay 風氣 *n. stampede*
fung hee, 風險 *n. risk*
fung heen 奉獻 *v. t. dedicate*
fung heen 奉獻 *n dedication*
fung ho 風口 *n. vent*
fung ju 封住 *v.t bar*
fung ju 封住 *v.i. stem*
fung kam 風琴 *n. harmonium*
fung kwong 瘋狂 *a. frantic*
fung low wan see 風流韻事 *n. romp*
fung mat jow 蜂蜜酒 *n. mead*
fung may 風味 *n. cuisine*
fung meen 封面 *n. cover*
fung mun dow 豐滿度 *n. fullness*
fung mun geh 豐滿嘅 *a. voluptuous*
fung sap 風濕 *n. rheumatism*
fung sap beng geh 風濕病嘅 *a. rheumatic*
fung seen 風扇 *n fan*
fung sing 奉承 *n adulation*
fung sing 奉承 *n flattery*
fung sing 豐盛 *a. luxuriant*
fung sor 封鎖 *n blockade*
fung tao 蜂巢 *n. honeycomb*
fung tee 諷刺 *a. ironical*
fung tee 諷刺 *v.t. lampoon*
fung tee 諷刺 *n. sarcasm*
fung tee 諷刺 *n. satire*
fung tee 諷刺 *v.t. satirize*
fung tee 諷刺 *a. wry*
fung tee geh 諷刺嘅 *a. sarcastic*

fung tee geh 諷刺嘅 *a. satirical*
fung tee jok ga 諷刺作家 *n. satirist*
fung tee man jeurng 諷刺文章 *n. lampoon*
fung tee wah 諷刺畫 *n. caricature*
fung ter 風車 *n. windmill*
fung way gway juk 封爲貴族 *v. t. ennoble*
fung...way jeurk see 封...爲爵士 *v.t. knight*
fut fut 狒狒 *n. baboon*
fut lung 弗隆 *n. furlong*
fuy 灰 *n. ash*
fwun dai 寬大 *n. lenience, leniency*
fwun dai 寬大 *n. magnanimity*
fwun dai geh 寬大嘅 *a. merciful*
fwun doy 款待 *n treat*
fwun fu 歡呼 *n acclamation*
fwun fu seng 歡呼聲 *n. cheer*
fwun horng 款項 *n. payment*
fwun kworng 歡狂 *n. spree*
fwun lok 歡樂 *n. frolic*
fwun lok 歡樂 *n. jollity*
fwun lok 歡樂 *n. merriment*
fwun shu 寬恕 *n. condonation*
fwun shu 寬恕 *n. mercy*
fwun siew 歡笑 *n. mirth*
fwun tang 歡騰 *n. jubilation*
fwun teen hay day 歡天喜地 *n. rapture*
fwun torng 寬敞 *a. capacious*
fwun torng 寬敞 *a. spacious*
fwun torng geh 寬敞嘅 *a. roomy*
fwun wang 寬宏 *a. magnanimous*
fwun wang dai leurng 寬宏大量 *n. generosity*
fwun ying 歡迎 *a. welcome*
fwun ying 歡迎 *n welcome*
fwun ying 歡迎 *v.t welcome*
fwun yung 寬容 *a. lenient*
fwut 闊 *a broad*
fwut 闊 *a. wide*

fwut 闊 *adv. wide*
fwut dow 闊度 *n breadth*
fwut dow 闊度 *n. width*
fwut ngoy pow 闊外袍 *n. toga*
fwuy fuk 恢復 *v.t. recover*
fwuy fuk 恢復 *n. recovery*
fwuy fuk 恢復 *v.t. rehabilitate*
fwuy fuk 恢復 *v.t. restore*
fwuy fuk 恢復 *n. resumption*
fwuy fuk ting chun 恢復青春 *n. rejuvenation*
fwuy hai doon see 詼諧短詩 *n epigram*
fwuy lay 灰泥 *v.t. mortar*
fwuy ling 奎寧 *n. quinine*
fwuy sam 灰心 *v. t deject*
fwuy sik geh 灰色嘅 *a. grey*

G

ga 加 *v.t. add*
ga 嫁 *v.t. marry*
ga 架 *n. rack*
ga 架 *n. shelf*
ga ban 假扮 *v.t. pretend*
ga biew deem fu ho 加標點符號 *v.t. punctuate*
ga cheet 假設 *v.t. assume*
ga cheet 假設 *n. assumption*
ga cheurng 加長 *v.t. lengthen*
ga chuk 加速 *v.t accelerate*
ga chuk 加速 *n acceleration*
ga chuk 加速 *v.i. speed*
ga deen 加墊 *v.t. pad*
ga deng 加釘 *v.t. stud*
ga fan 加粉 *v.t. powder*
ga fat 假髮 *n. wig*
ga feh 咖啡 *n coffee*
ga feh deem 咖啡店 *n. cafe*

ga ga seng siew 嘎嘎聲笑 *v. i cackle*
ga gak tung jeurng 價格通脹 *n. inflation*
ga geh 假嘅 *a sham*
ga heurng liew 加香料 *v.t. spice*
ga ho joot 加後綴 *v.t. suffix*
ga hoy 加害 *v.t. inflict*
ga huy 嘉許 *n commendation*
ga iew may liew 加調味料 *v.t. season*
ga jee seng 嘎吱聲 *v. i creak*
ga jee seng 嘎吱聲 *n creak*
ga jeh 家姐 *n. sister*
ga jeurng 假象 *n. pretence*
ga jeurng 假象 *n. semblance*
ga jeurng 假象 *n sham*
ga jik 價值 *n. value*
ga kam 家禽 *n. fowl*
ga kam yuk 家禽肉 *n. poultry*
ga kay 假期 *n. vacation*
ga keurng 加強 *v. t. cement*
ga keurng 加強 *v. t. consolidate*
ga keurng 加強 *v.t. intensify*
ga keurng 加強 *v.t. reinforce*
ga keurng 加強 *v.t. strengthen*
ga lun 加侖 *n. gallon*
ga meen 加冕 *v. t crown*
ga meen deen lay 加冕典禮 *n coronation*
ga mow hang peen 假冒行騙 *n. imposture*
ga pwuy 加倍 *v. t. double*
ga pwuy 加倍 *v.t. redouble*
ga san man 假新聞 *n canard*
ga say chorng 駕駛艙 *n. cock-pit*
ga say jeh 駕駛者 *n. motorist*
ga see 家私 *n. furniture*
ga seurng 加上 *n. addition*
ga seurng 加上 *a. additional*
ga sik 假釋 *n. parole*
ga sik 假釋 *v.t. parole*
ga tang 加層 *v.t. line*
ga teen 價錢 *n. price*

ga teet 假設 *n. hypothesis*
ga teet 假設 *a. hypothetical*
ga teet 假設 *n. presumption*
ga teet 假設 *n. presupposition*
ga tiew man 加條紋 *v.t. stripe*
ga ting luy gao see 家庭女教師 *n. governess*
ga torng 加糖 *v.t. sugar*
ga tow 加圖 *v.t. illustrate*
ga wu jiew fan 加胡椒粉 *v.t. pepper*
ga yap 加入 *v.t. incorporate*
ga yat jee larm 假日指南 *n brochure*
ga yeem 加鹽 *v.t salt*
ga yeet 加熱 *v.t heat*
ga yoon sik 加緣飾 *v.t fringe*
gah jik 價值 *n. worth*
gai 戒 *v.i. abstain*
gai 鎅 *v.t groove*
gai 鎅 *v.t. lacerate*
gai 鎅 *v.t. slit*
gai 街 *n. street*
gai chuy 解除 *v.t absolve*
gai doon 階段 *n. gradation*
gai doon 階段 *n. phase*
gai dung 解凍 *v.i thaw*
gai fo hook 解剖學 *n. anatomy*
gai forng 解放 *n. emancipation*
gai forng 解放 *v.t. liberate*
gai forng 解放 *n. liberation*
gai forng 解放 *n. manumission*
gai forng jeh 解放者 *n. liberator*
gai forng low day 解放奴隸 *v.t. manumit*
gai fow 解剖 *v.t dissect*
gai fow 解剖 *n dissection*
gai gu 解雇 *n dismissal*
gai hot 解渴 *v.t. slake*
gai hoy 解開 *v.t. solve*
gai hoy 解開 *v.t. undo*
gai jee 戒指 *n. ring*
gai koot 解決 *v.t. resolve*
gai koot 解決 *v.i. settle*

gai koot ban fat 解決辦法 *n. solution*
gai lai 戒奶 *v.t ablactate*
gai lai 戒奶 *n ablactation*
gai lai 戒奶 *v.t. wean*
gai mwut 芥末 *n. mustard*
gai san 解散 *v.t. dismiss*
gai see 街市 *n market*
gai seen 界線 *n. demarcation*
gai seen 疥癬 *n. scabies*
gai siew 介紹 *v.t. introduce*
gai siew 介紹 *n. introduction*
gai sik 解釋 *v.t define*
gai sik 解釋 *n definition*
gai sik 解釋 *v.t. explain*
gai sik 解釋 *n explanation*
gai sik 解釋 *n. paraphrase*
gai sik 解釋 *v.t. paraphrase*
gai tee 介詞 *n. preposition*
gai toot 解脫 *n. relief*
gai yap 介入 *v.i. intervene*
gai yap 介入 *n. intervention*
gai yee 介意 *v.t. mind*
gai yeurk 解藥 *n. antidote*
gai yeurk 解藥 *n. mithridate*
gak 鎘 *n cadmium*
gak dow 格鬥 *n. grapple*
gak gak siew 格格笑 *v.i. giggle*
gak gor yoot geh 隔個月嘅 *adj. bimonthly*
gak hoy 隔開 *v.t. space*
gak jay muk ga 格仔木架 *n. lattice*
gak joot 隔絕 *n. isolation*
gak lay 隔籬 *a. adjacent*
gak lay 隔離 *n. insulation*
gak lay 隔離 *v.t. isolate*
gak lay 隔籬 *a. next*
gak lay 隔離 *v.t. seclude*
gak lay 隔離 *v.t. sequester*
gak lay cho see 隔離措施 *n. segregation*

gak lay lun she 隔籬鄰舍 *n.* *neighbour*

gak lut geh 格律嘅 *a. metrical*

gak ming 革命 *n. revolution*

gak sik 格式 *n format*

gak yeen 格言 *n. adage*

gak yeen 格言 *n aphorism*

gak yeen 格言 *n dictum*

gak yeen 格言 *n. maxim*

gak yeen 格言 *n. motto*

gak yeen 格言 *n. proverb*

gak yeet 隔熱 *v.t. insulate*

gam 金 *n. gold*

gam *v.t. press*

gam 咁 *adv. that*

gam biew choy 錦標賽 *n. tournament*

gam doon 錦緞 *n brocade*

gam dow bat on 感到不安 *v.t. perturb*

gam dow ging kay 感到驚奇 *v.i marvel*

gam duk 監督 *v.t. oversee*

gam duk 監督 *n. superintendence*

gam duk 監督 *v.t. supervise*

gam duk 監督 *n. supervision*

gam far yoon 感化院 *n. reformatory*

gam fay 減肥 *v.i. slim*

gam gai 尷尬 *a. awkward*

gam gai 尷尬 *v. t embarrass*

gam gey 禁忌 *n. taboo*

gam gey 禁忌 *a taboo*

gam gik 感激 *n. appreciation*

gam gik 感激 *a. grateful*

gam gik 感激 *n. gratitude*

gam gik 感激 *a. indebted*

gam gok 感覺 *n feeling*

gam gok 感覺 *n. sensation*

gam gok dow 感覺到 *a. appreciable*

gam gok dow 感覺到 *v.t. sense*

gam gok geh 感覺嘅 *a. sensuous*

gam gok sing 感覺性 *n. sentience*

gam gung 監工 *n. overseer*

gam gwun geh 感官嘅 *a. sensual*

gam gwun yan 監管人 *n. superintendent*

gam hao 監考 *v.t. invigilate*

gam hao 監考 *n. invigilation*

gam hao gwun 監考官 *n. invigilator*

gam heng 減輕 *v.t. alleviate*

gam heng 減輕 *n. alleviation*

gam huy 敢去 *v.t. venture*

gam jay ling 禁制令 *n. injunction*

gam jay ling 禁制令 *n. prohibition*

gam jee 禁止 *n. ban*

gam jee 禁止 *v. t. debar*

gam jee 禁止 *v.t forbid*

gam jee 禁止 *v.t. prohibit*

gam jee 禁止 *v.t. taboo*

gam jee geh 禁止嘅 *a. prohibitive*

gam jee geh 禁止嘅 *a. prohibitory*

gam jee tap 金字塔 *n. pyramid*

gam jeh 感謝 *a. thankful*

gam jeurng 金匠 *n. goldsmith*

gam lam 橄欖 *n. olive*

gam ling 禁令 *n ban*

gam man 今晚 *n. tonight*

gam man 今晚 *adv. tonight*

gam may geh 甘美嘅 *a. mellow*

gam mo 感冒 *n cold*

gam see 監視 *v.i. spy*

gam see 監視 *n. surveillance*

gam sik geh 金色嘅 *a. golden*

gam suk 金屬 *n. metal*

gam suk geh 金屬嘅 *a. metallic*

gam suk see 金屬絲 *n. tinsel*

gam tan tee 感歎詞 *n exclamation*

gam tan tee 感歎詞 *n. interjection*

gam tat geh 監察嘅 *a. monitory*

gam teen geh 金錢嘅 *a. pecuniary*

gam ting 感情 *n. affection*

gam ting 感情 *n emotion*

gam ting fung fu 感情豐富 *a emotional*

gam ting yung see geh 感情用事嘅 *a. sentimental*
gam wu 監護 *n. wardship*
gam yat 今日 *adv. today*
gam yat 今日 *n. today*
gam yeem 感染 *n. infection*
gam yeem jor geh 感染咗嘅 *a. septic*
gam yeem lik 感染力 *n. pathos*
gam yow 甘油 *n. glycerine*
gam yuk 禁慾 *n. ascetic*
gam yuk 禁慾 *a. ascetic*
gam yuk 監獄 *n. nick*
gam yuk 監獄 *n. prison*
gam yung ga 金融家 *n financier*
gan 鹼 *n alkali*
gan 揀 *v. t. choose*
gan 揀 *v.i. opt*
gan 揀 *v.t. pick*
gan 根 *n. root*
gan 揀 *v.t. select*
gan 緊 *a. tight*
gan ban 跟班 *n. lackey*
gan dan 簡單 *a. brief*
gan dan 簡單 *a. simple*
gan dan 簡單 *n. simplicity*
gan dan geh 簡單嘅 *a. plain*
gan deep 間諜 *n. spy*
gan doon yee mo lay 簡短而無禮 *a curt*
gan far 簡化 *n. simplification*
gan far 簡化 *v.t. simplify*
gan gai 簡介 *n. profile*
gan gai 簡介 *n. prospsectus*
gan gak 間隔 *n. compartment*
gan gak 間隔 *n. interval*
gan gak see gan 間隔時間 *n lapse*
gan gan 僅僅 *adv. barely*
gan gan 僅僅 *a. mere*
gan gao gwan tow 緊急關頭 *n. conjuncture*
gan gap 緊急 *n emergency*

gan gap 緊急 *a. urgent*
gan geet 簡潔 *n brevity*
gan geet 簡潔 *a concise*
gan geet geh 簡潔嘅 *a. laconic*
gan geh 奸嘅 *a. treacherous*
gan gey 根基 *n. base*
gan hm jung 間唔中 *a. occasional*
gan ja hang way 奸詐行爲 *n duplicity*
gan jeep 間接 *a. indirect*
gan jeurng 緊張 *a. intense*
gan jeurng 緊張 *a. nervous*
gan jeurng 緊張 *a. tense*
gan jeurng 緊張 *n. tension*
gan ju 跟住 *v.t follow*
gan ju 跟住 *adv. next*
gan ju 跟住 *adv. then*
gan jung 跟蹤 *v.i. stalk*
gan jung 跟蹤 *v.t. trace*
gan kap 分級 *v.t grade*
gan keet 間歇 *n. interim*
gan keet 間歇 *n. interlude*
gan keet 間歇 *n. lull*
gan lan 艱難 *n. hardship*
gan lan 艱難 *n. thick*
gan lan 艱難 *a. tough*
gan leurk 簡略 *a crude*
gan lik 簡歷 *n. resume*
gan pai 近排 *a. recent*
gan pai 近排 *adv. recently*
gan pay lik jun 筋疲力盡 *v. t. exhaust*
gan san 謹慎 *a. cautious*
gan san 謹慎 *n discretion*
gan san 謹慎 *a. wary*
gan san geh 謹慎嘅 *a. prudential*
gan see 近視 *n. myopia*
gan see geh 近視嘅 *a. myopic*
gan seurng 奸商 *n. profiteer*
gan suk 緊縮 *n. stringency*
gan tek 間尺 *n. ruler*
gan ting 簡稱 *v.t. abbreviate*

gan ting 簡稱 *n abbreviation*
gan yiew 緊要 *v.i. matter*
gan yiew geh 簡要嘅 *a. terse*
gang 耕 *v. t cultivate*
gang 耕 *v.i plough*
gang 耕 *v.t. till*
gang dor 更多 *a. more*
gang dor 更多 *adv more*
gang ga 更加 *adv much*
gang goy 更改 *v. t correct*
gang goy 更改 *n. modification*
gang ho 更好 *adv. better*
gang jun yat bo 更進一步 *a further*
gang leen kay 更年期 *n. menopause*
gang san 更新 *v.t. renew*
gang san 更新 *n. renewal*
gang shu sik 更舒適 *n. cosier*
gang siew 更少 *a. lesser*
gang yoon 更遠 *adv. beyond*
gang yoon geh 更遠嘅 *adv. further*
gao 攪 *v. t. & i. churn*
gao 教 *v. t educate*
gao 攪 *v.i. stir*
gao 交 *v.t. submit*
gao 教 *v.t. teach*
gao bay 父畀 *v.t. consign*
gao cher 絞車 *n. winch*
gao chor 搞錯 *v.t. mistake*
gao deem 搞掂 *v.t. accomplish*
gao deem 交點 *n. intersection*
gao deem jor 搞掂咗 *a accomplished*
gao fwuy 教誨 *a didactic*
gao gey 攪機 *n whisk*
gao gway geh 搞鬼嘅 *a. mischievous*
gao heurng kuk 交響曲 *n. symphony*
gao ho 較好 *a better*
gao hok dai gorng 教學大綱 *n. syllabus*
gao jay ban 救濟品 *n. alms*
gao jeen 交戰 *n belligerency*
gao jeen 鉸剪 *n. scissors*
gao jeen gwok 交戰國 *n belligerent*

gao jung 教宗 *n. pope*
gao jung geh 教宗嘅 *a. papal*
gao jung geh jik way 教宗嘅職位 *n. papacy*
gao kuy 教區 *n. parish*
gao kuy 郊區 *n. suburb*
gao kuy geh 郊區嘅 *a. suburban*
gao leen 教練 *n. instructor*
gao loon 搞亂 *v.t. muddle*
gao lorng jorng 膠囊狀 *adj capsular*
gao low 交流 *n. intercourse*
gao pai geh 教派嘅 *a. sectarian*
gao pwuy 交配 *v.i. copulate*
gao pwuy 交配 *v.t. mate*
gao pwuy fan jik 交配繁殖 *v.t breed*
gao sang 搞生 *v. t. enliven*
gao see 教師 *n. pedagogue*
gao see 教師 *n. tutor*
gao siew 搞笑 *n. funny*
gao sing jeurng 攪成漿 *v.t. pulp*
gao sor fan 教唆犯 *ns. barrator*
gao sow 教授 *n. professor*
gao suk gam 交贖金 *v.t. ransom*
gao suy 膠水 *n. adhesive*
gao suy 膠水 *n. glue*
gao suy 絞碎 *v.t. mince*
gao suy 膠水 *n. mucilage*
gao ta 較差 *a. inferior*
gao ta 交叉 *v.t. intersect*
gao ta low ho 交叉路口 *n. junction*
gao tiew 教條 *n dogma*
gao tong 教堂 *n. church*
gao tong mo day 教堂墓地 *n. churchyard*
gao tubg gung guy 交通工具 *n. vehicle*
gao tung 交通 *n. traffic*
gao tung gung guy 交通工具 *n. transport*
gao tung gung guy 交通工具 *n. transportation*
gao wat 狡猾 *a crafty*

gao wat 狡猾 n cunning
gao wat 狡猾 n. knavery
gao wat 狡猾 a. sly
gao wat geh 狡猾嘅 a cunning
gao wat geh 狡猾嘅 a. wily
gao wat geh luy jay 狡猾嘅女仔 n. minx
gao wu cher 救護車 n. ambulance
gao wun 交換 n. barter2
gao wun 交換 n exchange
gao wun 交換 v. t exchange
gao wun 交換 n. interchange
gao wun 父換 v. interchange
gao yik 交易 n deal
gao yik 交易 v.i trade
gao yik 交易 n. transaction
gao ying ga 絞刑架 n. . gallows
gao yow 郊遊 n. outing
gao yu gey 攪乳機 n. churn
gao yuk 教育 n education
gao yuk hok 教育學 n. pedagogy
gap 急 a desperate
gap 鴿 n dove
gap 急 v.t. jabber
gap 鉀 n. potassium
gap ban 甲板 n deck
gap chung 甲蟲 n beetle
gap geh 急嘅 a. imperative
gap ju 急住 n hurry
gap low 急流 n. torrent
gap low tang 夾樓層 n. mezzanine
gap see 急事 n. urgency
gap sing 急升 v.i. soar
gap tiew 急跳 v.i. palpitate
gar 假 a false
gar ban 假扮 v. t disguise
gar ban 嘉賓 n. guest
gar ban 加班 adv. overtime
gar ban 加班 n overtime
gar chuk 加速 v. t. expedite
gar deem 加點 v. t dot
gar gak 價格 n. cost

gar geh 假嘅 a bogus
gar gung jay see 假公濟私 n. jobbery
gar jorng 嫁妝 n dowry
gar ting geh 家庭嘅 a domestic
garm 減 v.t. reduce
garm 減 v.t. subtract
garm 減 n. subtraction
garm 減 n. reduction
garm chuy 減除 prep. minus
garm day 減低 v.t. abate
garm day 減低 n. abatement
garm ga 減價 n. sale
garm gam 監禁 n. confinement
garm gum 監禁 n. captivity
garm hao gwun 監考官 n. proctor
garm heng 減輕 v.t. allay
garm heng 減輕 v.t. assuage
garm heng 減輕 v.i. lighten
garm heng 減輕 v.t. mitigate
garm heng 減輕 n. mitigation
garm heng 減輕 v.t. relieve
garm heng 減輕 v.t. soothe
garm low 監牢 n. jail
garm siew 減少 v. t decrease
garm siew 減少 v. t dwindle
garm wu koon 監護權 v custody
garm wu yan 監護人 n custodian
garm yeurk 減弱 v.i. recede
garm yeurk 減弱 v.i. subside
garm ying 減刑 v. t commute
garn lan 艱難 a. arduous
garn siew 減少 v. t diminish
gat 拮 v.t. jab
gat 拮 v.t. prick
gat cheurng mat 吉祥物 n. mascot
gat choon 拮穿 v.t. puncture
gat jat 甲由 n cockroach
gat jee jeurng 橘子醬 n. marmalade
gat lay geh 吉利嘅 a. auspicious
geem 劍 n. sword
geem cha 檢查 v. t. check

geem cha 檢查 *n check*
geem cha 檢查 *v. t examine*
geem ta 檢查 *n. inspection*
geem ta 檢查 *v.t. screen*
geem tat gwun 檢察官 *n. inspector*
geem tat gwun 檢察官 *n. prosecutor*
geem yu hay 檢乳器 *n. lactometer*
geen 見 *v.t. meet*
geen ding geh 堅定嘅 *a. spirited*
geen ding geh 堅定嘅 *a. staunch*
geen ding geh 堅定嘅 *a. steadfast*
geen dow 見到 *v.t. sight*
geen dow 見到 *v.t. spot*
geen dow geh 見到嘅 *a. visible*
geen gai 見解 *n. outlook*
geen horng 健康 *a fit*
geen horng 健康 *n. health*
geen horng 健康 *a. healthy*
geen horng 健康 *a. well*
geen jap sang 見習生 *n. probationer*
geen juk 建築 *n building*
geen juk hok 建築學 *n. architecture*
geen juk kwan 建築群 *n complex*
geen juk see 建築師 *n. architect*
geen keurng 堅強 *n. stoic*
geen keurng geh 堅強嘅 *a forceful*
geen koot 堅決 *a. adamant*
geen koot 堅決 *n. adamant*
geen koot 堅決 *a. insistent*
geen koot geh 堅決嘅 *a. resolute*
geen lap 建立 *n erection*
geen lay morng yee 見利忘義 *a. venal*
geen ngay bat wat 堅毅不屈 *a. indomitable*
geen tam 健談 *a. talkative*
geen tee 堅持 *v.t. insist*
geen tee 堅持 *n. insistence*
geen tee 堅持 *v.i. persevere*
geen tee 堅持 *n. persistence*
geen tee 堅持 *v.i. soldier*
geen tee geh 堅持嘅 *a. tenacious*

geen tee geh yan 堅持嘅人 *n. stickler*
geen yee 建議 *n. counsel*
geep 夾 *n. peg*
geep hay jung gan 夾喺中間 *v.t. sandwich*
geep ju 夾住 *v.t. peg*
geep keem 夾鉗 *n clamp*
geet 結 *n. knot*
geet cheurng 結腸 *n colon*
geet chuk 結束 *v. t conclude*
geet chuk 結束 *v. t end*
geet chut 傑出 *n. pre-eminence*
geet chut geh 傑出嘅 *a. pre-eminent*
geet chut geh 傑出嘅 *a. transcendent*
geet fan 結婚 *v.t. wed*
geet fan teen geh 結婚前嘅 *adj. antenuptial*
geet guk 結局 *n finish*
geet gwor 結果 *n. outcome*
geet gwor 結果 *n. upshot*
geet hap 結合 *v. t combine*
geet hap 結合 *adj. conjunct*
geet hap 結合 *v.t. fuse*
geet hap 結合 *n. fusion*
geet jok 傑作 *n. masterplece*
geet kow 結構 *n construction*
geet kow 結構 *n. structure*
geet kow geh 結構嘅 *a. structural*
geet lun 結論 *n. conclusion*
geet lun 結論 *n. inference*
geet mang 結盟 *v.t. ally*
geet mok 結膜 *n. conjunctiva*
geet sat 結實 *a firm*
geet ta 結他 *n. guitar*
geh ha meen 嘅下面 *a. nether*
geh jee teen 嘅之前 *a. prior*
geng 驚 *a. afraid*
geng 驚 *a dread*
geng 驚 *v.i fear*
geng 驚 *a. fearful*
geng 鏡 *n mirror*

geng 頸 *n. neck*

geng gan 頸巾 *n. muffler*

geng gan 頸巾 *n. scarf*

geng leen 頸鏈 *n. necklace*

geng leen 頸鏈 *n. necklet*

geng peen 鏡片 *n. lens*

geng tow 鏡頭 *n. scene*

geurk 腳 *n. leg*

geurng 姜 *n. ginger*

geurng ang 僵硬 *n. stiff*

geurng far 僵化 *v.t. ossify*

geurng guk 僵局 *n deadlock*

geurng guk 僵局 *n. stalemate*

geurng worng gan fan 薑黃根粉 *n. turmeric*

geurt 腳 *n foot*

geurt bo 腳步 *n. step*

geurt jang 腳踭 *n. heel*

geurt jee 腳趾 *n. toe*

geurt leen 腳鍊 *n anklet*

geurt ngan 腳踝 *n. ankle*

gey 計 *v. t. calculate*

gey 雞 *n. chicken*

gey 寄 *v.t. mail*

gey 寄 *v.t. post*

gey 幾 *adv. pretty*

gey 幾 *adv. quite*

gey 幾 *adv. rather*

gey 寄 *v.t. send*

gey 薊 *n. thistle*

gey 計 *v.t. total*

gey bun geh 基本嘅… *a elementary*

gey bwun 基本 *a. basic*

gey bwun geh 基本嘅 *a. fundamental*

gey bwun geh 基本嘅 *a. rudimentary*

gey bwun geh 基本嘅 *a staple*

gey bwun seurng 基本上 *adv. substantially*

gey cheurng 機場 *n aerodrome*

gey cheurng 幾長 *a. lengthy*

gey cheurng 機場 *n terminal*

gey chor 基礎 *adj. basal*

gey chor 基礎 *n. basis*

gey chor 基礎 *n. foundation*

gey chor 基礎 *n. rudiment*

gey dai geh 幾大嘅 *a. sizable*

gey dak 記得 *v.t. recollect*

gey dak 記得 *v.t. remember*

gey dan 雞蛋 *n egg*

gey dor 幾多 *a much*

gey duk gao 基督教 *n. Christianity*

gey duk gao tow 基督教徒 *n. Christendom*

gey duk tow 基督徒 *n Christian*

gey duk tow 基督徒 *a. Christian*

gey forng 飢荒 *n famine*

gey fu mow 幾乎無 *adv. hardly*

gey gan 雞姦 *n. sodomy*

gey gor 幾個 *a few*

gey gor 幾個 *a several*

gey gow 機構 *n. institute*

gey gow 機構 *n. institution*

gey hai geh 機械嘅 *a mechanic*

gey hai geh 機械嘅 *a. mechanical*

gey hai hok 機械學 *n. mechanics*

gey hai jorng jee 機械裝置 *n. mechanism*

gey hai see 機械師 *n. mechanic*

gey hai yan 機械人 *n. robot*

gey hao 技巧 *n. technique*

gey hm dow geh 計唔到嘅 *a. incalculable*

gey ho 記號 *n. marker*

gey hor hok 幾何學 *n. geometry*

gey hor hok geh 幾何學嘅 *a. geometrical*

gey jee 機智 *a. witty*

gey jee geh 機智嘅 *a. resourceful*

gey jee geh 機智嘅 *a. tactful*

gey jeh 記者 *n. correspondent*

gey jeh 記者 *n. journalist*

gey jeh 記者 *n. reporter*

gey jeurng yan 記帳人 *n book-keeper*

gey juk 繼續 *v. i. continue*

gey juk 繼續 *v.i. last*
gey juk 繼續 *a. lasting*
gey juk 繼續 *v.t. resume*
gey juk jow 繼續做 *v.i. proceed*
gey jung geh 幾種嘅 *a. various*
gey lang 技能 *n. skill*
gey leem 紀念 *v. t. commemorate*
gey leem 紀念 *n. commemoration*
gey leem 紀念 *n. remembrance*
gey leem ban 紀念品 *n. keepsake*
gey leem ban 紀念品 *n. memento*
gey leem bay 紀念碑 *n. memorial*
gey leem geh 紀念嘅 *a memorial*
gey leem yat 紀念日 *n. anniversary*
gey leurng hay 計量器 *n. meter*
gey luk 紀錄 *n. record*
gey luk 紀錄 *n. tally*
gey luk 記錄 *v.t. transcribe*
gey lut 紀律 *n discipline*
gey luy 妓女 *n. bawd*
gey luy 妓女 *n. prostitute*
gey luy 妓女 *n. strumpet*
gey luy 妓女 *n. whore*
gey mat 機密 *a. confidential*
gey or 飢餓 *n. starvation*
gey sang 寄生 *adj. adnascent*
gey sang chung 寄生蟲 *n. parasite*
gey see 技師 *n. technician*
gey see 計時 *v.t. time*
gey see 幾時 *adv. when*
gey see 幾時 *conj. when*
gey see hay 記時器 *n chronograph*
gey shoon 計算 *n. calculation*
gey shoon 計算 *n. computation*
gey shoon 計算 *v.t. compute*
gey sing 繼承 *v.t. inherit*
gey sing 記性 *n. recall*
gey sing 繼承 *n. succession*
gey sing yan 繼承人 *n. heir*
gey sing yan 繼承人 *n. successor*
gey so gey 計數機 *n calculator*
gey suk 寄宿 *v.t. lodge*

gey sut geh 技術嘅 *a. technical*
gey sut geh 技術嘅 *a. technological*
gey sut jing jam 技術精湛 *a. masterly*
gey sut joon ga 技術專家 *n. technologist*
gey sut sing say jeet 技術性細節 *n. technicality*
gey wak 計劃 *n. plan*
gey wak 計劃 *v.t. plan*
gey wak 計劃 *v.t. programme*
gey wak 計劃 *n. project*
gey wak 計劃 *n. proposal*
gey wak 計劃 *n. scheme*
gey wuy 機會 *n. chance*
gey wuy 機會 *n. opportunity*
gey wuy 機會 *n. scope*
gey wuy ju yee 機會主義 *n. opportunism*
gey yap jeurng wu 記入賬戶 *v. t debit*
gey yee hay 計議器 *n. gauge*
gey yeen 既然 *conj. now*
gey yik 記憶 *n. memory*
gey yik 記憶 *n. recollection*
gey yoon 妓院 *n brothel*
gcy yow hor lang 幾有可能 *a. likely*
gey yuk 肌肉 *n. muscle*
gey yuk tung 肌肉痛 *n. myalgia*
giew 叫 *v. t. call*
giew 叫 *v.i exclaim*
giew 叫 *v.i. scream*
giew cher 轎車 *n. sedan*
giew chor 叫錯 *v.t. miscall*
giew dung 撬動 *v.t. lever*
giew hai 繳械 *v. t disarm*
giew jing 矯正 *v.i. rectify*
giew jow 叫做 *v.t. term*
giew oh 驕傲 *n conceit*
giew oh geh 驕傲嘅 *a. proud*
giew ow 驕傲 *n. pride*
giew seng 叫聲 *n. bellows*

giew seng 叫聲 *n cry*
giew seng 叫醒 *v.i. rouse*
giew seng 叫聲 *n scream*
giew siew 嬌小 *a. dainty*
giew yeurng 嬌養 *v. t cocker*
gik 激 *v. t enrage*
gik 激 *v.t. infuriate*
gik bai 擊敗 *v. t. defeat*
gik bai 擊敗 *v.t. overwhelm*
gik ban 極品 *n. nonpareil*
gik dai geh 極大嘅 *a. stupendous*
gik day geh 極地嘅 *a polar*
gik doon 極端 *a drastic*
gik doon 極端 *n extreme*
gik doon fan jee 極端分子 *n extremist*
gik dung 激動 *v.t. agitate*
gik dung 激動 *v. t commove*
gik dung 激動 *a. giddy*
gik dung 激動 *n. panic*
gik fat 激發 *v.t. incite*
gik fat 激發 *v.t. stimulate*
gik gwong 極光 *n aurora*
gik hay 激起 *v.t. inflame*
gik hay 激起 *v.t. kindle*
gik hay 激氣 *v.t. resent*
gik hay 激氣 *v.i. seethe*
gik hay 激起 *v.t. stoke*
gik hay hing chuy 激起興趣 *v.t. intrigue*
gik hey 激起 *v.t. arouse*
gik jang 激增 *v.i. proliferate*
gik jang 激增 *n. proliferation*
gik jang 激增 *n. surge*
gik jun geh 激進嘅 *a. radical*
gik kow 擊球 *n stroke*
gik kow 擊球 *n. volley*
gik kow so 擊球手 *n. batsman*
gik lay 激勵 *n. goad*
gik lay 激勵 *v motivate*
gik lay 激勵 *v.t. uplift*
gik lay 激勵 *v.t. vitalize*

gik lo 激嬲 *v.t. aggravate*
gik lo 激嬲 *n. aggravation*
gik lorng 激浪 *n. surf*
gik low 激嬲 *v.t. nettle*
gik ta 極差 *a disastrous*
gik tuy 擊退 *v.t. repel*
gik tuy 擊退 *v.t. repulse*
gik wut 激活 *v. t enable*
giklay 激勵 *v.t. galvanize*
gikyan 激人 *v.t. incense*
ging 莖 *n. stem*
ging 經 *prep. via*
ging bo 警報 *n alarm*
ging bo hay 警報器 *n. siren*
ging deen 經典 *n classic*
ging dow 經度 *n. longitude*
ging dung 驚動 *v.t alarm*
ging fay 經費 *n. appropriation*
ging gai 警戒 *n. vigilance*
ging gey cheurng 競技場 *n. lists*
ging gey yan 經紀人 *n agent*
ging gey yan 經紀人 *n broker*
ging go 警告 *n. caution*
ging gok 警覺 *a. alert*
ging gok geh 警覺嘅 *a. vigilant*
ging gok sing 警覺性 *n. alertness*
ging gow 警告 *n. admonition*
ging gow 警告 *v.t. warn*
ging gow 警告 *n. warning*
ging gwor 經過 *adv by*
ging hak 驚嚇 *n. fright*
ging hay 驚喜 *v.t. impress*
ging hey 驚喜 *n. surprise*
ging hung 驚恐 *n. terror*
ging jang 競爭 *v. i compete*
ging jang 競爭 *n. rivalry*
ging jang duy sow 競爭對手 *n. rival*
ging jang lik 競爭力 *a competitive*
ging jay 經濟 *n economy*
ging jay geh 經濟嘅 *a economic*
ging jay geh 經濟嘅 *a economical*
ging jay hok 經濟學 *n. economics*

ging jay suy tuy 經濟衰退 n. recession

ging jung 敬重 n. venerate

ging kay 驚奇 v.t. amaze

ging kay 驚奇 n. amazement

ging kay 經期 n. menstruation

ging lay 經理 n. manager

ging lay 敬禮 v.t. salute

ging lay 敬禮 n salute

ging lay geh 經理嘅 a. managerial

ging lik 經歷 v. t. experience

ging lik 經歷 v.t. undergo

ging ngar 驚訝 v.t. astonish

ging ngar 驚訝 n. astonishment

ging ngar 驚訝 n wonder

ging sik 景色 n. vista

ging tat 警察 n constable

ging tat 警察 n. police

ging tat 警察 n. policeman

ging way 敬畏 n. awe

ging way 敬畏 v.t. overawe

ging yee 敬意 n. homage

ging yeem 經驗 n experience

ging yeem fung fu 經驗豐富 a expert

ging yeem fung fu geh 經驗豐富嘅 a. veteran

ging yeurng 敬仰 n. obeisance

go 告 n. charge

go 高 a. high

go 告 v.t. sue

go 高 a. tall

go beet 告別 n farewell

go dow 高度 n. height

go dow gey 高度計 n altimeter

go dow jan yeurng 高度讚揚 v. t exalt

go fung 高峰 n. apotheosis

go fung see kay 高峰時期 n. heyday

go hing 高興 a. cheerful

go hing 高興 n delight

go hing 高興 v. t. delight

go hing 高興 n. gaiety

go hing 高興 a. glad

go hing 高興 v.t. gladden

go hing 高興 n. glee

go hing 高興 n. hilarity

go jat leurng 高質量 a fine

go jung 告終 v.i. culminate

go san 高山 n. alp

go tiew 高潮 n. climax

go yee fu kow 高爾夫球 n. golf

gok 鉻 n chrome

gok 角 n. horn

gok dow 角度 n. angle

gok jee 各自 pron. each

gok jee 擱置 v.t. table

gok ji 擱置 n. abeyance

gok jung gok yeurng geh 各種各樣嘅 a. miscellaneous

gok jung gok yeurng geh 各種各樣嘅 a. multifarious

gok lok 角落 n corner

gok lok 角落 n. nook

gok low 閣樓 n. loft

gok mok 角膜 n cornea

gok sik 角色 n. character

gok sik 角色 n. role

gok sik fan pwuy 角色分配 n casting

gon 乾 n arefaction

gon 乾 a dry

gon 趕 v.t. hurry

gon cho 乾草 n. hay

gon jeng 乾淨 n. clean

gon jeng 乾淨 n cleanliness

gong 講 v.i. talk

gong 缸 n. tank

gong 講 v.t. tell

gong ga 講價 v.t. bargain

gong go lay yee 講究禮儀 a. ceremonious

gong gong seurng fan 剛剛相反 n. antipodes

gong jor 講座 n talk

gong lam dow 降臨到 v. t befall

gong mun 肛門 *n. anus*
gong siew 講笑 *v.t. banter*
goon 捐 *v. t contribute*
goon 捲 *v.t. convolve*
goon 捲 *n. curl*
goon 捐 *v. t donate*
goon 卷 *n. roll*
goon 捲 *v.i. roll*
goon fat 捲髮 *n. ringlet*
goon fwun 捐款 *n. benefaction*
goon fwun 捐款 *n. donation*
goon jang jeh 捐贈者 *n donor*
goon kuk 蜷曲 *v.t. crimple*
goon mai 捲埋 *v.t. furl*
goon sut 捐稅 *n. tithe*
goon tung 捲筒 *n. reel*
goon yap 捲入 *v. t entangle*
gor 歌 *n. song*
gor 嗰 *rel. pron. that*
gor been 嗰邊 *a. yonder*
gor been 嗰邊 *adv. yonder*
gor beet geh 個別嘅 *a. individual*
gor dow 嗰度 *adv. there*
gor dow fu gan 嗰度附近 *adv. thereabouts*
gor gor 嗰個 *a. that*
gor gor 嗰個 *dem. pron. that*
gor kek 歌劇 *n. opera*
gor mo biew yeen 歌舞表演 *n. cabaret*
gor sing 個性 *n. individualism*
gor sing 個性 *n. individuality*
gor sow 歌手 *n. singer*
gor sow 歌手 *n. songster*
gor sow 歌手 *n. vocalist*
gor tee 歌詞 *n. lyric*
gorn 肝 *n. liver*
gorn 趕 *adv. pell-mell*
gorn 杆 *n. rod*
gorn 趕 *v.t. rush*
gorn bwuy 乾杯 *v.t. toast*
gorn cho 乾燥 *adj. arid*

gorn cho duy 乾草堆 *n. rick*
gorn cho geh 乾燥嘅 *a. torrid*
gorn chut 趕出 *v. t. expel*
gorn hon 乾旱 *n drought*
gorn see gan 趕時間 *n. rush*
gorn yiew 干擾 *n. static*
gorn yu 干預 *v.i. interfere*
gorn yu 干預 *n. interference*
gorng 港 *n. harbour*
gorng 講 *v.t. remark*
gorng 講 *v.t. say*
gorng 講 *v.i. speak*
gorng 講 *n. spoke*
gorng 鋼 *n. steel*
gorng 講 *v.t. utter*
gorng dai wah 講大話 *v.i. lie*
gorng dai wah geh yan 講大話嘅人 *n. liar*
gorng dak gwor geh 講得過嘅 *a. tenable*
gorng day 降低 *n decrease*
gorng day 降低 *n. decrement*
gorng day 降低 *v.t. lower*
gorng day 降低 *v.t. windlass*
gorng day san fan 降低身分 *v. t degrade*
gorng dow 講道 *n. sermon*
gorng dow lay 講道理 *v.i. reason*
gorng fat 講法 *n. parlance*
gorng fay wah 講廢話 *v.i. prattle*
gorng for 講課 *v lecture*
gorng ga 降價 *v. t. cheapen*
gorng ga 降價 *v. t. debase*
gorng ga 講價 *v.i. haggle*
gorng gow 講究 *n. pedant*
gorng har 講下 *v.t. outline*
gorng ho 港口 *n. port*
gorng kam 鋼琴 *n. piano*
gorng kam ga 鋼琴家 *n. pianist*
gorng lok 降落 *v. i. descend*
gorng lok 降落 *n. descent*
gorng lok 降落 *v.i. land*

gorng lok 降落 n. landing

gorng lok sna 降落傘 n. parachute

gorng ming 講明 v.t. account

gorng ming 講明 v.t state

gorng see 講師 n. lecturer

gorng siew 講笑 v.i. jest

gorng siew 講笑 v.i. joke

gorng siew 講笑 n. raillery

gorng sut 講述 v.t. narrate

gorng sut 講述 v.t. recount

gorng tan 講壇 a. pulpit

gorng ting chor 講清楚 v. t elucidate

gorng toy 講台 n. rostrum

gorng wu yeet sut 江湖醫術 n. quackery

gorng yeh 講嘢 v.i. yap

got cho 割草 v.t. mow

gow 狗 n dog

gow 夠 a enough

gow 告 v.t. impeach

gow 告 n. impeachment

gow 九 n. nine

gow 救 v.t. rescue

gow 救 v.t. save

gow beng fuk fat 舊病復發 n. relapse

gow dam 夠膽 v. i. dare

gow day 高地 n. plateau

gow fan 糾紛 n row

gow fay seng 狗吠聲 n. woof

gow fay seng 狗吠聲 n yap

gow geh 高嘅 a. lofty

gow geh 舊嘅 a. old

gow gu 高估 v.t. overrate

gow gway geh 高貴嘅 a. noble

gow hing 高興 n. joyful, joyous

gow hing 高興 a. mirthful

gow hing 高興 v.i. rejoice

gow jay 狗仔 n. whelp

gow jing 糾正 v.t. redress

gow jing 糾正 v.t. right

gow jorng yan 告狀人 n sneak

gow kap gao see 高級教士 n. prelate

gow kap gwan gwun 高級軍官 n marshal

gow kiew 高蹺 n. stilt

gow kuk sap sam wan 九曲十三彎 adj anfractuous

gow ling 高齡 n. senility

gow mat jeh 告密者 n. informer

gow ngar geh 高雅嘅 a. tasteful

gow oh jee dai geh 高傲自大嘅 a. haughty

gow sap 九十 n. ninety

gow seurng 高尚 n. sublimity

gow sing 救星 n. messiah

gow sing 救星 n. saviour

gow sow 高手 n ace

gow uk 狗屋 n. kennel

gow yan 救恩 n. salvation

gow yeurng 羔羊 n. lamb

gow yoon 睪丸 n. testicle

gow yoot 九月 n. September

goy 改 v.t. alter

goy 蓋 n. lid

goy 改 v.t. modify

goy 改 v.t. reform

goy been 改變 v. t. change

goy been 改變 n. change

goy been ying tai 改變形態 v. transform

goy gak 改革 n. reformation

goy gak geh 改革嘅 a reformatory

goy gak jeh 改革者 n. reformer

goy gak jeh 改革者 n revolutionary

goy jing 改正 n correction

goy jing 改正 n. rectification

goy jow 改造 n. overhaul

goy leurng 改良 v.t. ameliorate

goy leurng 改良 n. amelioration

goy meng 改名 v.t. name

goy peen geh 改編嘅 n. adaptation

goy seen 改善 n betterment

goy seen 改善 v.t. meliorate

goy seen 改善 n. refinement

goy seen 改善 n. reform

gu 鈷 n cobalt

gu 鼓 n drum

gu 估 v. t estimate

gu 估 v.i guess

gu 估 v.t. presume

gu 估 v.t. suppose

gu ban geh 古板嘅 a. staid

gu dan 孤單 n. loneliness

gu dan 孤單 a. lonely

gu deen 古典 a classical

gu ding 固定 v.t. steady

gu ding geh 固定嘅 a. immovable

gu ding geh 固定嘅 a set

gu doy 古代 n. antiquity

gu doy geh 古代嘅 a. archaic

gu dung 古董 a. antique

gu fan 股份 n. share

gu fan 股份 n stake

gu fu ling ding 孤苦伶仃 a forlorn

gu ga 估價 n. valuation

gu gey 估計 n. estimate

gu gey 估計 n. prediction

gu gu giew 咕咕叫 v. i coo

gu gwai 古怪 n. oddity

gu gwai 古怪 a. strange

gu gwai geh 古怪嘅 a rum

gu gwai geh 古怪嘅 a. zany

gu horn 孤寒 n. miser

gu horn 孤寒 a. niggardly

gu horn geh 孤寒嘅 a. miserly

gu horn gway 孤寒鬼 n. niggard

gu jap 固執 n. obstinacy

gu jap 固執 n. provincialism

gu jap 固執 n. tenacity

gu jeurng 鼓掌 v.t. applaud

gu jeurng 故障 n breakdown

gu jeurng 鼓掌 n clap

gu jeurng 故障 n. hitch

gu joo 僱主 n employer

gu lap 孤立 n. insularity

gu lay 鼓勵 v. t encourage

gu lay 鼓勵 n. incentive

gu lor ma kek cheurng 古羅馬劇場 n amphitheatre

gu low 古老 a. ancient

gu low geh 古老嘅 a. immemorial

gu lung yoon huy 故弄玄虛 v.t. mystify

gu man 顧問 n. counsellor

gu man mat geh 古文物嘅 a. antiquarian

gu mat sow chong gar 古物收藏家 n antiquarian

gu mat sow chong gar 古物收藏家 n. antiquary

gu piew ging gey 股票經紀 n. jobber

gu see 故事 n. story

gu see 故事 n. tale

gu see ting jeet 故事情節 n. plot

gu sik gu heurng ghe 古色古香嘅 a. quaint

gu tay 固體 n solid

gu wak 蠱惑 n antic

gu wak 蠱惑 n. guile

gu wak geh 蠱惑嘅 a. roguish

gu wak jay 蠱惑仔 n. gangster

gu yee 故意 a. intentional

gu yee 孤兒 n. orphan

gu yee yoon 孤兒院 n. orphanage

gu yoon 僱員 n employee

gu yow geh 固有嘅 a. inherent

guk 焗 v.t. bake

guk 焗 a. humid

guk 局 n. innings

guk 局 n. round

guk 焗 a. stuffy

guk bo far 局部化 v.t. localize

guk chorng 穀倉 n. barn

guk gung 鞠躬 v. t bow

guk gung 鞠躬 n bow

guk low 焗爐 n. oven

guk luy 穀類 a cereal

guk mat 穀物 *n. cereal*

guk say yan 焗死人 *v.t. smother*

gung 拱 *n. arch*

gung 工 *n. job*

gung bo 公報 *n. communiqué*

gung bo 公報 *n. gazette*

gung cheurng 工場 *n. workshop*

gung choon 共存 *v. i co-exist*

gung choon 共存 *n co-existence*

gung chorng 工廠 *n factory*

gung dow 公道 *n. justice*

gung gey 公雞 *n cock*

gung gik 攻擊 *v. assail*

gung gik 攻擊 *v.t. mob*

gung gik 攻擊 *n offensive*

gung gik 攻擊 *n. onslaught*

gung gik sing 攻擊性 *n aggression*

gung go 公告 *n bulletin*

gung guy 工具 *n. implement*

gung guy 工具 *n. tool*

gung gwor yu kow 供過於求 *n glut*

gung hao 功效 *n efficacy*

gung heen 貢獻 *n contribution*

gung heurng geh 共享嘅 *a communal*

gung hey 恭喜 *v. t congratulate*

gung hoy gam 公開咁 *adv. openly*

gung hoy geh 公開嘅 *a. overt*

gung jay 公仔 *n doll*

gung jay geh 公制嘅 *a. metric*

gung jeen sow 弓箭手 *n archer*

gung jeurk 公爵 *n duke*

gung jeurng 工匠 *n. artisan*

gung jeurng 工匠 *n craftsman*

gung jeurng 工匠 *n. workman*

gung jik 功績 *n feat*

gung jing 公正 *a. candid*

gung jing 公正 *adv. justly*

gung jing geh 公正嘅 *a. just*

gung jing yan 公證人 *n. notary*

gung jok 工作 *n employment*

gung jok 工作 *n. work*

gung jok gwor dow 工作過度 *v.i.*
overwork

gung jok gwor dow 工作過度 *n.*
overwork

gung jok yan yoon 工作人員 *n. crew*

gung jok yan yoon 工作人員 *n. staff*

gung ju 公主 *n. princess*

gung jung 公眾 *n. public*

gung jung geh 公眾嘅 *a. public*

gung jung geh ju muk 公眾嘅注目 *n.*
limelight

gung jung jap wuy 公眾集會 *n rally*

gung lang 功能 *n. function*

gung long 拱廊 *n arcade*

gung man hok 公民學 *n civics*

gung man koon lay 公民權利 *n*
citizenship

gung man tow piew 公民投票 *n.*
plebiscite

gung mao 公貓 *n. tomcat*

gung mo jeh 共謀者 *n. conspirator*

gung muk 肱木 *n ancon*

gung ngay geh 工藝嘅 *a. polytechnic*

gung ping 公平 *a fair*

gung ping 公平 *adv. fairly*

gung ping 公平 *n. impartiality*

gung ping geh 公平嘅 *a equitable*

gung see 公司 *n. company*

gung see 公司 *n. firm*

gung see geh 公司嘅 *adj. corporate*

gung sik 共識 *n. consensus*

gung sik 公式 *n formula*

gung sing 公升 *n. litre*

gung tan ju yee 共產主義 *n*
communism

gung ting see 工程師 *n engineer*

gung tow 工頭 *n foreman*

gung tung geh 共同嘅 *a. mutual*

gung wor dorng dorng yoon 共和黨
黨員 *n republican*

gung wor dorng geh 共和黨嘅 *a.*
republican

gung wor gwok 共和國 *n. republic*

gung yan 工人 *n domestic*

gung yan 工人 *n. hireling*

gung yan 工人 *n. servant*

gung yan 工人 *n. worker*

gung yeep geh 工業嘅 *a. industrial*

gung yeurng 公羊 *n. ram*

gung ying 供應 *n. provision*

gung ying jeh 供應者 *n. supplier*

gung ying leurng 供應量 *n supply*

gung ying shoon 供應船 *n tender*

gung yoon 公園 *n. park*

guy 鋸 *n. saw*

guy been geh 巨變嘅 *a. revolutionary*

guy chee ying 鋸齒形 *a. zigzag*

guy chut 舉出 *v. t cite*

guy dai 巨大 *n. immensity*

guy dai geh 巨大嘅 *a. gigantic*

guy dai geh 巨大嘅 *a. immense*

guy dai geh 巨大嘅 *a. massive*

guy dai geh 巨大嘅 *a. tremendous*

guy dai geh 巨大嘅 *a. vast*

guy fat 句法 *n. syntax*

guy hang 舉行 *v.t. solemnize*

guy heurng 巨響 *n. bang*

guy jee 句子 *n. sentence*

guy ju 居住 *n. habitation*

guy ju geh 居住嘅 *a. resident*

guy ju yu 居住於 *v.t. inhabit*

guy kwong jing 懼曠症 *n. agoraphobia*

guy lorng 巨浪 *n billow*

guy man 居民 *n. inhabitant*

guy man 居民 *n resident*

guy sek 巨石 *n. megalith*

guy sek 巨石 *n. monolith*

guy sek geen jow geh 巨石建造嘅 *a. megalithic*

guy tay far 具體化 *v.t. incarnate*

guy yan 巨人 *n. giant*

gwa 掛 *v.t. hang*

gwa 瓜 *n. melon*

gwa fu 寡婦 *n. widow*

gwa gwa seng 呱呱聲 *v.i. quack*

gwa ju 掛住 *v.t. miss*

gwa low 寡佬 *n. widower*

gwa tow jing jee 寡頭政治 *n. oligarchy*

gwai 拐 *v.t. kidnap*

gwai geh 怪嘅 *a. odd*

gwai geh 怪嘅 *a. peculiar*

gwai jow 拐走 *v.t. abduct*

gwai pik 怪癖 *n. peculiarity*

gwak 摑 *v.t. slap*

gwak 摑 *n. smack*

gwak 摑 *v.i. smack*

gwan 郡 *n. shire*

gwan 棍 *n. stick*

gwan bay 軍備 *n. armament*

gwan dung geh 轟動嘅 *a. sensational*

gwan duy 軍隊 *n. army*

gwan duy 軍隊 *n battalion*

gwan duy 軍隊 *n military*

gwan for 軍火 *n. munitions*

gwan geen geh 關鍵嘅 *a decisive*

gwan geen geh 關鍵嘅 *a. momentous*

gwan hai fu 軍械庫 *n. armoury*

gwan hao sang 軍校生 *n. cadet*

gwan hay 關係 *n. affiliation*

gwan hay 關係 *n bond*

gwan hay 關係 *n. relation*

gwan hay 關係 *n. relevance*

gwan hay dow 關係到 *v.t. involve*

gwan jeet 關節 *n. joint*

gwan jeet yeem 關節炎 *n arthritis*

gwan jor 慣咗 *a. accustomed*

gwan ju 君主 *n. monarch*

gwan ju 君主 *n. sovereign*

gwan ju gway 君主制 *n. monarchy*

gwan leen 關連 *n connection*

gwan leen 關連 *n. link*

gwan sam 關心 *v. i. care*

gwan see ga 軍事家 *n. strategist*

gwan see geh 軍事嘅 *a. military*

gwan sing 慣性 *n. inertia*

gwan sum 關心 *n concern*

gwan toon 軍團 *n. legion*

gwan toon 軍團 *n. legionary*

gwan toon 軍團 *n. regiment*

gwan tow 關頭 *n. juncture*

gwan tung 滾筒 *n. roller*

gwan yu 關於 *prep about*

gwan yu 關於 *v.i. pertain*

gwan yung hay choy 軍用器材 *n. ordnance*

gwat 骨 *n. bone*

gwat 掘 *v.t. dig*

gwat 掘 *v.t. trench*

gwat day dow 挖地道 *v.i. tunnel*

gwat fwuy ang 骨灰甕 *n urn*

gwat jeet 骨折 *n. fracture*

gwat keurng 倔強 *n. perversity*

gwat tow horng 掘頭巷 *n. close*

gway 櫃 *n. ambry*

gway 貴 *a. costly*

gway 櫃 *n cupboard*

gway 鬼 *n. ghost*

gway 跪 *v.i. kneel*

gway 鬼 *n. phantom*

gway 龜 *n. tortoise*

gway been 詭辯 *n. sophism*

gway dow 軌道 *n. orbit*

gway dow 軌道 *n. track*

gway gey 詭計 *n dodge*

gway gey 詭計 *n. ruse*

gway gey 詭計 *n. wile*

gway gow yu 歸咎於 *v.t. impute*

gway jeen tung fan geh 貴賤通婚嘅 *a. morganatic*

gway jeet 季節 *n. season*

gway jeet geh 季節嘅 *a. seasonal*

gway juk 貴族 *n. aristocracy*

gway juk 貴族 *n. nobility*

gway juk 貴族 *n. noble*

gway juk 貴族 *n. nobleman*

gway juk koon lay 貴族權利 *n. lordship*

gway toy 櫃台 *n. counter*

gway tung 櫃桶 *n drawer*

gway wan 鬼魂 *n. wraith*

gway wan chut mwut 鬼魂出沒 *v.t. haunt*

gway yan yu 歸因於 *v.t. ascribe*

gway yan yu 歸因於 *v.t. attribute*

gwey 貴 *a expensive*

gwok ga 國家 *n. country*

gwok ga 國家 *n. nation*

gwok ga jap toon 國家集團 *n bloc*

gwok ga jow jik 國家組織 *n. polity*

gwok ga ju yee 國家主義 *n. nationalism*

gwok gor 國歌 *n anthem*

gwok jay 國際 *a. international*

gwok jay jeurng kay 國際象棋 *n. chess*

gwok jik 國籍 *n. nationality*

gwok worng 國王 *n. king*

gwok wuy 國會 *n congress*

gwok wuy 國會 *n. parliament*

gwok wuy geh 國會嘅 *a. parliamentary*

gwok yow far 國有化 *n. nationalization*

gwok yow far 國有化 *v.t. nationalize*

gwong 光 *a bright*

gwong 光 *n. light*

gwong bor 廣播 *n broadcast*

gwong bor 廣播 *v. t broadcast*

gwong choy 光彩 *n brilliance*

gwong jak 光澤 *n. gloss*

gwong morng say she 光芒四射 *a. radiant*

gwong seen 光線 *n beam*

gwong tow 光頭 *a. bald*

gwong wat geh 光滑嘅 *a. glossy*

gwong wing geh 光榮嘅 *a. glorious*

gwong yoon 光源 *n. illumination*

gwoon choy ga 棺材架 *n bier*
gwoon deem 觀點 *n angle*
gwoon jung 觀眾 *n. audience*
gwor 過 *v. t cross*
gwor 過 *adv over*
gwor 過 *prep. past*
gwor chor 過錯 *n fault*
gwor dor 過多 *n overload*
gwor dor 過多 *n. superabundance*
gwor dor geh 過多嘅 *a. superfluous*
gwor dow 過度 *a. lavish*
gwor dung 過冬 *v.i winter*
gwor fan 過分 *a. undue*
gwor hm dow 過唔到 *a. impassable*
gwor huy 過去 *n. past*
gwor huy geh 過去嘅 *a. past*
gwor jeurng 果醬 *n. jam*
gwor jeurng 果醬 *n. preserve*
gwor kay 過期 *v.i. expire*
gwor kay 過期 *a. overdue*
gwor leung fuk yung 過量服用 *v.t. overdose*
gwor leurng 過量 *n. overdose*
gwor leurng 過量 *n. surfeit*
gwor luy 過濾 *v.t filter*
gwor luy 過濾 *v.t. leach*
gwor luy hay 過濾器 *n filter*
gwor man 過敏 *n. irritation*
gwor sai see 過晒時 *n anachronism*
gwor sai see 過晒時 *a. antiquated*
gwor sai see geh 過晒時嘅 *a. outmoded*
gwor sam 果心 *n. core*
gwor sat 過失 *n demerit*
gwor see 過時 *a. outdated*
gwor see 過時 *v.t. stale*
gwor sok 過塑 *v.t. laminate*
gwor ting 過程 *n. proceeding*
gwor tow lap 過頭笠 *n. pullover*
gwor yan 果仁 *n nut*
gwor yoon 果園 *n. orchard*
gworng bor 廣播 *v.t. telecast*

gworng bor 廣播 *v.t. televise*
gworng gow 廣告 *v. advert*
gworng gow 廣告 *n advertisement*
gworng jak 光澤 *n. lustre*
gworng jak 光澤 *n shine*
gworng seen 光線 *n. ray*
gworng seen geh 光鮮嘅 *a. smart*
gworng wat geh 光滑嘅 *a. sleek*
gwun 獾 *n. badger*
gwun 滾 *v.i. boil*
gwun 罐 *n. can*
gwun 管 *n. pipe*
gwun 管 *n. pole*
gwun 罐 *n. pot*
gwun 鸛 *n. stork*
gwun 罐 *n. tin*
gwun 罐 *n. tub*
gwun 管 *n. tube*
gwun choy 棺材 *n coffin*
gwun deem 觀點 *n contention*
gwun deem 觀點 *n. perspective*
gwun dung 轟動 *adv. astir*
gwun ga 管家 *n chamberlain*
gwun gwan 冠軍 *n. champion*
gwun ho 管口 *n. nozzle*
gwun ja 轟炸 *v. t bombard*
gwun ja 轟炸 *n bombardment*
gwun jee bat dorng 管治不當 *n. misrule*
gwun jorng 管狀 *a. tubular*
gwun jung 觀眾 *n. spectator*
gwun jung jik 觀眾席 *n. auditorium*
gwun koy 灌溉 *n. irrigation*
gwun lay 管理 *v.t. manage*
gwun lay 管理 *n. management*
gwun lay bat seen 管理不善 *n. mismanagement*
gwun lay bat seen 管理不善 *n. mal administration*
gwun lay yan 管理人 *n. warden*
gwun liew 官僚 *n bureaucrat*

gwun liew ju yee 官僚主義 *n.* *Bureacuracy*
gwun meen 冠冕 *n. coronet*
gwun muk 灌木 *n. shrub*
gwun pang 棍棒 *n cudgel*
gwun shu 灌輸 *v.t. inculcate*
gwun shu 灌輸 *n. infusion*
gwun suy 灌水 *v.t. irrigate*
gwun tat 觀察 *n. observation*
gwun tat 觀察 *v.t. observe*
gwun tat lik keurng 觀察力強 *a. observant*
gwun tat lik keurng geh 觀察力強嘅 *a. perceptive*
gwun ying jun 管形樽 *n. vial*
gwun yoon 官員 *n. functionary*
gwun yoon 官員 *n. officer*
gwun yoon 官員 *n official*
gwun yoon ok duy 管弦樂隊 *n. orchestra*
gwun yoon ok geh 管弦樂嘅 *a. orchestral*
gwuy 劫 *v.t. tire*
gwuy 劫 *a. weary*
gwuy 劫 *v.t. & i weary*
gwuy gow 灰狗 *n. greyhound*

H

ha gong 下降 *n decline*
ha jeen geh yan 下賤嘅人 *n churl*
ha low geh 下流嘅 *a. obscene*
ha low geh hang way 下流嘅行為 *n. obscenity*
ha meen 下面 *adv below*
ha meen 下面 *adv beneath*
ha meen 下面 *prep beneath*
ha pa 下巴 *n. chin*
hai 蟹 *n crab*

hai 鞋 *n. shoe*
hai day 鞋底 *n. sole*
hai gwat 骸骨 *n. skeleton*
hai jeurng 鞋匠 *n cobbler*
hai lok 奚落 *v.t. ridicule*
hai lok 奚落 *n. ridicule*
hai sap sap 諧霎霎 *a. rough*
hak 刻 *v. t. carve*
hak 客 *n.. client*
hak 客 *n customer*
hak 黑 *a dark*
hak 嚇 *v. t daunt*
hak 刻 *v. t engrave*
hak 克 *n. gramme*
hak 嚇 *v.t. horrify*
hak 嚇 *n. scare*
hak 嚇 *v.t. scare*
hak 嚇 *n. shock*
hak 嚇 *v.t. shock*
hak 嚇 *v.t. startle*
hak 嚇 *v.t. terrify*
hak am 黑暗 *n dark*
hak bak wan hoot yee 黑白混血兒 *n. mulatto*
hak ban sang wut 刻板生活 *n. rut*
hak ban yan jeurng 刻板印象 *n. stereotype*
hak bok 刻薄 *a. harsh*
hak dow sor jor 嚇到傻咗 *a. aghast*
hak fuk 克服 *v.t. overcome*
hak fuk 克服 *v.t. surmount*
hak fuk hm dow geh 克服唔到嘅 *a. insurmountable*
hak gway 黑鬼 *n. nigger*
hak gwun geh 客觀嘅 *a. objective*
hak hay geh 客氣嘅 *a. mannerly*
hak hay shoot wah 客氣說話 *n. pleasantry*
hak jay 克制 *v.i. refrain*
hak loy jeurng 黑內障 *n amaurosis*
hak mak 黑麥 *n. rye*
hak pao 黑豹 *n. panther*

hak sik 黑色 *a black*
hak sing sing 黑猩猩 *n. chimpanzee*
hak tan 嚇 *v.t. frighten*
hak teng 客廳 *n drawing-room*
hak teng 客廳 *n. parlour*
hak yan 嚇人 *n bluff*
hak yan 黑人 *n. negro*
hak yan 客人 *n. visitor*
hak yan geh 嚇人嘅 *a. monstrous*
ham 喊 *n sob*
ham geen 坎肩 *n. jerkin*
ham giew seng 喊叫聲 *n howl*
ham jeng 陷阱 *n. pitfall*
ham jeng 陷阱 *n. snare*
ham jeng 陷阱 *n. trap*
ham jing 陷阱 *n. pl. toils*
ham low 喊路 *n. yawn*
ham seng 喊聲 *n whine*
ham tat 勘察 *n exploration*
ham wu 含糊 *n. obscurity*
ham wu bat ting 含糊不清 *v.i. gabble*
ham wu dow 含糊度 *n. vagueness*
ham wu seng 含糊聲 *n. slur*
ham yap 陷入 *v.t. mire*
ham yap heem ging 陷入險境 *v.t. imperil*
han 痕 *n. mark*
han 限 *v.t. restrict*
han 慳 *a. thrifty*
han 狠 *a. vicious*
han 行 *v.i. walk*
han dow 限度 *n. extent*
han duk geh 狠毒嘅 *a. virulent*
han ga 慳家 *a. frugal*
han ga 慳家 *n. thrift*
han jay 限制 *v. t confine*
han jay 限制 *v. t curtail*
han jay 限制 *v.t fetter*
han jay 限制 *n. limit*
han jay 限制 *v.t. limit*
han jay 限制 *n. limitation*

han jay 限制 *n. restriction*
han jay 限制 *n. stricture*
han jik 痕跡 *n. trace*
han jik 痕跡 *n. trail*
han ko 懇求 *n adjuration*
han kow 懇求 *n. entreaty*
han kow 懇求 *v.i. plead*
han san 閒散 *n. idleness*
han ting 懇請 *n. solicitation*
han wah 閒話 *n. gossip*
hang 行 *v.t ambulate*
hang 哼 *v. i hum*
hang 哼 *v.i. snort*
hang 哼 *n. snort*
hang 行 *v.i. step*
hang dak tung geh 行得通嘅 *a feasible*
hang ding 肯定 *v.t. affirm*
hang ding 肯定 *v.t. assert*
hang ding 肯定 *a. sure*
hang ding geh 肯定嘅 *a affirmative*
hang ding geh 肯定嘅 *a definite*
hang fat 行法 *n. gait*
hang fuk 幸福 *n felicity*
hang fuk 幸福 *n. welfare*
hang gai 行街 *v.i. shop*
hang jee 杏子 *n. apricot*
hang jing 行政 *n. administration*
hang jing geh 行政嘅 *a. administrative*
hang jing kuy 行政區 *n canton*
hang jing yan yoon 行政人員 *n. administrator*
hang lay 行李 *n. baggage*
hang lay 行李 *n. luggage*
hang lay yoon 行李員 *n. porter*
hang sam 恆心 *a. ambitious*
hang sing geh 行星嘅 *a. planetary*
hang tee 行刺 *v.t. assassinate*
hang tee 坑廁 *n. latrine*
hang way 行爲 *n. act*
hang way 行爲 *n behaviour*

hang way 行爲 n deed

hang way bat doon 行文不端 v.i. misbehave

hang way bat dorng 行爲不當 n. misbehaviour

hang way bat dorng 行爲不當 n. misdemeanour

hang way guy jee 行爲舉止 n conduct

hang way gwai yee geh yan 行爲怪異 嘅人 n. misfit

hang yan 杏仁 n. almond

hang yan 行人 n. pedestrian

hang yan low 行人路 n. pavement

hang ying jeh 行刑者 n. executioner

hao 敲 v.t. knock

hao 烤 v.t. roast

hao 敲 v.t. toll

hao choon 哮喘 n. asthma

hao geh 烤嘅 a roast

hao giew 吼叫 n. roar

hao giew 吼叫 v.i. roar

hao gwor 效果 n effect

hao gwun 考官 n examiner

hao ja 敲詐 v.t fleece

hao jeurng 校長 n principal

hao lut 效率 n efficiency

hao lut go 效率高 a efficient

hao luy 考慮 v. t consider

hao luy 考慮 v. t contemplate

hao luy dow 考慮到 prep. considering

hao luy dow 考慮到 a. mindful

hao luy gan 考慮緊 n contemplation

hao miew 巧妙 a. artful

hao miew 巧妙 n. subtlety

hao miew geh dap on 巧妙嘅答案 n. repartee

hao mo kwan 酵母菌 n. yeast

hao sang 考生 n examinee

hao see 考試 n. examination

hao yuk 烤肉 n roast

hao yung 效用 n. utility

haow 好 a. lash

hap 盒 n carton

hap 盒 n. cartridge

hap cheurng toon 合唱團 n choir

hap dong 恰當 n. adequacy

hap dong 恰當 a. apposite

hap fat 合法 a. lawful

hap fat geh 合法嘅 a. legal

hap fat sing 合法性 n. legality

hap fat sing 合法性 n. legitimacy

hap fat sing 合法性 n. validity

hap fu lor tap 合乎邏輯 a coherent

hap gam 合金 n. alloy

hap goy 盒蓋 v. t. cap

hap jok 合作 v. i collaborate

hap jok 合作 n collaboration

hap jok 合作 v. i co-operate

hap jok 合作 n co-operation

hap jok 合作 n. partnership

hap kwan geh 合群嘅 a. sociable

hap lay 合理 n. moderation

hap lay far 合理化 v.t. rationalize

hap lay geh 合理嘅 a. sound

hap lay sing 合理性 n. rationality

hap ngan gan 瞌眼瞓 v. i doze

hap ping 合併 v.t. amalgamate

hap ping 合併 n amalgamation

hap ping 合併 a. incorporate

hap ping 合併 v.t. merge

hap ping 合併 n. merger

hap sik 合適 a becoming

hap sik geng leen 盒式頸鏈 n. locket

hap sing mat 合成物 n synthetic

hap ting hap lay 合情合理 a. legitimate

hap tung 合同 n. compact

hap tung 合同 n. covenant

hap yeurk 合約 n contract

har chee 瑕疵 n flaw

har gong 下降 v.t. avale

har gorng 下降 a downward

har meen 下面 *prep down*
har ok 下顎 *n. jaw*
har ok 下顎 *n. maxilla*
har suk 下屬 *n. minion*
har tee 瑕疵 *n blemish*
har tee 瑕疵 *n. imperfection*
har teen 夏天 *n. summer*
har teen geh 夏天嘅 *adj aestival*
har wat 下滑 *n downfall*
har yan 蝦人 *v. t. bully*
har yat yeep 下一頁 *adv. overleaf*
harm 喊 *v. i cry*
harm 鹹 *a. salty*
hat 乞 *v. i cadge*
hat tee 乞嚏 *n sneeze*
hat tow 核桃 *n. walnut*
hat yan jang 乞人憎 *a. disagreeable*
hat yan jang 乞人憎 *a. loathsome*
hat yee 乞兒 *n beggar*
hay 係 *am*
hay 喺 *prep. at*
hay 喺 *pref. be*
hay 起 *v. t. construct*
hay 喺 *prep during*
hay 喺 *prep. in*
hay 喺 *conj. where*
hay 係 *adv. yes*
hay been dow 喺邊度 *adv. whereabout*
hay been dow 喺邊度 *adv. wherein*
hay cho jeh 起草者 *n draftsman*
hay choon 氣喘 *n. pant*
hay chorng dow 喺床度 *adv. abed*
hay far meng 起花名 *v.t. nickname*
hay fuk 起伏 *v.i. undulate*
hay guy 器具 *n. appliance*
hay gwun 器官 *n. organ*
hay hing geh 喜慶嘅 *a festive*
hay ho 氣候 *n. climate*
hay ho 喜好 *n. like*
hay ho 喜好 *n. preference*
hay ja geh 欺詐嘅 *a. fraudulent*

hay jat 氣質 *n. temperament*
hay jay 克制 *v.t. repress*
hay jeurk 喜鵲 *n. magpie*
hay jeurng hok 氣象學 *n. meteorology*
hay jeurng hok ga 氣象學家 *n. meteorologist*
hay jow 起皺 *n crimp*
hay kek 喜劇 *n. comedy*
hay kek 戲劇 *n drama*
hay kek 戲劇 *n. play*
hay kek fa 戲劇化 *a dramatic*
hay kek ga 喜劇家 *n. comedian*
hay kek geh 戲劇嘅 *a comic*
hay kek geh 戲劇嘅 *a. theatrical*
hay lap man 希臘文 *a Greek*
hay lap yan 希臘人 *n. Greek*
hay leet 系列 *n collection*
hay leet 系列 *n. range*
hay leet 系列 *n. series*
hay low 氣流 *n. turbulence*
hay low mow seurng 喜怒無常 *a. moody*
hay low mow seurng 喜怒無常 *a. temperamental*
hay may 氣味 *n. smell*
hay morng 希望 *a desirous*
hay morng 希望 *v.t. hope*
hay morng 希望 *n hope*
hay morng 希望 *n. prospect*
hay mun 氣門 *n. valve*
hay ngat gey 氣壓計 *n barometer*
hay po 起泡 *v.t foam*
hay sang 犧牲 *v.t. sacrifice*
hay sang geh 犧牲嘅 *a. sacrificial*
hay seurng meen 喺上面 *adv. aloft*
hay sik 稀釋 *v.t. thin*
hay so 係數 *n. coefficient*
hay sow 起訴 *v.t. indict*
hay sow 起訴 *v.t. prosecute*
hay toon 戲團 *n. troupe*
hay tung 系統 *n. system*

hay tung far 系統化 v.t. systematize

hay wok 起獲 n. seizure

hay yee 起義 n. uprising

hay yoon 戲院 a. multiplex

hay yoon yu 起源於 v.t. originate

hay yoot 喜悅 n bliss

hay yoot 喜悅 n. joy

hay yow 汽油 n. petrol

hay yow geh 稀有嘅 a. scarce

hay...geh ha meen 喺...嘅下面 prep. under

hay...geh ha meen 喺...嘅下面 a under

hay...geh ha meen 喺...嘅下面 adv. underneath

hay...geh ha meen 喺...嘅下面 prep. underneath

hay...geh seurng meen 喺...嘅上面 prep. on

hay...geh seurng meen 喺...嘅上面 adv. on

hay...teen meen ga 係...前面加 v.t. prefix

heem 欠 v.t owe

heem dan 欠單 n. chit

heem huy 謙虛 a. humble

heem huy 謙虛 n. humility

heem huy 謙虛 a. modest

heem huy 謙虛 n modesty

heem ok 險惡 a. sinister

heen dak 顯得 v.t. portray

heen fan 遣返 v.t. repatriate

heen fan 遣返 n. repatriation

heen fan yan 遣返人 n repatriate

heen fat 憲法 n constitution

heen gwa 牽掛 n. solicitude

heen hak 顯赫 n eminance

heen jak 譴責 v. t. censure

heen jak 譴責 n condemnation

heen jeurng 憲章 n charter

heen ju geh 顯著嘅 a dominant

heen leen 牽連 n. implication

heen leen 牽連 v.t. incriminate

heen may geng 顯微鏡 n. microscope

heen see 顯示 n. indication

heen see 顯示 n. manifestation

heen seen muk oh 牽線木偶 n. marionette

heen seep 牽涉 v.t. implicate

heep ding 協定 n. treaty

heep tiew 協調 a. co-ordinate

heep tiew 協調 v. t co-ordinate

heep tiew 協調 n co-ordination

heep wuy 協會 n. association

heep wuy 協會 n. guild

heep wuy 協會 n. union

heep yee 協議 n. pact

heep yee 協議 n. settlement

heep yee shu 協議書 n. agreement

hek lik bat tow ho 吃力不討好 a. thankless

heng 輕 a light

heng heng 輕輕 adv. lightly

heng heng gam deem 輕輕咁掂 v.t. tip

heng mor 輕摸 v.t. stroke

heng pak 輕拍 v.t. tap

heng tuy 輕推 v.t. nudge

heurng 響 v.i hoot

heurng 香 n. incense

heurng 響 v.i. resound

heurng 向 prep. towards

heurng bak 向北 adv. north

heurng choon sang wut 鄉村生活 n. rustication

heurng dung 向東 adv east

heurng geh 香嘅 a. fragrant

heurng gor dow 向嗰度 adv. thither

heurng ha geh 鄉下嘅 a. rural

heurng ha geh 鄉下嘅 a. rustic

heurng ha mang chung 向下猛衝 v.i. swoop

heurng ha yan 鄉下人 n rustic

heurng har 向下 adv down

heurng har 向下 *adv downward*
heurng har 向下 *adv downwards*
heurng ho 向後 *adv. aback*
heurng ho 向後 *adv. backward*
heurng jee 香脂 *n. balsam*
heurng jiew 香蕉 *n. banana*
heurng larm 向南 *adv south*
heurng leurng 響亮 *n. resonance*
heurng leurng 響亮 *n. sonority*
heurng leurng geh 響亮嘅 *a. resonant*
heurng liew 香料 *n. spice*
heurng lo 香爐 *n censer*
heurng loy 向內 *a. inward*
heurng loy 向內 *adv. inwards*
heurng mey 香味 *n. fragrance*
heurng ngoy 向外 *a. outward*
heurng ngoy 向外 *adv outwards*
heurng san 鄉紳 *n. squire*
heurng say 向西 *adv. west*
heurng say geh 向西嘅 *adv. westerly*
heurng seurng 向上 *adv. up*
heurng seurng geh 向上嘅 *a. upward*
heurng so 享受 *v. t enjoy*
heurng sow 享受 *v.t. relish*
heurng sow 享受 *n. sensuality*
heurng suy 香水 *n. perfume*
heurng teen 向前 *adv. forth*
heurng teen 向前 *adv forward*
heurng teen 向前 *a. onward*
heurng teen 向前 *adv. onwards*
heurng tow muk 香桃木 *n. myrtle*
heurng yan bo jing 向人保證 *v.t. reassure*
heurng yow 香油 *n. balm*
heurng yow 向右 *adv right*
hey 氣 *n breath*
hey 起 *v. t build*
hey choy 器材 *n equipment*
hey fan 氣氛 *n. atmosphere*
hey kow 氣球 *n. balloon*

hey sik 稀釋 *v. t dilute*
hey sik 稀釋 *a dilute*
hey tay far 氣體化 *v.t. aerify*
hey yan 起因 *n. cause*
hey yoon 戲院 *n. cinema*
hiew cheurng 囂張 *a. arrogant*
hing chuy 興趣 *n. interest*
hing day 兄弟 *n brother*
hing day 兄弟 *n mate*
hing day geh 兄弟嘅 *a. fraternal*
hing fan 興奮 *adj alacrious*
hing fan 興奮 *v. t electrify*
hing fan 興奮 *v. t excite*
hing fan 興奮 *v. i exult*
hing fan jay 興奮劑 *n agonist*
hing fan jay 興奮劑 *n. stimulant*
hing hay 氫氣 *n. hydrogen*
hing jorng 輕撞 *n dig*
hing juk 慶祝 *v. t. & i. celebrate*
hing juk wut dung 慶祝活動 *n. celebration*
hing juk wut dung 慶祝活動 *n festivity*
hing may geh 輕微嘅 *a. slight*
hing see 輕視 *a contemptuous*
hing see 輕視 *n. slight*
hing see 輕視 *v.t. slight*
hing see geh 輕視嘅 *a. sardonic*
hing sut 輕率 *a facile*
hing sut 輕率 *n flippancy*
hing sut 輕率 *adv. headlong*
hing sut 輕率 *a. impetuous*
hing sut 輕率 *n. imprudence*
hing tiew 輕佻 *a. frivolous*
hing tiew 輕佻 *n. levity*
hing worng 興旺 *v.i flourish*
hing worng 興旺 *n. prosperity*
hing worng 興旺 *v.i. thrive*
hing yee 輕易 *n ease*
hing yee gam chuy sing 輕易咁取勝 *v.i. romp*

hing yee seurng sun 輕易相信 *adj. credulity*

hing yow geh 輕柔嘅 *a. silken*

hing yow geh 輕柔嘅 *a. silky*

hm bao kwut 唔包括 *v. t except*

hm bay tay ho geh yan 唔被睇好嘅人 *n underdog*

hm dow 誤導 *v.t. misdirect*

hm dow 誤導 *n. misdirection*

hm dow 誤導 *v.t. mislead*

hm forng been 唔方便 *a. inconvenient*

hm gai 誤解 *v.t. misapprehend*

hm gai 誤解 *n misapprehension*

hm gai 誤解 *n. misconception*

hm gan san 唔謹慎 *a. indiscreet*

hm gan yiew 唔緊要 *a. immaterial*

hm gat lay geh 唔吉利嘅 *a. ominous*

hm geem deem geh 唔檢點嘅 *a. slatternly*

hm geem deem hang way 唔檢點行為 *n. indiscretion*

hm geeng mang geh 唔結盟嘅 *n. non-alignment*

hm gey dak 唔記得 *v.t forget*

hm gok ying 五角型 *n. pentagon*

hm gow 唔夠 *a. insufficient*

hm gow 唔夠 *v.t. lack*

hm gow 唔夠 *a. scanty*

hm gow 唔夠 *adv. short*

hm gung 蜈蚣 *n. centipede*

hm gung jing 唔公正 *n. injustice*

hm gung jing 唔公正 *v.t. wrong*

hm gung ping 唔公平 *a unfair*

hm gung ping geh 唔公平嘅 *a. unjust*

hm gway 唔貴 *a. inexpensive*

hm gwong choy geh 唔光彩嘅 *a. ignoble*

hm gwun 五官 *n. sense*

hm han ding 唔肯定 *a. uncertain*

hm hang ding geh 唔肯定嘅 *a. tentative*

hm hap dong 唔恰當 *a. indecent*

hm hap lor tap 唔合邏輯 *a. irrational*

hm hap lor tap geh 唔合邏輯嘅 *a. illogical*

hm hap see 唔合時 *a. inopportune*

hm hap sik geh hang way 唔合適嘅行為 *n. impropriety*

hm hay 唔係 *adv. nay*

hm hay 唔係 *a. no*

hm hay 唔係 *adv. no*

hm hay 唔係 *n no*

hm hay 唔係 *adv. not*

hm hay jok yung 唔起作用 *v.i. misfire*

hm heem huy 唔謙虛 *a. immodest*

hm heem huy 唔謙虛 *n. immodesty*

hm ho cheurng 午後場 *n. matinee*

hm ho choy 唔好彩 *a. luckless*

hm ho gorng yeh 唔好講嘢 *v.i hush*

hm ho yee see geh 唔好意思嘅 *a. sheepish*

hm hor kao geh 唔可靠嘅 *a. shifty*

hm hor sun geh 唔可信嘅 *a. suspect*

hm hor yi 唔可以 *a. unable*

hm how 唔好 *a. indifferent*

hm hoy sam 唔開心 *a. unhappy*

hm jee deem gai jow 唔知點解就 *adv. somehow*

hm jee juk geh 唔知足嘅 *a. insatiable*

hm jik dak 唔值得 *a. worthless*

hm jing dong geh 唔正當嘅 *a. improper*

hm jing dong geh 唔正當嘅 *a. wrongful*

hm jing seurng 唔正常 *n. aberrance*

hm jing seurng 唔正常 *a abnormal*

hm jing seurng 唔正常 *adj acentric*

hm jing seurng 唔正常 *adv. amiss*

hm joon ging 唔尊敬 *n disrespect*
hm jow yeh 唔做嘢 *n. inaction*
hm joy yee 唔在意 *a. unaware*
hm ju yee geh 唔注意嘅 *a. oblivious*
hm jun kok 唔準確 *a. inaccurate*
hm jun kok 唔準確 *a. inexact*
hm jun sow dow dak 唔遵守道德 *a. amoral*
hm jung sam 唔忠心 *a disloyal*
hm jung yee 唔鐘意 *v. t dislike*
hm jung yiew 唔重要 *n. insignificance*
hm jung yiew 唔重要 *a. insignificant*
hm jung yiew geh 唔重要嘅 *a. incidental*
hm jung yiew geh 唔重要嘅 *a. marginal*
hm jung yiew geh yan 唔重要嘅人 *n. pigmy*
hm kway jak 唔規則 *a. irregular*
hm kway jak sing 唔規則性 *n. irregularity*
hm lay 唔理 *v. t disregard*
hm loy fan geh 唔耐煩嘅 *a. restive*
hm ming bak see lay 唔明白事理 *a. witless*
hm ming heen geh 唔明顯嘅 *n. subtle*
hm ming jee geh 唔明智嘅 *a. imprudent*
hm mun yee 唔滿意 *v. t. dissatisfy*
hm on choon 唔安全 *a. insecure*
hm san seen geh 唔新鮮嘅 *a. stale*
hm sap jow leen gey leem 五十週年紀念 *n. jubilee*
hm sat jay geh 唔實際嘅 *a. quixotic*
hm shoon 誤算 *n. miscalculation*
hm shu fuk 唔舒服 *a crook*
hm shu fuk 唔舒服 *n discomfort*
hm shu fuk 唔舒服 *a. indisposed*
hm shu fuk 唔舒服 *n. malaise*
hm shu fuk 唔舒服 *a. unwell*

hm siew sam 唔小心 *a accidental*
hm sik hap geh 唔適合 *a. inapplicable*
hm sik hap ju geh 唔適合住嘅 *a. inhospitable*
hm sing sat 唔誠實 *a. corrupt*
hm sing sat 唔誠實 *a dishonest*
hm sing sat 唔誠實 *n. dishonesty*
hm sing sat 唔誠實 *a. insincere*
hm sing sat 唔誠實 *a. malafide*
hm sing sat 唔誠實 *adv malafide*
hm sun 唔信 *n distrust*
hm sun 唔信 *v. t. distrust*
hm sun 誤信 *n. misbelief*
hm sun 唔信 *v.t. mistrust*
hm sun chung geh 唔順從嘅 *a. insubordinate*
hm sun dak gwor geh 唔信得過嘅 *a. unreliable*
hm sun geet geh 唔純潔嘅 *a. impure*
hm suy yiew geh 唔需要嘅 *a. needless*
hm tam seurng geh 唔尋常嘅 *a. outlandish*
hm tay leurng 唔體諒 *a. inconsiderate*
hm tee 唔似 *prep unlike*
hm tee yeurng 唔似樣 *a. nefandous*
hm ting hm chor 唔清唔楚 *a. incoherent*
hm ting yoon 唔情願 *a. loath*
hm tow ming geh 唔透明嘅 *a. opaque*
hm tung 唔同 *a different*
hm tung 唔同 *a unlike*
hm tung geh 唔同嘅 *a diverse*
hm tung geh 唔同嘅 *a else*
hm tung yee 唔同意 *v. i disagree*
hm wai yee 唔懷疑 *a. implicit*
hm wan ding 唔穩定 *adj. astatic*
hm wan ding 唔穩定 *a critical*

hm wan ding sing 唔穩定性 n. instability
hm wan gu geh 唔穩固嘅 a. rickety
hm wan huy 唔允許 a. inadmissible
hm wan jan geh 唔穩陣嘅 a. shaky
hm wut yeurk 唔活躍 a. inactive
hm wuy 誤會 v.t. misconceive
hm wuy 誤會 v.t. misconstrue
hm wuy 誤會 v.t. misunderstand
hm wuy 誤會 n. misunderstanding
hm yam jow geh yan 唔飲酒嘅人 n. teetotaller
hm yap kay tow 誤入歧途 v.t. misguide
hm yat jee 唔一致 adj absonant
hm yeh 午夜 n. midnight
hm ying tung 唔認同 v.t. gainsay
hm yoon may 唔完美 a. imperfect
hm yoot 五月 n. May
hm yuk geh 唔喐嘅 a. stationary
hm yung 唔溶 n. insoluble
hm yung yan 唔容忍 a. intolerant
ho 後 a after
ho 蠔 n. oyster
ho 厚 a. thick
ho 好 adv. well
ho 蒿 n. wormwood
ho ah 好啊 interj. hurrah
ho bay 口鼻 n. muzzle
ho chee yoon gam 好似猿咁 a. apish
ho choy 口才 n eloquence
ho choy 好彩 a. fortunate
ho choy 好彩 a. lucky
ho chu 好處 n. advantage
ho chu 好處 n gain
ho chu 好處 n good
ho chu 好處 n plus
ho dai geh 好大嘅 a enormous
ho dai geh 好大嘅 a. huge
ho dor 好多 adv. galore
ho dor 好多 a. many
ho dor geh 好多嘅 a. manifold

ho dor geh 好多嘅 a. numerous
ho dow 好鬥 a belligerent
ho doy 口袋 n. pocket
ho doy 後代 n. posterity
ho fai 好快 adv. anon
ho fai 厚塊 n. slab
ho fai 好快 adv. soon
ho fan 好煩 a. irritant
ho fan 好煩 a. tiresome
ho fwuy 後悔 v.i. repent
ho fwuy 後悔 n. repentance
ho fwuy 後悔 v.t. rue
ho fwuy geh 後悔嘅 a. repentant
ho fwuy geh 後悔嘅 a. rueful
ho gao siew 好搞笑 a. hilarious
ho geep 浩劫 n. havoc
ho geh 好嘅 a. good
ho gey 後記 n epilogue
ho gik geh 好極嘅 a. superb
ho gok 號角 n bugle
ho gorng geh 口講嘅 a. verbal
ho gwor 後果 n consequence
ho gwor 後果 a consequent
ho gwor 後果 n. result
ho hak 好客 n. hospitality
ho hak geh 好客嘅 a. hospitable
ho ho 好好 a great
ho ho 好好 a. terrific
ho ho gam 厚厚咁 adv. thick
ho ho geh 好好嘅 a. marvellous
ho ho geh 好好嘅 a. wonderful
ho ho yan 好好人 a cordial
ho ho yan see 好好人士 a. affable
ho hok geh 好學嘅 a. studious
ho hot 口渴 a. thirsty
ho jak 豪宅 n. mansion
ho jeen geh 好戰嘅 a. militant
ho jeen geh 好戰嘅 a. warlike
ho jeen geh yan 好戰嘅人 n militant
ho joot 後綴 n. suffix
ho jung yiew geh 好重要嘅 a. vital
ho kay 好奇 a curious

ho kay sam 好奇心 *n curiosity*
ho la 好嘞 *a effeminate*
ho lay 後來 *adv after*
ho lay 後嚟 *a. subsequent*
ho leng 好靚 *a. attractive*
ho leng 好靚 *a. gorgeous*
ho leng 好靚 *a. lovely*
ho lung 喉嚨 *n. throat*
ho lung geh 喉嚨嘅 *a. guttural*
ho ma 號碼 *n. number*
ho may 好味 *a. tasty*
ho may geh 好味嘅 *a. palatable*
ho may geh 好味嘅 *a. toothsome*
ho meen 後面 *adv behind*
ho meen 後面 *prep behind*
ho mo bo low gam 毫無保留咁 *adv. outright*
ho pang yow 好朋友 *n chum*
ho sang 後生 *a. young*
ho sang geh 後生嘅 *a. youthful*
ho sao 口哨 *n whistle*
ho say geh 好細嘅 *a. minuscule*
ho say geh 好細嘅 *a. minute*
ho see 口試 *n viva-voce*
ho seh 後寫 *adj. adscript*
ho shu 厚書 *n. tome*
ho siew geh 好笑嘅 *a comical*
ho sik jeh 好色者 *n. sensualist*
ho sut 口述 *v. t dictate*
ho sut 口述 *n dictation*
ho sut geh 口述嘅 *adv. orally*
ho suy 好衰 *a. awful*
ho suy 口水 *n. saliva*
ho suy 口水 *n spit*
ho suy 口水 *n spittle*
ho tai yeurng 好太陽 *a. sunny*
ho tee bat ting 口齒不清 *v.t. lisp*
ho tee bat ting 口齒不清 *v.i. mumble*
ho teen sing 後天性 *adj adscititious*
ho tow geh 口頭嘅 *a. oral*
ho tow geh 口嘅嘅 *a viva-voce*
ho tow seurng geh 口頭上嘅 *adv.*

ho tow seurng geh 口頭上嘅 *adv. verbally*
ho tow yeem geh 好討厭嘅 *a. infernal*
ho wah 豪華 *a. lush*
ho wah 豪華 *a. luxurious*
ho wah geh 豪華嘅 *a. opulent*
ho wah geh 豪華嘅 *a. regal*
ho wan 好玩 *n. fun*
ho yam 口音 *n accent*
ho yiew 後腰 *n small*
ho yow 好油 *a. oily*
hok 學 *v.i. learn*
hok 殼 *n. shell*
hok hao 學校 *n. school*
hok hao geh 學校嘅 *a. scholastic*
hok jap 學習 *n. learning*
hok jeh 學者 *n. scholar*
hok jeurng 學長 *n. prefect*
hok jor 學咗 *a. learned*
hok juy chor 鶴嘴鋤 *n. mattock*
hok kay 學期 *n. semester*
hok kay 學期 *n. term*
hok lik 學歷 *n. qualification*
hok sang 學生 *n. learner*
hok sang 學生 *n. pupil*
hok sang 學生 *n. student*
hok sut geh 學術嘅 *a academic*
hok way 學位 *n degree*
hok yoon 學院 *n academy*
hok yoon 學院 *n college*
hon jeep 焊接 *v.t. solder*
hon koy 慷慨 *n bounty*
hon lang 寒冷 *n. chill*
hon lang geh 寒冷嘅 *a. wintry*
hon liew 焊料 *n. solder*
hon yow 罕有 *a. rare*
hon yow geh 罕有嘅 *a. sparse*
hong hung 航空 *n. aviation*
hoon 勸 *v. t. counsel*
hoon 勸 *v. t dissuade*

hoon giew seng 吠叫聲 v.t. bark
hoon jor 勸阻 v.i. dehort
hoot 血 n blood
hoot lum lum 血淋淋 a bloody
hoot tung 血統 n. lineage
hor 河 n. river
hor bay 可悲 a deplorable
hor hang geh 可行嘅 a. practicable
hor hang geh 可行嘅 a. workable
hor hang ghe 可行嘅 a. viable
hor jing 苛政 n. tyranny
hor ka yan 可卡因 n cocaine
hor kao geh 可靠嘅 a credible
hor lang 可能 v may
hor lang fat sang geh see 可能發生嘅 事 n. contingency
hor lang geh 可能嘅 a. possible
hor lang sing 可能性 n. likelihood
hor lang sing 可能性 n. odds
hor lang sing 可能性 n. possibility
hor lang sing 可能性 n. probability
hor leen 可憐 a. miserable
hor leen 可憐 v.t. pity
hor leen geh 可憐嘅 a. piteous
hor leen geh 可憐嘅 a. pitiful
hor leen geh say low 可憐嘅細路 n mite
hor ngoy 可愛 a. adorable
hor ngoy geh 可愛嘅 a darling
hor pa 可怕 a formidable
hor pa 可怕 a. terrible
hor sok geh 可塑嘅 a. malleable
hor tee geh 可恥嘅 a. shameful
hor yee 可疑 a. suspicious
hor yee chu lay geh 可以處理嘅 a. manageable
hor yee chuy geh 可以徐嘅 a. removable
hor yee dak dow geh 可以得到嘅 a. obtainable
hor yee fan hoy geh 可以分開嘅 a. separable

hor yee fan joon geh 可以翻轉嘅 a. reversible
hor yee forng wu 可以防護 a proof
hor yee gan geh 可以揀嘅 a. optional
hor yee geh 可疑嘅 a. questionable
hor yee joon geh 可以轉嘅 a. transferable
hor yee jung jee geh 可以終止嘅 a. terminable
hor yee juy sok geh 可以追溯嘅 a. traceable
hor yee leurng dok geh 可以量度嘅 a. measurable
hor yee teet wuy geh 可以撤回嘅 a. revocable
hor yee way choon geh 可以遺傳嘅 a. heritable
hor yee wun shu geh 可以寬恕嘅 a. venial
hor yee yoon leurng geh 可以原諒嘅 a. pardonable
hor yee yuk 可以郁 adj ambulant
hor yee yuk geh 可以郁嘅 a. movable
hor yee yung geh 可以溶嘅 a. soluble
hor yee yung geh 可以溶嘅 a. solvent
hor yi 可以 a able
hor yi 可以 v. t. can
hor yi jeep sow 可以接受 a acceptable
hor yi jeep sow 可以接受 a. admissible
hor yi jeep sow 可以接受 a. agreeable
hor yi say geh 可以洗嘅 a. washable
hor yi sik geh 可以食嘅 a eatable
hor yi sik geh 可以食嘅 a edible
hor yi tung horng geh 可以通航嘅 a. navigable

hor yi yee geh 可以醫嘅 *a curable*
horn 汗 *n. sweat*
horn dang 刊登 *v.t. publish*
horn hung hok 航空學 *n.pl. aeronautics*
horn jeep 焊接 *v.t. weld*
horn jeep deem 焊接點 *n weld*
horn ju 汗珠 *n. perspiration*
horng hang 航行 *n. voyage*
horng hang jeh 航行者 *n. voyager*
horng koy 慷慨 *n. liberality*
horng koy geh 慷慨嘅 *a. munificent*
horng leet 行列 *n. procession*
horng yeep 行業 *n. industry*
hot 渴 *n. thirst*
hot 渴 *v.i. thirst*
hot choy 喝彩 *v. t. cheer*
hot mong 渴望 *adj. agog*
hot mong 渴望 *adj. appetent*
hot mong 渴望 *adj. athirst*
hot morn gam 渴望咁 *adv avidly*
hot morng 渴望 *v.t. covet*
hot morng 渴望 *v.t. crave*
hot morng 渴望 *n desire*
hot morng 渴望 *v.t desire*
hot morng 渴望 *v.i. hanker*
hot morng 渴望 *n hunger*
hot morng 渴望 *v.i long*
hot morng 渴望 *n. longing*
hot morng 渴望 *v.i. yearn*
hot morng 渴望 *n. yearning*
hot morng geh 渴望嘅 *a. wishful*
how 好 *a. nice*
how choy 好彩 *adv. luckily*
how doy 後代 *n descendant*
how fai huy ha 好快去下 *v.t nip*
how fwut 後悔 *v.i. regret*
how geng 後頸 *n. nape*
how ho 口號 *n. slogan*
how ho 口號 *n. watchword*
how low 好嬲 *a. irate*
how meen 後面 *adv. back*

how meen 後面 *n. rear*
hoy 開 *v.t. prescribe*
hoy 海 *n. sea*
hoy bat 海拔 *n elevation*
hoy bat 海拔 *n. altitude*
hoy bo 海報 *n. poster*
hoy cheurng bak 開場白 *n. preamble*
hoy chorng geh 開創嘅 *a. inaugural*
hoy chung 害蟲 *n. pest*
hoy day geh 海底嘅 *a submarine*
hoy dow 海盜 *n. pirate*
hoy dung 開動 *v.t. activate*
hoy fa 開花 *v.i. bloom*
hoy fa 開花 *v.i blossom*
hoy far 開化 *v. t civilize*
hoy geh 海嘅 *a. marine*
hoy geh 海嘅 *a. maritime*
hoy gwan 海軍 *n. navy*
hoy gwan geh 海軍嘅 *a. naval*
hoy hap 海峽 *n. strait*
hoy jee 開支 *n. expense*
hoy jeurng 海象 *n. walrus*
hoy lai 海獺 *n. otter*
hoy lay 海狸 *n beaver*
hoy lor hok 海螺殼 *n. conch*
hoy lorng 海浪 *n. wave*
hoy meen 海綿 *n. sponge*
hoy ming 開明 *a. liberal*
hoy ngon 海岸 *n coast*
hoy ngon 海岸 *a. littoral*
hoy ow 海鷗 *n. gull*
hoy pao 海豹 *n. seal*
hoy sam 開心 *a. happy*
hoy sam 開心 *a. jubilant*
hoy see san low 海市蜃樓 *n. mirage*
hoy shoon geh 凱旋嘅 *a. triumphal*
hoy tee 開始 *n begin*
hoy tee 開始 *n. beginning*
hoy tee 開始 *v. t commence*
hoy tee 開始 *n commencement*
hoy tee 開始 *v. t embark*
hoy tee 開始 *n. inception*

hoy tee 開始 n. onset
hoy tee 開始 v.t. prelude
hoy tee 開始 v.t. start
hoy tee 開始 n start
hoy tok 開拓 n reclamation
hoy tok jeh 開拓者 n. pioneer
hoy tow 開頭 n. opening
hoy wan 海灣 n bay
hoy wan 海灣 n bight
hoy wan 海灣 n. gulf
hoy way geh 開胃嘅 a. piquant
hoy worng sing 海王星 n. Neptune
hoy yeurng 海洋 n. ocean
hoy yeurng geh 海洋嘅 a. oceanic
huk gey sang 槲寄生 n. mistletoe
huk sow 哭訴 v.i. sob
hung 空 a. bare
hung 熊 n bear
hung 胸 n breast
hung 空 a empty
hung 烘 v.t. parch
hung bak 空白 a blank
hung bo 胸部 n bosom
hung bo 恐怖 a. ghastly
hung bo 恐怖 n. horror
hung bo fan jee 恐怖份子 n. terrorist
hung bo geh 恐怖嘅 a. horrible
hung bo ju yee 恐怖主義 n. terrorism
hung bo sek 紅寶石 n. ruby
hung fan 空翻 n. somersault
hung gak 空格 n blank
hung gan 空間 n. space
hung gan 空間 a. spatial
hung gan 空間 n. void
hung geh 空嘅 a. vacant
hung giew 吼叫 v.i. growl
hung giew seng 吼叫聲 n growl
hung ging 孔徑 n. aperture
hung gow 控告 n accusation
hung gow 控告 v.t. accuse
hung gow 控告 n. indictment

hung guy 恐懼 n dread
hung guy 恐懼 n fear
hung guy 恐懼 n. spectre
hung hak 恐嚇 v. t. cow
hung hak 恐嚇 n. intimidation
hung hak 恐嚇 v.t. terrorize
hung hak 恐嚇 v.t. threaten
hung han 空閒 n. leisure
hung hey 空氣 n air
hung hey low tung 空氣流通 a. airy
hung hung day 紅紅哋 a. reddish
hung jay 控制 v. t control
hung jay 控制 n curb
hung jay 控制 v. t curb
hung jay 控制 v. t dominate
hung jay 控制 n domination
hung jay 控制 n grip
hung jay 控制 v.t harness
hung jay 控制 n. hold
hung jay gorn 控制桿 n. lever
hung jay koon 控制權 n control
hung jeurk 孔雀 n. peacock
hung jung 紅腫 n. weal
hung jung 紅腫 n. welt
hung jung geh 空中嘅 a. aerial
hung koot 空缺 n. vacancy
hung kuy jing 恐懼症 n. neurosis
hung lor bak 紅蘿蔔 n. carrot
hung luk 雄鹿 n. stag
hung or 雄鵝 n. gander
hung sam geh 空心嘅 a. hollow
hung sik 紅色 n. red
hung sik geh 紅色嘅 a. red
hung tan geh 兇殘嘅 a. murderous
hung way 雄偉 a. majestic
hung yan yu 雄人魚 n. merman
hung yun geh 紅潤嘅 a. rosy
hur 靴 n boot
huy 去 v.i. go
huy 去 v.t head
huy chuy jap jat 去除雜質 v.t. refine
huy ga 虛假 a. mendacious

huy ga geh 虛假嘅 *adj mock*
huy gou 虛構 *n figment*
huy ha lok yeen 許下諾言 *v.t. vow*
huy heurng ha 去鄉下 *v.t. rusticate*
huy hok 去殼 *v.t. shell*
huy hor jing 許可證 *n. permit*
huy jeurng sing say 虛張聲勢 *v. t bluff*
huy kow 虛構 *v.t fabricate*
huy kow geh 虛構嘅 *a fictitious*
huy luy hang 去旅行 *v.i. journey*
huy mow ju yee 虛無主義 *n. nihilism*
huy ngay 虛偽 *n. hypocrisy*
huy ngay 虛偽 *n. insincerity*
huy ngay geh 虛偽嘅 *a. hypocritical*
huy pay 去皮 *v.t skin*
huy pwuy 許配 *v. t betroth*
huy sey 去死 *adj. alamort*
huy wing 虛榮 *n. vainglory*
huy yee 虛擬 *a virtual*
huy yeurk 虛弱 *n debility*
huy yeurk 虛弱 *a feeble*
huy yoon 許願 *v.t. wish*

J

ja 揸 *v.t. pilot*
ja 搾 *v.t. squeeze*
ja 揸 *v.t. steer*
ja 炸 *v. t bomb*
ja cher 揸車 *v. t drive*
ja dan 炸彈 *n bomb*
ja ju 揸住 *v.t hold*
ja lai 揸奶 *v.t. milk*
ja lan 炸爛 *v.i blast*
ja soy 痄腮 *n. mumps*
ja yeurk 炸藥 *n dynamite*
ja yeurk 炸藥 *n. explosive*

ja yow teng 揸遊艇 *v.i yacht*
jai 債 *n.pl. arrears*
jai 債 *n debt*
jai gai 齋戒 *v.i fast*
jai gai kay 齋戒期 *n fast*
jai jok sing dung wah peen 製作成動畫片 *v.t. animate*
jai ju 債主 *n creditor*
jai mo yan 債務人 *n debtor*
jak 窄 *a. narrow*
jak been 側邊 *prep. beside*
jak fat 責罰 *v.t mete*
jak gwai 責怪 *v.t. admonish*
jak gwai 責怪 *v. t blame*
jak ngan koot ding 擲銀決定 *n toss*
jak yam 責任 *n blame*
jak yam 責任 *n duty*
jak yam 責任 *n. liability*
jak yam 責任 *n mantle*
jak yam 責任 *n. obligation*
jak yam 責任 *n. responsibility*
jak yiew 摘要 *n abridgement*
jak yiew 摘要 *n abstract*
jak yiew 摘要 *n. breviary*
jak yiew 摘要 *n. digest*
jak yiew 摘要 *n. precis*
jam 斬 *v. t chop*
jam 浸 *v.t flood*
jam 浸 *v.t. immerse*
jam 浸 *n. immersion*
jam 斬 *v.t. lop*
jam 針 *n. needle*
jam 針 *n. pin*
jam 浸 *v.t. swamp*
jam gat 針拮 *n. prick*
jam geurt 針腳 *n. stitch*
jam ngan 眨眼 *v. t. & i blink*
jam ngan 眨眼 *v.i. wink*
jam see 暫時 *a. transitory*
jam see geh 暫時嘅 *a. provisional*
jam see geh 暫時嘅 *a. temporary*
jam see sing 暫時性 *n. provisonality*

jam sow 禽獸 *n. sodomite*

jam ting 暫停 *n. pause*

jam ting 暫停 *v.i. pause*

jam ting 暫停 *v.t. suspend*

jam ting jik mow 暫停職務 *n. suspension*

jam tow 斬頭 *v. t. behead*

jam tow 枕頭 *n pillow*

jan 讚 *v.t acclaim*

jan 讚 *n acclaim*

jan 讚 *v. t compliment*

jan 賺 *v. t earn*

jan 讚 *v. t. extol*

jan 讚 *v.i hail*

jan 震 *a. jerky*

jan 震 *v.t. jolt*

jan 讚 *v.t. laud*

jan 讚 *v.t. praise*

jan 震 *v.i. quiver*

jan 震 *v.i. tremble*

jan 震 *v.i. vibrate*

jan dai teen geh 賺大錢嘅 *a. lucrative*

jan ding 鎮定 *n. composure*

jan ding geh 鎮定嘅 *a. sedate*

jan dung 震動 *n. jolt*

jan dung 震動 *n. pulsation*

jan dung 震動 *n. quiver*

jan dung 震動 *n. vibration*

jan geh 真嘅 *a. real*

jan gway geh 珍貴嘅 *a. precious*

jan hay 真係 *adv. really*

jan hung 真空 *n. vacuum*

jan jing 鎮靜 *v. t. calm*

jan jing geh 真正嘅 *a bonafide*

jan jing geh 鎮靜嘅 *adj calmative*

jan jing geh 鎮靜嘅 *a. sedative*

jan jing jay 鎮靜劑 *n. narcotic*

jan jing jay 鎮靜劑 *n sedative*

jan jor 贊助 *n. patronage*

jan jor 贊助 *v.t. sponsor*

jan jor seurng 贊助商 *n. sponsor*

jan jor yan 贊助人 *n. patron*

jan ju 珍珠 *n. pearl*

jan kuy 鎮區 *a. township*

jan kwan 真菌 *n. fungus*

jan may see 讚美詩 *n. psalm*

jan ngat 鎮壓 *v.t. quell*

jan ngat 鎮壓 *v.t. suppress*

jan ngat 鎮壓 *n. suppression*

jan sik 珍惜 *v. t. cherish*

jan sik 珍惜 *v.t. prize*

jan sik 珍惜 *v.t. treasure*

jan sik 珍惜 *v.t. value*

jan sing 贊成 *v.i. assent*

jan sing 真誠 *n. sincerity*

jan sing yan 贊成人 *n. seconder*

jan yeurng 讚揚 *n. compliment*

jan yeurng 讚揚 *n. glorification*

jan yeurng 讚揚 *n laud*

jang 憎 *v.t. abhor*

jang 憎 *v. t despise*

jang 憎 *v.t. hate*

jang 憎 *v.t. loathe*

jang 掙 *v.i. tussle*

jang 爭 *v.i. vie*

jang 增 *v.t. gain*

jang been 爭辯 *v. t contest*

jang dow 爭鬥 *n. tussle*

jang fwun 贈款 *n. largesse*

jang ga 增加 *v.t. accrete*

jang ga 增加 *v.t. augment*

jang ga 增加 *n. augmentation*

jang ga 增加 *v.t. increase*

jang ga 增加 *n increase*

jang ga 增加 *n. rise*

jang gow 增高 *v.t. heighten*

jang jap 爭執 *n affray*

jang jap 爭執 *n. skirmish*

jang jap 爭執 *v.t. skirmish*

jang jat 掙扎 *v.i. struggle*

jang jeurng 增長 *n accrementition*

jang jik 增值 *v.i. accrue*

jang jik 增值 *n. increment*

jang jun 增進 *v.t further*
jang keurng 增強 *v.t. fortify*
jang keurng hing chuy 增強興趣 *v.t.*
  whet
jang lun 爭論 *n. altercation*
jang lun 爭論 *n. conflict*
jang lun 爭論 *n controversy*
jang lun 爭論 *n. debate*
jang lun 爭論 *n dispute*
jang lun 爭論 *n. moot*
jang lun 爭論 *n. wrangle*
jao 爪 *n claw*
jao 爪 *n. paw*
jao 抓 *n. scratch*
jao 抓 *v.t. scratch*
jao 罩 *v.t. sheet*
jao fung 罩篷 *n. canopy*
jao gorng 驟降 *n. slump*
jao gorng 驟降 *v.i. slump*
jao siew 嘲笑 *v.i. jeer*
jao siew 嘲笑 *n taunt*
jao yan 抓人 *v.t. pay*
jao yee 罩衣 *n. smock*
jap 集 *n episode*
jap 閘 *n. gate*
jap 汁 *n juice*
jap 執 *v.t. tidy*
jap cho 雜草 *n. weed*
jap dat yoon 執達員 *n. bailiff*
jap fat yan 執法人 *n. martinet*
jap for deem 雜貨店 *n. grocer*
jap for deem 雜貨店 *n. grocery*
jap gey 雜記 *n. miscellany*
jap gey see 雜技師 *n. acrobat*
jap gik 襲擊 *n. assault*
jap gik 襲擊 *n. attack*
jap gik 襲擊 *v.t. attack*
jap gwan 習慣 *v.t. accustom*
jap gwan 習慣 *n. habit*
jap gwan 習慣 *n wont*
jap gwan geh 習慣嘅 *a. wonted*
jap gwan jor 習慣咗 *v. t. habituate*

jap gwan jor 習慣咗 *a. wont*
jap ha 執下 *v.t. retouch*
jap hang 執行 *v. t. enforce*
jap hang 執行 *v. t execute*
jap hang 執行 *v.t. implement*
jap hang lay 執行李 *v.t. pack*
jap hang ling 執行令 *n. warrant*
jap hap 集合 *v.t. rally*
jap horng ghe 雜項嘅 *a. sundry*
jap jat 雜質 *n. impurity*
jap jeurk geh 執著嘅 *a. persistent*
jap juk 習俗 *n. custom*
jap juk 習俗 *a customary*
jap jung 雜種 *n hybrid*
jap jung geh 雜種嘅 *a. hybrid*
jap jung gow 雜種狗 *a mongrel*
jap see 執事 *n. deacon*
jap tay 集體 *a collective*
jap wuy 集會 *n. convention*
jap wuy 集會 *n. convocation*
jar 炸 *v.t. fry*
jat 紮 *n bunch*
jat been 側邊 *n. side*
jat beng 疾病 *n. sickness*
jat day ta 質地差 *a flimsy*
jat gam 質感 *n. texture*
jat jat tiew 紮紮跳 *v.i scamper*
jat jay 姪仔 *n. nephew*
jat leurng 質量 *n. quality*
jat leurng geh 質量嘅 *a. qualitative*
jat liew 質料 *n material*
jat luy 姪女 *n. niece*
jat sat 紮實 *a. sturdy*
jat sik 窒息 *n apnoea*
jat sik 窒息 *v.t suffocate*
jat sik 窒息 *n. suffocation*
jat yee 質疑 *v. i dispute*
jat yee 質疑 *v.t. question*
jay 仔 *n. son*
jay 掣 *n. switch*
jay ban 祭品 *n. oblation*
jay ban 祭品 *n. offering*

jay ban 祭品 *n. sacrifice*

jay bay 責備 *n. reproof*

jay biew yoon 製表員 *n. tabulator*

jay choy 制裁 *n. sanction*

jay fuk 制服 *n. livery*

jay fuk 制服 *v.t. subdue*

jay fuk 制服 *n. subjection*

jay fuk 制服 *n. subjugation*

jay gak gung yan 製革工人 *n. tanner*

jay jee 制止 *v.t foil*

jay jee 制止 *v.t. restrain*

jay jok 製作 *n fabrication*

jay jok 製造 *n. production*

jay jow jeh 製造者 *n. maker*

jay jow seurng 製造商 *n manufacturer*

jay low 滯留 *v.i. strand*

jay low fay 滯留費 *n. demurrage*

jay luy 仔女 *n. offspring*

jay tan 祭壇 *n. altar*

jay yee 祭衣 *n. vestment*

jay yeurk gung see 製藥公司 *n. compounder*

jee 紙 *n. paper*

jee 指 *v.t. point*

jee 止 *v.t. quench*

jee 字 *n. text*

jee 枝 *n. withe*

jee 字 *n. word*

jee bay gam 自卑感 *n. inferiority*

jee bun ju yee jeh 資本主義者 *n. capitalist*

jee chan 資產 *n. asset*

jee chorng 痔瘡 *n. piles*

jee chu 支柱 *n. mainstay*

jee chu 支柱 *n strut*

jee chut 指出 *v.t. indicate*

jee dai 自大 *n. pomposity*

jee dan 子彈 *n bullet*

jee day 自大 *n. arrogance*

jee deen 字典 *n dictionary*

jee dow 知道 *a. aware*

jee dow 指導 *v. t direct*

jee dow 指導 *n. guidance*

jee dow 知道 *v.t. know*

jee dow 指導 *n. tuition*

jee fay gwun 指揮官 *n commander*

jee fey ga 指揮家 *n conductor*

jee forng 脂肪 *n fat*

jee fu 自負 *n egotism*

jee fu 自負 *a. vain*

jee fu 自負 *a. vainglorious*

jee fu 自負 *n. vanity*

jee gam 資金 *n. fund*

jee gam hok 冶金學 *n. metallurgy*

jee gam wu lay 指甲護理 *n. manicure*

jee gan 之間 *prep between*

jee gan 紙巾 *n. tissue*

jee gap chor 指甲銼 *n file*

jee gey 自己 *a. alone*

jee gey 知己 *n confidant*

jee gey 自己 *n. self*

jee gey geh 自己嘅 *a. own*

jee gey yat gor 自己一個 *adv. solo*

jee gok 知覺 *n. perception*

jee gung 子宮 *n. uterus*

jee gung 子宮 *n. womb*

jee hay 只係 *adv. only*

jee hay way teen geh 只係爲錢嘅 *a. mercenary*

jee heurng 志向 *n. aspiration*

jee hm seen 子午線 *a. meridian*

jee ho 之後 *prep. after*

jee ho 之後 *adv. thereafter*

jee hoot teep 止血貼 *n. plaster*

jee hung 指控 *n. allegation*

jee ja 吱喳 *v.i. twitter*

jee ja giew 吱喳叫 *v.i. chirp*

jee ja giew seng 吱喳叫聲 *n chirp*

jee jak 指責 *v. t. chide*

jee jak 指責 *v. t. condemn*

jee jak 指責 *v. t denounce*

jee jak 指責 n. denunciation

jee jak 自責 n. remorse

jee jak 指責 v.t. reproach

jee jee giew 吱吱叫 v. i cheep

jee jee seng 吱吱聲 n. twitter

jee jeh 智者 n. sage

jee jeh 智者 n. sophist

jee jeurng 紙漿 n. pulp

jee jeurng jorng geh 紙漿狀嘅 a. pulpy

jee ji 自治 a autonomous

jee joon 自傳 n. autobiography

jee jor 資助 v. t endow

jee jor 資助 v.t. subsidize

jee ju 蜘蛛 n. spider

jee ju mong 蜘蛛網 n. web

jee ju morng 蜘蛛網 n cobweb

jee juk 知足 v. t content

jee jung 之中 prep. among

jee jung 之中 prep. amongst

jee lam 指南 n. guide

jee larm jam 指南針 n compass

jee liew 飼料 n fodder

jee liew 資料 n. information

jee liew 治療 n. therapy

jee liew 治療 n. treatment

jee liew sow jao 資料收集 v.i. research

jee lik 智力 n. intellect

jee lik geh 智力嘅 a. mental

jee loon 自憐 n. narcissism

jee lor lan 紫羅蘭 n. violet

jee low 支流 n. tributary

jee low geh 支流嘅 a. tributary

jee loy 之內 prep. within

jee meen yee yi 字面意義 a. literal

jee ming 致命 a deadly

jee ming 致命 a. lethal

jee ming 自命 n. pretension

jee ming bat fan geh 自命不凡嘅 a. pretentious

jee ming dow 知名度 n. notability

jee ming geh 致命嘅 a fatal

jee mo 字母 n. alphabet

jee mo sun juy 字母順序 a. alphabetical

jee muk suk 紫苜蓿 n. lucerne

jee mwuy gam geh 姊妹咁嘅 a. sisterly

jee ngor 自我 n ego

jee on gwun 治安官 n. magistracy

jee pay 指派 v.t. assign

jee pay 紙皮 n. cardboard

jee piew 支票 n. cheque

jee sat 自殺 n. suicide

jee say 仔細 n. nicety

jee say 姿勢 n. pose

jee say 姿勢 n. posture

jee say 仔細 a thorough

jee say geem ta 仔細檢查 v.t. scrutinize

jee say geem ta 仔細檢查 n. scrutiny

jee say hao luy 仔細考慮 n consideration

jee say hao luy 仔細考慮 v. i deliberate

jee say hao luy 仔細考慮 v.t. ponder

jee see 芝士 n. cheese

jee see 指示 v.t. instruct

jee see 指示 n. instruction

jee see 指示 v.i. motion

jee see 自私 a. selfish

jee seurng mao tun geh 自相矛盾嘅 a. paradoxical

jee shoon 子孫 n. progeny

jee siew 至少 adv. least

jee sik 知識 n. knowledge

jee sik 紫色 adj./n. purple

jee sik fan jee 知識分子 n. intellectual

jee sik fan jee 知識分子 n. intelligentsia

jee sing 智勝 v.t. outwit

jee tang 支撐 v.t. prop

jee tay tan koot 肢體殘缺 *n. mutilation*
jee tee 支持 *n. advocacy*
jee tee 支持 *v.t. advocate*
jee tee 支持 *v.t. second*
jee tee 支持 *v.i. side*
jee tee 支持 *v.t. support*
jee tee 支持 *n. support*
jee tee 支持 *v.t uphold*
jee teen 之前 *prep. afore*
jee teen 之前 *adv. ago*
jee teen 之前 *prep before*
jee teen 之前 *conj before*
jee teen geh 之前嘅 *a. antecedent*
jee teen geh 之前嘅 *a. previous*
jee tiew 字條 *n. note*
jee ting 自稱 *v.t. purport*
jee way 智慧 *n. wisdom*
jee way 智慧 *n. wit*
jee way geh 自衛嘅 *adv. defensive*
jee way tee 智慧齒 *n. wisdom-tooth*
jee yan 指引 *v.t. guide*
jee yee way see 自以為是 *a dogmatic*
jee yeen gam 自然咁 *adv. naturally*
jee yeen san lun jeh 自然神論者 *n. deist*
jee yiew 紙鷂 *n. kite*
jee yoon 寺院 *n. monastery*
jee yoon 資源 *n. resource*
jee yoon 自願 *a. voluntary*
jee yoon 自願 *n. willingness*
jee yoon gam 自願咁 *adv. voluntarily*
jee yoon jeh 志願者 *n. volunteer*
jee yow 自由 *a. free*
jee yow 自由 *n. freedom*
jee yow 自由 *n. liberty*
jee yow 只有 *a. only*
jee yow ju yee 自由主義 *n. liberalism*
jee yow man 自由民 *n. yeoman*
jee yun 滋潤 *v.t. nourish*
jeem am 漸暗 *v.i. darkle*

jeem geh 尖嘅 *a. sharp*
jeem giew 尖叫 *adj argute*
jeem giew 尖叫 *v.i. shriek*
jeem giew seng 尖叫聲 *n. shriek*
jeem giew seng 尖叫聲 *n wail*
jeem hak geh shoot wah 尖刻嘅說話 *n acrimony*
jeem seng geh 尖聲嘅 *a. shrill*
jeem sing hok 占星學 *n. astrology*
jeem sing see 占星師 *n. astrologer*
jeem tap 尖塔 *n. steeple*
jeem tow 尖頭 *n. spike*
jeem uimg 佔用 *v.t. occupy*
jeem yow 佔有 *n. occupancy*
jeem yow say 佔優勢 *v.i. predominate*
jeem yow say 佔優勢 *v.i. preponderate*
jeem yow say geh 佔優勢嘅 *a. predominant*
jeem yow yan 佔有人 *n. occupant*
jeem yow yan 佔有人 *n. occupier*
jeem yu 尖銳 *adj. cultrate*
jeen 箭 *n arrow*
jeen 墊 *n cushion*
jeen 剪 *v. t cut*
jeen 剪 *v.t. shear*
jeen 煎 *v.i. sizzle*
jeen cher 戰車 *n chariot*
jeen chut 展出 *v. t exhibit*
jeen dan goon 煎蛋捲 *n. omelette*
jeen dow 戰鬥 *n battle*
jeen dow 戰鬥 *a. combatant*
jeen gak 賤格 *a. abject*
jeen jan geh 戰爭嘅 *a. martial*
jeen jang 戰爭 *n. warfare*
jeen lam 展覽 *n. exhibition*
jeen lam ban 展覽品 *n. exhibit*
jeen lan 展覽 *n display*
jeen lay ban 戰利品 *n. loot*
jeen leurk geh 戰略嘅 *a. strategic*
jeen luy yan 賤女人 *n bitch*

jeen see 戰士 *n combatant1*
jeen see 展示 *v. t display*
jeen see 展示 *v.t. model*
jeen sing 戰勝 *v.t. worst*
jeen yow 戰友 *n. comrade*
jeep 接 *n. catch*
jeep 摺 *n fold*
jeep 摺 *v.t fold*
jeep been 褶邊 *n. frill*
jeep bok deen seen 接駁電線 *v.t. wire*
jeep dang 褶凳 *n. stool*
jeep doy 接待 *v.t. serve*
jeep doy chu 接待處 *n. reception*
jeep fung 接縫 *v.t. seam*
jeep gan 接近 *v.t. approach*
jeep gan 接近 *v.i. near*
jeep han 摺痕 *n crease*
jeep hap chu 接合處 *n. commissure*
jeep juk 接觸 *n. contact*
jeep jung 接種 *n. vaccination*
jeep jung yoon 接種員 *n. vaccinator*
jeep lik choy 接力賽 *n. relay*
jeep lik pang 接力棒 *n baton*
jeep sow 接受 *& accept*
jeep sow 接受 *n acceptance*
jeep sow 接受 *n embrace*
jeep sow yan 接收人 *n. receiver*
jeet 節 *n. stanza*
jeet 擳 *v.t. tickle*
jeet bak 節拍 *n pulse*
jeet deem 節點 *n. node*
jeet hok 哲學 *n. philosophy*
jeet hok ga 哲學家 *n. philosopher*
jeet hok geh 哲學嘅 *a. philosophical*
jeet jeet giew 吱吱叫 *v.i. squeak*
jeet jeet seng 吱吱聲 *n squeak*
jeet jow 節奏 *v.i. pace*
jeet jow 節奏 *n rhythm*
jeet ju 截住 *v.t. intercept*
jeet mor 折磨 *v.t. afflict*
jeet mor 折磨 *v. t dog*

jeet mor 折磨 *n. ordeal*
jeet mor 折磨 *v.t. plague*
jeet mor 折磨 *n. purgatory*
jeet mor 折磨 *v.t. scourge*
jeet mor 折磨 *n. torment*
jeet mor 折磨 *v.t. torment*
jeet mor 折磨 *n. torture*
jeet mor 折磨 *v.t. torture*
jeet muk biew 節目表 *n. schedule*
jeet sang hoy jee 節省開支 *v.t. retrench*
jeet sang hoy jee 節省開支 *n. retrenchment*
jeet tee dung mat 齧齒動物 *n. rodent*
jeet toon 折斷 *v.t fracture*
jeet tow 折頭 *n discount*
jeet yat 節日 *n festival*
jeetmuk 節目 *n. programme*
jeh 借 *v. t borrow*
jeh 借 *v.t. lend*
jeh 借 *v.t. loan*
jeh 遮 *v.t. shade*
jeh 遮 *n. umbrella*
jeh 遮 *v.t. veil*
jeh gey 借記 *n debit*
jeh ju 遮住 *v. t. cover*
jeh ju 遮住 *v.t. shroud*
jeh lay 啫喱 *n. jelly*
jeh mwuy ting yee 姐妹情誼 *n. sisterhood*
jek gwat 脊骨 *n. spine*
jek gwat geh 脊骨嘅 *a. spinal*
jek gwut 脊骨 *n. backbone*
jeng jung sing ming 鄭重聲明 *n. protestation*
jerk sow 着數 *a. advantageous*
jeung gwun 掌管 *v.t. administer*
jeung ngar 象牙 *n. ivory*
jeurk 雀 *n bird*
jeurk 着 *v. t clothe*
jeurk 着 *v. t dress*

jeurk 着 *v.t garb*
jeurk 着 *v.t. wear*
jeurk chao 雀巢 *n. nest*
jeurk cheurng pow 着長袍 *v.t. robe*
jeurk for 着火 *adv. ablaze*
jeurk hm lok 着唔落 *v.t. outgrow*
jeurk may 着迷 *v. t enchant*
jeurk may 着迷 *v. t enrapture*
jeurk may 著迷 *n. infatuation*
jeurng 獎 *n. award*
jeurng 章 *n. chapter*
jeurng 獎 *v.t. reward*
jeurng 張 *n. sheet*
jeurng 漿 *v.t. starch*
jeurng 仗 *n. war*
jeurng ak 掌握 *n grasp*
jeurng ak 掌握 *v.t. master*
jeurng ban 獎品 *n. prize*
jeurng bay chung 象鼻蟲 *n. weevil*
jeurng bo 賬簿 *n. ledger*
jeurng fu 象夫 *n. mahout*
jeurng fung 帳篷 *n. tent*
jeurng gao 橡膠 *n. rubber*
jeurng gwan 將軍 *n checkmate*
jeurng gwor 橡果 *n. acorn*
jeurng hok gam 獎學金 *n. scholarship*
jeurng jap 醬汁 *n. sauce*
jeurng jeh 長者 *n elder*
jeurng jik sow fat 象徵手法 *n. symbolism*
jeurng jing 象徵 *v. i denote*
jeurng jing 象徵 *n emblem*
jeurng jing 象徵 *v.t. symbolize*
jeurng jor 獎座 *n. trophy*
jeurng jorng 獎狀 *n. certificate*
jeurng jow 將就 *v.t. lump*
jeurng lay 獎勵 *n. reward*
jeurng lo 樟腦 *n. camphor*
jeurng loy 將來 *n future*
jeurng ngar 象牙 *n. tusk*
jeurng ngoy 障礙 *n. barrier*

jeurng ngoy 障礙 *n. impediment*
jeurng ngoy mat 障礙物 *n. obstacle*
jeurng pai 獎牌 *n. medal*
jeurng pai wok dak jeh 獎牌獲得者 *n. medallist*
jeurng shu 橡樹 *n. oak*
jeurng sing 掌聲 *n. applause*
jeurng sing tee 象聲詞 *n. onomatopoeia*
ji dung 自動 *a. automatic*
ji ho 之後 *adv. afterwards*
ji jee kuy 自治區 *n. municipality*
ji yoon 寺院 *n. abbey*
jiew 照 *v.t. illuminate*
jiew *v.t. masticate*
jiew *v.t. munch*
jiew day 沼地 *n. swamp*
jiew deem 焦點 *n focus*
jiew gu 照顧 *n. care*
jiew gu 照顧 *v.t. mother*
jiew gu 照顧 *v.t nurse*
jiew gu ma pat 照顧馬匹 *v.t. agist*
jiew jak 沼澤 *n bog*
jiew jap 招集 *v.t. assemble*
jiew jap 召集 *v. t convene*
jiew jap 召集 *v.t. convoke*
jiew jap yan 召集人 *n convener*
jiew liew 鷦鷯 *n. wren*
jiew mow 招募 *v.t. recruit*
jiew sow 招手 *v.t hail*
jiew wan sut 招魂術 *n. spiritualism*
jik 織 *v.t. knit*
jik 直 *adv. straight*
jik 織 *v.t. weave*
jik bo gey 織布機 *n loom*
jik bo gung 織布工 *n. weaver*
jik cheurng 直腸 *n. rectum*
jik dak 值得 *v.t merit*
jik dak 值得 *a worth*
jik dak 值得 *a. worthy*
jik dak jan 值得讚 *a. laudable*

jik dak jan geh 值得讚嘅 *a.* commendable

jik dak jan geh 值得讚嘅 *a* creditable

jik dak jan geh 值得讚嘅 *a.* meritorious

jik dak jan geh 值得讚嘅 *a.* praiseworthy

jik dak joon jung geh 值得尊重嘅 *a.* venerable

jik dak jow geh 值得做嘅 *a desirable*

jik dak ju yee geh 值得注意嘅 *a.* noteworthy

jik dak tung ting geh 值得同情嘅 *a.* pitiable

jik dak wok jeurng 值得獲獎 *a.* laureate

jik dow 直到 *prep. till*

jik dow 直到 *n. conj. till*

jik dow 直到 *prep. until*

jik dow 直到 *conj until*

jik dow yee ga 直到而家 *adv.* hitherto

jik gam 織錦 *n. tapestry*

jik geh 直嘅 *a. straight*

jik ging 直徑 *n diameter*

jik gok 直覺 *n. hunch*

jik gok 直覺 *n. instinct*

jik gok 直覺 *n. intuition*

jik gok geh 直覺嘅 *a. instinctive*

jik hak 即刻 *a immediate*

jik hak 即刻 *a. instant*

jik hak 即刻 *adv. instantly*

jik hak 即刻 *a. prompt*

jik hak 即刻 *adv. straightway*

jik ho 藉口 *n excuse*

jik ho 藉口 *n pretext*

jik jak 職責 *n. onus*

jik jeep 直接 *a direct*

jik jeurng 跡象 *n. indicator*

jik jeurng fat sang 即將發生 *a.* imminent

jik jeurng fat sang 即將發生 *n.* offing

jik jeurng fat sang geh 即將發生嘅 *a.* forthcoming

jik lap geh 直立嘅 *a erect*

jik luy 積累 *v.t. accumulate*

jik luy gan 積累緊 *n accumulation*

jik man day 殖民地 *n colony*

jik man geh 殖民嘅 *a colonial*

jik mat 植物 *n. plant*

jik mat hok 植物學 *n botany*

jik mat kwan 植物群 *n flora*

jik mok 寂寞 *a. lonesome*

jik way 職位 *n post*

jik yeep 職業 *n. occupation*

jik yeep 職業 *n. profession*

jik yeep sang ngai 職業生涯 *n.* career

jik yoon 職員 *n. staff*

jing 整 *v. t create*

jing 整 *v.t. make*

jing 靜 *n. quiet*

jing 整 *n. scoff*

jing 正 *adv. sharp*

jing 整 *v.t sort*

jing 蒸 *v.i. steam*

jing 整 *v.t. mend*

jing bay 整跛 *v.t. lame*

jing been 政變 *n. coup*

jing bwun 正本 *n original*

jing choy 精彩 *a brilliant*

jing dak ju yee geh 值得注意嘅 *a.* notable

jing day 整低 *v.i. low*

jing day 剩低 *n. remainder*

jing day geh 淨低嘅 *a net*

jing doon 整短 *v.t. shorten*

jing dorng geh 正當嘅 *a. righteous*

jing dorng lay yow 正當理由 *n.* justification

jing dow sing san lay 整到成身泥 *v. t bemire*

jing fan 整返 *v.t. repair*
jing far 淨化 *n. purgation*
jing far 淨化 *n. purification*
jing far 淨化 *v.t. purify*
jing far geh 淨化嘅 *a purgative*
jing fat 蒸發 *v. i evaporate*
jing fat 蒸發 *v.t. vaporize*
jing forng mo liew 精紡毛料 *n. worsted*
jing fu 政府 *n. government*
jing fu bo mun 政府部門 *n. ministry*
jing fuk 征服 *v. t conquer*
jing fuk 征服 *n conquest*
jing fuk 征服 *v.t. overpower*
jing fuk 征服 *v.t. subjugate*
jing fwut 整闊 *v.t. widen*
jing gan 整緊 *v.t. tighten*
jing geet 貞潔 *n. virginity*
jing ging gwor dow geh yan 正經過度嘅人 *n. prude*
jing gon 整乾 *v. i. dry*
jing gor 整個 *n whole*
jing gu 整蠱 *v.t hoax*
jing gu 整蠱 *v.t. rag*
jing gu 整蠱 *v.t. tease*
jing guy 證據 *n evidence*
jing guy 證據 *n. proof*
jing guy 證據 *n. testament*
jing guy 證據 *n. testimony*
jing hak 整黑 *v. t. blacken*
jing hang 整坑 *v.t. pit*
jing hay 蒸氣 *n steam*
jing hay 蒸氣 *n. vapour*
jing heurng 正向 *adv due*
jing hm 正午 *n. noon*
jing ho 整好 *v.t fix*
jing ho 整厚 *v.i. thicken*
jing jan 淨賺 *v.t. net*
jing jay geh 精製嘅 *a. superfine*
jing jee 政治 *n. politics*
jing jee 精子 *n. sperm*
jing jee 靜止 *a. still*

jing jee 靜止 *n. stillness*
jing jee ga 政治家 *n. politician*
jing jee ga 政治家 *n. statesman*
jing jee geh 政治嘅 *a. political*
jing jee so dung 政治騷動 *n ferment*
jing jeem 整尖 *v.t. sharpen*
jing jik 整直 *v.t. straighten*
jing jorng 症狀 *n. symptom*
jing jorng geh 症狀嘅 *a. symptomatic*
jing kok 正確 *adv aright*
jing kok 正確 *a correct*
jing lap 整凹 *v.t hollow*
jing lik 精力 *n. verve*
jing lik chung pwuy 精力充沛 *a. sprightly*
jing lik chung pwuy 精力充沛 *a. vigorous*
jing lik hok 靜力學 *n. statics*
jing ling 精靈 *n elf*
jing loon 整亂 *v.t. jumble*
jing loon 整亂 *v.i mess*
jing low 蒸餾 *v. t distil*
jing lung 蒸籠 *n. steamer*
jing mak 靜脈 *n. vein*
jing man geh 正文嘅 *n. textual*
jing meen 正面 *n facade*
jing meen geh 正面嘅 *a. positive*
jing ming 證明 *v.t. justify*
jing ming 證明 *v.t. prove*
jing ming 精明 *a. sagacious*
jing ming 證明 *v.t. show*
jing ming 證明 *v.t. substantiate*
jing ming ghe 精明嘅 *a. shrewd*
jing ming mow juy 證明無罪 *n. vindication*
jing mo way yoon wuy 政務委員會 *n. council*
jing ping 整平 *v.t. smooth*
jing san 精心 *n. spirit*
jing san beng 精神病 *n. insanity*
jing san beng 精神病 *n. psychosis*

jing san beng hok 精神病學 *n.* *psychiatry*

jing san beng wan jeh 精神病患者 *n.* *psychopath*

jing san beng yoon 精神病院 *n* *asylum*

jing san chor loon 精神錯亂 *n.* *lunacy*

jing san for yee sang 精神科醫生 *n.* *psychiatrist*

jing san sing 精神性 *n. spirituality*

jing sap 整濕 *v. t. damp*

jing sap 整濕 *v.t. moisten*

jing sap 整濕 *v.t. soak*

jing sat 證實 *v.t. attest*

jing sat 證實 *v. t. certify*

jing sat 證實 *v.t. corroborate*

jing sat 證實 *n. substantiation*

jing sat 證實 *v.i. testify*

jing sat 證實 *v.t. validate*

jing sat 證實 *v.t. vindicate*

jing say 整細 *v.t. muffle*

jing seurng 正常 *n. norm*

jing seurng 正常 *a. normal*

jing seurng 正常 *n. normalcy*

jing seurng fan 正相反 *pref. contra*

jing seurng far 正常化 *v.t. normalize*

jing shoon geh 精選嘅 *a select*

jing shu 證書 *n. muniment*

jing sik 正式 *a formal*

jing sik 正式 *adv. officially*

jing sik geh 正式嘅 *a. official*

jing sik jow jik 正式就職 *v.t. induct*

jing sik luk chuy 正式錄取 *v.t. matriculate*

jing sik pay jun 證實批准 *v.t. ratify*

jing sow 徵收 *v.t. levy*

jing suy 精髓 *n essence*

jing suy 整碎 *v.t mash*

jing tak 政策 *n doctrine*

jing tam 偵探 *n. detective*

jing tam geh 偵探嘅 *a detective*

jing tao 整皺 *v.t. ruffle*

jing tay 整齊 *a. neat*

jing tay 整齊 *n. tidiness*

jing tay 整齊 *a. tidy*

jing teem 整甜 *v.t. sweeten*

jing toon 整斷 *v.t. snap*

jing tung 精通 *n. mastery*

jing tung 精通 *n. proficiency*

jing tung geh 正統嘅 *a. orthodox*

jing tung gwun leem 正統觀念 *n. orthodoxy*

jing uk deng 整屋頂 *v.t. roof*

jing wu jow 整污糟 *v.t. soil*

jing wu jow 整污糟 *v.t. stain*

jing yan 證人 *n. deponent*

jing yik 精液 *n. semen*

jing yoon 整軟 *v.t. soften*

jing yoon may 整完美 *v.t. perfect*

jing yu 剩餘 *n. surplus*

jing yung 徵用 *n. requisition*

jing yung 徵用 *v.t. requisition*

jo 做 *v. t do*

jo geen 組件 *n. component*

jo hap 組合 *n combination*

jo ho yee tow geh yeh 做好意頭嘅嘢 *v.t. auspicate*

jo pang yow 做朋友 *v. t. befriend*

jo seen 祖先 *n. ancestor*

jo seen 祖先 *n. ancestry*

jo seen 祖先 *n forefather*

jo seen geh 祖先嘅 *a. ancestral*

jo sing yat duy 組成一對 *v.t. pair*

jo tan 早餐 *n breakfast*

jo yu 遭遇 *n. encounter*

jok 鑿 *n chisel*

jok 作 *v. t compose*

jok ban 作品 *n composition*

jok ban 作品 *n creation*

jok fan 作反 *n. rebel*

jok fan jeh 作反者 *n. insurgent*

jok fay 作廢 *v.t. invalidate*

jok fay 作廢 *v.t. nullify*

jok jeh 作者 *n. author*
jok jeh 作者 *n. writer*
jok oh 作嘔 *v.t. gag*
jok oh 作嘔 *n. nausea*
jok ok geh 作惡嘅 *a. maleficent*
jok see 作詩 *v.t. versify*
jong 撞 *v.t. bang*
joo 煮 *v. t cook*
joon 磚 *n brick*
joon 鑽 *n drill*
joon 鑽 *v. t. drill*
joon 轉 *v.i. rotate*
joon 轉 *v.i. spin*
joon 轉 *n. spin*
joon 轉 *v.t. switch*
joon 轉 *n. transfer*
joon 轉 *v.t. transfer*
joon 轉 *v.i. turn*
joon 轉 *n.i. whirl*
joon been 轉變 *n. transition*
joon been 轉變 *n. twist*
joon cheurng 專長 *n. forte*
joon cheurng 專長 *n. speciality*
joon day 轉遞 *n. transitive*
joon day gung see 專遞公司 *n. courier*
joon dung 轉動 *n. rotation*
joon dung geh 轉動嘅 *a. rotary*
joon fat 轉發 *v.t. relay*
joon ga 專家 *n expert*
joon ga 專家 *n. luminary*
joon gar 專家 *n. specialist*
joon gey 轉寄 *v.t forward*
joon gey 傳記 *n biography*
joon gey jok ga 傳記作家 *n biographer*
joon ging 尊敬 *n esteem*
joon ging 尊敬 *v. t esteem*
joon ging 尊敬 *v. t honour*
joon ging 尊敬 *v.t. revere*
joon ging 尊敬 *n. reverence*
joon ging 尊敬 *n. veneration*

joon ging geh 尊敬嘅 *a. reverend*
joon gung 專攻 *v.i. specialize*
joon jee 轉子 *n. armature*
joon jow 轉租 *v.t. sublet*
joon ju 專注 *v.t focus*
joon jung 尊重 *n deference*
joon jung 尊重 *v.t. respect*
joon jung 尊重 *n. respect*
joon jung gao geh yan 轉宗教嘅人 *n convert*
joon jung geh 尊重嘅 *a. respectful*
joon kay 傳奇 *n. legend*
joon lay koon 專利權 *n patent*
joon lun 專論 *n. monograph*
joon mun ming tee geh 專門名詞嘅 *a. terminological*
joon mwun far 專門化 *n. specialization*
joon sam 專心 *v. t concentrate*
joon sam 專心 *n. concentration*
joon sam 專心 *v. t devote*
joon say 轉世 *n. transmigration*
joon sek 鑽石 *n diamond*
joon sek geen juk 磚石建築 *n. masonry*
joon tap 專輯 *n. album*
joon wan mwut gok 轉彎抹角 *a. oblique*
joon wan mwut got 轉彎抹角 *v.t hedge*
joon wang 專橫 *a autocratic*
joon wun 轉換 *n conversion*
joon yee 轉移 *v.t. & i. deflect*
joon yee 轉移 *v. t divert*
joon yee 轉移 *v.t. shift*
joon yeem 尊嚴 *n dignity*
joon yeep geh 專業嘅 *a. professional*
joon yeep yung tee 專業用詞 *n. jargon*
joon ying jeh 專營者 *n. monopolist*
joon yow geh 專有嘅 *a. proprietary*
joot 啜 *v.t. suck*

joot dow 決鬥 v. i duel
joot duy 絕對 a absolute
joot duy 絕對 adv absolutely
joot duy 絕對 a. categorical
joot duy 絕對 adv. stark
joot jung geh 絕種嘅 a extinct
joot morng 絕望 n despair
joot morng 絕望 v. i despair
joot morng 絕望 n. slough
jor 左 a. left
jor 左 n. left
jor 阻 v.t. obstruct
jor dorng 阻擋 n. obstruction
jor jec 阻止 v.i bog
jor jee 阻止 v. t. discourage
jor jee 阻止 v.t. impede
jor jee 阻止 v.t. inhibit
jor jee 阻止 a. obstructive
jor jee 阻止 v.t. thwart
jor jeet 阻截 v.t. tackle
jor lan 災難 n disaster
jor larn 災難 n. calamity
jor lun cheurng 左輪槍 n. revolver
jor ngoy 阻礙 v. t. encumber
jor ngoy 阻礙 v.t. handicap
jor ngoy 阻礙 v.t. hinder
jor ngoy 阻礙 v.t. retard
jor ngoy sang jeurng 阻礙生長 v.t. stunt
jor pai fan jee 左派分子 n leftist
jor sang 再生 v.t. regenerate
jor sat 阻塞 v.t block
jor sow 助手 n. assistant
jor way 座位 n. seat
jorng 撞 v. t. clash
jorng 撞 v. i crash
jorng 裝 v.t. load
jorng 裝 v.t. mount
jorng 撞 v.t. smack
jorng 撞 v.t. ram
jorng ban 裝扮 v.t. adorn
jorng bay 裝備 v.t. arm

jorng bay 裝備 v. t equip
jorng bay 裝備 n. kit
jorng bay 裝備 v.t outfit
jorng bay 裝備 n. pl paraphernalia
jorng cher 撞車 n smash
jorng chuk 裝束 n. outfit
jorng forng 狀況 n. state
jorng gwun 裝罐 v. can
jorng gwun 壯觀 a. spectacular
jorng gwun 裝罐 v.t. tin
jorng gwun geh 壯觀嘅 a. stately
jorng hung far fan 藏紅花粉 n. saffron
jorng joy 裝載 v.t. lade
jorng jun gey 裝樽機 n bottler
jorng lay 葬禮 n burial
jorng lay geh 壯麗嘅 a. grand
jorng ma on 裝馬鞍 v.t. saddle
jorng mat 臟物 n booty
jorng mat 臟物 n spoil
jorng mun 裝滿 v.t fill
jorng sik 裝飾 v.t. apparel
jorng sik 裝飾 v.t. bedight
jorng sik 裝飾 n decoration
jorng sik 裝飾 v.t. grace
jorng sik 裝飾 v.t. ornament
jorng sik 裝飾 n. ornamentation
jorng sik ban 裝飾品 n. ornament
jorng sik geh 裝飾嘅 a. ornamental
jorng sow 裝修 v. t decorate
jorng yao pwun dow 裝入盆度 v.t. pot
jorng yoon geh 莊園嘅 a. manorial
jorng yoon jak day 莊園宅第 n. manor
jow 做 prep.. as
jow 走 adv. away
jow 做 v. t. commit
jow 洲 n continent
jow 咒 n curse
jow 早 adv early
jow 早 a early

jow 租 *v.t hire*
jow 咒 *n. invective*
jow 走 *v.t. leave*
jow 酒 *n. liquor*
jow 租 *v.t. rent*
jow 酒 *n. wine*
jow 皺 *v.t. wrinkle*
jow ba 酒吧 *n. saloon*
jow ba 酒吧 *n. bar*
jow bwuy 酒杯 *n. goblet*
jow chor 做錯 *v.i blunder*
jow choy pwun 做裁判 *v.t., umpire*
jow dak gwor fan 做得過分 *v.t. overdo*
jow deem 酒店 *n. hotel*
jow gam 租金 *n. rent*
jow geh forng 租嘅房 *n. lodging*
jow gway 酒鬼 *n bibber*
jow gwun 酒館 *n. tavern*
jow hap sai 組合晒 *v.t. piece*
jow hay 就係 *adv. namely*
jow ho 袖口 *n cuff*
jow horn 週刊 *n. weekly*
jow jeurng 州長 *n. governor*
jow jik 就職 *n. inauguration*
jow jik 組織 *n. organization*
jow jing 酒精 *n alcohol*
jow kay 租期 *n. tenancy*
jow lo geh 走佬嘅 *a. fugitive*
jow long 走廊 *n. corridor*
jow luy yam ban 酒類飲品 *n. intoxicant*
jow man 皺紋 *n. furrow*
jow man 皺紋 *n. wrinkle*
jow may tow 皺眉頭 *v.i. scowl*
jow may tow 皺眉頭 *n. scowl*
jow mey 皺眉 *n. frown*
jow mey 皺眉 *v.i frown*
jow san geh dung mat 走散嘅動物 *n stray*
jow sat 酒塞 *n. cork*
jow sat geh 走失嘅 *a stray*

jow see 走私 *v.t. smuggle*
jow see jeh 走私者 *n. smuggler*
jow seen fung 做先鋒 *v.t. pioneer*
jow shoon 就算 *conj. albeit*
jow shoon hai gam 就算係咁 *adv. nonetheless*
jow shoon hai gam 就算係咁 *adv. notwithstanding*
jow sing 組成 *adj. constituent*
jow sing 組成 *v.t. group*
jow sing 造成 *v.i. result*
jow sing 造成 *v.i. spawn*
jow tan geh 早產嘅 *a. premature*
jow toon 組團 *v.t. regiment*
jow way 周圍 *n. periphery*
jow way 周圍 *n. surroundings*
jow way geh 周圍嘅 *adj. ambient*
jow wey 周圍 *prep. around*
jow wu 租戶 *n. lessee*
jow wu 租戶 *n. tenant*
jow yam 就任 *n accession*
jow yam 就任 *n. induction*
jow yeem 酒宴 *n. wassail*
jow yeh 做嘢 *v.t. work*
jow yeurk 租約 *n. lease*
jow yu 咒語 *n. spell*
jow yung 租用 *n. hire*
jow yung 租用 *v.t. lease*
jow...geh deen fa 做...嘅典範 *v.t. typify*
joy 再 *adv. again*
joy fat sang 再發生 *v.i. recur*
joy geen 再見 *n. adieu*
joy geen 再見 *interj. adieu*
joy geen 再見 *interj. good-bye*
joy jow 再造 *v.t. reproduce*
joy pwuy 栽培 *n. nurture*
joy pwuy 栽培 *v.t. nurture*
joy sang 在生 *a alive*
joy say lay 再洗禮 *n anabaptism*
joy tee ying sing 再次形成 *adj anamorphous*

ju 珠 *n bead*
ju 住 *v. i dwell*
ju 住 *v.i. live*
ju 豬 *n. pig*
ju 住 *v.i. reside*
ju 豬 *n. swine*
ju bay 豬鼻 *n. snout*
ju bay chorng 鑄幣廠 *n mint*
ju bo seurng 珠寶商 *n. jeweller*
ju cheurng 豬場 *n. sty*
ju ding sat bai 注定失敗 *v. t. doom*
ju dung geen yee 主動建議 *v.t. volunteer*
ju dung sing 主動性 *n. initiative*
ju fu gan geh 住附近嘅 *a. neighbourly*
ju gao 主教 *n bishop*
ju gu lik 朱古力 *n chocolate*
ju gwun 主觀 *a. subjective*
ju gwun 主管 *v.t. superintend*
ju gwun 主管 *n. supervisor*
ju jak kuy 住宅區 *n estate*
ju jik 主席 *n chairman*
ju jow 鑄造 *v.t. mint*
ju jow chorng 鑄造廠 *n. foundry*
ju jung siew see 注重小事 *adj. anal*
ju koon 主權 *n. sovereignty*
ju ming geh 著名嘅 *a eminent*
ju mwun yan 住滿人 *v.t. people*
ju sar 朱砂 *n cinnabar*
ju seh hay 注射器 *n. syringe*
ju she 注射 *v.t. inject*
ju shu chung 蛀書蟲 *n. bookish*
ju sor 住所 *n abode*
ju sor 住所 *n domicile*
ju sor 住所 *n dwelling*
ju sor 住所 *n. residence*
ju sor 住所 *n. shelter*
ju sow for ting 主修課程 *n major*
ju suk 住宿 *n. accommodation*
ju tay 主題 *n. motif*
ju tay 主題 *n. subject*

ju tay 主題 *n. theme*
ju tay geh 主題嘅 *a. thematic*
ju tee 主持 *n. host*
ju tee 主持 *v.i. officiate*
ju tee 主持 *v.i. preside*
ju teet 鑄鐵 *n cast-iron*
ju yam 主任 *n. dean*
ju yan 主人 *n. master*
ju yap 注入 *v.t. infuse*
ju yee 注意 *n. attention*
ju yee 注意 *v.t. heed*
ju yee 注意 *v.t. notice*
ju yee 注意 *v.t. perceive*
ju yeen 主演 *v.t. star*
ju yiew 主要 *adv. mainly*
ju yiew 主要 *adv. primarily*
ju yiew geh 主要嘅 *a main*
ju yiew geh 主要嘅 *a. major*
ju yiew geh 主要嘅 *a. prime*
ju yow 豬油 *n. lard*
ju yu 侏儒 *n. pygmy*
ju yuk 豬肉 *n. pork*
juk 竹 *n. bamboo*
juk 捉 *v. t. capture*
juk 捉 *n. capture*
juk 俗 *a. gaudy*
juk 捉 *v.t. noose*
juk 捉 *v.t. trap*
juk 族 *n. tribe*
juk chao 築巢 *v.t. nest*
juk chut 逐出 *v. t evict*
juk chut 逐出 *n eviction*
juk chut gao wuy 逐出教會 *v. t. excommunicate*
juk chut gao wuy 逐出 *n. expulsion*
juk fuk 祝福 *n benison*
juk fuk 祝福 *v. t bless*
juk gan 捉緊 *n clasp*
juk gan 捉緊 *v. i. cling*
juk go 足夠 *a. sufficient*
juk gok 觸覺 *a. tactile*
juk gok 觸覺 *n touch*

juk gor jee 逐個字 *a. verbatim*
juk gor jee 逐個字 *adv. verbatim*
juk gow 足夠 *a. ample*
juk gow 足夠 *adv enough*
juk gow 足夠 *v.i. suffice*
juk hor 祝賀 *n congratulation*
juk hor 祝賀 *v.t felicitate*
juk jap 續集 *n. sequel*
juk jeem 逐漸 *a. gradual*
juk jeen garm yeurk 逐漸減弱 *v.t. undermine*
juk ju 捉住 *v.t. grab*
juk ju 捉住 *v.t. grasp*
juk ju 捉住 *v.t. nab*
juk ju 捉住 *v.t. seize*
juk pow 族譜 *n. pedigree*
juk sam 燭芯 *n. wick*
juk sat 捉實 *v.t. grip*
juk sat 捉實 *v.t. poise*
juk so 觸鬚 *n. antennae*
juk yan 俗人 *n. worldling*
juk yu 竹芋 *n. arrowroot*
juk yu 俗語 *n byword*
jun 準 *v.t. allow*
jun 樽 *n bottle*
jun 樽 *n. jar*
jun bay 準備 *v.t. gird*
jun bay 準備 *n. preparation*
jun bay 準備 *v.t. prepare*
jun bay 準備 *n. readiness*
jun bay 準備 *a. ready*
jun bay geh 準備嘅 *a. preparatory*
jun bo 進步 *v.t. improve*
jun bo 進步 *n. improvement*
jun bo 進步 *v.i. progress*
jun chung 遵從 *v.t. obey*
jun dow 進度 *n. progress*
jun far 進化 *n evolution*
jun far 進化 *v.t evolve*
jun gung 進攻 *v.t. advance*
jun hang gan 進行緊 *adv. afoot*
jun jak 準則 *n. precept*

jun jik geh 盡職嘅 *a dutiful*
jun kok 準確 *a. accurate*
jun kok dow 準確度 *n. precision*
jun kok geh 準確嘅 *a exact*
jun kok geh 準確嘅 *a. precise*
jun kok sing 準確性 *n. accuracy*
jun lik 盡力 *v.i endeavour*
jun ma 駿馬 *n. steed*
jun see geh 準時嘅 *a. punctual*
jun see lut 準時率 *n. punctuality*
jun sing 晉升 *n. advancement*
jun sow 遵守 *v.i. adhere*
jun sow 遵守 *n. adherence*
jun sow 遵守 *n. conformity*
jun teep 津貼 *n. allowance*
jun teep 津貼 *n benefit*
jun teep 津貼 *n. subsidy*
jun ting gam 盡情咁 *adv. heartily*
jun yap 進入 *v.t. import*
jung 中 *prep. amid*
jung 鐘 *n. clock*
jung 種 *n. kind*
jung 種 *v.t. plant*
jung 腫 *n sore*
jung 種 *v.t. sow*
jung 仲 *adv. still*
jung 腫 *v i. swell*
jung 腫 *n swell*
jung 仲 *adv. yet*
jung bai 鐘擺 *n. pendulum*
jung bo day kuy 中部地區 *n. midland*
jung choy 仲裁 *n. arbitration*
jung choy yan 仲裁人 *n. arbitrator*
jung dai geh 重大嘅 *a. signal*
jung dang geh 中等嘅 *a. middling*
jung deem jam 終點站 *n. terminus*
jung deen 中殿 *n. nave*
jung dor 眾多 *n. multitude*
jung duk 總督 *n. viceroy*
jung duy 中隊 *n. squadron*
jung for juy 縱火罪 *n arson*

jung gan 中間 *n middle*
jung gan 中間 *n. midst*
jung gan geh 中間嘅 *a. intermediate*
jung gan geh 中間嘅 *a. median*
jung gan geh 中間嘅 *a. mid*
jung gan geh 中間嘅 *a. middle*
jung gan yan 中間人 *n. intermediary*
jung gan yan 中間人 *n. middleman*
jung gao 宗教 *n. religion*
jung gao doon man 宗教短文 *n tract*
jung gao hok 宗教學 *n. theology*
jung gao ye sik 宗教儀式 *n. observance*
jung geet 總結 *v.t. sum*
jung geet 總結 *v.t. summarize*
jung geet 總結 *n. summary*
jung geet sing geh 總結性嘅 *a summary*
jung gey 總計 *v.i amount*
jung gey geh 總計嘅 *a. total*
jung gik geh 終極嘅 *a. ultimate*
jung gor 頌歌 *n carol*
jung gor 頌歌 *n. ode*
jung ha 仲夏 *n. midsummer*
jung hap 綜合 *n. synthesis*
jung hm 中午 *n. midday*
jung ho 中號 *a medium*
jung hor yee 仲可以 *a. tolerable*
jung jee 終止 *v.i abort*
jung jee 終止 *v. i. cease*
jung jee 中子 *n. neutron*
jung jee 種子 *n. seed*
jung jee 終止 *v.t. terminate*
jung jee 終止 *n. termination*
jung jik jeh 種植者 *n. grower*
jung jik yoon 種植園 *n. plantation*
jung jing 忠貞 *n. chastity*
jung juk geh 種族嘅 *a. racial*
jung juk kay see 種族歧視 *n. racialism*
jung lap geh 中立嘅 *a. impartial*
jung lap geh 中立嘅 *a. neutral*

jung lay 總理 *n. chancellor*
jung lo 腫瘤 *n. tumour*
jung luy 種類 *n. category*
jung luy 種類 *n classification*
jung luy 種類 *n. sort*
jung luy 種類 *n. species*
jung luy 種類 *n. specimen*
jung luy shu 棕櫚樹 *n. palm*
jung ma 種馬 *n. stallion*
jung man 頌文 *n. panegyric*
jung mow 鬃毛 *n. manes*
jung peen siew shoot 中篇小說 *n. novelette*
jung sam 中心 *n center*
jung sam 中心 *a. central*
jung sam 中心 *n centre*
jung sam 中心 *n. locus*
jung sam 忠心 *a. loyal*
jung sam 忠心 *n. loyalty*
jung sam deem 中心點 *n. pivot*
jung sam geh yan 忠心嘅人 *n. loyalist*
jung sang geh 終身嘅 *a. lifelong*
jung sao yap 總收入 *n. gross*
jung sat 忠實 *n fidelity*
jung sat geh 忠實嘅 *a. stalwart*
jung sat yung wu jeh 忠實擁護者 *n stalwart*
jung say gey geh 中世紀嘅 *a. medieval*
jung seurng 中傷 *v.t. backbite*
jung seurng 中傷 *v. t. defame*
jung seurng 中傷 *v.t. vilify*
jung seurng 中傷 *v.t. libel*
jung seurng geh 中傷嘅 *a. slanderous*
jung sik 棕色 *a brown*
jung sik 棕色 *n brown*
jung sing 忠誠 *n. allegiance*
jung sing geh 忠誠嘅 *a faithful*
jung sing geh 中性嘅 *a. neuter*
jung so 總數 *v.t. aggregate*

jung so 總數 n. sum

jung sor jow jee 眾所周知 a. proverbial

jung sow 總數 n. total

jung tay geh 總體嘅 a overall

jung ting heurng yung 盡情享用 v.i feast

jung toon 中斷 n abruption

jung tow 鐘頭 n. hour

jung tung 總統 n. president

jung tung geh 總統嘅 a. presidential

jung worng sik 棕黃色 n., a. tan

jung yee 鐘意 v.t fancy

jung yee 鐘意 a fond

jung yee 鐘意 v.t. like

jung yee gorng siew geh yan 鐘意講笑嘅人 n. joker

jung yew geh 重要嘅 a focal

jung yiew 重要 a. important

jung yiew geh 重要嘅 a. monumental

jung yiew geh 重要嘅 a. significant

jung yiew sing 重要性 n. importance

jung yiew sing 重要性 n. significance

jung yu ying sing 終於應承 v.i. relent

jung yung 縱容 n. connivance

jung yung 縱容 n. indulgence

jung yung 縱容 a. indulgent

jung yung 縱容 v.t. pamper

jut 捽 v.t. rub

juy 追 v. t. chase1

juy 罪 n crime

juy 序 n foreword

juy 最 pron. most

juy 嘴 n. mouth

juy 罪 n. offence

juy 序 n. prologue

juy 嘴 n. spout

juy 醉 n. intoxication

juy bo 追捕 n. chase2

juy chor 最初 a. initial

juy chuy jeh 追隨者 n follower

juy dai geh 最大嘅 a. utmost

juy dai han dow 最大限度 a. maximum

juy dai han dow 最大限度 n maximum

juy dai koon lik 最大權利 n. supremacy

juy dai leurng 最大量 n utmost

juy day deem 最低點 n. nadir

juy day han dow 最低限度 n. minimum

juy dor 最多 adv. most

juy dor 最多 n most

juy fan 罪犯 n convict

juy fan 罪犯 n criminal

juy fan 罪犯 n culprit

juy fan 罪犯 n. malefactor

juy gai geh 最佳嘅 a optimum

juy gan 最近 lately

juy gow geh 最高嘅 a. supreme

juy gow kap 最高級 n. superlative

juy hang 罪行 n. vice

juy hay juy sun 撮起嘴唇 v.t. purse

juy ho 最後 a final

juy ho 最後 a. last1

juy ho 最後 adv. last

juy ho 最後 adv. lastly

juy ho 最好 n. optimum

juy ho 最後 adv. ultimately

juy ho geh 最後嘅 a. latter

juy ho geh yan 最後嘅人 n last

juy ho tung deep 最後通牒 n. ultimatum

juy jap 聚集 v. i. cluster

juy jap 聚集 v.i mass

juy jap 聚集 v.t. muster

juy jap geh yan kwan 聚集嘅人群 n muster

juy jeep gan geh 最接近嘅 a. proximate

juy jow 詛咒 v. t curse

juy jow 詛咒 n. malediction

juy jow low 醉酒佬 n drunkard
juy jow low 醉酒佬 n. reveller
juy jung 最終 adv. eventually
juy jung 追蹤 v.t. track
juy jung yee geh 最鐘意嘅 a favourite
juy jung yee geh yan 最鐘意嘅人 n favourite
juy jung yiew 最重要 a. cardinal
juy jung yiew geh 最重要嘅 a foremost
juy jung yiew geh 罪重要嘅 a. paramount
juy jung yiew geh 最重要嘅 a. primary
juy jung yiew geh 最重要嘅 a principal
juy jung yiew geh 最重要嘅 a. salient
juy kow 追求 n. pursuance
juy kow 追求 v.t. pursue
juy kow 追求 n. pursuit
juy kow 追求 v.t. woo
juy kuk 序曲 n. prelude
juy ok 罪惡 n. sin
juy san geh 最新嘅 a. up-to-date
juy siew 最少 a. least
juy siew geh 最少嘅 a. minimal
juy siew geh 最少嘅 a minimum
juy sorng 沮喪 n dejection
juy sorng 沮喪 v. t dishearten
juy sorng 沮喪 v. t embitter
juy sorng geh 沮喪嘅 a. sombre
juy sun 嘴唇 n. lip
juy wai 最壞 n. worst
juy wai geh 最壞嘅 a worst
juy yan 罪人 n. sinner
juy yeen 序言 n. preface

K

ka 卡 n. carat
ka 卡 n. card
ka cher 卡車 n. truck
ka leen wah 嘉年華 n carnival
ka lo lay 卡路里 n. calorie
ka ta seng 喀嗒聲 n rattle
ka way 卡位 n booth
kam so 禽獸 n brute
kan 近 adv. anigh
kan 近 a. close
kan 近 a. near
kan 近 prep. nigh
kan 近 n. proximity
kan lik 勤力 a diligent
kan lik 勤力 a. industrious
kang 哽 v. t. choke
kao gan 靠近 prep by
kap 級 n. grade
kap 級 n. level
kap 級 n. notch
kap 吸 n. puff
kap 吸 n. suck
kap 級 n. tier
kap beet gow geh 級別高嘅 a. senior
kap gorn 吸乾 v. t blot
kap gwun 吸管 n. straw
kap see 及時 a. timely
kap see 及時 a. well-timed
kap see geh 及時嘅 a. providential
kap see yu 及時雨 n. manna
kap sow 吸收 v.t absorb
kap sow 吸收 v. assimilate
kap sow 吸收 n assimilation
kap yan 吸引 v.t. appeal
kap yan 吸引 v.t. attract
kap yan 吸引 n. attraction
kap yan 吸引 v.t. beckon
kap yan 吸引 v. t. charm2

kap yan 吸引 *v. t engage*
kap yan ik 吸引力 *n. glamour*
kap yan ju 吸引住 *v.t. rivet*
kap yan lik 吸引力 *n. fascination*
kap yan lik 吸引力 *n. lure*
kap yap 吸引 *v.t fascinate*
kap yap 吸入 *v.i. inhale*
kat 咳 *n. cough*
kat 咳 *v. i. cough*
kay 鰭 *n fin*
kay 旗 *n flag*
kay 企 *v.i. stand*
kay dak 奇特 *n. singularity*
kay fat 啓發 *v. t. enlighten*
kay fat 啓發 *v.t. inspire*
kay gan 期間 *n duration*
kay gan 期間 *adv. meanwhile*
kay gwai 奇怪 *adj bizarre*
kay gwai 奇怪 *a. weird*
kay gwai geh 奇怪嘅 *a. queer*
kay horn 期刊 *n. periodical*
kay jik 奇蹟 *n. marvel*
kay jik 奇蹟 *n. miracle*
kay jung yat gor 其中一個 *a., either*
kay kuy 崎嶇 *adj bumpy*
kay kuy geh 崎嶇嘅 *a. rugged*
kay low 溪流 *n. rivulet*
kay see 歧視 *v. t. discriminate*
kay see 歧視 *n discrimination*
kay ta 其他 *adv else*
kay ta 其他 *a. other*
kay tow 企圖 *v. t. essay*
kay tow 祈禱 *n. invocation*
kay tow 祈禱 *v.i. pray*
kay yee geh 奇異咗 *a. wondrous*
kay yeep 企業 *n enterprise*
kay yeep 企業 *n. venture*
kay yu 其餘 *n rest*
keem 鉗 *n. pl. tongs*
keen sing 虔誠 *n. piety*
keen sing geh 虔誠嘅 *a. godly*
keen sing geh 虔誠嘅 *a. pious*

keen sing geh 虔誠嘅 *a. religious*
keet hung geh 褐紅色嘅 *a maroon*
keet hung sik 褐紅色 *n. maroon*
keet jee 蝎子 *n. scorpion*
keet low 揭露 *n. revelation*
keet mwuy 褐煤 *n. lignite*
keh 騎 *v.t. ride*
keh bing 騎兵 *n. cavalry*
keh bing 騎兵 *n. trooper*
keh jap 茄汁 *n. ketchup*
keh jee 茄子 *n brinjal*
keh mah man pao 騎馬慢跑 *n canter*
keh see 騎士 *n chevalier*
keh see 騎士 *n. knight*
keh sow 騎手 *n. rider*
kek been 劇變 *n. upheaval*
kek bwun 劇本 *n. script*
kek jiew 劇照 *n. still*
kek leet 劇烈 *a. tempestuous*
kek leet geh 劇烈嘅 *a. violent*
kek tung 劇痛 *n. throe*
kek yoon 劇院 *n. theatre*
keurng bik 強迫 *v. t compel*
keurng bik 強迫 *n compulsion*
keurng bik 強迫 *v.t force*
keurng bik tuy yow 強迫退休 *v.t. pension*
keurng cheurng 強搶 *n abaction*
keurng cheurng jeh 強搶者 *n abactor*
keurng diew 強調 *v.t accent*
keurng diew 強調 *v. t belabour*
keurng diew 強調 *n emphasis*
keurng diew 強調 *v. t emphasize*
keurng diew 強調 *v.t stress*
keurng diew geh 強調嘅 *a emphatic*
keurng dow 強盜 *n. bandit*
keurng dow 強度 *n. intensity*
keurng fa 強化 *n consolidation*
keurng far 強化 *n. reinforcement*
keurng far 強化 *v.t. toughen*
keurng gan 強姦 *v.t. rape*

keurng gan juy 強姦罪 *n. rape*

keurng hang geh 強行嘅 *a forcible*

keurng jorng 強壯 *a. lusty*

keurng jorng geh 強壯嘅 *a. manly*

keurng jorng geh 強壯嘅 *a. muscular*

keurng jorng geh 強壯嘅 *a. robust*

keurng jorng geh 強壯嘅 *a. virile*

keurng leet 強烈 *n. vehemence*

keurng leet 強烈 *a. vehement*

keurng leet fan duy 強烈反對 *a. hostile*

keurng leet geh yuk morng 強烈嘅慾望 *n. lust*

keurng leet korng yee 強烈抗議 *a. outcry*

keurng leet may dow 強烈味道 *a. pungent*

keurng leet yiew kow 強烈要求 *v. t demand*

key morng 期望 *n. expectation*

key sat 其實 *adv. actually*

kiew 橋 *n bridge*

kiew 轎 *n. palanquin*

kik tan 棘嘅 *v.i. stumble*

kik tan 棘嘅 *v.t. trip*

king 傾 *v.t. converse*

king 傾 *v.t. negotiate*

king gey 傾偈 *n. chat1*

king gey 傾偈 *v. i. chat2*

king gey 傾偈 *n conversation*

king heurng 傾向 *v.i. incline*

king heurng 傾向 *n. tendency*

king sam 傾心 *v. t enamour*

king seh geh 傾瀉嘅 *a. torrential*

king so 鯨鬚 *n. baleen*

king sow 傾訴 *v.t. unburden*

king ter 傾斜 *v.t. slant*

king ter 傾斜 *v.i. slope*

king ter geh 傾斜嘅 *adj. declivous*

king yu 鯨魚 *n. whale*

kok ding 確定 *n confirmation*

kok ding sing 確定性 *n. certainty*

kok ding way jee 確定位置 *v.i. navigate*

kok jok geh 確鑿嘅 *a conclusive*

kok sat geh 確實嘅 *a concrete*

kok ying 確認 *v. t confirm*

kok ying 確認 *n. verification*

kong shoon jay 抗酸劑 *adj. antacid*

koon 權 *n right*

koon chung 權重 *n. weightage*

koon da 拳打 *v.t. punch*

koon gik 拳擊 *n boxing*

koon gik 拳擊 *n. punch*

koon gway 權貴 *n. magnate*

koon jeurng 權仗 *n. sceptre*

koon lik 權力 *n. authority*

koon lin 權力 *n. power*

koon tow 拳頭 *n fist*

koon way geh 權威嘅 *a. magisterial*

koon yee jee gey 權宜之計 *a expedient*

koot deem 缺點 *n defect*

koot deem 缺點 *n drawback*

koot ding 決定 *v. t decide*

koot ding 決定 *n decision*

koot ding 決定 *v. t determine*

koot ding forng hay 決定放棄 *v.t. jack*

koot ding sing 決定性 *adj. crucial*

koot dow 決鬥 *n duel*

koot fat 缺乏 *n dearth*

koot fat 缺乏 *n. lack*

koot fat 缺乏 *n. scarcity*

koot fat 缺乏 *a. void*

koot fat 缺乏 *prep. without*

koot ham 缺陷 *n disability*

koot sam 決心 *n. determination*

koot tik 缺席 *n absence*

koot tik 缺席 *a absent*

koot tik 缺席 *v.t absent*

korng yee 抗議 *v.t. picket*

korng yee 抗議 *n. protest*

kow 求 *v. t. beg*
kow 求 *v. t. entreat*
kow 扣 *v.t fasten*
kow 求 *v.t. implore*
kow 溝 *v.i mix*
kow 求 *v.t. solicit*
kow 溝 *n. trench*
kow cheurng 球場 *n. pitch*
kow chuy 扣除 *v.t. deduct*
kow chuy 扣除 *prep. less*
kow fan 求婚 *v.t. propose*
kow jor yeh 溝咗嘢 *v.t. adulterate*
kow ju 扣住 *v.t. shackle*
kow low 扣鈕 *v. t. button*
kow low 扣留 *v. t detain*
kow low 扣留 *v.t. intern*
kow mai 購買 *n. purchase*
kow ngat koon 扣押權 *n. lien*
kow ngoy kay 求愛期 *n. courtship*
kow pak 球拍 *n bat*
kow see 構思 *n conception*
kow tay 球體 *n. orb*
kow tung 溝通 *v. t communicate*
kow wan 溝勻 *v. t blend*
kow yeh 溝嘢 *n. adulteration*
kow ying 球形 *n. sphere*
kow ying geh 球形嘅 *a. spherical*
kowju 扣住 *n buckle*
koy 鈣 *n calcium*
koy leem 概念 *n concept*
koy yiew 概要 *adv. summarily*
koy yiew 概要 *n. synopsis*
kuk 軸 *n. axis*
kuk 曲 *n. tune*
kuk jeet teen hang 曲折前行 *v.i. snake*
kuk jeet teen jun 曲折前進 *v.i. zigzag*
kuk seen 曲線 *n curve*
kun gwan kow 曲棍球 *n. hockey*
kung 窮 *a. poor*
kung geh 窮嘅 *a. needy*

kung yan 窮人 *n. pauper*
kuy 渠 *n ditch*
kuy 佢 *pron. he*
kuy 佢 *pron. her*
kuy 佢 *pron. him*
kuy 佢 *pron. it*
kuy 佢 *pron. she*
kuy chut 舉出 *v.t. adduce*
kuy day 佢哋 *pron. them*
kuy dey 佢哋 *a. their*
kuy dey 佢哋 *pron. theirs*
kuy gan 拘謹 *n. inhibition*
kuy geh 佢嘅 *a her*
kuy geh 佢嘅 *pron. his*
kuy joot 拒絕 *v. t. decline*
kuy joot 拒絕 *v.t. negative*
kuy joot 拒絕 *n. rebuff*
kuy joot 拒絕 *n. refusal*
kuy joot 拒絕 *v.t. refuse*
kuy joot 拒絕 *n. refuse*
kuy joot 拒絕 *v.t. reject*
kuy joot 拒絕 *n. rejection*
kuy joot 拒絕 *v.t. repudiate*
kuy joot 拒絕 *n. repudiation*
kuy joot 拒絕 *n. repulse*
kuy joot 拒絕 *v.t. spurn*
kuy juk 驅逐 *v.t. banish*
kuy juk 驅逐 *n. banishment*
kuy lay 距離 *n distance*
kuy low 拘留 *n. arrest*
kuy low beng 佝僂病 *n. rickets*
kuy wik geh 區域嘅… *a. zonal*
kwa dai 誇大 *v. t. exaggerate*
kwa dai geh 誇大嘅 *a. melodramatic*
kwa dai geh 誇大嘅 *a. pompous*
kwa jeurng 誇張 *n. exaggeration*
kwa jeurng 誇張 *n. hyperbole*
kwa jeurng 誇張 *v.t. overact*
kwa lan 跨欄 *n. hurdle1*
kwan 裙 *n dress*
kwan 群 *n flock*
kwan 裙 *n. skirt*

kwan chung 昆蟲 *n. insect*

kwan chung hok 昆蟲學 *n. entomology*

kwan dai gwan hay 裙帶關係 *n. nepotism*

kwan ging 困境 *n dilemma*

kwan ging 困境 *n. predicament*

kwan jap 群集 *v.t. throng*

kwan ju 困住 *v.t maroon*

kwan lan 困難 *n. plight*

kwan tay 群體 *v. t commune*

kwan tay 群體 *n. fraternity*

kwan wak 困惑 *n. quandary*

kwan yiew 困擾 *v. t. baffle*

kwan yiew 困擾 *v. t bemuse*

kwan yiew 困擾 *v.t. nonplus*

kwan yiew 困擾 *v.t. perplex*

kwan yiew 困擾 *n. perplexity*

kwang 框 *n frame*

kway dai 攜帶 *adj. borne*

kway ding 規定 *v.t. stipulate*

kway ding 規定 *n. stipulation*

kway ding geh 規定嘅 *a. mandatory*

kway fan 規範 *n. specification*

kway gap 盔甲 *n. armour*

kway guy 規矩 *n. rule*

kway jak 規則 *n. regulation*

kway lut sing 規律性 *n. regularity*

kway mo 規模 *n. scale*

kway wak 規劃 *v.t formulate*

kwong dai 擴大 *n amplification*

kwong dai 擴大 *v.t. expand*

kwong jeurng 擴張 *n. expansion*

kwong may 狂迷 *n fanatic*

kwong yam hey 擴音器 *n amplifier*

kwong yam jow 狂飲酒 *v. i booze*

kwong yeet 狂熱 *n. frenzy*

kworng 礦 *n mine*

kworng fwun 狂歡 *n. revel*

kworng fwun jok lok 狂歡作樂 *n. revelry*

kworng gung 礦工 *n. miner*

kworng gung 礦工 *n. pitman*

kworng jee 礦脂 *n. vaseline*

kworng mat hok 礦物學 *n. mineralogy*

kworng mat hok ga 礦物學家 *n. mineralogist*

kworng mat jat 礦物質 *n. mineral*

kworng mat jat geh 礦物質嘅 *a mineral*

kworng pao 狂跑 *v.i stampede*

kworng sek 礦石 *n. ore*

kworng yeet 狂熱 *n mania*

kwun 群 *n cluster*

kwun 裙 *n. frock*

kwun chung 昆蟲 *n. bug*

kwun ging 困境 *n. adversity*

kwun ging 困境 *n fix*

kwun yiew 困擾 *v.t. ail*

kwuy jay day tow 繪製地圖 *v.t. map*

kwuy lo 賄賂 *n bribe*

kwuy lo 賄賂 *v. t. bribe*

kwuy wah geh 繪畫嘅 *a. graphic*

kwuy yeurng 潰瘍 *n. ulcer*

kwuy yeurng geh 潰瘍嘅 *a. ulcerous*

L

la 罅 *n gap*

la 罅 *n. loop-hole*

la ba 喇叭 *n. clarion*

la ba 喇叭 *n. speaker*

la ba 喇叭 *n. trumpet*

la ba seng 喇叭聲 *n. hoot*

la ba tung 喇叭筒 *n. megaphone*

la ma 喇嘛 *n. lama*

lai 拉 *v.t. apprehend*

lai 拉 *v.t. arrest*

lai 拉 *v. t drag*

lai 奶 *n. milk*

lai 拉 v.t. pull
lai 拉 n. pull
lai 拉 v.t. stretch
lai 拉 v.t. trail
lai 拉 v.t. tug
lai 拉 v.t. zip
lai geh 奶嘅 a. milky
lai hay 氖氣 n. neon
lai leen 拉鍊 n. zip
lai lik 拉力 n. traction
lai luy 奶類 n dairy
lai may jee pai 拉米紙牌 n. rummy
lai piew 拉票 v. t. canvass
lai seurng 拉傷 v.t. strain
lai seurng 拉傷 n strain
lai ter 拉扯 v.t. manhandle
lai yow 奶油 n cream
lai yow dung 奶油凍 n custard
lak gwat 肋骨 n. rib
lak gwat geh 肋骨嘅 adj. costal
lak ju 勒住 v.t. rein
lak say 勒死 v.t. strangle
lak say 勒死 n. strangulation
lak say 勒死 v.t. throttle
lak sing 勒繩 n. rein
lak sok 勒索 n blackmail
lak sok 勒索 v.t blackmail
lam ban kow 籃板球 n. rebound
lam bo sek 藍寶石 n. sapphire
lam duy 艦隊 n. armada
lam fan hay 諗返起 v.t. recall
lam gwa 南瓜 n. pumpkin
lam mo gwun 林務官 n forester
lam suy 淋水 v.t. water
lam yeep 林業 n forestry
lan 欄 n column
lan 難 a. hard
lan 懶 a. indolent
lan 懶 n. lazy
lan bo 爛布 n. rag
lan dak 難得 adv. seldom
lan dow 難倒 v.t stump

lan duk 難讀 a. illegible
lan geh 懶嘅 a. sluggish
lan geh 難嘅 a. tricky
lan gorn 欄杆 n. rail
lan gwor 難過 v.i. pine
lan gwor 難過 v.i smart
lan ham 難堪 v.t. mortify
lan hung jay geh 難控制嘅 a. unruly
lan jeet 攔截 n. interception
lan ju 攔住 v.t. waylay
lan kow 攔球 v.t volley
lan man 難民 n. refugee
lan man geh 難聞嘅 a rank
lan may 闌尾 n. appendix
lan morng geh 難忘嘅 a. memorable
lan san 懶散 n. laziness
lan san gam chor 懶散咁坐 v.i. loll
lan san gam chor 懶散咁坐 v.i. lounge
lan san geh 懶散嘅 n. slothful
lan siew far 難消化 a. indigestible
lan tak 難測 n. vagary
lan tay 難題 n. conundrum
lan tay 難題 n struggle
lan tee kay gow 難辭其咎 a culpable
lan yee jee sun 難以置信 a. incredible
lan yee jeep sow 難以接收 a. insupportable
lan yee ying yung 難以形容 a. indescribable
lan yee ying yung 難以形容 a. intangible
lang dam 冷淡 adv. aloof
lang dam 冷淡 a. frigid
lang dam 冷淡 a. impersonal
lang dung 冷凍 n. refrigeration
lang geen dow 能見度 n. visibility
lang huk mo ting 冷酷無情 a. callous
lang huk mo ting 冷酷無情 a. inhuman

lang huk mo ting 冷酷無情 a. ruthless

lang jing 冷靜 n. calm

lang jing geh 冷靜嘅 a. nonchalant

lang keurk hay 冷卻器 n cooler

lang lik 能力 n ability

lang lik 能力 n. capability

lang lik 能力 n competence

lang lok 冷落 v.t. snub

lang lok 冷落 n. snub

lang mok 冷漠 n. apathy

lang tam 冷杉 n fir

lao 鬧 v.t. scold

lao 鬧 v.t upbraid

lao gao 鬧交 n. argument

lao kek 鬧劇 n farce

lao see 鬧事 v.t. riot

lap 蠟 n. wax

lap bat 蠟筆 n. pastel

lap cheurng 立場 n. standpoint

lap fat 立法 v.i. legislate

lap fat 立法 n. legislation

lap fat geh 立法嘅 a. legislative

lap fat gey gwan 立法機關 n. legislature

lap fat way yoon 立法委員 n. legislator

lap forng tay 立方體 a cubical

lap forng ying 立方形 n cube

lap forng ying 立方形 adj. cubiform

lap hak 立刻 adv. forthwith

lap jee jo 立志做 v.t. aspire

lap jik 立即 a. instantaneous

lap juk 蠟燭 n. candle

lap sap 垃圾 n. garbage

lap sap 垃圾 n. junk

lap sap 垃圾 n. litter

lap sap 垃圾 n. rubbish

lap sap 垃圾 n. trash

lap sap 垃圾 n. waste

lap sap hang 垃圾坑 n. cesspool

lap yap 納入 n. incorporation

larm 籃 n. basket

larm 南 n. south

larm day yam 男低音 n. bass

larm duy 艦隊 n fleet

larm fay ling yeurng 南非羚羊 n bontebok

larm forng geh 南方嘅 a. south

larm forng geh 南方嘅 a. southerly

larm forng geh 南方嘅 a. southern

larm gik 南極 a. antarctic

larm jai 男仔 n boy

larm jay 男仔 n. lad

larm jee hay koy 男子氣概 n manliness

larm jee hon geh 男子漢嘅 a. masculine

larm luy tung hao 男女同校 n. co-education

larm sik 藍色 n blue

larm sing 男性 n male

larm sing geh 男性嘅 a. male

larm yan 男人 n. man

larm yan 男人 n. manhood

larm yan por 男人婆 n. tomboy

larm yung 濫用 n abuse

larm yung 濫用 n. misapplication

larm yung 濫用 n. misuse

larm yung 濫用 v.t. misuse

larn 難 a difficult

larn dow 難度 n difficulty

larn sam 冷衫 n woollen

larn seen 冷線 n. yarn

larn sow 難受 a. wretched

larn yee juk mor 難以捉摸 a elusive

larn yee sing dam 難以承擔 a burdensome

larng sam 冷衫 n. sweater

lat 辣 a. spicy

lat jiew 辣椒 n capsicum

lat jiew 辣椒 n. chilli

lat tat 邋遢 a. squalid

lat tat 邋遢 n. squalor

lat tat geh 邋遢嘅 *a. slovenly*

lat tat geh luy yan 邋遢嘅女人 *n. slattern*

lay 嚟 *v. i. come*

lay 泥 *n dirt*

lay 泥 *n. mud*

lay 梨 *n. pear*

lay 犁 *n. plough*

lay 泥 *n. soil*

lay 脷 *n. tongue*

lay bai 禮拜 *n. week*

lay bai yee sik geh 禮拜儀式嘅 *a. liturgical*

lay bo 彌補 *v.i. atone*

lay dow 犁刀 *n colter*

lay fai 泥塊 *n. clod*

lay fan 離婚 *n divorce*

lay fan 離婚 *v. t divorce*

lay fat see 理髮師 *n. barber*

lay fwuy 泥灰 *n. marl*

lay gai 理解 *v. t comprehend*

lay gai 理解 *v.t fathom*

lay ging 離境 *v.t. deport*

lay gu am 尼姑庵 *n. nunnery*

lay gu ding 尼古丁 *n. nicotine*

lay gung hok yoon 理工學院 *n. polytechnic*

lay hap 離合 *n clutch*

lay hay 離棄 *v.t. forsake*

lay hoy 離開 *v. i. depart*

lay hoy 離開 *n departure*

lay hoy 離開 *n. leave*

lay jat 痢疾 *n dysentery*

lay jee 例子 *n example*

lay jee 例子 *n. instance*

lay jee 理智 *a. intellectual*

lay jee 理智 *n. sanity*

lay jee geh 理智嘅 *a. sane*

lay jeet 禮節 *n etiquette*

lay jeurng 泥漿 *n. ooze*

lay jiew 泥沼 *n. mire*

lay ling geh 泥濘嘅 *a. slushy*

lay lun 理論 *n. theory*

lay lun far 理論化 *v.i. theorize*

lay lun ga 理論家 *n. theorist*

lay lun seurng 理論上 *a. notional*

lay lun seurng 理論上 *a. theoretical*

lay lung 尼龍 *n. nylon*

lay mao 禮貌 *n. courtesy*

lay mao 禮貌 *n. manner*

lay mao 禮貌 *n. politeness*

lay mat 禮物 *n. gift*

lay mat 禮物 *n. present*

lay ming 黎明 *n dawn*

lay ngoy 例外 *n exception*

lay sa 泥沙 *n. silt*

lay sam 離心 *adj. centrifugal*

lay seurng 理想 *n. ambition*

lay seurng 理想 *n ideal*

lay seurng far 理想化 *v.t. idealize*

lay seurng geh 理想嘅 *a. ideal*

lay seurng gwok 理想國 *n . utopia*

lay seurng ju yee 理想主義 *n. idealism*

lay seurng ju yee 理想主義 *a. idealistic*

lay seurng ju yee jeh 理想主義者 *n. idealist*

lay sing 理性 *a. rational*

lay ting bay 里程碑 *n. milestone*

lay tong 禮堂 *n. hall*

lay tow 泥土 *n clay*

lay yee 禮儀 *a. ceremonial*

lay yee 禮儀 *n decency*

lay yik 利益 *n. lucre*

lay yu 俚語 *n. slang*

lay yun 利潤 *n. profit*

lay yung 利用 *v. t exploit*

lay yung 利用 *n. utilization*

leay 餌 *n bait*

lee dow 呢度 *adv. here*

lee tow fu gan 呢頭附近 *adv. hereabouts*

leem dow 鐮刀 *n. sickle*

leem forng 殮房 *n. morgue*
leem forng 殮房 *n. mortuary*
leem gow 念舊 *n. nostalgia*
leem tow 黏土 *n. adobe*
leem yik 黏液 *n. mucus*
leem yik 黏液 *n. slime*
leen 鍊 *n chain*
leen 年 *n. year*
leen biew 年表 *n. chronology*
leen far 蓮花 *n. lotus*
leen gam sut 煉金術 *n. alchemy*
leen gan bat hay 連根拔起 *v.t. uproot*
leen gwan sing 連貫性 *n. consistence,-cy*
leen jap 練習 *v.t. practise*
leen jap sang 練習生 *n. trainee*
leen jee sow tow 連指手套 *n. mitten*
leen jeep 連接 *v. t. connect*
leen jeep 連接 *v. t couple*
leen jeep 連接 *v.t link*
leen jeep gen 連接緊 *adj. annectant*
leen jeep ju 連接住 *v abutted*
leen jeurng 年長 *a elder*
leen jeurng 年長 *n. seniority*
leen juk 連續 *adj. consecutive*
leen juk 連續 *adj. continual*
leen juk da 連續打 *v.t. thrash*
leen juk gam 連續咁 *adv consecutively*
leen juk geh 連續嘅 *a. serial*
leen juk geh 連續嘅 *a. successive*
leen juk kek 連續劇 *n. serial*
leen juk pao gwun 連續炮轟 *n. v. & t cannonade*
leen juk sing 連續性 *n continuity*
leen ling 年齡 *n. age*
leen lo 煉爐 *n forge*
leen mai 連埋 *v.t. adjoin*
leep *n. lift*
leep 鎳 *n. nickel*
leep gow 鬣狗 *n. hyaena, hyena*
leep hoon 獵犬 *n. hound*

leep mat 獵物 *n. prey*
leep yan 獵人 *n. fowler*
leep yan 獵人 *n. hunter*
leep yan 獵人 *n. huntsman*
leep ying 獵鷹 *n falcon*
leet biew 列表 *n. tabulation*
leet dan 列單 *v.t. list*
leet duy hang 列隊行 *v.i troop*
leet fung 裂縫 *n. rift*
leet fung 裂縫 *n. slit*
leet guy 列舉 *v. t. enumerate*
leet han 裂痕 *n crack*
leet han 裂痕 *n fissure*
leet han 裂痕 *n. tear*
leet ho 裂口 *n cleft*
leet ho 裂口 *n split*
leet hoy 裂開 *v. i crack*
leet see 烈士 *n. martyr*
leet sing biew gak 列成表格 *v.t. tabulate*
lek 叻 *a. clever*
lek gwor 叻過 *v. t better*
lem *v.t. lick*
leng 靚 *a beautiful*
leng 領 *n collar*
leng geh 靚嘅 *a pretty*
leng jay 靚仔 *a. handsome*
leng luy 靚女 *n belle*
leurk gwor 掠過 *v.i. whiz*
leurk jee 略知 *n. inkling*
leurng 涼 *a cool*
leurng 糧 *n emolument*
leurng 糧 *n. salary*
leurng 兩 *a. two*
leurng 糧 *n. wage*
leurng chorng 糧倉 *n. granary*
leurng day jow 兩地走 *v.t. shuttle*
leurng dok 量度 *v.t measure*
leurng gor 兩個 *pron both*
leurng gor jee mo geh 兩個字母嘅 *adj biliteral*
leurng gor lay bai 兩個禮拜 *n. fort-*

night

leurng hai 涼鞋 *n. sandal*

leurng jee 量子 *n. quantum*

leurng juk dung mat 兩足動物 *n biped*

leurng leen yat chi geh 兩年一次嘅 *adj biennial*

leurng pwuy 兩倍 *n double*

leurng sam 良心 *n conscience*

leurng sing kay yat tee 兩星期一次 *adj bi-weekly*

leurng tee 兩次 *adv. twice*

leurng ting 涼亭 *n bower*

leurng ting 涼亭 *n. pavilion*

leurng tok 梁托 *n. corbel*

liew 尿 *n. urine*

liew cho geh jee 潦草嘅字 *n scrawl*

liew cho geh jee 潦草嘅字 *n. scribble*

liew dow 尿兜 *n. urinal*

liew fwuy 鳥喙 *n beak*

liew gai 瞭解 *v.t. acquaint*

liew gai 瞭解 *n. insight*

liew gao 鳥膠 *n birdlime*

liew geh 尿嘅 *a. urinary*

liew ha 鳥蛤 *v. i cockle*

liew ming 鳥鳴 *n warble*

liew yeurng yoon 療養院 *n. sanatorium*

liew yu jee jeurng 瞭如指掌 *adv pat*

lik dai mo bay geh 力大無比嘅 *a. herculean*

lik hay 力氣 *n. strength*

lik horng gey 力行雞 *n. leghorn*

lik leurng 力量 *n. energy*

lik leurng 力量 *n. might*

lik leurng 力量 *n. virility*

lik ming 匿名 *n. anonymity*

lik ming 匿名 *a. anonymous*

lik see 歷史 *n. history*

lik see geh 歷史嘅 *a. historical*

lik see gey joy 歷史記載 *n.pl. annals*

lik see hok ga 歷史學家 *n. historian*

lik see sing geh 歷史性嘅 *a. historic*

lik see way jik 歷史遺跡 *n. monument*

lik teng 瀝青 *n. tar*

ling 鈴 *n bell*

ling 零 *n. nil*

ling 零 *n. nought*

ling 令 *n. ream*

ling 零 *n. zero*

ling chut 擰出 *v.t wring*

ling dow 令到 *v.t cause*

ling dow choy lang 領導才能 *n. leadership*

ling dow hm hoy sam 令到唔開心 *v.t. upset*

ling dow mow hao 令到無效 *v. t disable*

ling dow...ging ngar 令到...驚訝 *v.t astound*

ling duy 領隊 *n. leader*

ling duy 領隊 *n. spearhead*

ling gam 靈感 *n. inspiration*

ling gam 靈感 *n muse*

ling hao 靈巧 *adj. deft*

ling hm 同族 *n cognizance*

ling hm 領悟 *n. realization*

ling hm lik 領悟力 *n comprehension*

ling mow 陵墓 *n. mausoleum*

ling mung 檸檬 *adj. citric*

ling mung 檸檬 *n. lemon*

ling mung suy 檸檬水 *n. lemonade*

ling ngoy 另外 *a another*

ling ngoy 另外 *pron. other*

ling seen 領先 *n. lead*

ling sik 零食 *n. snack*

ling sow 零售 *n. retail*

ling sow geh 零售嘅 *a retail*

ling sow seurng 零售商 *n. retailer*

ling wik 領域 *n domain*

ling wik 領域 *a. realm*

ling wut 靈活 *a. nimble*

ling yan bay ngoy 令人悲哀嘅 *adj*
melancholy

ling yan bay tarm 令人悲慘 *a.*
poignant

ling yan dam sam 令人擔心 *v.t.*
misgive

ling yan dor lok 令人墮落 *v. t.*
debauch

ling yan fan gam geh 令人反感嘅 *a.*
objectionable

ling yan fan gam geh 令人反感嘅 *a.*
repugnant

ling yan fan gam geh 令人反感嘅 *a.*
repulsive

ling yan fan geh 令人煩嘅 *v.t.* puzzle

ling yan fan low 令人煩惱 *a.*
irksome

ling yan fan low 令人煩惱 *a.*
troublesome

ling yan forng sung 令人放鬆 *v.t.*
lull

ling yan ging hay 令人驚喜 *v.t.*
surprise

ling yan ging ngar 令人驚訝 *v.t.*
stupefy

ling yan jan ging 令人震驚 *v.t.*
scandalize

ling yan jok oh geh 令人作嘔嘅 *a.*
obnoxious

ling yan jok oh geh 令人作嘔嘅 *a.*
odious

ling yan lan gwor 令人難過 *v.t.*
sadden

ling yan mwun yee 令人滿意 *v.t.*
please

ling yan seen mo 令人羨慕 *a*
enviable

ling yan sow fu 令人受苦 *v.t.*
victimize

ling yan tow yeem geh 令人討厭嘅 *a.*
repellent

ling yan tung fu 令人痛苦 *a.*
grievous

ling yan tuy gu 令人退股 *a.* invalid

ling yan way ham 令人遺憾 *a.*
lamentable

ling yan yam juy 令人飲醉 *v.t.*
intoxicate

ling yan yan jeurng sam hak 令人印
象深刻 *a.* imposing

ling yan yan seurng 令人欣賞 *a.*
admirable

ling yeurng 羚羊 *n.* antelope

ling yeurng 領養 *v.t.* foster

ling yeurng low gam yam 領養老金
人 *n* annuitant

lo 驢 *n.* ass

lo 腦 *n* brain

lo 褸 *n* coat

lo 爐 *n* cooker

lo day 爐低 *n.* hearth

lo fu 老虎 *n.* tiger

lo giew seng 驢叫聲 *n* bray

lo gung 老公 *n* husband

lo jeurng 路障 *n.* barricade

lo jor 老咗 *a.* aged

lo lik 努力 *n* effort

lo por 老婆 *n.* wife

lo say 老細 *n* boss

lo see 老師 *n.* teacher

lo suy 露水 *n.* dew

lo tee 鸕鷀 *n.* cormorant

lo teen yow lok cheurng 露天遊樂場
n. fair

lo tiew 爐條 *n.* grate

lo ting 路程 *n* drive

lo yan 老人 *a* elderly

lo yik 奴役 *v.t.* enslave

lo ying 露營 *v. i.* camp

lok 落 *v.t.* shed

lok chuy 樂趣 *n* relish

lok gak 落格 *n.* misappropriation

lok gwun 樂觀 *a.* jovial

lok gwun 樂觀 *n.* optimism

lok gwun 樂觀 *a. optimistic*
lok gwun 樂觀 *a. sanguine*
lok gwun geh yan 樂觀嘅人 *n. optimist*
lok ho 落後 *v. t benight*
lok ho geh 落後嘅 *a. medieval*
lok ho geh 落後嘅 *a. primitive*
lok ho geh yan 落後嘅人 *n. straggler*
lok how 落後 *v.i. lag*
lok meen 落面 *v.t. humiliate*
lok morng 落網 *v.t. net*
lok sai yu 落細雨 *v. i drizzle*
lok shoot 落雪 *v.i. snow*
lok suy seng 落水聲 *n splash*
lok tor 駱駝 *n. camel*
lok yee 樂意 *adv. readily*
lok yee 樂意 *a. willing*
lok yu 落雨 *v.i. rain*
lok yu jor yan 樂於助人 *a. helpful*
long 狼 *n. wolf*
look ap 亂噏 *v. t. chatter*
loon 亂 *v. t clutter*
loon 亂 *n. mess*
loon 聯 *v.t. stitch*
loon 暖 *a. warm*
loon ap 亂噏 *v. t. & i blab*
loon borng 聯邦 *n federation*
loon borng geh 聯邦嘅 *a federal*
loon duy 亂堆 *n. jumble*
loon fan 聯返 *v.t. sew*
loon fan 暖返 *v.t. warm*
loon forng 亂放 *v.t. misplace*
loon gao 亂搞 *v.i fiddle*
loon geh 暖嘅 *a. lukewarm*
loon geh 亂嘅 *a. motley*
loon gorng 亂講 *v.t. ramble*
loon hap 聯合 *n. unity*
loon hap day 聯合地 *adv. jointly*
loon hap jing fu 聯合政府 *n coalition*
loon hap ju yee jeh 聯合主義者 *n. unionist*
loon hay 聯繫 *n. liaison*

loon hay 聯繫 *v.t. relate*
loon lao 亂鬧 *n. rampage*
loon lok 聯絡 *v. t contact*
loon mang 聯盟 *n. alliance*
loon mang 聯盟 *n. league*
loon mor 亂摸 *v.i. fumble*
loon ngoy geh 戀愛嘅 *adj amatory*
loon seurng 聯想 *v.t. associate*
loon she 亂寫 *v.t. scrawl*
loon suy wu 暖水壺 *n. thermos (flask)*
loon tat bat jow geh 亂七八糟嘅 *a. topsy turvy*
loon wak 亂畫 *v.t. scribble*
loop ap ya say 亂噏廿四 *v.i. rave*
lor 攞 *v. t. carry*
lor 攞 *v.t fetch*
lor 攞 *v.t. get*
lor 鑼 *n. gong*
lor 攞 *v.t take*
lor bak 蘿蔔 *n. radish*
lor bak 蘿蔔 *n. turnip*
lor dow 攞到 *n acquest*
lor fan 攞返 *v.t. reclaim*
lor fan 攞返 *v.t. recoup*
lor fan 攞返 *v.t. retrieve*
lor hay 攞起 *v.t. lift*
lor jee 騾子 *n. mule*
lor jee geh 騾似嘅 *a. mulish*
lor lak 羅勒 *n. basil*
lor morng jee 羅望子 *n. tamarind*
lor see 螺絲 *n. screw*
lor shoon ying 螺旋型 *n. spiral*
lor shoon ying geh 螺旋形嘅 *a. spiral*
lor sor 囉唆 *v. i blether*
lor sor 囉唆 *n. tedium*
lor sor 囉唆 *a. verbose*
lor sor 囉唆 *n. verbosity*
lor sor 囉唆 *a. tedious*
lor tap 邏輯 *n. logic*
lor tap joon ga 邏輯專家 *n. logician*
lor tay 裸體 *a. naked*

lor tay 裸體 *n nude`*
lor tay 裸體 *n. nudity*
lorng dong jeh 浪蕩者 *n debauchee*
lorng fay 浪費 *n. prodigality*
lorng fay 浪費 *n. profligacy*
lorng fay 浪費 *a. wasteful*
lorng ha lorng ha 浪下浪下 *v.i. lurch*
lorng ho 口 *v.i. gargle*
lorng jung 朗誦 *n. recitation*
lorng jung 朗誦 *v.t. recite*
lorng kang 狼哽 *v. t devour*
lorng man 浪漫 *n. romance*
lorng man geh 浪漫嘅 *a. romantic*
lorng mow jow 朗姆酒 *n. rum*
lorng tun fu yeen 狼吞虎嚥 *n. gobble*
lorng tun fur yeen 狼吞虎咽 *v.i. scoff*
low 嬲 *a. angry*
low 鈕 *n button*
low 嬲 *a cross*
low 驢 *n donkey*
low 流 *v. t drain*
low 流 *v.i flow*
low 漏 *v.i. leak*
low 漏 *n. leakage*
low 路 *n. road*
low 留 *v.i. stay*
low 流 *v.i. stream*
low 扭 *v.t. twist*
low 路 *n. way*
low ba han 留疤痕 *v.t. scar*
low bay 盧比 *n. rupee*
low bing 溜冰 *v.t. skate*
low bing hai 溜冰鞋 *n. skate*
low bo 盧布 *n. rouble*
low cheurng 流暢 *a fluid*
low chut 流出 *v.i. well*
low da 扭打 *v.i. grapple*
low day 奴隸 *n. slave*
low day 奴隸 *n. thralldom*
low day jay 奴隸制 *n. slavery*
low dung 流動 *n flow*

low dung 漏洞 *n. lacuna*
low dung 漏洞 *n. leak*
low dung 扭動 *n wriggle*
low dung 扭動 *v.i. writhe*
low dung geh 流動嘅 *a. mobile*
low dung sing 流動性 *n. mobility*
low for 怒火 *n. anger*
low for 怒火 *n. fury*
low for 怒火 *n. wrath*
low forng 流放 *n. exile*
low fu la 老虎乸 *n. shrew*
low fu la 老虎乸 *n. tigress*
low gam 流感 *n. influenza*
low gu por 老姑婆 *n. spinster*
low gung 勞工 *n. labour*
low gung 勞工 *n. labourer*
low gwun 瘺管 *n fistula*
low hang 流行 *n. vogue*
low hang beng 流行病 *n epidemic*
low hang geh 流行嘅 *a current*
low hang geh 流行嘅 *a fashionable*
low hang kuk 流行曲 *n pop*
low ho 嘍口 *v.i. stammer*
low ho 嘍口 *n stammer*
low hoot 流血 *v. i bleed*
low horn 流汗 *v.i. sweat*
low kuk 扭曲 *v. t distort*
low lay 流利 *a eloquent*
low lay 流利 *a fluent*
low lay low huy 扭嚟扭去 *v.i. wriggle*
low lik 努力 *n diligence*
low lik jow 努力做 *v.i. labour*
low lorng 流浪 *v.i. rove*
low lorng geh 流浪嘅 *a vagabond*
low lorng hon 流浪漢 *n. vagabond*
low lorng jeh 流浪者 *n. rover*
low luy 流淚 *v.i. weep*
low meen 露面 *v.i surface*
low mok yeem 腦膜炎 *n. meningitis*
low por 老婆 *n.. missis, missus*
low sa 流沙 *n. quicksand*

low sam 留心 *a. attentive*

low sam 留心 *n heed*

low seen 路線 *n. route*

low seng gey 留聲機 *n. gramophone*

low seurng 扭傷 *n. sprain*

low seurng 扭傷 *n wrick*

low shoon 硫酸 *a. sulphuric*

low shu 老鼠 *n. mouse*

low shu 老鼠 *n. rat*

low shu 柳樹 *n. willow*

low sing geh 流星嘅 *a. meteoric*

low sow 牢騷 *n. moan*

low tan 扭哯 *v.t. sprain*

low tang 樓層 *n. storey*

low tay 樓梯 *n. stair*

low tiew 柳條 *n. wicker*

low tik 怒斥 *v.t. rail*

low tow 爐頭 *n. stove*

low wong 硫磺 *n. sulphur*

low wu tow geh 老糊塗嘅 *a. senile*

low yeep dow 柳葉刀 *a. lancet*

loy bo geh 內部嘅 *a. internal*

loy deen jeh 來電者 *n caller*

loy fuk cheurng 來福槍 *n rifle*

loy gow 內疚 *n. compunction*

loy gow 內疚 *n. guilt*

loy gow 內疚 *a. guilty*

loy hm jung 耐唔中 *adv. occasionally*

loy jak 內側 *n. inside*

loy jorng 內臟 *n. entrails*

loy joy geh 內在嘅 *a. intrinsic*

loy lik 耐力 *n. endurance*

loy lik 耐力 *n. fortitude*

loy lik 耐力 *n. stamina*

loy lik 耐力 *n. tolerance*

loy sam sam chu 內心深處 *a. inmost*

loy sam sam chu 內心深處 *a. innermost*

loy sing 耐性 *n. patience*

loy tan 內襯 *n lining*

loy yee 內衣 *n. underwear*

loy yeurk 懦弱 *n. cowardice*

loy yoon 來源 *n. source*

loy yung 內容 *n content*

loy yung 耐用 *a durable*

loy yung geh 耐用嘅 *a endurable*

luk 鹿 *n deer*

luk 錄 *v.t. record*

luk 六 *n., a six*

luk 錄 *v.t tape*

luk 轆 *a. wheel*

luk bo sek 綠寶石 *n emerald*

luk day 陸地 *a. inland*

luk day 陸地 *adv. inland*

luk dow 綠豆 *n. pea*

luk far 綠化 *v.t. afforest*

luk forng 氯仿 *n chloroform*

luk gok 鹿角 *n. antler*

luk gwan 陸軍 *n. brigade*

luk gwan jun jeurng 陸軍準將 *n brigadier*

luk hap choy 六合彩 *n. lottery*

luk hay 氯氣 *n chlorine*

luk sap 六十 *n., a. sixty*

luk sik 綠色 *n green*

luk sik geh 綠色嘅 *a. green*

luk sik jik mat 綠色植物 *n. greenery*

luk yam dai 錄音帶 *n. cassette*

luk yam gey 錄音機 *n. recorder*

luk yam sat 錄音室 *n. studio*

luk ying 錄影 *v.t film*

luk ying dai 錄影帶 *n. tape*

lum 諗 *v.t. think*

lum 諗 *n thought*

lun 磷 *n. phosphorus*

lun 卵 *n. spawn*

lun ju cheurng 輪住唱 *n. antiphony*

lun jun 輪盡 *v. t botch*

lun jun 輪盡 *a clumsy*

lun jun 輪盡 *a. maladroit*

lun kok 輪廓 *n contour*

lun low 輪流 *a. alternate*

lun low 輪流 *v.t. alternate*

lun man 論文 *n discourse*
lun man 論文 *n. essay*
lun man 論文 *n. thesis*
lun man 論文 *n. treatise*
lun sek 卵石 *n. pebble*
lun shoon yeem 磷酸鹽 *n. phosphate*
lun tan 論壇 *n. forum*
lun tao 卵巢 *n. ovary*
lun tee 輪齒 *n cog*
lun ying 卵形 *n oval*
lun ying geh 卵形嘅 *a. oval*
lung 籠 *n. cage*
lung 窿 *n. cavity*
lung 聾 *a deaf*
lung 龍 *n dragon*
lung 窿 *n hole*
lung 膿 *n. pus*
lung 窿 *n. apex*
lung cheurng 農場 *n. barton*
lung cheurng 農場 *n farm*
lung duk beng 膿毒病 *n. sepsis*
lung fu 農夫 *n farmer*
lung fu 農夫 *n. ploughman*
lung goon fung 龍捲風 *n. tornado*
lung har 龍蝦 *n. lobster*
lung hok 農學 *n. agronomy*
lung jok mat 農作物 *n crop*
lung jung 膿腫 *n abscess*
lung low 膿漏 *n. pyorrhoea*
lung low 農奴 *n. serf*
lung lung seng 隆隆聲 *n. rumble*
lung man 農民 *n. peasant*
lung man 農民 *n. peasantry*
lung mat 濃密 *a dense*
lung muk yeep 農牧業 *n. husbandry*
lung tong 濃湯 *n bisque*
lung yeep 農業 *n agriculture*
lung yeep ga 農業家 *n. agriculturist*
lung yeep geh 農業嘅 *a. agrarian*
lung yeep geh 農業嘅 *a agricultural*
lup 凹 *adj. concave*
lut 率 *n. rate*

lut jee 栗子 *n. chestnut*
lut see 律師 *n. lawyer*
lut see 律師 *n. solicitor*
lut sik 甩色 *v.i fade*
luy 鋁 *n. aluminium*
luy 女 *n daughter*
luy 鐳 *n. radium*
luy 雷 *n. thunder*
luy bat yeep sang 女畢業生 *n alumna*
luy buk 女僕 *n. maid*
luy day yam 女低音 *n alto*
luy gwun 旅館 *n. motel*
luy hak 旅客 *n. tourist*
luy hak 旅客 *n. wayfarer*
luy hak yan 女黑人 *n. negress*
luy hang 旅行 *n. holiday*
luy hang 旅行 *n. tour*
luy hang 旅行 *n travel*
luy hang 旅行 *n. trip*
luy hang tor cher 旅行拖車 *n. caravan*
luy hao 旅客 *n. traveller*
luy jay 女仔 *n. girl*
luy jay 女仔 *n. lass*
luy jay see 女祭司 *n. priestess*
luy jeurk see 女爵士 *n. dame*
luy jik 累積 *v.t. amass*
luy ju gok 女主角 *n. heroine*
luy juk jeurng 女族長 *n. matriarch*
luy lay fuk 女禮服 *n. gown*
luy meen 裡面 *adv. within*
luy meen geh 裡面嘅 *a. inner*
luy mo 女巫 *n. witch*
luy mow seurng 女帽商 *n. milliner*
luy mow teek gey see 女帽設計師 *n. milliner*
luy mow yeep 女帽業 *n. millinery*
luy san 女神 *n. goddess*
luy see geh 蕾絲嘅 *a. lacy*
luy see joon 螺絲鑽 *n. auger*
luy see yan 女詩人 *n. poetess*
luy see ying 女侍應 *n. waitress*

luy she 旅舍 *n. hostel*
luy shoon yeem 鋁酸鹽 *n. aluminate*
luy sing fa 女性化 *a. girlish*
luy sing far 女性化 *v.t. womanise*
luy sing geh 女性嘅 *a female*
luy sing geh 女性嘅 *a feminine*
luy sow dow yoon 女修道院 *n convent*
luy tee 類似 *a. akin*
luy ting 旅程 *n. journey*
luy ting 旅程 *n ride*
luy worng 女王 *n. queen*
luy wu see jeurng 女護士長 *n. matron*
luy xing 女性 *n female*
luy yan 女人 *n. lady*
luy yan 女人 *n. woman*
luy yan 女人 *n. womanhood*
luy yan geh 女人嘅 *n. womanish*
luy yeen yoon 女演員 *n. actress*
luy ying 類型 *n. type*
luy ying far tay fat 類型化睇法 *v.t. stereotype*
luy yow 旅遊 *v.i. travel*
luy yow sing day 旅遊勝地 *n resort*
luy yow yeep 旅遊業 *n. tourism*

M

ma 馬 *n. horse*
ma 媽 *n mum*
ma 馬 *n. nag*
ma 碼 *n. yard*
ma bao doy 麻包袋 *n. sack*
ma bay 痲痹 *n. palsy*
ma cher 馬車 *n. barouche*
ma cher 馬車 *n. cart*
ma cher 馬車 *n chaise*
ma cher 馬車 *n. wagon*

ma cher fu 馬車夫 *n coachman*
ma cho 馬槽 *n. manger*
ma choy hak 馬賽克 *n. mosaic*
ma dang 馬鐙 *n. stirrup*
ma dat 馬達 *n. motor*
ma fan 麻煩 *v. t bother*
ma fan 馬販 *n. coper*
ma fan 麻煩 *n. fuss*
ma fan 麻煩 *a. trying*
ma fan see 麻煩事 *n. nuisance*
ma fan yan 麻煩人 *n. gadfly*
ma feh 嗎啡 *n. morphia*
ma forng 馬房 *n stable*
ma fu geh 馬虎嘅 *a. slipshod*
ma fung 痲瘋 *n. leprosy*
ma fung beng wan jeh 痲瘋病患者 *n. leper*
ma fung geh 痲瘋嘅 *a. leprous*
ma giew seng 馬叫聲 *v.i. neigh*
ma giew seng 馬叫聲 *n. neigh*
ma guy 馬具 *n. harness*
ma hay toon 馬戲團 *n. circus*
ma jeurk 麻雀 *n. sparrow*
ma juy 麻醉 *n anaesthesia*
ma juy 麻醉 *n. narcosis*
ma juy yeurk 麻醉藥 *n. anaesthetic*
ma kow 馬球 *n. polo*
ma lai chung 馬拉松 *n. marathon*
ma luk 馬陸 *n. millipede*
ma ma 媽媽 *n. mamma*
ma mi 媽咪 *n. mummy*
ma mow tay teem jow 馬姆齊甜酒 *n. malmsey*
ma muk geh 麻木嘅 *a. nerveless*
ma on 馬鞍 *n. saddle*
ma tan 麻疹 *n measles*
ma tee 馬刺 *n. spur*
ma tow 碼頭 *n. dock*
ma tow fay 碼頭費 *n. wharfage*
mah fu 馬虎 *a. lax*
mah lak 馬勒 *n bridle*
mai 埋 *v. t bury*

mai 買 *v. t. buy*

mai 賣 *v.t flog*

mai 買 *v.t. purchase*

mai 賣 *v.t. retail*

mai 賣 *v.t. sell*

mai fuk 埋伏 *n. ambush*

mai fuk 埋伏 *v.i. lurk*

mai ga 買家 *n. buyer*

mai ga 賣家 *n. seller*

mai mai 買賣 *n. trade*

mai yam 賣淫 *v.t. prostitute*

mai yam 賣淫 *n. prostitution*

mak 墨 *n. ink*

mak bok 脈搏 *n. pulse*

mak dai gor ho 擘大個口 *adv., agape*

mak kay 默契 *n. rapport*

mak lap jung 麥粒腫 *n. stye*

mak lok mok 脈絡膜 *n choroid*

mak ngar 麥芽 *n. malt*

mak ngar beh jow 麥芽啤酒 *n ale*

mak ngar cho 麥芽醋 *n alegar*

mak pay 麥皮 *n. porridge*

mak sang yan 陌生人 *n. stranger*

mak see 默示 *a. tacit*

mak yeen jeep sow 默然接受 *n. acquiescence*

man 問 *v.t. ask*

man 蚊 *n dollar*

man 紋 *n. groove*

man 蚊 *n. mosquito*

man 聞 *v.t nose*

man 問 *v.t. quiz*

man 慢 *a slow*

man 慢 *v.i. slow*

man 聞 *v.t. smell*

man 聞 *v.i. sniff*

man 聞 *n sniff*

man 燜 *v.t. stew*

man bing 民兵 *n. militia*

man bo 漫步 *v.i. meander*

man bo 漫步 *v.i. roam*

man chuk 慢速 *n crawl*

man dow 聞到 *v.t. scent*

man dow 慢度 *n. slowness*

man dow 聞到 *v.t. smelt*

man far 文化 *n culture*

man far geh 文化嘅 *a cultural*

man fat 文法 *n. grammar*

man fat ga 文法家 *n. grammarian*

man gam 敏感 *n. allergy*

man gam geh 敏感嘅 *a. sensitive*

man gam sing 敏感性 *n. sensibility*

man geen 文件 *n document*

man geen gap 文件夾 *n. portfolio*

man geh choy 燜嘅菜 *n. stew*

man gene 文件 *n file*

man goon 問卷 *n. questionnaire*

man gor 民歌 *v.t. lay*

man guy 文具 *n. stationery*

man guy seurng 文具商 *n. stationer*

man hao 吻合 *v.t mesh*

man hap 吻合 *v.t. tally*

man ho 問候 *n. regard*

man ho 問候 *n. salutation*

man hok 文學 *n. literature*

man hok ga 文學家 *n. litterateur*

man hok geh 文學嘅 *a. literary*

man jeet 敏捷 *a. agile*

man jeet dow 敏捷度 *n. agility*

man jeet sow fat 敏捷手法 *n. sleight*

man jeurng 文章 *n article*

man ju 民主 *n democracy*

man ju 民主 *a democratic*

man juk ju yee jeh 民族主義者 *n. nationalist*

man lang jee gey 萬能之計 *n. panacea*

man leen geh 晚年嘅 *a. late*

man man 慢慢 *adv. slowly*

man man gam 慢慢咁 *adv. leisurely*

man man gwun shu 慢慢灌輸 *v.t. instil*

man man hang 慢慢行 *v.t. saunter*

man man sam chut 慢慢滲出 *v.i.* *ooze*

man mang 文盲 *n.* *illiteracy*

man mang 文盲 *a.* *illiterate*

man may por 問米婆 *n.* *necropolis*

man ming seh wuy 文明社會 *n.* *civilization*

man mow yat sat 萬無一失 *a.* *infallible*

man ngar 文雅 *n.* *urbanity*

man pang for ting 文憑課程 *n* *diploma*

man pao 慢跑 *v.t.* *jog*

man san 紋身 *n.* *tattoo*

man san 紋身 *v.i.* *tattoo*

man sing 慢性 *a.* *chronic*

man sow guk 萬壽菊 *n.* *marigold*

man tay 問題 *n.* *issue*

man tay 問題 *n.* *question*

man tay 問題 *n* *rub*

man tay 問題 *n.* *snag*

man tay 問題 *n.* *trouble*

man tay 問題 *n.* *problem*

man tun tun 慢吞吞 *v.i.* *dawdle*

man wah 漫畫 *n* *comic*

man yoon 文員 *n* *clerk*

man yuy 敏銳 *n.* *acumen*

mang 盲 *n* *ablepsy*

mang 盲 *a* *blind*

mang 錳 *n.* *manganese*

mang 搖 *v.t.* *pluck*

mang cheurng yeem 盲腸炎 *n.* *appendicitis*

mang gik 猛擊 *v.t.* *wallop*

mang gwok 盟國 *n.* *ally*

mang leet dung jok 猛烈動作 *n.* *jerk*

mang man 盲文 *n* *braille*

mang muk geh 盲目嘅 *a.* *mindless*

mang muk joon chung 盲目遵從 *a.* *slavish*

mang tuy 猛推 *v.t.* *thrust*

mao 錨 *n.* *anchor*

mao 貓 *n.* *cat*

mao 矛 *n.* *spear*

mao da fu low 貓打呼嚕 *v.i.* *purr*

mao fu low seng 貓呼嚕聲 *n.* *purr*

mao giew seng 貓叫聲 *n.* *mew*

mao ngan sek 貓眼石 *n.* *opal*

mao tow ying 貓頭鷹 *n.* *owl*

mao tun 矛盾 *n.* *antinomy*

mao tun 矛盾 *n* *contradiction*

mao tun 矛盾 *n.* *paradox*

mao uk 茅屋 *n.* *hut*

mao yow 貓鼬 *n.* *mongoose*

mar low 馬騮 *n.* *monkey*

mat 抹 *v.t.* *dust*

mat 密 *a.* *frequent*

mat 襪 *n.* *sock*

mat 抹 *v.t.* *wipe*

mat ban 物品 *n.* *ware*

mat dow 密度 *n* *density*

mat fung 蜜蜂 *n.* *bee*

mat geen 物件 *n.* *item*

mat jap geh 密集嘅 *a.* *intensive*

mat jat 物質 *n.* *substance*

mat jat geh 物質嘅 *a.* *material*

mat jat ju yee 物質主義 *n.* *materialism*

mat ju 物主 *n,* *owner*

mat lay hok 物理學 *n.* *physics*

mat lay hok ga 物理學家 *n.* *physicist*

mat luy 襪類 *n.* *hosiery*

mat ma 密碼 *n* *code*

mat ma hok 密碼學 *n.* *cryptography*

mat mo 密謀 *v. i.* *conspire*

mat mow 密謀 *v.t.* *plot*

mat mow 密謀 *v.i.* *scheme*

mat see 密使 *n* *emissary*

mat sik 物色 *v.i* *scout*

mat tay 物體 *n.* *object*

mat teet 密切 *a.* *intimate*

mat teet geh gwan hay 密切嘅關係 *n* *affinity*

mat torng 蜜糖 *n.* *honey*

may 謎 *n enigma*
may 醚 *n ether*
may 米 *n. metre*
may 咪 *n. microphone*
may 迷 *n. mystery*
may 謎 *n. puzzle*
may 米 *n. rice*
may bat juk dow 微不足道 *a. negligible*
may bor low 微波爐 *n. microwave*
may dak 美德 *n. goodness*
may dak 美德 *n. virtue*
may dow 味道 *n. savour*
may dow 味道 *n. scent*
may fan yan see 未婚人世 *n agamist*
may far 美化 *v. t beautify*
may fung 微風 *n breeze*
may fung 微風 *n. zephyr*
may gam 美感 *n.pl. aesthetics*
may gung 迷宮 *n. labyrinth*
may gung 迷宮 *n. maze*
may gung ngay hok 微工藝學 *n. micrology*
may hok geh 美學嘅 *a. aesthetic*
may jan 微震 *n. tremor*
may ju 迷住 *v. t. captivate*
may ju yee dow 未主義到 *adv. unawares*
may juy 未醉 *n. sobriety*
may kwan 黴菌 *n. mildew*
may kwan 黴菌 *n mould*
may lap 微粒 *a. particle*
may lay 美麗 *n. prettiness*
may lay chao geh jeurk 未離巢嘅雀 *n. nestling*
may lik 魅力 *n. charm1*
may lik 魅力 *n. seduction*
may lik 魅力 *n spell*
may loon 迷戀 *v.t. infatuate*
may loon 迷戀 *v.t. obsess*
may loon 迷戀 *v.i swoon*
may loy 未來 *a. would-be*
may loy geh 未來嘅 *a. future*
may morng 迷茫 *n daze*
may say geh 微細嘅 *a. microscopic*
may sik 美食 *n. dainty*
may sing leen 未成年 *n. immaturity*
may sing leen yan 未成年人 *n minor*
may wak 迷惑 *v.t bewitch*
may wak 迷惑 *n dazzle*
may wak 迷惑 *v. t. dazzle*
may wak 迷惑 *v.t. mesmerize*
may yan yu 美人魚 *n. mermaid*
may yeurk 微弱 *a faint*
may ying wah 微型畫 *n. miniature*
may yoon sing 未完成 *a. incomplete*
may yu 謎語 *n. riddle*
may yu tow mow 未雨綢繆 *a. provident*
meen 棉 *n. cotton*
meen 面 *n face*
meen 面 *n. visage*
meen bao 麵包 *n bread*
meen bao jing geh 麵包整嘅 *v. t. & i breaden*
meen bao pay 麵包皮 *n. crust*
meen bao see 麵包師 *n. baker*
meen bo geh 面部嘅 *a facial*
meen chuy 免除 *v. t. exempt*
meen chuy 免除 *a. exempt*
meen duy 面對 *v.t face*
meen duy 面對 *v.t. orientate*
meen duy meen 面對面 *n. tete-a-tete*
meen fan 麵粉 *n flour*
meen fan chorng 麵粉廠 *n. mill*
meen fay geh 免費嘅 *adv. gratis*
meen guy 面具 *n. mask*
meen heurng 面向 *v.t front*
meen hung 面紅 *adv ablush*
meen hung 面紅 *n blush*
meen hung 面紅 *v.i blush*
meen hung 面紅 *n flush*
meen jak 免責 *n. impunity*

meen ju 面珠 *n cheek*

meen keurng 勉強 *n. reluctance*

meen keurng 勉強 *adv. scarcely*

meen keurng geh 勉強嘅 *a. reluctant*

meen keurng jo 勉強做 *v.t. grudge*

meen keurng way tee sang wut 勉強
維持生活 *n. subsistence*

meen pay 棉被 *n. quilt*

meen sa 棉紗 *n. veil*

meen see 面試 *n. interview*

meen sik 面色 *n. countenance*

meen toon 麵團 *n dough*

meen yik 免疫 *v.t. immunize*

meen yik lik 免疫力 *n. immunity*

meet 搣 *v.t. peel*

meet 捏 *v.t. pinch*

meet 捏 *v. pinch*

meh 咩 *a. what*

meh 咩 *pron. what*

meh 咩 *interj. what*

meh meh giew 咩咩叫 *v. i bleat*

meng 名 *n. name*

meng 名 *n. title*

mey 尾 *n. tail*

mey dow 味道 *n flavour*

mey lay 美麗 *n beauty*

mey mey 美味 *a delicious*

mey sun 迷信 *n. superstition*

mey sun 迷信 *a. superstitious*

miew 喵 *v.i. mew*

miew 秒 *n second*

miew 廟 *n temple*

miew jun 瞄準 *v.i. aim*

miew kwuy 描繪 *v. t. depict*

miew kwuy 描繪 *n. portrayal*

miew kwuy 描繪 *n. sketch*

miew kwuy 描繪 *v.t. sketch*

miew see 藐視 *v. t. disdain*

miew sut 描述 *n description*

miew sut 描述 *a descriptive*

miew sut 描述 *n. narrative*

miew sut geh 描述嘅 *a. narrative*

miew tiew 苗條 *n. slender*

miew tiew 苗條 *a. trim*

miew tiew geh 苗條嘅 *a. slim*

miew tiew suk luy 窈窕淑女 *n. sylph*

miew yu 妙語 *n. witticism*

ming bak 明白 *v.t. understand*

ming fu kay sat geh 名副其實嘅 *a. veritable*

ming hay 名氣 *n fame*

ming hay 名氣 *n. repute*

ming heen 明顯 *a. apparent*

ming heen 明顯 *adv clearly*

ming heen 明顯 *a. conspicuous*

ming heen 明顯 *a distinct*

ming heen 明顯 *a. obvious*

ming heen geh 明顯嘅 *a. manifest*

ming heen geh 明顯嘅 *a. palpable*

ming heen geh 明顯嘅 *a. patent*

ming jee geh 明智嘅 *a. politic*

ming jee geh 明智嘅 *a. sensible*

ming ling 命令 *v.t. adjure*

ming ling 命令 *n command*

ming ling 命令 *v. t command*

ming ling 命令 *n. mandate*

ming ming fat 命名法 *n. nomenclature*

ming morng 名望 *n. renown*

ming muk jeurng darm 明目張膽 *a flagrant*

ming seurng 冥想 *v.t. meditate*

ming seurng 冥想 *n. meditation*

ming seurng 冥想 *v.i. muse*

ming suy teen gu 名垂千古 *v.t. immortalize*

ming tee 名詞 *n. noun*

ming wan 命運 *n destiny*

ming yan 名人 *n celebrity*

ming yan 名人 *n. personage*

ming yee seurng geh 名義上嘅 *a. nominal*

ming yu 名譽 *n. reputation*

ming yu 明喻 *n. simile*

mo 帽 *n. cap*

mo 舞 *n dance*

mo 霧 *n fog*

mo 毛 *n. fur*

mo 帽 *n. hat*

mo 墓 *n. tomb*

mo 無 *adv. without*

mo chung 毛蟲 *n caterpillar*

mo chung 冒充 *v.i. sham*

mo dak ao 無得拗 *a. indisputable*

mo dak bay 無得比 *a. incomparable*

mo dak yee 無得醫 *a. incurable*

mo dak yee 模特兒 *n. model*

mo dan sing 無彈性 *a. inflexible*

mo day 無低 *a. baseless*

mo day 踎低 *v. i. crouch*

mo day 踎低 *v.i. duck*

mo deet juy 無秩序 *a. haphazard*

mo doon 武斷 *a. arbitrary*

mo fa gwor 無花果 *n fig*

mo fan tow fan 模範囚犯 *n. trusty*

mo fat forng sow 無法防守 *a. indefensible*

mo fat sat see 無法事實 *n. impracticability*

mo fat yan sow 無法忍受 *n. intolerance*

mo fong 模仿 *v.t. ape*

mo forng 模仿 *v. t emulate*

mo forng 模仿 *v.t. imitate*

mo forng 模仿 *n. imitation*

mo forng 模仿 *v.t. impersonate*

mo forng 模仿 *n. impersonation*

mo forng jeh 模仿者 *n. imitator*

mo gam gok geh 無感覺嘅 *a. numb*

mo gan 毛巾 *n. towel*

mo geh 毛嘅 *a. woollen*

mo gey 母雞 *n. hen*

mo gey meng tow piew 無記名投票 *v.i. ballot*

mo gey sing 無記性 *a forgetful*

mo ging yeem 無經驗 *n. inexperience*

mo han geh 無限嘅 *a. immeasurable*

mo han kay 無限期 *a. indefinite*

mo heem 冒險 *n adventure*

mo heem 冒險 *v.t hazard*

mo hey 武器 *n. weapon*

mo hing chuy 無興趣 *a. weary*

mo hing chuy 無興趣 *v.t. weary*

mo ho 冒號 *n colon*

mo jee 無知 *n. ignorance*

mo jee 無知 *a. ignorant*

mo jeen 毛氈 *n blanket*

mo jeurng 毛象 *n. mammoth*

mo jing fu 無政府 *n anarchy*

mo jing fu juu yee jeh 無政府主義者 *n anarchist*

mo jow leen yee kwan 無袖連衣裙 *n chemise*

mo lai 無賴 *n cad*

mo lai 毛拉 *n. mullah*

mo lang 無能 *n. impotence*

mo lang lik 無能力 *n. inability*

mo lang lik 無能力 *a. incapable*

mo lang lik 無能力 *n. incapacity*

mo lang lik 無能力 *a. incompetent*

mo larn 毛冷 *n. wool*

mo liew 無聊 *a dull*

mo loy sing 無耐性 *n. impatience*

mo loy sing 無耐性 *a. impatient*

mo lun 謬論 *n fallacy*

mo lun 無論 *pron. whatever*

mo lun been gor 無論邊個 *pron whichever*

mo lun...ding hay 無論...定係 *conj. whether*

mo may 無味 *adj. bland*

mo morng 無望 *a. hopeless*

mo ngow 犛牛 *n. yak*

mo sam jorng joy 無心裝載 *a. inattentive*

mo san lun 無神論 *n atheism*

mo san lun jeh 無神論者 n atheist
mo see 武士 n. warrior
mo seen 無線 a. wireless
mo seen 無線 n wireless
mo sik geh 無色嘅 adj achromatic
mo so 無數 a. countless
mo sow ling geh 無首領嘅 adj. acephalous
mo sut 巫術 n. witchery
mo ting fu ju yee 無政府主義 n. anarchism
mo tow 無頭 n. acephalus
mo toy 舞台 n arena
mo wu 模糊 v. t blear
mo wu 模糊 n blur
mo wu 模糊 a. hazy
mo yee jung teng dow 無意中聽到 v.t. overhear
mo yeh jow 無嘢做 a. idle
mo yeurk hor gow 無藥可救 a. incorrigible
mo yeurng 母羊 n ewe
mo yik 貿易 n commerce
mo yik 無益 n. futility
mo yik seurng 貿易商 n dealer
mo ying geh 無形嘅 adj. aeriform
mo yoon 墓園 n. cemetery
mo yuk 侮辱 v.t. affront
mo yuk 侮辱 n affront
mo yuk 侮辱 n gibe
mo yung 無用 a. futile
mo yung geh 無用嘅 a. helpless
mo yung geh 無用嘅 a. waste
mok 膜 n. membrane
mok doot 剝奪 v. t deprive
mok bat gwan sam 漠不關心 n. indifference
mok bat gwan sam 漠不關心 n. nonchalance
mok gwong 剝光 v.t. denude
mong 忙 a busy
mong ju 望住 adv agaze

mong kow 網球 n. tennis
mong yoon geng 望遠鏡 n. binocular
mor 摸 v.t feel
mor chat lik 摩擦力 n. friction
mor fat 魔法 n. witchcraft
mor fat pang 魔法棒 n. wand
mor fat see 魔法師 n. wizard
mor forng gung yan 磨坊工人 n. miller
mor gu 蘑菇 n. mushroom
mor gway 魔鬼 n. demon
mor gway 魔鬼 n devil
mor gway 魔鬼 n. satan
mor keet jor 魔羯座 n Capricorn
mor shoon 磨損 n fray
mor sing fan 磨成粉 v.t. mill
mor sut see 魔術師 n. magician
mor suy 磨碎 v.t grate
mor suy 磨碎 v.i. grind
mor suy gey 磨碎機 n. grinder
mor tat 摩擦 v. t brustle
mor wan 魔幻 a. magical
morng 望 v.i. glance
morng 忙 v.i. moil
morng 網 n. net
morng ging low 望景樓 n belvedere
morng gwor 芒果 n mango
morng jorng geh 網狀嘅 a. webby
morng jorng mat 網狀物 n. mesh
morng ju 望住 v.t. gaze
morng lok 網絡 n. network
morng she 蟒蛇 n. python
morng yan fu yee 忘恩負義 n. ingratitude
morng yoon geng 望遠鏡 n. telescope
mow 帽 n. hood
mow 哞 v.i moo
mow ban 模板 n. stencil
mow been far 無變化 a. stagnant
mow chuy may 無趣味 a. lacklustre

mow dak bay geh 無得比嘅 *a.*
matchless

mow dak bay geh 無得比嘅 *a.*
nonpareil

mow dak bay geh 無得比嘅 *a.*
peerless

mow dam 無膽 *n. timidity*

mow day 踎低 *v.i. squat*

mow deng 無埞 *adv. nowhere*

mow dik geh 無敵嘅 *a. invincible*

mow fan 模範 *n. paragon*

mow fan 謀反 *n. rebellion*

mow fan ying 無反應 *a. insensible*

mow fat far gai 無法化解 *a.*
irreconcilable

mow fat gai sik 無法解釋 *a.*
inexplicable

mow forng 模仿 *n. mimesis*

mow forng 模仿 *v.t mimic*

mow forng 模仿 *n mimicry*

mow forng 模仿 *n. parody*

mow forng 模仿 *v.t. parody*

mow forng ghe 模仿嘅 *a. mimic*

mow gey lut 無紀律 *n. indiscipline*

mow gor day forng 某個地方 *adv.*
somewhere

mow gu 無辜 *a. innocent*

mow guy 模具 *n. mould*

mow gwan 無關 *a. irrelevant*

mow gwan 無關 *a. irrespective*

mow gwor geh jik mat 無果嘅植物
adj. acarpous

mow ha tee 無瑕疵 *a. stainless*

mow han 無限 *n. infinity*

mow han geh 無限嘅 *a. infinite*

mow han geh 無限嘅 *a. limitless*

mow han geh 無限嘅 *a. measureless*

mow hao 無效 *a. ineffective*

mow hao 無效 *a. inoperative*

mow hao 無效 *a. invalid*

mow hao 無效 *n. nullification*

mow hao geh 無效嘅 *a. null*

mow hay 武器 *n. arsenal*

mow heem 冒險 *v.t. risk*

mow heem 冒險 *v.t. stake*

mow hor bay meen 無可避免 *a.*
inevitable

mow hor fow ying 無可否認 *a.*
irrefutable

mow hor lang 無可能 *a. impossible*

mow hor lang sing 無可能性 *n.*
impossibility

mow hung 毛孔 *n. pore*

mow jee 無知 *n. nescience*

mow jee gok geh 無知覺嘅 *a.*
senseless

mow jing da choy 無精打采 *n.*
lethargy

mow jing da choy 無精打采 *a.*
listless

mow ju 母豬 *n. sow*

mow juk heng chung 無足輕重 *a.*
lowly

mow kwan geh 無菌嘅 *a. sterile*

mow lai 無賴 *n. knave*

mow lai 無賴 *n. rascal*

mow lai 無賴 *n. rogue*

mow lai 無賴 *n. scoundrel*

mow lay 無禮 *n. insolence*

mow lay 無禮 *a. insolent*

mow lay geh 無禮嘅 *n. impertinence*

mow lay mao 無禮貌 *a. impolite*

mow lay mao geh 無禮貌嘅 *a. rude*

mow lay moa geh 無禮貌嘅 *a*
unmannerly

mow liew geh 無聊嘅 *a. prosaic*

mow lik wan 無力還 *a. insolvent*

mow ma 母馬 *n. mare*

mow may 無味 *a. insipid*

mow may 無味 *n. insipidity*

mow meh hor lang 無咩可能 *a.*
unlikely

mow ming for siew 無明火燒 *v.i.*
smoulder

mow por 巫婆 n. necromancer

mow san lun jeh 無神論者 n antitheist

mow sang hay geh 無生氣嘅 a. lifeless

mow sang ming geh 無生命嘅 a. inanimate

mow sat 謀殺 n. murder

mow sat 謀殺 v.t. murder

mow see 母獅 n. lioness

mow see geh 無私嘅 a. selfless

mow seng 無聲 n. silence

mow seng gam gorng 無聲咁講 v.t. mouth

mow seng geh 無聲嘅 a. mute

mow seng geh 無聲嘅 a. silent

mow sik 暮色 n twilight

mow sing 母性 n. motherhood

mow sing geh 母性嘅 a. motherly

mow sing jow geh yan 無成就嘅人 n. nonentity

mow sor bat jee geh 無所不知嘅 a. omniscient

mow sor bat joy 無所不在 n. omnipresence

mow sor bat joy geh 無所不在嘅 a. omnipresent

mow sor bat lang geh 無所不能嘅 a. omnipotent

mow sow 無數 n. myriad

mow sow geh 無數嘅 a. innumerable

mow sow geh 無數嘅 a myriad

mow sow geh 無數嘅 a. numberless

mow sut 巫術 n. sorcery

mow tan 母親 n mother

mow tan geh 母親嘅 a. maternal

mow tee ghe 無恥嘅 a. shameless

mow ting geh 無情嘅 adj. merciless

mow ting geh 無情嘅 a. pitiless

mow toy 舞台 n. stage

mow wu 模糊 n. ambiguity

mow wu 模糊 a. ambiguous

mow wu 模糊 a. indistinct

mow wu bat ting 模糊不清 n. illegibility

mow yan 無人 pron. nobody

mow yan cho jok geh 無人操作嘅 a. unmanned

mow yee gam 無意咁 adv. unwittingly

mow yee see 無意思 a. meaningless

mow yee sik 無意識 n. oblivion

mow yeh 無嘢 n. nothing

mow yeh 無嘢 adv. nothing

mow yik cheurng sor 貿易場所 n. mart

mow yoot 墓穴 n. vault

mow yuk 侮辱 n. insult

mow yuk 侮辱 v.t. insult

mow yuk geh 侮辱嘅 a abusive

mow yung geh 無用嘅 a. pathetic

mow yung ghe 無用嘅 a. paltry

muk 木 n. timber

muk 木 n. wood

muk ban 木板 n. plank

muk biew 目標 n. aim

muk biew 目標 n. goal

muk biew 目標 n. target

muk cheurng 牧場 n. pasture

muk di dey 目的地 n destination

muk dik 目的 n. intent

muk dik 目的 n. intention

muk dik 目的 n. objective

muk dik 目的 n. purpose

muk ding ho ngoy 目定口呆 v.i. gape

muk gik 目擊 v.i. witness

muk gik ting yan 目擊證人 n. witness

muk gung 木工 n. carpentry

muk gung 木工 n. joiner

muk gwun 牧冠 n. mitre

muk jeurng 木匠 n. carpenter

muk jow geh 木造嘅 a. wooden

muk kam 木琴 *n. xylophone*
muk lai yee 木乃伊 *n mummy*
muk luk 目錄 *n. catalogue*
muk luk 目錄 *n. content*
muk mah 木馬 *n. hobby-horse*
muk man geh 牧民嘅 *a. pastoral*
muk mow fat gey 目無法紀 *a. lawless*
muk sang geh 木生嘅 *a. xylophilous*
muk see 牧師 *n clergy*
muk see 牧師 *n. oracle*
muk see 牧師 *n. parson*
muk see 牧師 *n. vicar*
muk see lam gwun yoon 穆斯林官員 *n. nabob*
muk sing 木星 *n. jupiter*
muk tee 木刺 *n. splinter*
muk tiew 木條 *n taper*
muk tow 木頭 *n. log*
muk tung 木桶 *n cask*
muk yan 牧人 *n. herdsman*
muk yeurng jor 牡羊座 *n aries*
muk yeurng yan 牧羊人 *n. shepherd*
muk yuk 沐浴 *n ablution*
mun 悶 *v. t bore*
mun 門 *n door*
mun 滿 *a. full*
mun geh 滿嘅 *adv. full*
mun ho 門口 *n. threshold*
mun juk 滿足 *a. content*
mun juk 滿足 *n. satiety*
mun juk 滿足 *v.t. satisfy*
mun juk gam 滿足感 *n. gratification*
mun juk geh 滿足嘅 *a. satiable*
mun mun bat lok 悶悶不樂 *a. sullen*
mun san 門閂 *n bolt*
mun tan beng yan 門診病人 *n. outpatient*
mun wai hay morng 滿懷希望 *a. hopeful*
mun way 門衛 *n. usher*
mun yee 滿意 *n contentment*

mun yee 滿意 *n. satisfaction*
mun yee geh 滿意嘅 *a. satisfactory*
mun yeet 悶熱 *a. sultry*
mung 夢 *n dream*
mung 夢 *v. i. dream*
mung ju ngan 蒙住眼 *v. t blindfold*
mung yow beng 夢遊病 *n. somnambulism*
mung yow beng wan jeh 夢遊病患者 *n. somnambulist*
mut so 沒收 *n confiscation*
mwun 蟎 *n. mite*
mwun kwang 門框 *n. lintel*
mwun lorng 門廊 *n. porch*
mwun mwun bat lok 悶悶不樂 *v.i. mope*
mwun mwun bat lok geh 悶悶不樂嘅 *a. morose*
mwun yeet 悶熱 *a. muggy*
mwut kay geh 末期嘅 *a. terminal*
mwut lay far 茉莉花 *n. jasmine, jessamine*
mwut sow 沒收 *v.t forfeit*
mwut yeurk 沒藥 *n. myrrh*
mwuy 每 *prep. per*
mwuy fan jung geh 每分鐘嘅 *adv. minutely*
mwuy gor 每個 *a each*
mwuy gor 每個 *a every*
mwuy gor lay bai 每個禮拜 *adv. weekly*
mwuy gor lay bai geh 每個禮拜嘅 *a. weekly*
mwuy gor yoot 每個月 *a. monthly*
mwuy gor yoot 每個月 *adv monthly*
mwuy gway 玫瑰 *n. rose*
mwuy gway dow geh 每季度嘅 *a. quarterly*
mwuy hay 煤氣 *n. gas*
mwuy leen geh 每年嘅 *a. yearly*
mwuy leurng gor yoot 每兩個月 *adj bimensal*

mwuy man 每晚 *adv. nightly*
mwuy yat 每日 *adv. daily*
mwuy yat geh 每日嘅 *a daily*
mwuy yow 煤油 *n. kerosene*

N

ng 五 *n five*
ng sap 五十 *n. fifty*
ngai shu 矮樹 *n bush*
ngam 啱 *adv. aright*
ngam geh 啱嘅 *a. right*
ngam jing 癌症 *n. cancer*
ngan 眼 *n eye*
ngan 銀 *n. silver*
ngan bao 銀包 *n. purse*
ngan fan 眼瞓 *a. lethargic*
ngan fan 眼瞓 *a. sleepy*
ngan fan 眼瞓 *n. somnolence*
ngan fan 眼瞓 *n. somnolent*
ngan for yee sang 眼科醫生 *n. oculist*
ngan gam gam 眼甘甘 *v.t. ogle*
ngan gao 晏覺 *n. nap*
ngan geh 眼嘅 *a. ocular*
ngan geh 眼嘅 *a. optic*
ngan geng 硬頸 *n. obduracy*
ngan geng 硬頸 *a. obstinate*
ngan geng 眼鏡 *n. spectacle*
ngan geng geh 硬頸嘅 *a. obdurate*
ngan geng seh 眼睛蛇 *n cobra*
ngan geng seurng 眼鏡商 *n. optician*
ngan goa 晏覺 *n. siesta*
ngan gwat gwat 眼倔倔 *n. glare*
ngan gwat gwat gam morng 眼倔倔 咁望 *v.i glare*
ngan hung 眼孔 *n eyelet*
ngan jeet mo 眼睫毛 *n eyelash*
ngan jow 晏晝 *n. lunch*

ngan kow 眼球 *n eyeball*
ngan lay 眼利 *a. watchful*
ngan luy 眼淚 *n. tear*
ngan sap sap 眼濕濕 *a. tearful*
ngan sik 顏色 *n colour*
ngan sik 眼色 *n wink*
ngan sik geh 銀色嘅 *a silver*
ngang geh 硬嘅 *a. solid*
ngang geng 硬頸 *a. stubborn*
ngap tow 岌頭 *v.i. nod*
ngar 牙 *n. tooth*
ngar 瓦 *n. watt*
ngar ba 啞巴 *n. mute*
ngar fai 瓦塊 *n. slate*
ngar giew 鴉叫 *v. i. caw*
ngar giew seng 鴉叫聲 *n. caw*
ngar kek biew yeen 啞劇表演 *n. mime*
ngar kek yeen yoon 啞劇演員 *n. mummer*
ngar ku 牙箍 *n brace*
ngar mar bo 亞麻布 *n. linen*
ngar mar jee 亞麻子 *n. linseed*
ngar meen 瓦面 *n. roof*
ngar peen 鴉片 *n. opium*
ngar tung 牙痛 *n. toothache*
ngar yee 牙醫 *n dentist*
ngar yuk 牙肉 *n. gum*
ngarm 啱 *a. true*
ngarm ngarm 啱啱 *adv. just*
ngat been 壓扁 *v.t. squash*
ngat bik jeh 壓迫者 *n. oppressor*
ngat dow 壓倒 *v.t. outnumber*
ngat dow 壓倒 *v.i. prevail*
ngat jay 壓制 *v.t muzzle*
ngat jay 壓制 *v.t. oppress*
ngat jay 壓制 *n. oppression*
ngat jay 壓制 *n. repression*
ngat jay 壓制 *v.t. stifle*
ngat jay geh 壓制嘅 *a. oppressive*
ngat lik 壓力 *n. pressure*
ngat lik 壓力 *n. stress*

ngat wan 押韻 n. rhyme
ngat wan 押韻 v.i. rhyme
ngat yan 壓印 n. imprint
ngay gey 危機 n crisis
ngay gorn 桅杆 n. mast
ngay gwan jee 偽君子 n. hypocrite
ngay heem 危險 n. danger
ngay heem 危險 a dangerous
ngay heem 危險 n. hazard
ngay heem 危險 n. insecurity
ngay heem 危險 n. jeopardy
ngay heem 危險 n. peril
ngay heem geh 危險嘅 a. perilous
ngay heem geh 危險嘅 a. risky
ngay jing juy 偽證罪 n. perjury
ngay jo 偽造 v.t forge
ngay jo ban 偽造品 n forgery
ngay jorng 偽裝 n disguise
ngay jow geh 偽造嘅 a. spurious
ngay kap 危及 v. t. endanger
ngay lik 毅力 n. perseverance
ngay sut 藝術 n. art
ngay sut ga 藝術家 n. artist
ngay sut geh 藝術嘅 a. artistic
ngay yan 矮人 n. midget
ngok toon 樂團 n. band
ngor 我 pron. I
ngor 我 pron. me
ngor day 我哋 pron. our
ngor geh 我嘅 pron. mine
ngor geh 我嘅 a. my
ngor jee gey 我自己 pron. myself
ngor po 臥鋪 n bunk
ngow 牛 n bull
ngow 牛 n. cattle
ngow 牛 n. cow
ngow 牛 n. ox
ngow jay fu 牛仔褲 n. jean
ngow pang 牛棚 n byre
ngow tow hoon 牛頭犬 n bulldog
ngow yow 牛油 n butter
ngow yuk 牛肉 n beef

ngoy 愛 v.t. adore
ngoy 愛 n. endearment
ngoy 愛 v.t. love
ngoy been geh 外邊嘅 a. outer
ngoy biew 外表 n appearance
ngoy biew 外表 n. guise
ngoy for yee sang 外科醫生 n. surgeon
ngoy gan 愛緊 a. loving
ngoy gao 外交 n diplomacy
ngoy gao geh 外交嘅 a diplomatic
ngoy gao gwun 外交官 n diplomat
ngoy gwok geh 外國嘅 a foreign
ngoy gwok geh 愛國嘅 a. patriotic
ngoy gwok jeh 愛國者 n. patriot
ngoy gwok jing san 愛國精神 n. partiotism
ngoy gwok yan 外國人 a. alien
ngoy gwok yan 外國人 n foreigner
ngoy ho 愛好 n. liking
ngoy ho jeh 愛好者 n buff
ngoy ho jeh 愛好者 n devotee
ngoy hok 外殼 n. husk
ngoy horng 外行 n. layman
ngoy horng geh 外行嘅 n lay
ngoy loy yan 外來人 n. outsider
ngoy meen 外面 adv outward
ngoy meen geh 外面嘅 a external
ngoy mo 愛慕 n. adoration
ngoy ting 愛情 n love
ngoy tow 外套 n. jacket
ngoy tow 外套 n. overall
ngoy way geen juk 外圍建築 n. outhouse
ngoy yee lan geh 愛爾蘭嘅 a. Irish
ngoy yee lan yan 愛爾蘭人 n. Irish
ngoy ying 外型 n. outline

O

oh 鉤 *n. hook*
oh 嘔 *v.t. vomit*
oh 嘔 *n vomit*
oh jeurng 偶像 *n. idol*
oh jow dai luk geh 歐洲大陸嘅 *a continental*
oh may ga 歐米加 *n. omega*
oh wan wuy 奧運會 *n. olympiad*
oi dow 哀悼 *v. i. condole*
ok 惡 *a ferocious*
ok 惡 *a fierce*
ok ba 惡霸 *n bully*
ok duk 惡毒 *a. nefarious*
ok duk geh 惡毒嘅 *a evil*
ok duk geh 惡毒嘅 *a. malicious*
ok fa 惡化 *v. i compound*
ok far 惡化 *v.t. sour*
ok geh 顎嘅 *a. palatal*
ok geh 惡嘅 *a. savage*
ok hang 惡行 *n. infamy*
ok hang 惡行 *n. misdeed*
ok hay 樂器 *n. instrument*
ok hay ga 樂器家 *n. instrumentalist*
ok hay yeen jow 樂器演奏 *a. instrumental*
ok jok kek 惡作劇 *n. hoax*
ok jok kek 惡作劇 *n mischief*
ok jok kek 惡作劇 *n. prank*
ok jok kek 惡作劇 *n. roguery*
ok ming 惡名 *n. notoriety*
ok mor 惡魔 *n fiend*
ok mung 惡夢 *n. nightmare*
ok sing 惡性 *n. malignancy*
ok sing geh 惡性嘅 *a. malignant*
ok tow 惡臭 *n. stench*
ok tow 惡臭 *n stink*
ok yee 惡意 *n. malice*
ok yee 惡意 *n. malignity*

ok yee geh 惡意嘅 *a. wanton*
ok yu 鱷魚 *n crocodile*
on 岸 *n. shore*
on (puy) 安(培) *n ampere*
on choon 安全 *a. safe*
on choon 安全 *n. safety*
on choon geh 安全嘅 *a. secure*
on fu 安撫 *v.t. appease*
on fu 安撫 *v.t. conciliate*
on gam 按金 *n. deposit*
on jiew 按照 *adv. accordingly*
on jing 安靜 *a. tranquil*
on jing geh 安靜嘅 *a. peaceful*
on jorng 安裝 *v.t. install*
on jorng 安裝 *n. installation*
on jorng see fu 安裝師傅 *n fitter*
on mor 按摩 *n. massage*
on mor 按摩 *v.t. massage*
on mor see 按摩師 *n. masseur*
on pai 安排 *v.t. arrange*
on pai 安排 *n. arrangement*
on pai 安排 *v. t conduct*
on pai 安排 *v.t. organize*
on pai 安排 *v.t. schedule*
on see 安士 *n. ounce*
on sik yat 安息日 *n. sabbath*
on wan kuk 安魂曲 *n. requiem*
on way 安慰 *v. t comfort*
on way 安慰 *n consolation*
on way 安慰 *v. t console*
on way 安慰 *v.t. solace*
on way 安慰 *n. solace*
or 鵝 *n. goose*
or 哦 *v.t. nag*
or liew 屙尿 *v.i. urinate*
or liew 屙尿 *n. urination*
ow da 毆打 *v.t. assault*
oy diew 哀悼 *v.i. mourn*
oy diew 哀悼 *n. mourning*

P

pa 爬 *v.i climb*
pa 爬 *v. t crawl*
pa 爬 *v. i creep*
pa 爬 *v.i. scramble*
pa 爬 *n scramble*
pa cho 怕醜 *a. bashful*
pa go 爬高 *n. ascent*
pa hang dung mat 爬行動物 *n. reptile*
pa jee 怕擮 *a. ticklish*
pa lo por 怕老婆 *a. henpecked*
pa san ga 爬山家 *n alpinist*
pa seep 跋涉 *v.i. wade*
pa tow 爬頭 *v.t. overtake*
pa tow 怕醜 *n. shy*
pa tow 怕醜 *v.i. shy*
pai 派 *n faction*
pai 派 *v.i. issue*
pai 排 *n. platoon*
pai 牌 *n. sign*
pai 牌 *n. tag*
pai 牌 *n. licence*
pai ban see 排版師 *n. compositor*
pai beet 派別 *n. sect*
pai beet geh 派別嘅 *a factious*
pai cheurng 排場 *n. pomp*
pai duy 派對 *n. party*
pai jee 牌子 *n brand*
pai jee 牌子 *n make*
pai ju 派駐 *v.t. station*
pai leen 排練 *v.t. rehearse*
pai leet forng sik 排列方式 *n. permutation*
pai sing yat horng 排成一行 *v.i. file*
pai suy 排水 *n drainage*
pai suy gwun 排水管 *n. culvert*
pai suy gwun 排水管 *n drain*
pai suy hay tung 排水系統 *n. sewerage*
pai tik 排斥 *v.t. ostracize*
pai tik 排斥 *a outcast*
pai yam mow 派任務 *v.t. task*
pai yan 派人 *v.t. post*
pak 拍 *v. i bat*
pak 拍 *v. t cuff*
pak 泊 *v.t. park*
pak 拍 *v.t. pat*
pak 拍 *n pat*
pak 拍 *v.t. whack*
pak dong 拍檔 *n co-partner*
pak dorng 拍檔 *n. partner*
pak jee 拍子 *n beat*
pak mai 拍賣 *n auction*
pak mai 拍賣 *v.t. auction*
pak seng 啪聲 *n. smack*
pak shu 柏樹 *n cypress*
pak sow 拍手 *v. i. clap*
pak tor 拍拖 *v. t date*
pan 噴 *v.i. spout*
pan 噴 *v.t. spray*
pan 噴 *v.i. spurt*
pan chut 噴出 *v. t. eject*
pan chut 噴出 *v.i. puff*
pan dang 攀登 *v. i clamber*
pan dang 攀登 *n. climb*
pan dang 攀登 *v.t. scale*
pan hay sik fay gey 噴氣式飛機 *n. jet*
pan ho suy 噴口水 *v. t beslaver*
pan hoot 貧血 *n anaemia*
pan jay 噴劑 *n. spray*
pan kung 貧窮 *n. poverty*
pan kwan 貧困 *n. privation*
pan lut 頻率 *n. frequency*
pan man fat 貧民窟 *n. slum*
pan suy tee 噴水池 *n. fountain*
pan yoon jik mat 攀緣植物 *n creeper*
pang 嘭 *n. bam*
pang 棚 *n shed*
pang ga 棚架 *n. scaffold*

pang jik gog geh 憑直覺嘅 a. intuitive
pang uk 棚屋 a. shanty
pang uk 棚屋 n. wigwam
pang yow 朋友 n. friend
pang yow 朋友 n. mate
pang yow 朋友 n. pal
pao 豹 n. leopard
pao 刨 v.t. plane
pao 跑 v.i. run
pao bo 跑步 n. run
pao choy 泡菜 n. pickle
pao hay 拋棄 v. t. desert
pao hay 拋棄 v.t. slough
pao lap sap 拋垃圾 v.t. litter
pao pao 泡泡 n bubble
pao sow 跑手 n. runner
par day 趴低 v.t. prostrate
par day geh 趴低嘅 a. prostrate
pay 批 n batch
pay 皮 n. leather
pay 皮 n. peel
pay 脾 n. spleen
pay dai 皮帶 n belt
pay fat 批發 n. wholesale
pay fat 批發 a wholesale
pay fat 批發 adv. wholesale
pay fat seurng 批發商 n. wholesaler
pay fu 皮膚 n. cutis
pay fu 皮膚 n. skin
pay fu hak geh 皮膚黑嘅 a. swarthy
pay gak chorng 皮革廠 n. tannery
pay geen 披肩 n. cape
pay geen 被肩 n. shawl
pay gu 屁股 n buttock
pay hay 脾氣 n. temper
pay jun 批准 v.t approbate
pay jun 批准 n. approval
pay jun 批准 v.t. approve
pay jun 批准 v.t. authorize
pay jun 批准 v.t. license
pay jun 批准 n. permission

pay lo 疲勞 n fatigue
pay pa 琵琶 n. lute
pay ping 批評 n. censure
pay ping 批評 n criticism
pay ping 批評 v. t criticize
pay ping 批評 v.t. rebuke
pay ping 批評 n. rebuke
pay ping 批評 n. reproach
pay ping ga 批評家 n critic
pay see 鄙視 n contempt
pay see 鄙視 n disdain
pay see 鄙視 n. scorn
pay see 鄙視 v.t. scorn
pay seurng 砒霜 n arsenic
pay tan 皮疹 a. rash
peen fuk 蝙蝠 n bat
peen geen 偏見 n. prejudice
peen gik 偏激 a extreme
peen guk 騙局 n deception
peen guk 騙局 n fiddle
peen guk 騙局 n trick
peen ho 編號 v.t. number
peen jee 騙子 n. cheat
peen jee 騙子 n. fraud
peen jee 騙子 n. impostor
peen jee 騙子 n. sharper
peen jee 騙子 n. trickster
peen jeh 騙子 n. swindler
peen kap 遍及 v.t. pervade
peen kap 遍及 adv. throughout
peen kek 編劇 n dramatist
peen lay 偏離 v. i deviate
peen lay 偏離 n deviation
peen leen see 編年史 n. chronicle
peen sam 偏心 n bias
peen she 編寫 v. t compile
peen tan 偏袒 n. partiality
peen tan geh 偏袒嘅 a. partisan
peen top 編輯 n editor
peen top geh 編輯嘅 a editorial
peen tow tung 偏頭痛 n. migraine
peen yoon geh 偏遠嘅 a. remote

peet chuy 撇除 *v. t* exclude

peet ho 撇號 *n.* apostrophe

pek 劈 *v.t.* hew

pek 劈 *v.t.* slash

pek 劈 *n* slash

peng 平 *a* cheap

peng for 平貨 *n.* bargain

pi lee pa la 劈里啪啦 *v.t.* crackle

piew 漂 *v.i* float

piew 票 *n.* ticket

piew bak suy 漂白水 *v. t* bleach

piew dorng 漂蕩 *v.t.* waft

piew dung 飄動 *n* flutter

piew ga 票價 *n* fare

piew ga 票價 *n* fee

piew geh 漂嘅 *a.* natant

pik ho 癖好 *n.* proclivity

pik pak 噼拍 *n. & v. i* clack

ping dang 平等 *n* equality

ping dang 平等 *n.* parity

ping day 平地 *n.* plain

ping fan 平凡 *a.* banal

ping fan 平分 *v. t* bisect

ping fan geh 平凡嘅 *a.* mundane

ping forng 平房 *n* bungalow

ping forng 平方 *v.t.* square

ping ga 評價 *v.t.* appraise

ping ga 評價 *n.* assessment

ping ga 評價 *n* review

ping geh 平嘅 *a* even

ping geh 平嘅 *a* flat

ping geh 平嘅 *n* flat

ping geh 平嘅 *a* level

ping geh 平嘅 *a.* plane

ping gu 評估 *v.t.* assess

ping gu 評估 *v. t* evaluate

ping gu 評估 *v.t.* rate

ping gwan sow 平均數 *n.* mean

ping gwor 蘋果 *n.* apple

ping gwun 平均 *a.* average

ping gwun so 平均數 *n.* average

ping gwun way 平均爲 *v.t.* average

ping hang 平衡 *v.t.* balance

ping hang geh 平行嘅 *a.* parallel

ping hang say gok ying 平行四角型 *n.* parallelogram

ping jing 平靜 *n.* calm

ping jing 平靜 *v.t.* quiet

ping jing 平靜 *n.* serenity

ping jing 平靜 *n.* tranquility

ping jing geh 平靜嘅 *a.* pacific

ping jing geh 平靜嘅 *a.* serene

ping lun 評論 *n* comment

ping lun 評論 *n* commentary

ping lun 評論 *n* editorial

ping lun yoon 評論員 *n* commentator

ping man 平民 *n* civilian

ping man 平民 *n.* commoner

ping man bak sing 平民百姓 *n.* populace

ping man geh 平民嘅 *a* civil

ping man say bo 平紋細布 *n.* muslin

ping meen 平面 *n* plane

ping mok 屏幕 *n.* screen

ping see 平時 *a.* usual

ping see gam 平時咁 *adv.* ordinarily

ping seurng 平常 *a.* casual

ping sik 平息 *v.t.* pacify

ping yam geh 拼音嘅 *a.* phonetic

ping yee gan yan 平易近人 *a.* amiable

po 抱 *v. t.* embrace

po day ban 鋪地板 *v.t* floor

po gung ying 蒲公英 *n.* dandelion

po mut 泡沫 *n* foam

po peen geh 普遍嘅 *a.* commonplace

po peen geh 普遍嘅 *a.* general

po poeen 普遍 *a.* widespread

po tee joon 鋪瓷磚 *v.t.* tile

po tow tong 葡萄糖 *n.* glucose

po tung 普通 *a.* ordinary

po tung geh 普通嘅 *a.* workaday

po way 鋪位 *n* berth

po yoon 抱怨 *v. t* cavil

pok 撲 *n. lunge*

pok 撲 *v.i lunge*

pok sik 撲熄 *v.t extinguish*

pok so 樸素 *a. austere*

pok sow 樸素 *n. rusticity*

pong been 旁邊 *n. aside*

pong dai 龐大 *a bulky*

pong gwong 膀胱 *n bladder*

pong lo 旁路 *n bypass*

por gow 破舊 *a. threadbare*

por gow geh 破舊嘅 *a. shabby*

por leet 破裂 *n. rupture*

por leet 破裂 *v.t. rupture*

por por ma ma 婆婆媽媽 *a maudlin*

por por ma ma 婆婆媽媽 *a. mawkish*

por shoon 破損 *n breakage*

por tan 破產 *n. bankrupt*

por tan 破產 *n. bankruptcy*

por tan 破產 *n. insolvency*

por wai 破壞 *v. t. corrupt*

por wai 破壞 *v. t. damage*

por wai 破壞 *v. t destroy*

por wai 破壞 *v.t. mar*

por wai 破壞 *v.t. ruin*

por wai 破壞 *v.t. spoil*

por wai 破壞 *v.i. tamper*

por wai 破壞 *n. wrack*

por wai 破壞 *v.t. wreck*

por wai geh 破壞嘅 *a. subversive*

por wai jeh 破壞者 *n. wrecker*

porng bak 旁白 *n. narration*

porng ban jeh 旁白者 *n. narrator*

porng dai geh 龐大嘅 *a mammoth*

porng gwun jeh 旁觀者 *n. on-looker*

pow 鋪 *a. lay*

pow 抱 *v.i. nestle*

pow 鋪 *v.t. pave*

pow bat ping geh 抱不平嘅 *a. malcontent*

pow mwun yow yeen 鋪滿油煙 *v.t. soot*

pow mwut 泡沫 *n. lather*

pow peen 普遍 *n. prevalence*

pow peen geh 普遍嘅 *a. prevalent*

pow peen sing 普遍性 *n. universality*

pow tow tang 葡萄藤 *n. vine*

pow tung 普通 *n. mediocrity*

pow tung geh 普通嘅 *a standard*

pow tung ghe 普通嘅 *a. mediocre*

pow tung yan 普通人 *n mortal*

pung 砰 *v.i. thud*

pung jorng 碰撞 *v. i. collide*

pung jorng 碰撞 *n collision*

pung jorng 碰撞 *n crash*

pung seng 砰聲 *n. thud*

pwun 盆 *n. basin*

pwun 盤 *n. tray*

pwun doon 判斷 *n estimation*

pwun doon 判斷 *v.i. judge*

pwun doon 判斷 *n. judgement*

pwun gwok juy 叛國罪 *n. treason*

pwun juy 判罪 *n conviction*

pwun koot 判決 *v.t. sentence*

pwun loon 叛亂 *n. insurrection*

pwun loon geh 叛亂嘅 *a. insurgent*

pwun man 盤問 *n. inquisition*

pwun man 盤問 *v.t. probe*

pwun mow juy 判無罪 *v.t. acquit*

pwun shoon 盤算 *n. preoccupation*

pwut 潑 *v.i. splash*

pwut fwun 撥款 *n grant*

pwuy 賠 *v.t. recompense*

pwuy ak 配額 *n. quota*

pwuy ak 配額 *n. ration*

pwuy geem 佩劍 *n. sabre*

pwuy hap 配合 *a co-operative*

pwuy oh 配偶 *n. consort*

pwuy oh 配偶 *n. spouse*

pwuy sam toon 陪審團 *n. jury*

pwuy sam yoon 陪審員 *n. juror*

pwuy sam yoon 陪審員 *n. juryman*

pwuy seurng 賠償 *v.t compensate*

pwuy seurng 賠償 *n compensation*

pwuy seurng 賠償 *n. recompense*
pwuy seurng 賠償 *n redress*
pwuy seurng 賠償 *n. repayment*
pwuy sow 倍數 *n multiple*
pwuy wuy 徘徊 *v.i. linger*
pwuy wuy 徘徊 *v.i. loiter*
pwuy wuy 徘徊 *v.t. maunder*

S

sa 沙 *n. sand*
sa 灑 *v.t. scatter*
sa 灑 *v. t. sprinkle*
sa geh 沙嘅 *a. sandy*
sa jap sa 耍雜耍 *v.t. juggle*
sa jeen 沙展 *n. sergeant*
sa lut 沙律 *n. salad*
sa mok 沙漠 *n desert*
sa mok geh luk jow 沙漠嘅綠洲 *n. oasis*
sa ngar 沙啞 *a. husky*
sa sek fwuy 傻石灰 *v.t lime*
sa tan 沙灘 *n beach*
sa yu 鯊魚 *n. shark*
sai 曬 *n brag*
sai 曬 *v.i. sport*
sai 嘥 *v.t. squander*
sai 嘥 *v.t. waste*
sai choon jorng 細村莊 *n. hamlet*
sai geh 嘥嘅 *a. profligate*
sai hak 曬黑 *v.i. tan*
sai hay geh 嘥氣嘅 *adv. vainly*
sai lik gey 晒力嘅 *a. onerous*
sai meng 曬命 *v.i boast*
sai meng 曬命 *n boast*
sai see geh 世事嘅 *a. worldly*
sai tai yeurng 曬太陽 *v.i. bask*
sai tai yeurng 曬太陽 *v.t. sun*
sai yu 細雨 *n drizzle*

sak 塞 *v.t. jam*
sak 塞 *v.t. silt*
sam 衫 *n. attire*
sam 衫 *n. clothes*
sam 衫 *n clothing*
sam 深 *a. deep*
sam 衫 *n. garment*
sam 心 *n. heart*
sam 三 *n. three*
sam 三 *a three*
sam cha 審查 *n. censorship*
sam cha gwun 審查官 *n. censor*
sam chu 深處 *n abyss*
sam dow 深度 *n depth*
sam dow 深度 *n. profundity*
sam fu kap 深呼吸 *n. gasp*
sam gao tung 心絞痛 *n angina*
sam gap 心急 *a eager*
sam geh 深嘅 *a. profound*
sam geurt ga 三腳架 *n. tripod*
sam gey 審計 *v.t. audit*
sam gey yoon 審計員 *n. auditor*
sam gok jow 三角洲 *n delta*
sam gok ying 三角形 *n. triangle*
sam gok ying 三角形 *a. triangular*
sam gor 三個 *a. triplicate*
sam gor bo fan 三個部份 *a. triple*
sam gor yam 三個人 *n. trio*
sam guk 深谷 *n. ravine*
sam gway 心悸 *n. palpitation*
sam hang 深坑 *n. pit*
sam ho 心口 *n chest*
sam hoot loy tiew 心血來潮 *n. whim*
sam hung sik 深紅色 *n crimson*
sam jee leen 甚至連 *adv even*
sam jorng geh 心臟嘅 *adjs cardiacal*
sam jow 衫袖 *n sleeve*
sam lam 森林 *n forest*
sam lam geh 森林嘅 *a. sylvan*
sam lay hok 心理學 *n. psychology*
sam lay hok ga 心理學家 *n. psychologist*

sam lay jee liew 心裡治療 *n.*
psychotherapy
sam ling 心靈 *n. psyche*
sam ling 心靈 *n. soul*
sam ling gam ying 心靈感應 *n.*
telepathy
sam ling gam ying geh 心靈感應嘅 *a.*
telepathic
sam ling gam ying jeh 心靈感應者 *n.*
telepathist
sam ling geh 心靈嘅 *a. psychological*
sam ling geh 心靈嘅 *a. spiritual*
sam lun cher 三輪車 *n. tricycle*
sam man 審問 *v.t. interrogate*
sam man 審問 *n. interrogation*
sam man jee 三文治 *n. sandwich*
sam ngoy geh 深愛嘅 *a beloved*
sam ngoy geh yan 心愛嘅人 *n*
beloved
sam ping hay wor 心平氣和 *adj.*
amicable
sam pwuy 三倍 *v.t., triple*
sam pwuy 三倍 *v.t. triplicate*
sam san 審慎 *n. prudence*
sam san geh 審慎嘅 *a. prudent*
sam sap 三十 *n. thirty*
sam sap 三十 *a thirty*
sam see geh 深思嘅 *a. meditative*
sam see suk luy 深思熟慮 *n*
deliberation
sam sik geh 三色嘅 *a. tricolour*
sam sik kay 三色旗 *n tricolour*
sam sun 審訊 *n. inquest*
sam sun 審訊 *n. trial*
sam ta 審查 *n. audit*
sam tai 心態 *n. mentality*
sam tee 三次 *adv. thrice*
sam ting 心情 *n. mood*
sam ting geh 深情嘅 *a. affectionate*
sam way yat tay 三位一體 *n. trinity*
sam yap 滲入 *v.i. seep*
sam ying 心形 *adj. cordate*

sam yoot 三月 *n. March*
san 身 *n body*
san 閂 *v. t close*
san 神 *n. deity*
san 山 *n. hill*
san 腎 *n. kidney*
san 山 *n. mount*
san 山 *n. mountain*
san 新 *a. new*
san 閂 *v.t. shut*
san 拴 *n. tether*
san 鋅 *n. zinc*
san bay geh 神祕嘅 *a. mysterious*
san bay geh 神祕嘅 *a. mystic*
san bay geh 神祕嘅 *a. occult*
san bay geh 神祕嘅 *a. secretive*
san bay ju yee 神主義意 *n.*
mysticism
san bay ju yee jeh 神祕主義者 *n*
mystic
san bo 散佈 *v. t bestrew*
san bo 散步 *n ramble*
san bo 散步 *v.i. stroll*
san bo 散步 *n stroll*
san bo 散步 *n walk*
san bor 散播 *n bruit*
san bow 散佈 *v.i. struggle*
san cheurng sow 神槍手 *n.*
marksman
san chuy 刪除 *v. t delete*
san chuy 刪除 *v. t erase*
san deng 山頂 *n. summit*
san dung 山洞 *n. cave*
san fan 身分 *n. identity*
san fan jing ming 身分證明 *n.*
indentification
san fat chut 散發出 *v. t emit*
san fat chut 散發出 *v.t. radiate*
san fu 辛苦 *a. laborious*
san fu 辛苦 *a. laboured*
san fu 神父 *n. priest*

san fu gam jow yeh 辛苦咁做嘢 *v.i.* slave

san fu geh 辛苦嘅 *a. painstaking*

san fu geh 辛苦嘅 *a. strenuous*

san fu jik way 神父職位 *n. priesthood*

san fu jow 辛苦做 *v.i. toil*

san fuk 臣服 *v.t. subject*

san ging 神經 *n. nerve*

san ging for yee sang 神經科醫生 *n. neurologist*

san ging hok 神經學 *n. neurology*

san gow 身高 *n. stature*

san guk 山谷 *n dale*

san guk 山谷 *n. vale*

san guk 山谷 *n. valley*

san hok 神學 *n divinity*

san hok ga 神學家 *n. theologian*

san hok geh 神學嘅 *a. theological*

san ja shu 山楂樹 *n. hawthorn*

san jeen 刪剪 *v. t. censor*

san jek 山脊 *n. ridge*

san jung 慎重 *adj. circumspect*

san kay geh 神氣嘅 *a. miraculous*

san koon jing jee 神權政治 *n. theocracy*

san lat 辛辣 *n. pungency*

san leurng 新娘 *n bride*

san lo 山路 *n. defile*

san long 新郎 *n. bridegroom*

san lorng 新郎 *n. groom*

san man 散漫 *n. laxity*

san man 新聞 *n. news*

san man 散文 *n. prose*

san man ga 散文家 *n essayist*

san man yeep 新聞業 *n. journalism*

san mo guy 山毛櫸 *n. beech*

san ngar 新芽 *n sprout*

san see 紳士 *n. gentleman*

san see seurng 新思想 *n. innovation*

san seen 新鮮 *a. fresh*

san sek hay see doy geh 新石器時代 嘅 *a. neolithic*

san sing 拴繩 *v.t. tether*

san sing bat hor tam fan 神聖不可侵 犯 *a. sacrosanct*

san sing far 神聖化 *n. sanctification*

san sing far 神聖化 *v.t. sanctify*

san sing geh 神聖嘅 *a divine*

san sing geh 神聖嘅 *a. holy*

san sing geh 神聖嘅 *a. sacred*

san sing geh 神聖嘅 *n. sanctity*

san sow 新手 *n. novice*

san suk 伸縮 *v. t contract*

san tan doy jeh 新陳代謝 *n. metabolism*

san tay geh 身體嘅 *a bodily*

san tay geh 身體嘅 *a corporal*

san tay geh 身體嘅 *a. physical*

san ting 申請 *v.t. apply*

san ting biew 申請表 *n. application*

san ting joon lay 申請專利 *v.t. patent*

san ting yan 申請人 *n. applicant*

san ting yan 申請人 *n. candidate*

san wah 神話 *n. myth*

san wah 神話 *n. mythology*

san wah geh 神話嘅 *a. mythical*

san wah geh 神話嘅 *a. mythological*

san wing 新穎 *n. novelty*

san wing geh 新穎嘅 *a. novel*

san wu 珊瑚 *n coral*

san wuy 晨會 *n. assembly*

san yam seng 呻吟聲 *n groan*

san yan 新人 *n. recruit*

san yeurk geh 孱弱孱弱 *a. puny*

san yeurng 山羊 *n. goat*

san ying 身形 *n figure*

sang 生 *v.t. grow*

sang 省 *n. province*

sang chiew 生肖 *n zodiac*

sang choon 生存 *n. survival*

sang choon 生存 *v.i. survive*

sang choy 生菜 *n. cabbage*

sang geh 生嘅 *a. live*
sang geh 生嘅 *a. living*
sang geh 省嘅 *a. provincial*
sang geh 生嘅 *a. raw*
sang gey 生計 *n. livelihood*
sang gey 生計 *n living*
sang gwor 生果 *n. fruit*
sang jik geh 生殖嘅 *a. reproductive*
sang mat 生物 *n being*
sang mat 生物 *n creature*
sang mat 生物 *n. organism*
sang mat 生物 *n. wight*
sang mat hok 生物學 *n biology*
sang mat hok ga 生物學家 *n biologist*
sang ming 生命 *n life*
sang ngar 生牙 *v.i. teethe*
sang sow 生鏽 *v.i rust*
sang sow 生鏽 *a. rusty*
sang tan 生產 *v.t. produce*
sang tan lut 生產率 *n. productivity*
sang wut jun teep 生活津貼 *n. stipend*
sang yee 生意 *n business*
sang yee yan 生意人 *n businessman*
sang yuk lik 生育力 *n fertility*
sao bing 哨兵 *n. sentinel*
sao bing 哨兵 *n. sentry*
sao may yeem 稍微染 *v.t. tint*
sap 濕 *a damp*
sap 十 *n., a ten*
sap 濕 *a. wet*
sap 濕 *v.t. wet*
sap bat 十八 *a eighteen*
sap day 濕地 *n. marsh*
sap day geh 濕地嘅 *a. marshy*
sap dow 濕度 *n. humidity*
sap dow 濕度 *n. wetness*
sap gey suy 十幾歲 *n. pl. teens*
sap gow 十九 *n. nineteen*
sap jee ga 十字架 *n cross*
sap jee ga 十字架 *n. rood*

sap jee gan 濕紙巾 *n. wipe*
sap jun way 十進位 *a decimal*
sap leen 十年 *n decade*
sap leep 十年 *n. decennary*
sap luk 十六 *n., a. sixteen*
sap ng 十五 *n fifteen*
sap sai 濕晒 *v. t drench*
sap sai 濕晒 *v.t. saturate*
sap sai 濕晒 *n. soak*
sap sam 十三 *n. thirteen*
sap sam 十三 *a thirteen*
sap say horng see 十四行詩 *n. sonnet*
sap sey 十四 *n. fourteen*
sap tat 十七 *n., a seventeen*
sap yat 十一 *n eleven*
sap yat yoot 十一月 *n. November*
sap yee yoot 十二月 *n december*
sap yeet 十二 *n. twelve*
sap yik 十億 *n billion*
sap yoot 十月 *n. October*
sap yun geh 濕潤嘅 *a. moist*
sar ngar 沙啞 *a. hoarse*
sat 塞 *v. t cram*
sat 蚤 *n. flea*
sat 殺 *v.t. kill*
sat 殺 *n. kill*
sat 蝨 *n. louse*
sat 殺 *v.t. sabre*
sat 殺 *v.t. slay*
sat bai 失敗 *adv abortive*
sat bai 失敗 *v. t bungle*
sat bai 失敗 *n defeat*
sat bai 失敗 *v.i fail*
sat bai 失敗 *n failure*
sat chung jay 殺蟲劑 *n. insecticide*
sat chung jay 殺蟲劑 *n. pesticide*
sat chung jay 殺蟲劑 *n repellent*
sat fu mow juy 殺父母罪 *n. parricide*
sat hao 失效 *v.t. vitiate*

sat hing day jee mwuy juy 殺兄弟姊妹罪 n. fratricide

sat hing day jeh 殺兄弟者 n cain

sat hm 失誤 n bungle

sat huy gworng jak 失去光澤 v.t. tarnish

sat jay geh 實際嘅 a. practical

sat jay hang dung 實際行動 n. practice

sat jik 失職 n. misconduct

sat joy geh 實在嘅 a. tangible

sat jung 失蹤 n disappearance

sat kwan jay 殺菌劑 n. germicide

sat lay 失禮 a discourteous

sat loy 室內 adv. indoors

sat loy 室內 n. interior

sat loy geh 室內嘅 a. indoor

sat loy geh 室內嘅 a. interior

sat meen 失眠 a. wakeful

sat ming 失明 n blindness

sat morng 失望 v. t. disappoint

sat morng 失望 v.i. lament

sat mun 塞滿 2 v.t. stuff

sat see 實施 n. imposition

sat tay 實體 n entity

sat ter 刹車 n brake

sat ter 刹車 v. t brake

sat tiew 失調 n disorder

sat tiew 失調 n. mal adjustment

sat tow gor 膝頭哥 n. knee

sat yan hung sow 殺人兇手 n. murderer

sat yan juy 殺人罪 n. homicide

sat yeem 實驗 n experiment

sat yeem sat 實驗室 n. laboratory

sat yeen 實現 v.t. materialize

sat yik 失憶 n amnesia

sat ying juy 殺嬰罪 n. infanticide

sat yung geh 實用嘅 a. pragmatic

sat yung geh 實用嘅 a. utilitarian

sat yung ju yee 實用主義 n. pragmatism

sat yung sing 實用性 n. practicability

say 死 a dead

say 死 v. i decease

say 細 a. little

say 死 v.i. perish

say 篩 n. sieve

say 篩 v.t. sieve

say 篩 v.t. sift

say 細 adv. smallness

say 洗 v.t. wash

say 洗 n wash

say 西 n. west

say 使 v.t. spend

say ban geh 死板嘅 a. rigid

say ban ngar geh 西班牙嘅 a. Spanish

say ban ngar leep gow 西班牙獵狗 n. spaniel

say ban ngar yan 西班牙人 n. Spaniard

say ban ngar yan 西班牙人 n. Spanish

say bao 細胞 n. cell

say bao geh 細胞嘅 adj cellular

say bo lay gwun 細玻璃管 n. cuvette

say dam 細膽 a. timid

say dam 細膽 a. timorous

say day jeen 細地氊 n. mat

say day jeen 細地氊 n. rug

say doy 細袋 n. pouch

say fan yam fu 四分音符 n. crotchet

say fan yat 四份一 n. quarter

say for 死火 v.t. stall

say forng 西方 n. occident

say forng 西方 a. western

say forng geh 西方嘅 a. occidental

say forng geh 西方嘅 a. west

say forng geh 西方嘅 a. westerly

say forng ying 四方形 n. square

say forng ying geh 四方形嘅 a square

say forng yoon 四方院 *n. quadrangle*
say gan geh 世間嘅 *a. temporal*
say gao tong 細教堂 *n. chapel*
say geep 洗劫 *v.t. ransack*
say geh 細嘅 *a. small*
say gey 世紀 *n. century*
say gey ngang bwuy 死記硬背 *n. rote*
say gok ying 四角型 *a. & n. quadrilateral*
say gok ying geh 四角型嘅 *a. quadrangular*
say gwa 西瓜 *n. water-melon*
say hap 細盒 *n casket*
say ho geh 死後嘅 *a. posthumous*
say ho geh 死後嘅 *a. post-mortem*
say jeet 細節 *n detail*
say jeet 細節 *n. particular*
say jeurng 誓章 *n affidavit*
say jorng 西裝 *n. suit*
say juk dung mat 四足動物 *n. quadruped*
say ka mok 西卡莫 *n. sycamore*
say kan 西芹 *n. leek*
say lan far 西蘭花 *n. broccoli*
say lap 細粒 *a. tiny*
say lay 洗禮 *n. baptism*
say lay geh 勢利嘅 *v snobbish*
say lay gway 勢利鬼 *n. snob*
say leng jay 死仔 *n. thug*
say lo 細路 *n. bantling*
say lo jai 細路仔 *n child*
say low 死路 *n. impasse*
say low jay 細路仔 *n. infant*
say low jay 細佬仔 *a. infantile*
say low jay 細佬仔 *n. kid*
say low jay 細路仔 *n. youngster*
say low jay pay hay 細路仔脾氣 *n. petulance*
say lung 細窿 *n. puncture*
say luy gwun 細旅館 *n. inn*
say ma 細馬 *n. pony*

say mao 細貓 *n. kitten*
say may tar beet 細微差別 *n. nuance*
say morng 死亡 *n death*
say morng 死亡 *n decease*
say morng lut 死亡率 *n. mortality*
say ngan yik 洗眼液 *n eyewash*
say ngow 犀牛 *n. rhinoceros*
say pay 洗牌 *n. shuffle*
say pwuy geh 四倍嘅 *a. quadruple*
say sarm 洗衫 *n. laundry*
say say dam sik 細細啖食 *v.t. nibble*
say say dam yam 細細啖飲 *v.t. sip*
say say dam yam 細細啖飲 *v.i. sup*
say seng 細聲 *n coo*
say seng 細聲 *n. undertone*
say seng geh 細聲嘅 *a. quiet*
say seng gorng 細聲講 *n whisper*
say sing 細繩 *n cord*
say sow 世仇 *n. feud*
say sow gan 洗手間 *n. lavatory*
say sow pwun 洗手盤 *n sink*
say tan 細鏟 *n. trowel*
say torng 洗燙 *v.t. launder*
say tow 洗頭 *v.t. shampoo*
say tow suy 洗頭水 *n. shampoo*
say yee gey 洗衣機 *n. washer*
say yee hay 洗耳器 *n. aurilave*
say yee luy gung 洗衣女工 *n. laundress*
say yeen 誓言 *n. oath*
say yeurk jun 細藥樽 *n. phial*
say ying geh 死刑嘅 *a. capital*
see 事 *n. ado*
see 試 *v.t. delibate*
see 事 *n favourl*
see 事 *n. happening*
see 事 *n. incident*
see 事 *n. matter*
see 詩 *n. poem*
see 詩 *n. poesy*
see 試 *n. taste*

see 試 *v.t. taste*
see 試 *v.t. test*
see 試 *v.i. try*
see ba la 士巴拿 *n. spanner*
see ban 私奔 *v. i elope*
see bing 士兵 *n. soldier*
see bing 士兵 *n. troop*
see dai 絲帶 *n. ribbon*
see dor 士多 *n. store*
see dor beh lay 士多啤梨 *n. strawberry*
see doy 時代 *n epoch*
see doy 時代 *n era*
see fan 示範 *v. t demonstrate*
see fan 示範 *n. demonstration*
see fat 司法 *n. judicature*
see fat 司法 *a. judicial*
see fat koon 司法權 *n. jurisdiction*
see fay 施肥 *v.t. manure*
see fu juy 弒父罪 *n. patricide*
see gan 時間 *n. time*
see gao 市郊 *n.pl. outskirts*
see geh 詩嘅 *a. poetic*
see gey 司機 *n. chauffeur*
see gey 司機 *n driver*
see gok geh 視覺嘅 *a. visual*
see gwan juy 弒君罪 *n. regicide*
see gworng 絲光 *v.t. mercerize*
see gwun 史官 *n. annalist*
see gwun 使館 *n embassy*
see gwun gwun yoon 使館館員 *n. attache*
see hao 思考 *n. mull*
see hao 思考 *n. rumination*
see har 試下 *v.t. sample*
see hay 士氣 *n. morale*
see ho 嗜好 *n. hobby*
see hok 詩學 *n. poetics*
see hoy 撕開 *v.t. tear*
see jan 市鎮 *n. town*
see jap 詩集 *n. poetry*
see jee 獅子 *n lion*

see jee geh 獅子嘅 *a leonine*
see jee jor 獅子座 *n. Leo*
see jeet 詩節 *n. verse*
see jeurng 市長 *n. mayor*
see jing geh 市政嘅 *a. municipal*
see jorng 時裝 *n fashion*
see kay 時期 *n. period*
see lan 撕爛 *v.t. rip*
see lan 撕爛 *v.t tatter*
see leep 獅鬣 *n. mane*
see leet 撕裂 *n. avulsion*
see lik 視力 *n. sight*
see lik 視力 *n. vision*
see ling 司令 *n. admiral*
see ling 司令 *n commandant*
see low 司爐 *n. stoker*
see lut 詩律 *n. versification*
see man 市民 *n citizen*
see mat 絲襪 *n. stocking*
see ming gam 使命感 *n. calling*
see ming gam 使命感 *n. vocation*
see mo chu 事務處 *n. bureau*
see morng mok 視網膜 *n. retina*
see mow geh 弒母嘅 *a. matricidal*
see mow juy 弒母罪 *n. matricide*
see ngar geh 嘶啞嘅 *a. throaty*
see ngat 施壓 *v.t. pressurize*
see sang geh 私生嘅 *a. illegitimate*
see sang jee 私生子 *n. bastard*
see sat 事實 *n fact*
see see seng 嘶嘶聲 *n hiss*
see see seng 嚇嚇聲 *n. sizzle*
see seen 事先 *adv. beforehand*
see seurng ga 思想家 *n. thinker*
see sseurng 時尚 *n cult*
see tai 時態 *n. tense*
see tat 視察 *v.t. inspect*
see tay 屍體 *n corpse*
see teen geh 史前嘅 *a. prehistoric*
see ting 私情 *n amour*
see tow 絲綢 *n. silk*
see tun 私吞 *v.t. misappropriate*

see way 視爲 *v.t. regard*
see yan 時人 *n. bard*
see yan 詩人 *n. poet*
see yan 私隱 *n. privacy*
see yan geh 私人嘅 *a. personal*
see yan geh 私人嘅 *a. private*
see yee yoon 市議員 *n. councillor*
see ying 侍應 *n. waiter*
see ying chu say 私刑處死 *v.t. lynch*
see yung 絲絨 *n. velvet*
see yung geh 絲絨嘅 *a. velvety*
see yung kay 試用期 *n. probation*
seem 閃 *v. i. dash*
seem 閃 *v.t flash*
seem 閃 *n flicker*
seem 閃 *v.i. glitter*
seem 閃 *n. scintillation*
seem 閃 *v.i. sparkle*
seem 閃 *n. sparkle*
seem 閃 *v.i. twinkle*
seem deen 閃電 *n. lightening*
seem geh 閃嘅 *a. shiny*
seem gwong 閃光 *n flash*
seem ha 閃閃下 *v.t flicker*
seem lap 閃粒 *n glitter*
seem leurng 閃亮 *n. twinkle*
seem yam 閃人 *v.i flee*
seen 仙 *n cent*
seen 腺 *n. gland*
seen 線 *n. line*
seen 癬 *n. ringworm*
seen 跣 *v.i. skid*
seen 跣 *n. slip*
seen 跣 *a. slippery*
seen 線 *n. thread*
seen been 善變 *a. capricious*
seen cheurng 擅長 *n. adept*
seen deet 跣跌 *v.i. slip*
seen dow hm seen ha 仙都唔仙下 *a. penniless*
seen dung 煽動 *v.t. instigate*
seen dung 煽動 *n. instigation*

seen dung bwun loon geh tee 煽動叛亂嘅詞 *n. sedition*
seen dung sing geh 煽動性嘅 *a. seditious*
seen fat jay yan 先發制人 *v.t forestall*
seen geen jee ming 先見之明 *n foresight*
seen hung sik 鮮紅色 *n. vermillion*
seen hung sik geh 鮮紅色嘅 *a. vermillion*
seen jee tam yap 擅自侵入 *v.i. trespass*
seen kow 線毯 *n. clew*
seen kuy 先驅 *n. precursor*
seen lay 先例 *n. precedent*
seen leurng 善良 *adj benign*
seen leurng 善良 *a kind*
seen leurng gam 善良咁 *adv benignly*
seen leurng gam 善良咁 *adv. kindly*
seen ling 先令 *n. shilling*
seen lo 線路 *n. circuit*
seen low 線路 *n. wiring*
seen luy 仙女 *n. nymph*
seen mo 羨慕 *v envy*
seen sam 善心 *n benevolence*
seen sang 先生 *n. Messrs*
seen sang 先生 *n. mister*
seen sang 先生 *n. sir*
seen yan jeurng 仙人掌 *n. cactus*
seen yee 善意 *n. goodwill*
seen yeurng fey 贍養費 *n. alimony*
seen yu 先於 *v. precede*
seep kap 涉及 *v. t concern*
seep see 攝氏 *a. centigrade*
seep way 楔位 *v.t. wedge*
seep ying 攝影 *n. photography*
seep ying geh 攝影嘅 *a. photographic*
seep ying see 攝影師 *n. photographer*
seet 楔 *n. wedge*
seet juk 褻瀆 *n. sacrilege*
seet juk 褻瀆 *a. sacrilegious*

seet juk san ling 褻瀆神靈 *v.t. profane*

seet juk san ling geh 褻瀆神靈嘅 *a. profane*

seh 蛇 *n. serpent*

seh 蛇 *n. snake*

seh 瀉 *n spill*

seh day 寫低 *v.t. jot*

seh day 寫低 *v.t. note*

seh gan gai 寫簡介 *v.t. profile*

seh gao 社交 *n. sociability*

seh gik 射擊 *n. shot*

seh jee low 寫字樓 *n. office*

seh meen 赦免 *v.t. assoil*

seh wuy 社會 *n. community*

seh wuy 社會 *n. society*

seh wuy day way 社會地位 *n caste*

seh wuy geh 社會嘅 *n. social*

seh wuy hok 社會學 *n. sociology*

seh wuy ju yee 社會主義 *n socialism*

seh wuy ju yee jeh 社會主義者 *n,a socialist*

seh ying 射影 *v.t shadow*

sek 錫 *n. kiss*

sek 錫 *v.t. kiss*

sek 錫 *n. peck*

sek fwuy 石灰 *n. lime*

sek fwuy suy 石灰水 *n. whitewash*

sek gwun 石棺 *n cist*

sek jeurng 石匠 *n. mason*

sek jeurng 石像 *n. statue*

sek lap 石蠟 *n. paraffin*

sek meen 石棉 *n. asbestos*

sek tow 石頭 *n. rock*

sek tow 石頭 *n. stone*

sek yow 石油 *n. petroleum*

seng 醒 *v.t. awake*

seng 醒 *a awake*

seng 聲 *n. noise*

seng 聲 *n sound*

seng 聲 *n. voice*

seng 醒 *v.t. wake*

seng geh 聲嘅 *a. vocal*

ser 寫 *v.t. write*

ser heurng 麝香 *n. musk*

ser juy 寫序 *v.t. preface*

ser meen 赦免 *v.t. pardon*

ser wuy wan ging 社會環境 *n matrix*

ser yeurk 瀉藥 *a laxative*

ser yeurk 瀉藥 *n. purgative*

seurk yeurk 削弱 *v.t. & i weaken*

seurng 雙 *pref bi*

seurng 上 *v. t. board*

seurng 箱 *n box*

seurng 箱 *n. case*

seurng 箱 *n. casing*

seurng 雙 *a dual*

seurng 鑲 *v.t. frame*

seurng 霜 *n. frost*

seurng 傷 *n. injury*

seurng 相 *n photo*

seurng 相 *n photograph*

seurng 相 *n snap*

seurng 上 *prep upon*

seurng 傷 *n. wound*

seurng ak 上軛 *v.t. yoke*

seurng ban 鑲板 *n. panel*

seurng ban 鑲板 *v.t. panel*

seurng bao toy jee yat 雙胞胎之一 *n. twin*

seurng bay 相比 *a comparative*

seurng bay 傷悲 *n. melancholy*

seurng been 鑲邊 *v.t border*

seurng beet 想必 *adv. surely*

seurng chun tang 常春藤 *n ivy*

seurng dang yan 上等人 *n. gentry*

seurng dang yu 相等於 *v. t equate*

seurng dang yu 相等於 *a equivalent*

seurng day 上帝 *n. god*

seurng day 上帝 *n. godhead*

seurng day 上帝 *n. providence*

seurng dong dai geh 相當大嘅 *a considerable*

seurng dow 想鬥 *a bellicose*

seurng fan 相反 *a contrary*

seurng fan 相反 *n reverse*

seurng fan geh 相反嘅 *a. reverse*

seurng fat 想法 *n. idea*

seurng forng 雙方 *a both*

seurng ga 上架 *v.t. shelve*

seurng gam 傷感 *a. wistful*

seurng gao 上校 *n. colonel*

seurng geen 常見 *a. common*

seurng geh 上嘅 *a. upper*

seurng gey 相機 *n. camera*

seurng gok 雙角嘅 *adj. biangular*

seurng gwan 相關 *n. correlation*

seurng gwan yu 雙關語 *n. pun*

seurng har man 上下文 *n context*

seurng hm 上午 *n forenoon*

seurng ho 傷口 *n cut*

seurng hon 傷寒 *n. typhoid*

seurng hoy 傷害 *v.t harm*

seurng hoy 傷害 *v.t. injure*

seurng hoy 傷害 *v.t. wound*

seurng jee 想知 *v.i. wonder*

seurng jeurng 想像 *v. t conceive*

seurng jeurng 想像 *v.t. picture*

seurng jeurng 想像 *v.t. visualize*

seurng jeurng ha 想像下 *v.t. imagine*

seurng jeurng lik 想像力 *n. imagination*

seurng jor 上咗 *adv aboard*

seurng jow 上晝 *n. morning*

seurng kap 上級 *n. senior*

seurng kuk geh 雙軸嘅 *adj biaxial*

seurng leen 相連 *v.t. interlock*

seurng leen 相連 *a twin*

seurng leen 上鏈 *v.t. wind*

seurng leen beng 上鏈柄 *n. winder*

seurng lor see 上螺絲 *v.t. screw*

seurng luk geh 常綠嘅 *a evergreen*

seurng luk shu 常綠樹 *n evergreen*

seurng ma 上馬 *n mount*

seurng meen 上面 *prep. above*

seurng meen 上面 *prep. over*

seurng meen 上面 *n. top*

seurng meen 上面 *adv. upwards*

seurng mong 傷亡 *n bloodshed*

seurng ngon 上岸 *adv. ashore*

seurng pwuy geh 雙倍嘅 *a double*

seurng sam 傷心 *v.t. grieve*

seurng sam 傷心 *a. sad*

seurng san 上身 *n bodice*

seurng see 嘗試 *v.t. attempt*

seurng see 嘗試 *n. attempt*

seurng see 嘗試 *n endeavour*

seurng see 嘗試 *n try*

seurng sing loon 雙性戀 *adj. bisexual*

seurng so 上訴 *n. appeal*

seurng so yan 上訴人 *n. appellant*

seurng sow 商數 *n. quotient*

seurng tee 相似 *a. analogous*

seurng tee 相似 *n. likeness*

seurng tee dow 相似度 *n. parallelism*

seurng tee dow 相似度 *n. similarity*

seurng tee dow 相似度 *n. similitude*

seurng ting tat 上清漆 *v.t. varnish*

seurng tow 商討 *v. i confer*

seurng tow wuy 商討會 *n consultation*

seurng tung 相同 *a. alike*

seurng tung geh 相同嘅 *a equal*

seurng way 上尉 *n. lieutenant*

seurng yan 上癮 *v.t. addict*

seurng yan 商人 *n. merchant*

seurng yan 商人 *n. monger*

seurng yan 商人 *n. trader*

seurng yan 商人 *n. tradesman*

seurng yan jeh 上癮者 *n. addict*

seurng yeen 上演 *v.t. stage*

seurng yeep geh 商業嘅 *a commercial*

seurng yeep geh 商業嘅 *a. mercantile*

seurng yiew 想要 *v.t. want*

seurng yiew 想要 *n want*

seurng yow 上油 *v.t. lubricate*

seurng yow 上油 *v.t oil*

seurng yu 雙語 *a bilingual*

seurng yu 相遇 *v. t encounter*

sey 死 *v. i die*

sey 四 *n. four*

sey gai 世界 *n. world*

sey kwun 細菌 *n. bacteria*

sey sap 四十 *n. forty*

she 寫 *v.t. pen*

she 射 *v.t. shoot*

shoon 酸 *n acid*

shoon 船 *n boat*

shoon 選 *v. t elect*

shoon 船 *n. ship*

shoon 酸 *a. sour*

shoon bo 宣佈 *v.t. announce*

shoon bo 宣佈 *n. announcement*

shoon bo 宣佈 *v. t. declare*

shoon bo 宣佈 *v.t. proclaim*

shoon bo 宣佈 *n. herald*

shoon bo forng hay 宣佈放棄 *v.t. renounce*

shoon bo forng hay 宣佈放棄 *n. renunciation*

shoon choon 宣傳 *v. t. endorse*

shoon choon 宣傳 *v.t. popularize*

shoon choon 宣傳 *v.t. promote*

shoon choon 宣傳 *n. promotion*

shoon choon 宣傳 *n. propaganda*

shoon choon 宣傳 *n. propagation*

shoon choon 宣傳 *v.t. publicize*

shoon choon jeh 宣傳者 *n. propagandist*

shoon chor 算錯 *v.t. miscalculate*

shoon chorng 船艙 *n. cabin*

shoon fan 船帆 *n. sail*

shoon fung 旋風 *n. cyclone*

shoon fung 旋風 *n. whirlwind*

shoon geh 船嘅 *a. nautic(al)*

shoon guy 選舉 *n. vote*

shoon ho 損耗 *n. wastage*

shoon hoy 損害 *n blight*

shoon hoy 損害 *n. harm*

shoon hoy 損害 *v.t. jeopardize*

shoon jak 選擇 *n. choice*

shoon jak 選擇 *n. option*

shoon jak 選擇 *n. pick*

shoon jak 選擇 *n. selection*

shoon jap 選集 *n. anthology*

shoon jeurng 船槳 *n. oar*

shoon jeurng 船槳 *n paddle*

shoon jeurng 船長 *n. skipper*

shoon jik 船跡 *n wake*

shoon joon 旋轉 *v.t. pivot*

shoon joon 旋轉 *n whirl*

shoon joon muk ma 旋轉木馬 *n. whirligig*

shoon kuy 選區 *n constituency*

shoon kuy 選舉 *n election*

shoon lay tap 宣禮塔 *n. minaret*

shoon lut 旋律 *n. melody*

shoon man 選民 *n. constituent*

shoon may 酸味 *a acid*

shoon may bay choy 選美比賽 *n. pageant*

shoon ngoy 船外 *adv. overboard*

shoon piew 選票 *n ballot*

shoon pwun yow juy 宣判有罪 *v. t. convict*

shoon sat 損失 *v.t. cost*

shoon sat 損失 *n. loss*

shoon shoon 宣傳 *n. publicity*

shoon sing 酸性 *n. acidity*

shoon sut 算術 *n. arithmetic*

shoon sut geh 算術嘅 *a. arithmetical*

shoon ting 宣稱 *n claim*

shoon wai 損壞 *n. damage*

shoon wai 損壞 *n. ravage*

shoon wor 旋渦 *n. whirlpool*

shoon yeen 宣言 *n. manifesto*

shoon yeurng 宣揚 *v.i. preach*

shoon yeurng 宣揚 *v.i. trumpet*

shoon yoon 船員 *n. sailor*

shoon yung 蒜蓉 *n. garlic*
shoot 雪 *n. snow*
shoot gao 說教 *v.i. sermonize*
shoot gway 雪櫃 *n. fridge*
shoot gway 雪櫃 *n. refrigerator*
shoot ka 雪茄 *n. cigar*
shoot ka yeen 雪茄煙 *n cheroot*
shoot lay 雪泥 *n. slush*
shoot ming shu 說明書 *n manual*
shoot wah mo wu 說話模糊 *a equivocal*
shu 書 *n book*
shu 輸 *v.t. lose*
shu 樹 *n. tree*
shu bao 書包 *n. satchel*
shu chung 書蟲 *n book-worm*
shu chung 雪松 *n. cedar*
shu chung 樹叢 *n. thicket*
shu dun 樹墩 *n. stump*
shu fat 書法 *n calligraphy*
shu forng 書房 *n. study*
shu fuk 舒服 *n. comfort1*
shu fuk 舒服 *a comfortable*
shu fuk 舒服 *n. snug*
shu gey ju gao 樞機主教 *n. cardinal*
shu goon 書卷 *n scroll*
shu jay 薯仔 *n. potato*
shu jay lay 薯仔泥 *n. mash*
shu jee 樹枝 *n branch*
shu jee 樹枝 *n. twig*
shu jing gwun teet chuy sow sut 輸精管切除手術 *n. vasectomy*
shu kam 豎琴 *n. harp*
shu kwang 豎框 *n. mullion*
shu lam 樹林 *n. woods*
shu lam 樹林 *n. woodland*
shu lan 樹懶 *n. sloth*
shu lay 樹籬 *n. hedge*
shu meen ming ling 書面命令 *n. writ*
shu muk peen ju jeh 書目編著者 *n bibliographer*

shu pay 樹皮 *n. bark*
shu seurng 書商 *n book-seller*
shu sik 舒適 *a. cosy*
shu sik 舒適 *a. cozy*
shu teem 書籤 *n. book-mark*
shu ting geh 抒情嘅 *a. lyric*
shu ting geh 抒情嘅 *a. lyrical*
shu toy 書枱 *n desk*
shu wun 舒緩 *v. t ease*
shu yap 輸入 *v.t key*
shuy suy gwun 輸水管 *n aqueduct*
si see 史詩 *n epic*
siem chuy 蟾蜍 *n. toad*
siew 燒 *v. t burn*
siew 燒 *n burn*
siew 笑 *v. i chuckle*
siew 燒 *v.i flare*
siew 笑 *n. laugh*
siew 笑 *v.i laugh*
siew 笑 *v.i. mock*
siew 笑 *v.i. smile*
siew 笑 *n. smile*
siew beng 小病 *n. ailment*
siew beng 笑柄 *n. mockery*
siew bo fai pao 小步快跑 *n trot*
siew bo fan 小部份 *n. fraction*
siew buk bo 小瀑布 *n. cascade*
siew bwuy 燒杯 *n beaker*
siew cho 小丑 *n buffoon*
siew cho 小丑 *n clown*
siew chuy 消除 *v. t efface*
siew chuy 消除 *n. removal*
siew duk 消毒 *n. sterilization*
siew duk 消毒 *v.t. sterilize*
siew duy 小隊 *n. squad*
siew fan 小販 *n hawker*
siew fan 小販 *n. vendor*
siew far 消化 *v. t. digest*
siew far 消化 *n digestion*
siew far bat leurng 消化不良 *n. indigestion*
siew fay 消費 *n consumption*

siew fay 消費 *n expenditure*

siew fay suy 消費稅 *n excise*

siew gam ling 宵禁令 *n curfew*

siew gan 燒緊 *adv. aflame*

siew gan 燒緊 *v.i. alight*

siew gwor duk geh 消過毒嘅 *a. antiseptic*

siew gwun 小罐 *n. canister*

siew hay geh 小器嘅 *a. stingy*

siew heen 消遣 *n. pastime*

siew heen wut dung 消遣活動 *n. recreation*

siew ho 消耗 *v. t consume*

siew ho leurng 消耗量 *n consumption*

siew hok sang 小學生 *n. junior*

siew hok sang geh 小學生嘅 *a. junior*

siew hong 小巷 *n. alley*

siew jeh 小姐 *n. miss*

siew kay 小溪 *n. beck*

siew kay 小溪 *n. brook*

siew kay 小溪 *n. creek*

siew kay 小溪 *n. stream*

siew kay 小溪 *n. streamlet*

siew leen 少年 *n. youth*

siew leep hoon 小獵犬 *n. terrier*

siew leurng 少量 *n lick*

siew leurng 少量 *n. little*

siew leurng 少量 *n. morsel*

siew leurng 少量 *n. paucity*

siew leurng geh 少量嘅 *n. modicum*

siew leurng geh jow 少量嘅酒 *n dram*

siew low 小路 *n. lane*

siew low 小路 *n. path*

siew lung 燒燶 *v.t. scorch*

siew lung 燒燶 *v.t. singe*

siew luy 少女 *n. damsel*

siew luy 少女 *n. wench*

siew mak 小麥 *n far*

siew mak 小麥 *n. wheat*

siew meet 消滅 *v.t. obliterate*

siew meet 消滅 *n. obliteration*

siew mor see gan 消磨時間 *v.t. while*

siew ping 燒瓶 *n flask*

siew sam 小心 *a careful*

siew sat 消失 *v. i disappear*

siew sat 消失 *v.i. vanish*

siew say 消逝 *v. t elapse*

siew seen luy 小仙女 *n fairy*

siew seng 笑聲 *n. laughter*

siew seurng 燒傷 *n singe*

siew shoot 小說 *n fiction*

siew shoot 小說 *n novel*

siew shoot ga 小說家 *n. novelist*

siew siew 少少 *adv. little*

siew siew 少少 *a. scant*

siew siew 少少 *a. sightly*

siew siew 少少 *n. tinge*

siew siew juy 少少醉 *a. tipsy*

siew siew may 少少味 *n. whiff*

siew sik 消息 *n. pl. tidings*

siew sow 少數 *n. handful*

siew sow 少數 *n less*

siew sow 少數 *n. minority*

siew tak jee 小冊子 *n booklet*

siew tak yeem 小測驗 *n. quiz*

siew tan 小產 *n. miscarriage*

siew tan 小產 *v.i. miscarry*

siew tay kam 小提琴 *n. violin*

siew tay kam ga 小提琴家 *n. violinist*

siew tiew 小潮 *a. neap*

siew tuy 小腿 *n. calf*

siew tuy 小腿 *n. shin*

siew uk 小屋 *n. cote*

siew uk 小屋 *n cottage*

siew uk 小屋 *n. lodge*

siew wah 笑話 *n. gag*

siew wah 笑話 *n. jest*

siew wah 笑話 *n. joke*

siew wan 小環 *n annulet*

siew way yan jee geh 少爲人知嘅 *a. obscure*

siew yam hay 消音器 *n. silencer*

siew yeh 宵夜 *n. supper*

siew yiew fat ngoy 逍遙法外 *adv. scot-free*

siew ying geh 小型嘅 *a. miniature*

siew yow 小丘 *n. hillock*

siew yu 少於 *prep below*

siew yu 少於 *adv under*

sik 骰 *n. dice*

sik 食 *v. t eat*

sik cho 食草 *v.i. graze*

sik dak 食得 *v.t. stomach*

sik dong 適當 *a. appropriate*

sik dong geh 適當嘅 *a. apt*

sik dong sing 適當性 *n advisability*

sik dor jung yu yeen geh yan 識多種 語言嘅人 *n. polyglot1*

sik dorng geh 適當嘅 *adv duly*

sik fan 食飯 *v. t. dine*

sik fan geh 適婚嘅 *a. marriageable*

sik forng 釋放 *v. t discharge*

sik fu yuk geh dung mat 食腐肉嘅動 物 *n. scavenger*

sik geh yan 識嘅人 *n. acquaintance*

sik hap 適合 *a. adequate*

sik hap 適合 *a. applicable*

sik hap 適合 *adj apposite*

sik hap 適合 *a congenial*

sik hap 適合 *a. suitable*

sik hap gang jung geh 適合耕種嘅 *adj arable*

sik hap geh 適合嘅 *a. opportune*

sik hap ju geh 適合住嘅 *a. habitable*

sik hap ju geh 適合住嘅 *a. inhabitable*

sik hap sing 適合性 *n. suitability*

sik jee 食指 *n forefinger*

sik leurng geh 適量嘅 *a. moderate*

sik lorng 色狼 *v.t. pervert*

sik mat 飾物 *n accessory*

sik mat 食物 *n food*

sik mat 事務 *n. sustenance*

sik mat sat 食物室 *n. pantry*

sik mow forng geh yan 識模仿嘅人 *n mimic*

sik muk geh 蝕木嘅 *a. xylophagous*

sik ngan 食晏 *v.i. lunch*

sik po 食譜 *n. recipe*

sik tong 食堂 *n. canteen*

sik yan juk 食人族 *n. androphagi*

sik yat geh 昔日嘅 *a former*

sik yee 適宜 *a. advisable*

sik yeen 食煙 *v.i. smoke*

sik yik 蜥蜴 *n. lizard*

sik ying 適應 *v.t acclimatise*

sik ying 適應 *v.t. adapt*

sik ying 適應 *v.t. orient*

sik ying lik keurng 適應力強 *adj. hardy*

sik yung 食用 *n. eatable*

sing 升 *v.t. ascend*

sing 乘 *v.t. multiply*

sing 升 *v. rise*

sing 繩 *n. rope*

sing 繩 *n. string*

sing 姓 *n. surname*

sing ban seurng 承辦商 *n contractor*

sing bay lay geh 成比例嘅 *a. proportional*

sing bay lay geh 成比例嘅 *a. proportionate*

sing beet 性別 *n. gender*

sing bo 城堡 *n. castle*

sing bo 城堡 *n. fortress*

sing cheurng 城牆 *n. rampart*

sing chuy heurng 性取向 *n. sexuality*

sing dam 承擔 *v.t. shoulder*

sing dan jeet 聖誕節 *n Christmas*

sing dan jeet 聖誕節 *n. Xmas*

sing day 聖地 *n. shrine*

sing fa 聖化 *v.t. consecrate*

sing for 星火 *n. spark*

sing forng 盛況 *n. pageantry*

sing fung 聖俸 *n benefice*

sing gak 性格 *n. personality*
sing gam 性感 *n. sexy*
sing gam geh 性感嘅 *a. nubile*
sing gam geh 性感嘅 *a seductive*
sing geet geh 聖潔嘅 *a. saintly*
sing geh 性嘅 *a. sexual*
sing geh 星嘅 *a. stellar*
sing ging 聖經 *n bible*
sing ging 聖經 *n. scripture*
sing gor 聖歌 *n. hymn*
sing gung 成功 *v.i. succeed*
sing gung 成功 *a successful*
sing gwor 勝過 *v.t. outdo*
sing gwor 勝過 *v.t. outshine*
sing hak 乘客 *n. passenger*
sing han 誠懇 *n. candour*
sing hang way 性行爲 *n. sex*
sing hay 星系 *n. galaxy*
sing ho 星號 *n. asterisk*
sing ho 成口 *n. mouthful*
sing jeurng 成長 *n. development*
sing jeurng 成長 *n. germination*
sing jow 成就 *n. accomplishment*
sing jow 成就 *n. achievement*
sing jow 成就 *n. attainment*
sing jow 成就 *n. success*
sing jow 成就 *n. triumph*
sing jow gam 成就感 *n. fulfilment*
sing kay luk 星期六 *n. Saturday*
sing kay ng 星期五 *n. Friday*
sing kay sam 星期三 *n. Wednesday*
sing kay say 星期四 *n. Thursday*
sing kay yat 星期一 *n. Monday*
sing kay yat 星期日 *n. Sunday*
sing kow 星球 *n. planet*
sing kwan 星群 *n. constellation*
sing kwun 星群 *n. asterism*
sing lap 成立 *v. t. establish*
sing lap 成立 *n establishment*
sing lay 聖禮 *n. sacrament*
sing lay 勝利 *n. victory*
sing lay geh 勝利嘅 *a. victorious*

sing lay jeh 勝利者 *n. victor*
sing leen 盛年 *n. prime*
sing leen yan 成年人 *n. adult*
sing lok 承諾 *v.t. pledge*
sing lok 承諾 *n promise*
sing lok 承諾 *n. vow*
sing ming 聲明 *v.t. avow*
sing ming 聲明 *n declaration*
sing ming 聲名 *n. proclamation*
sing ming lorng jik 聲名狼藉 *a. infamous*
sing ming lorng jik geh 聲名狼藉嘅 *a. notorious*
sing mo lang geh 性無能嘅 *a. impotent*
sing ngon yan 承按人 *n. mortagagee*
sing ngoy geh 性愛嘅 *a erotic*
sing sat 誠實 *a. honest*
sing sat 誠實 *n. honesty*
sing sat 誠實 *a. truthful*
sing sat 誠實 *n. veracity*
sing sat geh 誠實嘅 *adv bonafide*
sing see 城市 *n city*
sing see geh 城市嘅 *a civic*
sing see geh 城市嘅 *a. urban*
sing sing 猩猩 *n. gorilla*
sing sing 星星 *n. star*
sing sow 承受 *v.t bear*
sing sow 乘數 *n. multiplication*
sing sow yiew 性騷擾 *v.t. molest*
sing sow yiew 性騷擾 *n. molestation*
sing suk 成熟 *a adult*
sing suk 成熟 *v.i mature*
sing suk 成熟 *n. maturity*
sing suk 成熟 *v.i. ripen*
sing suk geh 成熟嘅 *a. mature*
sing ting 聲稱 *v.t. allege*
sing ting 聲稱 *v. t claim*
sing ting 聲稱 *v. i contend*
sing ting 聲稱 *v.t. profess*
sing tow 繩套 *n. noose*
sing wah 昇華 *v.t. sublimate*

sing wan 星雲 *n. nebula*
sing way gu yee 成爲孤兒 *v.t orphan*
sing wun 聲援 *v. t. champion*
sing yam geh 聲音嘅 *a. sonic*
sing yan 承認 *v.t. admit*
sing yan 承認 *v. t. confess*
sing yan 聖人 *n. saint*
sing yat 成日 *adv always*
sing yat ai sap 成日嗌諗 *a. quarrelsome*
sing yat chor geh 成日坐嘅 *a. sedentary*
sing yat huy geh day forng 成日去嘅 地方 *n haunt*
sing yat joon tai 成日轉軚 *v.i. vacillate*
sing yat yow 成日有 *a. stock*
sing ying 承認 *v. acknowledge*
sing ying 承認 *n. acknowledgement*
sing ying 承認 *v.t. concede*
sing yu 成語 *n. idiom*
sing yu 成語 *n. phrase*
sing yuk 性慾 *a. amorous*
siu hang sing 小行星 *adj. asteroid*
so 掃 *n brush*
so 數 *v. t. count*
so 瘦 *a. thin*
so bar 掃把 *n broom*
so fay 收費 *v. t. charge*
so fu 受苦 *v.t. suffer*
so jang 手踭 *n elbow*
so jap 收集 *v. t collect*
so jap ga 收集家 *n collector*
so jee 手指 *n finger*
so long 嗉囊 *n. craw*
so loon 騷亂 *n commotion*
so top 修葺 *v. t edit*
so way 數位 *n digit*
so yiew 騷擾 *v. t disturb*
sok jow 塑造 *v.t. mould*
sok jow 塑造 *v.t shape*
sok yan 索引 *n. index*

song fai 爽快 *n. alacrity*
song lay 喪禮 *n. funeral*
song ow 喪偶 *v.t. widow*
song sat 喪失 *v. t. bereave*
song sat tan yow 喪失親友 *n bereavement*
sor 梳 *n comb*
sor 鎖 *v.t handcuff*
sor 鎖 *n. lock*
sor 鎖 *v.t lock*
sor 梭 *n. shuttle*
sor bai 唆擺 *v.t. abet*
sor bai 唆擺 *n. abetment*
sor choy 蔬菜 *n. vegetable*
sor fa 梳化 *n. couch*
sor fa 梳化 *n. sofa*
sor fat 疏忽 *n. negligence*
sor fat 疏忽 *n. oversight*
sor fat geh 疏忽嘅 *a. negligent*
sor geh 傻嘅 *a. silly*
sor gwa 傻瓜 *n. simpleton*
sor low 傻佬 *n. pantaloon*
sor mun 鎖門 *v. t bolt*
sor san 疏散 *v. t evacuate*
sor san 疏散 *n evacuation*
sor see 鎖匙 *n. key*
sor suy 瑣碎 *a. trivial*
sor suy geh 瑣碎嘅 *a. petty*
sor yee 所以 *adv. so*
sor yee 所以 *conj. so*
sor yi 所以 *adv. therefore*
sor yi 所以 *adv. thus*
sor yoon 疏遠 *v.t. alienate*
sor yow 所有 *pron all*
sormo 梳毛 *v.t groom*
sorng sat 喪失 *n forfeiture*
sorng sat ming yu 喪失名譽 *n disrepute*
sorng shu 桑樹 *n. mulberry*
sow 收 *n. admission*
sow 手 *n hand*
sow 收 *v.t. receive*

sow 掃 v.i. sweep
sow 掃 n. sweep
sow 鬚 n. whisker
sow ak 數額 n amount
sow ak 手鈪 n. bangle
sow ak ngoy fay 收額外費 v.t. surcharge
sow an yoon 收銀員 n. cashier
sow ban 手板 n. palm
sow bay 手臂 n. arm
sow beng 手柄 n. handle
sow biew 手錶 n. watch
sow bo jeurng 修補匠 n. tinker
sow cheurng 手槍 n. pistol
sow doon 手段 n. artifice
sow dor teen 收多錢 v.t. overcharge
sow dor teen 收多錢 n overcharge
sow dow 首都 n. capital
sow dow 首都 n. metropolis
sow dow sang wut 修道生活 n monasticism
sow dung 騷動 n. pandemonium
sow dung 騷動 n. turmoil
sow dung 騷動 n unrest
sow dung 騷動 n. uproar
sow fay biew 收費表 n. tariff
sow for yoon 售貨員 n. salesman
sow fwun yan 收款人 n. payee
sow fwun ying 受歡迎 v.t endear
sow fwun ying dow 收歡迎度 n. popularity
sow fwun ying geh 受歡迎嘅 a. popular
sow gak lan geh 蘇格蘭嘅 a. scotch
sow gak lan way see gey 蘇格蘭威士忌 n. scotch
sow gak lan yan 蘇格蘭人 n. Scot
sow gan 手巾 n. handkerchief
sow gap 豆莢 n. pod
sow geen yan 收件人 n. addressee
sow geen yan 收件人 n. recipient
sow go 手稿 n. manuscript

sow got gey 收割機 n. havester
sow got gey 收割機 n. reaper
sow goy 修改 n alteration
sow goy 修改 v.t. amend
sow goy 修改 n. amendment
sow goy 修改 n.pl. amends
sow gung 手工 n. handiwork
sow gung ngay 手工藝 n. handicraft
sow han 仇恨 n animosity
sow han 仇恨 n enmity
sow han 仇恨 n. hate
sow ho 收好 v.t. stow
sow hok 數學 n mathematics
sow hok ga 數學家 n. mathematician
sow hok geh 數學嘅 a. mathematical
sow hoy jeh 受害者 n. victim
sow jap 收集 v.t. gather
sow jap 收集 v.t marshal
sow jee 數字 a. numeral
sow jee geh 數字嘅 a. numerical
sow jee gung 手指公 n. thumb
sow jeen 修剪 v.t. prune
sow jeen 修剪 n trim
sow jeen 修剪 v.t. trim
sow jing 受精 v.t fertilize
sow ju 數珠 n. rosary
sow juk jee ting 手足之情 n brotherhood
sow jun jeet mor 受盡折磨 v.t. rack
sow jung 訴訟 n. litigation
sow jung 訴訟 n. prosecution
sow koon 授權 v. t depute
sow koon 授權 v. t empower
sow koon tow piew 授權投票 v.t. enfranchise
sow koon yan 受權人 n. attorney
sow kow 手扣 n. handcuff
sow kow 手扣 n. shackle
sow kow jeh 收購者 n. suitor
sow lay 修理 n. repair
sow leen 手鏈 n bracelet
sow leurk 搜掠 v.i. rummage

sow leurng 數量 n. quantity

sow leurng geh 數量嘅 a. quantitative

sow ling 首領 n. chieftain

sow ling 守靈 n wake

sow loon 騷亂 n. riot

sow loon 騷亂 n. tumult

sow low dan 手榴彈 n. grenade

sow luy 修女 n. nun

sow luy yoon yoon jeurng 修女院院長 n. prioress

sow mai 收埋 v.t hide

sow mai hay sow ban 收埋係手板 v.t. palm

sow miew 掃描 v.t. scan

sow muk 數目 n toll

sow ngay 手藝 n craft

sow ngay 手藝 n. workmanship

sow peen jeh 受騙者 n gull

sow say 手勢 n. gesture

sow say 受洗 +v.t. baptize

sow seen 首先 adv first

sow seurng 受傷 v.t. hurt

sow seurng 首相 n premier

sow seurng sut 手相術 n. palmistry

sow seurng sut see 手相術士 n. palmist

sow sik 首飾 n. jewellery

sow sik geh 素食嘅 a vegetarian

sow sik jeh 素食者 n. vegetarian

sow sing 收成 n. harvest

sow sok 搜索 n browse

sow sok 搜索 n. search

sow sun 手信 n. souvenir

sow sut 手術 n. operation

sow sut 手術 n. surgery

sow suy 收稅 v.t. tax

sow ta 搜查 v.t. raid

sow tak 手冊 n brochure

sow tak 手冊 n. handbook

sow tak 手冊 n. pamphlet

sow tak jok jeh 手冊作者 n. pamphleteer

sow tam 搜尋 n rummage

sow tee 修辭 n. rhetoric

sow tee 羞恥 n. shame

sow tee 羞恥 v.t. shame

sow tee geh 首次嘅 a maiden

sow tok yan 受託人 n. assignee

sow tok yan 受託人 n. trustee

sow tow 手套 n. glove

sow way 守衛 v.i. guard

sow way 守衛 n. warder

sow way wat 受委屈 v.t. aggrieve

sow wok 收穫 v.t. reap

sow wu jeh 守護者 n. guardian

sow wun 手腕 n. wrist

sow yam 手淫 v.i. masturbate

sow yam gey 收音機 n. radio

sow yap 收入 n. income

sow yap 收入 n. proceeds

sow yee 壽衣 n. shroud

sow yee geh 獸醫嘅 a. veterinary

sow yeh 守夜 n. vigil

sow yeurng 收養 v.t. adopt

sow yeurng 收養 n adoption

sow yeurng yan 受養人 n dependant

sow yiew 騷擾 v.t. harass

sow yiew 騷擾 n. harassment

sow yiew geh 首要嘅 a. chief

sow yiew geh 首要嘅 a. premier

sow yiew joon 手搖鑽 n. wimble

sow ying 首映 n. premiere

sow yoon 修院 n. cloister

sow yuk 瘦肉 n. lean

sow yung 收容 v.t house

suk 熟 adj. conversant

suk 熟 a familiar

suk 粟 n. millet

suk doon 縮短 v.t abridge

suk fan 贖返 n. redemption

suk fong 縮放 n. zoom

suk fuk 馴服 v.t. tame

suk gam 贖金 *n. ransom*
suk geh 熟嘅 *a ripe*
suk jak 縮窄 *v.t. constrict*
suk jak 縮窄 *v.t. narrow*
suk leen 熟練 *a. adept*
suk leen geh 熟練嘅 *a. versed*
suk may 粟米 *n corn*
suk may 粟米 *n. maize*
suk may gao gwun 縮微膠卷 *n. microfilm*
suk ming lun 宿命論 *n. predestination*
suk say 縮細 *v.t. minimize*
suk say 縮細 *v.i shrink*
suk say 縮細 *n. shrinkage*
suk sik 熟悉 *a conversant*
suk sing 屬性 *n. attribute*
suk sow geh 熟手嘅 *a. proficient*
suk tung jing 縮瞳症 *n. myosis*
suk yu 屬於 *v. i belong*
suk yu 屬於 *v.t. subordinate*
suk yu 屬於 *v.t. vest*
sun 信 *v. t believe*
sun 信 *n letter*
sun 信 *n. missive*
sun 信 *v.t trust*
sun bai jeh 崇拜者 *n. worshipper*
sun chuk 迅速 *n. rapidity*
sun chuk geh 迅速嘅 *a. swift*
sun chung 順從 *a amenable*
sun chung 順從 *adj. complaisant*
sun chung 順從 *n. compliance*
sun chung 順從 *adj. compliant*
sun chung 順從 *v.t. toe*
sun chuung 順從 *v.i. acquiesce*
sun dak gwor 信得過 *a. trustful*
sun dak gwor 信得過 *a. trustworthy*
sun dak gwor geh 信得過嘅 *a. liable*
sun dak gwor geh 信得過嘅 *a. reliable*
sun fung 信封 *n envelope*
sun fung 信奉 *n. worship*

sun geet 純潔 *a. chaste*
sun geet 純潔 *n. purity*
sun geh 純嘅 *a pure*
sun ho 信號 *n. signal*
sun jiew wan geh yan 信招魂嘅人 *n. spiritualist*
sun jik 殉職 *n. martyrdom*
sun ju 順住 *prep. along*
sun leem 信念 *n creed*
sun leem 信念 *n faith*
sun leem 信念 *n. notion*
sun man 詢問 *v. t consult*
sun man 詢問 *n. inquiry*
sun sam 信心 *n confidence*
sun sik 訊息 *n. message*
sun suy ju yee jeh 純粹主義者 *n. purist*
sun tow 信徒 *n. apostle*
sun tow 信徒 *n disciple*
sun tow 信徒 *n. votary*
sun yam 唇音 *a. labial*
sun yam 信任 *n. trust*
sun yeurng 信仰 *n belief*
sun yow yee geh 純友誼嘅 *a. platonic*
sun yu 信譽 *n credit*
sung 送 *v. t deliver*
sung bai jeh 崇拜者 *n. idolater*
sung beet 送別 *interj. farewell*
sung bok 聳膊 *v.t. shrug*
sung bok 聳膊 *n shrug*
sung geh 鬆嘅 *a. loose*
sung ging 崇敬 *v.t. hallow*
sung go 鬆糕 *n. trifle*
sung gow geh 崇高嘅 *a. sublime*
sung gow geh see 崇高嘅事 *n sublime*
sung hoy 鬆開 *v.t. loose*
sung hoy 鬆開 *v.t. loosen*
sung jorng jeh 送葬者 *n. mourner*
sung sun yan 送信人呢 *n. messenger*
sung tee 鬆弛 *a flabby*
sung tee geh 鬆弛嘅 *a. slack*

sup yee 十二 *a. twelve*
sur *v.i. slide*
sur wat tay 滑梯 *n slide*
sut gao 摔跤 *v.i. wrestle*
sut gao shoonsow 摔跤選手 *n. wrestler*
sut jik 率直 *a. outspoken*
sut jik 率直 *a. straightforward*
sut sam 裇衫 *n. shirt*
sut see 術士 *n. sorcerer*
sut yu 術語 *n. terminology*
suy 碎 *adv. asunder*
suy 碎 *n crumb*
suy 碎 *v. t crumble*
suy 衰 *a. mean*
suy 碎 *v.t. splinter*
suy 稅 *n. tax*
suy 稅 *n. taxation*
suy 水 *n. water*
suy an 水銀 *n. mercury*
suy an 水銀 *n. quicksilver*
suy ba 水壩 *n dam*
suy bo 碎布 *n. tatter*
suy bo lay 碎玻璃 *n. cullet*
suy cho 水槽 *n. gutter*
suy diew 水貂 *n. mink*
suy dow cheet mey 衰到徹尾 *n. arrant*
suy fan 水分 *n. moisture*
suy far 水花 *n spray*
suy fu 水庫 *n. reservoir*
suy fuk 說服 *v. t convince*
suy fuk 說服 *v.t. persuade*
suy fuk lik 說服力 *n. persuasion*
suy fwun 稅款 *n. levy*
suy gak 衰格 *a. nasty*
suy gung 水工 *n. plumber*
suy gwun 水管 *n. hose*
suy ho 水候 *n. tap*
suy jam 水浸 *n flood*
suy jap 水閘 *n. sluice*
suy jat 水蛭 *n. leech*

suy jeng 水井 *n. well*
suy jik geh 垂直嘅 *a. perpendicular*
suy jik seen 垂直線 *n. perpendicular*
suy jing 水晶 *n crystal*
suy juk gwun 水族館 *n. aquarium*
suy keet 衰竭 *n. prostration*
suy kow 需求 *n demand*
suy lay 水泥 *n. cement*
suy lok 衰落 *v.i. wane*
suy low 水流 *n current*
suy luk leurng chay 水陸兩棲 *adj amphibious*
suy mat geh 水密嘅 *a. watertight*
suy ngow 水牛 *n. buffalo*
suy pao 水泡 *n blain*
suy pao 水泡 *n bleb*
suy pao 水泡 *n blister*
suy peen 碎片 *n. fragment*
suy peen 碎片 *n. scrap*
suy ping jor 水瓶座 *n. aquarius*
suy see geh 瑞士嘅 *a Swiss*
suy see yan 瑞士人 *n. Swiss*
suy seen far 水仙花 *n narcissus*
suy sek 碎石 *n. rubble*
suy sow 水手 *n. mariner*
suy sow 對手 *n. opponent*
suy tam 水窪 *n. puddle*
suy tung 水桶 *n bucket*
suy tuy 衰退 *v.i falter*
suy wu 水壺 *n. kettle*
suy yan 衰人 *a bastard*
suy yan 衰人 *n. villain*
suy yee 睡衣 *n. nightie*
suy yeen 雖然 *conj. although*
suy yeen 雖然 *prep. notwithstanding*
suy yeen 雖然 *conj. though*
suy yeurk 衰弱 *v. i ebb*
suy yeurk 衰弱 *v.i. lapse*
suy yiew 需要 *n. need*
suy yiew 需要 *adv. needs*
suy yiew 需要 *v.t. require*
suy yiew 需要 *n. requirement*

suy yiew geh 需要嘅 *a necessary*
suy yiew geh 需要嘅 *a. needful*
suy yiew geh yeh 需要嘅嘢 *n. acquirement*

T

ta 差 *a. bad*
ta 差 *adv. badly*
ta 搽 *v. t. daub*
ta 差 *adv. ill*
ta 搽 *v.t. smear*
ta 茬 *n. stubble*
ta 茶 *n tea*
ta ak 差額 *n. variance*
ta beet 差別 *n distinction*
ta deep 茶碟 *n. saucer*
ta geh see yan 差嘅詩人 *n. poetaster*
ta geh see yan 差嘅詩人 *n. rhymester*
ta heurng suy 搽香水 *v.t. perfume*
ta hm dor 差唔多 *adv. nearly*
ta ngow yow 搽牛油 *v. t butter*
ta yee 差異 *n disparity*
tai 踩 *v.t. conculcate*
tai 踩 *v.t. pedal*
tai 呔 *n tie*
tai 踩 *v.t. tread*
tai ba 柴把 *n faggot*
tai cheurng 太長 *a. interminable*
tai day 踩低 *v.t. abase*
tai day 踩低 *n abasement*
tai dow 態度 *n. attitude*
tai dow say lay 態度勢利 *n. snobbery*
tai duy 柴堆 *n. pyre*
tai fay torng 太妃糖 *n. toffee*
tai fwun 貸款 *n. loan*
tai fwun 貸款 *n. mortgage*

tai garm 太監 *n eunuch*
tai gwor 太過 *adv. too*
tai gwor gorng gow 太過講究 *a. pedantic*
tai gwor suy tam 踩過水漥 *v.t. puddle*
tai ho la 太好啦 *a fabulous*
tai ho la 太好啦 *a fantastic*
tai hung yan 太空人 *n. astronaut*
tai lorng 豺狼 *n. jackal*
tai see 差事 *n errand*
tai siew 太少 *a. meagre*
tai sun chung geh 太順從嘅 *a. servile*
tai suy 踩碎 *v.t. trample*
tai tak 猜測 *n conjecture*
tai tak 猜測 *n. guess*
tai yeurng 太陽 *n. sun*
tai yeurng geh 太陽嘅 *a. solar*
tai yeurng yoot 太陽穴 *n. temple*
tak 賊 *n burglar*
tak 賊 *n. dacoit*
tak 賊 *n. robber*
tak 賊 *n. thief*
tak chuy 拆除 *v. t. demolish*
tak leurk 策略 *n. manoeuvre*
tak leurk 策略 *n. stratagem*
tak leurk 策略 *n. tactics*
tak see 策士 *n. tactician*
tak see 測試 *n test*
tam 碳 *n. carbon*
tam 氹 *v. t coax*
tam 沈 *v.i drown*
tam 沈 *v.i. sink*
tam 痰 *n. sputum*
tam 氹 *v.t. wheedle*
tam chung gam hang 沈重咁行 *v.i. plod*
tam deen mat 沈澱物 *n. sediment*
tam fan 侵犯 *v.t. infringe*
tam fan 侵犯 *n. intrusion*
tam ga 參加 *v.t. join*

tam gow 探究 *n probe*
tam guy 寢具 *n. bedding*
tam gwun 痰罐 *n. spittoon*
tam gwun 參觀 *n. visit*
tam jeem 侵佔 *v. i encroach*
tam jeem 侵佔 *n. usurpation*
tam jung geh 沈重嘅 *a. massy*
tam koon 侵權 *v.t. usurp*
tam leurk 侵略 *v.t. invade*
tam leurk 侵略 *n. invasion*
tam leurk jeh 侵略者 *n. aggressor*
tam ma 蕁麻 *n. nettle*
tam mak geh 沈默嘅 *a. reticent*
tam mak gwa yeen 沈默寡言 *n. reticence*
tam mak gwa yeen 沈默寡言 *a. taciturn*
tam may 沈迷 *v.t. indulge*
tam may 沈迷 *n. obsession*
tam may 沈迷 *v.t. steep*
tam may jow sik geh 沈迷酒色嘅 *n. voluptuary*
tam mwun 沈悶 *a. leaden*
tam pwun 談判 *v.i parley*
tam pwun yan 談判人 *n. negotiator*
tam sam 貪心 *n cupidity*
tam sam 貪心 *a. greedy*
tam see geh 沈思嘅 *a. pensive*
tam shoon 沈船 *n. wreck*
tam sik 侵蝕 *v. t erode*
tam sik 侵蝕 *n erosion*
tam sok 探索 *v.t explore*
tam sok 探索 *n. quest*
tam sok 探索 *v.t. quest*
tam wu 貪污 *n. corruption*
tam yan 氹人 *v.t. amuse*
tam yap 侵入 *v.t. hack*
tam yat 尋日 *n. yesterday*
tam yat 尋日 *adv. yesterday*
tam yee yoon 參議院 *n. senate*
tam yee yoon 參議員 *n. senator*

tam yee yoon geh 參議員嘅 *a. senatorial*
tam yee yoon geh 參議員嘅 *a senatorial*
tam yeet jam 探熱針 *n. thermometer*
tam yuk 貪慾 *n. greed*
tam yuk 貪慾 *a. lustful*
tan 炭 *n coal*
tan 塵 *n dust*
tan 撢 *n duster*
tan 襯 *v.t. line*
tan 塵 *n. mote*
tan 鏟 *v.t. shovel*
tan 鏟 *n. spade*
tan 鏟 *v.t. spade*
tan 襯 *v.t. suit*
tan bak 坦白 *a. frank*
tan ban 產品 *n. produce*
tan ban 產品 *n. product*
tan bo hang way 殘暴行爲 *n cruelty*
tan bo hang way 殘暴行爲 *n. savagery*
tan chuy 鏟除 *v. t eradicate*
tan doon 診斷 *v. t diagnose*
tan doon 診斷 *n diagnosis*
tan far mat 碳化物 *n. carbide*
tan fay 殘廢 *a disabled*
tan gan 餐巾 *n. napkin*
tan geh 真嘅 *a. genuine*
tan hai 殘骸 *n debris*
tan hai 殘骸 *n. wreckage*
tan heurng yow 檀香油 *n. sandalwood*
tan huk 殘酷 *a. barbarous*
tan jat 殘疾 *n handicap*
tan jee 題字 *n. inscription*
tan jing geh 真正嘅 *a. authentic*
tan jing geh 真正嘅 *a. proper*
tan koon 產權 *n. ownership*
tan kwan 襯裙 *n. petticoat*
tan lan geh 燦爛嘅 *a. refulgent*
tan leurng 產量 *n yield*

tan low geh 殘留嘅 *a. residual*

tan low man jat 殘留物質 *n. residue*

tan mat 親密 *n. intimacy*

tan ngoi 親愛 *a dear*

tan pai 餐牌 *n. menu*

tan sai 殘晒 *a. worn*

tan sam 襯衫 *n blouse*

tan sang 產生 *v.t. generate*

tan seurng 真相 *n. truth*

tan shoon gap 碳酸鉀 *n. potash*

tan sik 歡息 *v. t bewail*

tan sik 嘆息 *v.i. groan*

tan sor 診所 *n. clinic*

tan suk gwan hay 親屬關係 *n. kinship*

tan sun 親信 *n. henchman*

tan teet sing 親切性 *n. amiability*

tan teng 餐廳 *n. restaurant*

tan tik 親戚 *n. kin*

tan tik 親戚 *n. relative*

tan tik pang yow 親戚朋友 *n. kith*

tan ting geh 真正嘅 *a. actual*

tan way 攤位 *n. stall*

tan wun 癱瘓 *n. paralysis*

tan wun geh 癱瘓嘅 *a. paralytic*

tan yan 殘忍 *n barbarity*

tan yan 殘忍 *a brutal*

tan yan 殘忍 *a cruel*

tang 曾 *adv ever*

tang 層 *n. layer*

tang 橙 *n. orange*

tang 層 *n ply*

tang 撐 *v.t. row*

tang 層 *n. stratum*

tang shoon 撐船 *v.i boat*

tang shoon 撐船 *v.i. paddle*

tang sik geh 橙色嘅 *a orange*

tang teng sow 撐艇手 *n. oarsman*

tang tiew 藤條 *n. cane*

tang worng sik 橙黃色 *a saffron*

tang wu 藤壺 *n barnacles*

tao 炒 *v.t. sack*

tao lao 吵鬧 *n. racket*

tao lao seng 吵鬧聲 *n clamour*

tao seh 抄寫 *n. transcription*

tap 插 *v.t. insert*

tap 塔 *n. pagoda*

tap 插 *v.t. plug*

tap 插 *v.t. spike*

tap 插 *n thrust*

tap 塔 *n. tower*

tap jor 插座 *n. socket*

tap juy 插嘴 *v.t. interrupt*

tap sor 插鎖 *n. latch*

tap sow 插蘇 *n. plug*

tap tow 插圖 *n. illustration*

tap tow shoot ming 插圖說明 *n. caption*

tap yap 插入 *n. insertion*

tap yap 插入 *v.t. penetrate*

tap yap 插入 *n. penetration*

tap yap yu 插入語 *n. parenthesis*

tar yee 差異 *n difference*

tarm 探 *v.t. visit*

tarm bai 慘敗 *n fiasco*

tarm hao shu muk 參考書目 *+n bibliography*

tarm kwai 慚愧 *v.t. abash*

tarm kway 慚愧 *a. ashamed*

tarm teen 貪錢 *n. avarice*

tarm yu 參與 *v.i. partake*

tarm yu 參與 *v.i. participate*

tarm yu 參與 *n. participation*

tarm yu jeh 參與者 *n. participant*

tarn bo hang way 殘暴行爲 *n atrocity*

tarn yan 殘忍 *a. atrocious*

tat 擦 *v.t. polish*

tat 七 *n. seven*

tat 七 *a seven*

tat gao hur 膝膠靴 *n. wellington*

tat gworng jay 擦光劑 *n polish*

tat hai jay 擦鞋仔 *n. sycophant*

tat sap 七十 *n., a seventy*

tat seurng 擦傷 *n graze*
tat yoon kam 七弦琴 *n. lyre*
tat yow 擦油 *v.t grease*
tat yow 漆油 *n. paint*
tay 堤 *n embankment*
tay 蹄 *n. hoof*
tay 提 *v.t. inscribe*
tay 梯 *n. ladder*
tay 睇 *v.i look*
tay 提 *v.t. prompt*
tay 提 *v.t. remind*
tay 睇 *v.t. see*
tay 剃 *v.t. shave*
tay 剃 *n shave*
tay 睇 *v.t. view*
tay 睇 *v.t. watch*
tay bar 堤壩 *n. weir*
tay bo jow 齊步走 *n march*
tay cho 體操 *n. gymnastics*
tay cho geh 體操嘅 *a. gymnastic*
tay cho yoon 體操員 *n. gymnast*
tay chor 睇錯 *v.t. misjudge*
tay chung 體重 *n. weight*
tay chut 提出 *v.t. propound*
tay chuy mat 提取物 *n extract*
tay dak chut geh 睇得出嘅 *adj perceptible*
tay dow 睇到 *v. t behold*
tay dow 堤道 *n causeway*
tay dow 剃刀 *n. razor*
tay dow 提到 *n. reference*
tay dow 睇到 *v.t. saw*
tay dow 剃度 *n. tonsure*
tay forng 提防 *v.i. beware*
tay gak 體格 *n build*
tay gao 提交 *v.t file*
tay go 提高 *v. t elevate*
tay gow 提高 *v.t. raise*
tay gow 提高 *n uplift*
tay gung 提供 *v.t. offer*
tay gung 提供 *v.i. provide*
tay gung jee gam 提供資金 *v.t finance*
tay gung jee sun geh 提供資訊嘅 *a. informative*
tay gung yam sik 提供飲食 *v. i cater*
tay hay 提起 *v.t. refer*
tay jee 提子 *n. grape*
tay jee gon 提子乾 *n. currant*
tay jee gon 提子乾 *n. raisin*
tay kap 提及 *v.t. invoke*
tay kap 提及 *n. mention*
tay kap 提及 *v.t. mention*
tay kap 梯級 *n. rung*
tay lay 睇來 *v.i. seem*
tay leen chorng 提煉廠 *n. refinery*
tay man 提問 *a. interrogative*
tay muk 題目 *n. topic*
tay sam 提審 *v. arraign*
tay see 提示 *n clue*
tay see 提示 *n cue*
tay see 提示 *n. hint*
tay see yan 提示人 *n. prompter*
tay seng 提醒 *v.t. refresh*
tay seng 提醒 *n. reminder*
tay siew 睇小 *v.i trifle*
tay sik 棲息 *v.i. roost*
tay sik chu 棲息處 *n. perch*
tay sik chu 棲息處 *n. roost*
tay sik day 棲息地 *n. habitat*
tay sing 提升 *v. t boost*
tay sing 提醒 *v. t. caution*
tay teep 體貼 *a. chivalrous*
tay teep 體貼 *n. chivalry*
tay teep 體貼 *a. considerate*
tay teep 體貼 *a. thoughtful*
tay yee 提議 *n offer*
tay yee 提議 *n. proposition*
tay yee 提議 *n. recommendation*
tay yee 提議 *n. suggestion*
tay yee 提議 *v.t. tender*
tay yeurk 體弱 *a. infirm*
tay yeurk 體弱 *n. infirmity*

tay ying 體型 *n. physique*
tay yuk cheurng 體育場 *n. stadium*
tay yuk gwun 體育館 *n. gymnasium*
tee 黐 *a. adhesive*
tee 遲 *adv. late*
tee 似 *a. like*
tee 似 *prep like*
tee 肢 *n. limb*
tee 似 *n. resemblance*
tee 似 *v.t. resemble*
tee 似 *a. similar*
tee 黐 *v.t. stick*
tee 黐 *a. sticky*
tee 刺 *v.t. sting*
tee 似 *a. such*
tee 刺 *n. thorn*
tee deen peen mow 詞典編纂 *n. lexicography*
tee deep 磁碟 *n. disc*
tee dow 刺刀 *n bayonet*
tee dun 遲鈍 *n. laggard*
tee dun geh 遲鈍嘅 *a. obtuse*
tee dun gen yan 遲鈍嘅人 *n dunce*
tee gang 匙羹 *n. spoon*
tee gik 刺激 *n. provocation*
tee gik 刺激 *n. stimulus*
tee gik 刺激 *n. thrill*
tee gik 刺激 *v.t. thrill*
tee gik mat 刺激唔 *n. irritant*
tee hak 刺客 *n. assassin*
tee hay 瓷器 *n. china*
tee hay 瓷器 *n. porcelain*
tee hung jeurk 雌孔雀 *n. peahen*
tee jang 賜贈 *v. t bestow*
tee jik 辭職 *n. conge*
tee jik 辭職 *v.t. resign*
tee jik 辭職 *n. resignation*
tee joon 瓷磚 *n. tile*
tee jor geh 遲咗嘅 *adj. belated*
tee ju 黐住 *n. adhesion*
tee ju leem yik geh 粘住黏液嘅 *a. slimy*

tee juk 持續 *n. continuation*
tee juk 持續 *v.t. perpetuate*
tee juk 持續 *v.t. ply*
tee juk 持續 *v.t. span*
tee juk geh 持續嘅 *a. perennial*
tee juk geh 持續嘅 *a. relentless*
tee juy 次序 *n. order*
tee lay gan 黐脷根 *n lisp*
tee lik 磁力 *n. magnetism*
tee luk 雌鹿 *n doe*
tee ma mi 似媽咪 *a. motherlike*
tee pai yan 持牌人 *n. licensee*
tee sat 刺殺 *n assassination*
tee seen 慈善 *n. charity*
tee seen 黐線 *a crazy*
tee seen 黐線 *a. insane*
tee seen 慈善 *n. philanthropy*
tee seen ga 慈善家 *n. philanthropist*
tee seen geh 慈善嘅 *a. charitable*
tee seen geh 黐線嘅 *a. lunatic*
tee seen geh 慈善嘅 *a. philanthropic*
tee sek 磁石 *n. loadstone*
tee sek 磁石 *n. magnet*
tee sor 廁所 *n bogle*
tee sor 廁所 *n. toilet*
tee sow 刺繡 *n embroidery*
tee suy geh 似水嘅 *a. watery*
tee tong 池塘 *n. pond*
tee worng jee gam geh 似王子咁嘅 *a. princely*
tee wu 雌狐 *n. vixen*
tee wuy 詞彙 *n. lexicon*
tee wuy biew 詞彙表 *n. glossary*
tee yam far 齒音化 *v. assibilate*
tee yee 刺耳 *v. i bray*
tee yee geh 刺耳嘅 *a. strident*
tee yee geh seng 刺耳嘅聲 *v. t blare*
tee yeurng 似樣 *a decent*
tee yiew 次要 *a. subservient*
tee yiew geh 次要嘅 *a. secondary*
tee yoon hok 詞源學 *n. etymology*
tee yuk 恥辱 *v.t. attaint*

tee yuk 恥辱 *n dishonour*
tee yuk 恥辱 *n. humiliation*
tee yuk 恥辱 *n. stigma*
teem 簽 *v.t. sign*
teem 甜 *a. sweet*
teem choy 甜菜 *n beet*
teem chu forng 簽署方 *n. signatory*
teem fuk 潛伏 *a. latent*
teem jat 潛質 *n. potential*
teem lik 潛力 *n. potentiality*
teem man hok 天文學 *n. astronomy*
teem may 甜味 *n. sweetness*
teem may geh 甜美嘅 *a. luscious*
teem meng 簽名 *n. autograph*
teem meng 簽名 *n. signature*
teem sik 甜食 *n confectionery*
teem sik seurng 甜食商 *n confectioner*
teem suy 潛水 *v. i dive*
teem suy 潛水 *n dive*
teem suy teng 潛艇 *n. submarine*
teem way 纖維 *n fibre*
teem yap suy dow 潛入水裡度 *v.i. submerge*
teen 田 *n field*
teen 前 *a. forward*
teen 前 *n. front*
teen 錢 *n. money*
teen 淺 *a pale*
teen 天 *n. sky*
teen 一千 *a thousand*
teen bay 前臂 *n forearm*
teen choy 天才 *n. genius*
teen chung 填充 *v.t. populate*
teen fan tek 千分尺 *n. micrometer*
teen far 天花 *n. smallpox*
teen far ban 天花板 *n. ceiling*
teen fu 天賦 *n. aptitude*
teen fung 前鋒 *n. striker*
teen gan ding 千斤頂 *n. jack*
teen geh 淺嘅 *a. shallow*

teen geh sap yat sing forng 千嘅十一乘方 *n. decillion*
teen geurt 前腳 *n foreleg*
teen ging wan dung 田徑運動 *n. athletics*
teen hay leen 千禧年 *n. millennium*
teen heen 天譴 *n. damnation*
teen hey 天氣 *n weather*
teen jan 天真 *a. artless*
teen jan 天真 *n. innocence*
teen jan 天真 *a. naive*
teen jan 天真 *n. naivete*
teen jan 天真 *n. naivety*
teen jeh 前者 *pron former*
teen jow kuk 前奏曲 *n. overture*
teen ju gao geh 天主教嘅 *a. catholic*
teen juy 前綴 *n. prefix*
teen king 前傾 *n. lurch*
teen man hok ga 天文學家 *n. astronomer*
teen man toy 天文台 *n. observatory*
teen meen 前面 *adv. ahead*
teen meen 前面 *a front*
teen ngan geh 錢銀嘅 *a. monetary*
teen ngor 天鵝 *n. swan*
teen sang geh 天生嘅 *a. inborn*
teen sang geh 天生嘅 *a. innate*
teen sao 前哨 *n. outpost*
teen see 天使 *n angel*
teen see jeurng 天使長 *n archangel*
teen seen 天線 *n. aerial*
teen seurng geh 天上嘅 *adj celestial*
teen sik 淺色 *n. tint*
teen tan 淺灘 *n shoal*
teen tee yan 填詞人 *n. lyricist*
teen tee yat kay 填遲日期 *v.t. post-date*
teen teng 前廳 *n. lobby*
teen tong 天堂 *n. heaven*
teen tong geh 天堂嘅 *a. heavenly*
teen torng 天堂 *n. paradise*
teen tow 鞦韆 *n swing*

teen yam 前任 *n. predecessor*
teen yan 前因 *n. antecedent*
teen yeen geh 天然嘅 *a. natural*
teep 妾 *n concubine*
teep 貼 *v.t. paste*
teep biew teem 貼標籤 *v.t. label*
teep jee 貼紙 *n. sticker*
teep ju 貼住 *v.t. affix*
teep see 貼士 *n. gratuity*
teep see 貼士 *n. tip*
teep teet 貼切 *adv appositely*
teet dat nay ho 鐵達尼號 *a. Titanic*
teet day 徹底 *a utter*
teet day da bai 徹底打敗 *v.t. rout*
teet day da bai 徹底打敗 *n rout*
teet day gam 徹底咁 *adv downright*
teet day gam 徹底咁 *adv. utterly*
teet day geh 徹底嘅 *a outright*
teet day gik bai 徹底擊敗 *v.t. vanquish*
teet fai 切塊 *v.t. slice*
teet gey 設計 *v. t. design*
teet gey 設計 *n. design*
teet ham jeng 設陷阱 *v.t. snare*
teet ham jing 設陷阱 *v. t. entrap*
teet hay 設喺 *v.t. base*
teet jap 鐵閘 *n. shutter*
teet jee 設置 *v.t set*
teet jeurng 鐵匠 *n blacksmith*
teet jeurng 鐵匠 *n. smith*
teet lap 切粒 *v. i. dice*
teet low 鐵路 *n. railway*
teet see 設施 *n facility*
teet seen 切線 *n. tangent*
teet siew 撤銷 *v.t. countermand*
teet siew 撤銷 *v.t. decontrol*
teet sow 鐵鏽 *n. rust*
teet sow tow 鐵手套 *n. gauntlet*
teet tam 鐵砧 *n. anvil*
teet tan 鐵鏟 *n. shovel*
teet toon 切斷 *v. t disconnect*
teet toon 切斷 *v.t. sever*

teet tuy 撤退 *v.i. retreat*
tek 踢 *n. kick*
tek 踢 *v.t. kick*
tek choon 尺寸 *n dimension*
tek dow 赤道 *n equator*
tek jee 赤字 *n deficit*
tek lor geh 赤裸嘅 *a. nude*
teng 請 *v. t employ*
teng 聽 *v.t. hear*
teng 聽 *v.i. listen*
teng choy 青菜 *a. vegetable*
teng dow geh 聽到嘅 *a audible*
teng gwa 青瓜 *n cucumber*
teng gwong ngan 青光眼 *n. glaucoma*
teng hay lay 聽起嚟 *v.i. sound*
teng hm dow 聽唔到 *a. inaudible*
teng jeh 聽者 *n. listener*
teng ling 青檸 *n. lime*
teng tung 青銅 *n. & adj bronze*
teng tung 聽筒 *n. stethoscope*
teng wah geh 聽話嘅 *a. obedient*
teng wah geh 聽話嘅 *a. submissive*
ter 呷 *interj fie*
ter 斜 *a. steep*
ter 斜 *v.i. tilt*
ter 斜 *n. tilt*
ter bor 斜坡 *n slant*
ter bor 斜坡 *n. slope*
ter ok 邪惡 *n evil*
ter ok 邪惡 *n. immorality*
ter ok geh 邪惡嘅 *a. sinful*
ter ok geh 邪惡嘅 *a. vile*
ter ok geh 邪惡嘅 *a. wicked*
ter see 斜視 *n squint*
ter seen gung jay 扯線公仔 *n. puppet*
ter tay 斜體 *a. italic*
ter tay jee 斜體字 *n. italics*
ter tee 奢侈 *n. luxury*
ter tee ban 奢侈品 *n. superfluity*
ter tee geh 奢侈嘅 *a. sumptuous*

tey gung 提供 *v.t. supply*

tey leen 提煉 *v. t extract*

tey yee 提議 *v.t. suggest*

tiew 跳 *n. bound*

tiew 跳 *v.i. dap*

tiew 跳 *n. jump*

tiew 跳 *v.i jump*

tiew 跳 *v.i. leap*

tiew 鞘 *n. scabbard*

tiew 潮 *n. tide*

tiew 跳 *v.i. vault*

tiew chut 超出 *prep. beyond*

tiew chut seurng yan geh 超出常人嘅 *a. superhuman*

tiew dai say 調大細 *v.t. size*

tiew doy 朝代 *n dynasty*

tiew dung 跳動 *v.i. pulse*

tiew dung 跳動 *n. throb*

tiew fwun 條款 *n clause*

tiew gai 調解 *n. mediation*

tiew geen 條件 *n condition*

tiew geen 條件 *n prerequisite*

tiew geh 潮嘅 *a. tidal*

tiew gow 跳高 *n leap*

tiew gwor 超過 *v.i excel*

tiew gwor 跳過 *v.t hurdle2*

tiew gwor 超過 *v.t. surpass*

tiew gwor 超過 *v.t. top*

tiew gwor 超過 *v.i. tower*

tiew hay 挑起 *v.t foment*

tiew jay 調製 *v. t concoct*

tiew jay ban 調製品 *n. concoction*

tiew jee yeen geh 超自然嘅 *a. supernatural*

tiew jeen 挑戰 *n. challenge*

tiew jeen 挑戰 *v. t. challenge*

tiew jeet hay 調節器 *n. regulator*

tiew jeurng 肖像 *n. portrait*

tiew jing 調整 *v.t. adjust*

tiew jing 調整 *n. adjustment*

tiew jing 調整 *v.t. modulate*

tiew joy 超載 *v.t. overload*

tiew leurng gung ying 超量供應 *v.t. glut*

tiew liew 調料 *n dressing*

tiew lo 潮流 *n. trend*

tiew low 超嬲 *a. furious*

tiew man 條紋 *n. stripe*

tiew may jeurng 調味醬 *n. dip*

tiew mo 跳舞 *v. t. dance*

tiew pay 調皮 *a arch*

tiew san 朝臣 *n. courtier*

tiew san jeh 跳傘者 *n. parachutist*

tiew sap 潮濕 *n damp*

tiew sat 跳蚤 *n. lop*

tiew see 超時 *v.t overrun*

tiew seen ging 朝鮮薊 *n. artichoke*

tiew sik ban 調色板 *n. palette*

tiew sing 跳繩 *v.i. skip*

tiew sing jee luy 朝聖之旅 *n. pilgrimage*

tiew sing jeh 朝聖者 *n. pilgrim*

tiew suy 憔悴 *a. haggard*

tiew suy 憔悴 *a. wan*

tiew ta 調查 *v.t. investigate*

tiew ta 調查 *n. investigation*

tiew ta 調查 *n research*

tiew ta 調查 *n. survey*

tiew ta 調查 *v.t. survey*

tiew ting 調情 *n flirt*

tiew ting 調停 *v.i. mediate*

tiew ting 調情 *v.t. pet*

tiew ting jeh 調停者 *n. mediator*

tiew yam 調音 *v.t. tune*

tiew yam bor geh 超音波嘅 *a. supersonic*

tiew yan 超人 *n. superman*

tiew yan geh 挑釁嘅 *a. provocative*

tiew yeh 招惹 *v.t goad*

tiew yoot 超越 *v.t exceed*

tiew yoot 超越 *v.t. outrun*

tiew yoot 超越 *v.t. overhaul*

tiew yoot 超越 *v.t. transcend*

tik 剔 *n. tick*

tik 剔 *v.i. tick*
tik jak 斥責 *n. reprimand*
tik jak 斥責 *v.t. reprimand*
ting 停 *v.t. stop*
ting bok 停泊 *v.t moor*
ting chor 清楚 *a clear*
ting chor 清楚 *a. evident*
ting chor 清楚 *a. explicit*
ting chor 清楚 *a. legible*
ting chor biew dat 清楚表達 *a. articulate*
ting chun kay 青春期 *n. adolescence*
ting chun kay 青春期 *n. puberty*
ting chuy 清除 *n clearance*
ting chuy 清除 *v.t. purge*
ting chuy 清除 *v.t. remove*
ting dan 清單 *n. list*
ting fat 懲罰 *v.t. penalize*
ting fat 懲罰 *n. penalty*
ting fat 懲罰 *n. punishment*
ting fat 懲罰 *v.t. sanction*
ting fat geh 懲罰嘅 *a. punitive*
ting forng 情況 *n circumstance*
ting forng 情況 *n. situation*
ting fu 稱呼 *v.t. address*
ting fu 情婦 *n. courtesan*
ting gao tow 清教徒 *n. puritan*
ting gao tow sik geh 清教徒式 嘅 *a. puritanical*
ting geet 清潔 *v. t clean*
ting geet gung 清潔工 *n. sweeper*
ting gok geh 聽覺嘅 *adj. auditive*
ting gor 情歌 *n. ballad*
ting jan 稱讚 *n. praise*
ting jan jee 清真寺 *n. mosque*
ting jap cho 請雜草 *v.t. weed*
ting jay 停滯 *v.i. stagnate*
ting jay 停滯 *n. stagnation*
ting jay 停滯 *n. standstill*
ting jee 停止 *v. t discontinue*
ting jee 停止 *v. t. halt*
ting jee 停止 *n halt*

ting jee tung yung 停止通用 *v.t. demonetize*
ting jeen heep ding 停戰協定 *n. truce*
ting jeet kek 情節劇 *n. melodrama*
ting jik geh 挺直嘅 *a. upright*
ting juy 程序 *n. procedure*
ting juy 程序 *n. process*
ting kow 請求 *n. plea*
ting kow 請求 *n request*
ting lan 整爛 *v. t break*
ting leem 清廉 *a. incorruptible*
ting leen yan 青年人 *n young*
ting pak chu 停泊處 *n anchorage*
ting pwun 清盤 *v.t. liquidate*
ting pwun 清盤 *n. liquidation*
ting sat 證實 *n affirmation*
ting sat 證實 *v.t. verify*
ting say 清洗 *v. t cleanse*
ting shoon chu 停船處 *n. moorings*
ting siew leen 青少年 *a. adolescent*
ting siew leen 青少年 *n. teenager*
ting sik 清晰 *n clarity*
ting sik dow 清晰度 *n. lucidity*
ting sik dow 清晰度 *n. resolution*
ting sik geh 清晰嘅 *a. vivid*
ting sing 清醒 *a conscious*
ting sing geh 清醒嘅 *a. sober*
ting suy 情緒 *n. sentiment*
ting suy far 情緒化 *a. saccharine*
ting suy gik dung 情緒激動 *a. hysterical*
ting tai 情態 *n. modality*
ting tat 清漆 *n. varnish*
ting ting 澄清 *v. t clarify*
ting ting 澄清 *n clarification*
ting wa 青蛙 *n. frog*
ting wa seng 青蛙聲 *n. croak*
ting yan 情人 *n. lover*
ting yan 情人 *n. paramour*
ting yat 聽日 *n. morrow*
ting yat 聽日 *n. tomorrow*

ting yat 聽日 *adv. tomorrow*
ting yeep 停業 *n. closure*
ting yoon 庭院 *n. courtyard*
ting yoon 請願 *v.t. petition*
ting yoon jeh 請願者 *n. petitioner*
ting yoon shu 請願書 *n. petition*
tong 糖 *n. candy*
tong 糖 *n. comfit*
tong 糖 *n. sugar*
tong 糖 *n sweet*
tong jay gwan 糖仔棍 *n. lollipop*
tong jeurng 糖漿 *n. syrup*
tong jing 糖精 *n. saccharin*
tong liew beng 糖尿病 *n diabetes*
tong meng yan 同名人 *n. namesake*
tong ting 同情 *v.i. sympathize*
tong yee 躺椅 *n chaise*
toon bo 臀部 *n hip*
toon geet 團結 *n. solidarity*
toon geet 團結 *v.t. unite*
toon joot 斷絕 *n. severance*
toon tay 團體 *n. confraternity*
toon toon juk juk 斷斷續續 *a fitful*
toon toon juk juk 斷斷續續 *a.*
　spasmodic
toon toon juk juk 斷斷續續 *a.*
　sporadic
toon tow 源頭 *n. origin*
toot jee lai 脫脂奶 *n buttermilk*
toot lap 脫粒 *v.t. thresh*
toot lay 脫離 *v.i. secede*
toot lay 脫離 *n. secession*
toot lay ju yee jeh 脫離主義者 *n.*
　secessionist
tor 拖 *v.t. mop*
tor bwuy 駝背 *n stoop*
tor hai 拖鞋 *n. loafer*
tor hai 拖鞋 *n. slipper*
tor heep 妥協 *v. t compromise*
tor heep 妥協 *n concession*
tor ju geurt hang 拖住腳行 *v.i.*
　shuffle

tor lai gey 拖拉機 *n. tractor*
tor lun 舵輪 *n. helm*
tor mo bo 駝毛布 *n camlet*
tor yeen 拖延 *v.i. procrastinate*
torliew 鴕鳥 *n. ostrich*
torng 燙 *v.t. iron*
torng 堂 *n. lesson*
torng 堂 *n. session*
torng 劏 *v.t. slaughter*
torng 湯 *n. soup*
torng 糖 *n. sweetmeat*
torng dow 燙斗 *n. iron*
torng hok 湯殼 *n. ladle*
torng jeurng 糖漿 *n molasses*
torng lik suy 湯力水 *n. tonic*
torng worng geh 堂皇嘅 *a. palatial*
tow 肚 *n belly*
tow 頭 *n. head*
tow 桃 *n. peach*
tow 偷 *v.t. pilfer*
tow 偷 *v.t. rifle*
tow 偷 *v.t. rob*
tow 吐 *v.i. spit*
tow 偷 *v.i. steal*
tow 臭 *v.i. stink*
tow 肚 *n. stomach*
tow 頭 *n. tip*
tow 醜 *a. ugly*
tow bay 逃避 *n elusion*
tow bay 逃避 *n escape*
tow bay 逃避 *n evasion*
tow bay 逃避 *v.t. shirk*
tow bay jeh 逃避者 *n. shirker*
tow biew 投標 *n bid*
tow biew 圖表 *n. chart*
tow biew 圖表 *n diagram*
tow biew 圖表 *n. graph*
tow biew 投票 *n tender*
tow bo 投保 *v.t. insure*
tow chee 陶瓷 *n ceramics*
tow chuk 抽搐 *n. spasm*
tow chuk 抽搐 *v.i. throb*

tow chut 抽出 v.t abstract
tow chut 抽出 v.t. spare
tow day 徒弟 n. apprentice
tow fan 逃犯 n. outlaw
tow far 醜化 v.t. uglify
tow far muk 桃花木 n. mahogany
tow fat 頭髮 n hair
tow fat 頭髮 n lock
tow forng 套房 n. suite
tow fu 屠夫 n butcher
tow ga 投家 n bidder
tow gan 頭巾 n coif
tow gan 頭巾 n. wimple
tow gow 禱告 n. prayer
tow gung 陶工 n. potter
tow gwat 頭骨 n. skull
tow hay 陶器 n. crockery
tow hay 陶器 n. pottery
tow hey 唞氣 v. i. breathe
tow ho 討好 v. t. court
tow ho 討好 v.t flatter
tow horng 投降 v.t. surrender
tow horng 投降 n surrender
tow jay 兔仔 n. rabbit
tow jay geh 土製嘅 a earthen
tow jee 投資 v.t. invest
tow jee 透支 n. overdraft
tow jee 透支 v.t. overdraw
tow jee 投資 n. investment
tow jeurng 抽象 a abstract
tow jeurng geh koy leem 抽象嘅概念 n. abstraction
tow jor lap geh 塗咗蠟嘅 adj. cerated
tow jow 逃走 v.i abscond
tow jow 逃走 v. i decamp
tow jow 逃走 v.i escape
tow juy 陶醉 v.i. revel
tow kow 投球 v.i bowl
tow kow sow 投球手 n. pitcher
tow kow sow geh jor ho 投球手左後 n. mid-off

tow kow sow geh teen yow 投球手嘅前右 n. mid-on
tow kway 頭盔 n. helmet
tow lan 偷懶 v.i. laze
tow liew 塗料 n. daub
tow lo 透露 v. i confide
tow low 透露 v. t disclose
tow low 頭腦 n. mind
tow low 醜陋 n. ugliness
tow lun 討論 v. t. debate
tow lun 討論 v. t. discuss
tow lun 討論 n. nagotiation
tow lun wuy 討論會 n. symposium
tow luy 醜女 n. hag
tow man 醜聞 n scandal
tow ming 透明 a. transparent
tow ming dow 透明度 n. opacity
tow morng 偷望 n peep
tow or 肚屙 n diarrhoea
tow or 肚餓 a. hungry
tow pay 頭皮 n dandruff
tow pay 頭皮 n scalp
tow peen 圖片 n. image
tow piew 投票 n. poll
tow piew 投票 v.i. vote
tow piew koon 投票權 n. suffrage
tow piew yan 投票人 n. voter
tow poon 頭盤 n appetizer
tow sat 屠殺 v. t butcher
tow sat 屠殺 v.t. massacre
tow sat 屠殺 n. slaughter
tow seet 盜竊 n burglary
tow seet 偷竊 n. theft
tow she 投射 v. t. cast
tow she mat 投射物 n. projectile
tow shu gwun 圖書館 n. library
tow shu gwun gwun jeurng 圖書館館長 n. librarian
tow so 投訴 v. i complain
tow so 投訴 n complaint
tow tai jor geh 淘汰咗嘅 a. obsolete
tow tay 偷睇 v.i. peep

tow tow 陶土 *n argil*
tow tow gam jow 偷偷咁走 *v.i. sneak*
tow tung 頭痛 *n. headache*
tow wah 圖畫 *n. picture*
tow wah geh 圖畫嘅 *a. pictorial*
tow yap 投入 *n. input*
tow yeem 討厭 *a abominable*
tow yeem gway 討厭鬼 *n. sod*
toy 台 *n channel*
toy 台 *n. dais*
toy 台 *n. platform*
toy 枱 *n. table*
toy fung 颱風 *n. gale*
toy fung 颱風 *n. hurricane*
toy fung 颱風 *n. typhoon*
toy seen 苔蘚 *n. moss*
toy tee 台詞 *n. speech*
toy tow ting hung hang 抬頭挺胸行 *v.i. strut*
tteen tee jee mat 天賜之物 *n. godsend*
tuk bay wu ngar 禿鼻烏鴉 *n. rook*
tuk jow 禿鷲 *n. vulture*
tun 盾 *n. shield*
tun 吞 *v.t. swallow*
tun mwut 吞沒 *v.t engulf*
tun ping 吞併 *v.t. annex*
tun ping 吞併 *n annexation*
tung 痛 *n. ache*
tung 痛 *v.i. ache*
tung 桶 *n. barrel*
tung 銅 *n copper*
tung 桶 *n. pail*
tung 痛 *v.t. pain*
tung 捅 *v.t. stab*
tung 捅 *n. stab*
tung 同 *prep. with*
tung been geh 通便嘅 *n. laxative*
tung dang 同等 *n equal*
tung dow 通到 *n. passage*
tung for gan suk 通貨緊縮 *n. deflation*

tung fu 痛苦 *n. affliction*
tung fu 痛苦 *n. agony*
tung fu 痛苦 *n. misery*
tung fu 痛苦 *n. pain*
tung fu 痛苦 *a. painful*
tung fu 痛苦 *n. tribulation*
tung fu 痛苦 *n. woe*
tung fung 通風 *n draught*
tung fung 通風 *v.t. ventilate*
tung fung 通風 *n. ventilation*
tung fung beng 通風病 *n. gout*
tung fung ho 通風口 *n. ventilator*
tung garn 通姦 *n. adultery*
tung gey 統計 *n. statistics*
tung gey geh 統計嘅 *a. statistical*
tung gey hok ga 統計學家 *n. statistician*
tung gowr 通過 *v.i. pass*
tung guy 同居 *v. t cohabit*
tung guy 同居 *n. concubinage*
tung gwor 通過 *v. t enact*
tung gwor 通過 *adv. through*
tung han 痛恨 *n. abhorrence*
tung hang fay 通行費 *n. toll*
tung hang jing 通行證 *n pass*
tung huk 痛哭 *v.i. wail*
tung jee 通知 *v.t. apprise*
tung jee 統治 *v.t. govern*
tung jee 通知 *v.t. impart*
tung jee 通知 *v.t. inform*
tung jee 通知 *n. notice*
tung jee 通知 *n. notification*
tung jee 通知 *v.t. notify*
tung jee 統治 *n reign*
tung jee 統治 *v.t. rule*
tung jee forng sik 統治方式 *n. governance*
tung jee forng sik 統治方式 *n. regime*
tung jee gwan 童子軍 *n scout*
tung jee kay 統治期 *v.i. reign*

tung jee koon 統治權 *n dominion*

tung ju jeh 同住者 *n. inmate*

tung juk 同族 *adj cognate*

tung jung liew fat 同種療法 *n. homeopathy*

tung jung liew fat see 同種療法師 *n. homoeopath*

tung kay ta yan yat yeurng 同其他人一樣 *n. conformity*

tung leen 童年 *n boyhood*

tung leen 童年 *n. childhood*

tung ling geh 通靈嘅 *a. psychic*

tung luy geh 同類嘅 *a. homogeneous*

tung mai 同埋 *conj. and*

tung pwuy 同輩 *n. peer*

tung see 同事 *n. associate*

tung see 同事 *n colleague*

tung see 同事 *n fellow*

tung see fat sang 同時發生 *v. i coincide*

tung see fat sang 同時發生 *v.t. parallel*

tung see fat sang 同時發生 *a. simultaneous*

tung seurng 同上 *n. ditto*

tung seurng 通常 *adv. generally*

tung seurng 通常 *adv. oft*

tung seurng 通常 *adv. often*

tung seurng 通常 *adv. usually*

tung seurng wuy 通常會 *v.i. tend*

tung sing 通勝 *n. almanac*

tung sing loon 同性戀 *a. gay*

tung sun 通訊 *n. communication*

tung sun 通信 *n. correspondence*

tung tap fan 通緝犯 *n. fugitive*

tung ting 同情 *v. t commiserate*

tung ting 同情 *n compassion*

tung ting 同情 *n. pity*

tung ting geh 同情嘅 *a. sympathetic*

tung ting sam 同情心 *n. sympathy*

tung wah kek 童話劇 *n. pantomime*

tung yat 統一 *n. standardization*

tung yat 統一 *v.t. standardize*

tung yat 統一 *n. unification*

tung yee 同意 *v.t. accede*

tung yee 同意 *v.i. agree*

tung yee 同意 *n. assent*

tung yee 同意 *v. i consent*

tung yee tee 同義詞 *n. synonym*

tung yeurng day 同樣地 *adv. likewise*

tung yung yu 通用語 *n. lingua franca*

tung...yat yeurng 同...一樣 *adv. as*

tuy 推 *v.t. push*

tuy 推 *n. push*

tuy 退 *v.t. refund*

tuy 推 *v.t. shove*

tuy 推 *n. shove*

tuy 推 *v.t. wheel*

tuy bo 退步 *v.i. backslide*

tuy chut 退出 *v.t. quit*

tuy chut 退出 *v.t. withdraw*

tuy chut 退出 *n. withdrawal*

tuy doon 推斷 *v.t. infer*

tuy dung 推動 *n. motivation*

tuy dung 推動 *v.t. propel*

tuy dung lik 推動力 *n. momentum*

tuy fan 推翻 *v.t. overthrow*

tuy fan 推翻 *n overthrow*

tuy fan 推翻 *v.t. subvert*

tuy fwun 退款 *n. rabate*

tuy fwun 退款 *n. refund*

tuy gworng 推廣 *v.t. advertise*

tuy hang 推行 *v.t. impose*

tuy hm gwan yan 退伍軍人 *n. veteran*

tuy ho 退後 *a. backward*

tuy hoy 推開 *n. jostle*

tuy hoy 推開 *v.t. jostle*

tuy jeen 推展 *v.t. nominate*

tuy jeen 推展 *n. nomination*

tuy jeen 推薦 *v.t. recommend*

tuy jeen sun 推薦信 *n. testimonial*

tuy mow 蛻毛 *v.i. moult*
tuy pay 蛻皮 *n. slough*
tuy siew 推銷 *v.t market*
tuy siew 推銷 *n. merchandise*
tuy suk 退縮 *v.i. cower*
tuy suk 退縮 *v.i. recoil*
tuy suk 退縮 *adv. recoil*
tuy tak 推測 *v. t conjecture*
tuy tak 推測 *v.i. speculate*
tuy tak 推測 *n. speculation*
tuy tak 推測 *n. supposition*
tuy tak 推測 *n. surmise*
tuy tak 推測 *v.t. surmise*
tuy tiew 退潮 *n ebb*
tuy yow 退休 *v.i. retire*
tuy yow 退休 *n. retirement*
tuy yow gam 退休金 *n. pension*
tuy yow yan see 退休人士 *n. pensioner*

uk 屋 *n house*
uk kay 屋企 *n. home*
uk kay yan 屋企人 *n family*

wah 畫 *n drawing*
wah 畫 *n. painting*
wah gar 畫家 *n. painter*
wah jeurng 畫像 *n. portraiture*
wah lay 華麗 *n. splendour*
wah lorng 畫廊 *n. gallery*
wah shu 樺樹 *n. birch*
wah tai dor 話太多 *v.t word*

wah tai dor 話太多 *a. wordy*
wai geh 壞嘅 *a faulty*
wai kuk 歪曲 *v.t. misrepresent*
wai yan 懷孕 *n. maternity*
wai yan 懷孕 *n. pregnancy*
wai yee 懷疑 *v.t query*
wai yee 懷疑 *v.t. suspect*
wai yee geh 懷疑嘅 *a. sceptical*
wai yee tai dow 懷疑態度 *n. scepticism*
wak 畫 *v.t draw*
wak 畫 *v.t. pencil*
wak gey ho 畫記號 *v.t mark*
wak jeh 或者 *adv. either*
wak jeh 或者 *adv. perhaps*
wak seen 畫線 *v.t. underline*
wan 彎 *n bend*
wan 彎 *v. t bend*
wan 雲 *n. cloud*
wan 彎 *v. t curve*
wan 玩 *v. i. dabble*
wan 暈 *v.i faint*
wan 搵 *v.t find*
wan 玩 *v.i. frolic*
wan 搵 *n hunt*
wan 玩 *v.i. play*
wan 搵 *v.i. root*
wan 搵 *v.t. search*
wan 搵 *v.t. seek*
wan 運 *v.t. ship*
wan 暈 *n. swoon*
wan 玩 *v.i. toy*
wan 彎 *n turn*
wan chut kok ding way jee 搵出確定位置 *v.t. locate*
wan day 暈低 *v. i collapse*
wan ding 穩定 *n. stabilization*
wan ding 穩定 *v.t. stabilize*
wan ding geh 穩定嘅 *a. stable*
wan ding sing 穩定性 *n. stability*
wan ding sing 穩定性 *n. steadiness*
wan dow 搵到 *v.t. found*

wan dow 溫度 *n. temperature*
wan dung 運動 *n. exercise*
wan dung 運動 *n. sport*
wan dung sam 運動衫 *n. jersey*
wan dung say bao 運動細胞 *a. sportive*
wan dung wuy 運動會 *n. meet*
wan dung ying 運動型 *a. athletic*
wan dung yoon 運動員 *n. athlete*
wan dung yoon 運動員 *n. sportsman*
wan fan 還返 *v.t. repay*
wan for ma cher 運貨馬車 *n. wain*
wan ga 玩家 *n. player*
wan ging 環境 *n. environment*
wan ging 環境 *n. milieu*
wan gor 輓歌 *n. monody*
wan gu 頑固 *n bigot*
wan gu 頑固 *n bigotry*
wan gu geh 穩固嘅 *v.t. stable*
wan hap 混合 *a compound*
wan hap 混合 *v.t. intermingle*
wan hap 混合 *v.t. mingle*
wan hap ban 混合品 *n blend*
wan hap ban 混合品 *n. mixture*
wan hap tay 混合體 *n amalgam*
wan hay 運氣 *n. luck*
wan hor 運河 *n. canal*
wan huy 允許 *n. consent*
wan huy 允許 *v.t. consent3*
wan huy 允許 *v.t. permit*
wan huy 允許 *v.t. vouchsafe*
wan jan geh 穩陣嘅 *a. steady*
wan jap 溫習 *v.t. revise*
wan jap 溫習 *n. revision*
wan jeurk 雲雀 *n. lark*
wan jiew wu 環礁湖 *n. lagoon*
wan jok 運作 *v.i function*
wan jor 彎咗 *n bent*
wan jorng san wu dow 環狀珊瑚島 *n. atoll*
wan kuk 弯曲 *v.t. arch*
wan kuk 彎曲 *v.t. crankle*

wan kuk 彎曲 *n. zigzag*
wan kuk geh 彎曲嘅 *a. sinuous*
wan look 溫暖 *n. warmth*
wan loon 混亂 *v. t bewilder*
wan loon 混亂 *n. chaos*
wan loon 混亂 *adv. chaotic*
wan loon 混亂 *v. t confuse*
wan loon 混亂 *n confusion*
wan loon 混亂 *n. melee*
wan loon 混亂 *n. muddle*
wan loon geh 混亂嘅 *a. turbulent*
wan low 環流 *n. circumfluence*
wan lut 韻律 *n. prosody*
wan mow 雲母 *n. mica*
wan ngat 還押 *n remand*
wan ngat ho sam 還押候審 *v.t. remand*
wan por 穩婆 *n. midwife*
wan see 輓詩 *n elegy*
wan sek 雲石 *n. marble*
wan sek 隕石 *n. meteor*
wan seurng 幻想 *n fancy*
wan seurng 幻想 *a. imaginary*
wan seurng 幻想 *n. reverie*
wan shu 運輸 *n. transit*
wan shu fay 運輸費 *n. cartage*
wan shu gung see 運輸公司 *n. carrier*
wan sun 溫順 *a docile*
wan sun 溫順 *a. tame*
wan sun geh 溫順嘅 *a. meek*
wan sung 運送 *v.t. transport*
wan sung for 運送貨 *n. consignment*
wan sung geh for 運送嘅貨 *n. shipment*
wan tung 頑童 *n. urchin*
wan wan kuk kuk 彎彎曲曲 *a. serpentine*
wan wan kuk kuk geh 彎彎曲曲嘅 *a. tortuous*
wan wo geh 溫和嘅 *a. placid*
wan wor geh 溫和嘅 *a. mild*

wan wor geh 溫和嘅 a. temperate

wan wuy 挽回 v.t. redeem

wan yiew 環繞 v. i. circulate

wan yiew 環繞 v.i. revolve

wan yiew 環繞 adv. round

wan yiew 環繞 v.t. skirt

wan yiew 彎腰 v.i. stoop

wan yiew 環繞 v.t. wind

wan yik 瘟疫 n. pestilence

wan ying tow 混凝土 n concrete

wan yow 溫柔 a. gentle

wan yow 溫柔 a tender

wan yung 運用 v.t. wield

wang ak 橫額 n. banner

wang chung jik jorng 橫衝直撞 v.i. rampage

wang gwor 橫過 adv. across

wang gwor 橫過 prep. athwart

wang way 宏偉 n. grandeur

wang way 宏偉 a. lordly

wang way 宏偉 a. magnificent

wat 滑 v.t. glide

wat 核 n. kernel

wat ban cher 滑板車 n. scooter

wat cheurng gey 滑翔機 n. glider

wat chung 屈從 n. servility

wat dat 核突 a gross

wat dat 核突 a. hideous

wat fuk 屈服 v. t capitulate

wat fuk 屈服 n. submission

wat fuk 屈服 v.i. succumb

wat fuk 屈服 v.t. yield

wat gam heurng 鬱金香 n. curcuma

wat geh 滑嘅 a. smooth

wat gwut 挖掘 v. t. excavate

wat gwut 挖掘 n. excavation

wat hang 滑行 v.i. taxi

wat kay doon kek 滑稽短劇 n. skit

wat lun 滑輪 n. pulley

wat sam 核心 n. hub

way 餵 v.t feed

way bwuy 違背 v. t dishonour

way cheurng 圍牆 n. bawn

way choon 遺傳 n. heredity

way choon geh 遺傳嘅 n. hereditary

way dow 緯度 n. latitude

way fan 違反 n. infringement

way fan 違反 n. transgression

way fan 違反 v.t. violate

way fan 違反 n. violation

way fat 違法 n breach

way geh 胃嘅 a. gastric

way gung 圍攻 v. t besiege

way han 遺憾 n regret

way heep 威脅 v.t. intimidate

way heep 威脅 n menace

way heep 威脅 n. threat

way heep dow 威脅到 v.t menace

way hey 遺棄 v.t. abandon

way ho 胃口 n. appetite

way jee 位置 n. position

way jik 遺跡 n. relic

way jik 遺跡 n. remains

way jik 遺跡 n. vestige

way jor 為咗 n. sake

way ju 圍住 v. t encase

way ju 圍住 v.t fence

way ju 圍住 v.t. surround

way ju 圍住 v.t. wall

way juk 遺囑 n. will

way korng 違抗 n defiance

way korng 違抗 v. t disobey

way kwun 圍裙 n. apron

way lai 餵奶 v.t. suckle

way lan 圍欄 n fence

way lan 圍欄 n. raling

way lik 威力 n. prowess

way low 遺留 v. t. bequeath

way low 遺漏 n. omission

way man 慰問 n condolence

way meet 毀滅 v.t. annihilate

way meet 毀滅 n annihilation

way meet 毀滅 v.t. decimate

way meet 毀滅 n destruction

way sang 衛生 *n. hygiene*
way sang geh 衛生嘅 *a. hygienic*
way sang geh 衛生嘅 *a. sanitary*
way see gey 威士忌 *n. whisky*
way sik geh yan 為食嘅人 *n. glutton*
way sing 彗星 *n comet*
way sing 衛星 *n. satellite*
way sow 維修 *n. maintenance*
way suk 畏縮 *v. i. cringe*
way suk 畏縮 *v.i. wince*
way sun 威信 *n cachet*
way sun 威信 *n. prestige*
way ta ming 維他命 *n. vitamin*
way tan 遺產 *n. heritage*
way tan 遺產 *n. inheritance*
way tan 遺產 *n. legacy*
way tee 維持 *v.t. maintain*
way tee 維持 *n. retention*
way tee 維持 *v.t. sustain*
way tee sang wut 維持生活 *v.i. subsist*
way tok 委託 *v. t delegate*
way tok 委託 *v. t entrust*
way wai 毀壞 *v.t. ravage*
way wat 委屈 *n. grievance*
way wat 委屈 *n hurt*
way yam 委任 *v.t. accredit*
way yam 委任 *v.t. appoint*
way yat geh 唯一嘅 *a sole*
way yeem 威嚴 *n august*
way yeem 威嚴 *n. stateliness*
way yeurk 違約 *n. default*
way yiew 圍繞 *v.t. begird*
way yiew 圍繞 *v. t. encircle*
way yiew 圍繞 *v.t girdle*
way yiew 圍繞 *v.t. wreathe*
way yoon 委員 *n. commissioner*
way yoon wuy 委員會 *n committee*
way yu 謂語 *n. predicate*
way...yee giew oh 為...而驕傲 *v.t. pride*
wik 減 *v.t. moat*

wing gow geh 永久嘅 *a. permanent*
wing gow sing 永久性 *n. permanence*
wing han geh 永恆嘅 *a abiding*
wing hang 永恒 *n eternity*
wing hang geh 永恆嘅 *a. everlasting*
wing sang 永生 *n. immortality*
wing yoon 永遠 *a. eternal*
wing yoon 永遠 *adv forever*
wing yoon dow hm wuy 永遠都唔會 *adv. never*
wing yu 榮譽 *n. glory*
wing yu 榮譽 *n. honour*
wok chuy bo lay 獲取暴利 *v.i. profiteer*
wok dak 獲得 *v.t. attain*
wok dak 獲得 *v.t. procure*
wok jeurng jeh 獲獎者 *n. laureate*
wok jun lay hoy 獲准離開 *n. discharge*
wok lo 鍋爐 *n boiler*
wong day 皇帝 *n emperor*
wong fan 黃昏 *n dusk*
wong gwun 皇冠 *n crown*
wong ho 皇后 *n empress*
wong sik 黃色 *n yellow*
wong sik geh 黃色嘅 *a. yellow*
wong suy chorng 黃水瘡 *n boil*
wong suy seen 黃水仙 *n. daffodil*
wong tung 黃銅 *n. brass*
wong wong day 黃黃地 *a. yellowish*
woo ngoy geh 戶外嘅 *a. outdoor*
woon jor 援助 *n aid*
wor chorng 窩藏 *v.t harbour*
wor deng 鍋釘 *n. rivet*
wor gai 和解 *n compromise*
wor gai 和解 *v.t. reconcile*
wor gai 和解 *n. reconciliation*
wor hai 和諧 *n. concord*
wor hai geh 和諧嘅 *a. harmonious*
wor hoy 禍害 *v.t. peril*
wor hoy 禍害 *n. scourge*
wor lun gey 渦輪機 *n. turbine*

wor muk 和睦 *n. amity*
wor muk 和睦 *n. harmony*
wor ngoy 蝸牛 *n. snail*
wor ping 和平 *n. peace*
wor ping geh 和平嘅 *a. peaceable*
wor seurng 和尚 *n. monk*
wor yam 和音 *n. consonance*
wor yoon 和弦 *n. chord*
worng bo seng 黃寶石 *n. topaz*
worng chung 蝗蟲 *n. locust*
worng dan 黃疸 *n. jaundice*
worng day geh 皇帝嘅 *a. imperial*
worng fung 黃蜂 *n. wasp*
worng gung 皇宮 *n. palace*
worng gwok 王國 *n. kingdom*
worng gwun 皇冠 *n. tiara*
worng jee 王子 *n. prince*
worng ma 黃麻 *n. jute*
worng pai 王牌 *n. trump*
worng sat geh 王室嘅 *a. royal*
worng sat sing yoon 王室成員 *n. royalty*
worng way 王位 *n. throne*
wu 弧 *n. arc*
wu 壺 *n. jug*
wu 湖 *n. lake*
wu bo 互補 *a complementary*
wu deep 蝴蝶 *n butterfly*
wu deep geet 蝴蝶結 *n bow*
wu fat fwuy fuk 無法恢復 *a. irrecoverable*
wu fuk yik 護膚液 *n. lotion*
wu gway 烏龜 *n. turtle*
wu ho 戶口 *n. account*
wu jiew 護照 *n. passport*
wu jiew fan 胡椒粉 *n. pepper*
wu jik 污漬 *n. blot*
wu jik 污漬 *n. smear*
wu jik 污漬 *n. stain*
wu jo 污糟 *a filthy*
wu jorng mat 糊狀物 *n. mush*
wu jow 污糟 *a dirty*

wu jow ghe 污糟嘅 *a. seamy*
wu lam yan 護林人 *n. ranger*
wu lay 狐狸 *n. fox*
wu lay yoon 護理員 *n. orderly*
wu low 葫蘆 *n. gourd*
wu mat 污物 *n filth*
wu muk 烏木 *n ebony*
wu ngan geng 護眼鏡 *n. goggles*
wu ngar 烏鴉 *n crow*
wu san fu 護身符 *n. amulet*
wu san fu 護身符 *n. talisman*
wu see 護士 *n. nurse*
wu seurng yee lai 互相依賴 *v.t. correlate*
wu seurng yee lai 互相依賴 *n. interdependence*
wu seurng yee lai 互相依賴 *a. interdependent*
wu seurng ying heurng 互相影響 *n. interplay*
wu sing hor 護城河 *n. moat*
wu so 鬍鬚 *n beard*
wu sow 鬍鬚 *n. moustache*
wu sow 鬍鬚 *n. mustache*
wu sung 護送 *v. t escort*
wu sung jeh 護送者 *n escort*
wu suy 污水 *n. sewage*
wu suy dow 污水道 *n sewer*
wu tow 糊涂 *adj addle*
wu way 護衛 *n. guard*
wu way wu lay 互惠互利 *a. reciprocal*
wu yeem 污染 *v.t. contaminate*
wu yeem 污染 *v.t. pollute*
wu yeem 污染 *n. pollution*
wu yeem 污染 *n. taint*
wu yeem 污染 *v.t. taint*
wu yeen lun yu 胡言亂語 *n. babble*
wu yeen lun yu 胡言亂語 *v.i. babble*
wu ying 烏蠅 *n fly*
wun 碗 *n bowl*
wun 換 *v. t convert*

wun gai kay 緩解期 *n. remission*
wun guy 玩具 *n. toy*
wun gwat 腕骨 *n. carpal*
wun hai day 換鞋底 *v.t sole*
wun jeurng 腕杖 *n. maulstick*
wun siew 玩笑 *n. banter*
wun wor 緩和 *v.t. moderate*
wun wor jorng gik 緩和撞擊 *v. t cushion*
wung wung seng 嗡嗡聲 *v. i buzz*
wung wung seng 嗡嗡聲 *n. buzz*
wung wung seng 嗡嗡聲 *n hum*
wung wung seng 嗡嗡聲 *n. whir*
wut dung 活動 *n. activity*
wut dung 活動 *n. campaign*
wut dung 活動 *n event*
wut lik 活力 *n. vitality*
wut pwut 活潑 *n. vivacity*
wut pwut geh 活潑嘅 *a. vivacious*
wut sat 活塞 *n. piston*
wut yeurk 活躍 *a. active*
wuy 會 *n club*
wuy 會 *n. meeting*
wuy 會 *v.t. will*
wuy bo 回報 *v.t. reciprocate*
wuy bo 回報 *v.t. requite*
wuy dap 回答 *v.t answer*
wuy dap yan 回答人 *n. respondent*
wuy fuk 回覆 *v.i. reply*
wuy fuk 回覆 *n reply*
wuy fuk 回復 *v.i. revert*
wuy fwun 匯款 *v.t. remit*
wuy fwun gam ak 匯款金額 *n. remittance*
wuy gey 會計 *n. accountancy*
wuy gey see 會計師 *n. accountant*
wuy gu 回顧 *v.t. review*
wuy hap 匯合 *adj. confluent*
wuy jeurng 會長 *n prior*
wuy low chu 匯流處 *n confluence*
wuy loy 回來 *n. return*
wuy say geh 會死嘅 *a. mortal*

wuy seurng 回想 *n. retrospect*
wuy sor 猥瑣 *v.t. grope*
wuy sor 猥瑣 *a. lewd*
wuy yam 回音 *n echo*
wuy yam 回音 *v. t echo*
wuy yee 會議 *n conference*
wuy yee teng 會議廳 *n. chamber*
wuy yik 回憶 *n. reminiscence*
wuy yik 回憶 *n. retrospection*
wuy yik fan 回憶返 *a. reminiscent*
wuy yik luk 回憶錄 *n. memoir*
wuy yoon 會員 *n. member*
wuy yoon san fan 會員身分 *n. membership*

Y

yam 飲 *v. t down*
yam 飲 *v. t drink*
yam 陰 *n. fringe*
yam 陰 *n. shade*
yam am 陰暗 *a cheerless*
yam am 陰暗 *a. gloomy*
yam am geh 陰暗嘅 *a. shadowy*
yam ban 飲品 *n beverage*
yam ban 飲品 *n drink*
yam ban 飲品 *n. refreshment*
yam cho day fu 陰曹地府 *n. underworld*
yam dorng 淫蕩 *a. lascivious*
yam dorng geh luy yan 淫蕩嘅女人 *n. slut*
yam dow 陰道 *n. vagina*
yam gan geh ju san 陰間嘅諸神 *a. manful*
yam ging 陰莖 *n. penis*
yam hao 音效 *n. acoustics*
yam hor 任何 *a. any*
yam hor 任何 *adv. any*

yam hor yeh 任何嘢 *n. aught*

yam jeet 音節 *n. syllable*

yam jeet geh 音節嘅 *a. syllabic*

yam kay 任期 *n. tenure*

yam leurng 音量 *n. volume*

yam mo 任務 *n. task*

yam mow 陰謀 *n. conspiracy*

yam mow 陰謀 *n intrigue*

yam mow 任務 *n. mission*

yam ok 音樂 *n. music*

yam ok ga 音樂家 *n. musician*

yam sap 陰濕 *adj. dank*

yam sik 飲食 *n. pl victuals*

yam sing 任性 *n. caprice*

yam sing 任性 *a. wayward*

yam sing geh 任性嘅 *a. perverse*

yam sing geh 任性嘅 *a. petulant*

yan 癮 *n. addiction*

yan 忍 *v.t. endure*

yan 印 *v.t. imprint*

yan 人 *n. people*

yan 人 *n. person*

yan 印 *v.t. print*

yan 印 *v.i. stamp*

yan 引 *v.t. tantalize*

yan 忍 *v.t. tolerate*

yan chor 印錯 *n. misprint*

yan chor 印錯 *v.t. misprint*

yan chorng 隱藏 *v. t bemask*

yan dow 引導 *v.t. usher*

yan dow geh 印度嘅 *a. Indian*

yan dow ju yee geh 人道主義嘅 *a humanitarian*

yan fat 引發 *v. t beget*

yan fat 引發 *v.i. spark*

yan gak far 人格化 *n. personification*

yan gan geh 人間嘅 *a earthly*

yan gung 人工 *n pay*

yan guy 隱居 *n. seclusion*

yan guy chu 隱居處 *n. hermitage*

yan gwor gwan hay 因果關係 *adj. causal*

yan gwor gwan hay 因果關係 *n causality*

yan hang wang dow 人行橫道 *n. crossing*

yan hay 引起 *v. t evoke*

yan hay 引起 *v.t. induce*

yan hey 引起 *v. t effect*

yan ho 人口 *n. population*

yan ho jung dor geh 人口眾多嘅 *a. populous*

yan ho tiew ta 人口調查 *n. census*

yan jee 人質 *n. hostage*

yan jeurng 印象 *n. impression*

yan jeurng 印章 *n. seal*

yan jeurng sam hak 印象深刻 *a. impressive*

yan jeurng sam hak 印象深刻 *v.t. lavish*

yan jo geh 人造嘅 *a. artificial*

yan jow geh 人造嘅 *a. synthetic*

yan jow lai yow 人造奶油 *n. margarine*

yan jow way sing 人造衛星 *n. sputnik*

yan jun 引進 *n. import*

yan kan 殷勤 *n. complaisance*

yan king 引擎 *n engine*

yan king goy 引擎蓋 *n bonnet*

yan lik 引力 *n. gravitation*

yan lik cher 人力車 *n. rickshaw*

yan luy 人類 *a. human*

yan luy 人類 *n. humanity*

yan luy 人類 *n. mankind*

yan mun 隱瞞 *v. t. conceal*

yan ok geh 音樂嘅 *a. musical*

yan san bo wu ling 人身保護令 *n. habeas corpus*

yan see 隱士 *n. hermit*

yan see 隱士 *n. recluse*

yan see bo 人事部 *n. personnel*

yan seurng 欣賞 *n. admiration*

yan seurng 欣賞 *v.t. admire*

yan seurng 欣賞 *v.t. appreciate*

yan so 因素 *n factor*

yan sow dow geh 忍受到嘅 *a. tolerant*

yan suy 人瑞 *n centenarian*

yan tan 姻親 *n. in-laws*

yan tat gey 印刷機 *n. printer*

yan tay far geh 人體化嘅 *a. incarnate*

yan tay mow ying 人體模型 *n. mannequin*

yan tee 仁慈 *a. gracious*

yan tee 因此 *adv. hence*

yan tee 因此 *adv. thereby*

yan way 因為 *conj. as*

yan way 因為 *conj. because*

yan way 因為 *a due*

yan way 因為 *conj. for*

yan yap 引入 *v.t. adhibit*

yan yap 引入 *v.t. innovate*

yan yee tan sang 因而產生 *v.i ensue*

yan ying 隱形 *a. invisible*

yan yow 引誘 *v. t. entice*

yan yow 引誘 *n. inducement*

yan yung 引用 *v.t. quote*

yao see suy 入市稅 *n. octroi*

yap 入 *v. t enter*

yap 入 *n entry*

yap 入 *prep. into*

yap been 入邊 *prep. inside*

yap been 入邊 *a inside*

yap been 入邊 *adv. inside*

yap been 入邊 *n. within*

yap doy 入袋 *v. i. bag*

yap hm 入伍 *v. t enlist*

yap ho 入口 *n entrance*

yap ho 入口 *n. portal*

yap hok 入學 *v. t enrol*

yap huy 入去 *n. admittance*

yap jik 入籍 *v.t. naturalize*

yap may 入迷 *a fanatic*

yarn yan ju muk geh 引人注目嘅 *a. remarkable*

yat 一 *a. a*

yat 一 *art an*

yat 一 *a. one*

yat 一 *pron. one*

yat ba jeurng 一巴掌 *n. slap*

yat ba jeurng 一巴掌 *n smack*

yat bak 一百 *n. hundred*

yat bak jow leen 一百週年 *n. centenary*

yat bak jow leen 一百週年 *adj. centennial*

yat ban 一班 *n. gang*

yat ban yan 一班人 *n crowd*

yat bao 一包 *n. pack*

yat bao 一包 *n. packet*

yat been 一邊 *adv. aside*

yat bo 日報 *n. daily*

yat bwun 一半 *n. half*

yat chai 一切 *n all*

yat chai 一齊 *adv. along*

yat chai 一齊 *adv. altogether*

yat chay 一齊 *adv. together*

yat choon 一串 *n strand*

yat da 一打 *n dozen*

yat dai ban yan 一大班人 *n. horde*

yat dai ban yan 一大班人 *n. throng*

yat dai dam 一大啖 *n. gulp*

yat dai duy 一大堆 *n. welter*

yat dai duy yeh 一大堆嘢 *n. hotchpotch*

yat dai kwan 一大群 *n. swarm*

yat dam 一啖 *n bite*

yat dap 一沓 *n. sheaf*

yat dat 一笪 *n patch*

yat dee 一啲 *n bit*

yat dee 一啲 *n. jot*

yat dee dow mow 一啲都無 *pron. none*

yat dee dow mow 一啲都無 *adv. none*

yat dee yeh 一啲嘢 *pron. something*

yat dee yeh 一啲嘢 *adv. something*

yat ding 一定 *v. must*

yat ding 一定 *n must*

yat ding geh 一定嘅 *adv. perforce*

yat ding yiew 一定要 *a compulsory*

yat ding yiew geh 一定要嘅 *a. obligatory*

yat dow 一竇 *n brood*

yat doy yan 一代人 *n. generation*

yat duy 一對 *n couple*

yat duy 一堆 *n. heap*

yat duy 一堆 *n. mound*

yat duy 一對 *n. pair*

yat duy 一堆 *n. pile*

yat duy lap sap 一堆垃圾 *n. tip*

yat fai 一塊 *n. slice*

yat fan 一份 *n portion*

yat fan 一份 *n share*

yat fu dor tay 一夫多妻 *n. polygamy*

yat fu dor tay geh 一夫多妻嘅 *a. polygamous*

yat fu yat tay jay 一夫一妻制 *n. monogamy*

yat gey 日記 *n diary*

yat gey 日記 *n. journal*

yat gor gway juk 一個貴族 *n. aristocrat*

yat gow 一嚿 *n block*

yat gow 一嚿 *n. lump*

yat gow 一嚿 *n. mass*

yat gu 一股 *n waft*

yat hak 一刻 *n. instant*

yat hak 一刻 *n. moment*

yat hak 一刻 *a. momentary*

yat hay leet 一系列 *n. sequence*

yat ho kuy joot 一口拒絕 *v.t. rebuff*

yat hoon 一圈 *n. lap*

yat horng 一行 *n. row*

yat horng yan 一行人 *n file*

yat jak fa 一紮花 *n bouquet*

yat jan 一陣 *adv. awhile*

yat jan 一陣 *n bout*

yat jan 一陣 *adv. shortly*

yat jan 一陣 *n. while*

yat jan fung 一陣風 *n. gust*

yat jan kek tung 一陣劇痛 *n. pang*

yat jat 一紮 *n. skein*

yat jay 一劑 *n dose*

yat jee 一致 *n. accord*

yat jee 一致 *n. oneness*

yat jee geh 一致嘅 *a. unanimous*

yat jee tung yee 一致同意 *n. unanimity*

yat jik 一直 *a consistent*

yat jik 一直 *a constant*

yat jow 一組 *n. group*

yat kay 日期 *n date*

yat kay fu fwun 一期付款 *n. instalment*

yat kwan 一群 *n. herd*

yat lap 一粒 *n. grain*

yat leen choon 一連串 *n. spate*

yat leen yat dow geh 一年一度嘅 *adv. yearly*

yat leen yat tee geh 一年一次嘅 *a. annual*

yat lik 日曆 *n. calendar*

yat lun tow kow 一輪投球 *n over*

yat ngan 一眼 *n. glance*

yat ngan 一眼 *n. glimpse*

yat pai 一排 *n. row*

yat pay 一批 *n lot*

yat san gao 一神教 *n. monotheism*

yat san gao sun tow 一神教信徒 *n. monotheist*

yat san sung bai 一神崇拜 *n. monolatry*

yat say dam 一細啖 *n nibble*

yat say dam 一細啖 *n. sip*

yat say deem 一細點 *n. speck*

yat say gow 一細嚿 *n. nugget*

yat say jat 一細紮 *n. wisp*

yat say jat far 一細紮花 *n. nosegay*

yat seurng 日常 *a. ingrained*

yat seurng geh 日常嘅 *a. informal*
yat seurng geh 日常嘅 *a routine*
yat seurng see mow 日常事務 *n. routine*
yat seurng yam sik 日常飲食 *n diet*
yat sik 日蝕 *n eclipse*
yat sik sam fan 一式三份 *n triplicate*
yat tan 一餐 *n feed*
yat tan 一餐 *n. meal*
yat tan bat yeem 一塵不染 *a. spotless*
yat tay 一齊 *n. unison*
yat tay jay geh 一妻制嘅 *a. monogynous*
yat tee 一次 *adv. once*
yat tee gang 一匙羹 *n. spoonful*
yat teen 一千 *n. chiliad*
yat teen 一千 *n. thousand*
yat tiew 一條 *n. loaf*
yat tiew 一條 *n. strip*
yat tiew cheurng lung 一條長龍 *n. queue*
yat tow 日頭 *adv adays*
yat tow 日頭 *n day*
yat tow 一套 *n set*
yat wak 一劃 *n. stroke*
yat yeh jee gan 一夜之間 *adv. overnight*
yat yeh jee gan 一夜之間 *a overnight*
yat yeh see hao 日夜思考 *v.t. preoccupy*
yat yeurng geh 一樣嘅 *a. identical*
yat yeurng geh 一樣嘅 *a. same*
yat yoon 日元 *n. Yen*
yay 拽 *a. naughty*
yee 姨 *n. aunt*
yee 耳 *n ear*
yee 醫 *v.t. physic*
yee 醫 *v.t remedy*
yee 二 *n. two*
yee 而 *conj. whereas*

yee bak jow leen 二百週年 *adj bicentenary*
yee been 易變 *a fickle*
yee been gorng 耳邊講 *v.t. whisper*
yee been jat geh 易變質嘅 *a. perishable*
yee cher 而且 *adv. also*
yee cher 而且 *adv besides*
yee chuy 耳垂 *n. lobe*
yee dai lay geh 義大利嘅 *a. Italian*
yee dai lay yan 義大利人 *n. Italian*
yee duk 易讀 *adv. legibly*
yee dung 移動 *v.i. manoeuvre*
yee ga 而家 *adv. now*
yee ga 而家 *adv. presently*
yee ga geh 而家嘅 *a. present*
yee geen 意見 *n advice*
yee geen 意見 *n. opinion*
yee ging 已經 *adv. already*
yee go 耳垢 *n cerumen*
yee guy 移居 *v.i. migrate*
yee guy 移居 *n. migration*
yee gway 衣櫃 *n. wardrobe*
yee harm 易喊 *a. lachrymose*
yee hay 儀器 *n device*
yee hey 儀器 *n. apparatus*
yee ho 以後 *conj. after*
yee ho 醫好 *v.t. cure*
yee ho 醫好 *v.i. heal*
yee jay yoon 耳仔軟 *a. inexorable*
yee jee 以致 *conj. that*
yee jee lik 意志力 *n. volition*
yee jee siew tam 意志消沉 *v.t. demoralize*
yee jeurng 意象 *n. imagery*
yee jeurng gwun 儀仗官 *n. beadle*
yee jik 移植 *v.t graft*
yee jik 移植 *v.t. transplant*
yee jik mat 移植物 *n. graft*
yee jorng 耳狀 *adj. auriform*
yee jun jay 二進制 *adj binary*
yee kao 依靠 *n. recourse*

yee kao 依靠 *v.i. resort*

yee kao geh 依靠嘅 *a dependent*

yee lai 依賴 *n anaclisis*

yee lai 依賴 *v. i. depend*

yee lai 依賴 *n dependence*

yee lai 二奶 *n. mistress*

yee lai 依賴 *n. reliance*

yee lai 依賴 *v.i. rely*

yee liew geh 醫療嘅 *a. medical*

yee ling sow forng sik 以零售方式 *adv. retail*

yee low 易嬲 *a. touchy*

yee luy 疑慮 *n. misgiving*

yee luy 疑慮 *n. mistrust*

yee man 疑問 *n doubt*

yee man 移民 *n. immigrant*

yee man 移民 *v.i. immigrate*

yee man 移民 *n. immigration*

yee man 移民 *n. migrant*

yee man 疑問 *n. query*

yee man 移民 *n. settler*

yee man tee 疑問詞 *n interrogative*

yee mat wun mat 以物換物 *v.t. barter1*

yee ming geh 易明嘅 *a. intelligible*

yee ming geh 易明嘅 *a. lucid*

yee mo geh 義務嘅 *a. honorury*

yee ngoy 意外 *n accident*

yee ngoy geh 意外嘅 *a. untoward*

yee ngoy so wok 意外收穫 *n bonus*

yee sang 醫生 *n doctor*

yee sang 醫生 *n. medico*

yee sap 二十 *a. twenty*

yee see 意思 *n. meaning*

yee see 醫師 *n. physician*

yee see 意思 *n. signification*

yee seurng 以上 *adv above*

yee seurng 異常 *n anomaly*

yee seurng geh 異常嘅 *a anomalous*

yee seurng geh 異常嘅 *a. extraordinary*

yee seurng geh 異常嘅 *a. uncanny*

yee seurng teen hoy geh 異想天開嘅 *a. whimsical*

yee sik 儀式 *n. ceremony*

yee sik 儀式 *n. rite*

yee sik 儀式 *n. ritual*

yee sik dow 意識到 *v.t. realize*

yee sik seurng geh 儀式上嘅 *a. ritual*

yee sup 二十 *n twenty*

yee tai 儀態 *n poise*

yee tan 遺產 *n. patrimony*

yee teen 以前 *adv. before*

yee teen 以前 *adv formerly*

yee teen geh 以前嘅 *a. retrospective*

yee ter 而且 *conj both*

yee ter 而且 *adv. moreover*

yee ter 而且 *adv. withal*

yee ting biew 議程表 *n. agenda*

yee tow 意圖 *n. conation*

yee tow gey 二頭肌 *n biceps*

yee way ping day 夷為平地 *v.t. raze*

yee yan far 擬人化 *v.t. personify*

yee yeen 易燃 *a. inflammable*

yee yoon 醫院 *n. hospital*

yee yoon 意願 *n. inclination*

yee yoon 議員 *n. parliamentarian*

yee yoot 二月 *n February*

yeem 染 *v. t dye*

yeem 厭 *v.t fatigue*

yeem 閹 *v.t. geld*

yeem 鹽 *n. salt*

yeem 厭 *v.t. satiate*

yeem 染 *v.t. tincture*

yeem cho 煙草 *n. tobacco*

yeem gak 嚴格 *a. strict*

yeem gak geh 嚴格嘅 *a. rigorous*

yeem geh 鹽嘅 *a. saline*

yeem got 閹割 *n neuter*

yeem jeem 奄尖 *adj censorious*

yeem jung 嚴重 *a. acute*

yeem jung 嚴重 *a dire*

yeem jung geh 嚴重嘅 *a serious*

yeem jung geh 嚴重嘅 *a. severe*

yeem jung shoon wai 嚴重損壞 *v.t. mangle*

yeem jung sing 嚴重性 *n. severity*

yeem koy 掩蓋 *v.t. overshadow*

yeem lay 嚴厲 *n. rigour*

yeem lay 嚴厲 *n. stark*

yeem lay 嚴厲 *n. stern*

yeem lay geh 嚴厲嘅 *a. stern*

yeem lay geh 嚴厲嘅 *a. stringent*

yeem lay pay ping 嚴厲批評 *v. t. castigate*

yeem liew 染料 *n dye*

yeem mwut 淹沒 *v.t. whelm*

yeem ngow 閹牛 *n bullock*

yeem say jeh 厭世者 *n. misanthrope*

yeem see 驗屍 *n. post-mortem*

yeem shu 鼴鼠 *n. mole*

yeem siew siew 染少少 *v.t. tinge*

yeem sik 染色 *v. t colour*

yeem sik 掩飾 *v.t. mask*

yeem sik 掩飾 *n. masquerade*

yeem sik 掩飾 *v.t. whitewash*

yeem sing 鹽性 *n. salinity*

yeem suk 嚴肅 *a. grave*

yeem suk 嚴肅 *n. solemnity*

yeem suk geh 嚴肅嘅 *a. solemn*

yeem suy 鹽水 *n brine*

yeem tay 掩體 *n blindage*

yeem yee 嫌疑 *n. suspicion*

yeem yee fan 嫌疑犯 *n suspect*

yeen 演 *v.i. act*

yeen 煙 *n. cigarette*

yeen 煙 *n. smoke*

yeen cheurng 延長 *v. t extend*

yeen cheurng 現場 *n. locale*

yeen cheurng 延長 *v.t. prolong*

yeen cheurng 延長 *n. prolongation*

yeen cheurng 現場 *n. site*

yeen cheurng wuy 演唱會 *n. concert*

yeen chut 演出 *n. performance*

yeen doy 現代 *a contemporary*

yeen doy far 現代化 *v.t. modernize*

yeen doy geh 現代嘅 *a. modern*

yeen doy sing 現代性 *n. modernity*

yeen fat 研發 *v. t. develop*

yeen gam 現金 *n. cash*

yeen gey 演技 *n. acting*

yeen gorng 演講 *n. lecture*

yeen gorng 演講 *n. oration*

yeen gorng 演講 *n. presentation*

yeen gorng ga 演講家 *n. orator*

yeen gorng geh 演講嘅 *a. oratorical*

yeen gorng sut 演講術 *n. oratory*

yeen han guy jee 言行舉止 *n. mannerism*

yeen ho 然後 *adv. thence*

yeen jay 延滯 *n. retardation*

yeen jee 燕子 *n. swallow*

yeen jik 筵席 *v.t. banquet*

yeen jow wuy 演奏會 *n. recital*

yeen kay 延期 *n. adjournment*

yeen kay 延期 *n. postponement*

yeen liew 燃料 *n. fuel*

yeen lun 言論 *n. remark*

yeen lun 言論 *n. utterance*

yeen mak 燕麥 *n. oat*

yeen mow 煙霧 *n. smog*

yeen sat 實現 *v.t. achieve*

yeen sat ju yee jeh 現實主義者 *n. realist*

yeen sat sang wut 現實生活 *n. reality*

yeen siew 燃燒 *v.i blaze*

yeen siew 燃燒 *v.i flame*

yeen tee 延遲 *v.t. & i. delay*

yeen tee 延遲 *v.t. postpone*

yeen tee 延遲 *n. procrastination*

yeen tow 煙頭 *n. stub*

yeen tow wuy 研討會 *n. seminar*

yeen tung 煙囪 *n. chimney*

yeen wuy 宴會 *n. banquet*

yeen wuy 宴會 *n feast*

yeen yam jeh 現任者 *n. incumbent*

yeen yoon 演員 *n. actor*
yeen yuk 煙肉 *n. bacon*
yeep 醃 *v.t. condite*
yeep 葉 *n foliage*
yeep 葉 *n. leaf*
yeep 頁 *n. page*
yeep 醃 *v.t pickle*
yeep been 頁邊 *n. margin*
yeep beng 葉柄 *n stalk*
yeep ju 業主 *n. proprietor*
yeep yu ngoy ho jeh 業餘愛好者 *n. amateur*
yeet 熱 *n. heat*
yeet 熱 *a. hot*
yeet dai 熱帶 *n. tropic*
yeet dai 熱帶 *a. tropical*
yeet dai sam lam 熱帶森林 *n. jungle*
yeet leet 熱烈 *a fervent*
yeet leet 熱烈 *a. tumultuous*
yeet leet 熱烈 *a. uproarious*
yeet leet fwun ying 熱烈歡迎 *n. ovation*
yeet ngoi 熱愛 *adj. avid*
yeet sam 熱心 *n devotion*
yeet sam 熱心 *n enthusiasm*
yeet sam 熱心 *a. keen*
yeet san 熱身 *v.t. limber*
yeet teet 熱切 *a. intent*
yeet tiew 熱潮 *n craze*
yeet ting 熱情 *a. ardent*
yeet ting 熱情 *n. ardour*
yeet ting 熱情 *adv. avidity*
yeet ting 熱情 *a enthusiastic*
yeet ting 熱情 *n fervour*
yeet ting 熱情 *n. keenness*
yeet ting 熱情 *n. passion*
yeet ting 熱情 *a. passionate*
yeet ting 熱情 *n. zeal*
yeet ting 熱情 *n. zest*
yeet ting geh 熱情嘅 *a. zealous*
yeh 惹 *v.t. incur*
yeh 惹 *v.t. provoke*

yeh 嘢 *n. stuff*
yeh 嘢 *n. thing*
yeh ang 夜鶯 *n. nightingale*
yeh choy fa 椰菜花 *n. cauliflower*
yeh gan wut dung geh 夜間活動嘅 *a. nocturnal*
yeh hok teem way 椰殼纖維 *n coir*
yeh jee 椰子 *n coconut*
yeh ju 野豬 *n boar*
yeh man 野蠻 *a. barbarian*
yeh man 野蠻 *n. barbarism*
yeh man 夜晚 *n. night*
yeh man yan 野蠻人 *n. barbarian*
yeh man yan 野蠻人 *n savage*
yeh ngow 野牛 *n bison*
yeh sang geh 野生嘅 *a. wild*
yeh so 野獸 *n beast*
yeh so 耶穌 *n. Christ*
yeh so gam geh 野獸咁嘅 *a beastly*
yeh tan 野餐 *n. picnic*
yeh tan 野餐 *v.i. picnic*
yeh tow 野兔 *n. hare*
yeh yan ngoy 惹人愛 *a. lovable*
yeng 贏 *v.t. win*
yeng 贏 *n win*
yeng ga 贏家 *n. winner*
yeurk 藥 *n cure*
yeurk 弱 *a. frail*
yeurk 藥 *n. medicament*
yeurk 藥 *n. medicine*
yeurk 藥 *n. physic*
yeurk 藥 *n. remedy*
yeurk 藥 *n. tablet*
yeurk 弱 *a. weak*
yeurk cho 藥草 *n. herb*
yeurk chuk 約束 *v.t. regulate*
yeurk chuk geh 約束嘅 *a. restrictive*
yeurk deem 弱點 *n. weakness*
yeurk doy 虐待 *v.t. abuse*
yeurk doy 虐待 *n. mal-treatment*
yeurk doy 虐待 *v.t. mistreat*
yeurk doy kwong 虐待狂 *n. sadism*

yeurk doy kwong 虐待狂 *n. sadist*
yeurk forng 藥房 *n dispensary*
yeurk forng 藥房 *n. pharmacy*
yeurk forng 藥方 *n. prescription*
yeurk geh 藥嘅 *a. medicinal*
yeurk gow 藥膏 *n. ointment*
yeurk ho geh 約好嘅 *a. promissory*
yeurk jat 瘧疾 *n. malaria*
yeurk jay see 藥劑師 *n druggist*
yeurk jeh 弱者 *n. weakling*
yeurk jow 藥酒 *n. tincture*
yeurk wuy 約會 *n. rendezvous*
yeurk yoon 藥丸 *n. pill*
yeurng 癢 *n. itch*
yeurng 癢 *v.i. itch*
yeurng 養 *v.t. rear*
yeurng 羊 *n. sheep*
yeurng ban 樣板 *n. prototype*
yeurng bwun 樣本 *n. sample*
yeurng fung cheurng 養蜂場 *n. apiary*
yeurng fung yeep 養蜂業 *n. apiculture*
yeurng gan jing 羊癇症 *n epilepsy*
yeurng giew seng 羊叫聲 *n bleat*
yeurng hay 氧氣 *n. oxygen*
yeurng jow chorng 釀酒廠 *n distillery*
yeurng jow leen fan 釀造年份 *n. vintage*
yeurng low gam 養老金 *n. annuity*
yeurng mo 羊毛 *n fleece*
yeurng pay 羊皮 *n. lambkin*
yeurng shu 楊樹 *n. poplar*
yeurng tow 陽台 *n. veranda*
yeurng tow cheurng 養兔場 *n. warren*
yeurng toy 陽台 *n. balcony*
yeurng wuy heurng 洋茴香 *n aniseed*
yeurng yuk 羊肉 *n. mutton*
yiew 要 *v.t. acquire*
yiew 窰 *n. kiln*

yiew 要 *v.t. need*
yiew 搖 *v.i. rattle*
yiew 搖 *v.t. rock*
yiew 搖 *v.i. shake*
yiew 搖 *v.i. swing*
yiew 搖 *v.i. wag*
yiew 腰 *n. waist*
yiew 搖 *v.i wobble*
yiew bai 搖擺 *v.i. sway*
yiew bai 搖擺 *n sway*
yiew bai 搖擺 *v.i. waddle*
yiew bai 搖擺 *n wag*
yiew bay geh 要畀嘅 *a. payable*
yiew bee bee 搖BB *v.t. dandle*
yiew dai 腰帶 *n. girdle*
yiew deem 要點 *n. gist*
yiew dung 搖動 *n shake*
yiew forng 搖晃 *n. stagger*
yiew gwai 妖怪 *n. monster*
yiew gwor 繞過 *v.t. round*
yiew ha yiew ha 擺下擺下 *v.i. reel*
yiew hung 遙控 *n. controller*
yiew kow 要求 *v.t. request*
yiew kow jeh 要求者 *n claimant*
yiew lam kuk 搖籃曲 *n. lullaby*
yiew larm 搖籃 *n cradle*
yiew seen gorn 繞線杆 *n. spindle*
yiew so 要素 *n element*
yiew ting 邀請 *v. invitation*
yiew ting 邀請 *v.t. invite*
yiew tow 腰頭 *n. waistband*
yiew yeen 謠言 *n. rumour*
yiew yiew bai bai 搖搖擺擺 *v.i. stagger*
yiew yuk 腰肉 *n. loin*
yik 液 *n. sap*
yik 翼 *n. wing*
yik at 抑壓 *v.t. withhold*
yik beng 疫病 *a. plague*
yik dow hm 亦都唔 *conj. neither*
yik dow hm 亦都唔 *conj nor*
yik far 液化 *v.t. liquefy*

yik jeurng 腋杖 *n crutch*
yik miew 疫苗 *n. vaccine*
yik tay 液體 *n fluid*
yik tay 液體 *n liquid*
yik tay geh 液體嘅 *a. liquid*
yik wat jing 抑鬱症 *n depression*
ying 鷹 *n eagle*
ying 鷹 *n hawk*
ying 影 *v.t. photograph*
ying 影 *n. shadow*
ying 影 *n. silhouette*
ying borng 英鎊 *n. pound*
ying borng 英鎊 *n. sterling*
ying dak 應得 *v. t. deserve*
ying dak 認得 *v.t. recognize*
ying dak geh yeh 應得嘅嘢 *n due*
ying fat geh 刑罰嘅 *a. penal*
ying fu 應付 *v. i cope*
ying fu 應付 *n. tackle*
ying geet 凝結 *v. t clot*
ying geh 營嘅 *adj castral*
ying gwok 英國 *n albion*
ying gwok geh 英國嘅 *adj british*
ying gworng mok 螢光幕 *n. monitor*
ying heurng 影響 *v.t. affect*
ying heurng 影響 *n. influence*
ying heurng 影響 *v.t. influence*
ying heurng 影響 *v.t. jaundice*
ying heurng 影響 *v.i. militate*
ying heurng 影響 *n. thrall*
ying heurng geh 影響嘅 *a subject*
ying heurng lik 影響力 *n. impact*
ying heurng lik 影響力 *n. leverage*
ying heurng lik 影響力 *n. potency*
ying heurng sam yoon geh 影響深遠嘅 *a. seminal*
ying hor 認可 *n. approbation*
ying hor 認可 *n. recognition*
ying hung 英雄 *n. hero*
ying hung jing san 英雄精神 *n. heroism*

ying jan see hao 認真思考 *v.i. ruminate*
ying jorng 形狀 *n. shape*
ying lap suy geh 應納稅嘅 *a. taxable*
ying larm 型男 *n gallant*
ying lay 英里 *n. mile*
ying lay sow 英里數 *n. mileage*
ying loon bong 英聯邦 *n. commonwealth*
ying man 英文 *n English*
ying morng 凝望 *n ogle*
ying mow 英畝 *n. acre*
ying mow 鸚鵡 *n. parrot*
ying see 凝視 *v. t daze*
ying see 凝視 *n gaze*
ying see 凝視 *n. stare*
ying she 影射 *n. insinuation*
ying sik 形式 *n medium*
ying sing 形成 *v.t. form*
ying sing 應承 *v.t promise*
ying sing jik seen 形成直線 *n. alignment*
ying tam 英尋 *n fathom*
ying tan 認真 *a earnest*
ying way 認爲 *v.i. deem*
ying way 認爲 *v.t figure*
ying way 認爲 *v.t. opine*
ying way 認爲 *v.t. reckon*
ying way 認爲 *v.t. repute*
ying yan gey 影印機 *n. xerox*
ying yeurng 營養 *n. aliment*
ying yeurng 營養 *n. nutrition*
ying yeurng ban 營養品 *n. nourishment*
ying yeurng bat leurng 營養不良 *n. malnutrition*
ying yeurng geh 營養嘅 *a. nutritive*
ying yu 凝乳 *n curd*
ying yung 形容 *v. t describe*
ying yung geh 英勇嘅 *a. heroic*
ying yung hang way 英勇行爲 *n exploit*

ying yung tee 形容詞 *n. adjective*
yoom jee 原子 *n. atom*
yoom jee geh 原子嘅 *a. atomic*
yoon 遠 *adv. afar*
yoon 猿 *n ape*
yoon 縣 *n. county*
yoon 完 *n. end*
yoon 遠 *adv. far*
yoon 遠 *a far*
yoon 鉛 *n. lead*
yoon 軟 *n. soft*
yoon ai 懸崖 *n. cliff*
yoon bat 鉛筆 *n. pencil*
yoon bat pao 鉛筆刨 *n. sharpener*
yoon choon 完全 *adv all*
yoon choon 完全 *a downright*
yoon choon 完全 *adv entirely*
yoon choon 完全 *adv. fully*
yoon choon 完全 *adv. wholly*
yoon choon geh 完全嘅 *a. sheer*
yoon choon mo 完全無 *a devoid*
yoon chu 遠處 *adv. afield*
yoon chu ying 圓柱型 *n cylinder*
yoon deng uk 圓頂屋 *n dome*
yoon fan 緣份 *n fate*
yoon gam 軟禁 *v.t. imprison*
yoon geh 遠嘅 *a distant*
yoon gow 原告 *n. plaintiff*
yoon han 怨恨 *n grudge*
yoon han 怨恨 *n. rancour*
yoon han 怨恨 *n. resentment*
yoon han 怨恨 *n. spite*
yoon hang 遠行 *v.i. voyage*
yoon hok 玄學 *n. metaphysics*
yoon hok geh 玄學嘅 *a. metaphysical*
yoon hoon 圓圈 *n. circle*
yoon hoon 圓圈 *n. loop*
yoon jak 原則 *n canon*
yoon jak 原則 *n. creed*
yoon jak 原則 *n. principle*
yoon jak 原則 *n. tenet*

yoon jee lang geh 原子能嘅 *a. nuclear*
yoon jee wat 原子核 *n. nucleus*
yoon jing 完整 *a complete*
yoon jing 遠征 *n expedition*
yoon jing 完整 *a. intact*
yoon jing 完整 *n. integrity*
yoon jok geh 原作嘅 *a. original*
yoon joot mat 緣絕物 *n. insulator*
yoon jow 圓周 *n. circumference*
yoon ju 沿着 *prep. up*
yoon ju man 原住民 *n. pl aborigines*
yoon juk 遠足 *n. excursion*
yoon juy ying 圓錐形 *n. cone*
yoon lay 原理 *n. rationale*
yoon leem 懸念 *n. suspense*
yoon leurng 原諒 *v.t excuse*
yoon leurng 原諒 *v.t forgive*
yoon may 完美 *n. perfection*
yoon may geh 完美嘅 *a. perfect*
yoon miew geh 玄妙嘅 *a. oracular*
yoon mong 願望 *n. wish*
yoon ngay 園藝 *n. horticulture*
yoon ngay ga 園藝家 *n. gardener*
yoon on 懸案 *n. subjudice*
yoon say 芫荽 *n. coriander*
yoon seng 原聲 *a acoustic*
yoon sing 完成 *v. t complete*
yoon sing 完成 *completion*
yoon sing 完成 *v.t finish*
yoon tee geh 原始嘅 *a. primeval*
yoon yam 元音 *n. vowel*
yoon yan 原因 *n. reason*
yoon yee ling ting geh 願意聆聽嘅 *a. receptive*
yoon ying 圓形 *a circular*
yoon ying geh 圓形嘅 *a. round*
yoot 月 *n. month*
yoot ging 月經 *n. menses*
yoot ging bat tiew 月經不調 *n amenorrhoea*
yoot ging geh 月經嘅 *a. menstrual*

yoot gway 越軌 *n. pale*
yoot gway 越軌 *v.t. transgress*
yoot gway shu 月桂樹 *n laurel*
yoot hon 月刊 *n monthly*
yoot leurng 月亮 *n. moon*
yoot leurng geh 月亮嘅 *a. lunar*
yow 有 *v.t. contain*
yow 釉 *n glaze*
yow 有 *v.t. have*
yow 油 *n. oil*
yow 油 *v.t. paint*
yow 疣 *n. wart*
yow am 幽暗 *n. gloom*
yow bay dak 邱比特 *n Cupid*
yow bay mo wan 有備無患 *v.t forearm*
yow beng geh 有病嘅 *a. sick*
yow cheen 有錢 *a. affluent*
yow cho cher 油槽車 *n. tanker*
yow chorng yee 有創意 *a. inventive*
yow chorng yee 有創意 *a. visionary*
yow choy wah geh 有才華嘅 *a. gifted*
yow chuy geh 有趣嘅 *a. laughable*
yow dak jing geh 有得整嘅 *a. raparable*
yow dak king geh 有得傾嘅 *a. negotiable*
yow dan xing 有彈性 *a elastic*
yow day 郵遞 *n mail*
yow day geh 郵遞嘅 *a. postal*
yow day korng lik 有抵抗力 *a. resistant*
yow dee 有啲 *adv. some*
yow dee 有啲 *pron. some*
yow dee 有啲 *adv. somewhat*
yow deem 優點 *n excellency*
yow deem 優點 *n. merit*
yow dorng 遊蕩 *v.i. wander*
yow dow lay 有道理 *a. reasonable*
yow doy biew sing geh 有代表性嘅 *a. representative*

yow doy luy dung mat 有袋類動物 *n. marsupial*
yow duk geh 有毒嘅 *a. poisonous*
yow duk geh 有毒嘅 *a. venomous*
yow fay 郵費 *n. postage*
yow ga jik 有價值 *a. valuable*
yow gam gok geh 有感覺嘅 *a. sentient*
yow geen 郵件 *n. mail*
yow geen day 有見地 *a. judicious*
yow gey geh 有機嘅 *a. organic*
yow gey sing 有記性 *a. retentive*
yow gey sut geh 有技術嘅 *a. skilful*
yow gik duy yoon 游擊隊員 *n. partisan*
yow gik jeen 游擊戰 *n. guerilla*
yow gok geh 有角嘅 *a. angular*
yow gow yow sow 又高又瘦 *a. lank*
yow guk 郵局 *n. post-office*
yow gwan geh 有關嘅 *a. pertinent*
yow gwan geh 有關嘅 *a. relevant*
yow gwan geh 有關嘅 *a. topical*
yow gwan hay geh 有關係嘅 *a. associate*
yow gwan hay geh 有關係嘅 *a. relative*
yow gworng jak 有光澤 *a. lustrous*
yow hai 遊戲 *n. game*
yow han 休閒 *a fallow*
yow han fu 休閒褲 *n. slacks*
yow han gam 休閒咁 *a. leisurely*
yow han geh 有限嘅 *a finite*
yow han geh 休閒嘅 *a leisure*
yow han geh 有限嘅 *a. limited*
yow hang 遊行 *v.i march*
yow hang 遊行 *n. parade*
yow hang 遊行 *v.t. parade*
yow hao 有效 *a effective*
yow hao 有效 *a. fruitful*
yow hao 有效 *a. valid*
yow hao geh 有效嘅 *a. potent*

yow hao lut geh 有效率嘅 a. productive

yow hay morng geh 有希望嘅 a. promising

yow hing chuy 有興趣 a. interested

yow hing chuy 有興趣 a. interesting

yow hm tung geh 有唔同嘅 v.t. vary

yow ho dor 有好多 v.i. abound

yow hok ham geh 有學問嘅 a. scholarly

yow hoon 幼犬 n. puppy

yow hor lang 有可能 adv. probably

yow hor lang geh 有可能嘅 a. probable

yow hoy 有害 a. injurious

yow hoy geh 有害嘅 a malign

yow hoy geh 有害嘅 a. negative

yow hoy geh 有害嘅 a. noxious

yow hoy geh 有害嘅 a. pernicious

yow jak yam 有責任 a accountable

yow jak yam 有責任 a incumbent

yow jak yam gam 有責任感 a. responsible

yow jee 幼稚 adj callow

yow jee 幼稚 a. childish

yow jee 油脂 n grease

yow jee 幼稚 a. immature

yow jee gak 有資格 a eligible

yow jee gak 有資格 v.i. qualify

yow jee geh 幼稚嘅 a. juvenile

yow jee geh 幼稚嘅 a. puerile

yow jee sat king heurng 有自殺傾向 a. suicidal

yow jee wey 有智慧 a. wise

yow jee yoon 幼稚園 n. kindergarten ;

yow jee yoon 幼稚園 n. nursery

yow jeen 休戰 n. armistice

yow jeet jow geh 有節奏嘅 a. rhythmic

yow jing 郵政 n. post

yow jing guk jeurng 郵政局長 n. postmaster

yow joon yem 有尊嚴 v.t dignify

yow jor 有咗 a. pregnant

yow jun dow geh 有進度嘅 a. progressive

yow koon 有權 v. t. entitle

yow koon geh 有權嘅 a. powerful

yow koon way 有權威 a. authoritative

yow koot ham geh 有缺陷嘅 adj. deficient

yow kuk seen ghe 有曲線嘅 a. shapely

yow lai geh 有奶嘅 a. milch

yow lam 遊覽 v.i. tour

yow lam jee hay koy 有男子氣概 a. manlike

yow lang lik 有能力 a. capable

yow lang lik 有能力 a. competent

yow lay 有利 v.t. advantage

yow lay 有利 a favourable

yow lay geh 有利嘅 a beneficial

yow lay mao 有禮貌 a. courteous

yow lay mao 有禮貌 a. polite

yow lay yow geh 有理由嘅 a. justifiable

yow lay yu 有利於 v. t. benefit

yow lay yu 有利於 n boon

yow lay yun geh 有利潤嘅 a. profitable

yow leurng gor bo fan 有兩個部份 a. twofold

yow liew hao geh 有療效嘅 a curative

yow loy sing geh 有耐性嘅 a. patient

yow lun 郵輪 n ferry

yow luy 憂慮 n agitation

yow luy 憂慮 a anxiety

yow luy 憂慮 a. anxious

yow luy 憂慮 n distress

yow luy 憂慮 v. t distress

yow mak 幽默 *a. humorous*
yow mak 幽默 *a. jocular*
yow mak gam 幽默感 *n. humour*
yow mak jok ga 幽默作家 *n. humorist*
yow man far geh 有文化嘅 *a. literate*
yow man tay geh 有問題嘅 *a. problematic*
yow may 優美 *n. grace*
yow may geh 有味嘅 *a. odorous*
yow may geh 優美嘅 *a. picturesque*
yow may lik 有魅力 *a. winsome*
yow meen yik lik geh 有免疫力嘅 *a. immune*
yow meng geh 有名嘅 *a. renowned*
yow miew 幼苗 *n shoot*
yow ming mow sat 有名無實 *a. titular*
yow morng geh 有望嘅 *a. prospective*
yow muk 柚木 *n. teak*
yow muk dik 有目的 *v.t. purpose*
yow muk geh 遊牧嘅 *a. nomadic*
yow muk man 遊牧民 *n. nomad*
yow mun 油門 *n. throttle*
yow mwuy may geh 有霉味嘅 *a. musty*
yow ngan lik geh yan 有眼力嘅人 *n. visionary*
yow ngar 優雅 *n elegance*
yow ngar 優雅 *adj elegant*
yow ngoy sam 有愛心 *a benevolent*
yow ok yee 有惡意 *a. baleful*
yow peen geen 有偏見 *v. t bias*
yow piew 郵票 *n. stamp*
yow sam gor bo fan geh 有三個部份 *a. tripartite*
yow san lun 有神論 *n. theism*
yow san lun jeh 有神論者 *n. theist*
yow sang hey 有生氣 *a. lively*
yow say 優勢 *n. predominance*

yow say 優勢 *n. preponderance*
yow see 有時 *adv. sometime*
yow see 有時 *adv. sometimes*
yow seen geh 優先嘅 *a. preferential*
yow seen koon 優先權 *n. precedence*
yow seen koon 優先權 *n. priority*
yow seurng geh 憂傷嘅 *a mournful*
yow seurng jeurng lik 有想像力 *a. imaginative*
yow seurng jun sam geh yan 有上進心嘅人 *n. aspirant*
yow shoon jak geh 有選擇嘅 *a. selective*
yow shu 幼樹 *n. sapling*
yow sik 休息 *n break*
yow sik 休息 *n. repose*
yow sik 休息 *v.i. repose*
yow sik 休息 *v.i. rest*
yow sow 幼獸 *n cub*
yow sow 優秀 *n. excellence*
yow sow 優秀 *a. outstanding*
yow sow geh 優秀嘅 *a. excellent*
yow sow geh 優秀嘅 *a. sterling*
yow sow ho han 遊手好閒 *v.i. loaf*
yow sow ho han geh yan 遊手好閒嘅人 *n. idler*
yow sow ho han geh yan 遊手好閒嘅人 *n. sluggard*
yow sun sam 有信心 *a. confident*
yow suy 游水 *v.i. swim*
yow suy 游水 *n swim*
yow suy fuk lik 有說服力 *adj. cogent*
yow tai 郵差 *n. postman*
yow tai yan 猶太人 *n. Jew*
yow tar yee 有差異 *v. i differ*
yow tee 有刺 *a. barbed*
yow tee jee jung 由始至終 *prep. throughout*
yow tee lik geh 有磁力嘅 *a. magnetic*
yow teem lang 有潛能 *a. potential*
yow teen 有錢 *a. wealthy*

yow teen 有錢 *a. well-to-do*

yow teen geh 有錢嘅 *a. rich*

yow teng 遊艇 *n. yacht*

yow tiew lay geh 有條理嘅 *a. methodical*

yow tiew lay geh 有條理嘅 *a. orderly*

yow tiew lay geh 有條理嘅 *a. systematic*

yow wak 誘惑 *v.t. allure*

yow wak 誘惑 *n allurement*

yow wak 誘惑 *v.t. lure*

yow wak 誘惑 *v seduce*

yow wak 誘惑 *v.t. tempt*

yow wak 誘惑 *n. temptation*

yow wak jeh 誘惑者 *n. tempter*

yow wat 憂鬱 *a blue*

yow wat 憂鬱 *v. t depress*

yow wat geh 憂鬱嘅 *a. melancholic*

yow wat jing 憂鬱症 *n. melancholia*

yow way goon 優惠券 *n. coupon*

yow way goon 優惠券 *n. voucher*

yow way morng geh 有威望嘅 *a. prestigious*

yow wing jeh 游泳者 *n. swimmer*

yow wut lik geh 有活力嘅 *a dynamic*

yow wut lik geh 有活力嘅 *a energetic*

yow wuy 休會 *v.t. prorogue*

yow wuy 幽會 *n. tryst*

yow wuy kay 休會期 *n. recess*

yow yan 有人 *pron. somebody*

yow yan 有人 *n. somebody*

yow yan 有人 *pron. someone*

yow yan 蚯蚓 *n. worm*

yow yan sing geh 有人性嘅 *a. humane*

yow yee 猶豫 *n demur*

yow yee 猶疑 *v. i doubt*

yow yee 猶豫 *v.i. hesitate*

yow yee 猶豫 *n. hesitation*

yow yee 猶豫 *v.i. shilly-shally*

yow yee 猶豫 *n. shilly-shally*

yow yee chorng 幼兒床 *n. cot*

yow yee chorng 幼兒床 *n. crib*

yow yee geh 猶豫嘅 *a. hesitant*

yow yee see 有意思 *a. meaningful*

yow yee yee geh 有意義嘅 *a. allegorical*

yow yeen 油煙 *n. soot*

yow yik 有益 *a. wholesome*

yow yik geh 有翼嘅 *adj. aliferous*

yow yik geh 有益嘅 *a. salutary*

yow ying heurng lik 有影響力 *a. influential*

yow ying juy lik 有凝聚力 *adj cohesive*

yow ying yeurng 有營養 *a. nutritious*

yow yoon 柔軟 *a flexible*

yow yoon 柔軟 *n limber*

yow yoon 柔軟 *a. supple*

yow yoot 優越 *a. superior*

yow yoot 優越 *n. superiority*

yow yow gwa doon 優柔寡斷 *n. indecision*

yow yung 有用 *v.t. avail*

yow yung 有用 *a. useful*

yow yung geh 有用嘅 *a. invaluable*

yow yung geh 有用嘅 *a. serviceable*

yu 瘀 *n bruise*

yu 魚 *n fish*

yu 雨 *n rain*

yu ak 餘額 *n. balance*

yu bay cho see 預備措施 *n preliminary*

yu chun hang way 愚蠢行為 *n. idiocy*

yu deng 預訂 *n. reservation*

yu fai 愉快 *n enjoyment*

yu fai 愉快 *a. jolly*

yu fai 愉快 *n. pleasure*

yu fai geh 愉快嘅 *a merry*

yu fai geh 愉快嘅 *a. pleasant*

yu forng 預防 *n. precaution*

yu forng 預防 *n. prevention*

yu forng 乳房 *n. udder*

yu forng geh 乳房嘅 *a. mammary*

yu forng geh 預防嘅 *a. precautionary*

yu forng jeem jung 預防接種 *n. inoculation*

yu forng sing geh 預防性嘅 *a. preventive*

yu fu 迂腐 *n. pedantry*

yu gam 預感 *n. premonition*

yu geen 預見 *v.t foresee*

yu gey 預計 *n. anticipation*

yu gey 預計 *n bet*

yu gey 預計 *v. t expect*

yu gey 預計 *v.t. predict*

yu go 預告 *n forecast*

yu go 預告 *n. trailer*

yu gow 預告 *v.t. prophesy*

yu gway 雨季 *n. monsoon*

yu gwor 如果 *conj. if*

yu gwor hm hay 如果唔係 *conj. otherwise*

yu hao 愈合 *v.t. conglutinate*

yu hap 愈合 *n. concrescence*

yu hay 語氣 *n. tone*

yu jee 預知 *n. foreknowledge*

yu jee 預知 *n. prescience*

yu jee 魚子 *n. roe*

yu jow 宇宙 *n. universe*

yu jow geh 宇宙嘅 *adj. cosmic*

yu kay 預期 *n antedate*

yu kwan 魚群 *n. shoal*

yu lan jeh 遇難者 *n. casualty*

yu liew 預料 *v.t. anticipate*

yu liew 預料 *v.t. presuppose*

yu lok 娛樂 *n amusement*

yu lok 娛樂 *v. t entertain*

yu lok 娛樂 *n. entertainment*

yu luy 魚雷 *n. torpedo*

yu miew 魚苗 *n fry*

yu mo 羽毛 *n feather*

yu mo kow 羽毛球 *n. badminton*

yu mow 預謀 *n forethought*

yu mow 預謀 *n. premeditation*

yu mow kow 羽毛球 *n. shuttlecock*

yu say gak joot geh 與世隔絕嘅 *a. secluded*

yu see 於是 *conj. whereat*

yu see 於是 *conj. whereupon*

yu seen 預先 *n. advance*

yu seen ging go 預先警告 *v.t forewarn*

yu seen hao luy 預先考慮 *v.t. premeditate*

yu seen koot ding 預先決定 *v.t. predetermine*

yu shoon 預算 *n budget*

yu siew 預兆 *n. auspice*

yu siew 預兆 *n forerunner*

yu siew 預兆 *v.t herald*

yu siew 預兆 *n. omen*

yu siew 預兆 *v.t. portend*

yu tak 預測 *v.t forecast*

yu torng 乳糖 *n. lactose*

yu tow 乳頭 *n. nipple*

yu tow 乳頭 *n. teat*

yu wan 雨雲 *n. nimbus*

yu yam hok 語音學 *n. phonetics*

yu yan 漁人 *n fisherman*

yu yee 寓意 *n. allegory*

yu yeen 寓言 *n apologue*

yu yeen 寓言 *n. fable*

yu yeen 預言 *v.t foretell*

yu yeen 語言 *n. language*

yu yeen 語言 *n. lingo*

yu yeen 寓言 *n. parable*

yu yeen 預言 *n. prophecy*

yu yeen fung gak 語言風格 *n. locution*

yu yeen ga 預言家 *n. prophet*

yu yeen ga 預言家 *n. seer*

yu yeen geh 語言嘅 *a. lingual*

yu yeen geh 語言嘅 *a. linguistic*

yu yeen geh 預言嘅 *a. prophetic*

yu yeen hok 語言學 n. linguistics
yu yeen hok 語言學 a. philological
yu yeen hok 語言學 n. philology
yu yeen hok ga 語言學家 n. linguist
yu yeen hok ga 語言學家 n. philologist
yu yeurk 預約 n. appointment
yu yeurk 預約 v.t. reserve
yuk 嘟 v. i. & n budge
yuk 肉 n flesh
yuk 玉 n. jade
yuk 肉 n. meat
yuk 嘟 v.t. move
yuk dow hm yuk ha 嘟都唔嘟下 a. motionless
yuk gong 浴缸 n bath
yuk gway fan 肉桂粉 n cinnamon
yuk jeurng 肉醬 n. paste
yuk jut 獄卒 n. jailer
yuk ma 辱罵 v.t. taunt
yuk mong 慾望 n. appetence
yuk mong 慾望 n. appetite
yuk sow yuk geurk 嘟手嘟腳 v.t. paw
yuk tong 肉湯 n broth
yun wat 潤滑 n. lubrication
yun wat yow 潤滑油 n. lubricant
yung 用 n access
yung 溶 v.i. melt
yung 湧 v.i. surge
yung 用 v.t. use
yung 用 v.t. utilize
yung bay mor 用鼻摸 v. nuzzle
yung bo sek jorng sik 用寶石裝飾 v.t. jewel
yung chu 用處 n. use
yung chut geh 湧出嘅 n spurt
yung dai leem dow got 用大鎌刀割 v.t. scythe
yung fan gan say 用番梘洗 v.t. soap
yung far geh 熔化嘅 a. molten
yung far gway jeet 熔化季節 n thaw

yung fat 用法 n. usage
yung fwuy lay pow 用灰泥鋪 v.t. plaster
yung gai 溶解 v.t dissolve
yung gai dow 溶解度 n. solubility
yung gam 佣金 n. commission
yung gam 勇敢 a. courageous
yung gam 勇敢 a. gallant
yung gam 勇敢 n. gallantry
yung gam 勇敢 a. interpid
yung gam geh 勇敢嘅 a daring
yung gam geh 勇敢嘅 a dauntless
yung gam geh 勇敢嘅 a. mettlesome
yung gam geh 勇敢嘅 a. valiant
yung gan geh 用緊嘅 a. operative
yung guy 用具 n. utensil
yung gwong wun fat 容光煥發 v. i beam
yung gwong wun fat 容光煥發 n. radiance
yung gwun shu sung 用管輸送 v.i pipe
yung hay 勇氣 n. mettle
yung hay 勇氣 n. valour
yung hey 勇氣 n. courage
yung hoy meen mat 用海綿抹 v.t. sponge
yung huy geh 容許嘅 a. permissible
yung jay 溶劑 n solvent
yung ju seh hay say 用注射器洗 v.t. syringe
yung lap 容納 v.t accommodate
yung leurng 容量 n. capacity
yung lik bai 用力擺 v.t. plank
yung lik deng 用力掟 v.t. pitch
yung lik teng pow 用瀝青鋪 v.t. tar
yung lo 熔爐 n. crevet
yung mai 擁埋 v.i flock
yung mao 容貌 n. physiognomy
yung mao cho jing uk deng 用茅草整屋頂 v.t. thatch
yung mao gat 用矛拮 v.t. spear

yung mo gan mat 用毛巾抹 *v.t. towel*

yung mow ban yan 用模板印 *v.i. stencil*

yung ngam 熔岩 *n. lava*

yung ngar kek dung jok 用啞劇動作 *v.i mime*

yung seurng gwan yu 用雙關語 *v.i. pun*

yung shoon wan sung 用船運送 *v.t ferry*

yung shu 榕樹 *n. banyan*

yung so jee mor 用手指摸 *v.t finger*

yung sow geh 用手嘅 *a. manual*

yung sow jee gung ping 用手指公評 *v.t. thumb*

yung tang tiew da 用藤條打 *v. t. cane*

yung tee 用詞 *n diction*

yung tee bat dorng 用詞不當 *n. misnomer*

yung tong ju 用糖煮 *v. t. candy*

yung wan ying tow 用混凝土 *v. t concrete*

yung wu jeh 擁護者 *n exponent*

yung wu jeh 擁護者 *n. protagonist*

yung yan 容忍 *v.i abide*

yung yan 容忍 *n. toleration*

yung yao 湧入 *n. influx*

yung yee 容易 *a easy*

yung yee fat low 容易發嬲 *a. irritable*

yung yee gam yeem dow 容易感染到 *a. prone*

yung yee seurng chu 容易相處 *adj. convivial*

yung yow 擁有 *v.t. own*

yung yow 擁有 *v.t. possess*

yung yu luy jap gik 用魚雷襲擊 *v.t. torpedo*